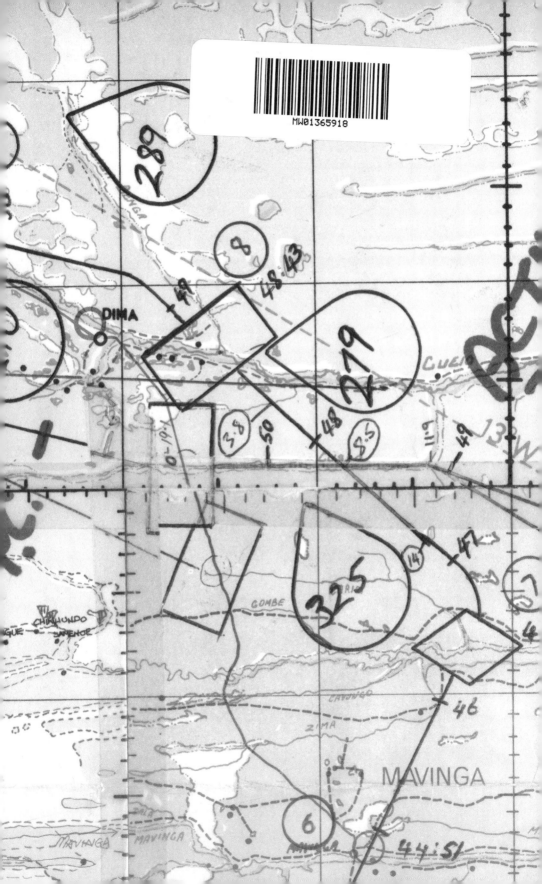

Praise for Dick Lord's previous books:

"*Vlamgat* deserves a place of pride in the long history of this, the second oldest air force in the world."—**Lt-Gen Willem Hechter**, former Chief of the South African Air Force

"*Vlamgat* is a superb book … my congratulations to Brigadier Dick Lord for the outstanding work he has done."—**Serge Dassault** (builder of the Mirage) in a letter to General Willem Hechter, former commander of the SAAF.

"Should *Vlamgat* have been written three years earlier, I would have made it compulsory reading for my pilots … I was CO of Sqn 2/33 from September '96 to May '99, after getting my wings in 1982. I flew in the Gulf, and I had some experience of Africa in Chad, Central Africa … but we French were not fighting there for our country, as you did in SWA."—**Vincent Gojon**, former F1 pilot and Squadron CO in the French Air Force

"I wanted to tell you that I thoroughly enjoyed reading *From Tailhooker to Mudmover*. As a former tailhooker in the U.S. Navy, it made me break out the old logbooks and review some mutual South China Sea dates."—**Thomas A. Kamm**, Rear Admiral U.S. Naval Reserve (Ret.)

"I read *From Tailhooker to Mudmover* from cover to cover over the weekend and really enjoyed it. It is a superb book."—**William Hare**, former Fleet Air Arm pilot, UK

"As a former Officer of the Reserve of the Netherlands Air Force I have to congratulate you on writing this fine book [*Fire, Flood and Ice*], which I have been reading with great pleasure and interest."—**W. P. J. Schuiten**, Holland

"*Vlamgat* is outstanding! If you have any interest in air combat this book is a must-read … the best book I have read about the South African Air Force."
—**E. Burke, Lauderhill**, Florida, USA

"*Vlamgat* is an eye opener on the skills, professionalism and training of the South African Air Force. If you thought that all African air forces were 'Third-World', then this book shows you are mistaken. Air-to-air combat, ground strikes far away from home base into the hornets' nest, SAMs chasing your tail, AAA fire from hell, odds 100-to-1 against you—you'll find it all here."—**Michiel Erasmus**, Netherlands

BRIG-GEN DICK LORD
FOREWORD BY COL JAN BREYTENBACH

FROM FLEDGLING TO EAGLE
THE SOUTH AFRICAN AIRFORCE DURING THE BORDER WAR

Also by Dick Lord

Fire, Flood and Ice—Search and Rescue Missions of the South African Air Force

Vlamgat—The Story of the Mirage F1 in the South African Air Force

From Tailhooker to Mudmover—An Aviation Career in the Royal Naval Fleet Air Arm, United States Navy, and South African Air

Published in 2008 by 30° South Publishers (Pty) Ltd.
28, Ninth Street, Newlands
Johannesburg 2092, South Africa
www.30degreessouth.co.za
info@30degreessouth.co.za

Copyright © Dick Lord, 2008
dicklord@mweb.co.za

Design and origination by 30° South Publishers (Pty) Ltd.

Printed and bound by Pinetown Printers, Durban

All rights reserved. No part of this publication may be reproduced, stored, manipulated in any retrieval system, or transmitted in any mechanical, electronic form or by any other means, without the prior written authority of the publishers. Any person who engages in any unauthorized activity in relation to this publication shall be liable to criminal prosecution and claims for civil and criminal damages.

ISBN 978-1-920143-30-5

June

You have shared the trials, tribulations and joy
of
the SAAF,
the Border War
and the recording of its history

I thank and salute you

For those who served

and

for their loved ones

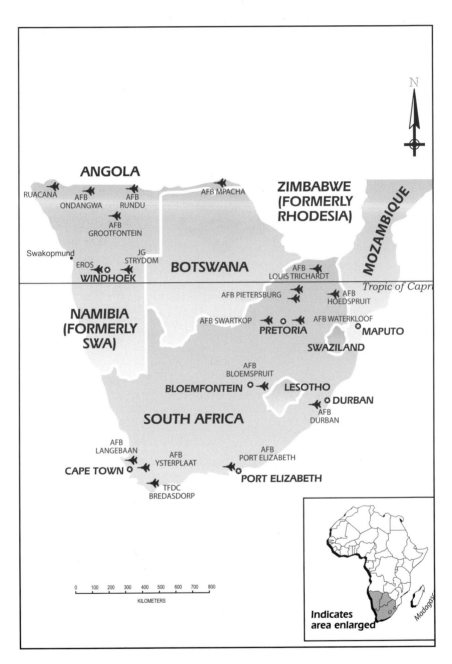

SOUTHERN AFRICA

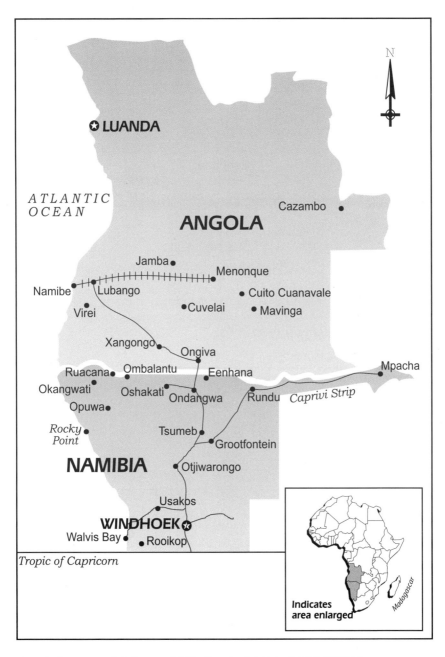

ANGOLA and SOUTH WEST AFRICA (NAMIBIA)

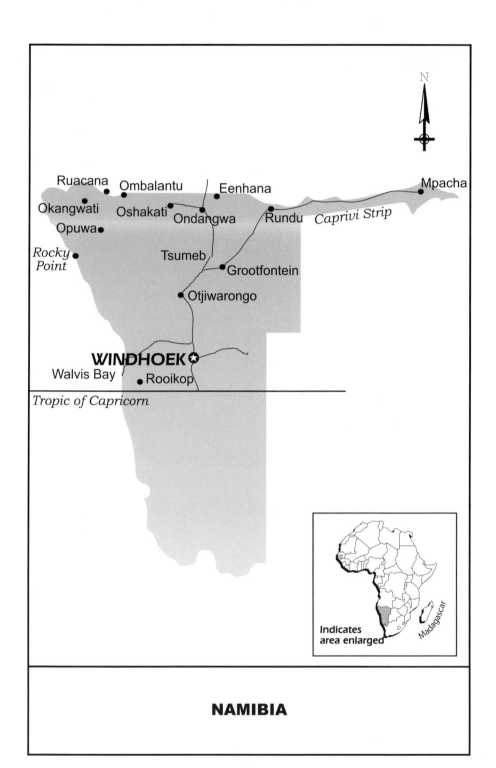

Contents

Foreword by Colonel Jan Breytenbach		12
Author's notes		16
Chapter 1	Setting the scene	20
Chapter 2	1966–1974: Provocation evolves into incursion	42
Chapter 3	1975–1977: Aftermath of *Savannah*	64
Chapter 4	1978: Cassinga	81
Chapter 5	1979: Learning the ropes	94
Chapter 6	1980: Establishing a pattern	138
Chapter 7	1981: Taking the war to the host nation	164
Chapter 8	1982: Cross-border operations	200
Chapter 9	1983: Anti-insurgency campaign	223
Chapter 10	1984: Uneasy peace	309
Chapter 11	1985: Internationalization	342
Chapter 12	1986: Taking a breather	367
Chapter 13	1987: Conventional warfare	385
Chapter 14	1988: Negotiated settlement	435
Chapter 15	1989: Breach of promise	456
Chapter 16	Conclusion	470
Glossary		479
Appendix 1	"One of our aircraft is missing" —SAAF aircraft and crew losses to the enemy during the bush war	491
Appendix 2	Chronology of operations	501
Appendix 3	ACM diagrams	508
Appendix 4	V3 air-to-air missiles	513
Appendix 5	The Billy Boys' Song	514
Bibliography		516
Index		517

Foreword

I can think of nobody more qualified to write a book about the South African Air Force during the so-called bush war than Dick Lord. He contributed immensely towards turning the already professional air- and ground crews into the most operational-ready, air-combat arm in the world at that time. The operationally deployed SAAF elements may not have been the strongest because of their limited size and outdated equipment, but they were certainly the most effective in a combat zone where they were not only heavily outnumbered but also outclassed in the field of combat 'kit'. We ended the war with F1AZs and CZs; the enemy with MiG-21s and the formidable MiG-23s. Yet they lost several aircraft in air-to-air combat and thereafter avoided crossing swords with the SAAF. Their gunships literally bristled with guns and missiles, veritable flying fortresses, while we soldiered on with the venerable Alouette III armed only with a 20mm gun … and so we can go on, comparing other types of aircraft on both sides. But the fact remains that our own SAAF brilliantly supported the army from the very beginning in 1966 right up to the final day when an armistice was signed in 1988—and beyond when a few gunships were hastily scrambled to sort out Sam Nujoma's swarm of terrorists which had crossed the Namibian–Angolan cut-line, arrogantly breaching the ceasefire conditions. Once again they got a bloody nose from the same gunships which had been the bane of Nujoma's ambitions while the bush war was raging.

Dick Lord contributed, on the ground, perhaps more than anybody else in forging a wide spectrum of SAAF elements, albeit sparsely manned and equipped, into a highly efficient combat force that became the envy of all air forces worldwide. He was successfully able to integrate the SAAF into the battle being waged on the ground by the 'pongos' (infantry, 'grunts'). The SAAF thus became a 'force multiplier' in the bush war operational area, out of all proportion with its size, manpower and equipment.

Foreword

So who is this Dick Lord and what is his background?

Richard Lord trained as a pilot with the Royal Navy's Fleet Air Arm and, one way or another, elected to specialize in all-weather fighters, probably the 'hairiest' of all occupations in the Royal Navy. He flew Sea Venoms and Sea Vixens while serving in various frontline, 'night-fighter' squadrons, operating from aircraft carriers which remained depressingly small while the jets they launched became ever faster and bigger with time. Imagine, as a night-fighter pilot, landing at uncomfortably high speeds on small, pitching decks in total darkness when the weather had clamped in and when only a slight mistake could pitch plane and crew into the drink, alongside or ahead of the carrier, at speeds of 130 knots or more. And please spare a thought for the poor, twittering observer/navigator whose fate rested in the hands of his pilot at such moments. Well, Dick always made it without a hitch, at least in the Royal Navy, which underlines his superb airmanship.

Because of this superior airmanship he was cross-attached to the US Naval Air Force's fighter school near San Diego, in California, which featured in the famous movie *Top Gun* with the unconvincing Tom Cruise as the gung-ho pilot and hero. In fact, while there, Dick wrote a treatise about the intricate but 'instinctive' manoeuvres a fighter pilot had to execute to get on the tail of an opponent in order to shoot him down with his guns. This was at a time when guns had been discarded in favour of only air-to-air missiles—big mistake as the Americans soon found out over North Vietnam when Viet pilots came at the Yanks with both missiles and guns and when friendly missiles sometimes failed to lock on to an adversary. The concept of 'dog fighting' had been dismissed as frivolous exhibitionism. Dick had to re-introduce this to the high-tech pilots who had lost the art of jousting with an opponent in an aerial display of G-pulling ballet.

Dick came to the end of his 'trick' (a navy term) in the RN and returned to South Africa with June Rosalind, his English wife, sometime after I had returned (after my own service in the RN's Fleet Air Arm) with my own English wife, Rosalind June, in tow. He joined the SAAF as a fighter pilot while I had elected to jump out of aeroplanes, an occupation less hazardous than pushing the envelope with gung-ho, all-weather fighter pilots. Dick was, without any doubt, a prime catch for the SAAF having clocked up thousands of hours in frontline naval squadrons, mostly at sea from carriers deployed operationally all over the world. He was soon 'deployed' (as MK, the ANC's armed wing would grandly say) into positions where he could transfer his experience to the SAAF's own *vlamgatte* [SAAF slang for jet pilots—from the Afrikaans *vlamgat*, literally 'flaming hole', in reference to the tail-end of a Mirage F1].

However, his ability and experience soon led to postings to the operational area, the so-called bush-war theatre, where he set about integrating the air force combat power with the army's, to form a combined offensive capability that made short shrift of any enemy attempts at forcing the South African Defence Force (SADF) to quit a theatre of war that was of prime importance, not only to South Africa but also to the West. Further postings followed, via TF101, SWA Territorial Force and Air Force HQ, which kept him at the cutting edge in developing tactics and procedures for SAAF squadrons to support the ground war in a hostile environment where the enemy had a distinct advantage in superior equipment—and a tactical air-defence system considered, at the time, to be the best in the world. The enemy, nevertheless, still had to face the best air crews in the world, placed at Dick's disposal, which he could mould and use to even the odds and clear the skies of any air threats aimed at the bundu-bashing 'pongo' forces below.

Being an AWF pilot himself he very successfully introduced night-flying operations for Impalas, known as 'moonlight sorties' to intercept enemy convoys under cover of darkness to move logistics and troops by road. Air transport support for UNITA allies and own forces required C-130s and choppers to fly at night to satisfy their demands. Thus C-130s were used at night, as just one example, to urgently shift a UNITA brigade from the Cazombo Bight in the far north to Mavinga in the south to face off a FAPLA attack from Cuito Cuanavale. They flew into old Portuguese bush strips, barely lit by paraffin lamps improvised from empty bully beef tins with home-made wicks, each crew flying several sorties every night for almost a week to get the job done.

Dick, with Deon Ferreira, commander of 32 Battalion, successfully developed a technique called 'butterfly ops' that flushed SWAPO guerrillas from their bases inside Angola by using speculative fire from gunships followed by the rapid deployment of ground forces by Puma helicopters, already standing by, to hem them in and destroy them. During daylight hours Dick used low-flying Impalas to deliver all sorts of ordnance (rockets, gunfire and bombs) deep into Angola, to support ground forces locked in battle with FAPLA/Cuban adversaries. At one time a couple of Impalas were used to shoot a string of MI-24 helicopters out of the sky in broad daylight while they were clattering along on a mission in support of their own troops. This required quick reaction but Dick's system allowed for the rapid scrambling of Impalas or gunships to exploit any opportunistic targets. I suspect that he also introduced toss-bombing techniques for the Mirage F1AZs to enable them to fly in at tree-top level, to avoid the MiGs and AA fire, to attack FAPLA/Cuban supply columns on the move between Menongue and Cuito Cuanavale.

He used Pumas to infiltrate Recce teams deep into Angola at night and to extract them after mission was accomplished, or in any emergency, both day and night. At one stage a small, two-man Recce team kept the railway between Namibe and Lubango cut for three months only because Pumas could clandestinely resupply them with water, rations and explosives. Of course, the favourite capability of

Pumas, usually accompanied by Alouette gunships and Impalas, in the minds of paratroopers, Recces and 32 Battalion troops, was the dicey evolution called a hot extraction. Some Pumas and air crews were lost carrying out this very dangerous function, as were some paratroopers, but they never flinched from coming to the aid of the 'pongos' who might be facing almost certain annihilation.

As a grand finale Dick was heavily involved during 1987/88 in launching Mirage and Buccaneer air strikes against FAPLA supply columns along the Menongue–Cuito Cuanavale supply line and against FAPLA/Cuban brigade formations on the Lomba River. These air strikes contributed significantly to the destruction of three brigades' worth of tanks (94 in all) and huge personnel losses (approximately 4,700 enemy troops), forcing the survivors to withdraw and skulk behind a belt of mines on the east bank of the Cuito River. This, together with the battle at Calueque, led to an end of the bush war.

The SAAF and the army came out of this twenty-year conflict with a reputation unequalled anywhere by any other armed force, largely due to men like Dick Lord who, at the sharp end, forged the two arms of the SAAF and the army into a formidable strike weapon that defeated, even wiped out, numerically far superior enemy forces.

During his service on the border Dick was made an honorary member of 32 Battalion, a unit I had formed, by Eddie Viljoen because we considered him to be one of us, a soldier to the core while also having proved himself an airman of impeccable credentials. It gave me great joy, as a former AWF naval observer/navigator to see a former AWF naval pilot being accepted into my own unit as just another beetle-crushing 'pongo'.

Jan Breytenbach
October 2008

Author's notes

Presently, those of us living in South Africa enjoy the benefits of peace and prosperity brought about by a democratic system that governs the well-being of the country. Unfortunately, it was not always so.

For 23 years, between 1966 and 1989, a bitter struggle between proponents of opposing ideologies took place in the remote far north of Namibia and in the southern portion of Angola. The rights and wrongs of the struggle have been documented by those more able than I, and will remain subjects for debate for many years to come.

In this historical account of that military conflict I have tried to avoid being judgemental and apportioning blame to any one faction. It was a war that the soldiers of both sides fought to the best of their abilities. Only those who have experienced the terror of a live fire fight understand the courage it takes to stand up and be counted, when all reason is telling you to dive for the nearest cover. Political propagandists, on both sides, should take cognizance of the guts it takes to enter into combat day after day and, when tributes are paid to those who died during conflict, suitable acknowledgements should be made to the combatants of both sides.

Although names have changed since those days I have employed the jargon in common use in the Defence Force at the time. For instance, I refer to Namibia as South West Africa and refer to the SWAPO cadres as 'terrorists' or 'terrs'. 'Politically incorrect' by today's standards—that is how it was then.

I have followed the course of the war, from the first clash at Ongulumbashe, Owamboland, to the eventual signing of the peace agreement that ended the struggle. I have concentrated on the actions of the South African Air Force, as that was my field of expertise. All the operations the SAAF were involved in are recorded in this book as accurately as I was able to achieve.

I thank the many air force and army personnel who supplied me with contributions detailing their own personal involvement. They are great stories that tell of tremendous courage, determination and outstanding professionalism. Detailed aircrew logbooks have enabled me to be extremely confident regarding the authenticity of this book. I insisted on accurate dates and times from all the contributors, to ensure fading memories had not altered or embroidered their stories. I am proud to have served in the SAAF and enjoyed every minute of it.

I have concentrated on operations and, therefore, on the aircrew who flew the missions. I realize by doing this I am doing a disservice to the vast majority of SAAF personnel. The ratio of aircrew to supporting staff is of the order 1:20. For every pilot or navigator I mention there were 20 other servicemen or women who were required to ensure that one crew member was able to fly. Like all aviators I too relied on aircraft fitters, electricians, radio technicians, engine mechanics, electronics boffins, flight-safety personnel, parachute packers, radar technicians, GCI and ATC controllers, aircraft handlers, pay clerks, aviation doctors and medics, intelligence teams, armourers, dog-handlers, security guards, map-makers, photographic interpreters, oxygen handlers, caterers—the list is never-ending. Every one of you deserves the acknowledgement for a duty well and truly done. I hope I have done you justice.

'At her call you did not falter,
Oh! South Africa, dear land'

The compilation of a history like this relies heavily on the contributions of many different people and it is my duty to acknowledge each and every one. I single out Rynier Keet because it was he who, unknowingly, is responsible for this book—I was initially on another track completely. Manuel Ferreira, also a historian, allowed me to use his photographs of Angolan military equipment. Riem Mouton was my gopher offering welcome assistance when I found myself up against a brick wall. He kindly spent many hours finding and assembling the maps which were readily available during the war but are now as rare as hen's teeth.

I have also included stories and photographs from the following people, in random order:

Charlie Wroth, George Snyman, Anton Kriegler, Cobus Toerien, Adrian Woodley, Hobart Haughton, Richard Cornelius, Steve Ferreira, Gert Havenga, Bart Hauptfleish, Daantjie Beneke, Mario Vergottini, Martin Louw for his contribution and allowing me to use photographs from his book, Lee le Crerar, Vlooi van Rooyen, Thinus du Toit, Rassie Erasmus, Daan Nel, Steyn Venter, Peter Kirkpatrick, Derek Lord, Johan 'Oppies' Opperman, Paul Dubois, Ollie Holmes, Neil Napier, Lappies Labuschagne, Koos Botha, Herman du Plessis, Eddie Viljoen, Eddie Brown, Derek Kirkland, Paddy Carolan, Graham Rochat, Marius

Whittle, Elmarie Dreyer and David Goodhead. Any errors are theirs!

It was a pleasure and a privilege to have served alongside people like this.

Chris and Kerrin Cocks of 30° South Publishers have been terrific to work with as publishers and as good friends.

Also to Aulette Goliath at 30° South Publishers for her administration and to Peter E. Butler who has worn his DTP teeth down on this project.

I am privileged and honoured to have had my old shipmate, Jan Breytenbach, write the foreword to this book. We both served in the Fleet Air Arm and in the SADF together—he as a Brown and I as a Blue. As well as being a most respected soldier, he is a conservationist and military historian. Thanks for the kind words, Jan.

In the two years it has taken to write this book I have been wonderfully supported by Richard, Michael, Keegan and a team of lovely ladies, Heather, Courtney and Tayla.

Dick Lord
Somerset West
October 2008
dicklord@mweb.co.za

Chapter 1

Setting the scene

The cut-line

The international border between South West Africa (SWA) and Angola was decided upon during the 'Scramble for Africa'—the heyday of colonialism in the 1880s. In the west, the winding Cunene River provided a convenient physical barrier for the first 300-odd kilometres until, showing no consideration for real-estate planners in Europe, it suddenly turned northward. This dilemma was solved in Berlin in 1884 when a cartographer misinterpreted a letter sent to him by the land surveyor in far-off Deutsch-Südwestafrika. The surveyor told them to draw a line due east from the falls, meaning the Epupa Falls, until it met the Cubango River, some 420 kilometres away.

This German military map drawn in 1904 has very different place names from those found on present-day map.

Unfortunately, the draughtsman found the Ruacana Falls and drew the line from there. This small bureaucratic glitch had major repercussions as it neatly divided the Owambo people, the largest homogenous group in the entire area, into German and Portuguese citizens. Initially this had little effect on the customs and way of life of the Owambo. However, the ever-efficient Germans decided to demarcate this arbitrary border by clearing the bush and erecting a four-strand, barbed-wire fence to separate the two countries over the entire distance. This was how the 420-kilometre gash through the bush acquired the aptly named sobriquet—cut-line.

Had the east–west line been drawn from Epupa Falls almost the entire Owambo tribe would have been in South West Africa. All the Angolan rivers were impressively large. The mass of water from the Cubango and Cuito rivers disappears into the desert of Botswana in the fabulous Okavango Delta.

At Katwitwi the border meets the Cubango River, which then becomes the border for the next 300 kilometres before joining the Cuito River to become the Okavango River. At Andara, where this mighty river turns southward towards Botswana, the map-maker ruled a straight line to Singalamwe on the Kwando River and continued along the ruler until it bisected the Zambezi at Sesheke. The border then continues along the Zambezi to Kazungulu, near Kasane, where no fewer than four countries, Zambia, Zimbabwe (formerly Rhodesia), Botswana and South West Africa (now Namibia) meet. The southern border with Botswana runs along the Kwando River to Sikosi, where a neat bit of parallel-ruler work brought it back past Shakawe in Botswana. All these place names became significant focal points during the border war.

It is easy to see why many of the initial SWAPO incursions took place into the Caprivi Strip—there was a safe haven within a few kilometres to the north or the south. SAAF aircraft straying off course in the Caprivi were often fired at by Botswana AAA gunners stationed on the hills at Shakawe. From the Cunene Mouth to Kasane is a distance of 1,500 kilometres.

Herds of cattle and goats, migrating across Owamboland to better grazing areas, had destroyed the fence many moons ago, and in most places there was no physical barrier between the countries. Originally, the surveyors had built marker beacons every ten kilometres along its length, from Ruacana eastwards. This aided ground navigation; people uncertain of their position only needed to

The cut-line can be clearly seen below this Impala.

locate one of these beacons. For example, Beacon 20 was 200 kilometres east of Ruacana, just north of Ondangwa.

Crossing an international border in peacetime means another stamp in one's passport, however, during a war, crossing the border—in our case the cut-line—could be much more traumatic. To the local Owambo it meant nothing at all—he went where the grazing was best. To the men of the South African Police Koevoet unit it meant that their presence was illegal, as the police only had jurisdiction on South African soil. It gave the army ground troops a chance to find out exactly where they were, because navigation through the bush is by no means easy. Aircrew reacted slightly differently. They knew, when crossing the cut-line, that if their aircraft were spotted they could be brought down. Returning from an attack mission one experienced a feeling of relief crossing back into friendly territory.

I believe though, that everyone experienced some degree of anxiety when they crossed the border for the first time. I well remember thinking on my first cross-border mission, "Here we go into the unknown." On one of the first Mirage F1 strike sorties of the war a pilot, who shall remain nameless, was heard to whisper every time he used the radio.

After the novelty of operations wore off the cut-line no longer held any fears; however, everyone was always very conscious of the artificial cut-lines imposed on every mission. The forward line of own troops (FLOT) is one such line. If a mission was planned to approach and return from the target behind the FLOT, the time exposed to enemy fire was greatly reduced. In addwition, if an aircraft was damaged during the strike, the sooner it returned behind the FLOT the safer it was.

I clearly remember planning an Impala strike to attack a target north of Mulondo, just west of the Cunene River. Because our troops were east of the river we planned the sortie so the strike leader, Commandant Chris Eksteen, and his formation would only be over 'Injun territory' for one minute and 35

Setting the scene

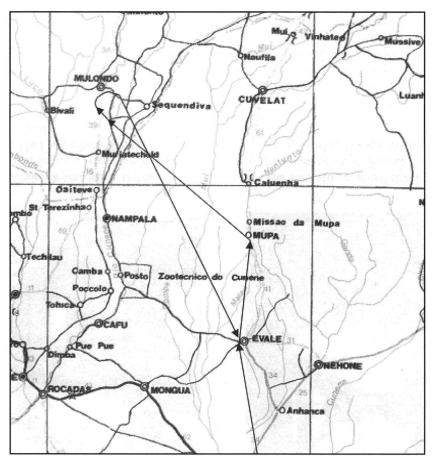

The Cunene River runs through Mulondo, Nampala and Rocadas (now Xangongo). West of the river was controlled by the MPLA and was thus considered 'Injun territory'. All the land east of the river was controlled by UNITA and was friendly territory. Therefore, in the strike described here, the Cunene was the FLOT.

seconds; a nice safe sortie or so I thought at the time. In the event, the enemy saw him coming and he drew heavy anti-aircraft artillery (AAA) fire, none of which hit any of the aircraft. He breathed a huge sigh of relief when once again safely behind the FLOT.

Radar cover produces another artificial cut-line. A radar beam is limited by the line of sight. When approaching a target, pilots tend to fly lower and lower to ensure their aircraft remains 'under the lobe'—the bottom limit of the radar beam. Initially, the introduction of SA-7 Strela heat-seeking missiles by the South West Africa People's Organization (SWAPO) forced the South African Air Force (SAAF) to fly above 15,000 feet, above missile range. However, the introduction of the more sophisticated SA-6, SA-8 and SA-9 missile systems forced our 'cut-line' down as low as it was safe to fly.

Governance

The border war took place either side of the cut-line, although the border was never the cause of the conflict. There were as many reasons for the conflict as there were perceptions about the cause. Basically, the problem began because of poor governance. The people had genuine grievances which the South African government did not address or correct. This discontent was the thin edge of the wedge, creating an opening into which many other malcontents were happy to squeeze.

Anti-colonialists, proponents of the liberation theory, communists of both red and yellow persuasion and the US State Department, all saw opportunities in Africa to advance their own agendas. The Soviets wanted world domination and Angola was a suitable stepping stone. The Chinese wanted to create a 'yellow belt' across sub-Saharan Africa from Tanzania, through Zimbabwe to the Atlantic Ocean via Angola. Cuba, for years under the hammer from America, wanted to flex her muscles and achieve a 'glorious victory'.

Left: A division of four Impalas return to the circuit after a mission.
Right: Major Chris Eksteen, leader of the Mulondo strike.

All conflicts are supposed to be solved by 80 per cent political will and 20 per cent military force. In the case of South Sest Africa the politicians seemed quite happy to hand the problem to the South African Defence Force (SADF) to solve. We could, and did, contain the military situation. However, it was a war we could not win because of poor governance.

Climate and terrain

The terrain varies from mountainous desert in the west, to an absolutely flat plain in the centre and thick, riverine bush in the east. At 17° 30′ south of the equator, northern SWA/Namibia has a tropical climate with very high summer temperatures. Dry, clear air over deserts allows maximum heat radiation to escape from the surface almost every night. Temperatures in the low single digits, or even below 0° Centigrade, are quite common. However, as soon as the tropical sun rises above the horizon temperatures soar, often peaking at around 40°C. At night, placing one's hand on the steel of military vehicles can chill the entire body—at midday the same vehicle becomes too hot to touch. Fortunately, humidity is low so temperatures are bearable, provided one has water to drink.

The plain of Owamboland is as flat as a pancake. There are no vertical features over an area 500 by 500 kilometres, making navigation extremely difficult—everything looks identical. An interesting geological anomaly is that on this plain there are no rocks or even stones—the surface is sandy, similar to that found on any beach. On the beach one needs protection from the sun and reflection off the white sand—the same applies in Owamboland. Oshakati was commonly referred to as Oshakati-by-the-Sea. Walking on loose sand on the beach is both difficult and tiring and is equally so in Owamboland. Four-wheel-drive vehicles have to be used for off-road driving to prevent getting stuck in the sand during winter and in the mud during the tropical rainy season.

Taken from a Buccaneer cockpit as the aircraft descends down the side of the Brandberg in South West Africa. The terrain is similar to that in the mountainous area of Kaokoland farther north.

Water is extremely scarce in the desert and on the plain, except from February to April when the 'Big Rains' saturate the entire area. I remember one of our more eloquent helicopter pilots describing Owamboland after a particularly heavy deluge: "It looks just like a tall cow shitting on a flat rock." However, in the east, thick bush and trees are nourished by the abundant water available from the mighty rivers which flow southeastwards out of Angola. Here again, off-road driving is limited to strongly built 4WD vehicles that can withstand 'bundu-bashing'—driving through, and over, bush and trees. Horizontal visibility decreases as one moves eastwards and the bush thickens.

The dot in the centre of the frame is a Buccaneer in battle formation as it passes down the dunes at Sossusvlei. Note the complete absence of vegetation.

Heat exhaustion, sunburn and sunstroke were constant threats as were malarial mosquitoes. Hygiene was a chronic problem as flies were an ever-present menace. Nutria uniform shirts soaked through with perspiration attracted the flies, which settled on one's back like a black carpet.

Within the tropics rainfall accompanies the movement of the area of low pressure directly under the sun, as it moves from one hemisphere to the other for the seasonal changes. This belt of low pressure is called the Inter-Tropical Convergence Zone (ITCZ). As the name implies, moist air from both tropics is sucked in and converges into the low pressure belt. The excessive temperatures, caused by the sun being directly overhead, cause the converging air to rise and form cumulo-nimbus clouds. These clouds build upwards to the tropopause, which in the tropics can be as high as 50,000 feet. These huge clouds then unload their moisture in a monsoon-type deluge accompanied by the usual lightning, thunder and very often heavy hailstorms.

The absence of any vertical features on the enormous Owamboland plain is clear to see in this sunset photo of a Puma landing.

One factor common to all three areas was dust. Sand was everywhere, in clothing, vehicles and engines. Driving in a military convoy was fine provided you were the leader; anywhere further back was a nightmare. Landing a helicopter was a tricky business as the pilot had to get the wheels firmly on the ground before his entire helicopter was enveloped in a cloud of dust. Aircraft engines sucked up prodigious quantities of sand which tended to grind away at bearings and other moveable parts, shortening engine life. Army food was renowned for its gritty texture, to the extent that some pilots were convinced the 'browns' (air force jargon for soldiers) added a spoonful or two to every dish.

This photo illustrates the dangers of dust. The second helicopter can barely be seen behind the tail rotor of the nearest Puma.

South Africa's neighbours

I have described the Angolan border in some detail because it was the main theatre of operations. However, during the border war, South Africa was also threatened by nefarious activities emanating from all the neighbouring countries. While countering these threats elements of the SA Defence Force were active, to a greater or lesser degree, in Zambia, Rhodesia/Zimbabwe, Mozambique, Lesotho, Swaziland and Botswana. As I will explain later this was the strategy, planned in Moscow, for the communist onslaught against South Africa.

Communism

Nowadays it has become fashionable to deride people like myself who, at that time 'saw a communist behind every bush'—people are entitled to their own opinions. I need to explain how I came to develop my anti-communist feelings. Bear in mind that the over-riding world political situation then was the Cold War, the delicate balance between Western capitalism and Eastern communism. Failure of the status quo might have resulted in nuclear holocaust.

Communism had spread through the African continent like wildfire. Recently independent countries were flexing their muscles and calls of, 'Africa for the African' were widespread. To their everlasting credit the SADF was not caught napping; programmes had been initiated to ensure our forces were prepared when, and wherever, the inevitable war broke out.

The threat facing South Africa was two-pronged. We were faced with an insurgency situation on the northern border between SWA and Angola and growing internal unrest within South Africa.

Both threats had their origins in bad governance, as people in SWA and South Africa had genuine grievances. Despite grandiose political rhetoric the standing in society of these people was not equal to that of the governing party. Therefore, situations were created which would inexorably lead to bloodshed. These grievances should have been properly addressed by the politicians. They were not and inevitably turmoil, violence and hostility erupted in both countries. However, whenever politicians are 'surprised' by erupting discontent the global tendency is to reverse the 80/20 balance and resort post-haste to a military option, as occurred in our case.

Both prongs of the threat were multi-faceted involving military, economic, religious, educational and racial elements. There were remarkable similarities between the SWAPO insurgency and the African National Congress (ANC)–Pan Africanist Congress (PAC) unrest. The reason was the willingness of the Soviet communist party to aid and support 'liberation organizations' and their struggles anywhere in the world. These organizations all received similar indoctrination, training and equipment from their Soviet masters. The Soviets were the acknowledged global experts in the art of fomenting political grievances into full-scale guerrilla wars.

The USSR made no secret of the fact that her ultimate aim was world domination. A glance at a world atlas will highlight the advance of Soviet imperialism between 1945 and 1995. During this period world headlines were dominated by militant struggles in Eastern Europe 1945, Korea 1950, Indochina 1946, Malaya 1948, Kenya Mau Mau terror 1952, Aden 1963, Algeria 1954, Hungary 1956, Congo 1960, Castro's Cuban revolution 1956, Portuguese Africa 1961, South America 1960–80, Vietnam 1954, Rhodesia 1959, Horn of Africa 1974, Northern Ireland, the Gulf wars of 1980 and 1993 and the growth of international terrorism. While Soviet troops were not involved in most of these struggles the communist technique was to subvert and train surrogates to shoulder the brunt of the fighting.

Choke-point theory

In the long list above it is interesting to see how many of those struggles took place in strategic world 'choke-points'. The flow of world trade around the globe has to pass through geographic choke-points, the Suez and Panama canals being the two most obvious examples. This explains the countless struggles centred around the Suez Canal in the Middle East—for example, Egypt, the Horn of Africa, Eritrea, Yemen and Aden. Similarly, countries like Nicaragua, Honduras and Panama, surrounding the Panama Canal, have also seethed with unrest.

A large portion of the world's oil passes through the Gulf of Hormuz at the mouth of the Persian Gulf which explains the almost unceasing unrest in this area of the globe. The Strait of Sumatra, between Malaysia and Indonesian Sumatra, explains the cause of their confrontation in the 1960s. In a like manner, the western entrance to the Mediterranean has seen trouble boil over in Algeria, Morocco and farther east in Libya.

The other great choke-point is the southern tip of Africa. Super-tankers, too large to transit Suez, pass round Cape Point. All sea traffic converges into a narrow sea lane around the Cape; therefore, whoever controls the Cape can control all shipping rounding the tip of Africa.

South Africa's natural resources include many strategic minerals used in the manufacture of aircraft engines and other hi-tech products. Control of these minerals, which occur only in southern Africa and Russia, would have given the communists a monopolistic advantage over her archrival America. These two factors combined to make South Africa a prize target in the Soviet Union's expansionist programme.

The Portuguese states of Angola and Mozambique were both in turmoil and Portuguese government forces were stretched to the limit trying to maintain a semblance of control. The next stop in the southward march of communism was South Africa, so it was in our own best interests to lend support to the Portuguese and the increasingly beleagured Rhodesians. These territories acted as a buffer zone between the peaceful south and the turbulent north. However, much of our population, living the good life in South Africa, behaved like ostriches, preferring to bury their heads in the sand rather than face the troubled future.

South West Africa had been mandated to South Africa after WWI and was administered from Pretoria like a fifth province. Unrest and dissatisfaction with their lack of autonomy stimulated the formation of anti-government protest groups in SWA, which eventually led to the formation of the South West Africa People's Organization (SWAPO). When the inevitable decision to turn to militancy was made SWAPO, with the blessing of neighbouring Angola, decided to establish bases in that country from which they could launch insurgency raids into SWA. So-called 'liberation' movements with their adherence to the Leninist/Marxist doctrine, which has such an appeal to the unsophisticated masses, were encouraged with the disintegration of Africa's colonies.

During historical research it is easy to see how all these factors had a direct bearing on the struggle for SWA's independence and for democracy in South Africa. However, for people caught up in the day to day problems of an expanding emergency situation it was not always easy to see the 'big picture'. We, in the defence force, had our suspicions that the increasing security problems were not haphazard, spontaneous outbursts. As the pressure built we could detect the orchestration behind the overall campaign.

One only has to compare a map of Africa in 1961 to one in 1985 to see how rapidly communism had spread throughout the continent.

Note also the Soviet's obsession with the choke-point theory. In 1961 they effectively controlled the Suez Canal through their affiliation with Egypt. When Egypt tired of their presence the Soviets immediately shifted their focus to Eritrea and Ethiopia, at the southern end of the Red Sea. To this day both these countries still suffer from the effects of communist influence.

Vital shipping transits the Mozambique Channel between mainland Africa and Madagascar. By 1985 this entire strait was under Soviet influence. Sea ports and air bases in Angola gave the Soviets a massive air/sea capability against the flank of shipping transiting in the Atlantic Ocean, between the Cape and the Bulge of West Africa. In exactly the same manner Soviet pressure could be exerted on Mediterranean shipping from bases in Algeria, Tunisia and Libya.

On a personal level, my own experience of the evils of communism stretch back to 1960. As a young rookie pilot on my first carrier tour, I was on board HMS *Centaur* when we passed through the Kattegat, between Denmark and Sweden, and entered the Baltic Ocean. As we rounded the southern point of Sweden we

 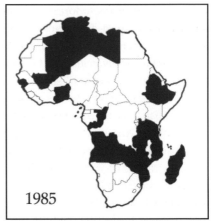

Note the completed ring on the second map, of Angola, Zambia, Zimbabwe and Mozambique encroaching on South West Africa and South Africa and remember that the Soviets' asserted aim was world domination. In Africa, in a mere 24 years, they had made spectacular progress with South Africa the final prize.

were intercepted by a Soviet destroyer which dropped in astern of our large carrier. Ten miles further on a West German Navy Fast Patrol Boat fell in astern of the Soviet ship, all abiding by the 'rules' of the Cold War and watching each other. As the Soviet ship crept ever closer under our stern our ship's tannoy system announced its presence to the entire 2,000-man crew. Immediately those not on duty streamed onto the flight deck to view our 'escort'. Jolly Jack and sailors the world over are well known as jovial coves and our matelots were soon waving and shouting ribald remarks at their Soviet counterparts. Unbelievably, the Soviets did not respond! They stood gazing at us without any acknowledgment in an astonishing display of churlish, ungracious behaviour. Then, I noticed one of their sailors standing in a tiny recess in the superstructure of the Soviet vessel. With a careful movement of his head to ensure that no one aboard his ship was watching him, he gave us a quick wave of his hand which was held low down near his hip. This was the only reaction I saw in the almost two hours they 'escorted' us. It was apparent that the communist commissar was one of the men on the forecastle and, not only had he briefed the crew, but was watching for any aberrant reactions from them. I realized then just how oppressive a communist-controlled system really is.

A few years later, while serving on board HMS *Ark Royal* in Norwegian waters off the Lofoten Islands, our radar detected an unidentified aircraft approaching the NATO fleet. As we were operating in international waters this was permissible but needed investigation, in the unlikely event it turned out to be hostile. During the Cold War military forces were always on high-alert status and on this occasion I was strapped into my Sea Vixen on cockpit standby. After the catapult launch I was given a heading to intercept the unidentified aircraft. About 80 miles from the fleet my observer picked up the bogey on our radar set and talked me round in a sweeping curve of pursuit. Normally, fighter aircraft move straight into the six o'clock position directly behind a target, but this was not advisable in tense Cold War situations as it could be interpreted as a hostile move. Instead, we drew up alongside the bogey and closed in until we positively identified it as a Soviet Tupolev TU-95 Bear. This huge aircraft was built as a long-range, heavy bomber, but the version I was in formation with was configured as a reconnaissance aircraft.

It was powered by four turbo-prop motors each driving two huge, contra-rotating propellers. It had a massive wingspan and was quite the largest aircraft I had ever formated on. It was important, from a morale aspect, to be in close formation with the intruder as it passed over the NATO fleet so observers on board would know that, had the 'war' been hot, then it would have been shot down. On the 80-mile flight towards the fleet I had a good chance to study the aircraft from all angles; I knew our intelligence officers would expect an extensive debriefing once I landed back aboard.

It was during my inspection of the aircraft that I noticed a crewman in the turret, situated under the tailplane. On closer inspection I saw he was waving to me in a 'come here' motion. This I did, and slid in close under the tailplane from where there was no more than 20 metres between us. He was smiling and waving enthusiastically and I responded in kind. After passing over the fleet, my job completed, I waved cheerio to the Russian. He immediately raised both hands, palms outwards, in the window to signify 'stay'. He disappeared for a few seconds and then returned into view unscrewing the top of a Thermos flask. He then poured a measure (which I took to be coffee but might well have been vodka!) into the cup and toasted me in a gesture of camaraderie. After downing his drink he gave me a salute which I returned, before breaking formation and returning to my ship.

Here was another example of the iniquity of the communist system. Obviously there was no political commissar on board the Bear so this man reacted like most

Traditionally, all photographs of Soviet aircraft have been blurry. However, a close inspection under the tail will reveal the dark shape of the blister turret.

servicemen the world over. He was a professional doing his duty as ordered, to the best of his ability, but without animosity. This display, along with the one on the forecastle of the Soviet destroyer, convinced me it was the system that was flawed not the men; further reason to vehemently oppose to the spread of communism in southern Africa.

South African military

After World War II, the military budget was understandably reduced to the bare minimum as the country tried to re-establish itself on a peace footing. The SADF had shrunk to a level where the professional core was barely sufficient to maintain expertise in military warfare. Under trying conditions the generals had built a training structure allowing for rapid expansion. The country had a conscription system; white youths were called up for military service for one year, following which they were required to stay on a reserve list attending military camps every year. This was the manpower pool available in times of tension or conflict.

PD-USGOV-Military-Navy. In this close-up, a crewman can be seen in the window above the blister turret

South Africa did not have a balanced military force as it was originally envisaged to be part of the British military structure. The army was equipped with British equipment which included Centurion tanks, 25-pounder and 5.5-inch artillery pieces.

Having operated in Korea in the early 1950s, the air force was in a slightly better position with Sabre jets having replaced the war-time Spitfires as the major strike fighter, and with Sikorsky helicopters, introduced in small numbers. The Active Citizen Force squadrons, positioned in all the major cities, operated Harvard aircraft—their pilots being utilized when required.

In the early 1960s, visionaries in the air force ordered C-130 Hercules transport aircraft from the USA, a squadron of Canberra bombers and 16 Buccaneers from Britain, with an option to purchase a further sixteen. As international pressure and isolation was enforced Britain's labour government cancelled the second order of 16 Buccaneers. Britain had been our traditional arms supplier but the French were quite happy to fill the void; through them we acquired C-160 Transall transport aircraft, Mirage III fighters, and Alouette, Puma and Frelon helicopters. This excellent relationship with France created an opportunity through which South Africa obtained 48 magnificent Mirage F1 fighters before the embargo curtain finally closed in the early 1970s.

The basis of SAAF flying training over nearly 50 years was the wonderful North American Harvard. It was easy to fly but difficult to fly well, making it an ideal tough, reliable trainer. From the 1960s onwards our advanced flying schools

This battery of 25-pounder howitzers was used by the cadets at Parktown Boys' High School in the 1950s, before military training at schools ceased.

Fifty SAAF Harvards make a pretty picture against the African sky. Professionals will tell you that on a bumpy highveld afternoon the place to be is either leader or tail-end Charlie, not number 37 or 43 somewhere in the middle.

were equipped with the tandem-seat Aero Macchi Impala. The only drawback of this superb aircraft was the cockpit air-conditioning system which struggled to cope with high South African temperatures.

Command and control

During the border war the SAAF, having limited resources, utilized a system of centralized control of all air bases from its headquarters in Pretoria, except for those situated within two regional commands. Southern Air Command, co-located with the navy at Silvermine in the Cape, was responsible for maritime matters over the seas surrounding our coast. Western Air Command (WAC), co-located with the army in the Bastion headquarters in Windhoek, SWA, was responsible for the air support of counter-insurgency operations in that theatre. An interesting fact was that both regional commands were co-located with other service arms to conduct joint operations, whereas, at the highest levels in Pretoria, all four service headquarters were separated. Lessons learned from World War II indicate that a joint approach is the most efficient way to counter any threat.

The bomb-proof structure built to house 310 AFCP at Oshakati. When I took up the commander's appointment the cement was still damp. Using a pencil I christened the establishment 'The House of Lords'.

Operational command and control improved dramatically during the course of the border war. A computerized, real-time system, known by the codename Jampot, was introduced in WAC during late 1981, to replace the 'hand-draulic' system that had its origins in the RAF control rooms during the Battle of Britain. 'King' Ferreira, the installation engineer, spent an anxious period dashing between Windhoek, Oshakati and Ondangwa sorting out hiccups in the system and training the operators. The clatter and inherent delays of tele-tape machines sending and receiving tasking signals, was replaced by the press of a button. After the successful installation throughout WAC the entire air force was linked into the network—the results were dramatic.

The commander at each level had an immediate display of the state of preparedness of all his assets. Turnaround times decreased, allowing aircraft to fly more missions every day. The philosophy of the system was to place all unit commanders in the direct command line in contact with one another. In combat commanders must be able to talk to one another. Direct and dedicated command lines between commanders, in the Jampot system, allowed executive decisions to be made rapidly—a vital element when keeping control of aircraft travelling at nine or ten miles per minute.

Aircraft give flexibility and rapid reaction to combat situations. At the drop of a hat they can be switched from one front to another if required. The downside is the considerable investment a country must make before introducing them into

From left: King Ferreira, Colonel Breyty Breytenbach, Brigadier Blackie de Swardt and Colonel Jan Nel photographed enjoying an Air Force Command Post's luncheon in 1991.

operational service. Correct utilization, in all its facets, is the only way to make the vast capital expenditure cost-effective:

- Aircrew and ground crew *must* be fully trained
- Servicing and logistical support *must* be readily available
- Air traffic control *must* handle air movements efficiently
- Fighter controllers, radar operators and telecommunication staff *must* be highly skilled
- Armourers *must* handle their explosives quickly and safely
- Air bases *must* be fully functional

The focus of the entire air force system is to get 'air-delivered weapons' on target, where and when required.

When one watches a Formula One race meeting one notices that pit stops are critical. Getting the driver back into the race is all-important. It is exactly the same with aircraft. If the ground crew can reload, rearm, top up the oxygen system and check through all the aircraft systems in 30 minutes, instead of the peacetime norm of one hour, a squadron could possibly fly four sorties in a day instead of three. Effectively, a quick turnaround is a force multiplier, in this case increasing productivity by 25 per cent.

Evolution of the South West African Territory Force

A most notable achievement during the course of the 23-year-long border war was the development of the South West African Territory Force (SWATF).

SWA was administered from Pretoria; military matters being the preserve of the SADF. However, after the initial armed contact with SWAPO took place at Ongulumbashe in Owamboland in 1966, it became apparent that the problem was not going to disappear. In fact, escalation of SWAPO activities made it clear that to counter the threat South African resources would be severely tested.

In its search for viable solutions to this problem the South African Army used the traditional British approach, very effectively, and raised ethnic battalions. In 1974, 1 Owambo Battalion was formed. Following closely the historical example set by the British in their forays around the world, officers and senior non-commissioned officers were drawn from the ranks of the SA Army but the soldiers were local Owambo men. From the very beginning this was a success story. It took hard work and discipline to train men from a particularly rural background to attain standards necessary to allow them to be used in combat. There were huge cultural, technological and language problems to overcome, but the Owambo proved himself to be an excellent soldier.

The advantage of using local men was that they possessed skills no ordinary soldier in the SADF had. They had grown up in the territory, could speak the local language and knew the habits of the foe—the Owambo SWAPO cadres. The other endearing characteristic common to these men was the pride they displayed in their units and the loyalty they showed to their own people and country.

In 1975, Commandant Jan Breytenbach, one of South Africa's great soldiers of modern times, gained permission from Pretoria to train FNLA fighters (Frente Nacional para a Libertação de Angola—opposed to the Marxist Angolan government). Under the most difficult circumstances he transformed this ragtag group of men into probably the best, and the most effective, army unit of the border war. This was the beginning of the famous 32 Buffalo Battalion, based at Bagani in the Caprivi Strip. This unit saw more action than any other battalion during the course of the war.

In Africa, the bush telegraph spreads news far and wide so it was no surprise when, early in 1975, a group of 50 Kavango men arrived in Rundu to volunteer for training in the Kavango Battalion.

Meanwhile, in the Caprivi Strip, a military base called Omega was established to accommodate the thousands of Bushmen who, in a great humanitarian operation, had been brought out of Angola to the safety of SWA. SA Army personnel had discovered, during their foray into Angola in 1975, that these Bushmen were unwanted by any of the three rival factions struggling for power in Angola (MPLA, UNITA and FNLA). Bushmen were routinely hunted and persecuted wherever they were found. At Omega they were settled securely in a base that catered for their needs and those of their entire extended families. The able-bodied men were also recruited into the SA Army, initially as 31 Battalion. These men were exceptional in the traditional bush-craft skills of survival and tracking of spoor, either animal or man.

A second Bushman battalion was centred on Mangetti Dunes in the arid heart of Bushmanland. This group was eventually to man eight bases spread throughout this harsh desert region.

On 15 August 1977, 33 Battalion was formed and subsequently based at the eastern end of the elongated Caprivi Strip. They were to protect the border against any SWAPO aggression emanating from the southeastern corner of Angola and from Zambian territory.

Setting the scene

On parade, the SWATF was smartly turned out. In the bush they were excellent.

SWAPO expanded their traditional infiltration routes through Owamboland and Kavangoland and in 1979/80 opened up more routes farther west, in the arid desert areas of Kaokoland. The immediate response to this threat was the raising of a company of three platoons of Himba and Herero men under the name Kaokoland Company.

The most interesting fact about this proliferation of locally raised units was that they were a truly representative force of the people of SWA. There were people from all eleven ethnic groups in the country—white, black, brown and yellow all fought together.

Eventually, SWA became an independent country (but without UN recognition), needing its own security force. Under a proclamation from the State President of South Africa, a Department of Defence for SWA was instituted on 1 August 1980—an unusual, but sensible arrangement, placed this force under the appointed General Officer Commanding (GOC) based in Windhoek. This man effectively wore three hats: GOC SA Army in SWA; GOC SWATF and Secretary for Defence in the Transitional Government of National Unity for SWA.

Under the proclamation all the locally raised units were re-organized into the SWATF with the exception of 32 Battalion which remained a South African Army unit. A Territory Force HQ was established in Windhoek with various sector headquarters to manage staff functions for personnel, intelligence, operations, logistics and finance.

Locally raised units became Full-time Force units. They formed the foundation of the new defence force and offered all SWA citizens the opportunity to undertake voluntary military service.

The Reaction Force (Citizen Force) constituted part of the SWA reserve force and was trained in both conventional and counter-revolutionary warfare.

An Area Force, based on the SA Commando system, was also part of the reserve force but provided protection mainly in counter-insurgency warfare against terrorist incursions and attacks.

The air force already existed in the form of 1 SWA Squadron. Air operations remained the responsibility of the SAAF.

SWA was divided militarily into sectors to provide cohesive control. The operational theatre bordering on Angola, in the north of the country, was demarcated by the so-called Red Line running east to west, just north of the huge Etosha Pan. Inside the Red Line were the following:

- Sector 10   HQ Oshakati
- Sector 20   HQ Rundu
- Sector 30   HQ Otjiwarongo (formerly Group 30) controlled the farming area just below the Red Line
- Sector 40   HQ Luipaardsvlei (formerly Group 29) just south of Windhoek
- Sector 50   HQ Gobabis (formerly Group 33) protected the country's eastern border with Botswana
- Sector 60   HQ Keetmanshoop
- Sector 70   HQ Katima Mulilo—this small sector had international borders with Zambia, Zimbabwe, Botswana and Angola

Name-changing under the re-organization, included the existing combat units as:

- 1 Owambo Battalion (Oshakati) – 101 Battalion
- Kaokoland Company (Opuwa) – 102 Battalion
- Bushman Battalion (Omega) – 201 Battalion
- Kavango Battalion (Rundu) – 202 Battalion
- Bushman Battalion (Mangetti Dunes) – 203 Battalion
- 33 Battalion (Caprivi) – 701 Battalion
- 41 Battalion (Luipaardsvlei) – 911 Battalion
- 1 SWA Specialist Unit (Otavi) was formalized as a specialist tracking unit
- 2 SWA Specialist Unit (Windhoek) was formed in 1978 as a parachute element

All these units were employed in combat in the defence of their country and all gave wonderful service. 101 Battalion became renowned as a most efficient anti-terrorist force when used in the motorized Reaction Force concept, initiated by SA Police Koevoet units. The Bushmen of 201 and 203 battalions were unsurpassed in finding and following enemy spoor, while two companies of specialist unit paratroopers were used alongside their SA counterparts in airborne operations against SWAPO.

The SWATF was demobilized with undue haste by the new power (Nujoma's SWAPO) on 27 May 1989. A final, interesting statistic is that by the end of the border war SWATF was providing up to 70 per cent of the personnel required during operations. A marvellous response from a country with limited personnel resources–epitomized in an emotional song popular at the time:

Life on the line

Green sunburnt grasslands, rivers that run dry
Grows on you daily, don't ask me why
From the barren red Namib to the green swamps in the east
It's a country in which a bold young heart can feast

Show me a young man in any South West town
Never mind his colour be it black, white or brown
And I'll show you a young man with his life on the line
For your and my freedom and peace for all time

Written and performed by Cmdt Russell Bartlett
Teal Record Co. 1986

Chapter 2

1966–1974: Provocation evolves into incursion

Increasing provocation

The southerly advance of communist imperialism through the African continent did not go unnoticed in South Africa and, by the mid-1960s, was perceived as a direct threat. Revolutionary organizations like SWAPO and the African National Congress (ANC) had involved themselves in troubles brewing in Rhodesia, Angola and Mozambique. It was this involvement that prompted South Africa's military assistance to these countries.

It really all began in July 1965 when six terrorists, trained in Tanzania, entered South West Africa in the Rundu area having crossed from Zambia and southeastern Angola. They eventually established a base at Ongulumbashe, in Owamboland. This initial group, and their successors, were responsible for the string of attacks, murders and mayhem that was to evolve into the conflict that came to be known as the 'border war'. The list of SWAPO provocation includes:

- On 27 September 1965, an attack on buildings and officials of the Department of Bantu Administration and Development in Oshikango.
- On 29 December 1965, they attacked a local headman's kraal and killed five of his entourage.
- In February 1966, they attacked a shop, killing the Portuguese owner.
- In March 1966, a further group of ten terrorists was arrested shortly after crossing the border.
- In December 1966, another group of ten attacked the Breedt family on their farm near Grootfontein. The SAP were responsible for countering these infiltrations and were given restricted assistance by the Defence Force who supplied advisors, logistic and transport support, as well as air support in

1966–1974: Provocation evolves into incursion

the form of helicopters and DC-3 Dakota transport aircraft.
- During March 1967, another group crossed into SWA from Botswana, near Bagani in western Caprivi. The SAP carried out a follow-up operation in which they killed one and captured five terrorists with the remaining four fleeing into Zambia.
- On 28 December 1969, a group consisting of seven terrorists was discovered in a follow-up operation; four were killed and three escaped into Botswana
- On 19 April 1971, terrorists fired over the border from Zambia, wounding five policemen.
- On 22 May 1971, a police vehicle detonated a landmine three kilometres from Singalamwe—two policemen were killed.
- In October 1971, not far from the same location, four policemen were seriously injured when their vehicle detonated a mine. The very next day another police vehicle was destroyed when it hit a landmine; fortunately none of the occupants was injured. However, after this incident a booby-trapped mine was activated, killing a policeman.
- On 7 January 1972, a police vehicle detonated a mine, with eight policemen suffering serious injuries. Only two metres from the scene a further mine was discovered and safely lifted.
- On 5 February 1972, a homemade landmine was discovered in the dry bed of the Kwando River. The name Nitrogen Chemicals of Zambia was printed on the plastic sack it was bound in.
- On 30 March 1972, a policeman and his patrol dog were killed in a mine explosion 16 kilometres east of Singalamwe. A further six members were seriously injured in this incident.
- On 22 May 1972, four Defence Force members and a Bushman tracker were severely injured in a mine detonation only 800 metres from the Singalamwe Base. Four days later two homemade landmines, weighing eight and 12kg respectively, were found 2,000 metres south of the same base.
- On 26 November 1973, a Defence Force truck detonated two mines near Wenela Base, 200 metres south of the cut-line. Two soldiers and an army chaplain were injured.

Documents captured during follow-up operations in late 1973 included a SWAPO operational plan contained in a report to a Chinese representative in Dar es Salaam. The plan detailed SWAPO's intention to attack SWA over six fronts—Owambo, Kavango, Kaokoland and the Caprivi, as well as two fronts in central SWA. On the last two fronts they were to concentrate on cutting communication lines, attacking white-owned farms and conducting urban terrorism in Windhoek, Walvis Bay, Tsumeb and other main towns. It was clear that SWAPO intended using Angola and Zambia as springboards for these attacks.

These incidents led to the SADF taking over the task of counter-insurgency operations in SWA from 1 April 1974. Initially, not wanting to escalate the conflict, the military adopted a defensive posture within SWA against SWAPO provocation. SWAPO took this as a sign of weakness and stepped up their campaign with quick-fire insurgency missions from the safety of Angola—even with periodic intrusions into central SWA. They concentrated on intimidation and the elimination of anti-SWAPO leaders, such as:

- Filemon Elifas, Chief Minister of Owambo was shot dead on 16 August 1975
- Toivo Shiyagaya, one of the Owambo Cabinet ministers was murdered on 7 February 1978
- Clemens Kapoo was murdered on 27 March 1978

SWAPO's ability to carry out these hit-and-run attacks was the provocation factor which decided the Defence Force to change their posture to offensive defence. This contradiction in terms meant that instead of having to wait inside South West Africa to react to deeds of violence, SWAPO would be aggressively hunted in their host countries.

SADF reaction

The SAP was responsible for border control and, to prevent the movement of trained terrorists in the Caprivi and within the northern borders of South West Africa, two SAAF Alouette IIIs were seconded to the police to increase their mobility. These helicopters were dismantled at AFB (air force base) Swartkop, loaded into the back of a C-130 and flown to J. G. Strydom Airport, outside Windhoek. The crews, who accompanied the helicopters, were lieutenants Daantjie Beneke and Tobie Winterbach (brother of Gawie, a Mirage pilot). To assist with the reassembly and maintenance of the aircraft four flight engineers, Stan Brits, Hoffie Hoffman, George Morton and Jan Delport, completed the SAAF complement.

The aircraft were assembled, test-flown and then ferried to Windhoek where they landed in the backyard of a police station. They operated from this temporary base for a few months until they were moved to permanent aircraft accommodation at Eros airfield.

The police had received information that a group of SWAPO terrorists were infiltrating from Zambia via southern Angola, to Owamboland, where they intended to establish a training camp. On 22 March 1966, the Alouettes flew to Andara on the Cuito River with the Inspector General of the Police, Colonel Pretorius. On landing they picked up Paul Oosthuizen, the owner of a small shop, who directed them to a hunting lodge near Luenge. The manager of the lodge

1966–1974: Provocation evolves into incursion

The famous Alouette III, sturdy workhorse of the border war and scourge of SWAPO.

confirmed that a group of heavily armed terrorists had recently passed through the area, robbing and murdering a shop owner to the west of the lodge.

This information was sent to Pretoria and a team under the leadership of Colonel Theuns 'Rooi Rus' Swanepoel was despatched to SWA. They set up a camp in Owamboland under the cover of Pascoe Engineering, a company that was supposed to survey and plan the building of a new road in the area. A group of locals was employed from which informers were identified and recruited.

On 21 April, a tragedy occurred. Tobie Winterbach and George Morton were killed when they flew into the sea, at night, off Terrace Bay. They were replaced by Vince van Buuren and Thys Snyman.

Meanwhile, in Pretoria, the first helicopter airborne assault in the history of the SAAF was being planned. Operation *Blouwildebees* was scheduled to take place in the early morning of 26 August 1966.

Six Alouette pilots were trained to operate without flight engineers, which would enable them to carry six paratroopers/police special-force personnel. If trees in the target area prevented the helicopter from landing the passengers would descend using knotted ropes, tossed out of the rear passenger door. An aluminium plate in the form of a V was bolted to the floor to allow the pilot, while flying with his right hand, to pull the rope back into the cockpit. The two pilots already in South West Africa, Beneke and van Buuren, missed this training.

On 24 August, the six Alouettes and crews were flown to AFB Rooikop, outside Walvis Bay, where the aircraft were reassembled and test-flown. The next day they flew to Kamanjab where they were joined by Beneke and van Buuren. After refuelling, the entire formation completed the ferry flight to Ruacana. Routing well away from the target area they approached the base from the west where three C-130s and the command and assault teams were waiting.

The SAAF operation was commanded by Brigadier Jan Blaauw, the police by General Pat Dillon and the SA Army by Brigadier Renfree and Major Paetzold. The assault teams comprised a mixture of SAP Reaction Force members and paratroopers. The entire force was briefed by Brigadier Blaauw and for the first time informed what the mission was about. That night, after receiving 'rat-packs' (rations) for their sustenance, they slept out under the clear, cold, sky of Owamboland. Daantjie Beneke and Vince van Buuren, the 'old' Southwest campaigners, were the only ones to sleep on stretchers as these had become part of their helicopters' night-stop kit.

During the night an informer slipped away from the terrorist camp near Ongulumbashe to join Swanepoel and his team to fly in the lead helicopter piloted by 'Gooks' Loubsher. The other three passengers were to be Blaauw, Dillon and Renfree. The following morning seven Alouettes lifted off, flying in line astern, each with their six-man assault team. The route took them north from Ruacana until they reached the cut-line, then along the cut-line until they reached the irrigation canal. Turning right they followed the canal until they located a small, single-spoor road which led into the terrorist camp. On reaching the camp centre Brigadier Blaauw fired off a red Verey-pistol flare.

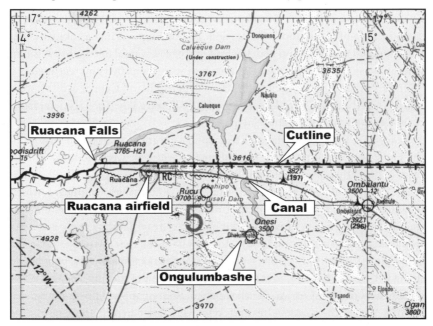

The SWAPO camp at Ongulumbashe was well constructed with a number of protected bunkers. Coincidentally, the final battles of the border war took place in the same area 23 years later.

Then, the seven helicopters spread out and dropped their troops at pre-planned positions. Where there were open spaces the helicopters air-landed their passengers while others descended the ropes. Because Daantjie Beneke's helicopter did not have the V bolt modification he hovered as low as he dared, between the bushes, and motioned to his passengers to abandon ship, by jumping. Fortunately, despite some pretty hard landings they all survived intact. After completing the drop six of the helicopters returned to Ruacana for refuelling.

All hell broke loose in the camp. Despite being fired at Loubsher remained overhead, his attackers being taken out by Swanepoel from the helicopter. Some of the terrorists were dug in in the trenches and, despite offering spirited resistance, they were soon overpowered. They were armed with Tokarev pistols, PPSh-41 sub-machine guns and, believe it or not, bows and arrows. I personally believe that these old-fashioned weapons were used by the terrorists in hunting expeditions, where the noise of gunfire would have attracted unwanted attention from the police.

Left: An early model Soviet Tokarev TT-33 pistol in common use with SWAPO. During the war we also came across later models, Chicom Type 51 and 54 copies, plus Hungarian, Polish and North Korean variants.
Right: An early model Soviet PPSh-41 sub-machine gun. The drum magazine held 71 x 7.62 rounds.

After refuelling, the Ruacana helicopters headed back to the target area—the most difficult part of the entire operation. There are no reference points in that part of Owamboland and all the *shonas* (pans) look alike. At one stage, during a right-hand turn, Daantjie Beneke looked back to see three Alouettes following him, not knowing that he was lost.

After the fire fight was over and the captured terrorists interrogated it was established that some occupants of the camp had escaped. Their dug-outs were outside the dropping circle the Alouettes had used and so it was decided to send four helicopters to search for them. At one stage, Beneke heard Joos Cloete trying to contact the ground forces to inform them he had spotted three terrorists. Beneke, racing to assist him, saw them under a thick clump of trees next to a *shona*. With Cloete giving top cover, Beneke moved away to drop off his passenger. Almost in the hover and just before landing he saw three terrorists, with their PPSh machine guns, firing at his aircraft. The passenger sitting behind Beneke immediately fired back hitting one of the terrorists in the neck, a shot which proved fatal. The other two terrorists managed to escape.

Total casualties in the operation were two terrorists killed, another seriously wounded, who was casevaced to Windhoek, and eight captured. An unknown number escaped or were not present in the camp when the assault took place.

That night, the success of the operation was celebrated around a big fire. The terrorists, under guard, were handcuffed together around the trunk of a large tree. The following morning the six 17 Squadron Alouettes flew back to Rooikop, to be returned to AFB Swartkop by C-130s. The C-130 pilots were Colonel Freeman, Commandant Eloff and Major Tinky Jones; one of the navigators was Gordon Lennox. Daantjie Beneke and Vince van Buuren returned to Eros airfield in Windhoek while Gooks Loubsher, Fred Frayne, Piet Snyman, Joos Cloete, Vossie Vos and John Wesley, the other Alouette pilots, returned to the South Africa.

Others who took part in this first operation were to become legends of the border war—soldiers Jan Breytenbach and Wim 'Kaas' van der Waals, policemen Johan Viktor, Des Weltehagen and Ben Badenhorst, and senior medic Dr Anton Klomp.

8 Squadron goes to war

On 29 July 1967, newly promoted second lieutenants Bart Haupfleisch and André 'Jinx' Botes were having lunch in the officers' mess, AFB Bloemspruit, when they received a message to report to 8 Squadron's Briefing Room at 14h00. They were also requested to inform as many other Harvard pilots as possible. Although 8 Squadron was the SAAF's designated squadron on operational standby the young pilots had no idea what the call-out was about.

Most of the other pilots were either on the base or in Bloemfontein. However, Boesman du Toit and Steyn Venter were at Ellis Park in Johannesburg, watching the rugby test match between France and the Springboks. At 14h00, Major Dizzy Deans, OC 8 Squadron, Captain Thys Branders and Lieutenant Faan Perold and other junior pilots gathered together for the briefing, along with technical and maintenance personnel. The directive stated, that by Sunday evening 8 Squadron was to have eight Harvards at AFB Runtu (the spelling was later changed to Rundu) configured for war, with the national and SAAF insignia removed. A further operational briefing would be carried out at Runtu and, as security was paramount, no word of the flight must be leaked to anyone.

With great excitement preparations for the journey northwards began. Bart Haupfleisch, as squadron navigation officer, had to prepare eight sets of maps for the aircrew involved. The planned route was Bloemfontein–Upington–Keetmanshoop–Windhoek–Grootfontein–Runtu. This task, pasting and cutting the required 54 maps, kept him busy late into Saturday night.

There was insufficient time to re-spray all the Harvards so the maintenance personnel decided to cover just the insignia with grey duco. All the aircraft were loaded with 400 rounds of .303 ammunition and six of them were fitted with two

1966–1974: Provocation evolves into incursion

This Harvard, also without SAAF or national insignia, was on loan to the Portuguese Air Force before it was returned to CFS Dunnottar.

SNEB 37mm rocket pods. The other two aircraft were fitted with two 3" rocket rails.

Boesman du Toit and Steyn Venter returned later that evening. Earlier, officials at Ellis Park had used the loudspeaker system, before the match and again at half-time, requesting them to return to Bloemfontein. However, they decided to watch the whole game, which incidentally the Springboks won. On their return to Bloemspruit they discovered that the preparations for the flight had been finalized. All they had to do was ensure they were ready for a 06h15 take-off the following morning.

Being winter it was still dark as the eight aircraft lifted off from Bloemfontein, crewed by nine pilots and five ground crew. Approaching Upington, at approximately 08h30, the pilots saw a cloud of dust as cars streamed from the town towards the airport. The noise of eight Harvards was sufficient incentive to attract onlookers from the sleepy town. At that time the runway and parking areas were sand. Refuelling was by means of a 'wobble-pump' from 44-gallon drums which the men had to roll to the aircraft. Pushing the aircraft and the drums through the sand proved very difficult. Most of the townsfolk had been on their way to church, dressed in suits and Sunday dresses and hats, when they diverted to the airfield. Many of them wanted to know where the squadron was heading and why the aircraft insignia had been obliterated. They probably received several different answers because the crews had not been briefed on a cover story—a lesson for the future.

Refuelling at Keetmanshoop was even more difficult than at Upington because the sand was softer. Some of the spectators assisted with pushing aircraft and rolling the drums. The squadron members were also better prepared to answer the inevitable questions. Fortunately, both Windhoek (Eros) and Grootfontein had asphalt runways and parking areas which speeded up the refuelling process.

At 19h15, after 8¼ hours flying, the squadron landed at AFB Runtu after a long, tiring day.

Runtu at that time had a white gravel runway. The ops room was a small prefab building and air traffic was controlled via a mobile radio. Two C-130s

AFB Rundu in the early 1970s. It had grown since the Harvard mission in 1967 and the runway and dispersal area had been hardened. However, the 16 x 16 tents were still there in military rows. All border military facilities grew like squatter camps with bits and pieces added on as the need arose.

and four or five Alouette helicopters were in the parking area. A few 16 x 16 tents served as stores, briefing rooms and the like. The helicopter pilots gave the newly arrived pilots a briefing on Runtu and the surrounding area and someone managed to arrange a few most welcome beers. Each man was issued with a *trommel* (Afrikaans for tin trunk but a word used commonly by all personnel) which contained a stretcher, sleeping bag and a few basic necessities. One of these was a *varkpan* (Afrikaans for the military 'pig-trough' eating dish).

Due to the shortage of tents they slept under the stars. A water truck, normally used to water the sand roads, was their designated bathroom, complete with a large zinc bath. Not having eaten since breakfast, at 04h30, they were famished. LAM Pierre Pretorius, in charge of the food, allowed them to eat their fill before they retired to bed. With no electric lights in Runtu the stars were exceedingly bright and they all slept well.

At 11h00 on Monday morning, both the Harvard and helicopter crews were briefed at the police station in Runtu town in the presence of senior police and SAAF officers, including Lieutenant-General Kalfie Martin, then Chief of the SAAF. Intelligence agencies had learned that a number of terrorist leaders were meeting the next morning at Sacatxai, some 80 miles north in Angola. The plan was for the Alouettes to drop the policemen on the outskirts of the huts, where the meeting was to take place, in an effort to capture some of the terrorist leaders. The Harvards were to escort the Alouette force to the target and be available for close air support if required. General Martin and a Bushman tracker would be in the leading Alouette to guide the force to Sacatxai.

At 08h45 on 1 August, five Alouettes and eight Harvards took off and headed north into Angola flying at 300 feet AGL. The Harvard pilots flew as escort for the helicopters but soon had difficulty staying in formation with the slow-flying helicopters. Eventually, the Harvard formation increased speed to make the handling of their loaded aircraft easier, and criss-crossed behind the helicopter formation—another lesson for the future.

Unfortunately, tracking from the air is vastly different from following spoor on the ground. The helicopters dropped the policemen at a circle of huts, which proved to be the wrong destination; they had to be uplifted and flown 15 minutes farther north to the correct target. The noise of the approaching formation was sufficient to ensure that the target was empty by the time the force arrived. The police found documentation which proved the terrorists had in fact been there earlier.

It was decided to destroy the empty huts to prevent their re-use by the enemy. Thys Branders and Faan Perold each blasted a hut with 3" rockets fired in salvo, followed by six Harvards each firing 72 x 37mm rockets, effectively destroying the settlement. Then they headed back to Runtu and the next day started their long flight back to Bloemfontein. By a remarkable coincidence the Harvard flown by Boesman du Toit and Steyn Venter, broke down in Windhoek. The necessary spare part had to be flown up a day or two later from Bloemfontein thus allowing the two pilots, both Southwesters by birth, the opportunity to see their families.

Although the mission had been unsuccessful valuable experience had been gained, thus starting the learning-curve that was to see the SAAF transformed from humble, fledgling beginnings to a highly proficient air force.

As a footnote to this story, I must mention that Faan Perold was later to become known as the scourge of the far northern Transvaal, regarding another 3" rocket sortie. While pulling out of a 30° dive on the Roodewal bombing range, in a Vampire, Perold experienced an inadvertent release and fired a salvo of 3" rockets. They were last seen describing a huge arc into the far distance. The salvo straddled a farmhouse, fortunately, without causing any harm or damage. However, as a result of this incident the farmer was irate and decidedly nervous. It turns out he was the only man in the district who had not voted for the government of the day in the previous general election and thought they were getting at him!

Christmas 1969

On 24 December 1969, Rundu was in crisis. The problem was beer—or the lack of it! Commandant Steve Armstrong, the base OC, was facing a dilemma and the prospect of Christmas without beer was unacceptable. After mulling over the few options available to him he made his decision.

Lieutenant Dave Knoesen, on his first bush tour, was summoned to the OC's office. There he was tasked, like Cecil John Rhodes, to look northwards for the answer. He was to fly his light Cessna-185 to Cuito Cuanavale, and buy beer from the Portuguese. All the seats were removed from the Cessna, except the pilot's, before take-off. After an hour's flight he landed at the Portuguese base to discover that, like Rundu, their logistics convoy had not arrived and they too faced the prospect of a beerless, cheerless Christmas.

Knoesen contacted Rundu by HF radio and was told, "Try Serpa Pinto" (now Menonque). Off he flew deeper into Africa. His luck was in as beer was available. Worried about the carrying capacity of his little aircraft he enquired what a case of beer weighed and was told the answer in kilograms. At that time South Africa was still on the Imperial system of weights and measures. Unfortunately, Knoesen didn't know the conversion factor to pounds, nor did any of the Portuguese soldiers, but they suggested that the fountain of all knowledge was the doctor. After an hour-long search the doctor was located who told them, "Two point two pounds to the kilogram".

Back at the airfield they loaded the aircraft, case after case, side by side, floor to ceiling. The calculated weight was within the operating parameters of the aircraft, but it just didn't look right. Knoesen unloaded ten cases, started up and did a take-off, circuit and landing to check the handling of the aircraft. It was

Lt Dave Knoesen alongside his C-185 dray.

good, so he re-loaded the ten cases and took off with the Cessna at max-all-up-weight. He landed back at AFB Rundu an instant superhero.

Combined operations with the Portuguese

At the request of the Portuguese government and, it must be said, in South Africa's best interest, the SAAF provided aircraft and crews to assist the hard-pressed Portuguese in Angola. Little was known about these operations because the SA government kept a tight rein on the media. Even the fighter fraternity was kept in the dark, although it was our air force helicopter and light transport squadrons involved.

In January 1971, SAAF helicopters and light aircraft operated alongside those of the Portuguese Air Force in Operation *Mexer* against the FNLA and UNITA, in the Cuito Cuanavale region of Angola. In February, it was Operation *Anniversaria*, around Nerequinha and in July, Operation *Dragon*, in the Mavinga region. Interestingly, the twist of fate was to reverse the situation a few years later. South Africa became an ally of UNITA and enlisted the remnants of the FNLA into 32 Battalion.

Photo-reconnaissance and JARIC

At this time, virtually the only available maps of sub-Saharan Africa were Michelin Road maps, completely unsuitable for the detail required in planning operations. The years 1972 to 1974, became the years of intensive photo-reconnaissance (PR) in the SAAF. Canberras of 12 Squadron were used extensively to improve existing coverage of all possible areas of conflict. With the co-operation of the Portuguese

Canberra crews of 12 Squadron in 1975. These men carried out most of the photographic-reconnaissance missions during the developing stages of the border war.
Back L to R: Keith Bailey, Stony Steenkamp, Riem Mouton, J. J. Strydom, Colin Campbell; *centre:* John Somerville, Errol Earp, Brick Steenkamp, Francois Oosthuizen, Daan Badenhorst; *front:* Sakkie Liebenberg, Hans Botha.

they filmed Dar es Salaam and Tanzania. In co-operation with the Rhodesian Air Force they covered the whole of Mozambique, including the Limpopo and Save rivers, where they looked for possible terrorist crossing points. They also overflew southern Zambia from Kariba to the Kwando River. They photographed the Caprivi Strip including Sangombe, Sitoti Ferry in Zambia and Katima Mulilo at the eastern end of the Caprivi and, at the request of the Portuguese in Angola, they operated out of Luanda filming the oil-rich enclave of Cabinda.

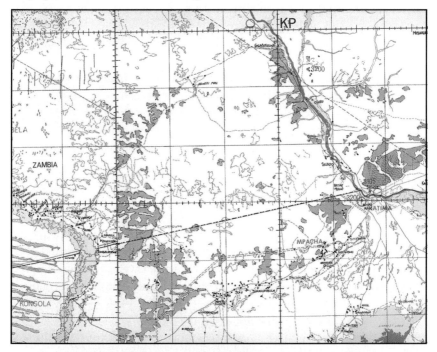

An aeronautical chart, the result of a photographic survey carried out by high-flying Canberras. Throughout the theatre there were few man-made features to ease navigation. Aircrew relied on the shapes of rivers and shonas which were accurately depicted. However, during the 'big rains' of February to April 70 per cent of the surface could be covered by water, making navigation extremely difficult.

The Joint Air Reconnaissance and Intelligence Centre (JARIC), situated at AFB Waterkloof, converted the miles and miles of film into a series of photo maps which were to prove invaluable during the bush war.

The survey flying had to be precise to ensure overlapping strips of film. Good, cloudless skies were prerequisite—conditions not too common in sub-tropical Africa. Each strip of film had to include some outstanding features, such as bends in rivers, to allow the strips to be correctly aligned. In each strip successive photos had to have a 60 per cent overlap to enable stereoscopic interpretation to be performed. The stereoscope gives depth to the images, allowing the photographic interpreter (PI) to see under trees and pick up shadows. Shadows with straight edges in the bush are unnatural. Footpaths and vehicle tracks are indications of human presence, especially when they disappear into areas of thick bush. The survey photography was used as reference material when a suspicious area was found on later photography. By comparison any new developments could be readily identified.

This vertical photo illustrates the adverse effects of clouds. The photographic interpreter (PI) had found a suspected terrorist camp but cloud obscured the main details.

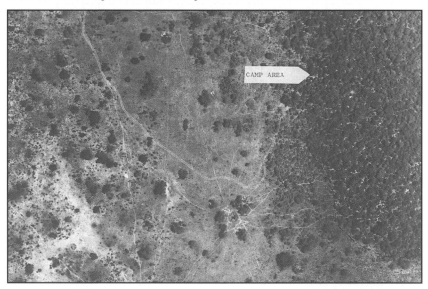

This vertical frame is a PI's dream. Laborious hours are spent examining every frame of film. Suddenly their efforts pay off when they see a frame like this. A waterhole can be identified at the bottom of the photo. Numerous footpaths can clearly be seen disappearing into the thick bush on the upper right-hand side. In addition, a well-used, twin-track vehicle spoor can be seen entering the bush from the top left of the photo—certain indications of an occupied terrorist camp.

All possible aircraft were fitted with PR pods. This close-up of terrorists' one-man shelters was taken by a low-flying Cessna 185, giving wonderful definition.

Casualty evacuation

From the earliest days of the war casualty evacuation (casevac) was always accorded the highest priority by the SAAF. Our aircrew, and the medical staff who accompanied every mercy mission, established a superb reputation and were instrumental in saving many lives. Medical staff determined the priority of each patient using the following guidelines:

- Priority 1: Life-threatening injuries requiring immediate resuscitation
- Priority 2: Injuries requiring resuscitation to maintain the stability of the patient
- Priority 3: Injuries not warranting resuscitation

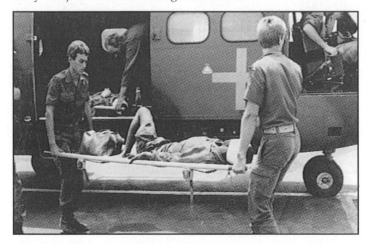

Unfortunately, this was an all-too-common scene at AFB Ondangwa.

The SAAF responded to priority 1 and 2 casualties with equal speed. If an injury occurred during a fire fight the unit involved was responsible for the extraction of the wounded personnel and to initiate the casualty-evacuation plan. Wounded soldiers were initially in the care of the 'ops medic' attached to the unit. Doctors accompanied all helicopters on 'casevac' missions to accept responsibility of the patient from the 'medic'. At AFB Ondangwa, a fully equipped intensive care unit was established to treat the patients straight from the helicopter.

Throughout the war the SA Medical Services (SAMS) were absolutely outstanding; however, I do have one tiny criticism—their choice of décor. In any naval wardroom you will find magnificent pictures of ships; in an air force mess the walls will be covered with breathtaking pictures of aircraft; the SA Army are a bit questionable, with photos of tanks and guns; but the SAMS' choice of pictures in any of their working areas is quite appalling—innards, private parts, colons and decaying teeth seem to adorn every wall.

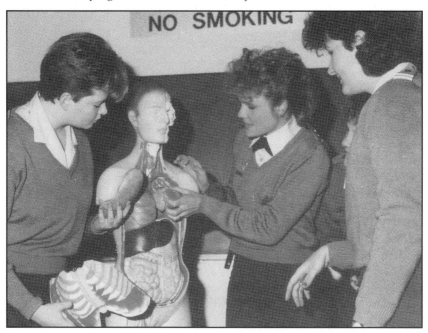

With the South African Medical Services (SAMS) if it was not disturbing pictures it was indecorous sculptures.

Emergency call-outs became a feature of life for the helicopter crews at AFB Ondangwa. On 15 October 1972, Lieutenant Visser and his flight engineer Mike Eksteen were called out to fly their Puma to Opuwa, in the remote vastness of Kaokoland. The patient was a black policeman who had been injured in a triangular domestic argument. The policeman, attacked by the husband of a Himba lady, had an axe imbedded into his skull. The man was still alive and

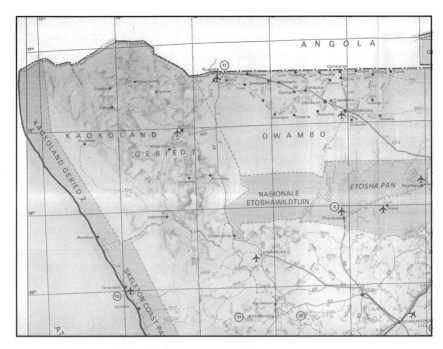

Opuwo, formerly Ohopoho, lies west of Ondangwa in the sparsely inhabited, arid, mountainous Kaokoland. At that time there were no tar roads and the only significant sand road was the one running south from Ruacana and west of Etosha, to Kamanjab.

they flew him back to Oshakati Hospital with the axe firmly in place. Amazingly, the policeman lived. The X-ray showed that the blade had entered the skull exactly between the two lobes of the brain. In the words made famous by Rocky Graziano—'somebody up there must have liked him'.

During 1973, the SAAF once again flew alongside the Portuguese in operations *Zorba*, *Zurzir* and *Zorro*, covering the areas around Lupire, Gago Coutinha and Cuito Cuanavale, in Angola.

Superpower intervention

Unfortunately, as is so often the case, these offensive operations proved to be too little too late, because by now the situation in Angola was ungovernable. Extreme internal pressure inside Mozambique added to the crisis which came to a head in 1974 when Portugal, almost overnight, withdrew from her African possessions. This left a power vacuum in countries with largely uneducated, unskilled populations and, as occurred in the rest of Africa, chaos was the inevitable result.

Like galleons of old, with full sails billowing in the wind, the world's two superpowers entered the fray. Just the slightest hint of an opportunity to gain further influence brought both the USA and USSR straight out of the starting blocks. Neither power was interested in the well-being of the local population; they wanted Angola to become firmly part of their region of influence.

The Portuguese decision in 1974 to return her African colonies to the indigenous people was made in undignified haste. One minute the Portuguese governor was in control of Angola and the next he departed with unseemly speed. In Angola, the resultant vacuum was an African's dream and a frenetic scramble for power ensued. The situation would have been limited to the usual tribal wars, so common throughout Africa, if the locals had been left to their own devices. Unfortunately, both world superpowers saw the chaos as an opportunity to extend their spheres of influence, expanding the conflict to one of international proportions.

The Portuguese departure left a three-way fight for power in Angola. The MPLA, by far the largest group, was centred in Luanda, the capital city, and was communist-inspired and communist-backed. They were opposed by two smaller anti-communist groups, the FNLA, led by Holden Roberto and UNITA, led by Jonas Savimbi.

At this stage, America, in the guise of the ubiquitous CIA, entered the Angolan arena. It appeared that the US State Department considered it would not be in America's best interest to allow the communists to establish a strong presence in mid-Africa. State Department thoughts had very little, if anything, to do with the rights and wishes of the local population. The Cold War was at its peak and its implications were paramount in American thinking. I hasten to add, that while this may seem an indifferent, even arrogant, way of dealing with world problems, it was no different from that used by the European powers a century earlier, as they arbitrarily divided Africa into suitable slices.

CIA operatives, skulking mainly in the Congo, Angola's northern neighbour, aided and abetted both smaller parties, attempting to create a suitable opposition to the more powerful MPLA. On the realization that this would not be possible without substantial outside support, America invited/persuaded/encouraged/tempted (depending on whose history one reads) the South African government to intervene in the Angolan struggle. America's aim was for a South African military force to enter Angola from the south and push towards Luanda. American political pressure via the State Department would then offer aid and assistance to the floundering population to force a negotiated settlement, which would ensure capitalistic domination of Angola.

Of course, this is the stuff dreams are made of and people in the real world are not as naïve as those in the US State Department were on this issue.

Combined operations with the Rhodesians

At this time the SAAF was also active in Rhodesia. Helicopters and their crews operated, initially in police uniform, alongside Rhodesian forces. Mount Darwin

Pupil Pilot Course 1/69.
Back row L to R: Buks Brits, Anton Botes, Glen Williams (CAA), Danie Ferreira, 'Flip' van Zyl (farming), Lewis Botes, Hobart Houghton (Gulf Air), Hans Koning.
3rd row: Kiewiet Marais (43 Flying School), John Ritchie (late), Ben van der Westhuizen (SAP helicopters), Gavin Foxcroft (SAA), Noel Minnaar (SAA), Roy Holland (Swissair), Johan Stroh (SAAF rtd).
2nd row: Howie Cook (SAA), Reg Schickerling, Piet Otto (Game Park helicopters), Rassie Erasmus (SAAF), Frits Pieksma (late), Jannie van der Merwe (insurance), Arthur Bradstreet.
Front: Gary Barron (late) Hojan Cronjé (SAAF rtd), Gerrie Botha (Comair), Piet Roos (SAAF rtd), Herman Viljoen, Rocky Walsh (priest), Mike Pearce (SAA).

is a small town near the Mvuradona Mountains, north of Salisbury (now Harare), about an hour's flight by Alouette. There was a contingent of Rhodesian Light Infantry (RLI) troopers based there with Alouette III helicopters. One or two of these aircraft were configured as 'K-Car' gunships with 20mm cannons and the rest as troopers ('G-Cars') mounted with .303 Browning machine guns on the left-hand side.

Ray 'Hobart' Houghton was based there with three other SAAF lieutenants, Johan 'Hojan' Cronjé, Johan 'Strawdog' Stroh and Lourens 'Rassie' Erasmus. These four had all gained their wings on Pupil Pilot Course 1/69.

At about 10h00 on 14 August 1974, ground troops reported a contact southwest of Mount Darwin, in the Madziwa Tribal Trust Land. After a quick briefing by the army Erasmus, Cronjé and Houghton took off in their troopers behind Flight Lieutenant Dave Thorne of the Rhodesian Air Force, who was flying a gunship.

They arrived at the contact area and, after much circling while talking to the ground forces, Thorne advised them to air-land their troops in an area where the terrorists had been sighted. Houghton, with his flight engineer Sergeant Ray Wernich, went into land in scrub country without much cover for anybody on the ground. The Rhodesian troops' helicopter drills were superb and, as Houghton entered the hover, they were already deploying before his wheels touched the ground.

However, as the helicopter touched down there was a massive explosion and a blast of orange flame just behind the cockpit; the crew were hurled forward. Houghton's first thought was that one of the soldiers had set off a grenade by mistake, but there were no dead troops behind him—just a gaping hole full of orange flame. The crew unstrapped, jumped out and ran at great speed to a shallow ditch about 20 yards in front of them, where they made themselves as small as possible. They were anticipating further explosions as there was the crack of small-arms fire whizzing overhead. With the rotors going full speed the burning helicopter was hopping around looking like a huge Catherine Wheel. On impulse, Wernich ran back to the wreck and turned the fuel off. This was to no avail as the linkages had probably been destroyed. He raced back into the ditch and suddenly everything went quiet as the engine stopped. However, the rotors continued to windmill with flames streaming off their trailing edges.

All that remained of the Alouette III after being struck by an RPG near Mt Darwin. Unbelievably, both crew and passengers escaped alive.

They could see the other helicopters circling overhead but there were no ground troops anywhere in the vicinity. The crew felt very vulnerable because their personal weapons had been lost in the burning wreck. They remained in the ditch for around ten minutes, which felt like an hour. Suddenly, another Alouette, dropped out of the orbit, stood on its tail and came to an ultra-quick stop before touching down. From the cover of the ditch the downed crew made a frantic dash to reach the helicopter, where they were pulled in and flown to Mount Darwin.

Left: Commandant Rassie Erasmus c. 1994.
Right: Captain Ray 'Hobart' Houghton c. 1976

During the return flight the pilot, Erasmus, told them how he had seen their helicopter hit by an RPG fired from a range of about 30 yards. The terrorist responsible had been hiding under a bush as Houghton flared to land his troops. The orange flame was caused by the ignition of the 300lbs of fuel remaining in the Alouette's tank. Combat incidents, as in this case, are often double-edged. The airmen were unlucky to take a hit but extremely fortunate that the RPG had not entered the cockpit further forward.

Houghton was bleeding heavily from wounds to his left shoulder and arm, down to his wrist. Oddly, he was also suffering a great deal of pain from his big left toe. It transpired that a tiny piece of shrapnel had gone through his *veldskoene* (suede bush shoes) and nicked his big toe, damaging all the nerve endings in the process.

At Mount Darwin the doctor set up a drip, then took Houghton's photograph with an instamatic camera (probably to enhance his 'war stories'). Houghton was flown to Salisbury by Flight Lieutenant Clive Ward in a Trog, the Rhodesian nickname for the Trojan light aircraft. By chance, a SAAF C-130 happened to be at the airport. Hobart was loaded aboard and flown back to AFB Waterkloof by

Captain Bill Bowie. An ambulance took him straight to 1 Military Hospital, still dressed in T-shirt and underpants—the rest of his clothing having been removed to allow the doctors to dress his wounds. Being August it was pretty chilly.

A nurse took one look at his dishevelled appearance and the blood seeping from his wrist and asked him why he had tried to commit suicide! The medics then discovered the extent of the injuries to his back and upper arm and a number of offending 'bits and pieces' were removed. By the next day his 'collective' arm (the left one) had turned black and blue. That night he was visited by Brigadier Dennis Earp, followed a short while later by 'Monster' Wilkins and Os de Waal. They came well stocked with bottles—the aviator's panacea for all ills.

Chapter 3

1975–1977: Aftermath of *Savannah*

Portuguese refugees from strife-torn Angola streamed southwards into South West Africa. Their arrival among this isolated population stirred feelings of unease within the territory. As a show of solidarity to the local population and of force to those harbouring anti-government feelings four Buccaneers, from 24 Squadron, flew up to Grootfontein on 15 May 1975. The aim of the deployment was to demonstrate the presence of the SAAF by carrying out low-level flights over the entire territory.

The formation was led by Commandant Dan Zeeman, OC of the squadron. Sandy Allison was the No 2, Gert Havenga with navigator Ken Snowball No 3 and Mathew Morton with Philip Rosseau as No 4. Approaching the airfield they intended to fly in battle formation onto initial, and then break onto a right-hand downwind leg. Unknown to the pilots the tower frequency had been changed from the one they were expecting, so no contact could be made. Closing the airfield at 420 knots Zeeman called the formation 'into box' as they started to turn onto the downwind leg.

Unfortunately, in the turn, Morton's aircraft collided with that of Gert Havenga. Morton's tail-plane broke off and he lost control. Although Morton and Rosseau ejected successfully from their aircraft, Morton was seriously injured and Rosseau damaged an ankle.

The collision removed the Pitot tube from Havenga's aircraft and so he was left without airspeed indication. He requested Dan Zeeman to lead him in close formation down to land. At that time the Grootfontein runway was still very short. Later, after the runway had been considerably lengthened, pilots loved operating from there. However, on this particular day it was still short so landing without airspeed was interesting to say the least. At this time the standard operating procedure (SOP) for this type of emergency was for the lead aircraft to break away just before touch-down, allowing the aircraft without airspeed indications to land on its own. However, Zeeman landed in front of Havenga who, without airspeed readings, landed a 'little hot' for safety's sake in Zeeman's slipstream. In his effort to stop he passed Zeeman's Buccaneer on the runway—this time without a collision.

Morton and Rosseau were stabilized and flown to 1 Military Hospital in a C-160 where they both made a full recovery.

The next few days were spent 'entertaining' the locals, as the three remaining aircraft flew all over the territory at treetop height. They then returned to Waterkloof. Nobody can say that the Buccaneers did not arrive in South West without a BANG. (Perhaps this was the origin of the 24 Squadron slogan: 'Hit the floor, its 24!')

Advance into Angola

In 1975, a small South African military force entered Angola on Operation *Savannah*. As requested by the Americans they advanced northwards until virtually in sight of Luanda. However, at this stage the 'ideal American solution' encountered problems. The Soviets did not take too kindly to what they saw happening in South West Africa and dramatically increased military matériel shipments to the MPLA. Soviet advisors arrived to 'professionalize' the Angolan armed forces and surrogate Cuban troops were rushed to the area.

The US had recently been forced out of Vietnam with a bloody nose and a decision was made in Washington that, in the interest of the Cold War, America would not become embroiled in Africa. The CIA operators and advisors, with their promises of aid, surreptitiously disappeared from the theatre overnight. At the same time, in the United Nations, the American political finger of accusation for all Africa's ills was pointed firmly at the 'invading' South Africans.

During *Savannah* the SAAF had two aircraft shot down. The first was on 25 November, when a Cessna-185, flown by Second Lieutenant K. Williamson, failed to return from a reconnaissance flight. Two days later an enemy radio message was intercepted in which they reported that the aircraft had been shot down north of Ebo. Williamson, Second Lieutenant Thompson and Captain Taljaard of the South African Army were all killed. To date (2008), despite many efforts, the remains of the three men still have not been returned to South Africa.

The other aircraft lost was a Puma flown by Captain John Millbank, co-pilot Chris Hartzenberg and Flight Sergeant Piet O'Neill du Toit. It was hit by Cuban AAA fire from a hillside 18 kilometres northwest of Cela. The pilots completed a successful forced landing less than three kilometres from the anti-aircraft site. For the following 22 hours they successfully evaded capture, before returning to safety.

Of course, this is a simplified version of the many secret meetings and political wrangling which took place around that time. In effect, this is precisely what happened—South Africa was vilified, political and arms embargoes were strengthened and the country was almost completely isolated from its traditional trading partners and allies.

The SADF had been ill-prepared for a military venture on this scale. The army, equipped with world-war-vintage 5.5" artillery, Unimog and Land Rover vehicles to transport troops and supplies and Panhard armoured cars, had achieved remarkable success. They were in sight of Luanda when America withdrew their promised support. The long withdrawal was fraught with danger because they were faced by superior numbers of Angolans and Cubans using Soviet D-30 artillery and BM-21 rocket-launchers that greatly outranged the South African guns.

The 4,000-kilometre trek to Luanda and back, under extreme conditions, was a military epic of courage and daring. However, it highlighted the shortcomings of our military preparedness for the type of fighting which was surely to come. The SAAF had not been able to provide offensive support to the ground forces—the distances involved were just too great. A Canberra bombing sortie was flown to support Holden's Roberto FNLA troops at the Bengo River. The medium-level bombing was ineffective and the FNLA attack fizzled out against superior MPLA and Cuban forces.

C-185 light aircraft were used in the light communications role and for reconnaissance purposes. Puma helicopters were used for battlefield support. Apart from the Cessna and Puma lost to enemy action a second Puma was lost in a tragic accident in which captains F. Immelmann and C. D. de Wit, and Sergeant G. W. Kellett were killed. A SAAF Wasp helicopter was used to extricate 26 SADF personnel from the beach at Ambrizete on 28 November 1975, to SAS *President Steyn*.

The one area where the SAAF played a major role was in air transport and resupply. C-130 and C-160 aircraft from 28 Squadron shuttled in and out of Angolan airstrips carrying personnel, ammunition, rations and casevacs. At one stage the huge aircraft were operating out of Cela airfield on a round-the-clock service. One crew was reported to have flown 100 hours in 12 days—way beyond the legal limit.

The Puma accident exposed the severe limitations of SADF command and control structures and communications. Overall, *Savannah* emphasized that courage and daring had to be supported by the correct organizational structures and superior equipment.

Building of an arms industry

In South Africa, the Afrikaners, with their long history of struggle against British

1975–1977: Aftermath of *Savannah*

imperialism had developed into a resourceful people. Whenever a seemingly insoluble problem arises there is a wonderful saying they use—*'n Boer maak 'n plan*, literally, a farmer makes a plan. By 1975, South Africa had been virtually cut off from the rest of the western world and it was at this crucial stage in its history that survival brought this wonderful characteristic to the fore.

Initially, South Africa created an armament industry to fill the gap left by traditional arms suppliers. Eventually, this burgeoning giant was to produce first-class armoured and mine-protected fighting vehicles to protect the lives of the young men sent to do battle in the remote areas of SWA and Angola. During the push towards Luanda, in Operation *Savannah*, South African forces were outgunned by Soviet-supplied D-30 artillery and BM-21 rocket launchers, known on the battlefield as 'Stalin's Organ'—from the peculiar sound it makes as the rockets fire. This deficiency was rectified by the development and quantity production of the long-range 155mm towed G-5 and self-propelled G-6 gun-howitzers.

The 122mm BM-21 multiple rocket launcher firing one of its 40 rockets. Each 78kg rocket has an effective range out to 20,500 metres. One of these units was captured intact during Operation *Savannah* and this was used to guide the designers of the South African 127mm system, known as Valkiri.

The draught G5 howitzer, possibly the best of its class in the world at the time.

The self-propelled G6 howitzer—the 'Rolls-Royce' of artillery pieces.

Self-protection devices for aircraft, unobtainable from western sources, were designed, developed and manufactured in South Africa. Of course, being designed from scratch, this equipment was extremely costly and took a long time to develop—some of the much-needed chaff and flare dispensers only becoming available at squadron level as the war was coming to an end. However, the *Boere* had made a plan and expanded South African armaments industry and capability to levels undreamed of before the war.

In addition to the fledgling arms industry South Africa set about making new friends among other 'pariah' states. Alliances, co-operation and trade agreements were formed, usually clandestinely, which benefited all partners. Taiwan, Chile and Israel stand out, among many others, as the nations most concerned with their own security. Therefore, it is not remarkable that the Cheetah, a South African conversion of the Mirage III aircraft, looks very like an Israeli Kfir.

Single-seat Cheetah E with canards and in-flight refuelling probe.

Cheetah Squadron

Twenty-three years after the cessation of the Korean War, 2 Squadron, the famed Cheetah Squadron of that conflict, was called on to fly their first operational mission of the border war. Intelligence reports on Angolan defence deployments were received at 301 FACP at AFB Grootfontein. The commander, Colonel Dan Zeeman, was granted authority for three cross-border PR missions and 2 Squadron was tasked to complete the job.

On 14 May 1976, Commandant Ollie Holmes led a formation of four Mirage IIIs on the ferry flight from AFB Waterkloof, via a refuelling stop at AFB Grootfontein, to AFB Ondangwa from where the operational flights would be flown. On the ferry flight, just after the Point of No Return (PNR), the belly-tank on Holmes's aircraft failed to feed. A most uncomfortable situation as the formation was almost in the centre of Botswana. Holmes punched off the under-wing tanks and started cruise climbing to gain maximum distance from the fuel he still had aboard. Pilots who have flown the Mirage III know that on every flight fuel is a critical commodity. He called for a precautionary landing at Grootfontein, which he executed safely. On refuelling for the next leg of the ferry, it was established that Holmes had landed with only 20 gallons of fuel remaining—a very close call indeed.

Fuel emergencies were not uncommon in the Mirage III aircraft and, during normal training flights, Bertus Burger, Spyker Jacobs and Roelf Beukes all had similar close calls. Fuel or the shortage thereof was probably the only major criticism of an otherwise very fine fighter.

Once at AFB Ondangwa the pilots carried out route planning for the three reconnaissance missions they were tasked to fly. Because MiG-21 activity was normal in the area they were to cover, it was decided that Holmes and Major Barry Moody would fly as escort for the photographic Mirage III R2Z to be flown by either majors Steve Ferreira or Skillie Hartogh.

They were tasked to cover the east-to-west route from Menonque, Kuchi, Kuvango, Matala, Lubango and Namibe, with a third of the long route being covered in each mission. The first sortie was flown on 16 May and the second two on 17 May.

During the second flight Barry Moody flew a Mirage R2Z aircraft in the escort position. These aircraft were newer models than the Mirage III CZs and were fitted with a radar warning receiver. Overhead one of the targets Moody picked up a 'locked-on' radar signal, which triggered some frantic manoeuvring by the escorts, while the unarmed R2Z flew at high speed out of the area. It turned out the warning was a spurious signal but it was many minutes before the pilots' breathing rate returned to normal.

After the final mission the aircraft landed at AFB Grootfontein where they spent the night, before returning to AFB Waterkloof on 18 May. The overall photographic results were very good and confirmed the intelligence inputs. Angola had received and deployed an entire series of SA-2 and SA-3 fixed missile sites and the question raised was 'Why?'

Two months later 2 Squadron flew their next PR mission, this time into Mozambique. The target was a place called Surgue, on the borders of Mozambique and Rhodesia. Once again the R2Z PR aircraft was escorted by Mirage III CZs. In fact, this was to become the normal practice throughout the conflict.

Around 1973, the decision had been made to establish a fully fledged PR unit within 2 Squadron, which worked in close co-operation with JARIC. This was to be one of the joint operations which paid off most handsomely in the entire war. Recognition must be given to the groundwork laid by the initial group namely, Major Blackie Swart OC JARIC, and recce pilots, Otto Schür, Steve Ferreira, Eric Schmulian and Skillie Hartogh.

Zambia

On 22 February 1977, an Alouette operating out of AFB Mpacha was struck by small-arms fire as it overflew a SWAPO detachment operating in Zambia. A bullet entered the floor of the aircraft and passed through the bottom of the pilot's seat. The pilot, although seriously injured, made a successful forced landing. Although Sergeant 'Flip' Pretorius, the flight engineer, ran off immediately for assistance Lieutenant Liddell succumbed to his wound before help arrived.

Close shave

During October, 32 Battalion and elements of the Reconnaissance Commandos were busy with Operation *Kropduif* when, on 28 October, they encountered stiff opposition from SWAPO cadres near Eheke. The fighting was fierce and both sides suffered heavy casualties. 32 Battalion and Special Forces recorded nine dead and four wounded; they radioed for helicopter support to lift out the their dead and wounded comrades.

Three helicopters approached the battle area; Gordon Roberts flying an Alouette and 'Muis' Pretorius and 'Hug' Paine flying two Pumas. As they approached Shona Oihapete, just southwest of the battle taking place around Shona Onalomona, Muis radioed 'Echo Victor' (famous call sign of then Major Eddie Viljoen) saying that he had the troops visual in trenches on the eastern side of the *shona*, and began circling prior to landing.

'Echo Victor', who was with his troops four kilometres away on the western side of the *shona*, yelled at him to "get the hell out of the area fast, because there are no Three Two troops on the eastern side". The helicopter formation turned west in a hurry, found the correct LZ, landed and evacuated the casualties as required.

Recently, Eddie Viljoen who now lives in Namibia had an interesting discussion

1975–1977: Aftermath of *Savannah*

Three fine army officers. *L to R:* Colonel MacGill Alexander (44 Parachute Brigade), Colonel Eddie Viljoen (32 Battalion) and Colonel Doug Wellington (Signals).

about the bush war with General Charles Namolo (known as 'Ho Chi Min' during the war), now Namibia's Minister of Defence and General Shalli, Chief of the Namibian Defence Force.

At the height of the battle Namolo was in command and Shalli was in charge of the battery of four 14.5mm anti-aircraft guns, sited in the trenches where the SAAF helicopters were about to land. When Shalli saw the three helicopters on approach he ordered his gunners to hold their fire until the helicopters had all landed. He intended to destroy them and hopefully take prisoners. He was disgusted when the three helicopters dropped below the tree line and disappeared to the west. Namolo was even angrier—the fortunes of war!

Left: Colonel Eddie Viljoen (Echo Victor) facing and Colonel Deon Ferreira (Falcon) on the river at Buffalo, the 32 Battalion base.
Right: Major Anton Kriegler and Brigadier Gert Nel. These army officers commanded 32 Battalion with distinction.

Oshakati border tour

My first 'border tour' lasted three months, which is quite a long time to be separated from one's family and away from one's current posting. However, it is insufficient time in which to assimilate all the nuances of a hostile insurgency. I felt I was just getting to grips with the war environment when it was time for another 'new boy' to replace me. This approach to running a low-intensity war was inefficient. To a large degree the American's utilized the same method in their Vietnam débâcle. Every 12 months the troops would be rotated so, instead of fighting one 12-year war, in effect they fought 12 one-year wars, with each new intake making the same mistakes as their predecessors and only reaching true fighting efficiency just before returning to the USA.

Very shortly after taking up my appointment Captain 'Lappies' Labuschagne, my operations officer, presented me with my first problem. In the services all Labuschagnes are known as 'Lappies,' therefore, each is given a prefix so people understand which Labuschagne is being referred to, such as 'Black' or 'Lang.' In this case it was '24 Lappies', a Buccaneer pilot from 24 Squadron.

An army patrol urgently required a helicopter to airlift a section member to hospital and we immediately tasked a Puma to fly to the scene. Casevacs were daily occurrences during the war and always received top priority. I considered it important to receive feedback on patients in order to inform the aircrews who had carried out the various flights.

At the order group the next morning I asked the doctor about the condition of this particular casevac. He told us that just about everything that could have been broken in the soldier's body had been broken. The good news was that, being young and fit, the patient would recover fully after a lengthy period of rehabilitation. The doctor then explained exactly how the injuries had been inflicted.

The youngster was only nineteen years old. He had started his national service straight from school and, like me, was on his first bush tour. He was a city boy, raised in the bright lights of Johannesburg. Being in the PBI ('poor bloody infantry') his introduction to the war was as a member of a ten-man section assigned the laborious task of patrolling a designated area of the border. The novelty of being in the bush, similar to the anxiety associated with a first live patrol, soon palled as they trudged kilometre after kilometre through the sand and heat, to be replaced by the fatigue only foot soldiers really understand.

Silence is a prerequisite for a patrol. No metallic clinking or other noises are permitted. The enemy must not be forewarned—surprise being a principle of war. Towards noon the sun's heat was nearing its maximum, exacting its toll on the stamina of the soldiers. Walking quietly in a tactical-spread formation, they entered an area of thick bush looking for a place under the shade of the trees where they could take a much-needed rest.

'Sol' or 'Spike,' as the sun was referred to by the troops, also sapped the energy of wild animals and they too sought refuge from the burning rays. With the same thought in mind as the soldiers a lone elephant had found an ideal spot in the shade of a *kameeldoring* tree and gone to sleep. Unlike humans elephants sleep standing upright, only the slightest to-and-fro sway of their enormous bodies indicating their state of repose.

Approaching soundlessly, the soldiers discovered the elephant had obtained first choice of the available shade. Not wanting to awaken the slumbering behemoth the patrol leader made signs for his men to withdraw, which they duly did. Once out of audible range the soldiers discussed their discovery. They knew that no enemy could be in the vicinity and they could relax for a while. During their break our 'casevac' produced an automatic camera from his rucksack. Cameras were forbidden in the operational area, for security reasons, but our city boy wanted to record his experiences for posterity.

He decided he wanted a photograph of the pachyderm but desperately wanted to be included in the picture. Mother and the girlfriend were bound to be impressed. He asked one of his buddies to hold the camera and, not wanting to awaken the elephant, asked him to take the picture only when he mouthed the word 'now'.

Approaching from the rear he crept towards the creature, ensuring he remained downwind. The midday heat is intense in those latitudes and Jumbo was sound asleep. Excitement among the rest of the soldiers was reaching fever pitch as our boy moved closer and closer. He reached a position that was, in the eyes of the rest of the section, much too close for comfort, or safety; they were unable to shout a warning for fear of disturbing the animal.

The excitement and success of his stalk aroused the daring spirit of our boy. To the dismay and horror of the rest of his section, while turning round to pose, he lifted the elephant's tail and silently articulated the word 'now'. I agree it would probably have made a wonderful snapshot, but I wasn't there. However, the elephant was and disagreed with the whole silly idea; he awoke immediately his tail was lifted. Presumably, this very rare occurrence has that effect on wild animals.

The elation of the moment was spoilt by the spiteful reaction of the elephant; it proceeded to extract revenge on the would-be model. The rest of the soldiers, firing into the air, chased the animal back into the bush but not before the beast had broken "just about everything that could be broken".

I can report, with relief that not only was my first 'casevac' successful but the doctor's prognosis of a "full recovery" was correct.

1 Squadron—'The Billy Boys'
I returned to my position as Commanding Officer of the Advanced Fighter School,

at AFB Pietersburg, with the realization that before very long fighter presence on the border would be required. In August 1980, I was pleasantly surprised to be given command of 1 Squadron SAAF, flying Mirage F1AZ ground-attack fighter-bombers. Surprised, because at 44 years of age I suspected my fighter flying days had come to an end. As it turned out I was extremely fortunate; my arrival at 1 Squadron coincided with the expected escalation in the border war. From then on we were utilized in all the major cross-border operations.

During my tenure at the helm, 1 Squadron deployed on nine occasions to either AFB Grootfontein or AFB Ondangwa. The shortest deployment was

1 Squadron members, obviously pleased with the interception of the defecting Mozambique Air Force MiG-15 flown by Lieutenant Bomba.
L to R: Frans Coetzee, Paddy Carolan, Frans Pretorius, Alan Knott-Craig, Dick Lord, Hennie Louw, Frik Viljoen, Jan Henning, Billy Collier, Norman Minne, Chris Venter, Dirk de Villiers, Budgie Burger; *front:* Theo Nell.

four days, during which we flew six ground-attack missions, while the longest lasted six weeks. At this time, 1980 to 1982, we flew virtually unopposed by enemy fighters. However, the targets we struck were well defended by AAA and heat-seeking surface-to-air missiles, all of which had been manufactured and supplied by the Soviets. On a personal level, it is hard not to become antagonistic towards a political system which actively encourages surrogates to attempt to kill you.

The SAAF was involved in the conflict during its entire duration. However, apart from some sporadic missions flown by Canberra crews, the jet fighter force

1975–1977: Aftermath of *Savannah*

Left: A distinctive 1 Squadron formation.
Right: Flaming hole!—the reason jet pilots in the SAAF are known as 'Vlammies'.

only entered the fray permanently during the last decade of the war, namely 1978 to 1988.

Prior to the jet deployment the ground forces had been supported by light tactical and reconnaissance aircraft (Bosbok, Cessna-185 and Kudu), and the transport fleet (Dakota, C-160 Transall and C-130 Hercules).

SAAF helicopters (Alouette, Puma and Frelon) supplied offensive support to both the army and police.

The early years of the war were characterized by the low-intensity incursion activities by SWAPO from Angola—their aim was to destabilize the situation in

While the helicopter crews fought the war, the fighter pilots pranced around in tutus.
L to R: Steyn Venter, Graham Rochat, Willem Hechter, Zach Repsold, Pete Vivier.

From Fledgling to Eagle

1. Cessna-185.
2. Kudu.
3. Bosbok.
4. DC-3 Dakota.
5. C-160 Transall.
6. C-130 Hercules.
The border conflict ensured that all our aircraft ended up in camouflage livery.

SWA. They endeavoured to avoid contact with the South African security forces preferring to plant vehicle and anti-personnel mines, sabotage telephone and electrical pylons, intimidate the local population by murdering local headmen and by abducting school children back into Angola as 'recruits', to swell their ranks.

During this period Canberra aircraft were employed extensively in PR flights over Angola and the entire African subcontinent. This mammoth task required hundreds of hours of precision flying which had the beneficial effect of honing the skills of the aircrew. During Operation *Savannah*, South Africa's move into Angola during 1975, the Canberras were also used in bombing missions.

1975–1977: Aftermath of *Savannah*

1. Alouette III. This helicopter was used as battlefield transport for up to six people. For command and control of the battle from the air it was adopted as a gunship and in this role became the most successful aircraft in the war against SWAPO.
2. The Puma was the undoubted workhorse of the aerial fleet. It was used to transport passengers, casevacs, Fireforce troops and in the supporting role it carried ammunition, rations, fuel and vehicle spares.
3. The Frelon had the largest lifting capacity. However, it was not suited to the hot, high and dusty conditions of the battle theatre and was soon withdrawn.

War preparation for the jet-fighter force

In 1974, recognizing that sooner or later the jet force would be required in earnest the SAAF set up 85 Advanced Flying School at AFB Pietersburg. The school consisted of three flights:

Impala Flight: equipped with 27 Impala Mk I and Mk II; where students were given sufficient instruction in combat flying and basic weaponry skills to qualify them to fly as wingmen on operational missions.

Sabre Flight: equipped with 16 Sabres; where selected students from the frontline Impala squadrons were given advanced weaponry and combat training. They qualified as section leaders and eventually could graduate to formation or flight leaders. At this stage of training, navigation, especially at low level, was a high priority.

Mirage Flight: equipped with 30 Mirage III dual- and single-seat fighters; where experienced Impala pilots received conversion training onto the Mirage III fast jet. In addition, they were taught ground-attack and air-fighting techniques. Pilots who qualified on this course were then posted to Mirage III, Mirage F1, Canberra or Buccaneer squadrons.

SAAF fighter pilots used to rotate every two years or so between their frontline squadrons and the school where their progress and skill levels were continually assessed. The result of this magnificent training scheme was that the SAAF's operational pilots who flew in the bush war were of the very highest calibre.

1. The school had dual- and single-seat Impala aircraft.
2. The Sabres were later camouflaged.
3. Mirage III single- and dual-seat aircraft equipped the Mirage flight.

Political developments and aircraft deployments

Developments in the border war during late 1977 instilled a new sense of urgency into the situation and a decision, taken at President John Vorster's holiday home during December 1977, had a galvanizing effect on the Defence Force. It was decided that purely defensive tactics could not stop terrorist incursions into SWA from Angola; there were not sufficient men available to effectively patrol the extensive border between the two countries. Pre-emptive attacks against SWAPO concentrations were deemed to be a more cost-effective method of protecting sovereignty. Cross-border raids required protective air cover—a further step up the escalation ladder.

In an effort to provide a rapid response to the increasing contact situations occurring in the bush between SWAPO and security force ground patrols, a small force of six single-seat Impala light jet strike-fighters was deployed to AFB Ondangwa in 1978. The air and ground crews manning these aircraft were selected from members of Impala squadrons based in South Africa, on a tour basis. This tour system allowed most of the aircrew to experience the rigours of

1975–1977: Aftermath of *Savannah*

bush flying and helped to build a wealth of bush experience.

Jet maintenance is a sophisticated procedure requiring specialized equipment and a dust-free environment. At all SAAF fighter bases in South Africa well-equipped hangars were set aside for proper maintenance. Inadequate facilities at the dusty forward bases in SWA were not conducive to long-term deployments of sophisticated jet fighters. This requirement was one of the main reasons why the Mirage, Canberra and Buccaneer fleets were never permanently deployed to the border area and why two-week deployments away from their main support bases were considered maximum for these jets. In the event, there were often occasions when much longer deployments were operationally necessary. These were managed, but the aircraft were generally in a relatively poor state when

A formation of Impala MkII fighters joins the AFB Mpacha circuit at low level.

they returned to their home base.

As a compromise, the relatively unsophisticated Impala was selected to provide the permanent jet presence on the border. Later, a further five Impalas were allocated to AFB Mpacha and the number at AFB Ondangwa was increased to eight. As the Mpacha aircraft were seldom required for operational use in that area they were often redeployed to AFB Ondangwa and AFB Rundu when serious fighting was taking place.

The main Ondangwa to Oshakati road runs fairly close to the runway at AFB Ondangwa, making the aircraft a viable target for anyone with evil intent. An earthen wall was scraped along the entire airfield boundary with this road to prevent AK-47 pot-shots being taken against the parked aircraft. In addition, large revetments were erected at the take-off end of the runway to give added protection and a quick scramble path onto the runway. These structures were covered with netting as a precaution against mortar or Katyusha rocket fire. The introduction of a permanent jet presence on the border was, without doubt, an escalation factor in the nature of the war.

Chapter 4

1978: Cassinga

There were strong indications that the inhabitants of the SWAPO camp close to Chetaquera, only 25 kilometres north of the cut-line, were actively pursuing an aggressive programme of incursions into Owamboland. In response, during April 1978, Operation *Bruilof* was planned as a cross-border raid by ground forces, to attack and destroy the base. At a late stage of the planning and preparation another active SWAPO camp was identified at Cassinga, nearly 250 kilometres inside Angola. A decision was made to cancel *Bruilof* and replace it with *Reindeer*, both bases to be attacked simultaneously in early May.

Reindeer
Chetaquera would be attacked by ground forces following a preliminary air strike by Buccaneers and Mirage IIIs. However, Cassinga presented a far more involved problem. The distance precluded the use of a mechanized ground force; the bush telegraph would ensure SWAPO cadres would be long gone before the invading force could reach it. It was decided to use the element of surprise and assault the camp from the air followed by an airborne landing of paratroops.

The air force was involved right from inception of the plan. Canberras and Buccaneers would perform the air attacks and C-130 and C-160 aircraft from 28 Squadron would drop the troops. Practice drops were carried out at the Roodewal bombing range, north of Pietersburg; I took the opportunity to fly in the back of a C-130 to experience a drop from the air and what an experience it was.

Most of the paratroopers were civilian members of the reserve force. These men had been called up from their office desks, fitted with parachutes and vast amounts of ammunition and then loaded into the huge transport aircraft. Because their equipment was so heavy many of them needed assistance to clamber up the

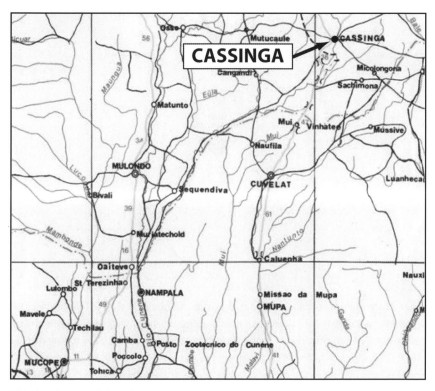

This dated map still uses the old names for Ongiva and Xangongo, however, it gives a clear indication of the great distance between Chetequera and Cassinga—the reason for using an airborne assault on Cassinga.

inclined ramp into the aircraft. I battled to lift some of the packs these men had to carry into action. When the ramp closed, prior to take-off, it was possible to feel and smell the tension in the crowded aircraft. Under tightly strapped-on helmets eyes were large and wide with apprehension. The men sat on the canvas seats, each one holding a mound of equipment on his lap which consisted of a normal and an emergency parachute, a personal weapon and ammunition, a mortar tube, mortar bombs or a radio. Under this pile of equipment their body temperatures soared and they emitted the distinctive odour that all combat troops recognize—the peculiar mix of perspiration and nerves.

The long taxi around the airfield perimeter also increased their visible anxiety and nervousness. However, the moment the pilot released the brakes and started his take-off roll the atmosphere inside the back of the aircraft changed like magic. The men started to clap in unison and chant: "ONE, TWO … ONE, TWO, THREE … ONE, TWO, THREE, FOUR … LET'S GO!" The chant grew louder and the tempo increased until the aircraft wheels finally left the ground. Looking from face to face I was amazed to see apprehension replaced by determination, focus and pride in belonging to the airborne elite.

1978: Cassinga

The flight from AFB Pietersburg to the drop zone (DZ) only took a few minutes. Orders were shouted and all the paratroopers stood, enabling each of them to check the condition of the parachute of the man ahead. On a following command the men hooked up their static lines to the overhead cable running down the length of the aircraft's cabin; side-doors were opened and, at the order 'Stand in the door!' they all used a one-two, one-two shuffle, to move up into close line astern of the first jumper standing in the doorway.

If magic had occurred at the commencement of the take-off roll I was now to witness a miracle. As the jump light turned green the dispatcher started shouting "Go, go, go" and within the blink of an eye the two long lines of heavily laden men had disappeared and the overloaded cabin was suddenly completely empty. The only hint of the paratroopers' presence was the long static lines hanging out of both the back doors. These were retrieved by the dispatcher, the doors closed and the aircraft returned to Pietersburg. I had experienced one of the most memorable events of my life. It takes courage to leap into the unknown burdened with an enormous amount of heavy equipment.

Left: Paratroopers jumping from the side doors of a C-160 Transall.
Right: Paratroopers ready to pick up their parachutes on a training jump. In combat, their packs were twice the size.

A day later I accompanied commandants Jan Breytenbach and Monty Brett to the Roodewal range to watch another practice jump, this time from the ground. I watched in awe as bodies tumbled out of the low-flying transport aircraft. Suddenly, someone in the watching group gave a shout and pointed at a falling paratrooper whose parachute had not opened properly and was descending at a much higher rate than the others. Radioing for the ambulance I joined the people who were now running to the scene.

Breathlessly we reached the DZ, to find the paratroopers neatly falling in as if on a parade ground. In answer to the question, "Where is the man whose 'chute failed to open properly?" a man in the back rank put up his hand. He explained that when he realized his parachute had candled he shouted out. One of the other men, falling at a normal rate, caught him, wrapped his legs around him and stayed like that until they hit the ground. If the question had not been asked it would have been 'just another day at the office' for these tough customers. I am full of admiration for those who wear the maroon beret of the paratroopers.

Training and planning went ahead and 4 May 1978 was chosen for the assault. A week before the attack Commandant Ollie Holmes, commander of 2 Squadron at AFB Waterkloof, was summoned to SAAF Headquarters. The latest intelligence warned that Angolan MiGs were very active in the Cassinga area. The planners decided to deploy Mirage III fighters as top cover for the transport aircraft during the para-drop and for the helicopters during the subsequent extraction of the soldiers from Angola. A secondary task was for offensive support of the ground troops, if required. For the operation Holmes's formation was assigned the aptly chosen call sign 'Sanlam' (a South African life insurance company), because they were the operation's insurance policy.

The first obstacle facing Commandant Holmes was one of air transportation for his ground crew and equipment to AFB Ondangwa. The entire C-130/C-160 fleet was required for the para-drop. All Holmes was offered was a Dakota returning to Pretoria from the border. This restricted 2 Squadron to sending only 12 maintenance personnel to service the Mirage IIIs. Under normal circumstances one Mirage takes seven qualified personnel to prepare it for the next flight. In this case, the 12 men would have to handle the four fighters being flown to Ondangwa.

The Dakota pilot landed at Pretoria after a long, six-hour flight from SWA expecting a restful night. Holmes was very impressed by the pilot's reaction when informed of the operation. The pilot calmly accepted the situation, had a meal, made a few apologetic phone calls and once the aircraft was loaded took off for the operational area—another six-hour flight, this time at night.

The four-ship formation took-off from AFB Waterkloof at 15h00 on 3 May. Major Gerrie Radloff was the deputy leader and the wingmen were captains Norman Bruton and John Orr, all good experienced aviators. A few months earlier, realizing their entry into the war was fast approaching, 2 Squadron had embarked on an intensive training programme. They had concentrated on air combat manoeuvring (ACM) and the new high-dive weapon-delivery profile. The four pilots were anxious to test their newly developed skills in actual combat. As planned, they landed at last light to give minimum time for the 'bush telegraph' to alert SWAPO of their presence.

At 07h45 the following morning, Holmes and Radloff took off for Cassinga where they arrived just in time to witness the combined Canberra and Buccaneer air strike. Immediately thereafter, they sighted the transport aircraft approaching from the north and positioned themselves to give top cover as planned. Remaining overhead Cassinga they watched as the ground battle developed. At one stage they were asked, by a Forward Air Controller (FAC), to give supporting fire against an enemy position that was delivering heavy fire on the advancing troops. Unfortunately, poor radio communications hindered the pilots in pinpointing the required target; Holmes was loath to open fire in an area where our own troops were fighting. Fortunately, the troops overcame the resistance and Mirage support was not required. When the aircraft reached minimum fuel the two Mirages returned to debrief at AFB Ondangwa. Meanwhile, captains Bruton and Orr had attacked the targets at Chetequera, the other phase of the *Reindeer* plan.

At 08h00, four Canberras dropped anti-personnel Alpha bombs and Buccaneers 1,000lb bombs to soften up the heavily fortified SWAPO stronghold at Cassinga. Within minutes more than 250 paratroopers were air-dropped from C-130 and C-160 transport aircraft in a pattern that surrounded the target.

There can be nothing more frightening than the shadow of a Canberra passing overhead at 300 feet AGL during wartime.

After hours of fighting the Parabats were extracted by a large force of helicopters, mainly from 19 Squadron, that had been flown into a pre-determined helicopter administration area (HAA). Nobody in the operational theatre referred to the helicopter area as anything other than a HAG, from the Afrikaans term *helikopter administrasie gebied*.

This evacuation was threatened by Angolan armoured fighting vehicles approaching from Tetchamutete and a flash call went out for fighter assistance. Mirage IIIs, piloted by Holmes and Radloff, were scrambled to attack these enemy vehicles. After a high speed dash they arrived to find an armoured convoy approaching Cassinga from the south and the leading vehicles were only a few kilometres from the town. Holmes led the pair straight into a high-angle strafing attack on the leading elements of the convoy. In the dive he noticed that three vehicles had already passed a bend in the road and were passing out of his line of sight. As his wingman was farther back Holmes asked him to attack these three vehicles which Radloff did, with accuracy and great effect.

On their second attack Holmes noticed most of the vehicles had turned off the road onto the verges. He scored heavily on a loaded troop carrier. After the second attack the pair of Mirages orbited the scene confirming that the convoy had suffered severe damage and had been brought to a stop. After ten minutes another troop carrier was seen approaching which they immediately attacked and destroyed. Approaching bingo fuel state they left the area as a Buccaneer arrived to take over air support duties.

After the Mirages had left pandemonium broke out on the ground—an unseen tank suddenly put in an appearance, close to the helicopter force waiting on the ground. This tank was attacked again and again by Dries Marais flying a Buccaneer. Even when his ammunition had been expended Marais still buzzed the tank at very low level. For this deed he was subsequently awarded the Honoris Crux. When captains Bruton and Orr arrived to patrol the scene all action had ceased.

The paratroopers suffered three dead and eleven wounded. SWAPO lost over 1,000 members. Puma pilot John Church was awarded the Honoris Crux for his actions under fire ensuring that all the paratroopers were recovered.

Left: This frame was taken from the gun-camera film of a 2 Squadron Mirage III attacking the armoured column sent to assist the defenders of Cassinga. The pilot was Commandant Ollie Holmes, the squadron commander. Notice the vehicles below his sight picture. These were the ones attacked by Gerrie Radloff.
Right: The sight picture is blurred due to the vibration from the 30mm Defa cannons. The white bursts clearly show the effects of the cannon fire.

To this day the success of the attack is disputed with SWAPO claiming the people killed were refugees. Afterwards, at the debrief, paratroopers told in detail how these 'refugees' used 23mm anti-aircraft cannons in the ground role against them; how hundreds of AK-47 rifles were found next to bodies; and how the 'refugees' offered stiff resistance from the extensive fortifications surrounding the village.

Soldiers who fought at Cassinga say it was a heavily defended target. Propagandists, not present at the fight, offered the 'refugee' story. It is a disgrace that SWAPO propaganda still dismisses, for petty political points, this stout-hearted defence by their forces. However, let history record that our paratroopers recognized their doughty opponents as worthy fighters.

This historic photo shows the four pilots and 12 ground crew of 2 Squadron who took part in Operation *Reindeer*.

The only indisputable result of Cassinga was the escalation of the bush conflict. The introduction of fighter aircraft, into what had been a helicopter-supported counter-insurgency struggle, raised the tempo and sophistication of the war.

Impala light strike fighter

Our small force of Impala aircraft became indispensable in the war against enemy incursion and they were used in a variety of roles, with reconnaissance probably being paramount. Inside South West Africa they carried out visual reconnaissance missions, reporting any suspect activity for the ground forces to follow up. Externally, they traversed the 'shallow' area of Angola (up to 60 kilometres north of the border) performing the same visual reconnaissance. However, on these sorties they were armed with 68mm rockets and 30mm cannon to be able to take on enemy positions and vehicles whenever they were spotted. The pilots became so adept in this role that even flying at 300 knots and only 50 feet AGL they could pick up recent vehicle tracks and, on many occasions, found and destroyed enemy vehicles.

Although small, the Impala Mk II packed a heavy punch. Here it is firing a full salvo of 68mm rockets. It could also carry bombs and fire a deadly burst of 30mm cannon fire.

As mentioned earlier, Owamboland is as flat as a pancake which severely restricted line-of-sight communications. In order to maintain crucial communication links between ground forces deep inside Angola and their headquarters in Oshakati, SAAF aircraft would fly as airborne relay stations. Flying at high altitudes over the border line the SAAF pilot could communicate through his VHF radio to both parties. The Impala was ideal for this role, particularly when our ground forces had penetrated long distances inside Angolan territory. Flying above 30,000 feet the Impala pilot could maintain vital communications in this role, known as Telstar.

Impalas were almost constantly on CAS standby throughout the ten years they were deployed on the border. The aircraft would stand fully armed and serviceable in their revetments; the pilots fully dressed and briefed to react immediately to radio calls from our ground patrols when they came under fire from SWAPO groups. Within minutes Impala jets could be flying to the contact area where they were 'talked' into firing positions by the ground troops. Often, ground troops would let off a smoke grenade at their position to assist the pilots. Fortunately, these grenades included coloured smoke which eliminated any possibility of confusion.

Impala aircraft were frequently used in the air-strike role once suitable enemy targets had been located. A strike by Impala jets would be followed by the advance of the ground troops through the target area, by an airborne assault by paratroopers, or forces inserted by Puma helicopters.

1978: Cassinga

Perhaps the most dominant role of the Impala fleet was during *Maanskyn* and *Donkermaan* operations, initiated in 1980. However, the operation for which the Impala aircraft was most famous occurred in 1985 when Impalas, operating out of AFB Rundu, shot down six Soviet-built helicopters in two separate engagements. The excellent manoeuvrability of the small fighter and the accuracy of its 30mm Defa cannons made it an ideal aircraft for this tricky job.

Fast jets

50-ship Mirage formation. For those who count, the 50th aircraft was the spotter.

The 50 crews.

The Mirage F1 entered the war almost by default. On 6 July, a 2 Squadron Mirage III R2Z flew on a reconnaissance mission into Zambia from AFB Mpacha, the base at the eastern end of the Caprivi Strip in South West Africa. It was escorted by a Mirage F1AZ, the first operational sortie performed by an F1.

In an attempt to stretch the South African defences SWAPO decided to open an eastern front along the border of the Caprivi Strip. On the night of 22 August, they launched a stand-off rocket bombardment on the military base at Katima Mulilo, from Zambia. One 122mm Grad-P rocket exploded in a barrack block killing ten South African soldiers and wounding another ten. This tragedy was to have drastic consequences for SWAPO's organization in Zambia.

Left: Soviet GRAD-P single-shot launcher fired a 122mm rocket with a warhead weighing 18.3kg over a distance up to 11,000 metres. Not very accurate, but with a rate of fire of 10 rounds per minute could, and did, cause damage.
Right: The barrack block received a direct hit from one of these missiles

Within half an hour of the completion of the bombardment South African forces launched a follow-up, named Operation *Cotton*, using ground forces supported by Alouette helicopter gunships. Then on 25 and 26 August, the SAAF retaliated by carrying out air strikes against two SWAPO camps, annotated 32 and 42 by our intelligence department, approximately 60 kilometres inside Zambian territory. Flying out of AFB Waterkloof, Canberras and Buccaneers bombed both camps.

Although only 16 SWAPO cadres were accounted for the cross-border follow-up achieved a far greater result. It crushed the insurgency campaign on the eastern front; SWAPO never regained a position of strength in the Caprivi.

No one could forecast what the enemy reaction to this cross-border operation was going to be, so a contingency factor was added to the plan. 4 Squadron, based at Lanseria, had deployed to Upington on 24 August, to continue tactical training. These training camps were attended by both Permanent and Citizen Force squadron members. The CF pilots, mostly employed by South African Airways, provided a strong core of professional, experienced operators and included people like Peter Cooke, Piet Kruger, Errol Schmidt, Laurie Kay (pilot of the Boeing 747 over Ellis Park in 1995), Aubrey Bell, Sarel van Eeden, Dave Martin, Punchy de Bruyn and Dawid van der Bijl.

During the afternoon of 24 August, Major Steyn Venter, commanding the squadron, received a message from Colonel Dan Zeeman at Strike Command to pack up and return to Lanseria immediately. The pilots flew the aircraft out that afternoon and the ground crew drove through the night to arrive at Lanseria early the next morning. At this stage, the Impala Mk II was experiencing malfunctions when the 30mm cannons were fired. Venter and his chief instrument fitter, Barend Esterhuizen, made up six modification packages and installed them into six of the Impalas. At this stage, because no authority had been granted for the modification, it was technically illegal.

At 07h00 the next morning, 26 August, six Impalas flown by Steyn Venter, Tristan la Grange, Piet Kruger, Errol Schmidt, Pete Cooke and Johan du Plessis took off from Lanseria for AFB Mpacha, stopping at AFB Pietersburg to refuel. The aircraft were armed with 36 x 68mm rockets in six F2 pods, three under each wing. On subsequent flights the routing was changed as the fuel specifics of the Impala allowed a direct flight between Lanseria and Mpacha. The procedure was to descend over Lake Liambezi and join the AFB Mpacha circuit at low level.

At the briefing they were told that the Buccaneers and Canberras would fly the strike and the Impalas to be on standby if required. The pilots were disappointed but benefited immensely from the deployment. They learned what to take with them to keep both the aircraft and themselves fit for operations. They realized the serious nature of warfare and introduced realistic training into their syllabus once they returned to Lanseria. The pilots refined the need for an operational SAR plan that was to pay dividends when Aubrey Bell, from their own squadron, was later shot down in Angola.

Impala pilots posing with one of their aircraft. *L to R:* Robbie Robinson, Johan du Plessis, Ronnie Knott-Craig, Cobus Toerien, Steyn Venter, Gene Kotze.

From Fledgling to Eagle

4 Squadron Impalas at AFB Mpacha armed with six F2 rocket pods.

The first of many Mirage F1 operational deployments began on 3 November, when five F1CZs deployed to AFB Ondangwa. These aircraft were used to escort Mirage III R2Zs from 2 Squadron, who were flying extensive PR missions over southern Angola.

On 11 November, one of the sorties flew close to the Angolan port of Namibe. On the return leg the escorts were notified by the 'Dayton' radar controller (Dayton was the call sign of the Marconi mobile radar system permanently deployed at AFB Ondangwa to give much-needed cover to our aircraft) that two high-speed blips were approaching from the north. Regretfully, having only minimum combat fuel available after their long flight the F1s could not engage the enemy fighters. The F1s accelerated towards Ondangwa and the interceptors gave up the chase and returned to their airfield at Lubango, 300 kilometres north of the border. The threat of MiG intervention in the bush war increased considerably with this attempted interception and was to continue throughout the remainder of the war.

It also gave added impetus to the production of the V3 series of South African-developed air-to-air missiles which were designed to be integrated with a helmet-mounted sight, also of South African design. Development of the helmets began in 1975 and the SAAF was the first air force to fly operationally with this type of system. One of these helmets was stolen by the spy Commodore Dieter Gerhard of the South African Navy. It was passed onto the Soviets and was part of the reason Gerhard was eventually apprehended. On completion of the Cold War, and when South Africa's diplomatic relations with Russia were established, it is interesting to note that the helmet sight used by the Russian Air Force was basically the same as the helmet stolen from the SAAF. The latest version of the

South African helmet is an integral part of the considerable weapons capability of the Rooivalk attack helicopter.

On 28 December, Commandant Gert Havenga and navigator Philip Rosseau flew an EW surveillance mission over Rhodesia as the final operational mission of the year.

SAAF aircrew on operations in Rhodesia. Identifiable are: Maj Daantjie Beneke *(standing 2nd from L)*, Maj Len Haasbroek, Frelon pilot *(standing 5th from L)*, Cmdt 'Breyty' Breytenbach, OC 19 Squadron and commander of the SAAF contingent *(standing 6th from L)*, Cmdt Gerrie Botha, OC 44 Squadron Dakota pilot *(standing 6th from R)*, F/Sgt Kenny van Straaten *(standing 4th from R)*, Lt Mark Dutton *(kneeling at L)*, Lt Frans Vermuelen *(kneeling middle)*.

Cmdt Breyty Breytenbach *(left)* talking to Air Commodore Frank Mussell, Rhodesian Air Force. Cmdt Breytenbach was awarded the HC for his role in in Operation *Uric*. Later, in Owamboland, he was to add a second HC to his impressive list of decorations.
Photos courtesy Craig Fourie

Chapter 5

1979: Learning the ropes

During January and February 1979, Foreign Minister Pik Botha was in contact with the United Nations. In a diplomatic note to the UN Secretary-General Kurt Waldheim he asked whether United Nations Transitional Agreement Group (UNTAG) troops would be arriving to commence the independence process for SWA. No significant reaction was received from the UN HQ to this peace initiative.

The situation in Rhodesia was nearing crisis point with the acceptance by Ian Smith of the principle of majority rule and a transitional administration being set up. The ferocity of the conflict was increased when a second Air Rhodesia Viscount, taking off from Kariba for Salisbury, was shot down by ZIPRA (Zimbabwe People's Revolutionary Army) using a Soviet-made SAM-7 missile. The Viscount's Commander, ex-SAAF pilot Jan André du Plessis, four crew and 54 passengers were all killed when the aircraft crashed in the Vuti African Purchase Area.

Fifteen minutes later Lieutenant-General Peter Walls, Rhodesian Commander of Combined Operations, took off from Kariba also in a Viscount. It was later reported that ZIPRA leader, Joshua Nkomo, had confirmed that General Walls had been the intended target.

Luso

A retaliation strike on a ZIPRA camp near Luso Angola, was called for and, because only four Rhodesian Air Force Canberra bombers were available, the assistance of 12 Squadron SAAF was requested.

Three SAAF Canberras took off from AFB Waterkloof at 18h15 on 25 February, crewed by Major Hannes Bekker and Lieutenant Riem Mouton; Captain Roly

1979: Learning the ropes

12 Squadron Canberra bombers in line-astern formation.

Jones with Lappies Labuschagne; and lieutenants Wally Marais and Owen Doyle.

Initially, the flight to Victoria Falls was flown in low-level battle formation until darkness forced the pilots to climb. At a late stage, on their approach to the Victoria Falls airfield the runway lights were switched on, allowing the aircraft to land and taxi to the dispersal area prior to the lights being extinguished again for security reasons. The crews were taken to the control tower where all the windows were covered. A 'black-out' policy was strictly enforced. They were met by the commander of 5 Squadron Rhodesian Air Force, Squadron Leader Chris Dixon and, among others, Flight Lieutenant Jim Russell, who had completed Navigators Wings Course No 22 in 1973/74 at AFB Ysterplaat.

After receiving intelligence, weather and mission briefings the SAAF navigators

The Canberra crews who took part in the Luso strike. *L to R*: Wally Marais, Roly Jones, Hannes Bekker, Riem Mouton, Owen Doyle, Lappies Labuschagne.

commenced their sortie planning, while the pilots were entertained on the lawn outside with welcoming Castle beers. Each SAAF navigator was allocated two steps on the stairway leading up to the control tower to serve as flight planning tables. This was the only area where lights were permitted because they were not visible from outside. Shortly after midnight, once their planning was completed, each navigator was permitted an ice-cold Castle before retiring.

Their target was situated outside and to the east of Luso, an Angolan town over 600 nautical miles northwest of Victoria Falls. An estimated 3,000 ZIPRA soldiers and their Cuban and East German advisors were accommodated in row upon row of flat-roofed bungalows with canvas sides.

The weapon chosen for the SAAF Canberras was Alpha bombs—loaded at AFB Waterkloof. Each aircraft had six steel-mesh baskets, known as 'hoppers', fitted in the bomb bay. Fifty Alpha bombs were loaded into each hopper making a total of 300 per aircraft. Three of the Rhodesian Canberras were similarly loaded, with their fourth Canberra armed with six 1,000 pounders fitted with delay fuses. During an operational attack it was usual to release all six hopper loads simultaneously.

The Alpha bombs were completely round in shape and measured about 15cm in diameter. The bomb consisted of two steel casings each about 8mm thick; the inner one being pre-fragmented. This inner casing was maintained in a centralized position within the outer casing by 250 high-density rubber balls of 15mm diameter. On impact with any surface the bright red Alpha bombs would bounce back into the air where, at three to four metres above the ground, they would explode. The air-burst detonation was achieved by a clever, all-ways pistol that allowed a 0.6-second delay after impact before triggering the bomb.

The aiming device for the release of these bombs was a simple SFOM-sight fitted in the nose of the Canberra. The navigator would 'patter' the pilot onto the target as it appeared in the clear-vision panel. The target was approached at 200 feet above ground level (AGL) with the aircraft flying at 360 knots groundspeed in a tight line-abreast formation. Just short of the target, the formation would step up to 300 feet AGL and open the bomb doors. This action decreased the groundspeed to 350 knots at the time of release—the ideal release parameters. The three Canberras, flying in tight line-abreast formation, could saturate an area approximately 300 metres by 1,000 metres with lethal rubber balls and pre-fragmented shrapnel.

As soon as the navigator pressed the bomb tit and called "Bombs gone" the pilot would count to five before descending to treetop level while closing the bomb doors. A rear-facing F95 oblique camera, mounted in the tail of the Canberra and controlled by the pilot, would photograph the Alpha bombs exiting the bomb bay all the way down to impact point and proved invaluable in assessing the success of a strike.

1979: Learning the ropes

The navigator's bomb-aiming position in the nose of a Canberra. The SFOM sight glass is just visible below the black protrusion from the top of the photograph.

The Alpha bomb was developed by the Rhodesians, namely Group Captain Peter Petter-Bowyer, and introduced into service in the latter part of 1976. The SAAF Canberras were modified in 1977. The first Alpha bomb trials were carried out by Captain Len Haasbroek and Lieutenant Riem Mouton at the Roodewal bombing range on 19 October 1977.

At dawn on 26 February 1979, the South African and Rhodesian crews walked out to pre-flight the waiting Canberras. Squadron Leader Chris Dixon and his navigator Flight Lieutenant Mike Ronne were the designated strike leaders; the mission would proceed under the call sign 'Green Formation'.

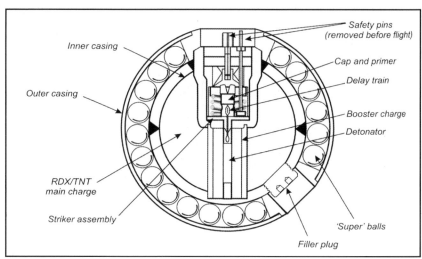

Alpha, the bouncing bomb

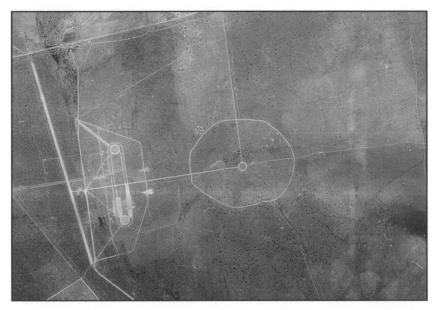

Roodewal bombing range, north of Pietersburg (now Polokwane). The Alpha and Bravo 'cokes' can be seen one above the other on the left of the photo. Charlie 'coke', used for Canberra medium- and high-level bombing, is in the centre of the frame. Two tactical targets can also be identified—an AAA site outside the ring-road around Charlie 'coke' and a SAM site inside the ring-road.

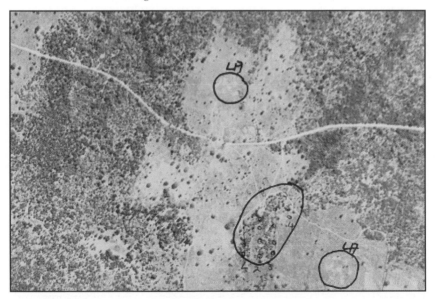

Neil McGibbon and I built the targets on the Roodewal bombing range with the help of AFB Pietersburg armourers. When compared to this actual target photograph we must have been visionaries. Four sticks of bombs have been circled inside the target area. The two circles marked LA (*Lugafweer*) are AAA sites, exactly as we practised at Roodewal.

1979: Learning the ropes

On start-up Dixon's radio wouldn't work, so the lead passed to Flight Lieutenant Ted Brent and his navigator Jim Russell. The formation was airborne at 06h30 and spiralled up to Flight Level 390 (39,000 feet) to allow the string of Canberras to join into formation. Two Rhodesian Hunters, armed with Sidewinder missiles, were launched to provide top cover for the bombers. In addition, a Command and Control Dakota was flown to monitor enemy radio frequencies.

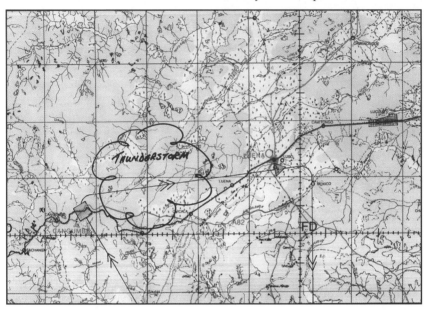

The attack route flown by the Canberra bombers. The square east of Cangumbe was the turning point and the target is marked with a triangle. The position of the large storm is clearly marked.

The formation routed westward from Victoria Falls towards Kazungula where they turned northwest towards Mongu. At this stage, Dixon called up on the radio to say his radio problem had been fixed and the formation was to orbit Mongu to allow him to join up. Riem Mouton was tasked to keep a listening watch on the Mongu Air Traffic Control (ATC) frequency in case of Zambian interceptor activity. Three times Mongu ATC transmitted: "Aircraft overflying Mongu, identify yourself." The requests were ignored.

Dixon's Canberra rejoined the formation and the aircraft continued northwest to intercept the Benguela railway line, west of Luso. On this leg, because low cloud cover obscured the ground, the navigators were kept busy plotting their position by dead-reckoning (DR). At top of descent (TOD) the formation was still above thick cloud, making for some exciting formation flying as the aircraft descended through it.

At 2,000 feet they cleared the cloud and continued down to 200 feet AGL. The navigators left their pilots and clambered down into the glass-nose. Tightening

An additional inherent hazard to navigators lying in the nose of the Canberra was the possibility of a bird strike. This particular Canberra was flown by Des Barker and Brett Schafer.

their Sabre parachute harnesses they crawled into a prone position to map-read and pinpoint their position. Jim Russell had brought the formation slightly west of track during the blind descent but a small correction to heading had the formation in perfect position as they hit the Initial point (IP), a prominent kink in the railway line, where the formation turned eastward towards their target. The Canberras had now split into two formations, a four-ship and a three-ship, with the latter dropping into a trail position to avoid flying through the debris and shrapnel from the first wave. At this crucial time they entered a tropical rainstorm. The pelting rain drops hitting the fuselage made such a noise it nearly drowned out the voices on the intercom. Hannes Bekker had to shout so Riem Mouton could hear the 'Vrystaat' check—perhaps the most common cry heard at Currie Cup rugby matches were the Orange Free State fans shouting "Vrystaat!" (Free State)—it was for this reason the SAAF had adopted this term, to ensure aircrew carried out all the proper checks prior to dropping live weapons.

Riem Mouton checked and re-checked the weapon selection switches, intervalometer setting and the 159 mils depression set on the SFOM sight. The Canberra, with its big wings, was riding the turbulence like a bucking bronco; Riem was flung about in the nose as he battled to dial in accurately the Doppler drift angle on the sight. Due to the rain, it was almost impossible for him to see anything through the clear-vision panel and he realized it was going to be very interesting trying to patter the pilot onto the target.

Then, two minutes before the attack, they flew out of the storm. The turbulence was gone, the noise ceased and through the clear-vision panel he had a perfect view of Vila da Luso and its surrounds. He reminded Hannes Bekker the bomb doors still had to be opened and the F95 camera switched on. Just then the formation started the gentle climb to 300 feet AGL. When the call "Bomb doors" came from Green Leader, the groundspeed was nicely pegged at 350 knots. The view through the clear-vision panel was a bomb aimer's dream. There, directly ahead, were row upon row of bungalows neatly aligned to the attack direction. Puddles of water indicated the camp had not escaped the storm the aircraft had just passed through. There was no sign of activity, no AAA firing at the aircraft, no vehicles moving around or troops on the parade ground. Mouton thought perhaps the camp was empty as the cross-hairs on his sight crept up towards the release point. He firmly pressed the bomb tit in his right hand as the sight moved over a small tree, 50 metres short of the first bungalow.

Then he saw him—a man with a bucket in his hand! He was walking between what must have been an ablution facility and his bungalow when he heard the aircraft. He stopped and looked up at the approaching formation. The very next second the bucket was hanging in mid-air as the man disappeared through the wall of the nearest bungalow at great speed. The rest of the camp slipped from view without Mouton seeing any further activity.

They cleared the target area and, because the Rhodesian B2 Canberras were limited in fuel, started a climb up to flight level 410 direct to Victoria Falls, where they landed. The SAAF B12 Canberras, with fuel tanks in the aircraft wings, continued on to Fylde, a tactical airfield 140 kilometres southwest of Salisbury near the small town of Hartley, where the participation of SAAF bombers would be less conspicuous.

Later that day, when Green Leader and his formation arrived at Fylde the problem with Chris Dixon's radio was clearly identified. A length of electric wire had been duct-taped from the cockpit, through the crew's entrance door and along the fuselage to the radio bay at the back of the bomb bay, to replace a broken wire in one of the looms. Desperate measures by a desperate air force!

The F95 films from the SAAF aircraft were removed and developed for the debriefing. Only then was it apparent how successful the strike had been. The best coverage came from Wally Marais' camera. It clearly showed the Alpha bombs leaving the bomb bay, hitting the ground and exploding with bright white flashes that ran through the full length of the target. One frame-by-frame sequence showed three enemy soldiers manning a 14.5mm AAA gun and firing at the Canberras. A bomb could be seen landing in their midst and exploding, leaving the three gunners lying incapacitated alongside their weapon.

There had been more than just the man with a bucket. On the photos it could be seen how the occupants of the camp bailed out through the canvas walls of the bungalows, only to be struck by the rubber balls or shrapnel. Altogether 1,800 Alpha bombs struck the target as well as five out of six 1,000lb delayed-fuse bombs. The sixth bomb hung up in the Canberra bomb bay, which caused a few anxious minutes at Victoria Falls. Flight Lieutenant Kevin Pienke and Jay Jay Strydom had to make an extremely soft touch-down with a live 1,000 pound bomb on board. The bomb was eventually defused and lowered onto a bed of mattresses for the army disposal unit to take care of. Operation *Vanity* had been a most memorable and successful Canberra strike. The attack received much attention in the Rhodesian media.

One sad feature was that two of the crews who took part in the operation were killed in separate incidents, very shortly thereafter. On 14 March 1979, just three weeks after the Luso strike, Wally Marais and Owen Doyle crashed after taking enemy fire during Operation *Rekstok*. On 3 October 1979, Kevin Pienke and Jay Jay Strydom were killed during a Rhodesian air strike on an AAA position on the ZANLA (Zimbabwe African National Liberation Army) base at Chimoio Circle (Operation *Miracle*) in Mozambique, east of Umtali.

Lieutenants Cobus Toerien and Vic Kaiser pose with Impala maintenance personnel.

Navigational error?

During February, Owamboland was in the grip of the 'big rains', with low clouds and showers occurring almost every afternoon. Water in the *shonas* covered about 70 per cent of the normally arid area. At 09h00 on 27 February, the Impala pilots were called to the briefing room at AFB Ondangwa. At the briefing they learned that army patrols had reported the presence of enemy vehicles just north of the cut-line, between Oshikango (Beacon 18) and Eenhana (Beacon 30). Steyn Venter with Henry Jackson as his number two, were tasked to fly an armed reconnaissance mission just south of the cut-line, to assess whether the enemy had crossed into SWA. Thirty minutes later a second pair of Impalas, flown by Cobus Toerien and Vic Kaiser, flew a similar pattern to maintain air force presence in the area.

On the leg between Eenhana and Oshikango the second pair joined up into a

1979: Learning the ropes

divisional battle formation of four aircraft with the pairs flying about 800 metres apart. The cloud base was at 500 feet and rain was observed towards the east. In these murky conditions Venter saw smoke curling up through the bush canopy a little way to the north and immediately altered heading to investigate.

During this turn the formation ended up almost in long line-astern as Venter overflew the smoke. Looking down he saw figures scattering in all directions. However, there was no sign of a village. He ordered the formation to select rockets and to follow him up in a pitch to the left. Cloud base prevented him from going higher than 400 feet. In order to remain visual with the target area he maintained a very tight turn, descending in to the attack under conditions which were far from ideal for rocketing. All the pilots fired while they were still in a descending left turn, each firing 24 x 68mm rockets and pulling out extremely low over the target. Henry Jackson reported several secondary explosions.

Cobus Toerien in the gunner's seat of a Soviet-built ZPU-1 14.5mm heavy machine gun. Used in a ground role it had a maximum range of 2,000 metres. In an anti-aircraft role the range decreased to 1,400 metres. The optical sight can be seen in front of Cobus's head.

While returning to Ondangwa Venter realized that the target had been about three kilometres *inside* Angolan territory and that something had to be done about it! After landing, for purposes of debriefing, the pilots agreed that the target was attacked three kilometres 'south' of the cut-line. Colonel Andy Kapp, who had driven over from Oshakati for the debrief, was very sceptical but eventually sent the debrief through to Windhoek.

Afterwards, in the pub, the Impala pilots suddenly remembered they had incorrectly said south when they really had meant north! This sortie was the first offensive Impala sortie into Angola—but by no means the last. The Impala was an ideal aircraft for this type of bush warfare—slow but agile enough to observe movement on the ground, yet fast enough not to be too vulnerable to ground fire. One interesting feature of armed recce sorties was that the pilots were taught to monitor the movement of cattle. If a herd did not have a number of locals guiding it, it immediately created suspicion because SWAPO often used cattle to obscure their footprints.

2 Squadron PR flight

On 5 March, the photo-reconnaissance (PR) flight of 2 Squadron left AFB Hoedspruit for AFB Ondangwa, via Upington. The formation was led by Major Steve Ferreira, commander of the recce flight. The briefing, shortly after their arrival at Oshakati, indicated that our intelligence picture of what was happening at Ongiva, just 50 kilometres north of the cut-line, was sketchy at best. The recce pilots were tasked to rectify this shortcoming.

During the internecine fighting between MPLA and UNITA forces that had raged since 1975, large amounts of infrastructural damage had affected most Angolan towns and facilities. The hardened runway at the Ongiva airfield had also suffered. Shortly before Ongiva changed hands MPLA forces had dynamited holes in the runway surface to prevent the runway being used against them. Now they were once again back in control of the airfield and our intelligence indicated that the runway had finally been repaired. This was viewed as an extremely serious development as a MiG force could be stationed within minutes of our large base at AFB Ondangwa. It was 2 Squadron's task to find out.

The mission was planned for the afternoon of 6 March. Two photographic Mirage III R2Zs would perform a low-level recce of the runway and environs.

This photo shows Ongiva airfield. Concrete repairs can be clearly seen in the circles in the hard surface of the runway. In the top half of the frame a cross-pattern of trench works can be seen, with a 14.5mm gun at the end of each trench. A cloud of smoke emanating from the top left-hand gun shows it firing at the photographic aircraft. Fortunately he missed.

This captured AAA site could well be the same one as in the previous photograph.

The approach to the target area would be at very low level. A quick pitch-up to 1,000 feet immediately short of the target would ensure the best photographic coverage of the area. The aircraft would be flying at 540 knots (1,000kph), which equates to nine miles per minute for navigational purposes. In those days, global positioning systems (GPSs) hadn't yet been invented and pilots flying at these very high speeds had their work cut out in maintaining track, especially being so very close to the treetops. The mission was, however, unopposed because of its complete surprise.

Very little activity was observed on the photos, probably because the target was overflown during siesta time. The intelligence officers were disappointed because they could not detect anything worthwhile and so requested Ferreira and his wingman Gavin Bornman to return to Ongiva early the following morning.

As the Mirage IIIs approached at 08h30 on 7 March, Ferreira glanced inside his cockpit to ensure his cameras had been switched on. As he looked up again he noticed tracer fire coming their way. When he saw the tracers dipping below the aircraft flight path he continued with the PR run, adjusting his flight attitude to ensure the anti-aircraft site appeared on the photos. Fortunately, neither aircraft was hit and the mission brought back a truly remarkable photo showing one of the guns of a 14.5mm AAA battery firing at them.

On 11 March, Ferreira and Bornman were busy with high-level reconnaissance in the Xangongo area flying, fortunately, within the coverage of the Dayton

Gavin Bornman and Steve Ferreira immediately before boarding their Mirage III R2Z aircraft for another PR mission.

radar station. Suddenly, the two pilots were galvanized by a warning shout from a fighter-controller that 'bogeys' were in the air. Neither of the Mirage III aircraft were armed and, when the 'bogey' call was changed to 'bandits', neither pilot hesitated—they turned onto a heading for base and plunged to very low level at a very high speed. This provocative action indicated that the Angolan Air Force seemed eager to get involved. (In air force parlance a bogey is an unidentified aircraft while a bandit is an identified hostile aircraft.)

The following morning, 12 March, the same pilots were carrying out a road recce between Ongiva and the cut-line, at low level. As they approached the old mission station at Omapande, about 12 kilometres south of Ongiva, Bornman yelled frantically, "Go low! Go low!" An interesting warning as they were already flying at low level. Ferreira wasted no time putting his Mirage among the treetops at 1,000kph. They saw grey-white puffs of AAA fire overhead, tell-tale signs of the dangerous 23mm anti-aircraft guns.

On 15 March, Ferreira and Bornman, flying another sortie near Ongiva, decided to even the score a little. Unarmed, they only had one trick up their sleeve and they played it. Both aircraft flew at very low level and supersonic speed over the Ongiva airfield. There is no sound warning ahead of aircraft flying faster than the sound barrier. However, they leave an unmistakable sonic boom as they pass, which is usually sufficient to induce a change of underpants for the recipients of the double boom.

Cut and thrust

In February and March SWAPO responded to the peace initiative by stepping up attacks on Owambo civilians and launching a stand-off bombardment on the security force base at Elundu. All 122mm Katyusha rockets and mortars missed the base. This did not stop them from claiming to have killed 300 South

1979: Learning the ropes

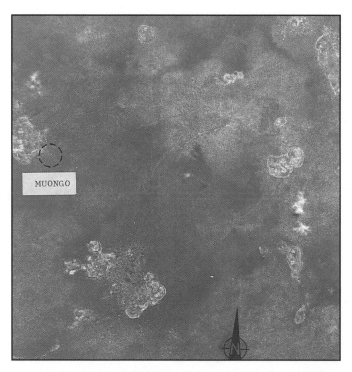

This picture was taken by a high-flying Canberra giving a scale of 1:60 000 or 1cm = 600 metres. The photographic interpreter (PI) identified the area marked Muongo as a possible SWAPO camp.

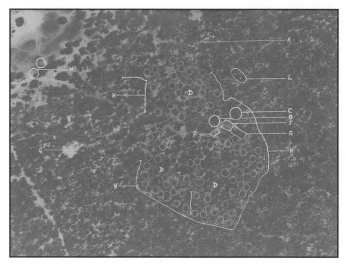

The identified area was then enlarged to a scale of 1:1,800 or 1cm = 25 metres. The PI identified a long defensive trench K and marked some rectangular structures and 67 circular shelters. At F, using stereoscopes and enlargements, he even identified four terrorists. A double-spoor track can be seen at bottom left of the photograph.

From Fledgling to Eagle

Exploding bombs shredded foliage from the thick bush allowing post-strike, damage-assessment photography to clearly show the extensive trench system that surrounded the base. When an air strike is planned aircrew are given copies of photos for orientation and attack purposes.

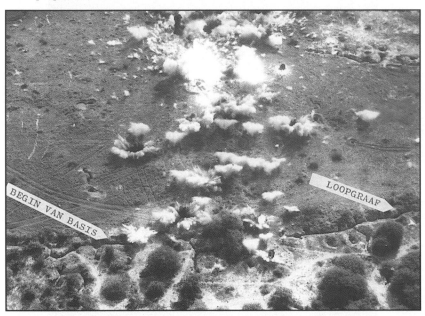

This photograph was taken from the tail camera of one of the Canberra bombers on the Cahama raid. A careful study of the photograph will show two long, defensive trench lines. In the left centre of the picture an anti-aircraft emplacement can be seen. The two U-shaped trenches were usually manned by crews firing SA-7 Strela heat-seeking missiles. The explosions are from the 300 Alpha bomblets dropped from the bomb bay of each Canberra.

1979: Learning the ropes

African soldiers in the previous three months, destroyed two military bases and 40 military vehicles—and shot down two SAAF reconnaissance aircraft. This posturing by SWAPO brought a swift riposte from South Africa. Authority was granted to carry out two cross-border military operations during March.

Between 6 and 13 March, ground forces crossed into southern Angola to destroy known SWAPO bases near Mongua, Oncocua and Henhombe, in Operation *Rekstok I*. The SAAF supported these attacks using aerial bombardment from Canberra bombers and photo-reconnaissance flights by Mirage III RZs.

As a safeguard for these vulnerable aircraft 3 Squadron was deployed to AFB Ondangwa until the end of March. Combat air patrols (CAPs), escort missions and low-level armed reconnaissance flights were flown and many long hours were spent on cockpit standby.

At 07h15 on 6 March, a Canberra attacked Muongo dropping 300 Alpha bombs. Later the same day two Canberras struck a target at Franca, while another two struck Capindi. These strikes were repeated the next day when a pair of aircraft attacked Henhombe. On 8 March, two Canberras attacked Huambango and another pair again struck Henhombe. On 9 March, two Canberras struck Oshono.

On 14 March, two Canberras, operating from AFB Ondangwa, attacked the ANC camp at Nova Catengue, 20 nautical miles southeast of Lobito. Later the same day four Canberras carried out an attack near Ediva. Immediately after bomb release from 500 feet the Canberras descended to low level. It was noticed that Lieutenant Wally Marais' aircraft, No 452, remained with its bomb doors open. Radio calls failed to establish contact with either occupant. Detaching from the formation Captain Roly Jones closed in on it but could see no outward sign of damage to the aircraft.

Flying above 452 he noticed the pilot slumped over the controls, as it climbed slowly up to 2,000 feet while decreasing speed to around 200 knots. The aircraft then banked gently to port before adopting a 10º nose-down attitude. It descended to extremely low level before suddenly pitching up into an almost vertical attitude and stalled, before plunging into the ground.

At 17h00, two Mirage F1CZs were scrambled from Ondangwa. En route, the Dayton radar controller informed them that a Canberra had been shot down. The F1 pilots were told to search for the wreckage and try to establish whether the crew had ejected successfully. Unfortunately, after a long search no signs of the wreckage, the pilot Lieutenant Dewald 'Wally' Marais or navigator Second Lieutenant Owen Doyle were found.

On completion of *Rekstok* the Canberras had flown 25 sorties, 75 flight hours and dropped 7,300 Alpha bombs.

Unfortunately, during an attack when aircraft overfly a target, the level delivery mode makes them very vulnerable, as happened on this strike. Surprise was the only safeguard for attacking aircraft.

Impala pilots. *Standing L to R*: Vic Kaiser, Glen Williams, Gene Kotze, Cobus Toerien, Jan Henning, Johan Nieuwoudt, Graham Rochat, Steyn Venter, Koos Kieck, Dave Fish; *seated*: Frans Vermaak, Henry Jackson, Mark Clulow.

Zambia

Operation *Saffraan* was launched to seek and destroy SWAPO terrorists known to have moved into Zambia. As a precaution the SAAF deployed 12 Impala Mk II aircraft to AFB Mpacha on 5 March. Four redeployed from AFB Ondangwa and the remainder came from 6 and 8 Squadrons. Commandant Speedy de Wet commanded the SAAF operation and the pilots, under Major Steyn Venter's command, were Johan Niewoudt (OC 8 Squadron), Graham Rochat (OC 6 Squadron), Cobus Toerien, Jan Henning, Koos Kieck, Dave Fish, Hannes Prinsloo, Vic Kaizer, Glen Williams, Gene Kotze, Henry Jackson and Mark Clulow.

At 08h00 on 6 March, Steyn Venter led a formation on an attack on Base 52, while a formation led by Graham Rochat attacked Base 55. All the aircraft were loaded with four 250kg bombs and full cannon ammunition. The flight to the attack point was uneventful. Rochat found his designated target and carried out the attack as planned.

However, it had been scheduled that Venter's formation would attack immediately after a strike by both Canberras and Buccaneers. After the attack C-130s were to drop Parabats into the area to clean up the target. On reaching his roll-in point Venter could not see any dust from the combined strike. He entered an orbit around the target. Just then one of his formation noticed dust clouds about five miles away—the bombers had struck the wrong target. Venter immediately ordered his formation into attack and they dropped all their bombs within the boundaries of the camp. Although the strike was accurate Venter decided that 16 bombs were insufficient to inflict the required damage on the target, so he called off the paradrop.

1979: Learning the ropes

The same morning, at 06h30, four Buccaneers, each loaded with eight 450kg bombs and full fuel, launched from AFB Waterkloof on the same combined mission as the Impalas and Canberras. Gert Havenga, with his navigator Koos Botha, led the formation. In that configuration, with AFB Waterkloof being over 5,000 feet above sea level, the take-off was a nightmare. The performance manual recommends that after take-off the recommended acceleration should be at least one knot per second. On this sortie, and on many others flown out of Waterkloof, the pilots had to settle for half that acceleration. In fact, they were on steady ADI (angle of attack indicator) and on the wrong side of the drag curve until they had passed Hartebeespoort Dam west of Pretoria.

The attack was to be from a pitch-up into a 30° dive. All went well until they rolled in. The target proved to be extremely difficult to recognize and the aircraft did not drop their bombs on the first pass. The second Buccaneer to roll in was flown by Major George Snyman, with Captain Hugh Baumgartner, an ex-RAF Vulcan navigator, in the back seat.

The formation did a 360° turn looking for the target, before the lead rolled in again. George Snyman, with less than 50 hours on type and still to complete the Buccaneer conversion course, was understandably nervous because he still couldn't see the briefed target. He decided to set his armament master switch to live during the roll-in to have more time in the dive to search for the target. He did this, but unfortunately, while manoeuvring the aircraft, put pressure on the trigger. The explosive ERUs (explosive release unit) fired and the bombs left the aircraft inadvertently. Hugh Baumgartner interpreted the sudden *thump-thump-thump* as anti-aircraft fire and called out over the intercom that the aircraft had been hit.

Meanwhile, Gert Havenga, in the lead aircraft, decided it wasn't the target after all, called off the attack and started a climbing turn to the left. A few seconds later Snyman's bombs hit Zambia. The formation leader, interpreting the explosions as the expected Canberra attack, proceeded to re-enter the attack dive and the remaining three Buccaneers released their bombs onto the smoke from Snyman's inadvertent release. Eventually, 32 bombs were dropped—the dust cloud Steyn Venter saw about five miles from the target. Later, Reconnaissance troops (Recces) on a ground patrol reported back that one unfortunate elephant had been killed. The formation landed at AFB Grootfontein.

At 12h30 they were airborne again, this time to attack targets designated as Franca 3 and 4. Thereafter, until 14 March, the squadron flew strikes against targets at Efitu, Senanga, Cahama and Nova Catenque.

Included in the list of targets was the first night operation, on 8 March. The late Tom Engela, the excellent radar controller at Dayton, guided the formation to the roll-in point for a 30° dive-bomb attack. The formation had split into a 30-second trail with the pilots dropping their bombs into the smoke and dust from the leader's bombs. The feedback received later was that six of the 32 bombs had fallen into the target area.

At 23h00 on the night of 11 March, a team from 4 Reconnaissance Commando was dropped from a C-160 flying at 27,000 feet approximately 15 kilometres north of a target at Lake Nayaya, in the Senanga district of Zambia. They were to reconnoitre the target area prior to an air strike by Buccaneers which would drop 450kg bombs and Canberras delivering Alpha bombs.

They spent two days in the area and found the base had been deserted, probably two or three days earlier. The Canberras and Buccaneers were already on their way to the target, when the Recces made contact with the C-160 Telstar to abort the air strike. The bombers returned to base.

At 19h30 on 13 March, two Frelons flew to a pre-arranged LZ three kilometres northeast of the camp and uplifted the recces—even though one of the Frelon rotors had clipped the trees during landing. The recces reported that the photographic interpretation of the camp had been 100 per cent accurate—only the inhabitants had been missing.

Lobito

On 14 March, a formation of four Buccaneers penetrated Angolan airspace en route to a target adjacent to the Benguela railway line, near Lobito. Because of the distance to the target the aircraft had to fly at medium level until, reaching latitude 21° south, they started their descent to low level for the final run-in, at treetop height. The aircraft pitched up and entered a standard 30° dive. The Canberras attacked after the Buccaneers had released their bombs, so their tail-mounted cameras could take photos for bomb-damage assessment purposes.

It was a well-executed combined strike with a little added excitement on the return leg. When the Buccaneers had to start climbing for fuel reasons someone in the formation spotted a bogey high in the six o'clock position. A minute or two later the bogey was positively identified as one of the Canberras pulling a condensation cloud—the Buccaneer crews relaxed. When the Canberra films were processed it revealed that the target, although well struck, had been deserted and the combined strike was therefore a 'lemon'.

'Lemons'

During the course of the war the SAAF had a number of strikes which could only be described as 'lemons' (an unsuccessful mission, or a waste of time). I personally led 16 Mirage F1s on perhaps the most perfect 'lemon' of the war. My formation ran in at low level, pitched up on time, on target. Commandant Deon Ferreira, leading 32 Battalion, talked me onto the target, which we bombed most successfully. Unfortunately, SWAPO had got wind of our intentions during the early hours of the morning and, by first light, had drifted away to watch the

1979: Learning the ropes

This RAM (radio-activated marker) is being placed on the range at Riemvasmaak. Under operational conditions it is not so easy. The RAM must be positioned, usually in the wee hours of the morning prior to the air attack. It must be disguised and hidden from view while ensuring that the aerials are still capable of picking up radio signals from aircraft. All this within sneezing distance of a hostile enemy.

show. Ferreira and I were unanimously elected 'Directors of the Citrus Board'.

In defence of these expensive failures let me explain that to strike a temporary base in the bush is no easy matter. Firstly, the base has to be found either by PR or ground reconnaissance. Then, Recce troops have to be inserted into the area to pinpoint the exact dimensions of the base. To do this some extremely brave individuals have to sneak right under the nose of the enemy to find the extremities of the camp. Often, these men would position RAMs (radio-activated marker beacons) close to the base. As the attacking aircraft pitched up the pilots would transmit on the RAM frequency, igniting the flare to mark the position of the camp. This was a great help to pilots flying at over 500 miles per hour. They would see the smoke billowing from the bush and quickly identify the target.

If the target was to be attacked by ground forces immediately after the air strike, the men would have to be within a kilometre or two of the enemy base. In the silence of the bush any unexpected noise could be heard from a great distance, giving the occupants of the base time to disappear into the thick foliage where horizontal visibility, at some points, could be down to 20 or 30 metres.

The *clap-clap* noise of heavily laden helicopter rotors can also be heard up to a minute before the helicopter arrives and in a minute or two a nervous terrorist can be many hundreds of metres away from the base.

If the target had been identified from photographs the chances of a 'lemon' were even greater. The time required to take the film and have it developed and interpreted can be quite lengthy, so by the time a strike was launched the inhabitants could be well gone. A temporary base in a combat zone is exactly that. Static bases are easier to find and strike, therefore. No good soldier will stay in one place longer than necessary. SWAPO had learned this lesson early in the war and were past masters in keeping on the move.

Given all these factors it is only good planning, excellent execution and a vast slice of luck, or sloppiness on the part of the enemy, that brings success. We had our failures, particularly earlier on but as we honed our skills our success rate soared dramatically.

On 24 March, 1 Squadron deployed to AFB Mpacha. The F1AZ pilots flew armed reconnaissance sorties without finding any worthwhile targets. Using standard dive attacks they also rocketed and strafed terrorist camp No 52, previously bombed by Steyn Venter's Impalas. The air-strike results throughout *Saffraan* were disappointing, mainly because intelligence covering that region was sketchy at best.

Helicopters from 15 and 19 Squadrons carried out trooping into Zambia, concentrating on areas in the vicinity of Selungu and Kalabelewe schools.

On 4 April, AFB Ondangwa was subjected to a mortar attack. Graham Rochat, who was there that evening, recalls:

>>During our tours of duty at Ondangwa, affectionately known as 'Ondangs', the pongos would fire their fire-plan each night. Two or three mortar rounds would be fired at random intervals from inside the base into 'safe' zones, in order to keep the terrs on their toes and prevent them from moving about freely. As these mortars were fired from within the base we became accustomed to a *doef* followed by a *wheeeee*—the sound of a mortar on its way out of the camp. Occasionally, the silence of the night would be broken by the sound of the anti-aircraft unit squirting off a number of rounds, causing spectacular airbursts which lit up the sky.

A number of sandbag bunkers had been built around strategic areas such as the mess, accommodation blocks and the pub as contingencies against a possible attack on the base. When the mortars were fired we were supposed to dash for the bunkers. However, this intruded on drinking time and was almost totally ignored by the SAAF. As a result, only a few new boys ran for shelter when the mortars were fired.

On 4 April, while we were in the pub, the mortars fired and hardly anyone batted an eyelid. After closing time, at 21h00, we all returned to our accommodation and went to bed.

At about 23h00, much to my annoyance, I was disturbed by the *wheeeee* and *doef* sounds of mortar fire. However, after the second *wheeeee* and *doef* something started to register in my sleepy head. The customary *doef* and *wheeeee* were actually a *wheeeee* and *doef.* "That's the wrong way round!" I said to myself.

The third *wheeeee* was followed by a very loud *doef* as a mortar exploded close by followed by the sound of hail falling on the 'terrapin' I was staying in. "Shrapnel from a mortar!" I registered. That awakened me very quickly and two seconds later I put into practice what we should have practised almost every night. I dived into the nearby bunker, in my birthday suit. To my horror, I found that I had landed among a bunch of naked or scantily clad men—the best dressed among us wearing underpants. On the way to the bunker I heard another mortar flying overhead and then exploding, thankfully a bit further away than the one that had rained shrapnel on my terrapin.

Quite a few of the occupants of the bunker had grabbed a trusty Castle on the way out of their rooms and the explosion was followed by cans popping and the proverbial 'cheers'.

With that I heard an unfamiliar voice, looked up, and saw a pongo captain (I think he was a captain). He was properly dressed in uniform and was setting an example with his rifle at his side. He had a full-on go at us using the following dialogue, as closely as I can remember, translated from Afrikaans:

"Where are your weapons? This is a mortar attack and you guys are all sitting here drinking beer and joking. Go and get your weapons."

At that point in time we had no intention whatsoever of moving out of the bunker.

"Where are your weapons?" he repeated.

Still no movement from any one of us, only a few comments and obscenities, but we were not going to move.

After another short lecture someone asked, "Who are you?"

"I am the OC of the mortar unit at Ruacana. Go and fetch your weapons; we are under attack," he stated.

A bit of chit-chat took place. The pongo was starting to get agitated by the lack of response from the SAAF aircrew he was sharing the bunker with. During this chit-chat the pongo asked why we were not going to fetch our weapons. The reason was that we were in the middle of the camp where our weapons could not be used. If the terrorists did attack the camp we had the army looking after the perimeter. If we heard any fighting taking place on the perimeter we would only then consider getting our weapons. This did not go down well with our new pongo friend. The next thing we saw was him exiting the bunker and leopard-crawling away with his rifle. This of course was very amusing to all of us and a number of comical comments were forthcoming from the SAAF occupants left behind in the bunker.

A few minutes later the pongo captain came leopard-crawling back. After sitting there without saying a word for a minute or two, he said, "Sorry guys,

I have to admit I was giving you all a mouthful because you did not have your weapons with you and when I looked down I noticed that I did not have a magazine in my rifle. I had to go and fetch it." That took guts after the lecture he had given us earlier and I take my hat off to him.

After a few minutes of silence after the fourth and last mortar had landed, we had a quick roll call and everyone was accounted for without injuries. We analyzed that the first mortar had landed outside the perimeter of the airfield, the second at the aircraft, the third between my terrapin and where the Parabats were accommodated and the fourth in no-man's land, close to the mess facilities and pub. We needed to make an assessment of the damage so hurried to the aircraft to see if they were okay. We had four Mk II Imps parked at the end of the taxiway near the runway threshold of runway 14, the most used runway at Ondangs.

It was dark and we were not too keen to turn on too many lights. The aircraft were parked quite close to the airfield perimeter and we had just been subjected to our first ground-to-ground attack. Arriving at the aircraft things looked bad. One of the Imps was standing with a wing almost touching the ground, the other one way up in the air—definitely damage of some sort as there was a lot of fuel lying on the apron as well. On closer inspection it was determined that one of the mortars had landed about five to ten metres directly behind and between Impalas 1054 and 1045. We found that shrapnel had punctured the tip tank. The fuel had drained out and the imbalance left the aircraft in an 'unusual attitude'. We were all relieved. Never be fooled by first impressions!

While we were standing around swapping 'war stories' someone leaned against one of the Mk II aircraft with an outspread palm. "Ouch!" he shouted, pulling his hand back, complaining that the aircraft had burnt it. Obviously there had been more damage than we could see in the dark and everybody jumped into action. The canopy was opened and it was discovered that a piece of shrapnel had penetrated the side of the cockpit, punctured the battery, which had shorted out and was in the process of overheating. The battery was quickly disconnected and removed from the aircraft.

In the morning all the aircraft were thoroughly inspected. Two had suffered minor damage—the other two were undamaged. Things were a lot better than expected. We were able to continue operations using two Imps and alternating crews, while the damaged aircraft were repaired.<<

Between 10 and 12 April, SAAF Canberras once again linked up with the Rhodesian Air Force for Operation *Mulungushi*. At 19h00 local time, two SAAF Canberras joined a formation of six RhAF Hunters and six Canberras in an air strike on the terrorist base at Mulungushi. The same formation re-struck the target at first light on 11 March. On both occasions 37mm anti-aircraft fire was drawn.

At 16h00, the aircraft were airborne once again; this time they struck a terrorist target at Shilende. On 12 April, after debriefing, the SAAF crews returned to Waterkloof. Unconfirmed Rhodesian media reports estimated over 1,000 casualties from these strikes.

Seek and destroy

At AFB Ondangwa, during the afternoon of 11 April, the Recces gave a demonstration of captured Soviet-manufactured weapons, some of which our pilots could come into contact with during operations inside Angola. One of the weapons demonstrated was an RPG (rocket-propelled grenade) fired at a vehicle parked on the temporary shooting range, created on Ondangwa airfield. Once this demonstration was completed a second RPG was fired into the air where the self-destruct fuse, which activates at about 1,000 metres after launch, was demonstrated. Major Graham Rochat who witnessed this demonstration subconsciously recorded the fact that a 'shockwave' was seen in the sandy surface around and ahead of the launcher.

The following morning, 12 April, he awoke to a normal day in the bush and by 07h30 was airborne with Hubs Füss, conducting an armed recce north of the area between beacons 3 to 12. They were looking for smoke from enemy cooking fires. On their return Rochat was tasked to lead a two-ship Impala Mk II sortie with Derek Sevenster, who was doing his first bush-tour flight. The briefing was for an armed recce of the area up to 40 nautical miles north of the cut-line starting from Ruacana in the west, then working their way eastward to a point more or less due north of Ondangwa, from where they would return to base.

The Impala Mk II aircraft were configured with four rocket pods with six 68mm rockets in each; the 30mm cannons were loaded with 180 rounds of a combination of ball (solid shot) and HE (high explosive) rounds.

Rochat briefed his No 2 to maintain radio silence after departing 'Ondangs'. As they were doing an armed reconnaissance he intended to fly at 300 knots on a heading of 360° for six minutes after crossing the cut-line, then turn south and fly back to the cut-line. The pattern would be repeated as they worked their way eastward. During the briefing he noted they would be passing two known MPLA bases—one just a few miles northeast of Ruacana—the other at a town named Cuamato, about 20 nautical miles north of the cut-line, northwest of Ondangwa.

Once airborne they departed as per SOP and crossed the cut-line just east of the Ruacana falls. Rochat called "Vrystaat live!" as they crossed the international border and proceeded north at 50–100 feet AGL. About a minute after crossing the cut-line he saw the first of the known MPLA camps a couple of kilometres away on the starboard side. Squinting into the morning sun he noted a few reflections which he took to be the sun reflecting off of a moving vehicle. Then he realized that the 'reflections' were in fact muzzle flashes from anti-aircraft guns. He was not unduly concerned, knowing that at that firing range and the fact the Impalas were down at 50–100 feet AGL, that it was virtually impossible for anything from the site to harm them.

They continued northward then, following the planned route, worked their way east. While on a northerly heading Rochat saw Cuamato coming up on the nose of his aircraft so turned slightly left to pass approximately a kilometre to the west. Abeam of the town he pulled up to 150 feet to get a better view of what military equipment was there. He noticed a dust cloud coming from the front of a house in the northwest corner of the village. This looked very much like the shockwave he remembered from the previous day's demonstration on the shooting range.

"Missile launch, missile launch! Get down, get down!" he called over the radio while pushing forward on the stick to get down to very low level. The shape of the shockwave coming from the launch position appeared to be oval, not round, and Rochat had the impression the missile was not aimed at his aircraft. Immediately he heard a loud thud behind him and, at the same time, felt the aircraft lunge slightly forward, which he believed was caused by the shockwave of a nearby explosion.

He heard his No 2 say, "Major, a big explosion just behind your aircraft. Are you okay?"

He answered, "No problems. Stay down."

They cleared the danger zone before commencing a climb to 20,000 feet. On crossing the cut-line he called "Vrystaat safe" and de-armed all weapons systems.

During the climb Rochat made contact with Dayton. He requested the controller to contact Oshakati Ops, advise them that he had been fired upon and was requesting permission to retaliate.

"Go for it, major. Go *klap* them," was the immediate reply from the corporal providing radar surveillance on Dayton frequency.

"I am not requesting your permission. Get the air force commander at Oshakati on the air for me."

Not too long after this the radar officer, a captain, came on the radio and Rochat again explained the situation.

"Go *klap* them, major," was once again the reply.

Rochat again answered with, "I am not asking your permission. I require permission from the Oshakati ops commander to retaliate as this could become an international matter."

Shortly thereafter the SAAF ops commander came on the air and granted permission to retaliate.

Rochat quickly briefed his No 2, telling him they were to prepare for a high-level RP (rocket projectile) attack with all RP pods selected to 'single' and cannons on 'both'. They then turned for the target area. Rochat decided to attack the left-hand row of buildings and told Sevenster to take the right-hand row. After weapons release they would break off to the left and return to low level.

Cuamato was easy to identify from the air. The road divided the small town, which consisted of two rows of between six and ten buildings orientated north to south, and nothing else. Rochat planned the route to the target so they could do a left-hand attack, as they had practised so many times on the weapons range at Pietersburg. He planned to enter a high-level academic RP attack. Crossing the cut-line he again called "Vrystaat live!" and continued navigating to the target.

They approached at 20,000 feet with the settlement on their left-hand side, exactly as taught on the Roodewal range. He adjusted his flight path to get the target appearing just above the left-hand canopy sill for a 30° dive. At the appropriate point just short of roll-in he throttled back to idle and rolled in to his planned 30° dive. As they rolled in he checked all four RP pods were selected 'on' and 'single', while the cannon selector was set to 'both'. He set the gun-sight depression to 48mils to ensure the correct sight-setting for the profile.

On the practice range things had always happened so quickly once the aircraft had rolled into the dive—there never seemed enough time to do all that was required. However, in this live attack everything appeared to be happening in slow motion.

Just before the Impala reached 10,000 feet Rochat fired a burst of 30mm cannon fire to keep enemy heads down. The fixed cross of his gun sight was above the target area but he raised it a bit more to allow for the additional height and squirted off three short bursts. After a few seconds, which felt like an eternity, he saw the 30mm rounds raking the left-hand row of buildings.

By this time he was approaching release height and aiming at the building from which the RPG had been launched, at the far end of the left-hand row. He squeezed the RP button three times at one-second intervals to spread the RPs through the buildings short of the target.

Sevenster, in the dive behind and to the right of his leader, came on the air calling, "They are all running to my side, major."

After sending off four salvos Rochat held back and concentrated on getting the pipper (the dot of light in the centre of the gun sight* *see* details on page 121) and aircraft into the correct parameters for the final launch. The dive angle was pretty close to the intended 30° and the speed was now very close to 300 knots, showing that all the academic training on the range had proved its worth.

Unlike the tiny 'coke' (air force jargon for a bull's eye) they were used to on the range this target was literally as big as a house. Aiming at the centre he squeezed off another salvo of four RPs. The four rockets jumped out of the pods with a *thump* and raced towards the target. When last seen they were still trailing smoke at the base of the house (the sign of an accurate attack). Instinctively, Rochat pulled 4–5G to recover from the dive and then applied 110° angle of bank to the left and exited the target area, while descending back to about 50 feet AGL. No 2 called off and they departed for their return to 'Ondangs'.

Southeast of Cuamato, Rochat looked back and saw black columns of smoke coming from the settlement. Foolishly he turned back to re-attack as he still had one salvo of rockets remaining. They changed their sight setting for a 10° dive. The top of the fixed cross was used for cannon attacks and they could fire their cannons or rockets without having to make any sight-setting changes. Rochat set the formation up for a pitch and fan to the left, using the smoke to guide him onto the target.

As soon as he pitched up and had broken the skyline the sky around him turned black from the flak of anti-aircraft fire from the town. He immediately called, "Stay down, stay down", while at the same time hearing Sevenster's warning call of the flak. Because Rochat was already at altitude and in his dive he continued his attack. He raised the fixed cross way above the building with a flag flying from a flagpole, probably the HQ, and squeezed the trigger to send off a stream of 30mm rounds. He held the trigger and after two to three seconds, while still firing, he rolled on bank to the left and manoeuvred until the 30mm rounds started hitting the building. As he was still in a bank he applied a bootful

Commandant Graham Rochat, SM.

of top rudder and squeezed off the last salvo of rockets. Where they went to he had no idea, however, he did see his 30mm HE rounds flashing on the wall of the building which then collapsed under the barrage.

As he exited the target area Sevenster formed up with him and they returned home at treetop level, having expended all their ammunition. Rochat admits to making some elementary errors on this sortie flown during the early stage of the 'jet-jocks' bush war. His major error was to carry out a re-attack on the same target and he almost came off second best.

On 3 June, 3 Squadron returned to AFB Ondangwa to escort Impalas on a strike against a SWAPO target near Humbe. The Impalas went through the target unimpeded and the Mirage F1CZs were not brought into action.

*A 'pipper' is the dot of light in the centre of the gun sight which is used to aim with. If you put the pipper on the cockpit of the aircraft you are trying to shoot down, the gun sight measures the G force being applied and computes the 'lead' you have to apply automatically. Put another way—to hit a moving target, you have to aim ahead of it. The harder or faster the target is turning the more lead that has to be applied. The gun sight system does all this for you, provided you can get the pipper onto the target and hold it there long enough for the sighting system to resolve the computation. If you are the unfortunate target, you are flying looking backwards at the aircraft threatening you. Provided you can't see his belly he can't hit you with guns as he has no lead. As soon as you see the aircraft's belly then it is time for a quick 'Ave Maria'.

All at sea

The previous day, Major Harry Anderson, one of the Alouette gunship pilots, was deployed to Tsumeb on standby, to thwart any attempt by SWAPO to gain a foothold in the farming area south of Grootfontein. The crews were on alert to respond to any summons for assistance.

An adrenaline rush always accompanied a phone call from the AFCP at Oshakati. Nine times out of ten it would be to bring the helicopter crews into action. The message that day was the tenth time. Nevertheless it was a call requesting a helicopter, but instead of going north into the war zone it was to go south.

A sailor on board a huge BP tanker was gravely ill and needed hospitalization. The ship's radio message for help was put through to WAC HQ in Windhoek. They decided to offer assistance and 310 AFCP in Oshakati was instructed to task an aircraft. With the war at a crucial stage the air boss in Oshakati, Colonel Ollie Holmes, decided he could not spare any Pumas so he tasked a Tsumeb aircraft to answer the call.

Anderson and Sergeant Johnny Smit, flying Alouette 615, took off from Tsumeb at 19h00 in the dark and set course for AFB Grootfontein. At the huge logistics base the 20mm cannon was removed from the gunship to allow space for a stretcher. Then they flew to Otjiwarongo to refuel before heading for Walvis Bay. There was no moon and the night was particularly dark. To avoid the Erongo mountains, which were on his direct track, Anderson climbed to a safe altitude of 10,000 feet. The lights of Usakos and Rössing Mine confirmed they were on course and shortly after midnight they arrived overhead their destination, AFB Rooikop.

Unfortunately, Rooikop was in total darkness and all the personnel were fast asleep. Anderson descended over the lights of Walvis Bay and air-taxiied up the Rooikop road to the base, using his landing light as a guide. Using the same method he found the base's aircraft dispersal area before selecting a spot to touch down. Fortunately, Smit was wide awake and, in the illumination of the landing beam, picked out a camouflaged Dakota directly underneath them. Moving away they landed without further incident and were met by the duty officer, who had been awakened by the noise of the aircraft.

They learned that the tanker would be 32 nautical miles off Pelican Point, the lighthouse near Walvis Bay, at 08h00 the following day. Gratefully the crew used the few remaining hours before daylight to get some well-earned sleep.

At the appointed time Anderson, with a feeling of trepidation, rendezvoused with the huge ship. The Alouette is a single-engined helicopter that, when operating alone, is forbidden by SAAF regulations from flying over the sea. It may only be flown within reach of the beach in the event of engine failure. Because Anderson had been authorized by Windhoek headquarters he was legally in the clear. However, this fact did nothing to ease the feeling of anxiety brought on by flying over the sea without maritime survival equipment, aircraft flotation gear or even Mae West lifejackets for the crew.

The ship had a marked landing area on which Anderson landed without difficulty. After shut-down the district surgeon and sister, who had accompanied them from Walvis Bay, disappeared into the bowels of the ship to find their patient. Meanwhile, the captain set course for his destination in Europe at 16 knots. The novelty of their unaccustomed surroundings soon wore off as Anderson watched the land vanish behind them.

This photograph taken a few years later shows Harry Anderson on the left enjoying a celebratory drink. It is a photograph of historic value as it shows, from left: Harry Anderson, HC, Mario Vergottini, HC, unknown, Arthur Walker, HCG and bar.

Despite Anderson's suggestion that the doctor "get a move on", it took the medical team two and a half hours to stabilize the patient who had serious injuries to his neck and head. The time equated to 40 nautical miles which, added to the original 32, meant an anxious sea passage of over an hour before the Alouette reached dry land.

The voyage was Anderson's first and, being out of sight of land, he confirmed the direction to Rooikop with the ship's chief mate before lifting off. After refuelling at Rooikop, at the request of the doctor they flew the casevac directly to the Windhoek state hospital. They topped up their tanks at Windhoek's Eros airfield before returning to the war in Tsumeb—stopping at AFB Grootfontein to have their cannon reinstalled. Total sortie time was ten hours and 30 minutes. In the 23-year bush war there were not many crews who could include a sea voyage among their list of operational experiences.

Operation *Rekstok II*

Cabinet approval was given for an air strike on SWAPO's Tobias Haneko Training Camp (THTC) on 6 July. This strike, originally part of operation *Rekstok* carried out between 6 and 13 March, became known as *Rekstok II*. Two Buccaneers and seven F1AZs attacked the target situated ten nautical miles northeast of Lubango. 'Gamblers', the Buccaneer formation, took off from AFB Grootfontein at 07h00. The Mirages took off from AFB Ondangwa and were planned to attack 40 seconds after the Buccaneers. Both approaches were without incident except for slight errors in timing. This resulted in the Buccaneers tossing 16 x 450kg bombs through the flight path of the approaching Mirage formation. Later, a captured SWAPO terrorist said that THTC had been cordoned off after the air strike and a stream of trucks had been required to take away the casualties.

Omapande

On the same day as the Buccaneer–Mirage attack, a combined air strike was planned on targets in the shallow area of Angola. Mirage F1AZ attacked a radio facility in the town of Ongiva, while four Impala jets simultaneously attacked a logistics depot in Chiede, a little town a few miles east of Ongiva.

A Mirage III R2Z was tasked to carry out post-strike damage-assessment photography of both targets, immediately after a low-level reconnaissance of Omapande. This little settlement had become a thorn in the side of air force operations. In the previous few weeks our patrolling aircraft had drawn gunfire every time they flew near it. Intelligence was urgently required for an assessment to be made of enemy activities in the town.

AFB Ondangwa operations staff conducted the strike briefing. Commandant Casey Lewis led the Mirage F1s and Captain Otto Schür, using the call sign 'Snoopy', was flying the Mirage III recce aircraft. Captain Trevor Schroeder led the Impalas with Lieutenant André Botha as No 2, Captain Nic Oosthuysen as deputy leader and Lieutenant Piet 'Pongo' van Zyl as No 4. Van Zyl's aircraft was also equipped with an F95 camera pod to take film of the Impala strike. Time on target (TOT) for both strikes was 11h00.

This was Schür's second flight of the day. Earlier that morning he had been on a recce sortie 350 kilometres into Angola, a high-risk mission. This second sortie just over the border was considered a routine flight. While taxiing out Schür noticed all the helicopter crews and Parabats who had been on cockpit alert for the first sortie, standing down; this registered in the back of his mind as a potential problem.

To increase his own safety he was to overfly Omapande 15 seconds before the simultaneous strikes on the other two targets. Speed, like low-level flying, was an aircraft safety feature in the bush. Schür approached Omapande from the southwest at 190 feet on the radio altimeter, travelling at 600 knots.

The air strikes went according to plan. At Chiede the Impalas did not draw any ground fire and, after ensuring they had destroyed the target, Schroeder and André departed for Ondangwa. As briefed, Oosthuysen and van Zyl carried out a further photographic run to film the results. After breaking off from the target on the way back to base Oosthuysen visually picked up an explosion in the direction of Omapande. His immediate reaction was that the Mirages had struck the wrong target. While thinking about the explosion, a nagging thought crept into Oosthuysen's mind. The explosion did not look like bomb blast and there appeared to be a white parachute against the black smoke.

It must be remembered that all these occurrences took place within milliseconds while Oosthuysen was turning off his own target. It was difficult for him to recall exactly what he had seen but the more he thought about it the more he suspected Snoopy had been hit. After all, Oosthuysen had been hit twice on previous sorties near the town. He broke the briefed radio silence and tried to call Snoopy, without success. The only reaction was a terse comment over the radio, from one of the more senior pilots flying in the strike formations, to maintain radio discipline.

Ondangwa is only a few minutes' flying time south of the border and Oosthuysen was soon on the ground. After switching off he was met by Trevor Schroeder and told him what he suspected. Together they ran to the operations room and reported the possibility of a downed aircraft. None of the senior staff believed the story. Schür still had another 15 minutes of flight time before he was due back at base.

However ... as Schür, in his Mirage, had switched on the cameras for the start of the photo run he heard a bang like that of a 30mm shell exploding. This was followed immediately by total electrical failure, an emergency not thought possible in a Mirage. Without electrical power he could not make an emergency radio call. He had the presence of mind to stay at low level until he had passed the town before starting a right-hand climbing turn to recover to Ondangwa. At 8,000 feet, 12 kilometres from the town and still moving at over 500 knots he rolled out, headed south, and reduced throttle. At that the engine seized and the delta-winged Mirage flicked into a high-G right-hand descending spiral. Schür could not recover as he had no emergency hydraulic pressure so he opted to eject. Because the G-force was so high he could not lift the seat-pan handle but with his left hand managed to grip and pull the face-blind. He blacked out momentarily as he shot through the canopy. When he regained his senses he remembers seeing his aircraft below him with a bright orange flame just behind the canopy. He watched as the Mirage plunged into the ground with a massive fuel explosion sending up clouds of black smoke.

The prevailing wind drifted the parachute just south of the impact point. Schür had time to stabilize his oscillation before he hit the ground 100 metres from the wreck. The impact was so great that his head hit the ground between his knees, causing a gash under his chin—amazingly the only injury he suffered. His helmet and mask, which might have prevented even this injury, had been lost in the blast of the high-speed ejection.

His first reaction was to hide his parachute. He was hastened by a rush of adrenaline triggered by the sound of machine-gun fire very close at hand. Luckily, it was only his own 30mm cannon ammunition cooking off in the conflagration. In his combat jacket he had all the emergency equipment he would need. After hiding his parachute he set off, running southward, to put as much distance between him and the wreck as he could. After about four kilometres Schür selected a suitable helicopter landing zone (LZ), with thick bush in close proximity where he could conceal himself until pick-up. He got rid of all incriminating documentation in case he was captured. One hour after ejection, the time he considered it would take to get the rescue started, he turned on his emergency Pelba beacon. To his delight he immediately received an answering call.

Back at Ondangwa, Schroeder, the senior Impala pilot, had told Oosthuysen that he believed him and would take the one available Impala, without waiting for authority, to go and verify the situation. Schroeder scrambled into the air while Oosthuysen rushed to have the refuelling completed on his own aircraft so he could fly and give Schroeder cover. As Schroeder crossed the cut-line he picked up Schür's Pelba beacon, confirming he had been shot down.

On the radio Schroeder raised Oosthuysen, who by this time was strapped into his Impala. He told Oosthuysen to wait and get Piet van Zyl ready so the pair of aircraft could take off together to relieve him on station over the crash scene when his fuel was down to bingo minimum—the fuel needed to return to base.

Schür could now talk to Schroeder and homed him into the smoke from the wreck. From there he talked the Impala onto his own position. Schroeder then went low level and Schür moved out into the open LZ so Schroeder could pinpoint his position accurately to inform the helicopter crew. Schür then asked Schroeder to hold off in a pattern away from his position so the enemy could not use the Impala as a guide.

Schroeder noticed an enemy truck leaving Omapande and turning south towards the wreck. He rolled in to attack the truck, which then left the narrow track and disappeared under thick bush. Approaching minimum fuel Schroeder called Oosthuysen to take off and relieve him on station. Within a few minutes Oosthuysen was on the scene and Schroeder set course for base.

Oosthuysen established Schür's position and set about guiding Ralph Platter, the Puma pilot, to the LZ. As both Omapande and Chiede had been stirred up by the air strikes the helicopter had to route around Chiede before approaching Schür from the north. At this time Schür heard the enemy approaching through the bush. Oosthuysen made a few fast, low-level passes to try and discourage them while the helicopter touched down in the LZ. Before the Parabats could even jump out of the helicopter Schür had dived into the cabin. The helicopter took off and headed south to AFB Ondangwa, with its escort of two Impalas.

Although apparently unhurt, apart from the cut chin, Schür was dispatched by C-160 Transall for a proper medical check at 1 Military Hospital in Pretoria. Over five years later, severe back pains revealed that he had compressed three vertebrae in an ejection which could have proved fatal.

Rhodesian operations

On 7 and 8 July, SAAF Canberras joined the Rhodesian Air Force to carry out Operation *Cucumber*. Three SAAF Canberras took off from the Fylde airfield to join three RhAF Canberras and six Hunters flying from New Sarum, Salisbury. In the target area the formation split; two Canberras and two Hunters each struck one of three targets. The strike was repeated at 08h30 on 8 July. The 12 Squadron Canberras flew 21.45 hours and dropped 1,800 Alpha bombs.

On 09h15 22 August, three SAAF Canberras joined forces with the Rhodesian Air Force for Operation *Placid I*. Once again operating out of the Fylde airfield, each Canberra carried two 1,000lb and nine 500lb bombs for attacks on ZIPRA bases in Zambia along Rhodesia's northern border. Hunters were used to escort the Canberras and, although Zambian Shenyang F-6 fighters were scrambled, they were too late to intercept the mission. By 12h15 the same formations were airborne for Operation *Sponge*. The bombers ran in at medium altitude (15,000 feet) and bombed a different set of targets 12 miles east of Rufunsa, on the Zambian Great East road. This time the Shenyang fighters were not scrambled as they were still on the ground being turned around.

At 15h40, the combined formations again took to the air on Operation *Placid II*, to re-strike the early morning targets. This time the Shenyang fighters were scrambled but were again too late to carry out an effective interception.

At 09h40 on 23 August, the formations rendezvoused over Victoria Falls, this time for Operation *Motel I*. From low level the aircraft bombed a ZIPRA target 20 miles south of Solwezi, in northern Zambia.

At 15h30, the combined formation rendezvoused over Wankie for a re-strike on the morning's target, on operation *Motel II*. Once again, low-level bombing

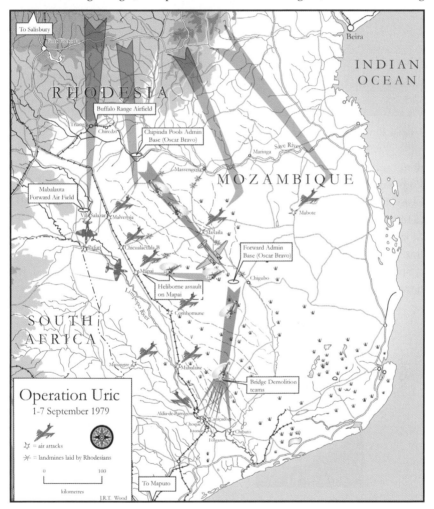

The Rhodesian Operation *Uric*. *Map by J. R. T. Wood*

was carried out. However, this time Canberra 451, flown by Major Bekker and Captain Labuschagne, picked up shrapnel damage from a Golf bomb dropped by one of the Hunters but the Canberra landed safely.

Between 1 and 8 September, the Rhodesians launched Operation *Uric*. The aim of this big operation was to destroy infrastructure in Mozambique, specifically

Twelve Pumas during a training exercise. Large formations are difficult to manage, especially when each crew has to select their own suitable LZ. Training is the answer.

dams and roads, and to destroy large concentrations of enemy at Mapai. Fifteen Pumas and two Frelons, from 19 and 15 Squadrons respectively, were deployed to assist the Rhodesian Special Air Service (SAS) and the Rhodesian Light Infantry (RLI). The battle arena covered Barragem, Mapai and Mabalane in western Mozambique, with SAAF aircraft operating from Rhodesian airfields at Buffalo Range and Chipinda Pools.

Strategic targets (bridges and railway lines) were successfully damaged and destroyed. However, the Rhodesian attack on Mapai was repulsed by very heavy

'Breyty' Breytenbach, HCS.

'Crow' Stannard, HC.

AAA fire and determined defenders in a formidable trench network, neither of which had been given much significance at the intelligence briefing. Because there were approximately 700 more enemy troops than anticipated the attack on Mabalane was called off. A SAAF Puma, flown by Captain Paul Vellerman, Lieutenant Nigel Osborne and Flight Sergeant Dick Retief was shot down, killing the three crew and 14 Rhodesian soldiers (eleven RLI paratroopers and

1979: Learning the ropes

three Rhodesian Engineers). A Rhodesian Bell (Huey) helicopter was also shot down in which one person was killed. Two Puma pilots were decorated after this battle. Commandant Breytenbach received the Honoris Crux (Silver) and Major Stannard the Honoris Crux. (Incidentally, Operation *Uric* was the first Rhodesian operation of their bush war in which they failed to fully achieve their objectives.)

On 25 and 26 September, an interesting air strike mission took place. AFB Waterkloof had cancelled flying while the main runway underwent a much needed resurfacing. 24 Squadron's aircraft had deployed to Jan Smuts International airport (now O. R. Tambo), and it was from here the mission originated—probably the only operational mission flown from that location.

Three Buccaneers flew from there to AFB Pietersburg to bomb up with six 450kg bombs in each aircraft in preparation for Operation *Driepoot*. The next day, in atrocious weather, they flew to AFB Rooikop, outside Walvis Bay, to refuel. Then they took off to attack a SWAPO ammunition dump and supply depot close to Lubango. The actual aiming point was a 30 x 19-metre building. During the last 30 seconds of run-in to release point the radar warning system (RWS) illuminated with multiple warnings. No 3's bombs hit the target and caused large secondary explosions.

Intelligence often determines the success or failure of operations. All forms of intelligence gathering are used to build an overall picture of enemy dispositions

The western end of the AFB Ondangwa runway. The living areas, aircraft hardstandings and maintenance area are at the bottom of the photo. At top centre the mobile radar station, 'Dayton', can be seen and at bottom left the tar road to Oshakati.

129

1. The Tsumeb–Ruacana main road running past AFB Ondangwa.
2. The base perimeter fence.
3. The Comint listening-post camp at the end of Ondangwa runway.
4. The eastern end of the main runway was too close for comfort when taking off with a fully loaded Mirage F1.

and intentions. Photographic intelligence, although not always the best method, is certainly the most convincing. PR work requires tremendous planning and precise flying. It is an exacting task. On missions over enemy territory the vulnerable PR aircraft are always given the protection of an accompanying escort thus allowing the PR crew to concentrate solely on their task. On 15 September, two Canberra reconnaissance missions overflew targets in Angola, escorted by F1CZs.

On 27 September, two SAAF Canberras again flew up to Fylde airfield to participate in Operation *Miracle*. After take off they rendezvoused with the Rhodesian force and attacked a combined ZANLA/Frelimo target 30 miles northeast of Umtali, at Chimoio in Mozambique. The profile used was a low-level bombing run with a 500 feet release height. All three Rhodesian Canberras took small-arms hits and one SAAF Canberra received an AK-47 bullet through the cockpit.

AFB Ondangwa

Over the years, AFB Ondangwa had developed into a large sprawling airfield. It became home to the medical intensive care unit; the Fireforce reaction unit; Special Forces had built their own HQ, named Fort Rev, halfway along the runway; the mobile radar unit; as well as all the air force supporting units. Ondangwa was active day and night throughout the war and bore the brunt of air-related operations.

1979: Learning the ropes

Left: Presentation of a water-cooler to the pub with James Wallace listening intently. 'Chopper Corner' can be seen in the background.
Right: CAF Lieutenant-General Mike Muller being entertained by AFB Ondangwa OC, Commandant Div de Villiers.

Being only 30 kilometres from the Angolan border it was constantly under threat from SWAPO insurgents; strict security precautions were therefore the order of the day. Road traffic to the south was often controlled in the form of convoys, while passenger air traffic was covered on landing and take-off by airborne helicopter gunships. It was a tense professional atmosphere that prevailed throughout the base.

Ondangwa developed in a similar manner to all the other military establishments that had sprung up, like mushrooms, throughout the entire operational theatre. An urgent operational requirement had been to get troops on the ground in the areas where they were needed using minimal planning and even less funding. Little wonder that practically all our bases and facilities resembled glorified squatters' camps. The renowned South African characteristic of *'n Boer maak 'n plan* brought numerous buildings into being mostly with begged, borrowed or stolen materials. Some grandiose structures were built, but none was more carefully discussed, or caringly constructed, than the one building that dominated AFB Ondangwa during its entire existence—the pub.

Luxuries in the operational area were scarce and opportunities for rest and recreation limited. The pub, therefore, became the focal point of life for those stationed at Ondangwa. It was decided that it would be a combined facility catering for all ranks; I believe this decision made it the success it undoubtedly was. Everybody was in the war together, sharing the same hardships and dangers, so why not share the same facility within which to relax? On Sundays the pub also served the community as a church.

The main aim of Commandant Ertjies Penzhorn and his team of pub-builders was to ensure the bar counter was the longest in the operational area, if not in the southern hemisphere. They got it right. It had a very long counter with a tight-angled bend towards the one end leading into an alcove, which was promptly christened 'Chopper Corner' because the helicopter crews were always the first in and the last out. It was aptly named.

The counter was under cover, as was a large area filled with garden tables and chairs where groups could converse in more private surroundings. Where the roof ended the branches of a large tree provided overhead shelter. This left the entrance side of the pub completely open. An ideal arrangement as it helped keep the tropical temperatures from becoming excessive as air conditioning was but a dream at that time.

'Hot Extractions Limited'

On 18 October 1979, I found them in the pub. Two big men, in physical stature and reputation, renowned for their deeds in the bush. They were seated facing each other across the right-angle of the counter. Normally, such men stand while in a pub. However, the number of empty glasses and bottles on the counter indicated they had been there for some time and I was glad they were seated. It would be indelicate of me to suggest they were drunk but I do believe they were probably very, very unsober.

They greeted me with widespread arms and invited me to join them for a drink. They were obviously celebrating but, because they were now speaking in *shackle,* it took me longer than normal to ascertain what they were celebrating. Shackle was a code used to obviate radio messages from being intercepted and understood by the enemy. A form of shackle also seems to be in common use in pubs worldwide and apparently becomes more readily understood nearer closing time. After repeated attempts I finally understood the reason for their determined and steadfast celebration.

Major Steyn Venter, a Southwester by birth, was a very experienced and dedicated fighter pilot. An instructor, who had flown Sabres and Mirages, he was at this time Commanding Officer of 4 Squadron. He was in his thirteenth year with the SAAF and was currently on a bush tour, flying Impalas.

Across the counter and appropriately seated in Chopper Corner was another veteran of the bush war, Major Paul Kruger, known as 'Polla' by all his associates. An experienced and devoted helicopter pilot, he considered any aircraft flying higher than fifty feet to be wasting helicopter fuel. These two celebrants had just come up with the idea of forming a company, to be called 'Hot Extractions Limited'; they were to become joint directors of this new firm. Later, from more sober sources, I unravelled the reason for the founding of this proposed new company.

While taxiing back to dispersal, after a cross-border sortie, Venter noticed two pilots, Aubrey Bell and Giep Vermeulen, strapping in to two Impalas. After shut-down he approached Bell to find out where they were going. He was told they had been tasked to look for enemy vehicles in the Cuamato, Chiede and Ongiva

1979: Learning the ropes

triangle. Venter felt uneasy about the mission and warned Bell that the whole area was thick with enemy air defence artillery. After his mission debriefing Venter was put on standby for SAR (search and rescue) for the remainder of the afternoon.

By October, the summer heat had arrived with a vengeance in Owamboland. It was customary for all the SAR crews, both fixed-wing and helicopter, to carry out their standby from the swimming pool—this being the coolest place on the base. Venter put on his costume, placed his damp flying overall out in the sun to dry and joined the rest of the aviators in the pool. A portable Becker VHF radio set, tuned to the SAR frequency, was conveniently placed within earshot to initiate any required call-out, all under the watchful eye of Major Koos Botha, the MAOT commander.

In the early years of the war SAR was a jointly planned operation involving Impala, Puma and Alouette crews, and soldiers from the Parachute Battalion. The Parabats accompanied the helicopters to fetch and carry rescued persons if necessary, while providing protection for the helicopter in the LZ. The plan was theoretically a good one but, for inexplicable reasons, had never been practised.

All hell broke loose when Giep Vermeulen's voice was heard on the Becker shouting "Mayday, Mayday, Mayday" and reporting that his leader had been shot down but had ejected. Aircrew dashed into the prefabricated terrapins in record time. Swimming costumes were swapped for flying gear and survival jackets donned while on the run to the operations centre.

The briefing given by the duty operations officer, Major Pete 'Vark' Harvey, was short and succinct. With a finger pointing to a spot on the wall map of Angola he told Kruger to "*Klap* it, cock!" (literally slap it or hit it). This well-known phrase was the answer to any problem relating to navigation, destination, enemy information—in fact, in the early days of the war it was the standard helicopter briefing.

Contrary to the apparent casual approach adopted by the helicopters the jet aircrew briefings and procedures were more formal. Venter and his number two, Second Lieutenant Charlie Rudnick, were in their aircraft ready to go when they heard Kruger checking in. After starting up, Venter had tuned his radio to the SAR frequency and was speaking to Giep Vermeulen.

Kruger had Lieutenant Andy Lithgow and Flight Sergeant 'Ziggie' Hoebel as his crew. Major Hugh 'Hug' Paine was captain of the second Puma. After a hurried start they checked in on the radio asking for take-off clearance. This call, informing the network that they were serviceable and ready to lift off, was the signal to allow the Impalas to start rolling. Co-ordination was necessary to ensure the jets did not run out of fuel before the helicopters arrived in the search area.

It would appear that a classic mistake had been made. During their armed reconnaissance sortie, Bell had led his pair of Impalas too near the Angolan village of Omapande. Noticing something unusual he returned for a second closer inspection and was met by severe flak from Angolan AAA. His aircraft was hit and started to burn, forcing him to eject. The aircraft crashed approximately three kilometres south of the town, but Bell's parachute could be seen on the ground only 200 metres south of the trench line surrounding the town. Vermeulen immediately went into an orbit around his downed leader, carrying out strafing attacks on the closest trench line. He then called Venter to say there was a lorry coming out of Omapande, obviously looking for the downed pilot. Because Vermeulen was now out of ammunition Venter told him to carry out a dummy attack on the vehicle, which he proceeded to do. This had the desired effect as the lorry stopped.

Venter and Rudnick were in attack formation as they raced to the scene. Venter took over from a much relieved Vermeulen, whose fuel tanks were almost empty. The new formation went into a circular pattern at 9,000 feet above the scene. At this height they were safe from the light AAA, while the medium-altitude cloud cover gave them protection from the SA-7s. Venter could see smoke from the burning wreck, the empty parachute, and flashes of gunfire and RPG rockets coming from the trenches.

Just then Bell came up on his emergency radio to report he was in thick bush about 60 metres north of his parachute. His neck was injured and his left leg was probably broken.

By this time, Kruger and Paine were approaching from the south. Venter told Rudnick to stay and orbit the scene while he dashed south to visually pick up the helicopters and lead them to the smoke. Assessing the situation Kruger then detached Paine to orbit away from the AAA while he went in to drop the Parabats. During the run-in heavy ground fire could be heard in the helicopter. Lieutenant Lithgow, on his first operational tour, asked Kruger what all the noise was. Kruger replied, "They are shooting at us, cock!" Deathly silence was Lieutenant Lithgow's acknowledgement. They dropped the Parabats close to the parachute and then lifted off, coming under intense ground fire. Kruger had hardly turned away when the Parabat leader called up on the radio to say they had reached the pilot.

During the helicopter approach Venter and Rudnick attacked the trenches with 68mm rockets and 30mm cannon. Kruger made his return to the LZ where the Parabats quickly loaded Bell into the helicopter. On lift-off the Puma again came under heavy and sustained fire. During the transition to forward flight two RPG-7s flashed underneath the helicopter, before a long burst of tracer struck the aircraft. Two shots came through the cockpit grazing Kruger's neck and knocking out his intercom.

After a rapid course in sign language he persuaded his co-pilot to call Paine and ask him to do a visual inspection of the damaged helicopter. Paine reported that fuel was streaming from the aircraft but, apart from holes, there was no further indication of problems. One of the holes had been caused by a bullet which entered the cabin wounding Rifleman Brian Gibson, one of the Parabats, in the hip and arm. The well-trained paras applied dressings to his wounds preventing further loss of blood. Kruger flew his two casualties to the forward medical facility in Oshakati (it was only in later years that the highly professional SAMS intensive care unit was established at AFB Ondangwa).

Venter and Rudnick landed their Impalas at Ondangwa, followed thereafter by Hug Paine in his Puma. Kruger detoured via Oshakati to drop off his casualties before returning to Ondangwa in his damaged helicopter. After the sortie debrief Venter and Kruger decided it would be criminal to waste their adrenaline rush and thus adjourned to the pub, along with the other aircrews and Parabats involved in the operation. During the evening the rescue was re-enacted many times growing in viciousness and stature at each telling. The adrenaline and alcohol-induced creativity gave birth to the idea of forming 'Hot Extractions Limited'.

Apart from Bell's lost Impala, his injured neck and broken leg, Vermeulen's aircraft also incurred a 7.62mm AK-47 bullet hole through the vertical tailplane. Kruger's Puma had 22 holes in it and required major repair; his neck required a band-aid. Brian Gibson spent the remainder of his national service in various hospitals before recovering fully from his injuries.

Two other noteworthy incidents occurred during this frenzied activity. A C-130 Hercules had landed at AFB Ondangwa with change-over personnel on board. Aircrew, completing their bush tours, were returning to South Africa and being replaced by the newcomers. Captain Mike 'Pez' Parsonson stepping out of the aircraft in his nutria uniform, was whisked away, dumped into an Impala and told to be on cockpit standby in case the rescue took longer than expected. Fortunately he was not required. However, it was certainly a quick start to his bush tour.

Against all regulations, the OC AFB Ondangwa, Major Basil Newham, himself an experienced helicopter bush-war veteran, met all the returning aircraft personally to hand over well-deserved, ice-cold bottles of beer. In a small way it was an acknowledgement of a job well done. Like Nelson putting his telescope to his blind eye—'I see no ships'—Basil saw no regulations.

Polla Kruger, Ziggie Hoebel, Brian Gibson and the five other Parabats were all awarded the Honoris Crux for their actions.

Zambia

On the same day, SAAF Canberras took part with a Rhodesian force in Operation *Tepid*. They attacked a ZIPRA target halfway between Kariba and Lusaka, in Zambia. All the aircraft bombed from medium altitude (15,000 feet) dropping 1,000 and 500lb bombs.

SWAPO still had a presence in Zambia, although they dared not approach close to the Caprivi Strip. Intelligence sources pinpointed a SWAPO camp on the edge of the Namafa pan, in the Senanga area of southwest Zambia, 850 nautical miles from Waterkloof. A combined air strike was planned for Guy Fawkes Day, 5 November 1979, using three Canberras to drop Alpha bombs, followed by four Buccaneers dropping a total of 24 x 460kg bombs.

On that day only three operationally qualified Buccaneer crews were available to fly. However, 24 Squadron was running a Buccaneer conversion course and, after 47 hours on type, Major Dave Knoesen and his 21-year-old navigator, Lieutenant Charlie Wroth, were doing well. They were whipped out from the course, given two 30° dive-bombing sorties and some live in-flight refuelling practice and found themselves in the No 2 position of the strike formation, under the watchful gaze of Commandant Gert Havenga, the squadron commander.

The Canberras took off from AFB Waterkloof followed at 05h30 by the Buccaneers. Because the aircraft were heavily loaded and Waterkloof is nearly a mile above sea level the formation took off in a stream, each aircraft ten seconds behind the other. It was the first of many heavy take-offs for the new crew. The aircraft joined into battle formation while climbing to altitude over Botswana.

As they approached the Caprivi Strip the new crew ran through their pre-attack checks, double-checking that they had remembered everything. Their big worry was to remember to roll open the bomb door prior to weapon release. Overhead Mpacha the formation turned northeastwards. The huge Zambezi River made

Buccaneer conversion course students, Dave Knoesen and Charlie Wroth, after their first operational mission.

navigation easy. Lead called "Target visual" and the new crew confirmed bomb checks complete, including the bomb door!

Sitting on the perch as No 2 it was easy to pick up the distinctly orange flashes of the Alpha bombs dropped from the Canberras which had attacked from low level. The Buccaneers then rolled in to a 30° high-dive. Charlie Wroth read out heights off the altimeter as it rapidly wound down until he felt, for the first time, the thuds of the ERUs which fired the bombs off the pylons.

There was no ground fire or missiles from the target as all the aircraft climbed to the south. The combined strike had been on target but had turned out to be a 'lemon' as the camp was empty during the attack. It was never proven but always suspected that Gerhard, the navy spy, could have leaked the information. He always seemed to be in the vicinity whenever the SAR plans for the mission were discussed. The Buccaneer formation landed back at Waterkloof three hours and 15 minutes after take-off.

The Rhodesian operation *Capsule* was planned to take place between 23 and 26 November, but bad weather foiled any attempt to carry out the strikes. They were re-flown on 9 December. A massive increase in ZANLA and ZIPRA incursions was expected into Rhodesia as a result of the imminent Lancaster House agreement. Rhodesian Canberras and Hunters were used in air strikes to prevent the terrorists being in a better position if talks broke down.

Three combined strikes were flown, the first hitting the CGT-2 target in southern Zambia. Then it was the turn of Nkume in Zambia followed by New Mavonde, in Mozambique. On each occasion the Rhodesian Canberras were armed with six 250kg bombs fitted with delay fuses; the SAAF Canberras each dropped two 1,000lb and nine 250kg bombs.

This successful series of combined strikes was to be the last joint effort before the ceasefire was signed between the Patriotic Front (Mugabe's ZANU and Nkomo's ZAPU) and Bishop Abel Muzorewa, the prime minister of the interim Zimbabwe-Rhodesia.

On 17 December, 3 Squadron deployed to AFB Ondangwa and the following day flew escort to a Mirage III R2Z on a PR deep into Angola, along the Lubango–Menonque railway line.

Chapter 6

1980: Establishing a pattern

The year started badly for the SAAF. On 7 January, and again on 15 January, a combined force of Canberras and Buccaneers, flying from AFB Waterkloof, were joined by Impalas flying out of AFB Ondangwa to strike a SWAPO target at Chitumba, in southern Angola. Both air strikes recorded poor results. The first, because the time on target (TOT) was too early and in the grey light of dawn the aircrew had difficulty identifying the target. The second air strike was affected by weather.

Late in the afternoon of 24 January, Captain Leon Burger was flying an Impala on a low-level armed reconnaissance flight. As he flashed past the little town of Aanhanca, in Angola, a heat-seeking SA-7 Strela missile entered the jet-pipe of his aircraft and detonated. The force of the explosion blew the entire vertical fin of the tailplane off the Impala. Despite the loss Captain Burger managed to fly the aircraft back to AFB Ondangwa.

Night had fallen by the time he arrived overhead the base and he was ordered to eject rather than attempt a landing. The airfield was crowded with aircraft and it was decided not to risk landing the Impala with severely reduced directional control. The ejection was successful.

SWAPO employed vehicles to carry the heavy mines, rockets and mortars used in their insurgency campaign, through Angola to caches just north of the SWA border. It was then comparatively easy for their cadres to stock up for a quick foray into Owamboland. As a counter-measure the SAAF launched a programme of low-level, armed reconnaissance flights by Impala fighters over the 'shallow area' in Angola, immediately adjacent to the cut-line. Success was almost immediate as the pilots attacked and destroyed vehicles moving anywhere close to the border. The enemy then switched to transporting their war matériel at night.

Night weaponry

The success of the visual armed recce flights created a problem for Colonel Ollie Holmes. The Impala pilots had successfully curtailed the movement of SWAPO's logistics by day, but the SAAF was almost impotent at night. The dilemma came to a head on 1 February—Lieutenant Frans Vermaak reported seeing a mass gathering of SWAPO insurgents just to the north of the cut-line, southeast of Ongiva. Apparently they had lit a number of fires and were 'feasting', prior to setting off on their mission into SWA.

None of the Impala pilots was trained for night weaponry and the practice had been banned following an accident in 1976. To Holmes, this situation was unacceptable and he initiated a 'chain reaction' requesting authority to launch a night strike. The request went to WAC, SAAF HQ, SADF HQ and finally to the cabinet, who granted permission.

At 23h45 that night, Lieutenant Pete Hollis and Captain Cobus Toerien took off from Ondangwa under a bright, full moon. Unfortunately, by this late hour SWAPO's fires had been extinguished so the target was difficult to see. The pair released their weapons and tried to avoid looking back towards the target. It was presumed that in the 1976 accident the pilots had lost their night vision in the brilliance of the bomb explosion, leading to the crash.

During the night of 5 February, the same pilots flew two more sorties against these SWAPO camps. On the second sortie they fired rockets which extinguished the fires burning in the camp. It was reports of these night missions that suddenly gave impetus to resolving the night-attack problem.

Attacking moving targets at night posed a huge problem for the SAAF. In 1976, a night weaponry trial was brought to an abrupt halt when a two-seat Impala crash at Riemvasmaak weapons range, in which majors Barry Moody and Jock Kerr, two highly experienced squadron commanders, were killed. Night weaponry required special equipment to reduce the inherent dangers in this activity.

Left: Major Barry Moody. *Right: Front L to R*: Jock Kerr, Brand Haasbroek, Dick Lord, Pieter Roos, John van Rooyen, Rudi Kritzinger; *back*: Piet Truter, Koos Vogel, Tristan la Grange, Paddy Carolan, Dave Stead.

Early in 1980, a SAAF brains trust consisting of Brigadier Bossie Huyser, Director of Force Preparation; Colonel Fred du Toit, SSO Attack; Colonel Willem Hechter, SSO Mirages and Major Steyn Venter, SO Impalas decided to re-initiate the trials. 8 Squadron, based at AFB Bloemspruit, was given the task as they were close to the De Brug weapons range, just west of Bloemfontein. The guidelines given to the squadron were that the trials had to be safe but completed urgently—which appeared to be conflicting objectives. Each trial pilot was required to have a minimum of 1,000 hours on Impala aircraft. Simon van Garderen, an ex-commanding officer of the Buccaneer squadron, was assigned to the trials as an advisor. 24 Squadron had developed an excellent night-attack capability; Simon was the right man to give advice.

The team assembled nine days after the SAAF ultimatum, during which time avionics specialists from the SAAF depot and Atlas Aircraft Corporation had been hard at work modifying five aircraft. These modified aircraft were then dubbed 'Maanskyn' aircraft. The attitude indicator, in the centre of the instrument panel, was the main reference instrument required by the pilot to recover from an unusual position or extreme attitude. The instrument had to be isolated from the rest of the cockpit illumination, allowing all the other lights to be dimmed to protect the night vision of the pilot. This would allow the pilot to see the lights of any target on the ground, with the easily visible attitude indicator providing his primary reference for recovery from a dive attack.

A further innovation was the fitting of an audio bomb-release device. According to the ground elevation of the target, the pilot could dial in the release altitude for the weapons being carried. As he entered the dive attack a low audio warning in his earphones started at 1,800 feet before the computed release altitude. This changed to a higher pitch at 500 feet above release and cut out completely at exactly the release altitude. This was a great improvement as it allowed the pilot to concentrate on the target without having to cross-refer to the altimeter, making the tracking of the target far more accurate.

The attack profile decided on was the standard 30° dive angle used when firing 68mm rockets, to utilize a proven gun-sight setting. Another advantage of this dive, over a steeper one, was that the height lost in the recovery after release was not too great—an important safety feature. Later it was discovered that if a burst of 30mm cannon fire was fired when the bomb-release audio warning first came on, there was still time to fire a salvo of 68mm rockets when the audio stopped. The bonus was that the same sight setting achieved impact accuracy.

The team began an intensive night-flying programme which included night formation because, for safety's sake, it was decided to operate in pairs. The crew room and briefing room underwent changes. All white light bulbs in the building were replaced by red ones to aid the achievement of good night vision. Night adaptation typically takes about an hour.

Maanskyn operations were planned to utilize the period of five days before a full moon until five days after. Cloud cover was not to exceed 3/8ths and, because the moon rises nearly an hour later every night, sorties flown after full moon had to be flown after midnight. Translucence, the level of moonlight, is greater before full moon. All these factors were taken into account.

On 22 February, the pilots flew their first night weapon's sortie at De Brug range and achieved quite credible results. Improvement in accuracy and confidence grew rapidly. On 27 February, SAAF headquarters staff was briefed on the progress of the trials. As the next full moon was only two days away the pilots were given authority to fly up to Ondangwa to put their new skills to the test.

The team was somewhat surprised by this sudden development as they had planned to do some additional training. That night, because the weather was bad over the Orange Free State, they flew down to AFB Langebaan and carried out two night sorties on the Tooth Rock range. Next day, configured with four rocket pods and external drop tanks they flew to Windhoek via Keetmanshoop, to refuel. After a well-earned night's sleep they flew the final leg to AFB Ondangwa. Later, they flew a day sortie to familiarize themselves with their strange new surroundings. That night, 3 March, the crews were tasked to fly the first of many operational sorties under the famous call sign 'Skunk'.

The patrol profile decided on was one that would keep the aircraft out of range of the Angolan 23mm, 37mm and 57mm anti-aircraft fire. The pilots would cruise at a low 200KIAS (knots indicated air speed) and select all their armament switches to 'live' as they crossed into Angola. When the lights of a vehicle were seen the pilot had to adjust his offset position for the roll-in-point. He would pull his throttle to idle and silence the undercarriage warning horn before rolling into the dive. The speed would build up and at 300KIAS he would extend the dive brake. Then, it was a matter of tracking the target through the gun sight and waiting for the audio cues from the bomb-release altimeter, before firing.

Before rolling in to the attack the pilot would check the direction in which the vehicle was driving and attack from astern. To achieve the correct release conditions it was established that an entry dive-angle of 37° was required. A spot was selected 50 to 60 metres ahead of the vehicle where the headlight beams stopped. This spot was tracked in the sight by the pilot as he flew down the 'shaft'. The forward velocity of the vehicle reduced the dive-angle to the required 30° at release.

The moment the pilot fired he initiated the pull-out concentrating solely on the illuminated attitude indicator. As the aircraft's nose rose through the horizon he selected 'dive brake in' and 'full throttle' to quickly climb out of small-arms range. He circled when climbing back up to cruising altitude watching his six o'clock for any surface-to-air (SAM) missile launch. Should this happen the drill was to break into the approaching missile, and disengage back down to low altitude and head for home base.

Safe separation of between four to five miles between aircraft was fairly simple to maintain using the air-to-air mode of the Tacan beacon. For safety, a vertical separation of 2,000 feet was also maintained between aircraft. The Mobile Radar Unit (MRU) at Ondangwa controlled all *Maanskyn* sorties with the radar controllers giving regular 'Clara' calls, signifying that there were no threats on the radar screen. The controllers also assisted with suitable heading changes for navigation and aircraft separation purposes.

An Impala Mk II, a great aeroplane for bush warfare.

By 5 March, the moon had waned and the Impala crews flew back to Bloemspruit, satisfied that the trials had been successful. Training was continued at De Brug and on 27 March they returned to Ondangwa. That night, on the very first sortie, a vehicle was spotted, attacked and destroyed. This success was repeated the following night. However, no further vehicles were seen during the rest of the full-moon period.

During the May and June periods very good results were achieved. It became obvious that the attacks were taking their toll when vehicles stopped driving at night with their headlights on; only parking lights were used and consequently drivers were forced to reduce their speed. However, this was not a problem for the Impala pilots because, in the blackness of Africa, even those lights were visible from a distance.

To reduce the risk of being hit by AAA fire after pulling up from an attack another profile was developed. The factor which has the greatest effect on armament fired from aircraft is the force of gravity. If a bullet or rocket is fired horizontally the gravity drop effect is at its maximum. However, in a 90° dive gravity drop is zero. The gun-sight setting was adjusted to correspond to the fuselage reference line giving an aiming index. It was then a simple manoeuvre to roll in to a vertical attack from 20,000 feet, place the pipper on the target and fire. The aircraft's speed and gravity drop were not a factor because the weapons were descending vertically. Because of the higher roll-in altitude recovery could be completed above effective small-arms range. This extreme profile was first proven during daytime before being tried at night and was called a VRD —vertical rocket delivery.

Repeated deployments every month became a drain on the *Maanskyn*-qualified pilots. The system was changed to allow other more inexperienced pilots to fly the missions within certain restrictions. The qualified leader would be the 'attack' pilot and his wingman would act as 'shepherd'. The leader's aircraft would be armed with 68mm rockets carried in pods under the aircraft's wings and a full load of 30mm cannon shells. The shepherd would be used for safety purposes, to watch for SAM missile launches or AAA fire during the leader's attack dive, and as a Telstar in the event his leader was shot down.

The pair would fly into the designated area at a medium level of approximately 20,000 feet. On sighting a vehicle's lights the leader would carry out a high-dive profile throttled right back to reduce engine noise and to achieve surprise. The shepherd would remain at altitude to cover the leader visually. These attacks were extremely effective. The enemy soon learned to avoid moonlight conditions and to only move during the dark moon periods. The flat terrain and light-coloured sand of southern Angola, allowed this form of attack to be performed.

The method was to fly at random times during the night, when moon conditions allowed, and to patrol the three main lines of road communication that existed through the Cunene Province of Angola. These were the Cahama–Xangongo tar road, the Mulondo–Quiteve sand road, and the Cuvelai–Ongiva sand road.

Maanskyn evolved into *Donkermaan* when it became obvious that the enemy was no longer driving vehicles during moonlight conditions. The modus operandi for the two Impalas was the same as for *Maanskyn*, with the exception that the attack pilots had received additional night-flying training allowing them to carry out attacks in conditions of no moon—a highly skilled operation requiring a great deal of nerve. The pilots had become so accustomed to night flying that the transition to conditions of 'dark moon', or even 'no moon', did not create too great a problem. More reliance was placed on maintaining aircraft separation using the Tacan air-to-air mode because close formation without a moon and with navigation lights turned off, was both difficult and dangerous.

Pilot rescue mission

On 22 March, a two-ship Puma formation had lifted off from Ombulantu for a routine flight back to AFB Ondangwa. The crews had been on casevac standby duty at the army base. A sudden radio call changed all that. Captain Ray Fitzpatrick, the mission commander, was given an in-flight call-out. They had to change direction to the north and fly across the Yati strip, the border between

South West Africa and Angola, and head towards Ongiva.

These were fairly alarming instructions for Fitzpatrick, co-pilot 'Lang Lappies' Labuschagne, and flight engineer Mike Eksteen because, in those days, Ongiva was definitely a no-go area. It was a heavily defended FAPLA garrison town ringed by temporary SWAPO bases, sheltering under the Angolan air defence system. They were told to climb to 200 feet AGL so that Dayton could guide them to the area where an Impala Mk II had been shot down. Lieutenant 'Moolies' Moolman, wingman to the downed Impala, passed information regarding the position of the wreck to the approaching helicopters. There was real danger from small-arms fire and SA-7 shoulder-launched infra-red missiles for the aircraft flying up at 200 feet AGL, therefore, they shared the risk. Captain Steel Upton, flying number two, would fly high for a minute or two before plunging to low level then Fitzpatrick would climb, to chance his luck, for an equally short period.

As they crossed the border they picked up the distress signal of the Impala pilot's Pelba beacon and started homing in on it. On the one hand this was a comfort, but on the other it could have been a trap if the enemy had already captured the pilot. However, as they neared the scene, which was actually closer to Anhanca than Ongiva, Captain Sarel Smal, the downed pilot, heard the approaching Puma and marked his position with red smoke to guide the helicopter in. After selecting a suitable LZ they touched down to be met by a very relieved Sarel Smal who, despite having to hobble on an injured ankle, scrambled quickly into the cabin of the helicopter. The flight back to Ondangwa was uneventful except for the continuous thanks Smal showered on Flight Sergeant Eksteen and the rest of the crew.

Smal was taken to 1 Military Hospital in Pretoria in a C-160 Transall. Apart from a damaged ankle caused by a protruding piece of canopy during the ejection sequence, he also suffered compression of the vertebrae in his neck.

The remains of Sarel Smal's Impala were later recovered by helicopter to prevent it being triumphantly displayed in Luanda.

1980: Establishing a pattern

These three photographs show an assortment of SADF military hardware put on display in the grounds of the fort overlooking Luanda Bay.

On 12 April, Smal ejected again. This time on a training exercise flying Mirage III 810, out of AFB Hoedspruit. In a dogfight with a Mirage F1CZ, flown by Captain Kenny Williams, Smal's Mirage flamed out. After repeated unsuccessful re-light attempts Smal ejected at 800 feet AGL.

It was early in the morning and he was only 25 nautical miles from AFB Hoedspruit, his home base, on a day with good visibility and weather. Ironically, his pick-up took three hours compared to the 15 minutes of his operational rescue.

Mine warfare

On 14 April, Mike Eksteen, now a WOI (warrant officer first class), was again on a casevac call-out from AFB Ondangwa—this time with Captain Robinson as the Puma commander. They flew to Kaokoland. Eight policemen had been on patrol in a Buffel armoured personnel carrier traversing the rugged, rocky terrain that is Kaokoland. The two-wheeled dirt track twisted through the hilly countryside.

From Fledgling to Eagle

L to R: Colonel Dick Lord, Brigadier 'Thack' Thackwray, Jeff Ethel (American aviation author), unknown and Sarel Smal who featured in both ejection stories.

At a place where the vehicle was forced to navigate between two stout trees, and therefore had to stay in the tracks, they detonated a triple cheese-mine.

South Africa had learned from early losses in the border war that all fighting vehicles had to be built to protect the occupants, as far as possible, from the effect of mine detonations. Mines were the favourite offensive weapons of the terrorists throughout the war. They could be laid without risk and the terrorist could be long gone by the time a detonation occurred, thereby successfully avoiding contact with the security forces. Despite all their heroic propaganda they were never too keen to actually come face to face with the military.

South Africa produced a range of fighting vehicles all of which embodied safety measures against mines. Most visible of these measures were the V-shaped armoured hull with protruding wheels. The theory being, that if a wheel detonated a mine, the wheel would be blown off and the main force of the blast would be deflected by the V-shaped hull. In addition, proper moulded seating and seat belts were fitted for each occupant. It is remarkable how successful these measures proved to be. In most detonations if any injuries were sustained it was usually because the occupants had not been strapped in.

As the war continued, SWAPO realized that they were not achieving favourable results from their mine-laying activities because of these counter-measures. The terrorists, therefore, started doubling up their mines by placing one on top of the other. In this case these unfortunate policemen had been blown up by a triple mine.

Arriving overhead the scene the Puma went into an orbiting pattern while the crew tried to gain radio contact with the men they could see on the ground. Operating rules for the safety of the aircraft declared 'that aircraft were not to

The mine-protected Buffel, the army's equivalent to the SAAF's 'Vomit Comet' Dakota.

land in hostile territory without clearance from the ground troops'. In this case no clearance came but it was obvious to the aircrew that the area was safe so they landed. It turned out that the reason no radio contact could be made was that all the men had been temporarily deafened by the noise of the explosion and none of them had heard the radio call.

The force of the triple explosion had broken the vehicle completely apart. The driver's cab was 100 metres away from the crew compartment—only one wheel was ever found. The crater caused by the explosion had a diameter of more than five metres. The driver had his right thumb driven all the way back into the upper part of his lower arm. Unbelievable as it may sound but that was the most serious injury. All eight men were suffering from aching ears and deafness. However, because they had all been correctly strapped in and wearing the proper helmets

This shows the effect of a single vehicle mine exploding beneath a civilian vehicle. Note the relatively small crater on the left of the photograph.

none of them was seriously injured. The aircrew loaded all eight into the Puma and flew them back to the Oshakati hospital.

Impala shoot-down

On 25 April, Lieutenant Pete Hollis was flying as one of a pair of Impala fighters carrying out an armed reconnaissance mission over Angola. His aircraft was struck by ground fire and flames were seen coming from his aircraft's tail section. He turned south for home base but his engine began to lose power and his flying speed started to drop. Moments before the aeroplane stalled Hollis ejected. The other Impala pilot saw a good 'chute develop and initiated the SAR actions by relaying through the Telstar aircraft. Despite the good parachute there was no call on the Sabre beacon which every pilot carried in his survival jacket. Running short of fuel the wingman had to leave his orbit and return to base.

The rescue helicopter crew finally recovered Hollis's body. Back at Ondangwa the doctors discovered that Hollis, who was nearly two metres tall, had broken his neck during the ejection sequence. Normally, the canopy-breaker on top of the Martin Baker ejection seat strikes and shatters the cockpit canopy as the seat is ejected. In a real tragedy, it appeared that his head had struck the canopy first.

Smokeshell

During their 1980 incursion SWAPO had demonstrated aggressive intent by attacking AFB Ondangwa with a stand-off bombardment of mortars. The long-distance attack was inaccurate and the facilities suffered only minor damage. By mid-May, 324 SWAPO terrorists and 30 South African personnel had been killed in numerous contacts. Intelligence pinpointed two large concentrations of SWAPO inside Angola, where retraining was taking place. Cabinet approval was given to attack these bases.

It had long been suspected that informants living in the exclusive Waterkloof Ridge suburb of Pretoria were notifying certain unfriendly embassies whenever large formations of armed aircraft took off from the Waterkloof air base. These departures often heralded the next series of operations into Angola. A deception plan was implemented to avoid the usual telltale signs when both F1 squadrons departed for operations *Smokeshell* and *Sceptic* on 6 June. Throughout the afternoon the aircraft took off in pairs at irregular intervals, without visible underwing stores.

At 12h45, a C-160 Transall left Waterkloof for AFB Hoedspruit, loaded with underwing tanks and wing-tip missiles for 3 Squadron. Between 13h00 and 14h00, 1 Squadron took off and flew to Upington for an overnight stop as if deploying for a routine weapons training camp. From 14h00 onwards 3 Squadron flew clean aircraft to AFB Hoedspruit. On landing, 3 Squadron maintenance personnel flown down in the C-160 configured all the F1CZs with external fuel tanks and Matra 550 missiles for the long ferry flight to AFB Ondangwa the next morning.

The next day both squadrons set out very early:

At 05h00, 1 Squadron F1AZs took off in the dark from Upington on a 75-minute ferry flight to AFB Grootfontein where each aircraft was refuelled and armed with four Mk 82 bombs.

At 05h15, 3 Squadron took off from AFB Hoedspruit on a 125-minute ferry flight to AFB Ondangwa. Because it was winter one hour 45 minutes of the route was flown in darkness. The formation leader, Jack Gründling, made a critical decision as his flight came abeam Grootfontein. Although their fuel states were on minimum he elected to continue to Ondangwa. Had they landed at Grootfontein the element of surprise would have been lost; it was suspected that informers were also operating near that airfield. On landing at AFB Ondangwa the belly tanks were removed and replaced with four Mk 82 bombs.

At 10h00, 1 Squadron took off from AFB Grootfontein to strike the SWAPO base QFL, as part of Operation *Smokeshell*. QFL was just north of the Angolan border and posed an immediate threat to Owamboland. SWAPO terrorists easily slipped into SWA from this camp on nefarious incursions to plant mines and intimidate the local population.

Because Norman Minne's AZ had starting problems he only took off after the formation had left. He flew the mission alone, just slotting into the No 5 position of the last four-ship formation as the aircraft pitched up from their low-level approach. The target was spread out on either side of a dry riverbed. 14.5mm and 23mm anti-aircraft fire was drawn from the camp but none of the aircraft was hit. The formation reformed after the attack and landed safely at AFB Ondangwa. Ground crew re-armed and refuelled the aircraft while the pilots planned the following strike.

At 12h30, Captain Otto Schür, a Mirage III R2Z reconnaissance pilot, took off from Ondangwa, with Pierre du Plessis and Darryl Lee flying escort in F1CZs. His mission was to photograph the airfield southeast of Lubango to confirm an intelligence report that SA-3 missile batteries had been deployed around the airfield. This confirmation was required before SAAF aircraft could strike the nearby SWAPO Tobias Haneko Training Camp (THTC). SWAPO sheltered under the umbrella of safety provided by the Angolan Defence Force anti-aircraft installations, positioning their camps and bases within range of these facilities. This ploy did not always help them as SAAF aircraft attacked SWAPO wherever they were found. However, it did escalate the war because their Angolan hosts were drawn into the fight by default.

The reconnaissance flight proceeded as planned with the three aircraft passing directly overhead the airfield. In transit through the critical zone the three pilots

Sidenet height-finding radar which was a part of every Angolan radar site. The nodding action of the aerial allows the radar to measure target height above ground level.

heard their BF1 radar-warning receivers (RWRs) pick up the ominous sounds of locked-on enemy radar. However, no fire was drawn and the aircraft landed safely back at Ondangwa. At the debriefing, Commandant Mossie Basson confirmed that the warning received on the RWR was the guidance radar of the SA-3 system.

This fact caused considerable debate among the crews who were busy planning the strike on THTC. Schür's photographs would have visually confirmed the situation but were not available at the time the attack decision had to be made. Major Theo Nell, the leader of the planned strike, was understandably deeply concerned about the situation. He suggested the strike be delayed until the following day so that the photographs could be studied beforehand. Theo was also worried that visibility at low level would cause problems en route, particularly looking up-sun late in the afternoon. However, the planners decided that if missiles had been deployed they would have been launched at the PR formation. In this case it would be better to fly the strike sortie *before* missiles were deployed. Unfortunate logic, as events were to prove. The advice of the operations and intelligence officers, as well as pressure from senior 3 Squadron pilots, outweighed and outranked the suggestions put forward by 1 Squadron aircrew. The decision was made to fly the strike.

At 16h45, Major Frans Pretorius, the leader of the last four-ship formation, had to stop the armourers from loading the last two bombs onto his aircraft so that he could taxi out. Loading 16 Mirages was a long, back-breaking job for the ground support personnel. The other 15 F1s were configured with two underwing drop tanks and six Mk 82 bombs; four under the belly and two under the wings. Buccaneers, flying a different route to the target, would drop their bombs following the Mirage attack.

Led by Major Nell the combined strike of 16 Mirage F1s lifted off from AFB Ondangwa at 17h00. Nell flew a large, teardrop pattern to allow all 16 fighters to join into their allotted positions. Leaders and deputy leaders of each four-ship flight were ground-attack F1AZs with CZ pilots flying as wingmen. If Angolan MiGs threatened the formation the wingmen would jettison their bombs and give air defence cover. The four flights were planned to fly in line astern.

Abeam Ombalantu a standard navigational check confirmed that Nell's navigation computer was giving 'duff gen' and so he handed overall lead of the strike to his No 3, Captain Dirk de Villiers. As predicted, visibility was appalling, especially towards the fast-setting sun. As time progressed, trying to maintain station within the formation became increasingly difficult. The concertina effect, usual in any large formation, assumed major proportions as the leaders jockeyed to keep position. As always, it was the tail-end Charlies' who suffered the extreme effects. Afterburner to catch up, dive brakes and idle throttle to avoid overtaking aircraft ahead, followed by quick dog-legs to fall back into position! A most uncomfortable situation which became progressively worse as the flight continued.

The planned route took the aircraft well west of the target to a pitch-up point that allowed the aircraft to attack from north to south. The advantage of this profile was the element of surprise because the enemy had their defensive positions facing south. The other advantage was that the run-out from the target was southwards towards base; an important consideration because all the aircraft would be low on fuel.

The formation pitched early, leaving the aircraft exposed to anti-aircraft fire for longer than planned. The first three flights of four aircraft were all in reasonable formation positions. The fourth flight, at the extended edge of the concertina effect, was left dangerously exposed. As the aircraft broke cover the SA-3 search radar immediately illuminated them. RWRs started screeching and Les Bennett, No 4 in the first flight, was heard to say over the radio, "They're looking at us."

The correct roll-in point was achieved and the F1s entered the attack dive. The first four aircraft had a trouble-free attack without drawing any defensive fire. Captains Hennie Louw and Darryl Lee, in the second formation, realized that their dive angle was too shallow and made bold corrections to their sight pictures before dropping their bombs. At release Darryl could see the entire camp area filling his windscreen. On pull-out he looked back to check where his bombs had fallen. He was in time to see a Soviet-built Gaz truck driving around the camp perimeter, disappear in a cloud of smoke from one of the bombs. Later, at the debriefing, Colonel Ollie Holmes confirmed that the truck had been destroyed—it was mentioned in damage assessment signals sent out by the SWAPO camp commander after the strike.

During the pitch to roll-in point Norman Minne, the No 3 of the third flight, could see his designated target through the haze as well as a number of smoke trails. As he rolled in he spotted three flaming missiles coming from his right-hand side. All three flames appeared to be standing still—the optical effect of missiles that are homing onto your aircraft. He managed to call "SAM-3s, right three o'clock ... *'n hele kakhuis vol*! [a whole shithouse full]" before selecting afterburner, bunting his aircraft and pickling his bombs, which he overtook on his way down to low level.

At treetop height and full power he proved that the aircraft's belly tank, which had only been cleared for flight up to M0.95, could exceed the speed of sound. Once out of missile range he climbed up to altitude and found himself among the lead formation. He had taken off as No 11 but landed No 3! On engine shut-down he had 300 litres of fuel remaining, only enough for three minutes' flying at full power.

As the second four-ship approached release point Norman Minne's warning was heard on the operational radio frequency. Captain Pierre du Plessis, seconds before release altitude ignored the call, dropped his bombs and only then looked out for the missiles.

Norman's missile call and the strident tones of the RWRs convinced most of the pilots to egress at low level from the target instead of climbing to altitude as planned. This low-level, fast run-out from the target combat zone played havoc with the planned fuel-flow figures. Consequently, all pilots became dangerously low on fuel during the return to base.

Flying on time and heading, the fourth formation arrived at pitch-up point for the attack. As they climbed, someone called "Smoke to the right!" while Frans Pretorius, the No 3, saw smoke to the left. Fortunately, the leader, I. C. du Plessis, chose to fly onto the right-hand smoke caused by explosions from bombs dropped onto the target by the previous formations.

At the apex of the pitch the SA-3 search radar audio signals changed to continuous lock-on mode. Pretorius saw the smoke trails of the missiles fired at the third formation. It took him a second or two to appreciate what they were. Looking up-sun he realized that the missiles were flying out of a dark, black hole near the town of Lubango. As he pulled his aircraft's nose down into the dive he saw two more thick beige/brown trails in front of him, passing from right to left.

Concentrating on his sight picture he released his bombs. He initiated the pull-out while at the same time selecting bomb jettison in case any of his bombs had hung up, then looked to his right again. He saw three smoke trails coming towards him; they appeared to be several miles away and travelling very slowly.

Quadruple SA-3 launchers allowed a high rate of missile fire as experienced by 1 Squadron Mirage F1 pilots over Lubango. These six-metre-long missiles have a range of 30km and are guided by Flat-Face and Low-Blow radars.

He could see that the right- and left-hand missiles had gone ballistic and were not guiding because their flight paths were straight. However, the centre missile had a curved smoke trail indicating that it was tracking Pretorius's aircraft. Waiting to turn sharply into the missile at the right moment seemed to take forever but suddenly the missile's speed appeared to treble. After breaking hard right, he had rolled on 90° of bank when he felt a jolt and heard a sound similar to that of a guitar string snapping. This was followed immediately by a cacophony of noise as all the emergency warnings were activated and the warning panel illuminated.

Ignoring the emergency warnings Pretorius dived to very low level away from the area. He did not want to eject over the target he had just bombed, and realized his aircraft was still handling correctly. The audio from the locked-on enemy radar was still blaring in his ears so he dared not gain height to sort out the emergencies. Approaching a ridge, he realized that if he could descend below the level of its summit the enemy radar would lose lock. Inverting his aircraft he pulled down into a valley, narrowly avoiding the treetops as he rolled out. Once he was safe he began to think rationally, accepting that if he were to make it back to base he would have to climb.

As he began a shallow climb he immediately picked up a missile audio warning. Checking for missiles he saw a thick smoke trail immediately behind him. He broke to the left but to his horror saw the trail following him so he snapped the aircraft into a reverse break to the right but the trail still followed him. Only when he glanced in his rear-view mirror did he realize the smoke was in fact the trail left by fuel leaking from his aircraft. The fuel gauges confirmed his serious predicament.

Cruise-climbing back towards base Pretorius was eventually joined by Captain

John Inggs. As he passed 30,000 feet he heard the voice of the fighter controller at Dayton on his radio. The controller was warning all the returning pilots about MiGs trying to intercept our aircraft. Pretorius knew that his leaking aircraft would attract interceptors like bees to a hive. However, it turned out that the controllers, expecting a neat formation, were reacting to the blips of the spread-out strike force appearing on their screens.

Captain Dirk de Villiers, in the first formation, checking to see what was happening behind, him immediately focused on the smoke trail left by Pretorius's leaking aircraft. He assumed it was a MiG formation approaching from six o'clock. De Villiers decided to plunge to low level but then checked his

Dayton radar station mounted on a ramp on the western side of the Ondangwa runway. Manned continuously, the staff played a major role in ensuring SAAF air superiority.

fuel gauges. He had 800 litres of fuel remaining but was 80 nautical miles from base. At low level, flying at ten miles per minute the F1 uses 100 litres per minute. Under these conditions he would have arrived overhead Ondangwa with zero fuel. Although the plunge call was given none of the aircraft responded—all the pilots had done the same calculation.

As Pretorius crossed the cut-line at 31,000 feet, still 28 nautical miles from Ondangwa, the engine flamed out. He set up a glide and then glimpsed the thin black strip of runway just left of his aircraft's nose. The aircraft, minus the fuel and underwing tanks, which he had jettisoned over Angola, was so light he realized he could make the runway. In fact, in the forced landing pattern he had to make a 360° turn to lose sufficient height. On the downwind leg he delayed lowering his undercarriage; he was alarmed at how long it took to lock into position using emergency procedures. He lowered half flap, then full flap, realizing he was still too high. To lose height he employed the old Harvard sideslip learned many years before at flying school, which worked too well. On rolling wings level he judged he was now too low.

At this critical time, after the sweat and trauma of trying to fly back to base, emergency warnings still ringing in his earphones and with all 16 Mirages calling low fuel states and asking for joining and landing instructions, Pretorius described how a guiding hand lifted his Mirage and placed it on the concrete strip at the very beginning of the runway. The drag 'chute worked and slowed the light aircraft quickly. Not wanting to block the runway Pretorius turned off into the veld and stopped. After re-inserting in his ejection seat pins he slid down the side of the fuselage onto the ground where he kissed the Owamboland sand. He walked back to the line hut on extremely rubbery legs. Pretorius was awarded the Southern Cross medal for the airmanship he displayed in saving F1AZ 234.

On hearing Pretorius's Mayday call, Major Errol Hart, the air traffic controller at AFB Ondangwa, instructed all the other approaching Mirages to clear the airfield while Pretorius carried out his forced landing. None of the pilots obeyed this call. They couldn't! Their fuel states were so low they were all in imminent danger of suffering the same fate.

Meanwhile Captain I. C. du Plessis in F1AZ 237, the leader of Pretorius's four-ship formation, was experiencing severe problems of his own. In the mayhem around the target du Plessis had been hit by two missiles and had lost hydraulic pressure and the use of the engine nozzle flaps. Although he had radioed that he had been hit none of the other pilots had sufficient fuel to go to his aid. After hearing over the radio of the misfortunes that had befallen the Mirages the Buccaneer crews aborted their attack. Disconcertingly, they were heard on the radio talking about du Plessis in the past tense.

Fortunately, Captain 'Budgie' Burgers, flying an Impala as Telstar radio relay for the mission, answered du Plessis's call for help. As I. C. struggled to keep his damaged F1 in the sky he realized that Ondangwa was out of reach and needed to divert to the forward airstrip at Ruacana. Having lost his navigational computer he was not sure of the headings and distances he had to fly. However, as the senior Impala pilot at Ondangwa, Burgers had built up a wealth of knowledge about the terrain and topography of the operational flying area. Using the visual references that du Plessis said he could see Burgers worked out where the damaged Mirage was and gave du Plessis headings and distances for Ruacana. Du Plessis found the airfield and carried out a flapless landing. Using the emergency undercarriage selection he managed to lower the two main wheels but not his nose wheel. As a result, because the aircraft's nose was scraping along the Ruacana runway, his landing run was much shorter than normal. Captain du Plessis was awarded the Honoris Crux for his airmanship

Captain I. C. du Plessis' Mirage at rest on the runway at Ruacana.

and courage saving an irreplaceable aircraft. Both damaged F1s were eventually repaired and returned to operations.

When all the aircraft and pilots had been accounted for a long debriefing was held in an attempt to sort out the root causes of the catastrophe. The intelligence officer produced the Mirage III R2Z photography from the midday reconnaissance flight which had not been available earlier. Exactly in the middle of an 8"x 8" photo was a picture of an SA-3 quad-launcher with four white missiles clearly visible. A hard lesson was learned; wartime sorties require that all intelligence inputs be available before embarking on a mission.

Fearing possible retaliation from the Angolan Air Force the planners decided to have the entire strike force ferry back to the safety of AFB Grootfontein. After debriefing the pilots manned their aircraft and took off in the dark. Most of them had been on the go since 03h00 that morning. They had ferried to the operational airfields before dawn, carried out two operational missions, the second of which had been an adrenaline-charged affair, and were now required to complete their 'longest day' with another night ferry flight.

AFB Grootfontein had a long runway, however, the runway lighting had not been completed. To solve the temporary problem emergency lights were used to mark the runway edges. Unfortunately, one of the first Mirage F1s to arrive landed a little short and dragged out the emergency lighting cable. The result was that, for the rest of the aircraft, the runway only had lights down one side.

The SA-2 had a range of 50km and could reach an altitude of 25km. Provided our pilots knew where the fixed launching sites were they could generally avoid these ten-metre-long missiles.

This was the straw that broke the camel's back. Not all of the pilots landed on the correct side of the lights. Captain Mark Clulow's plaintive voice was picked up on the radio saying "Hey, major, I think I've missed the runway." The next morning, after a visual check of the aircraft a number were found to have grass and sand stuck in the wheel rims. One aircraft had even flattened a runway marker lodged in its wheel but none of the Mirages had suffered major damage.

At about the same time as the strike sortie took off Major Gerrie Radloff taxiied out at AFB Waterkloof to ferry a spare F1CZ to Ondangwa. The ground crew had hung and filled three external fuel tanks under the aircraft for the long flight. Unfortunately, this exceeded the maximum all-up-weight of the aircraft. It was the middle of winter and temperatures were low and so Radloff decided to fly the aircraft in that configuration.

The F1 staggered into the air and climbed, albeit, slowly. However, for the first 400 miles it would not cruise without using mini-afterburner. Every time Radloff came back into dry power the speed would decay and the angle of incidence would increase. The problem was solved only after sufficient fuel had been burned off.

That evening, as the strike aircraft ferried to Grootfontein, ATC diverted Radloff to the same airfield to join up with his squadron. Upon arrival he had to descend to low level to burn off excess fuel before his aircraft was down to a safe landing weight.

Realistic training

In the SAAF we trained as realistically as possible. Earlier I compared the Roodewal range targets to real targets we encountered in Angola. Major Theo Nell went one further when he managed a project building lifelike enemy equipment out of fibreglass. These models were distributed on our ranges as exercise for both our PR and attack pilots. From the air it was almost impossible to tell the model from the real thing. Even from 100 metres away on the ground the fake was difficult to identify.

Air combat manoeuvring (ACM) training was progressed by the inclusion of top Israeli pilots in our ACM programmes. ACM clinics were regularly held to ensure all fighter pilots were involved.

Left: The T-55 'assembly line'.
Right: An uncomfortably realistic looking SA-2 on its launcher. These models were so light they could be moved easily by two men.

An ACM fighter clinic takes a break to pose for a group photo.
Standing L to R: Pierre du Plessis, Carlo Gagiano, John Orr, Jack Gründling, Israeli, Mac van der Merwe, Graham Rochat, Norman Bruton; *front:* Tinky Jones, Israeli, Mark Crooks.

Operation *Sceptic*

On 8 June, our ground forces launched Operation *Sceptic*. Our aim was to destroy a main SWAPO logistics base near Mulemba, north of beacons 20 to 26. Eenhana was used as the tactical HQ and a HAG was established near Mulemba.

Helicopters from 19 and 17 Squadrons were used, as well as Bosbok light aircraft for reconnaissance, with the Ondangwa Impalas on CAS standby. The operation was successful—the base destroyed and a great deal of enemy equipment captured. SWAPO's command and control system was seriously affected by the loss of this base. The enemy had developed new tactics using heavily fortified bunkers and employing optically guided anti-aircraft artillery

A further combined strike on 10 June saw captains Darryl Lee and Wassie Wassermann paired up in another 16-ship formation. This time each aircraft was armed with eight Mk 82 bombs, as the range to the selected SWAPO camp was much less than the Lubango raid. After an early morning take-off a perfect attack was carried out. All the pilots dropped their bombs on the designated targets.

After bomb release Lee pulled off to the left and looked back to check the fall of shot. What he saw was the smoke trail of an SA-7 missile curving towards Wassermann and himself. He called "Stand by for manoeuvring!" but the missile broke lock and dived towards the ground. Their relief was short-lived because a second missile appeared from the same area. Calling "Stand by to break left!" Lee watched as the heat-seeking missile broke lock and headed for the sun. A third missile curving in behind forced both aircraft to break to port. The missile then disappeared and exploded safely behind the F1s. To this day Wassermann recalls this story to a tune taken from the 1970s' *Rocky Horror Picture Show*—'It's just a jump to the left and then a jump to the right'.

Impala shoot-down

On 20 June, Lieutenant Neil Thomas was flying a close-support mission over Angola when his aircraft was hit by a 23mm shell. The shell struck the Impala on the lower nose in the region of the cannon barrel. Debris passed through the engine compressor and the damage immediately reduced the power. Even with 98 per cent power selected Thomas could not maintain height. The Impala descended and was striking the treetops when he ejected. The ejection was successful but the pilot's problems were still far from over.

The SAR plan worked well and Neil Thomas was picked up by an Alouette piloted by Lieutenant André Hattingh, and flown to the HAG situated near Evale, still inside Angola. Thomas had hardly breathed a sigh of relief when a red warning light on the Alouette's instrument panel suddenly illuminated, indicating a fuel filter blockage. After a hurried forced landing in enemy territory the crew cleared the filter and the rescue flight continued.

The Impala was recovered by a Frelon helicopter and returned to the Atlas Aircraft Corporation. It was repaired and eventually returned to service.

Alouette shoot-down

Three days later on 23 June, an Alouette III, crewed by Captain Thinus van Rensburg and Sergeant Koos Celliers, was struck by enemy fire. They had been providing top cover for Pumas landing in the bush 12 kilometres east of Xangongo. After exiting the burning wreckage Sergeant Celliers was shot by SWAPO terrorists. He was confirmed dead by Captain van Rensburg; no pulse could be found. Van Rensburg managed to escape, evade capture and reach safety on foot. He was found by South African ground forces near Cuamato, suffering from compression fractures of the vertebrae, superficial scratches and dehydration. Intercepts of enemy radio signals indicated that SWAPO had taken the body of Sergeant Celliers to Lubango.

On 29 June, Commandant Derek Kirkland led a two-ship Impala formation. It was scrambled at the urgent request of our ground forces close to Mongua. The troops were being threatened by an Angolan armoured convoy approaching from the west. On arrival, Derek and his wingman Captain 'Budgie' Burgers, found the convoy three nautical miles west of Mongua and confirmed that tanks were among the armoured vehicles. The Impalas immediately went into an attack using a very low 10° dive angle to reduce their exposure to enemy fire.

The 30mm cannons were loaded with a mixture of incendiary and armour-piercing ammunition. As Kirkland fired he could see the sparks made by the rounds striking the tank. After the Impalas' first pass the convoy came to a halt, making them easier targets. However, they had stopped to enable their gunners to defend themselves against the aircraft. Small-arms fire and rocket-propelled grenades (RPGs) started flying thick and fast. The pilots jinked their aircraft every time they pulled off an attack and stayed very low—below 50 feet when repositioning for the next attack.

Both pilots carried out four attacks on the convoy, selecting different targets each time, before running out of ammunition and rockets. By this stage the enemy had also had enough and the survivors turned tail, driving off into the west.

On 30 July, Puma helicopters, supported by Alouette gunships, landed 80 soldiers close to a SWAPO logistic/transit base at Chitado, five kilometres north of the cut-line and 35 kilometres west of Ruacana. The aim of Operation *Klipkop* was to discourage any further SWAPO attacks on the Ruacana hydro-electric scheme.

The assault began just after first light. Aircraft dropped pamphlets around the scene of battle warning the local population not to get involved in the fighting. A total of 27 enemy soldiers were killed but as they were all wearing identical uniforms it was difficult to tell whether they were MPLA or SWAPO men. After the battle, to counter enemy propaganda journalists were flown into the base.

1980: Establishing a pattern

Captain Budgie Burgers and Colonel Dick Lord at Rocky Point. No respecter of rank, Budgie's was the bigger fish.

Impala loss

On 10 October, the SAAF suffered another sad loss. Lieutenant Steve Volkerz, a Mirage III pilot on 2 Squadron, was still current on Impalas and volunteered to do an operational tour at AFB Ondangwa. During a mission 20 kilometres southwest of Mupa, Lieutenant. Skinner, the other pilot in the formation, saw Lieutenant Volkerz's Impala hit by two SA-7 missiles. He saw him eject and the aircraft explode as it hit the ground. Circling over the scene he saw Lieutenant Volkerz land in his parachute and stand up and wave, to indicate he was uninjured. Radio messages intercepted from the enemy the next day, confirmed that Steve Volkerz had been shot and killed by SWAPO.

On the night of 17 October, Steyn Venter and his wingman Pikkie Siebrits were tasked as 'Skunk 8' to carry out an armed *Maanskyn* reconnaissance north of Mupa. Venter reported to Pikkie that he had a visual on two pairs of lights heading northwards and was preparing to attack. Because the night was particularly calm Venter was able to enter an accurate dive from astern. During the dive he experienced an interesting visual phenomenon. At the point of entry the vivid white *shonas* of daytime appeared black. However, as the bomb-release altimeter started its noise, indicating the release height of 7,300 feet, the *shonas* once again changed to white.

Venter fired 12 rockets in salvo and immediately initiated his pull-out. Because he was focusing all his attention on his flying instruments he did not know the results of his attack. However, a few moments later Pikkie Siebrits broke radio silence with an excited call in Afrikaans of, *"Daar kak hy!"* (There's shit there!)—a quaint Afrikaans way of indicating that the target had been hit. When the first vehicle was hit and burning the second truck turned around. The formation did not make the fatal mistake of returning to the same target, a fundamental safety principle in aerial warfare.

Left: Even when released in salvo stores still leave the aircraft separately. These are cluster bombs being dropped from a Mirage F1AZ from level flight.
Right: The cluster bomb has opened explosively, freeing the smaller bomblets.

Operation *Wishbone*

The year ended with Operation *Wishbone* taking place on 19 December. Two air strikes were launched against SWAPO targets at Oshiheng, near Ongiva and Palela, towards Xangongo. Four formations of five aircraft were assembled at AFB Grootfontein and AFB Ondangwa respectively to deliver Mk 82 bombs from medium level. Each formation consisted of either four Mirage F1s or four Buccaneers led by a Canberra—with the aircraft to release their bombs on a call from the Canberra navigator. The results achieved on both these strikes were poor due to the inherent inaccuracy of medium-level bombing and bad intelligence. Both camps were later shown to be unoccupied.

1980 had been a bad year for the South African Air Force.

1980: Establishing a pattern

This operational photograph, taken during Operation *Wishbone*, illustrates very well the effect of the intervalometer affecting the sequence of bomb release. The intervalometer can be adjusted to vary the interval between each bomb in a stick.

Chapter 7

1981:
Taking the war to the host nation

At the end of 1980, grim statistics showed that 1,447 terrorists had been killed at the cost of 100 South African/South West African soldiers—the heaviest yearly casualty figure of the war. During the rains of 1981, despite their grievous losses, SWAPO once again embarked on incursions into SWA. In an effort to expand the war they sent infiltration units into Kavango as well as Owamboland. This SWAPO move achieved the desired result, effectively doubling the length of border which had to be defended. Army, police and air force units in Sector 20, the military area situated around the town of Rundu, were reinforced to cope with the additional threat.

Honoris Crux Gold

On 15 January, Lieutenant Arthur Walker and his flight engineer Sergeant 'Boats' Botes, led a two-ship formation to support hard-pressed ground forces engaged in a contact near Cuamato. Six Puma helicopters brought in troops to carry out an assault on a heavily defended Angolan base. During the Puma landings and throughout the fire fight Walker continued to expose his aircraft to heavy and continuous AAA fire displaying exceptional courage. The fighting lasted three days with the gunships giving accurate and effective cannon fire support. Lieutenant Walker was awarded the Honoris Crux Gold for his dedication and courage under fire.

*****

On 17 March, four Canberras and five Buccaneers took off from AFB Grootfontein on Operation *Interrupt*. They attacked the SWAPO 'Jumbo' camp situated nine kilometres southwest of Lubango. A ground reconnaissance team had infiltrated into Angola to verify that the camp was occupied at the time of the strike. The Canberras approached the target using a low-level profile, with each aircraft releasing 300 Alpha bombs. The Buccaneers, also using a low-level approach, delivered their bombs in a medium-toss attack. The attack was unsuccessful for a number of reasons, including poor weather. Commandant Gert Havenga was recalled from senior staff course for this particular sortie which he flew with Riem Mouton as his navigator. On 24 Squadron there was always a scarcity of aircrew.

By April, 365 terrorists had been killed. The first week of July became the bloodiest of the year when a further 93 SWAPO insurgents were killed.

Honoris cruxes

On 5 July, Commandant 'Borries' Bornman was leading a company in a 'hot-pursuit' follow-up operation of a group of SWAPO north of Elundu. Two Alouette gunships were in support, orbiting ahead of the spoor when Captain David Owen, one of the pilots, spotted a SWAPO ambush two kilometres ahead of the advancing ground forces. As he orbited overhead he noticed 40 SWAPO cadres lying motionless in a semi-circle. He notified Commandant Bornman and Captain André Hattingh, the pilot of the other Alouette, of the ambush.

Owen remained overhead while Hattingh flew in low, his gunner raking the area with 20mm cannon fire. Then all hell broke loose as SWAPO opened up on the helicopters with small arms, machine guns and RPGs. This allowed Bornman to charge into the contact with his troops. In the fighting which ensued Owen noticed the army's left flank advancing into another ambush. Because radio contact had ceased Owen dropped his Alouette into the heavy firing so that his engineer 'Whitey' van Heerden could hang out of the door and signal to the soldiers to withdraw. In this contact 17 out of the 40-strong SWAPO group were killed. Dave Owen and André Hattingh were both awarded the Honoris Crux for their actions.

*****

The situation prevailing along the SWA–Angolan border had become intolerable. Escalation in an expanded area and in the intensity of the war was not acceptable. Defence Force capabilities and resources were being stretched unnecessarily. SWAPO, using the protection and often the logistics capability offered by the Angolan army, could approach close to the SWA border with impunity.

With limited resources in equipment, and particularly manpower, it made little economic or military sense to attempt an impossible task. Imagine a 1.2-metre-high, broken, four-strand wire fence stretching from Brussels to Milan, northern Italy. All the NATO forces in Europe would have extreme difficulty trying to stop determined people crossing from one side to the other. In SWA the problem was compounded by dense bush and the visibility often being reduced to 30 metres or less.

After each wave of terrorist activity the security forces would apply different tactics, deploy more personnel, increase their mobility by vehicle or helicopter, speed up reaction times and increase the effectiveness of armaments. By 1981, the thinly spread security forces were assessed to be non-cost-effective—too much expended effort at too great a cost with little to show for it. In any conflict when one side starts gaining an advantage, confidence within the organization soars and there is an upsurge in activities. Pressure had to be applied by the security forces to regain the advantage.

The problem was the easy access SWAPO had to SWA. The solution was to deny the guerrillas freedom of movement within what came to be known as the 'shallow area' of Angola. This was the strip of land immediately adjacent to the border stretching 50 kilometres into Angola. The legality of this idea was based upon international law which prohibits host countries from allowing incursions from their territories into those of international neighbours. This 'shallow area' was to be cleared of all SWAPO presence. It was upon this premise that the planning for Operation *Protea* took place.

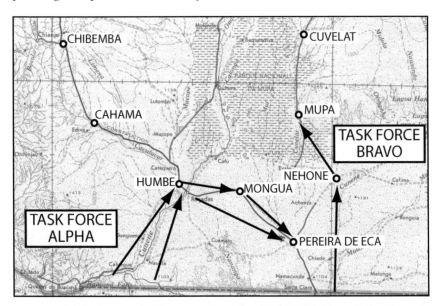

The ground force operation was carried out by TF A and TF B. The SAAF supported there groups, carrying out aerial bombardments of Xangongo (marked as Rocadas) and Ongiva (marked as Pereira de Eca).

Operation *Protea*

The aim of *Protea* was to destroy SWAPO's military forces and logistical supply lines in the central theatre of southern Angola, by means of ground forces supported by air force operations. Two mechanized armoured fighting groups, Task Forces Alpha and Bravo, would be involved. TF Alpha, equipped with armoured cars, artillery, Ratel and Buffel armoured personnel carriers, would bear the brunt of the operation, with the Angolan military establishments in Xangongo and Ongiva being the main targets. While these centres were being cleared TF Bravo would advance deeper into the eastern theatre to seek and destroy known and suspected SWAPO training and logistic bases and force them to positions north of Cassinga. SAAF MAOTs would be attached to each fighting group as air support advisors to the army commanders. They had the ability to control ground-attack missions in direct support of the army.

The air force support plan, Operation *Konyn*, was designed to achieve two distinct objectives:

- Firstly, the disruption and destruction of Angolan air force and SWAPO air defence systems in the central theatre, with air strikes targeting the radar installations at Chibemba and Cahama. These strikes were to be conducted independently of the ground operations and were designed to achieve air superiority and freedom of movement for the air force.
- Secondly, to provide air support to the ground forces to enable them to achieve their overall objectives.

To achieve these objectives the SAAF required the largest operational effort since the Second World War. The following aircraft were allocated for the duration of the operation:

- Air strikes, close air support (CAS), interdiction and air defence:
  12 x Mirage F1AZs
  8 x Mirage F1CZs
  7 x Mirage III CZs
  6 x Mirage III D2Zs
  16 x Impalas
  5 x Buccaneers
  5 x Canberras

- Photo-reconnaissance (PR):
  1 x Canberra
  3 x Mirage III RZ/R2Zs
  2 x Impalas

- Fire support, trooping and reaction force:
19 x Alouette gunships and troopers
17 x Pumas
2 x Frelons

- Communications:
8 x Kudus

- Paratrooping, transport, resupply and pamphlet-dropping:
7 x Dakotas (1 x ambulance Dakota)
3 x C160/130s

- Navigation, Telstar and reconnaissance:
11 x Bosboks

Operation *Knife* was to run concurrently with *Protea* with the aim of providing electronic-warfare (EW) support to all forces. A ground communication–intelligence (Comint) team based at Ruacana and ECM-equipped aircraft would build up assessments of enemy radar and air defence dispositions.

D-Day for the start of *Protea* was 24 August, but from D-4 planning details were finalized. Routine interdiction missions and road and photo-reconnaissance flights were flown to update intelligence information. On D-3, the fighter and bomber force aircraft, allocated for *Protea*, from air bases across South Africa, started to arrive at AFB Grootfontein. The bomber force of 12 Squadron (Canberra), 24 Squadron (Buccaneer) and 1 Squadron (Mirage F1AZ) were tasked to operate from AFB Grootfontein, while the fighters of 2 and 3 Squadrons and all the Impala light-attack-jet aircraft, were to be deployed at AFB Ondangwa from D-Day. There were just too many aircraft to be accommodated on one airfield.

2 Squadron was already in residence at AFB Grootfontein having arrived on 12 August from AFB Hoedspruit, via a refuelling stop at Upington. Flying the relatively short-ranged Mirage III delta-winged fighters, their primary role was air defence and were therefore skilled in the fields of interception and aerial combat. However, during *Protea* they would also be utilized in their secondary role of ground attack, and had arrived to hone their delivery techniques on a weapons range north of Etosha. As a counter to the threat posed by AAA and shoulder-launched SA-7 Strela missiles the SAAF had introduced the high-dive attack profile. Aircraft would enter a 30° dive from an altitude above 20,000 feet AGL, the height beyond the reach of the small missile. Weapon release would be at 10,000 feet and the pilot would recover from the dive in a nose-high attitude in full afterburner. The aircraft would bottom out at around 7,000 feet, well inside the missile envelope but, in theory, if aircraft speed was maintained above 450

1981: Taking the war to the host nation

knots then it would outdistance the missile.

Of course weapon accuracy is proportional to the range from the target at release. The closer you are the more accurate the result. From 10,000 feet pinpoint accuracy could not be guaranteed, which was compensated for by the release of full pods of rockets or a stick of bombs. The natural dispersion pattern of weapons fired in salvo caters for the reduced accuracy inherent with a high release. The thick bush of the battle area provided superb cover for enemy vehicles and facilities, especially when they were dispersed, making it extremely unlikely that pilots would spot individual targets. Area coverage was the answer.

2 Squadron's pilots exercised the profile under the direction of FAC, who would 'talk' the pilots onto the targets to be attacked. It was during this training that some of the Mirage IIIs were rushed to AFB Ondangwa to protect it from Angolan MiG interference during the assembly stage of the SAAF forces prior to the operation.

On 20 August, Rynier Keet found himself strapped into the cockpit of a Mirage III in the readiness shelter at the end of the Ondangwa runway. He was the wingman of a section led by Commandant Mac van der Merwe, 2 Squadron's commander. As the standby was just a precaution the aircraft were still configured with underwing rocket pods, totally unsuitable for any air defence activities. At 09h45, Dayton radar picked up fast-jet traffic on the Angolan side of the border heading directly towards Ondangwa. The Mirage pair was scrambled on an interception vector. The formations closed rapidly in the head-on approach. At 40 nautical miles, moments before van der Merwe ordered the jettisoning of the valuable rocket pods, to reduce drag and before the expected air fighting began, the MiGs turned a quick 180° degrees and headed back towards Lubango. This was Keet's first operational mission and, like every other pilot, he experienced the 'first night nerves' which accompanied every crossing of the cut-line into enemy territory.

On D-1, 23 August, air force participation in Operation *Protea* began in earnest with sustained attacks on the radar installations at Chibemba and Cahama. The attacks were initiated with a four-ship Buccaneer strike on the Barlock and Sidenet radars positioned at Cahama; TOT 11h00. The formation attacked from the northeast with the lead aircraft firing AS-30 guided missiles. It was a successful attack as both radar installations were damaged.

The Buccaneer could carry one AS-30 missile under each wing. The AS-30 had an all-up-weight of 520kg with a 50kg warhead. It had a boosted burn-time of approximately 20 seconds and was manually controlled by the pilot with a joystick on the left side of the cockpit. The pilot had to steer the missile through a UHF radio link into the target. As soon as the missile cleared the aircraft wing a red flare ignited at the back giving the pilot a good visual on the missile throughout its flight.

The attack profile was to fly to a pitch-up point about 20 nautical miles from the target, pitch-up to 15,000 feet AGL and then attack in a shallow 20° dive. The missile was launched at 13 nautical miles from the target at 480 knots and then steered to hit just in front of the target.

Prior to *Protea*, the Buccaneer crews had carried out an intensive AS-30 simulator training programme and flown practice sorties at the Riemvasmaak weapons range.

At 11h02 and 11h03, two waves, each comprising a single Canberra leading four Mirage F1CZs, attacked the same Cahama target flying from east to west. The ten aircraft were armed with long-delay and contact-fused 250/450kg bombs. No AAA ground fire or missile launches were observed during these strikes.

At 11h07, the Buccaneers attacked the Flatface and Spoonrest radar sites at Chibemba from the southwest, firing their second AS-30 missiles. During this attack an SA-7 was launched but detonated at an estimated 18,500 feet above the ground. The leader of the formation was Gert Havenga, with Sandy Roy flying as his navigator.

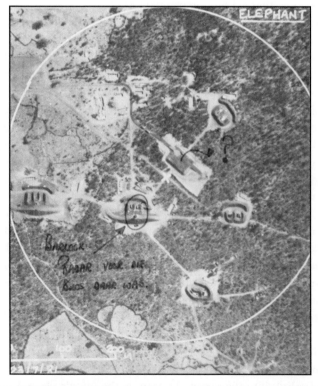

The radar and missile site at Chibembe, codenamed Elephant in *Protea* plans but known to aircrew as 'Die Wawiel' (wagon wheel) because of its distinctive shape. The Barlock radar can be seen as a black dot in the centre of the circle—it was surgically removed by a Buccaneer-launched AS-30 missile.

1981: Taking the war to the host nation

At 11h08, three composite waves of Canberra and Mirage aircraft, using a level-bombing delivery technique, attacked Chibemba from the west and dropped a total of 12 x 450kg and 72 x 250kg bombs. A release error in the leading Canberra resulted in all these weapons landing in virgin bush over two kilometres from the target.

At 16h45, I led a re-strike against the same target—not recommended by any war manuals—this time using 16 Mirage F1s. The profile differed from that flown by the composite formations. The approach was carried out at low level with the four formations pulling up into a right-hand high dive onto the clearly visible, revetment-protected radar sites. An SA-7 was launched against the Mirages; it missed and self-destructed at 20,000 feet. Pilots reported that 70 per cent of the bombs exploded within the target area and this was confirmed by EW operators. They reported that at strike time all radar signals went off the air. Eight days later a Flatface radar came back on air, this time operating out of the Cahama area. Subsequently, it too was eliminated in an air strike.

At 17h15, a formation of five Canberras carried out a medium-level attack on the Cahama installations, dropping ten 450kg and 45 x 250kg bombs. This attack was hampered by cloud cover over the target and only achieved an estimated 40 per cent coverage of the area.

At 20h00, a second attack was carried out by four Buccaneers against the radar installations at Chibemba. In the dark it was impossible to estimate target damage.

At 20h30 two Impalas, flown by Major Dick Lewer and Captain Kallie Knoetze, were diverted from a night reconnaissance mission to lend CAS to elements of Task Force Bravo. Captain Les Rudman and his company of Bushmen from 31 Battalion had been ambushed by a combined force of SWAPO and FAPLA. They were together with three seriously wounded soldiers, pinned down in the bush by a large group of terrorists at grid reference VM950320. The aircraft launched two very successful rocket attacks on the enemy position from a north-to-south direction, thus allowing our own troops to break contact and bring their wounded to safety. This was the first instance of Impala jets lending successful CAS to ground troops at night.

Dick Lewer was an experienced Citizen Force pilot attached to 8 Squadron. He had flown Mustangs in Korea while serving with 2 Squadron and had been awarded the American Distinguished Flying Cross. For the night attack in defence of 31 Battalion he was awarded the Honoris Crux Silver.

By the end of a long first day of operations no aircraft had been lost or damaged. AS-30 missiles had been used with success for the first time under operational conditions and no enemy radar at either centre was in operation. The only operational failure was in the mixing of formations, with Canberras 'mother-goosing' the Mirage F1s.

This photo from a squadron lines book, shows the effect of the Xangongo air strike.

On D-Day, 24 August, the focus of air attacks shifted to aerial bombardments of the military installations at Peu-Peu, Humbe and Xangongo in support of Task Force Alpha.

The day's air activity began at 11h05 when four Impalas attacked AAA sites at Peu-Peu with rockets. Ten minutes later the same formation attacked the AAA sites at Humbe from the northeast.

At 11h45 four Buccaneers attacked what was thought to be the Brigade HQ building in Peu-Peu with AS-30 missiles. No AAA was encountered and the building was completely destroyed by hits from three out of the four missiles fired. However, it was later found out to be the barracks, not the HQ.

At 11h50, the same Buccaneers initiated the first of six waves of aircraft to attack military installations and AAA sites around Xangongo. The leader's AS-30 scored a direct hit on the main military barracks building. Unfortunately, the other three AS-30 missiles all missed their targets, two because of technical malfunctions.

At 11h54 five Canberras dropped bombs from medium level. This was followed almost immediately by eight Mirage F1AZs, then six F1CZs and a formation of four Mirage III CZs, all dive-bombing their respective targets. The operation was completed at 12h10 when eight rocket-firing Impalas also attacked.

This aerial bombardment of the extensive installations surrounding both the town and airfield was followed by a ground-force assault. During the course of this battle two pairs of Mirage III aircraft were scrambled to attack pockets of stubborn resistance. The first pair took off at 14h30, to take on a 23mm AAA site which was being used effectively in the ground role against our assaulting troops. The second

1981: Taking the war to the host nation

The effects of the strikes can be judged from the palls of smoke billowing vigorously from the target area.

pair scrambled at 15h20 but could not be used in the target area because our own troops were at that stage too close to the enemy AAA site for safety.

Overall the day's operations were very successful and, in spite of heavy AAA fire, no aircraft were lost. Task Force Alpha was of the opinion that the heavy air strikes had kept enemy heads down and had done much to demoralize them. However, the troops' advance was held up by one 23mm gun which had remained in action after the aerial bombardment.

Captain Daan Laubscher was flying a Bosbok light reconnaissance aircraft as an artillery spotter during the attack on Xangongo. He saw the gun position which was holding up the advance and attacked it with 68mm rockets. His slow-flying aircraft was met by a barrage of enemy defensive AAA fire. The gun was put out of action, and the Ratels continued their advance to finally take Xangongo. Laubscher was awarded the Honoris Crux for his brave action.

D+1, 25 August, was spent by TF Alpha forces consolidating their position in Xangongo. The long road bridge over the Cunene River had been seriously damaged, preventing FAPLA units from using the crossing to reinforce their colleagues in Xangongo. The main occurrence of the day was the tragic loss of Lieutenant Bertus Roos and Sergeant Clifton Stacey who were killed when their Alouette gunship was shot down by 23mm AAA fire near Mongua. The gunners had shown an improvement in gunfire discipline and held their fire until the unsuspecting helicopter was within easy range. Smoke was seen coming from the helicopter as it crashed.

Task Force Bravo operating in the east captured the tiny town and sand

This photograph of a civilian-registered Bosbok was taken in 2007 by Elmarie Dreyer. The aircraft was flown by my nephew Derek Lord, an airline captain. Apart from the red spinner and the ZS registration it is in authentic SAAF livery. Laubsher's aircraft would have had rocket pods suspended under the wings.

airfield of Ionde. This added considerably to the flexibility of our forces because, although the runway was found to be bumpy, it was suitable for aircraft up to DC-3 Dakota size. This made logistical resupply to ground forces and evacuation of casualties considerably easier.

On D+2, 26 August at 15h30, formations of Buccaneers and Canberras carried out a re-strike on the installations at Chibembe. For this attack some of the bombs were fitted with long-delay fuses to discourage any attempts to repair the site. Both formations drew 23mm AAA fire but no aircraft were hit.

Dave Knoesen was one of the Buccaneer pilots on this sortie. While taxiing out he developed a serious nose-bleed. He told his navigator Charlie Wroth but insisted on completing the mission. He stuffed his scarf into his oxygen mask and flew the 105-minute flight without any other problems. However, while shutting down at Grootfontein, the bloody scarf caused pandemonium among the ground crew up the ladder. They thought he had been wounded.

The airfield at Ionde was brought into full use during the day. Three Dakotas flew in bringing supplies, equipment and a mortar team for Task Force Bravo. Twelve Puma helicopters were stationed there for the day, as well as a Bosbok that flew an intelligence-gathering reconnaissance mission over Caiundo.

At 22h00, a 55-man-strong reconnaissance team was dropped by parachute from a C-130, slightly north of the required XN100964 grid reference. Apart from this small error it was a successful operation.

The main feature of D+3, 27 August, was the sustained air attacks on military installations and AAA sites surrounding both the town and airfield at Ongiva. This aerial assault was in support of the ground attack launched from the west by Task Force Alpha, which had commenced at sunrise.

Protea—Strela hit

The day started well before dawn for the aircrews who had to brief and prepare for the day's missions. Captain Rynier Keet was appointed to lead the first strike in Mirage III 811 with a dual-seat Mirage III D2Z, crewed by Major Ben Arnoldi and Lieutenant Frans Vermaak as his No 2. Their target was an AAA site on the northern side of the Ongiva runway and each aircraft was armed with two pods of 68mm rockets. They planned to approach it at 20,000 feet and roll in from the east, out of the sun.

The evening prior to the attack everyone was busy planning their respective missions, discussing tactics and co-ordinating with operations, intelligence and the other involved squadrons—the normal pre-mission activities associated with any tactical flight. Keet well recalls the main subject under discussion. HQ had decided it was necessary to send in a Skyshout light aircraft during the afternoon to warn the enemy by voice and a pamphlet drop, that from 07h00 the next day we were going to attack Ongiva. In the light of what the crews had been tasked to do they were understandably agitated.

Keet's formation took off on time, on a typical SWA August day. Visibility directly downwards was zero as they flew eastwards towards the rising sun in the winter haze, ruling out map-reading as a viable option. Therefore, he flew on the old standby of heading and time which worked well. However, to accomplish this he had to fly past the Ongiva airfield on the northern side, giving the enemy ample time to prepare for the coming attack. Because the sun was still very low his aircraft was probably silhouetted against the lightening sky.

Keet concentrated on acquiring his assigned target visually and rolling in at the correct dive angle. He did this and fired the 36 rockets at release height. His next action was to fly out of the SA-7 envelope as quickly as possible as no one, Keet included, believed the enemy would have abandoned their positions without a fight. He applied 6G, lit his afterburner and while climbing looked back to see whether he had hit the target and if his tail was clear. He cannot remember seeing where his rockets hit but vividly recalls seeing a little red dot in front of the airfield control tower. There was no relative movement of the dot except that it grew bigger and bigger. He immediately realized it was a missile and pulled in towards it as hard as he could while cutting the afterburner to reduce the heat signature of his engine. This action was too late and he felt a thump as the missile struck his aircraft.

His overtaxed body received an additional adrenaline boost as the audio warning system began ringing in his earphones. Looking down he could see the alarm panel lighting up like a Christmas tree and felt the stiffening of his controls as the hydraulic control dampers popped. His immediate thought was to try and put some distance between himself and some understandably angry people on the ground that he had just attacked.

Just then Arnoldi slid his Mirage into close formation with Keet and Frans Vermaak gave him a running commentary on the condition of his damaged aircraft. He had lost hydraulic pressure and could not re-set his dampers. The clam-shell, which controls the afterburner section of the Atar engine, was also damaged and Vermaak advised him not to attempt to use it. However, by flying with very smooth stick movements and reducing speed Keet found he could still control the aircraft and turned onto a heading for AFB Ondangwa.

The fifteen minutes' transit to Ondangwa was a fairly anxious time for Keet, even though his aircraft was flying relatively well. Having lost hydraulic pressure he knew that he would have to land without brakes. Because the delta-winged Mirage III does not have flaps it has a high landing speed of over 250km per hour. In the event of a drag-'chute failure there was nothing to stop Keet's aircraft from careering off the end of the short Ondangwa runway, except the airfield fence.

He had just cause for concern. A few years earlier, flying in the back of a twin-seat Mirage III under the control of Piet Roos (known throughout the SAAF as Sir Peter Rose for his long, flowing locks), they had run out of hydraulics, options and ideas while landing on the long runway 01 at AFB Pietersburg. Leaving the end of the runway the speeding Mirage cut a swathe through the veld and over the huge antheaps that dot the highveld plains. The aircraft finally came to rest, after breaking off its nose gear, in a tangle of barbed wire security fencing. Fortunately, the Mirage III is a very strong aircraft and neither pilot was injured. However, events like this tend to linger in the back of a pilot's mind and it was a situation Keet did not wish to repeat.

His other fear was that the oil lines to his engine might have been damaged. Oil pressure from the engine is used to regulate throttle movements and an oil failure is considered a very serious emergency. After landing, close inspection of the damage showed that one of the oil pipes was in fact damaged but fortunately had not ruptured.

On requesting landing instructions from Ondangwa Tower Keet was ordered to orbit before making his approach until all twelve Ondangwa aircraft involved in the strike had landed. The ATCs dared not risk having his damaged aircraft blocking the only usable runway. Fortunately Keet made a good approach and the drag 'chute deployed correctly. By his skilful use of aerodynamic braking and keeping the aircraft's nose very high he managed to bring the aircraft to a stop without further damage.

Emergency services were waiting to replace the safety pins in his seat which allowed him to leave the cockpit, before the aircraft was towed back to its place on the hardstanding. By keeping a cool head Keet had saved an expensive and, because of the international arms embargo, irreplaceable asset. All credit to 2 Squadron's ground crew; they replaced the Mirage's tail section and engine and

1981: Taking the war to the host nation

With a relieved smile Rynier Keet surveys the damage to the tailpipe of his aircraft after being hit by a shoulder-launched SA-7 Strela missile.

returned the aircraft to operational service within three days.

Meanwhile, over Ongiva the sky had erupted in a maze of diving aircraft and telltale puffs of black and grey smoke from exploding anti-aircraft shells. At 07h45, the same time as Keet had attacked, four Mirage F1AZs were diving on another of the AAA sites close to the airport, firing full pods of 68mm rockets. Heavy AAA fire was drawn from two positions, one 700 metres south and the other a mile or so west of the target. The pilots reported a number of SA-7 missile trails as well as larger puffs of 57mm AAA fire.

At 07h48, four Mirage IIIs attacked a target close to the town, releasing pods of 68mm rockets. The natural dispersion of rockets fired from pods gives good area coverage on anti-aircraft sites providing a pilot's aim is accurate.

At 07h52, four Mirage IIIs attacked sites north of the target which drew AAA and several SA-7 missiles but none of the aircraft was hit.

At 08h00, five pairs of aircraft streamed in at medium altitude to drop sticks of bombs on the area north of Ongiva. Each pair consisted of one Canberra leading one Buccaneer. Each Canberra dropped two 450kg bombs, carried on the wing stations and eight 250kg bombs carried in their bomb bays. The Buccaneers dropped sticks of eight 250kg bombs. This wave of aircraft had problems contacting the MAOT on their radios and consequently bombed the wrong target. Fortunately, the bombing seemed to have the desired effect because after the attack the rate of AAA fire slackened off markedly.

At 08h10, six F1AZs attacked targets on the airfield dropping air-bursting Mk 82 bombs and at 08h15, six F1CZs attacked the brigade HQ complex with the

The army assault force waits while the SAAF pounds the military defences of Ongiva.

same type of weapons. Both these attacks were assessed as successful as the targets received over 80 per cent coverage.

Task Force Alpha then initiated the ground assault, working their way through the huge target complex from west to east. CAS missions were scrambled several times during the day to attack tank, mortar and 122mm rocket positions which were hampering the ground-force advance. At 11h45, two F1AZs were scrambled to attack a tank in a hull-down position. AAA fire was still being drawn but the target was effectively neutralized. Often, when the enemy had adopted defensive positions they would dig large holes allowing their armoured vehicles protection right up to turret height. This was known as a hull-down position. It is extremely difficult to damage vehicles when they are in this position as the more vulnerable tracks, or wheels, are protected by sand.

At 12h45, a pair of F1AZs flown by Norman Minne and Paddy Carolan was called in to attack an artillery fire control position in Ongiva. The ground troops were taking a bit of a hammering; it was suspected that the enemy observation post responsible was positioned on top of the water tower in the town—a good site bearing in mind how flat the entire terrain was. For those who remember the old Ongiva it was the tower with the large 'Cuca' advertisement on the top.

Minne, the leader, decided that as the target was in the centre of the town and ringed by AAA defences the best attack profile to use was a high dive and release, firing all 72 x 68mm rockets in salvo. Sight settings were set and the Mirage F1AZs rolled into the high dive, meeting some heavy resistance on the way down. As Paddy, the No 2, reached his release height he noticed that Minne was still merrily heading earthwards. He reminded Minne over the radio of the decision to do the high release. In the excitement Minne had forgotten and

1981: Taking the war to the host nation

replied, "Oh shit! Let's make it an academic dive." Paddy hastily changed sight settings, realigned the aircraft and fired all 72 rockets at the tower.

The pull-out was quite exciting as a great deal of dangerous metal was flashing past both aircraft. Looking rearwards, Carolas saw an SA-7 missile trail approaching from the starboard side and pulled into it from what was already a high-G recovery. The missile vanished into his 6 o'clock so he reversed his turn. Having lost sight of the missile he assumed it had detonated behind him.

Once clear of the target Paddy surveyed his aircraft for damage and noticed that both wing-tip-mounted air-to-air missile heads were damaged. Minne suggested he jettison both missiles. However, Mossie Basson, the MAOT with the ground forces, overhearing the radio exchange between the pilots advised against this procedure, intimating that there could be a proximity detonation as the missiles left the pylons. He further recommended that Paddy return to AFB Ondangwa, avoid flying into birds and insects on the return flight and land with missiles attached.

Needless to say Paddy flew very carefully back to base avoiding, as he put it, "all items of interest to ornithologists and entomologists", where he carried out an extremely smooth touch-down. The tower ordered him to taxi to the deserted eastern end of the runway where he was to await the arrival of the armourers—the tower authorities did not want any premature explosions which could harm anybody else—a comforting thought.

After a patient, although tense wait the armourers arrived to make-safe the missiles. With a feeling of relief Paddy watched as the men carefully approached the aircraft from the rear. Before reaching the missiles the pair of armourers did an abrupt about-turn and high-tailed it into the middle distance; they had obviously decided that the exercise was too dangerous—Paddy was left completely alone.

He shut down the engine and considered his next move. Would the missiles detonate if he opened the canopy? He decided to try anyway. He unstrapped and then opened the canopy. Nothing happened. Climbing out of the cockpit he gingerly made his way onto the back of the aircraft staying behind the missiles and jumped from the tail. He joined the armourers who were taking cover some distance from the aircraft. After Paddy had informed them that he had switched everything off one of the armourers sprinted to the aircraft, ripping out the connector cable as he passed. After taking a breather he repeated the performance to make-safe the second missile.

On investigation it was discovered that the missile heads had collapsed under the application of the high G force used to avoid the surface-to-air missile. Because this was only Paddy's second strike mission in an F1AZ the memory is still clear in his mind. On a later trip to Ongiva as an MAOT Paddy had time to inspect the water tower—the target for his attack. Only one of the rockets had

The target was the OP on top of the water tower on the left. However, most of the rockets hit the building on the right.

hit the top of the tower, with the remaining 143 hitting the building directly behind it. However, the one hit had been sufficient to dislodge the unfortunate artillery spotter.

*****

At 13h01, three 1 Squadron Mirages neutralized a mortar pit and a rocket launching site.

At approximately 15h00 a convoy consisting of some 20 enemy vehicles broke free of the fighting in and around Ongiva and started moving northeastward along the road leading out of the town. Fifteen kilometres from the town the convoy was stopped by C Company, 32 Battalion. This unit was part of Task Force Bravo which had been deployed as a stopper group for this type of eventuality. The convoy was halted 100 metres in front of the stopper group and two Mirages were called in to the attack. They did not fire however, as the two opposing groups were too close together for safety. This allowed some of the convoy to sneak through the bush around the stopper group.

These vehicles were found by a Bosbok reconnaissance aircraft and the pilot called in two Impala aircraft to initiate an attack. When the Impalas were out of ammunition they were replaced by four Alouette gunships from the deployment at Ionde. These in turn were replaced by a further three Alouette gunships from the group allocated to support Task Force Alpha. During these attacks the Impalas accounted for one vehicle, the Alouette gunship twelve and the ground forces three. Included among the shot-up vehicles were two Soviet-built T-34 tanks and several BTR armoured personnel carriers. Four Russians (two men and two women) were killed during the air attack while one Soviet sergeant-

Soviet-supplied T-54 tank being inspected by the crew of a Ratel.

major was captured by ground forces.

The MAOT attached to TF Bravo set up another HAG in the east which was to stay in operation for the remainder of *Protea*. By day this HAG was large enough to accommodate six Puma and five Alouette helicopters. At night the large Pumas withdrew to AFB Ondangwa.

The combined air attacks launched throughout the day on the Ongiva target complex did not succeed in neutralizing all the enemy AAA sites and bunkers. Various strongpoints continued to resist and, although a Bosbok landed at the airfield earlier, two Puma helicopters were fired upon while flying over the airfield late in the afternoon. Nevertheless, the air attacks had made the ground forces' job very much easier and the outstanding work done by Lieutenant Jakes Venter, the pilot of the Bosbok, allowed co-ordinated air attacks to be made on the escaping convoy. The capture of the Russian proved to be of immense propaganda value—no longer could the active presence of Soviets be dismissed as the imagination of overzealous 'securicats'.

*****

At 08h05 on D+4, 28 August, the final CAS mission was flown in support of ground forces mopping up in Ongiva. Six Impalas each armed with four 250kg bombs attacked the last remaining strongpoints. No AAA fire was drawn as enemy resistance had finally been broken.

A lot of air activity occurred in the TF Bravo area of operations with little in the way of success. A number of SWAPO bases were attacked, the majority of which proved to be empty as SWAPO had fled in time.

At 10h03, four Buccaneers attacked what was thought to be newly installed Barlock radar at Chibemba. This site was known to the aircrew as '*die wawiel*' because from the air the layout of the target resembled the wheel of a wagon.

History, like beauty, is in the eye of the beholder. I received an account of this mission from two sources:

>>Source 1 (Archival records). In the initial attack the aircraft used AS-30 missiles and then re-attacked dropping 460kg bombs. The accuracy of these attacks varied between 50 and 75 per cent coverage as heavy AAA was drawn from the entire area and at least two SA-7 smoke trails were sighted by the aircrew.<<

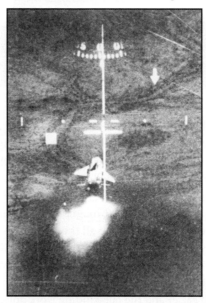

A good shot of an AS-30 missile just after firing. A bright flare ignites in the tail of the missile allowing the pilot to keep it in sight as it speeds away. By moving a mini-control stick in the cabin the missile can be steered accurately into the selected target.

>>Source 2 (Major George Snyman [*ed*. It was his 32nd birthday]). The formation was led by Commandant Gert Havenga and Major Sandy Roy. No 2 was Major Lappies Labuschagne and Lieutenant Dewald Pretorius. George Snyman and Captain Riem Mouton were No 3 and No 4 was crewed by Major Trevor Schroeder and Lieutenant Charlie Wroth. Because it was suspected that the target complex was defended by SA-9 systems the formation's initial attack was with AS-30 missiles to take advantage of the surprise element. After firing their missiles the first pair broke off to the left while 3 and 4 broke right to split the enemy defences.

At this break-off point Lead and 2 were 20 seconds ahead and about 300 metres to the left of 3 and 4. They were attacking with the sun directly behind them. Suddenly Lead called a SAM launch. The pilots of Buccaneer 3 and 4 did not have time to look for the missile as they were still steering their AS-30 missiles towards the designated targets. After the AS-30 impact George broke right telling Schroeder to go low. George then looked over his shoulder for the first time and noticed the smoke trail the SAM had left—he had not seen it streak by.

However, he did see it had originated from an open area about 2km away, in his 10 o'clock position, and there was a vehicle parked there. Immediately the word SAM-9 flashed through his mind and he realized that their right-hand break had presented the missile launcher with a wonderful view up the tail of the two Buccaneers. He levelled out and dived for the treetops at 550 knots to present the missile launcher with a maximum crossing-speed problem to solve.

As he reached treetop level he saw a SAM fired, which streaked straight towards him, followed seconds later by a second missile. George had only a few seconds available to decide on what evasive action he must make. A thousand thoughts went through his mind. Should he break towards the threat or not? Crazily, he remembered someone telling him once that the CSIR (Council for Scientific and Industrial Research) had done tests and determined that the turbofan engines of the Buccaneer had the heat signature of a Cessna 150. Whether that was at full power as he was now, or not, he couldn't remember. He decided not to break towards the missile while reducing power (and his heat signature) because that would have left him idling straight towards the missile launcher and a sitting duck for the next missile.

He sat watching the missiles approach hoping that the CSIR had been correct in their estimation. He followed the leading missile all the way until it passed about 15 metres behind the Buccaneer. It was so close he clearly remembers seeing the short, square fins on its fuselage as it flashed by. Suddenly as it broke lock the missile pulled up into a steep climb towards the sun and detonated at altitude. Fortunately, the second missile did exactly the same although it had passed a little farther away. The two very fortunate Buccaneers sped away and a few minutes later rejoined the formation at the pre-planned RV point. From there they ran in at 30-second intervals in line astern and at low level to carry out an IPMT (initial point medium toss) attack.

During the run-in George saw Lead and 2 pulling up for the toss followed by their right-hand break towards SWA. Rushing after the Buccaneers was the trail of another SAM which also missed as the two aircraft reached ultra-low level. Then it was the turn of George and Schroeder to release their bombs and break right and downwards, closing throttles to idle to reduce their heat signature. This time, however, they were not fired at and 105 minutes after take-off they landed safely back at AFB Grootfontein. During the crew debriefing the intelligence analysis was that the missiles fired were SA-7s not SAM-9s. Whatever they were they had given George Snyman the most exciting birthday he had ever experienced.<<

By 10h30 the airfield at Ongiva was finally secured. The runway was found to require only minor repairs before being brought into commission by the SAAF. A formation of ten Mirage F1s struck a SWAPO temporary base identified as target 57 with 250kg bombs. Although the target was well covered ground troops who followed up the strike reported that the base had been deserted some four to six weeks earlier.

*****

D+7, 31 August, was another quiet day for the air forces involved with *Protea*. By this time Combat Teams (CBT) 10 and 20 of TF Alpha had withdrawn from Angola and TF Bravo was planning its return to SWA. Thirty-six SAAF members were withdrawn from the HAG and returned to AFB Ondangwa. A visual reconnaissance flight followed by a photo reconnaissance indicated a large concentration of enemy vehicles about six kilometres south of Cahama. In all probability these were vehicles belonging to the SWAPO battalion which, reports indicated, had been sent as reinforcements from Lubango. An air strike was planned for the next day.

At 07h30 on D+8, 1 September, five Canberras attacked the vehicle concentration from the northeast. This line of attack with the sun behind the aircraft worked well as the target was clearly visible. No AAA was drawn and it appeared the attack achieved complete surprise. However, stronger-than-forecast southerly surface winds caused most of the bombs to land to the right of the proposed bomb line. Three formations of Mirage F1s then dive-bombed the target at two-minute intervals. These attacks were met with light 14.5mm AAA fire and a number of SA-7 missiles but no aircraft was damaged.

On D+9, 2 September, *Protea* was in the final withdrawal stages and the Canberras and Buccaneers were released to their home base at AFB Waterkloof.

On D+10, 3 September, interest was aroused by the appearance of fast MiG traffic on SAAF radar screens. At 09h36, three MiGs were seen approaching the theatre of operations of TF Bravo. Two Mirage F1CZs of 3 Squadron were detached from an escort mission and vectored towards the MiG formation, without success. The MiG formation disappeared off our radar screens before the Mirage pilots could get within range. It was noted that the pilots in the MiG formation spoke Spanish, giving a clear indication that the air war had escalated, with the Cubans now actively involved.

At 15h28, the MiGs reappeared on radar. No attempt was made to intercept them as they did not pose a threat to our ground forces; also, the time lag between reports would have given our interceptors little chance of success.

At 16h25, three formations of four Mirage aircraft attacked the large vehicle park just north of Cahama with a mixture of 68mm rockets and 250kg bombs. Very little AAA fire was noticed and no telltale missile smoke trails were seen.

1981: Taking the war to the host nation

*****

On D+11, 4 September, *Protea* officially ended when TF Bravo withdrew over the cut-line back into SWA. The only non-routine mission flown was a photo reconnaissance over the enemy airfield at Menonque just before 11h00 by two Mirage III R2Zs escorted by four Mirage F1CZ fighters. The object of this flight was to update intelligence concerning this airfield. No opposition was encountered and all the aircraft returned safely to AFB Ondangwa.

Apart from the major missions a full-scale interdiction programme was carried out around the clock by Impala and Mirage aircraft, with the aim of disrupting the enemy's logistical supply routes. Numerous radio messages from SWAPO forces in the field were intercepted indicating serious food shortages which testified to the success of the interdiction programme.

Other routine flights, which went almost unnoticed during the entire operation, were those carried out by the helicopter, transport and light aircraft crews. They flew missions as diverse as casualty evacuation, trooping and para-trooping, fire support, resupply, communications navigation and Telstar for ground forces, as well as pamphlet-dropping and skyshout.

Protea had been a huge operation, the largest the SAAF had carried out since the end of the Second World War in 1945. It was an undoubted success as all our objectives were achieved. Radar installations at Chibemba and Cahama were destroyed and AAA sites around Xangongo, Ongiva, Peu-Peu and Humbe had been neutralized. Ground forces attacked and occupied Xangongo, Mongua, Ongiva, Omupanda, Namacunde and Santa Clara, thus SWAPO could no longer be protected by the defensive umbrella provided by Angolan forces sited around these towns. The 50-kilometre 'shallow area' had been cleared of SWAPO combatants including the area east of the Cassinga–Santa Clara road where Task Force Bravo had operated.

These facts were noted on both sides of the border. SWAPO, the Angolans, the Cubans, and their political masters in the USSR realized their military plans for southern Africa were doomed to fail unless, and until, the combined strengths of the South African ground forces and the SAAF had been nullified. But the success of *Protea* was a double-edged sword. With the raising of the South Africans' confidence level came the realization that subsequent operations would become much harder as captured or destroyed enemy equipment was replaced by newer and better weapons.

The aims of *Protea* had been achieved, with the Cunene Province of Angola cleared of both SWAPO and FAPLA forces and South African forces firmly in control of Ongiva and Xangongo. UNITA forces were introduced into the area to help prevent SWAPO from re-establishing a presence. Short, sharp incursions by mine-laden terrorists became a thing of the past. Future insurgencies became physically more difficult for them. Before crossing the border they had to trudge 200 kilometres carrying their weapons and supplies. If they survived they had to return the same way. One has to admire their courage as every year they tried again and again.

During Operation *Protea* SADF troops captured and occupied the Angolan town of Xangongo on the Cunene River. Quoting from the Sector 10 official document giving details of the operation it is apparent that 'in their haste to escape, the Russians left behind personal possessions and a huge quantity of documents, which military intelligence sources say point to a growing Soviet involvement in the war situation in southern Angola'. At the Soviet headquarters in an old house in Xangongo, charts and maps were on the walls setting out command structures and strategy in Russian script. The Soviets were billeted in a house next to their HQ, some of them apparently with their wives and children.

During the eleven days of *Protea*, 1,112 individual sorties were flown from Grootfontein and Ondangwa, 333 tons of bombs were dropped, 1,774 68mm rockets and 18 AS-30 missiles fired. A Mirage III CZ was damaged by a SA-7 missile but landed safely. The air force lost an Alouette helicopter and crew shot down near the town of Mongua, Angola.

Protea set the trend that was to last until the end of the border war. The actual insurgency war against SWAPO was supported throughout the entire 23 years by the SAAF. However, it was the helicopter, transport and light aircraft crews who bore the brunt of the conflict. The 'fast jets' were only summoned from

Soviet advisors provided the impetus for all Angolan operations.

1981: Taking the war to the host nation

Over the years vast amounts of war matériel were captured from the Angolans, including armoured vehicles, logistic trucks, anti-aircraft guns and mines. The downside of this was that the Soviets kept replacing this equipment with more modern equivalents,

their home bases in South Africa for specific operations such as *Protea*. At no time were Canberra, Buccaneer, Mirage III or Mirage F1 aircraft ever permanently deployed to SWA. That would have happened only in the event of an all-out war and the Angolan conflict never reached that stage.

Intelligence-gathering is an ongoing process using all forms of humint (human intelligence), sigint (signal intelligence), elint (electronic intelligence) and reconnaissance (both photographic and visual). A combination of these inputs evaluated after *Protea* indicated that SWAPO had moved their military command post to a position in thick bush northeast of Techamutete. Further information showed that despite their losses sustained during *Protea* they were planning another large-scale infiltration during the rainy season, early in 1982.

Operation *Daisy*

In an endeavour to disrupt these plans the SADF decided to seek and destroy the enemy HQ by means of a ground force assault assisted by the air force. Because

1 Squadron, known as the 'Billy Boys' since the Desert Air Force days of 1941. Hannes Faure, the then OC, used to shout "*Jou Bielie!*" over the radio every time a 1 Squadron pilot shot up an enemy truck. The RAF squadrons seconded to the same wing attached the name Billy Boys to the squadron. 1 Squadron OC is always known by his call sign 'Billy'. *Back left to right:* Dirk de Villiers, Hennie Louw, Frik Viljoen, I. C. du Plessis, Theo Nell, Dick Lord, Frans Pretorius, Wassie Wasserman, Bill Einkamerer, Norman Minne; *front:* Mark Clulow, Ronnie Knott-Craig, Vic Kaiser, Frans Coetzee, Bill Collier, Ed Every.

the theatre of operation was extremely deep into Angola, up to 150 kilometres, the decision was made to provide adequate fighter back-up for the ground forces. The main Angolan defence line was centred on the east–west railway line that stretched from Namibe on the Atlantic coast to Menonque in the east. Two major Angolan airfields were positioned at Lubango and Menonque, putting the theatre of operations well within their MiG striking range.

Air force participation in *Daisy* was to last from 1 November to 14 November. The following aircraft were allocated for the operation:

- Army support:
  15 x Impalas
  9 x Pumas
  2 x Frelons
  10 x Alouettes

- Air transport, trooping, resupply and casualty evacuation:
  4 x DC-3 Dakotas
  6 x C-130/160s
  1 x DC-4

- Telstar, navigation and reconnaissance support:
  9 x Bosboks

1981: Taking the war to the host nation

This map, with the cut-line as the southern border, shows how deep the *Daisy* combat area was inside Angola. The area our ground forces had to search was between Cassinga, Jamba and Cuchi. The Ionde airfield was approximately half way.

- Photo-reconnaissance:
  2 x Mirage III RZs

- Air superiority:
  20 x Mirage F1s from both 1 and 3 Squadrons

- Enemy airfield attack (if required):
  3 x Buccaneers

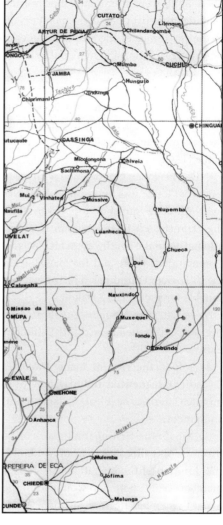

Colonel Ollie Holmes was in charge of the air force contingent at 10 AFCP Oshakati. He was assisted by Colonel Mickey Brand as SSO Fighters, Commandant Koos Botha SO1 Elint and Buccaneers, Commandant Johan Louw SO1 140 Squadron Radar, and majors Otto Schür and Zack Zunckel in charge of reconnaissance and helicopters respectively.

The forward HQ of the ground forces was to position at Ionde airfield once it had been secured. The air force MAOT team co-located with this HQ, consisting of Commandant Dudley Foote, Major Mitz Maritz and Captain Ian Solomon. The army task force was divided into three elements, each one having an air advisor team as part of their HQ contingent. Major Rod Penhall was with Alpha, Captain H. P. Cook with Bravo and Major Knoppies Coetzer with X-Ray.

On D-3 (1 November), all forces moved into Angola to position themselves prior to the start of *Daisy*. A HAG was established by ground troops and two Pumas and two Alouette gunships were deployed, as well as Major Coetzer. He laid strobe lights marking the position of the HAG for use later that evening.

These lights were illuminated shortly after 22h00 as a position marker for a C-130 Hercules that dropped eight members of a reconnaissance team by parachute in the proximity of the suspected enemy HQ. This team was to establish the prevailing situation and mark out a suitable DZ for a large-scale paradrop on the morning of D-Day.

On D-2 (2 November), a reconnaissance team from 32 Battalion, commanded by Captain Willem Ratte, was trooped in to the HAG. He and his small team were to reconnoitre the Ionde airfield and environs in preparation for the assault the next morning. By last light eight Alouettes and eight Pumas were positioned at the HAG.

D-Day (3 November) dawned with reports coming in from the reconnaissance team that Ionde was unoccupied. This was confirmed at 06h15 when six Pumas, with Alouette gunship top cover, found the airfield deserted. Therefore, they transferred their attention to a suspected enemy base at Embundo, six kilometres to the southwest, which was worked through and secured. By 10h45, Commandant Foote and his MAOT team were established at Ionde in one of the dilapidated buildings. The runway was found to be in good condition, quite suitable for use by DC-3 Dakotas.

At 14h20, two Alouette gunships were detached to Captain Cook to lend fire support to members of 201 Battalion who had run into a contact with the enemy.

At 15h20, the first of many Dakota flights arrived at Ionde bringing in Brigadier Groenewald and his ComOps (communication operations) team. Five minutes later the next Dakota landed with the Tac HQ medical team and their equipment.

By 15h45, the first of three pairs of Bosbok light aircraft landed as part of the air forces allocated to Commandant Foote and were to remain at Ionde for the duration of the operation. At 16h00, two Pumas were sent to pick up four members of 201 Battalion wounded in the contact and to bring back a captured SWAPO member for interrogation. At 16h30, a third Dakota landed, bringing in 20 tyres for the Buffel armoured troop-carriers which were badly needed by 61 Mechanized Battalion. At 17h56 a fourth Dakota landed at Ionde with paratroopers who were to act as the Tactical HQ mobile reserve.

The other event of note took place away from the chosen theatre of operations at 08h35. Two Mirage III RZs escorted by two Mirage F1CZ fighters took off on a PR mission over Cahama. The radars at Cahama had been heavily bombed during *Protea* but indications were that they were once more in operation, which could severely compromise the SAAF's freedom of movement during *Daisy*. The PR mission was successful, confirming the re-activation of the radar sites. Based on this information a strike on the installations was planned for D+1.

Finally, when the MAOT team was established at Ionde the HAG was closed

1981: Taking the war to the host nation

down. A second administrative area was opened as HAG 2, supporting TF X-Ray close to 61 Mechanized Battalion.

On D-Day (4 November), air activities started at 03h00 when six C-130/C-160 transport aircraft took off from AFB Grootfontein with three companies of paratroopers; the DZ was at map reference XP47 095. They routed via Ionde and HAG 2, both of which were illuminated by strobe lights. However, the actual drop did not go according to plan. The DZ had not been illuminated on time by the reconnaissance team and the paratroopers were dropped a few kilometres from the desired position. Fortunately, no paratrooper was seriously injured despite landing in very bushy terrain.

At 05h45, the first pair of Bosboks was airborne from Ionde to the target area. Subsequent pairs followed at 07h30 and 07h45. These aircraft played an invaluable role throughout the day as navigational guides, artillery spotters and Telstar for 61 Mechanized Battalion, 201 Battalion and the paratroop companies.

At 08h15, three Buccaneers initiated the attack against the SWAPO HQ target with a low-level medium-toss profile, each aircraft tossing a stick of eight 460kg bombs. The bombs were fused alternately with air-burst and contact fuses. It was an early strike and the Buccaneer crews decided to attack from north to south. During their low-level run-in to the selected IP they passed approximately ten miles to the east of the target. A meteorological inversion had trapped the smoke from the enemy's breakfast fires thereby identifying their position. The navigators used this smoke to confirm the target information. They performed a 180° turn to overfly the IP and, during the run-in at 580 knots with steering signal selected, the target release signal (pipper) was sitting exactly over the area where the smoke was. The result was a very accurate strike.

One minute later, four Mirage F1AZs dived onto the target from the northeast with their four sticks of bombs all falling in the designated target area. No AAA fire was seen but the No 4 pilot reported an SA-7 trail and explosion as he was pulling out of his dive. This attack was followed 30 seconds later by three F1CZs releasing bombs onto the target, this time drawing AAA fire as well as a missile.

At 08h17, a further four F1s dived onto the target followed 30 seconds later by another four aircraft. These eight sticks of bombs also impacted well inside the target area and the pilots reported AAA fire and at least one missile trail. Puffs of what were taken to be 23mm AAA fire appeared at 10,000 feet.

Despite the heavy pounding they received SWAPO put up a stern defence. At 08h55, Major Penhall called two F1CZs in to rocket an AAA site that was still firing at Bosbok aircraft. As they pulled out from the attack both pilots noticed 23mm AAA fire as well as an SA-7, all of which missed. At 09h30, a pair of rocket-firing Mirage F1CZs was called in again by Major Penhall against two further AAA sites.

Between 10h00 and 12h00, Impala aircraft were used to attack AAA sites still giving resistance. Between 12h00 and 14h00, several interdiction- and road-reconnaissance missions were flown by both Impalas and Mirage F1s along the roads between Cassinga, Techamutete, Bambi and the target area, looking for possible reinforcements en route to aid SWAPO. However, no vehicles were seen at this time.

At 14h09, two Alouettes were tasked to search for two paratroopers who had been separated from their company during the drop. At 15h38, two Pumas left Ionde to recover a casualty whose leg had been broken when his vehicle detonated a landmine. At 15h40, a Dakota carrying the Chief of the Air Force and Brigadier Bossie Huyser flew in to Ionde where they spent the night.

At 16h30, news was received that three of our ground forces had been killed in a contact in the target area and two Pumas were dispatched to recover the bodies.

The disappointment of the day was when it was learned that of the three ground force task groups only one had found a worthwhile target, in which SWAPO's Bravo Battalion put up a gallant defence. The other two targets were found to be empty, emphasizing the need to improve the accuracy of our intelligence reporting.

An interesting feature of the day was the frequent appearance of MiG activity on our radars. However, although the frequency increased it became apparent they were flying combat air patrols to intercept SAAF aircraft dispatched to attack Angolan airfields.

D+1 (5 November) began with a 07h00 take-off of 14 Mirage F1 aircraft from AFB Ondangwa. Twelve were armed with air-burst fused 250kg bombs—their targets the Sidenet radar and fuel dumps at Cahama. The other two F1CZs, configured with air-to-air missiles and cannon, acted as a CAP protecting the ground-attack bombers.

At 09h00, five Pumas and six Alouettes were moved to HAG 3, established by Major Penhall, closer to the scene of activity. Between 09h00 and 11h00, Impalas and Mirage F1s were scrambled to seek and destroy enemy convoys which had been heard by our ground forces. After a great deal of flying and no sighting of an enemy convoy the mystery was unravelled. Two of our own task forces had passed in close proximity to each other and mistakenly identified the armoured noises as emanating from the enemy.

A Buffel armoured personnel carrier carrying ammunition exploded at HAG 3 at 12h10, forcing Major Penhall to evacuate all his helicopters back to HAG 2 to avoid aircraft damage. Fortunately, no one was injured in the explosion.

At 12h34, ground forces reported a high-flying, twin-engined aircraft passing over the *Daisy* target area. Fearing that it might be an enemy elint aircraft Oshakati ordered two Mirage F1CZs to scramble but the aircraft disappeared before an intercept could take place.

At 13h16, two Pumas arrived at Ionde from the target area carrying one body and three wounded engineers. A booby trap had detonated in a bunker in the SWAPO Bravo Battalion area and these men had taken the full force of the explosion.

Throughout the day MiGs had been active and at one stage it seemed as if they were set to intervene against our forces. Our Elint units intercepted an enemy radio call ordering, "MiGs to go for their targets". Fortunately, nothing came of this and the MiGs remained on the defensive.

Daisy—MiG kill

D+2 (6 November) turned out to be by far the most exciting day of the operation for the respective air forces as MiGs of the Angolan Air Force finally became aggressive. Increased MiG activity over the previous two days ensured that a comprehensive air defence programme had been initiated at AFB Ondangwa. Mirage F1CZs, armed with missiles and 30mm cannon, were on cockpit standby in the readiness shelters from first light. At 07h00, Major Marsh Facer, the Dayton radar fighter controller, detected two fast-moving tracks moving southwards from Lubango towards Quiteve and he scrambled two Mirages onto an intercept vector. Previously, during attempted interceptions the MiGs had always retired out of range whenever SAAF fighters were detected by their early warning radar. On this occasion the F1CZs used a low-level penetration up to the Cunene River to stay below enemy radar cover, while accelerating to combat speed.

Leading the formation was Major Johan Rankin with Lieutenant Johan du Plessis as his wingman. Both men were graduates of 85 Advanced Fighter School at AFB Pietersburg and were accomplished pilots. Their training in 3 Squadron had concentrated on interception techniques and ACM—the old-fashioned dogfighting—for exactly this moment. Marsh ordered the Mirage formation (Mission 269) to stay at low level until they had crossed the Cunene River.

Once across the river the two Johans pitched from 50 to 25,000 feet in fewer than 30 seconds and were undetected by the enemy radar controllers. Johan du Plessis sighted the enemy flying in the opposite direction between three and five miles away on the port beam. They identified the enemy as two MiG-21s flying in a fighting element formation at the same height as the Mirages.

Jettisoning their drop tanks the F1s entered a hard left turn bringing them in behind the unsuspecting MiGs. The enemy were flying 1,000 to 1,500 metres apart with the No 2 aircraft trailing 30 degrees behind the leader's beam. The MiGs were flying directly into the sun, precluding a shot with the Matra 550 heat-seeking missile. Rankin, closing from astern of enemy No 2, fired a burst of 30mm explosive shells from approximately 350 metres. Immediately, a puff of smoke appeared around the MiG and fuel started leaking from its fuselage.

The MiGs entered a tight, descending left-hand turn and jettisoned their external fuel tanks. Major Rankin, by now in missile range of the lead MiG attempted to launch his own missile which malfunctioned. Rankin re-entered a curve of pursuit on MiG No 2 telling Johan du Plessis to go after the leader. MiG No 2 then committed a cardinal sin of aerial combat and reversed his turn, allowing Rankin to close range rapidly and fire again with his cannons. The MiG exploded, immediately breaking in two behind the cockpit and forcing Johan to break away violently to avoid the debris. He watched as the stricken aircraft spiralled down in flames and saw the pilot eject.

Meanwhile, Johan du Plessis followed the MiG leader who had entered a last-ditch spiral manoeuvre. Twice du Plessis entered the firing parameters for a missile launch but his missiles failed to fire, the high-G descending turn possibly exceeding the Matra 550 launch limits.

Both pilots were fêted on their return to Ondangwa, the MiG-21 being the first aircraft shot down by the SAAF since the Korean War. However, the celebration was short-lived as all indications pointed to further encounters with MiGs and our air-to-air missiles had proved to be sub-standard. (*See* Appendix 3)

Daisy—clean and dirty

Pilots often talk about flying clean or dirty aircraft; this has nothing to do with the physical cleanliness of the aeroplane. It refers to the aircraft configuration. A clean aircraft is one that has nothing hanging beneath the wings or fuselage,

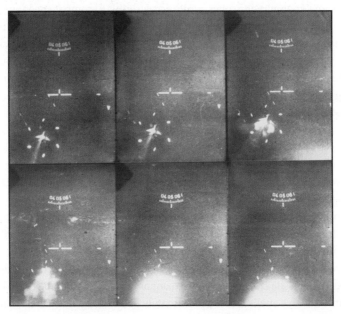

This sequence of camera-gun film shows the accurate pipper placement as Johan Rankin opened fire with his cannons. Subsequent frames show the rapid development of the fireball.

thereby presenting the most aerodynamic surface to the air. Consequently, the clean aircraft creates the least drag and will achieve the maximum design performance. In aerial combat maximum speed, G and manoeuvring capabilities are all important therefore fighters are generally flown 'clean'.

Often fighters are required to fly long distances when escorting bombers, or to loiter for lengthy periods when on CAP. On these occasions extra fuel is carried in drop tanks fitted on pylons under the wings or belly. Under normal circumstances the aircraft will return with these tanks. However, if it is necessary

Johan Rankin being congratulated by an obviously delighted Dries Wehmeyer.

to engage enemy fighters the pilot can jettison these tanks to rid his aircraft of the extra drag, as Rankin did.

Any aircraft approaching to land has its flaps and undercarriage lowered and is thus in a dirty configuration. Extra engine power is needed to counteract the effects of the increased drag. Similarly, ground-attack aircraft when loaded with bombs and rocket pods are in an extremely dirty configuration with a high drag index. Every extra bomb, pod or tank increases the drag index. When planning a mission the drag indices are used to plot the fuel usage which allows the pilot to check on the aircraft's progress at each navigation turning point.

After weapon delivery a fighter-bomber instantly becomes much 'cleaner', with a lower drag index. It can now perform as a 'fighter' if the pilot is forced into aerial combat provided the mission allowed sufficient 'combat allowance'—the extra fuel the aircraft has above the amount required to return safely to base. This combat allowance in pounds, or litres, of fuel is converted to minutes of combat using full power which a pilot can utilize before having to return to base.

If a pilot engaged in aerial combat has a greater combat allowance than his opponent it gives him a considerable advantage. He knows that sooner or later his opponent has to straighten his flight path to ensure he gets back to his base. Any time an aircraft flies a straight path during a dog-fight his chances of survival decrease immensely.

Between D+3 (7 November) and D+13 (17 November), *Daisy* petered out as far as the fast-jet force was concerned. A full air defence programme was maintained and fighters were scrambled on numerous occasions when Dayton detected MiG traffic. However, none of these sorties achieved any success and it appeared as if the Angolan Air Force was in fact flying only in defence of their air bases. On D+13, the Mirage force finally withdrew and returned to their bases in South Africa, the Buccaneers having returned somewhat earlier.

This quiet period for the fast jets was not shared by either the ground forces or the aircrews of the helicopters, transport or light aircraft. By contrast their work load increased as the ground forces entered the seek-and-destroy phase of the operation. After the heavy aerial bombardment of D-Day SWAPO realized what we were up to and melted away from their temporary bases into the bush.

This photograph shows a beautifully clean Mirage III D2Z in a dirty configuration. Once the wheels are retracted the aircraft shape would be aerodynamically clean. With the 'takkies hanging' the drag index is considerably increased.

This Mirage F1AZ is loaded with eight 1,000lb bombs, four under the fuselage and two under each wing. To carry the bombs ejection racks have to be fitted to the aircraft. Every protuberance increases the drag index of the aircraft making this a particularly dirty F1.

1981: Taking the war to the host nation

This is an interesting photograph of rocket pods hung on a pylon under the wing of a Mirage F1. Pylons and pods greatly increase the drag-index. To assist in reducing drag the pods are fitted with frangible nose cones. On firing, the rockets punch through the streamlined cone. Where the pilot is required to fight his way out from a target the pods can be jettisoned to reduce drag.

Foliage was thick and it was with relative ease that they avoided contact with the security forces. It must be remembered that SWAPO was a lightly armed guerrilla force who were outgunned by the South African forces. It was never their aim to engage in military confrontation with us. Their objective as a terrorist organization was to intimidate the local population inside SWA to ensure their support for SWAPO. In Africa the strong man usually rules and SWAPO was intent on establishing themselves at the top of the pile.

Transport aircraft shuttled to and from Ionde bringing in rations, ammunition and vehicle spares and ferrying casualties to AFB Ondangwa. Bosbok aircraft flew every day, lending navigation and communication support to elements of the ground teams who were searching the bush for SWAPO. The helicopter crews were continually used to shuttle in stopper groups and assault teams whenever a contact situation was anticipated.

On D+5 (9 November), Parabats were flown in to a target area from Ionde at 13h35. On arrival they deployed four Parabat sticks and, with four Alouette gunships overhead lending fire support, contact was made with the enemy. Out of a total of 40 SWAPO troops, 24 were killed and five wounded and captured. Twenty of the 24 were killed by the heavy fire put down by the gunships.

61 Mechanized Battalion was bogged down in a minefield and the next day at first light Bosbok aircraft were airborne to guide the mechanized force, the echelon troops and the artillery to a safe rendezvous point (RV). Three routes through the bush were used, avoiding all the open *shonas* which enabled the forces to re-assemble again at the selected RV.

Daisy finally ended on 17 November. The air force had flown 272 sorties out of AFB Ondangwa in direct support of the operation, while a further 207 helicopter and light aircraft missions were flown out of the Ionde airfield.

Honoris Crux and bar

During Operation *Vlinder* Alouette gunship helicopters were operating in support of ground forces near Evale. On 29 December, our troops were in contact with the enemy who were armed with SA-7 missiles and RPGs. A serious casevac, his injuries caused by an enemy 82mm mortar, needed to be picked up. Lieutenant Arthur Walker led a two-ship Alouette formation to the scene and provided top cover for Lieutenant Serge Bovey who was to carry out the pick-up.

After calling for the ground troops to mark the LZ with 'white phos', Lieutenant Bovy approached to land. During his approach he noticed Walker's helicopter veer sharply as it drew heavy AAA fire. Bovy also drew tracers as he flared to land. On touch-down two troops loaded the casevac into the helicopter while the rest of the platoon formed a defensive circle around the helicopter.

On lift-off, because of the extra weight, it took a long time for the Alouette to pass through the transition from vertical to forward speed. As Bovy started to bank away from the enemy positions he saw two 14.5mm AA guns firing at him from a little over 100 metres away. His aircraft was hit with rounds going through the door, another removing the top portion of his instrument panel and one passing through his flying overall but missing his leg.

Turning away from the AAA site Bovy tried to fly below tree level keeping his rotors just clear of the branches. There was a smell of burning and several electrical sparks in the cockpit. The AAA continued and further hits were felt in the port forward door and the co-pilot's seat. Bovy's armoured seat was also hit and he was bounced briskly forward several times.

The engine started losing power, causing the rotor blades to slow down. When the controls stiffened up he realized they were about to crash and flared harshly to dig the tail in. Looking up, he saw that the helicopter was going to hit a big tree and so deflected the cyclic and rudder to the right.

After impact the helicopter came to rest. Dolf van Rensburg, the flight engineer, was lying in the small space between Bovy's chair and the door. Although a lot of blood was streaming from his mouth he indicated that otherwise he was fine. Bovy unstrapped and despite a very sore back punched out a window and exited the helicopter. The casevac who was trapped in the wreckage showed no signs of life.

Seconds later mortars started falling around them and the two men ran off in a northerly direction. During their escape Bovy noticed a terrorist with an AK-47 about 50 metres away. Van Rensburg wanted to make a stand but Bovy persuade him to keep silent as the terrorist hadn't seen them; he was looking up at Walker's helicopter, firing upwards.

Soon AK-47 rounds and other larger calibre shells started bouncing off the trees around the two men. It appeared as if the enemy was following their spoor. Sergeant Botes, the gunner in Walker's helicopter, then spotted the two airmen on the ground. Arthur Walker, despite heavy AAA landed in a confined LZ and the two survivors jumped aboard. Pulling all the instrument panel needles into the red Walker managed to get his helicopter into the air and safely back to base.

Walker was awarded with the Honoris Crux (Gold) for this deed, becoming the only person with a double award of this coveted honour.

Chapter 8

1982: Cross-border operations

The new year began with the enemy still demonstrating aggressive intent, despite the debilitating effects of *Daisy*. On 5 January, a SAAF Puma helicopter was shot down and the three crew members, Captain Robinson, Lieutenant Earp and Sergeant Dalgleish were killed. All signs indicated that the yearly incursion into South West Africa was about to begin and the bloodshed continue. This close-contact, seek-and-destroy warfare was fought by troops on the ground with helicopter and light aircraft support. The fast fighters were not required, allowing much-needed time for aircraft maintenance and pilot training.

Armourers

In those early years at Hoedspruit a group who directly influenced the spirit of 1 Squadron were the armourers. It would be hard to find a more hard-working, enthusiastic and willing group of men. Always to the fore whenever hard work was called for were people like Daantjie Fourie, Willem Botha, Alan Dillon, 'Skippy' Scheepers and the rest of the team. So great was their contribution that Major Chris Venter informed Lieutenant Terry Crous on his first operation, "If you want to learn about the Mirage F1 work with the armourers."

Flight Sergeant Alan Dillon was in the habit of abbreviating ranks. He used to refer to a captain as 'capo' and a major as 'maj'. Once on deployment to AFB Ondangwa all the armourers immediately on disembarkation from the C-130 were taken directly to the bomb dump. An early-morning strike the next day called for 180 x 250kg bombs to be prepared, fused and hung under the F1s, which meant an all-night slog for them.

In the darkened surroundings of the bomb dump Dillon saw a 'capo' watching the activities. Being short-handed he invited him to assist with the humping and

1982: Cross-border operations

Humping and fusing bombs is very hard labour. Two bombs in the centre of the second row still require fuses.

lugging of the bombs. He promised that in the morning he would personally show the officer around the best aircraft in the SAAF. Capo was set to work and ably assisted the armourers until well into the early hours of the next morning. When the sky lightened he was back on the scene. Only then did Dillon see his shoulder boards. He saluted at the same time as he said, "Oh shit capo! You're a colonel." Capo was none other than Colonel Spyker Jacobs, the commanding officer of Ondangwa, who had willingly assisted with the night's hard labour while hugely enjoying the humour of the moment.

Going up to the bush was always easier than getting back. The planners at HQ always supplied the correct number of transport aircraft, at the right time, to deploy the squadron. However, after an operation transport aircraft were never as freely available.

On one occasion three C-130s were used to fly 1 Squadron to Ondangwa. On the return journey only two were available. Fortunately, Major Peter Gardiner, commanding one of the C-130s, realized how anxious everyone was to return to Hoedspruit. He divided the squadron's equipment from the three aircraft and somehow managed to load it all into the holds of two C-130s. The only seating for the personnel was on the floor. The heavily loaded aircraft managed to creep into the air and it was only after they were well south of the Etosha Pan that Gardiner was able to start the slow climb to cruising altitude. It was actions like this that welded all the air force's components into a formidable team.

*****

Early in March 1 Squadron deployed to AFB Bloemspruit, to carry out forward air controlling (FAC) training exercises with the army. Army officers were taught how to 'talk' pilots in, to attack targets in close proximity to a land battle. Training is required to alter the mindset of soldiers from the slow grind of an infantry assault to fighters moving at close to 14 kilometres per minute.

The army officer positions himself on a suitable vantage point overlooking the battlefield. When he has selected targets requiring immediate attention he requests air support. Fighter bombers, armed with the correct weapons, fly to pre-determined holding points within close proximity of the battle area. On arrival the pilots check in with the ground FAC officer by radio. While the aircraft orbits the holding point the officer describes the target and its defences to the pilot. He then passes a carefully worked-out heading and time for the pilot to fly from his holding position. Immediately after he pitches up the FAC describes the target and surrounding area and tries to orientate the pilot to acquire the target visually so he is able to carry out the desired attack.

This training is vital for success in the heat of battle. However, on the training range these flights often result in extreme frustration for the pilots. Trainee FAC officers often suffer stage fright the first time they find themselves in charge of jet fighters. Instead of the fast, accurate commentary that is required by the pilot to find his target the trainee frequently comes up with statements like: "As you pitch-up look for the tree in the big green field". Little does he realize that from 5,000 feet the pilot can see a thousand trees in hundreds of green fields. A good FAC can be the difference between life and death on a battlefield, hence the necessity for training.

Where the Marienflüss meets the Cunene River in Kaokoland. The tree line indicates the course of the river.

1982: Cross-border operations

Operation *Super*

On 13 March, a mobile Fireforce consisting of 45 men of 32 Battalion, transported in Puma helicopters and supported by Alouette gunships, was involved in a highly successful operation north of Kaokoland. Operation *Super* resulted from an accurate intelligence report that SWAPO was attempting to open up infiltration routes in the far western theatre. Their reason was twofold. Firstly, their casualty rate when trying to infiltrate through Owamboland was becoming prohibitive. Secondly, the opening up of routes through Kaokoland would stretch our resources and defensive capabilities.

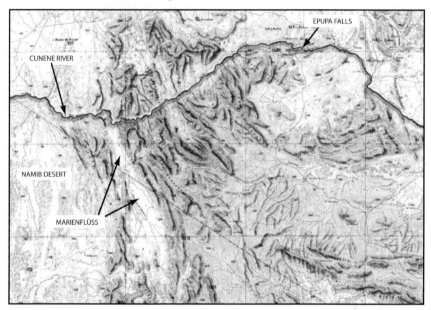

On this topographical map of Kaokoland the Cunene River can be seen running east–west across the top. On the left are the relatively flat sand dunes of the Namib Desert while rugged mountains cover the rest of the area. The flat Marienflüss can be seen running north–south on the western side of the mountainous area.

Kaokoland is rugged in the extreme. Its topography resembles the face of the moon. It is arid, with little vegetation or natural water and suffers the rigours of a desert climate—hot as Hades during the day and as cold as charity at night. The rocky, hilly terrain makes mobile vehicular warfare almost impossible. Perhaps this factor induced SWAPO to attempt their infiltration there. Intelligence pinpointed the base camp, north of the Cunene River, from where the incursion would start.

Puma helicopters flew men from 32 Battalion, under command of Commandant Jan Hougaard, into a temporary base established in the Marienflüss on the Cunene River. Alouette gunship helicopters, led by Captain Neall Ellis, arrived to support the assault and logistics were supplied by DC-3 Dakotas.

From Fledgling to Eagle

A Puma, Dakota and Bosbok on the sand strip in the Marienflüss. Apart from this flat, sandy valley, the rest of Kaokoland resembles the face of the moon.

The assault began when the gunships arrived overhead the enemy base. Ellis was unable to locate the enemy until Sergeant Stephen Coetzee, his flight engineer, drew his attention to the area immediately below. What Ellis had thought to be rocks turned out to be bivouacs, with each sparse bush having a distinctive star-shaped appearance. With the approach of the helicopters the enemy soldiers had dived under the bushes leaving their legs sticking out. This large base covered an area of 1,000 by 1,500 metres. Realizing they had been discovered the enemy opened fire on the helicopters.

Under air cover supplied by the gunships 45 soldiers were landed by Puma and the base attacked. The battle lasted for eight hours with the gunships actively

After the operation Pumas landed on the battlefield. This photo gives an idea of how rugged the terrain was.

supporting the ground troops. Two hundred and one SWAPO members were killed for the loss of three members of 32 Battalion. The base was destroyed and the infiltration route was never attempted again. Captain Ellis, who had directed the air assault from overhead, and Sergeant Stephen Coetzee were awarded the Honoris Crux. Three members of 32 Battalion, Second Lieutenant Petrus 'Nella' Nel, Temporary Sergeant Victor Dracula and Rifleman Bernardo Domingos received the same award.

Operation *Rekstok III*

However, this attempt by SWAPO to expand the area of the war worried the military planners and emphasized the need for PR throughout the operational theatre. Authority was granted for Mirage III and Canberra photographic aircraft to cross into Angola. Canberra coverage was required to update maps of southern Angola, while the Mirage III RZs obtained tactical intelligence of specific pinpoint targets. Because 3 Squadron was unavailable Mirage F1AZs of 1 Squadron were tasked to fly escort on these missions.

On 25 March, nine F1AZs arrived at AFB Ondangwa for Operation *Rekstok III*. Mission planners had scheduled the PR programme to be completed in two flying days. The climate on the western side of southern Africa is clearly divided into a predominantly long, dry season and four months of 'big rains'—when moist, tropical air produces huge, cumulo-nimbus thunderstorms. March is right in the middle of the 'big rains'. Twelve days later, after escorting a three-ship Canberra and a two-ship Mirage III RZ formation, 1 Squadron returned to Hoedspruit. Both escort missions were uneventful. The MiG pilots sensibly stayed on the ground—the threat posed by the weather probably being assessed as greater than that of the SAAF formations.

During the long Canberra sortie escorts were provided in relays. As the first pair of fighters reached bingo, minimum-fuel-to-reach-home fuel state, Captain 'Spook' Geraghty and I replaced them. Shortly afterwards my radio failed and, waggling my wings, I indicated Geraghty was to take over the leadership of our formation. This is standard procedure, except that our new boy Geraghty only had 20 hours experience on the aircraft, was on his first operational mission in the theatre and hadn't a clue where we were. Blissfully unaware of his predicament I maintained formation. Fortunately, the return route of the Canberras passed directly overhead AFB Ondangwa, the only place in Owamboland Geraghty recognized, and he led us down for a safe landing.

On 13 May, Captain Martin Louw and Lieutenant Jon Inggs were on ops room standby at AFB Ondangwa. These two excellent Mirage F1CZ pilots had arrived the day before with 3 Squadron, from AFB Waterkloof. At approximately 16h00, they were tasked by 310 AFCP to carry out an armed reconnaissance mission in the Cuvelai area. Oshakati had received 'hot' intelligence that a helicopter

From Fledgling to Eagle

3 Squadron.
Standing L to R: Clive Turner, Kenny Wiliams, Johan Ackerman, Ed van Ravenstein, Dolf Prinsloo, Johan du Plessis, John Inggs, Cobus Toerien, Les Bennett.
Seated: Pete Vivier, Johan Rankin, Israel Krieger (IAF), Dries Wehmeyer, Jack Gründling, Eddie Dert (Technical Officer), Gerry Radloff, Tristan la Grange, Martin Louw.

carrying senior military staff, Cubans or Angolans, was on its way to Cuvelai to attend a planning conference with the local military commanders. They were tasked to seek and destroy the helicopter.

Armed with R550 missiles and 30mm cannon the pair of Mirage F1CZs took off at 16h35, with Lieutenant Inggs as the leader. They climbed to 20,000 feet on a direct course for Cuvelai, arriving overhead about 15 minutes later. To stay above the range of Cuvelai's AAA defences they immediately set up a CAP at 16,000 feet while they searched for the helicopter. They expected to find it near the town but had great difficulty locating it from that height.

They descended to 10,000 feet on opposite sides of a circular CAP to be able to cover and support each other. Fifteen minutes later Inggs spotted an Mi-8 (Mi-17) in a field south of the town and just to the west of the S-bend, in the road heading south. They positioned themselves for an air-to-ground attack from the west, out of the sun, and Inggs rolled in first. His 30mm rounds exploded just past the front of the helicopter. Then Louw rolled in. His shells walked up into the helicopter and it exploded in a typical fuel fireball. After a flight of 55 minutes the pilots landed back at AFB Ondangwa.

Busy weekend

After nearly six weeks at home 1 Squadron flew into AFB Ondangwa on 14 May. SWAPO's 1982 incursion into Owamboland and the Kavango had again been costly for their organization. Five hundred and twelve terrorists had been killed since the beginning of the year. In the same period combined security forces had lost nearly 50 men. Despite operations *Protea* and *Daisy*, SWAPO was still operating hand in glove with FAPLA. The 'big rains' had ceased, therefore targets identified from the March photographic flights were to be attacked.

On the long flight northwards Captain Geraghty was flying in a three-ship formation led by Major Paddy Carolan. Crossing Botswana Geraghty realized that Carolan was drifting off course. Radio silence was a prerequisite to prevent enemy listeners from learning the strike force was once more heading into their region. Geraghty flew up alongside Carolan's aircraft and was perturbed to see Carolan's head slumped forward. Fearing anoxia he moved in for a closer inspection, which attracted Carolan's attention. Carolan looked up, raised the paperback novel he was engrossed in, nudged the auto-pilot to bring the formation back on track and resumed his reading.

Two hours after landing two F1AZs, flown by me and Captain Jan Henning, took off to strike the railhead at Jamba, a mining town north of Cassinga. Both aircraft pitched up from a low-level approach and we delivered our bombs from a high-dive profile. Surprise was complete and no enemy retaliation fire was experienced.

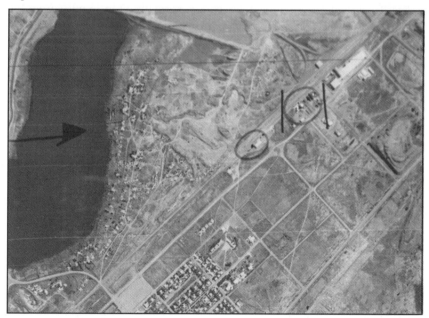

Target photos of the railhead at Jamba.

The following morning at 07h55, eight AZs and four CZs attacked a SWAPO log base northeast of Cassinga. Forty-eight Mk 82 bombs were released into the base, half armed with contact fuses and half with Limbo air-burst fuses. Once again the enemy was caught off guard and no return fire was drawn. Two secondary explosions indicated that damage had been inflicted to SWAPO's logistics.

At 14h30, nine AZs lifted off to attack another logistics base in the bush just south of Mulondo. The low-level approach caught the enemy napping and only limited AAA fire was drawn from the target area. Intelligence interceptions of the SWAPO communication system confirmed that both ammunition and arms had been destroyed.

Early in the afternoon three Buccaneers took off from AFB Grootfontein for a strike on a target located on Jamba airfield. Commandant George Snyman and Major Sandy Roy led the strike, Major Labuschagne and Captain Brian Daniel flew as No 2 and the third aircraft was crewed by Major Trevor Schroeder and Captain Riem Mouton.

The strike profile was to be an IPMT (initial point medium toss) and each aircraft was loaded with eight 460kg bombs. The IPMT attack was to be initiated from low level, between 100 and 200 feet, with a 4G pull-up approximately four nautical miles from the target; the bombs would be released automatically at the correct range and then the pilots would plunge back to the safety of low level. The elapsed time allowed for the formation attack from pull-up back to low level was between 30 to 40 seconds, making this a fairly safe method of delivery.

The IP selected for this type of attack was normally 12 to 15 miles from the target and was selected so the crews approaching at low level would be able to identify it—often difficult in the flat, featureless expanse of southern Angola. A few minutes before 15h00, the TOT selected for the attack, the formation approached the area where the IP was supposed to be. Unfortunately they missed it by a couple of hundred metres and, seeing as they were the only formation participating in the strike, George Snyman made a good decision to turn through 360° and start the attack run again. These Buccaneer attacks were initiated from the IP and an error there would give the same error to the fall of bombs. It was safe to manoeuvre the formation for the re-run because no warning signals had been heard on any of the radar warning receivers.

Passing over the correct position the attack sequence was initiated. The aircraft, now flying at 580 knots and 100 feet AGL, had assumed the attack formation. Lappies Labuschagne was in a left echelon 45° back and 200 to 300 metres from the leader. Suddenly, before pitch-up and to Labuschagne's surprise, bombs started falling from the wings and bomb bay of the lead aircraft and came flying past his cockpit.

The attack was aborted and the formation returned to Grootfontein. It was established that the lead aircraft's bomb system had failed and released the

1982: Cross-border operations

bombs shortly after the aircraft left the IP. Fortunately the bombs had not armed otherwise the result could well have been catastrophic. When Labuschagne relates this story his eyes become larger as he describes how just how enormous a half-ton bomb and tail-cone appear when just outside one's cockpit canopy.

On 16 May at 07h17, eight AZs and four CZs departed at low level on track for Ruacana. Fourteen minutes later, overhead Ruacana airfield, the formation turned northward across the border and accelerated to 540 knots. Abeam Techipa three minutes later, the pilots 'hacked' (reset the cockpit clocks) to accurately time the run-in to the PUP (pitch-up point). At the PUP the pilots pulled their aircraft in to a high nose-up attitude to climb rapidly to 18,000 feet. A left-hand roll-in ensured that the high dive came out of the rising sun, blinding the enemy gunners waiting on the ground. The pilots used the few seconds at the top of the dive to orientate themselves by checking the area photographs carried in each cockpit. During the dive each pilot concentrated on his individual aiming point to achieve a good bomb release.

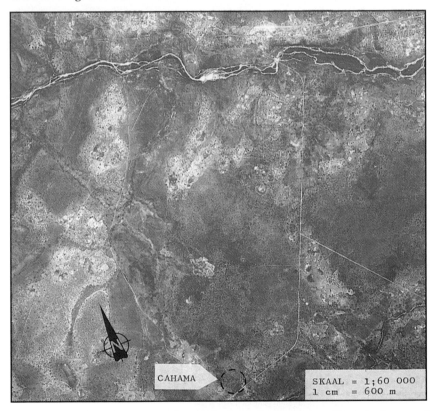

This photo of the Cahama area shows a target at bottom centre. The actual town of Cahama is north of the river at top right. The road running south from the town led to the aggressive little enclave of Ediva which threw everything at every SAAF aircraft that ventured within range.

Cahama was famous for its resistance whenever a SAAF aircraft was in the vicinity of the town. On this occasion they did not disappoint. Heavy 23mm and 57mm fire were seen exploding among the diving aircraft, but no aeroplane was hit. By 08h07, all the Mirage F1s had landed safely back at Ondangwa.

The hard-working ground crew had only three hours to prepare all the aircraft for the next strike, at 11h50 against a Cuban position south of Jamba airfield. The Cubans had been giving constant support to SWAPO and the aim of this strike was to persuade them this was an unhealthy practice.

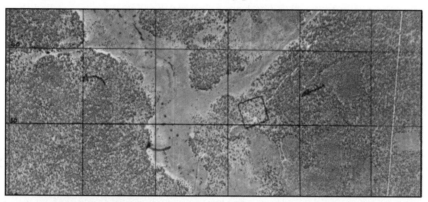

The Cuban camp is marked with the square and all the paths and tracks leading in from all directions is an almost certain indication of a large camp.

Three four-ship F1 formations attacked the Cuban positions from the west. The usual 57mm AAA was drawn but on this occasion the Mirages were faced, for the first time, with heavy fire from mobile ZSU 23-4 Shilka batteries. Fortunately these four-barrelled, rapid-firing cannons were off target. However, their effect increases a pilot's flow of adrenaline. When the shells exploded they formed an immediate thick white cloud bank. During the attack dive a Soviet-built, twin-engined AN-26 transport aircraft was observed on the airfield hardstanding, but it was not attacked.

Shilka on parade in Luanda. The firepower of these weapons is devastating.

The same afternoon four AZs and four CZs returned to Cahama, this time to pound the active AAA sites that had been seen firing during the morning attack. This strike had fighter protection from Mirage F1CZs so the procedure was altered. As the strike reached roll-in altitude only the leader rolled in—the other pilots orbited while watching the leader in his dive. When the expected AAA firing started Mirage No 2 attacked that particular AAA site. This pattern repeated itself until all eight aircraft had dropped their bombs; no enemy MiGs attempted to gate-crash the party. The following day all Mirages returned to their respective home bases after a most successful operation.

Ground crew packed and waiting for the Flossie to return them to home base. There were always plenty of transport aircraft to take you to the border but getting home was often a problem.

Impala shoot-down

On 1 June, Major Gene Kotze, flying an Impala Mk II, was hit by AAA fire while diving to attack a SWAPO target inside Angola. The aircraft crashed and Kotze was killed.

*****

During operational deployment ground crew often wrote derogatory anti-SWAPO messages on the aircraft's bombs before loading them. If the target range allowed, underwing or belly fuel tanks were removed and stored in rows at the edge of the hardstanding. One morning rude, suggestive and lewd remarks were found painted and scratched onto these tanks. The culprits were passing soldiers who thought the tanks were extra large bombs.

Once again the dry season, July and August, brought the usual security force push into Angola, this time on Operation *Meebos*. This operation was designed to disrupt Angolan/SWAPO plans to retake Xangongo and Ongiva which had

Message-writing became an occupational pastime.

been in South African hands since *Protea*. To do this it was planned to destroy the SWAPO Central and Eastern HQ, situated near Evale and Ionde respectively.

On 16 July, when ground forces attacked these SWAPO bases both were found to be empty. The SWAPO HQ had moved to the Mupa area. On 22 July, ground forces, supported by Puma and Alouette helicopters, attacked this base and 18 SWAPO were killed.

1 Squadron had been deployed to AFB Ondangwa for the duration of these ground activities as support in case of MiG interference. To reassure ourselves that we had air superiority over the combat zone we needed periodically to devote attention to the enemy's air defence system.

This entailed the obligatory air strike on the radar systems in the vicinity of Cahama. At 13h40 on 21 July, eight F1AZs escorted by two missile-armed CZs took off from Ondangwa and 23 minutes later attacked the radar site. For once no retaliatory AAA fire or missiles were fired by the defenders. As it was a Sunday it was assumed that, like South Africans, the Angolans also enjoyed their afternoon nap.

Despite tracking SWAPO all over the combat theatre the ground forces had extreme difficulty establishing the exact position of the SWAPO headquarters. The F1 pilots spent many hours on CAS standby but no really effective sorties were flown.

On 1 August, orders were issued from 10 AFCP for a strike the next day on a SWAPO base located 25 kilometres southeast of Tetchamutete. Eight AZs and four CZs loaded with Mk 82 bombs formed the strike formation. Two additional AZs, armed with 68mm rockets and 30mm cannon, accompanied the strike in a CAS role. The strike went through the target unopposed and returned to base. The pair of CAS F1s held above the target while helicopters moved ground forces into the target area. Suddenly, the operational radio channel burst into life as the helicopters started drawing heavy fire from the target area.

While the Mirage strike force was refuelling the helicopters engaged the enemy in a fierce battle, which included RPGs as well as a host of SA-7 missiles being fired at the helicopters. As the battle moved into its second day, Neall Ellis, by then a major, was again involved, ably assisted by Captain Harry Anderson and Lieutenant Mike Hill. When the helicopters again drew fire they called in the F1AZs and directed the Mirage rocket and cannon fire onto the target. Pairs of Mirages kept up a shuttle service to the target and were extremely successful, scoring many hits and destroying some of the AAA guns. The combined onslaught by all the SAAF aircraft and ground forces accounted for 106 terrorists.

South African ground forces were now deep into Angola. One task force was operating in an area northwest of Cuvelai while another was just south of Techamutete. Both groups were constantly engaged with pockets of enemy resistance. While the Mirage F1s remained on CAS standby at Ondangwa, Pumas and Alouette helicopters were used in support on the battlefields.

Puma shoot-down, *Meebos* and *Bravo*

On 9 August, Puma helicopters were used to leapfrog troops in a follow-up operation. While the helicopters were crossing a riverbed flying at very low level the sky was suddenly filled with clouds of smoke from exploding AAA and small-arms fire. One of the Pumas, apparently struck by an RPG-7 crashed, killing Captain John Twaddle, Lieutenant Chris Petersen, Sergeant 'Grobbies' Grobler and all 12 paratroopers on board.

A touching memorial fashioned in the workshop honouring the lives of the 15 men killed when the Puma was shot down.

Finally, on 23 August, Mirage F1s were used in earnest. Alouette gunships finally found the SWAPO Alpha Battalion west of Cassinga and attacked. CAS standby Mirage F1s were scrambled to the scene arriving 18 minutes later. Attacks using 68mm rocket and cannon were carried out on the fleeing enemy who launched SA-7s at the Mirages and fired inaccurate AAA. Having exhausted their ammunition the Mirages returned to Ondangwa. Pairs of fighters remained overhead the combat area for the rest of the afternoon.

Early the next morning, Captain Norman Minne and I, on cockpit readiness for CAS duties, were scrambled. Alouette pilots, majors Neall Ellis and Harry Anderson, had found a SWAPO camp 30 kilometres north of Cuvelai on the banks of the Calonga River. The enemy opened fire aggressively with 14.5mm AAA, RPG-7s and SA-7 Strela missiles. It wasn't long before they realized they had made a serious error. Instead of transport helicopters the Alouettes were gunships armed with 20mm cannons.

A serious fire fight began with the gunship pilots preventing the enemy from escaping by keeping them trapped against the riverbank. Arriving overhead the AZs were given targets by the circling Alouette pilots and amid missile smoke trails began decimating the enemy defenders. As on the previous afternoon the next pair of Mirages was on hand to take over the attack as ammunition was expended. A hectic day ensued with jets and helicopters acting in harmony. As resistance crumbled the fight petered out. When they cleared the target zone ground forces counted 118 SWAPO dead.

After these severe setbacks SWAPO retreated from the combat area. It took the army a long time to realize the battle was over. Finally, at the end of the month, *Meebos* was completed and the ground forces returned to SWA. On 28 August, after nearly three weeks of CAS standby duty and very little flying, the Mirages returned to Hoedspruit.

On 3 October, Operation *Bravo* was flown. This was a Canberra PR sortie over Virei—a direct result of intelligence inputs referring to the build-up of forces in the area. Virei was being developed as an advanced radar and possible missile base. The Canberra, with two F1CZ Mirages as escort, carried out a low-level penetration before climbing to Flight Level 240 for the photo run. On the egress from Virei a pass was made over Cahama to update our photography.

As the Canberra formation broke Angolan radar cover another pair of F1CZs, acting as a spoof raid, popped above the radar horizon to confuse the Angolan radar controllers. Two F1AZs were on SAR standby at Ondangwa; two armed Impalas were positioned at Ruacana along with four Pumas with Parabats for SAR; one EW equipped DC-3 Dakota flew from Grootfontein to monitor enemy radar and radio transmissions during the operation; and one Impala flying at high level from Ondangwa operated as the Telstar radio link.

All these activities must have excited the Angolan air defence authorities who brought their forces to a high state of readiness. This was to have a bearing on the operations which took place a few days later

Second MiG down

Between 3 and 8 October, it was 3 Squadron's turn to deploy to AFB Ondangwa. Canberras were required to carry out a photographic small-area coverage (SAC) of Cahama. The F1CZs were tasked to escort the vulnerable medium bombers during this task.

At 11h20 on 5 October, Major Johan Rankin and Captain Cobus Toerien rendezvoused with a Canberra flown by Commandant Bertus Burger and his navigator Captain Frans Conradie. Under positive control from Dayton radar the formation headed for Cahama. While monitoring the formation during the photographic runs, Captain Les Lomberg, Dayton radar fighter-controller, detected approaching enemy aircraft.

Detaching the Canberra to run southward for safety Lomberg turned the F1s northwards, instructing them to climb to 30,000 feet and accelerate to Mach 0.95, which was the limiting speed for external tanks. This turn placed the opposing formations nose to nose with each other, 12 nautical miles apart and closing at twice the speed of sound.

Rankin picked up two MiG-21s at the same level, approximately five nautical miles away, as they flashed down the right-hand side. The F1 pilots jettisoned their drop tanks, went into afterburner and started a hard right-hand turn in pursuit. Shortly before the formations crossed the enemy fired their missiles but they had no chance of guiding correctly.

Angolan Air Force (FAPA) MiG-21. The canopy shape and the delta-wing seriously restricted the pilot's look-out capability.

The F1s completed a 180° turn, while the MiGs were turning gently to the right maintaining supersonic speed. Radar confirmed they were outdistancing the F1s. Unable to close to firing range Rankin switched his intercept radar onto transmit, hoping the MiGs radar warning receiver would warn their pilots and force them to turn into the F1s. As was hoped the MiGs did reverse their turn. Whether this was a result of the radar warning or whether they were still intent on intercepting the Canberra was uncertain, but the manoeuvre allowed the F1s to cut the corner and close the range.

Unloading the G, the F1s performed an energy acceleration reaching Mach 1.3. Entering a curve of pursuit and judging the range to be correct—although his radar had not locked onto the target—Rankin fired a Matra 550 infrared missile. The missile tracked the MiG until it reached all-burnt range then dropped away. Subsequent examination of the gun-camera film showed that the missile had been fired at 3,000 metres, the extreme limit of its range at those speeds.

Closing range, Rankin fired his second missile from about 1,500 metres. This missile tracked the MiG which had entered a descending split-S manoeuvre and exploded right behind it. The MiG was hit but still controllable and continued its left-hand roll before heading back to base, trailing smoke. According to information acquired later, the MiG-21, although damaged, made it back to base. However, the pilot was unable to lower the undercarriage and the ensuing forced landing caused additional serious damage.

With one enemy aircraft out of the fight Rankin closed on the lead MiG, which entered a split-S to the left. Rankin followed, overtaking rapidly, and at 230 metres started firing his 30mm Defa cannons. The MiG exploded directly in front of him and he could not avoid flying through the fireball of the explosion. The heat and smoke caused the F1s engine to develop a compressor stall. Only after cutting the engine and performing a hot-relight did his engine return to normal. (*See* Appendix 3)

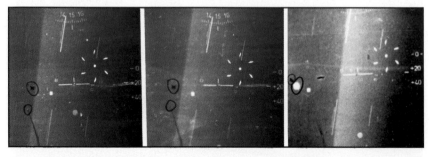

These three frames from the gun-camera film illustrate clearly the missile's shortcomings.
Left: Missile clearly on interception path. The circled tiny white dot is the flame from the missile motor.
Centre: The dot has gone, illustrating missile reached all-burnt range.
Right: The MiG can be seen ahead of the missile explosion which detonated in the heat-source astern of the jet-pipe.

1982: Cross-border operations

Left: The aiming pipper is on the intersection of wings and fuselage at open fire.
Centre: Immediately the effect of the hits can be seen.
Right: Rapid development of the fireball which caused the engine compressor to stall in the engine of the Mirage F1 as it passed through the smoke.

In contrast, Cobus Toerien found the sortie utterly depressing. He managed to get a MiG in his sights at 12 o'clock, but at 1,500 metres and 80° angle off he could do nothing about it.

On this flight Rankin was flying F1CZ 203. This aircraft was the first, and at that time, the only aircraft painted in the SAAF air superiority blue/grey colour scheme. The aircraft had been christened *'Le Spectre'*, French for ghost, by General Jan van Loggerenberg because of the effectiveness of the colour scheme. The camouflage was still being evaluated but was soon applied to the other F1CZ aircraft. (*See* last page of the colour picture section)

The aim of aircraft camouflage is to blur the outline of the aircraft. In this photo of 'Le Spectre', only the shadows have definite outlines.

Déjà vu

Captain Spook Geraghty took off from AFB Hoedspruit as target for a session of dusk, ground-controlled interceptions (GCIs). Flying on autopilot he watched the beautiful sunset while I acted as the attacker.

Many years before when I was flying a Phantom off the Californian coast over the sea at sunset I received the shock of my life. Heading eastward towards a dark sky I became the victim of a colleague's sense of humour.

Returning from a training sortie Lieutenant Jake Jacanin, USN, spotting my aircraft cruising gently back towards base, came up astern and at supersonic speed passed very closely underneath my aircraft. The shockwave buffeting my aircraft instantly roused me from my reveries. Then he pulled up directly in front of me with long flames issuing from the exhausts of the two J-79 engines. The bump and the flames silhouetted against the night sky caused an adrenaline surge I remember vividly to this day.

This photo of a Fleet Air Arm Phantom clearly shows the flaming exhausts that caused me such concern.

So it was, as I approached astern of Geraghty's aircraft I had a distinct feeling of déjà vu. In full afterburner I performed the same manoeuvre. Poor Geraghty had the impression of a missile explosion as I passed directly underneath his right wingtip.

The Mirage F1 proved to be a superb aircraft in the 'African' context in that it had excellent range and could carry large amounts of underwing armaments. While the 32 F1AZ aircraft of 1 Squadron were used in the ground-attack role, 3 Squadron's F1CZs were used mainly as air-defence fighters flying CAP and as escorts. They were superior to the Angolan Mig-17 and -21 but were outperformed by the MiG-23s introduced towards the end of the war.

12 Squadron

The elderly Canberra bombers of 12 Squadron were vulnerable to all the enemy fighters ranged against them but, because of superb mission planning and execution they were used very effectively throughout the war. They were the primary source of PR, often having to be escorted through dangerous target areas. They were used as low-level bombers, dropping 300 Alpha bombs

1982: Cross-border operations

A three-seater aircraft, but in SAAF service the Canberras were flown by a two-man crew.

from their cavernous bomb bay. They also dropped 250kg and 1,000lb general purpose bombs from medium altitude on to heavily defended targets. It was the Canberras that were involved in two of the most effective air strikes of the war. During Operation *Askari* a combined strike of Canberras and Impalas destroyed Angolan defences at Cuvelai, which allowed SA ground forces to capture the town at little cost. Later they combined with AS-30 missile-firing Buccaneers to destroy strong enemy fortifications at Cangamba, allowing UNITA to capture the town after an impasse of nine days of heavy fighting.

24 Squadron

The Buccaneer was perhaps the best aircraft in the SAAF arsenal in terms of an African war. It could fly fast and low over great distances while carrying everything plus the kitchen sink.

Buccaneers earned a proud reputation of being 'on time, on target'. These long-range bombers were used mainly to penetrate long distances into Angola on interdiction strikes against known enemy positions. These two-seater aircraft carried eight 1,000lb bombs, which packed a deadly punch. Earlier in the war they had delivered their weapons from a dive-bombing profile but later, when enemy defensive missiles and radar were widespread, they delivered bombs using a toss profile from a low-level approach. Not one of these valuable aircraft was lost to enemy fire although they were utilized on all the most dangerous missions.

2 Squadron

Perhaps the disappointment of the war, as far as aircraft were concerned, was the Mirage III. Unfortunately this superb fighter was limited in range which proved to be a decided disadvantage over the vast distances in SWA, although they were used effectively during Operation *Reindeer* and *Protea*. The longer range of the Mirage F1 was more suited to the requirements of the border war. One notable exception was the use of the Mirage III RZ and R2Z photo-reconnaissance aircraft. These aircraft and their skilful pilots provided tactical photographic coverage of heavily defended targets which were considered too dangerous for the more vulnerable Canberra.

The Mirage III was a wonderful fighter but limited fuel capacity restricted its use over the vast expanse of the combat area.

1982: Cross-border operations

This close-up of the Shilka shows the operators in the turret, the four-barrelled 23mm cannons and the Gun Dish radar guidance aerial.

Enemy defensive weapons

When discussing the role of South African jet fighters in the border war mention must be made regarding the formidable defensive system that opposed them. Although the fighting was ostensibly against SWAPO insurgents, armed with little more than small arms and SA-7 shoulder-launched infrared missiles, they were actively supported by the entire Angolan defence force which brought the

SA-3 missiles being paraded through Luanda.

SAAF into direct contact with these systems. Anti-aircraft artillery (AAA) was present in all its forms, from optically guided 12.7mm, 14.5 and 20mm weapons to radar-guided 37mm, 57mm and the deadly 23-4mm tank-mounted four-barrelled Shilka.

The complete range of Soviet-made SAM guided-missile systems was present in Angola: SA-2 and -3 which were launched from fixed sites and could thus be fairly easily avoided; mobile-tracked SA-6 and SA-13 were used as well as the mobile-wheeled SA-8 and SA-9. These mobile systems could pop up anywhere in the combat area so special low-level flying techniques had to be used in order to avoid them. Shoulder-launched missiles, including the SA-7, SA-14 and SA-16, were equally dangerous to unsuspecting pilots.

Enemy successes against our fighters using these AAA and SAM systems included a Canberra, a Mirage III RZ PR aircraft, a F1AZ, numerous Impala jets and three remote-controlled reconnaissance drones. A Bosbok light aircraft was also downed as were Alouette and Puma helicopters. Many aircraft returned with battle damage but most were repaired and returned to front-line service.

The year drew to a close with the final fast-jet activity being a four-Buccaneer strike. The target was SWAPO's special unit 'Volcano' training base situated 35 kilometres west of Lubango between the Umbria tunnel and the Leba Pass. The aircraft took off from Grootfontein at 07h30 and penetrated at low level. They approached the target from the west for a toss-bomb attack. Each aircraft delivered eight 460kg bombs. They landed back at Ondangwa for 'hot' refuelling and reported that 60 per cent of their bombs had landed in the target area.

At the end of 1982 my active flying career finally came to an end. I was promoted to colonel and posted as air force commander to 310 AFCP. This was basically the same post which I had assumed in 1978 for three months. However, this time it was on a permanent basis and the facility and its responsibilities had been expanded considerably.

Until now I had been an active participant in the front line with my thoughts focused on the very real day-to-day problems of safety, security and efficiency of pilots, crews and aircraft. This new appointment would require greater concentration on the 'bigger picture' of the war, its execution and solution.

Chapter 9

1983: Anti-insurgency campaign

In terms of the war, the first half of 1983 was comparatively quiet. This apparent lull in major operations gives me the opportunity to describe, in some detail, how the actual counter-insurgency campaign was carried out. It was a daily grind, plugging holes, launching follow-up, seek-and-destroy operations, all of which were designed to keep SWAPO on the hop, trying not to allow them a moment's respite. Their insurgency campaign against our security forces took guts and determination. Rhetoric and propaganda can initially put fire in the bellies of insurgents, however, the passion soon palls if they are continually harassed and suffer massive losses without achieving notable success, as was clearly the case with SWAPO.

It took very hard work and total commitment on the part of the security forces to achieve this situation. In modern parlance it was a 24/7 task, year in and year out, to outlast the insurgent. What I am about to describe are the details of security force activity in Sector 10 (Owamboland) from January to September 1983, in diary-type format. Bear in mind this activity also occurred in Sector 20 (Rundu) and Sector 70 (Katima Mulilo), albeit on a lower-intensity scale. These activities continued while the major cross-border operations were in progress but this was the 'real' war.

Military organization in SWA

In SWA, the army was under command of Major-General Charles Lloyd and the air force Brigadier Bossie Huyser. These two officers and their respective staffs were co-located at the Bastion building in Windhoek. War, as in every other walk of life, brings together people of all types. General Lloyd was meticulous, deep-thinking and painstakingly thorough. The decisions he made were always as a result of an in-depth appreciation of the situation and therefore were usually good decisions. Bossie Huyser was cast in a very different mould. An ex-fighter pilot, top gun of the air force, mercurial, dynamic, with a hustling-bustling personality, quick to make decisions based on an excellent foresight of operations and almost always with an ingredient of aggression. Two excellent officers but so diametrically opposed in personalities that clashes were bound to erupt that could, and did, affect the course of the war.

Left: Brigadier Bossie Huyser, the mercurial, commander of Western Air Command.
Right: Brigadier Joep (Juliet Juliet) Joubert in pensive mood with Major Johan Opperman, SAAF Intelligence Officer, in the foreground.

Sector 10 was commanded by Brigadier Joep Joubert, with me commanding 10 AFCP. Brigadier Joubert was a soldiers' soldier. He spent more time up front with his troops than in his HQ, he knew what was going on and didn't have to rely on his staff briefings. He was a good listener and made his decisions after analyzing the inputs from both his operational and intelligence staffs; a successful commander, always concerned for the wellbeing of his troops.

The order group of the joint HQ at Sector 10, Oshakati consisted of the following officers:

- Brig Joep Joubert   OC Sector 10
- Brig Hans Dreyer   OC Koevoet (SA Police)
- Col J. P. Durand   OC COIN (SA Police)
- Col Dick Lord   OC 310AFCP (SA Air Force)

- Maj Neels de Villiers — OC SA Medical Services
- Col Wouter Lombard — SSO OPS
- Col Clive Cloete — SSO LOG
- Col Wep Wepener — SSO PERS
- Cmdt Jackie Snyman — SSO INT
- Cmdt Borries Bornman — SO1 OPS
- Cmdt Barend van Heerden — SO2 OPS
- Cmdt Gene Basson — OC 51 Bn Ruacana
- Cmdt Tienie Smuts — OC 52 Bn Ogongo
- Cmdt Daan Nel — OC 53 Bn Ondangwa
- Cmdt Fred Burger — OC 54 Bn Eenhana
- Maj Anton Prins — OC 25 Field Regt

Staff of the Joint Headquarters, Sector 10, Oshakati, 1983.
Front: Col J. Wepener, Lt-Col H. J. van der Watt, Col C. C. Cloete, Col W. G. Lombard, Brig A. J. M. Joubert, Col J. P. Durand, Col R. S. Lord, Col P. J. Meyer, Lt-Col P. Viljoen. *Second row:* Cmdt A. S. J. Kleinhans, Chap J. J. Pretorius, Cmdt C. J. Bornman, Cmdt B. I. J. van Heerden, Cmdt P. H. du Plessis, Cmdt J. C. R. Croukamp, Maj W. B. van der Merwe, Maj J. J. Laas, Maj J. H. Coetzee. *Third row:* Maj A. J. L. Botes, Maj D. M. van Onselen, Capt J. C. Opperman, Maj W. J. Swanepoel, Maj G. J. Hoon, Maj B. G. B. Sharp, Maj C. H. Kruger, Capt G. Pansegrouw, Maj J. C. Flatow. *Back:* Cpt L. Nefdt, WOI F. H. Smit.

Counter-insurgency warfare

Until I took up my appointment in Oshakati, my involvement in the border war had been almost solely concentrated on the optimum utilization of the fast-jet force. In Sector 10 I found out how the war was really fought. It was a relentless day-after-day slog to contain and defeat the SWAPO incursion. It was fought over the barrel of a gun on the sands and in the bush of SWA and southern Angola. The true combatants were the foot soldiers of the security forces and the cadres of SWAPO. It was a 'no quarter asked, no quarter given' struggle. Support was given at the coal-face by helicopter and light aircraft aircrew who, like the infantrymen, were constantly within range of the ubiquitous AK-47 and RPG-7.

I feel it is important to highlight how much effort is required to win a war of attrition therefore I will include details of ongoing, everyday events that form the foundation of an anti-insurgency conflict. It requires vast sums of money and much personnel. Both factors negatively impact on a country's economy as people are kept out of the job market. It takes brainpower to outsmart and out-think the terrorist and force levels have to be utilized in the most cost-effective manner. Also, to beat the enemy, it takes personnel who are better trained and have a higher morale than one's opposition. Most importantly, it takes patience because you have to outlast the enemy and continually beat him until he runs out of stamina. This is exactly what happened in SWA.

A terrorist insurgency war is a war of the people. Chairman Mao, the doyen of revolutionary warfare, stated the terrorist "must be a fish who swims in the sea of the people". In SWA there was a population of a little over one million inhabitants divided unevenly between 12 ethnic groupings. The Owambo tribe accounted for approximately 500,000 people living in Owamboland, which borders SWA's boundary with Angola. If there was to be a terrorist war in the vast expanse of SWA then it had to have its centre in Owamboland. In fact, probably 90 per cent of all SWAPO activities which occurred during the war took place in

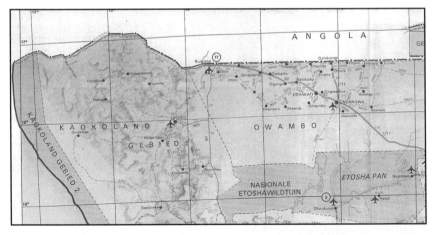

This map, taken from the excellent South West Africa Tourism pamphlet, shows Owambo and Kaokoland with only one tar road through this vast area. Population concentration on the Owambo plain can be clearly seen when compared to the desolation of mountainous Kaokoland.

1983: Anti-insurgency campaign

Owamboland or in the Angolan territory immediately north of it.

Our successes during the war can probably be ascribed to the remarkable ability of the staff at the co-located headquarters in SWA, to combine the talents of each service arm to carry out operations. This is directly contrary to inter-service rivalry prevalent during peacetime when each service arm is fighting for the biggest slice of the defence budget.

January

The day I started my new post plans were underway for Operation *Gepetto*. This area operation called for a sweep through the bush by security forces, between 24 and 31 January. The chosen area was selected because intelligence reports indicated that SWAPO had recently deployed there. The SWAPO bush telegraph was excellent and if possible they tried to avoid military contact by moving out of the area ahead of the sweeping troops. On 1 February, the plan was for Koevoet Zulu teams to sweep into the area from the south hoping to force SWAPO back into Angola. Between 2 and 10 February, army forces would deploy north of the border trying to trap SWAPO as the meat in the sandwich.

Planning then switched to Operation *Bantam*, which was to be an attack on a SWAPO base camp inside Angola. On 28 January, an air force HAG would be established within 20 minutes' flying time from the target and, just after first light the next day, six Pumas and four Alouette gunships would arrive to be refuelled, ready for a 09h40 take-off for the assault. Four Canberras, flying out of AFB Grootfontein, would strike the target at 10h00 with each aircraft dropping 300 Alpha bombs.

A good photo taken from the tail camera of a Canberra showing the effect of dropping 300 Alpha bombs.

227

Left: The crater caused by a 'bouncing' Alpha bomb.
Right: Bomb damage to the thick bush resulting from an Alpha bomb strike.

At 10h05, Alouette gunships would give top cover as Puma helicopters disgorged the assault troops in the target area. The Intelligence department was tasked to produce the exact co-ordinates of the target by 27 January, so a PR mission could be flown to obtain photographs of the target area required by the helicopter aircrew.

The planning for *Bantam* was no sooner finished than the operation was postponed and the forces allocated to Operation *Kwagga*, a sweep operation in the 'shallow area' of Angola. The air force resources allocated for this operation were two Pumas, one Kudu for casualty evacuation, four gunships, an Alouette trooper for aerial command and control and a Bosbok for reconnaissance duties. The Impala light-attack jets at AFB Ondangwa were to be on CAS standby. On 2 February, the final plan had to be presented to GOC SWA/OC WAC for approval.

Opportunities for rest and recreation on the border were few and far between. However, civilian residents of Oshakati had scraped a nine-hole golf course out of the sand. There was not one blade of grass on the course. Because tee boxes and fairways consisted of sand there was no need for bunkers. Naturally, the 'greens' were also built with sand, the only commodity in plentiful supply. The sand was mixed with oil to give substance to the 'green', or more correctly the 'slightly black'. After pitching the ball onto the 'green', usually with a sand wedge, the most useful club in one's bag, the putting ritual began. You had to lift your ball from the plug mark, drag a flat iron between it and the hole and then putt on the smoothed surface.

I played a few times on this course, as there were not many other forms of entertainment in the vicinity. Some wag, using a technique copied from the major circuits around the world, produced name boards for each hole. It was one of these boards, not the sand, which drastically reduced the active membership of the club. The hole at the far end of the course, where the players were farthest from the town's defensive perimeter had been named POMZ Corner, after one of these devices had been found there. The Soviet POMZ-2 was the notorious, anti-personnel widow-maker. Having taken so many risks during a long and exciting

1983: Anti-insurgency campaign

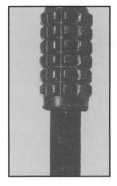

Left: Soviet POMZ-2 anti-personnel mine. The wooden stake is pushed into the ground to give an air-burst. The six rows of pre-fragmented casing explode outwards.
Right: Soviet TM-46 anti-tank mine has 5.9kg of moulded TNT as explosive. In South West Africa, SWAPO would often double-up these mines.

flying career I felt that this was just one chance too many so I temporarily hung up my clubs.

On 25 January, Bosbok aircraft were engaged with road reconnaissance flights covering the Chandelier road and Oom Willie se pad (Uncle Willie's road) near Eenhana. These two roads ran close to, and roughly parallel with, the international border and had become perennial targets for SWAPO's mine-laying teams. In fact, these roads could not be used by security forces before being swept by army mine-sweeping teams. Unfortunately local civilian drivers did not always heed security force warnings and consequently suffered severe penalties. Throughout the war civilian mine-related casualties far exceeded those suffered by security force personnel; these victims were always recovered by helicopter and treated by the SA Medical Service teams at Oshakati.

Below the Impala is a typical Owambo sand road, a target for many SWAPO mine-layers.

It is of interest to note that by this time all South African military vehicles were mine-protected, having the distinctive V-shaped armoured hull (the Rhodesians had been leaders in vehicle mine-protection design). This protected the occupants by deflecting the upward blast of a mine detonated by one of the protruding wheels. Most victims, provided they were strapped in correctly, suffered little more than burst eardrums and bruising. The occupants who suffered serious injuries were usually not strapped in.

The Buffel was the first of an entire series of mine-protected vehicles. The hull was V-shaped to deflect the mine blast as the wheels detonated the mine. All the windows were fitted with armoured glass and each seat was equipped with sturdy seat belts.

On 27 January, planning was carried out to see if the 'Rum Run' schedule could be improved. The 'Rum Run' was a DC-3 Dakota schedule which served all the front-line army bases and, in fact, proved to be the very lifeline that allowed the bases to remain operational. The threat to vehicular movement from both vehicle and anti-personnel mines was such that air delivery of supplies and personnel was the only viable option. The 'Rum Run' was flown three times a week by a Dakota based at Grootfontein, to deliver fresh rations. The route was Grootfontein, Opuwa, Ondangwa, Rundu, Ondangwa, Eenhana, Nkongo, Ondangwa then ferry back to Grootfontein. The repeated stops at Ondangwa were necessary to reload and refuel. It must be noted that, particularly during the summer months, the temperatures which affected take-off loads were often in the very high thirties or low forties centigrade.

The flying on this arduous route was physically exhausting for the aircrews. Another disadvantage was if the aircraft developed a fault along the route all the fresh rations ('rats') would be lost. The new schedule decided upon was to use two aircraft, one based at Grootfontein and the other at AFB Ondangwa, to split the responsibilities.

1983: Anti-insurgency campaign

There is a saying in aviation circles that the only replacement for a Dakota is another Dakota. This aircraft was designed and in service long before the majority of people involved in the war were even born, and was still giving excellent service.

Maanskyn

It was a full-moon period between 28 and 31 January. During that period we tasked Major Peter Cooke to carry out Operation *Maanskyn*. Cooke was one of a group of exceptional pilots who had trained for this particular operation.

Our initial success rate was on the decline. At this stage both SWAPO and the Angolan forces had learned that to travel in southern Angola at night using headlights was tantamount to committing suicide.

The result was the Impalas were flying almost every night, moon and weather permitting. However, it was only on rare occasions that they acquired a target which caused frustration and the lowering morale among the pilots.

Ever conscious of the need to keep them interested I decided to alter the system slightly. The primary target for all *Maansky/Donkermaan* operations never

Peter Cooke served the SAAF and later SAA with distinction.

231

changed; it was always vehicles. The major change was if the pilots reached the limit of their planned patrol without seeing any vehicles then they were tasked to deliver their weapons on selected targets.

In conjunction with Major Johan Opperman, we selected a pinpoint target for the rocket-armed leader and an area target for the shepherd pilot. The shepherd was armed with old-generation 115kg bombs known as 'Varkies' ('little pigs'). These obsolete bombs were not up to standard for normal ground-attack missions but ideal for this task.

Within a few nights of this type of operation we started to reap unexpected benefits. On the first night as the pinpoint target for the leader's rockets we had selected a newly built AAA site just outside Mulondo. The area target we chose for the shepherd was an area of thick bush just west of Quiteve, the type loved by SWAPO.

Imagine our delight when the following morning we picked up through intelligence channels that we had "attacked the Russians" outside Mulondo. Then, First Lieutenant Gomez of 2 Brigade reported that "the racists had bombed 600 metres west of his position". This type of radio chatter assisted in improving our own intelligence picture. As a footnote, let it be mentioned that our 600-metre error was adjusted the following night.

Realizing the potential value of a concerted campaign of this nature Opperman and I drew up a three-month plan covering all three logistical routes through Cahama, Mulondo and Cuvelai. In this plan we intended to fly one or two sorties every night while varying the times of the patrols. On each sortie we selected a pinpoint target from latest intelligence reports as well as suitable 'suspect' area targets. This plan was approved by WAC.

Within ten days, we had built up the best intelligence picture of southern Angola than any ever achieved throughout the war. Every unit, call sign or detachment in the whole of the Cunene Province was bitching and crying and soon we had identified their complete orbat (order of battle). With just eight Impalas we were dominating the entire province because the aircraft had freedom of action over the complete area, with the exception of the 57mm radar-guided anti-aircraft batteries within the defence perimeter of Cahama.

During the day armed reconnaissance flights by the same aircraft severely restricted enemy logistical movement. At night they could hardly move at all. Our intelligence picture was as near complete as one could hope for during a war. We had the initiative, the surprise, were flexible and carrying on a war of manoeuvre. It was an offensive campaign based on economy of effort and the principles of war. Eight Impala aircraft and their eight pilots were involved in a low-risk environment, as opposed to the inherent dangers to personnel and equipment when large-scale ground force operations were launched. An aim for the campaign had been selected and maintained which resulted in a tremendous

1983: Anti-insurgency campaign

boost of morale for the involved aircrew and ground personnel.

Using the punch-line from a familiar joke 'that was the good news'—the 'bad news' was due to the amount of complaining from the Angolan representative to the United Nations regarding this operation the United States government applied pressure on the South African government to have the campaign stopped, which it did.

It must be pointed out that a recognized communist tactic whenever they are losing, politically or militarily, is to call for *détente* or negotiations. History contains dozens of such instances: *Glasnost*, the Tet Offensive in Vietnam, the Lusaka Agreement and the Nkomati Accord being just a few.

They were on the losing end in Angola. They realized this after only ten nights of continuous *Maanskyn* operations. They persuaded the traditionally naïve Americans that they were prepared to negotiate. Of course, absolutely nothing came of these so-called negotiations but they did succeed in putting a stop to our programme. After a halt of two-weeks I requested permission to continue but was told "negotiations are at a delicate state". The same requests after a month's halt and then a second received the same answer.

In fact, the programme was never restarted because, true to form, the Angolans had used the 'negotiating period' as a tactic. With the cessation of Impala activities they used the opportunity to bring in all their air-defence equipment including radars, SAM missile and AAA systems which gave them some measure of control over their airspace—for the first time in the history of the war.

It can be said that *Maanskyn* provoked the Angolans into deploying that equipment. What is certain is that over the years the SADF involvement had forced this situation. Certain too, was the fact Soviet-supplied air-defence equipment was available in Angola; they just could not deploy it south of Lubango due to the presence of our Impalas.

I sincerely believe these day-and-night Impala operations were possibly the most cost-effective and efficient operations carried out during the war. In 1984, I had occasion to travel in a Ratel armoured vehicle from Xangongo to within seven kilometres of Cahama. This 70-kilometre stretch of road carried evidence of the accuracy of the air attacks. Within every kilometre were the wrecks of petrol tankers, BTR-152s and Gaz and Zil logistic trucks. Some were 70 metres off the road, many were in ditches alongside the tar macadam, while others were blocking one half of the roadway. All of them displayed shrapnel damage.

The campaign was planned and superbly executed in accordance with the principles of war and the aircraft well serviced and expertly flown; this was the recipe for success.

January ended with Cessna-185 aircraft being used on a comprehensive Skyshout programme. A loudspeaker system, with the addition of recording tapes or a live announcer, was flown in these light aircraft over areas identified by the

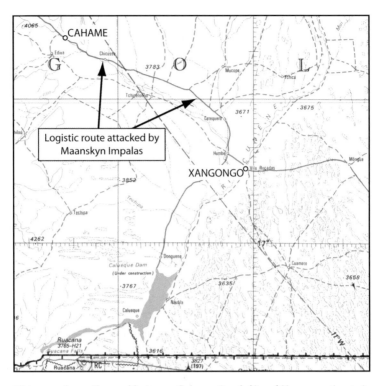

This map shows the road between Cahama (top left) and Xangongo (centre).

intelligence department and above small-arms range. Messages were broadcast aimed at particular audiences, sometimes our own troops but more often the local population. This was part of psychological operations (Psyops) introduced in an attempt to win the hearts and the minds of the locals. The army used groundshout equipment mounted in vehicles to do the same job. SAAF aircraft were often used to drop pamphlets to achieve the identical result. I was never convinced these efforts were of any real value as they were counter-balanced by the absence of good governance and severe intimidation by SWAPO.

Every month each HQ had to produce a statistical account of their activities to pass on to the next higher headquarters. At the end of January I was concerned at the number of Puma helicopter hours flown. Over the previous 12 months the Puma fleet in Owamboland had flown 2,798 hours, an average of 494 per month. The idea of a war of attrition was to 'bleed' your opponent to death. As it is well-nigh impossible to forecast the duration of a war conservation of assets is of vital importance.

One of the successful measures we introduced to curb the amount of Puma flying was to utilize DC-3 Dakota aircraft to resupply troops in the field instead of using the Puma in a delivery role. The DC-3 crews air-dropped supplies by parachute where and when requested by the ground forces.

1983: Anti-insurgency campaign

February
Early in February intelligence reported vehicular movement north of Kaokoland, travelling south to a place called Virei. The SAAF launched an EW reconnaissance sortie staying on our side of the border but tasked to confirm by electronic means this information. We also considered the use of *Maanskyn* and *Donkermaan* operations in that region. However, the terrain in the west differed vastly from the flat plains of the usual battle area. Kaokoland has been compared to the face of the moon—rugged, arid mountains with deep valleys—not conducive to low-level pull-outs so the idea was scrapped.

Initial planning was carried out for Operation *Trallies*, which was to take place during March and April. It was to be a large-scale, high-density operation to dislocate SWAPO command and control by attacking their base camps near Cahama, Cuvelai, Tetchamutete and Mulondo. It was decided that before we could launch a large operation like this we had to be certain our intelligence inputs were correct. A large ground and air reconnaissance effort would have to precede the main operation. *Trallies* would require three SAAF MAOTs, one to be attached to each of the army fighting groups.

Experience had shown that at all levels joint operations were the only certain way of finding and defeating the enemy. Windhoek and Oshakati both had permanent combined HQ. When the army moved into the bush for any operation of company size or greater the SAAF would always attach a MAOT. This team usually consisted of a major or senior captain as the commander, assisted by an operations officer and a clerk, an intelligence officer with his clerk and a communications team consisting of two senior NCOs. This team would travel in two command vehicles of the same type used by the ground forces. These vehicles could be Buffels, Ratels or Caspirs. They were armoured, mine-resistant and fitted out with communications that could connect with the army in the field, with 10 AFCP at Oshakati, on both operations and intelligence nets and with ground-to-air VHF radios to talk to the aircraft involved in the operation. These SAAF vehicles formed an integral part of the fighting group's command element. The SAAF officer in charge was the air advisor to the group commander.

Two further events ended the first day of February. A Bosbok was launched to carry out a reconnaissance survey in the east of Owamboland to search for lying water which could be used by the enemy in transit to the south of SWA. These heavily loaded men, trudging through the sands of Owambo, needed water to sustain their strength. As in any game reserve water sources were utilized by all inhabitants to sustain life in this arid, semi-desert. Water holes were always approached with great caution by both sides as one could never be certain who would be there.

The absence of a cannon and the number of aerials indicate that this Ratel has been modified as a command vehicle. In mechanized warfare two vehicles like this would be manned by the SAAF MAOT team and form part of the ground force command group.

The second event was a call I made to Colonel Bertus Burger, OC AFB Ondangwa, to inform him of an intelligence report I had just received. It indicated that Ondangwa airfield was the target of a group of SWAPO insurgents known to be in the area and armed with 122mm rockets. In fact, no attack was launched. Nevertheless, for the next three or four nights Burger had to ensure that precautionary drills were carried out, including the dispersal of aircraft. All this required additional effort from his personnel but was absolutely necessary.

We received word from Windhoek that our plans for Operation *Kwagga* had been approved with the proviso that an extra Bosbok was allocated as a dedicated Telstar aircraft at Eenhana. A tedious sortie for the pilot, who had to maintain a set height and position for up to three to four hours at a time. However, it often proved to be the vital link between the success and failure of an operation.

Skyshout and all military vehicles, both army and police, were prohibited from entering the *Kwagga* area of operations for the two weeks prior to the commencement of the mobile phase of this operation. This absence of our security force was designed to induce a feeling of relative safety in the enemy, the calm before the storm. Major Buck Buchanan was appointed as MAOT commander at Eenhana, where 20 drums of aviation fuel were to be placed. A further 12 drums were to be sited at the mini-HAG. Although our forward bases had fuel in storage for our aircraft, drums were usually placed at strategic points to reduce the ferry time for helicopters in the target area. A mini-HAG was a safe small area that could be used to refuel and re-arm helicopters for the duration of the immediate assault. This fuel was carried on logistic vehicles attached to the ground forces enabling the helicopters to refuel literally within minutes of the contact area.

Left: The battery of loudspeakers of the Skyshout system below the rear window.
Right: Major Buck Buchanan, MAOT at Eenhana.

On 4 February, SWAPO succeeded in blowing up a culvert under the tar road on the eastern approach to Oshakati. The same day a SWAPO bomb demolished a section of the Oshakati post office within the confines of the town. SWAPO were two up for that day.

During the early evening, after the threat from optically guided SA-7 Strela missiles had dissipated we sent a DC-3 down the entire length of the cut-line dropping pamphlets. Not believing in the value of these missions I termed it 'Operation Pollution'.

The majority of air force operations were carried out in radio silence. We knew that, like ourselves, the enemy monitored VHF and HF radio frequencies. Normally, only during emergencies were pilots cleared to use open text messages over the radio in an effort to expedite rescue operations. One particular night I broke my own rules, temptation getting the better of me. We had briefed a

This envelope survived the Oshakati bomb blast to become an interesting addition to my stamp collection.

Kudu pilot to carry out a night mission and his route brought him very close to Oshakati. As I entered the command post I heard the distinctive drone of the Kudu as it approached the overhead. Picking up the microphone I made a transmission that was to follow me for the rest of my career. Captain Mark Moses was the pilot and I could not waste the moment.

"Moses," I said, "this is the voice of the Lord."

On 10 February, I drove Nestor to Ondangwa to talk to available aircrew. Nestor was an Owambo migrant labourer who had worked in Walvis Bay. Whilst there he had learned to speak Afrikaans and been recruited by SWAPO with promises of a university education and a medical degree. What he got for his troubles was a limited training in guerrilla warfare and his leg blown off below the knee in his first contact with the security forces. He was nevertheless an intelligent and charming man who gave interesting and informative briefings on how SWAPO functioned in the field. It was with astonishment I learned that later during the war he had taken the opportunity to slip away from Oshakati back to SWAPO. A leopard never changes his spots.

At this time, Commandant Derek Kirkland was at AFB Ondangwa to fly *Donkermaan* sorties around Vinticette, Cuvelai, Mucope and Ediva over a period of five nights. During the day Impala pilots flew armed reconnaissance sorties to the Maquete area. All these sorties were flown to restrict the smooth flow of SWAPO logistics and munitions.

An interesting and experienced bunch of aviators.
Far side L to R: Derek Kirkland (Impala), Johan Niewoudt (Buccaneer), Hubbs Füss (Impala recce expert), Geoff Garrett (Mirage III), Dick Lord (F1AZ), Chris Brits (F1CZ), Bill Einkamerer (F1AZ); *near side L to R:* George Bester (Technical Officer), Johan Potgieter (Mirage III), J P Wessels (Mirage III).

1983: Anti-insurgency campaign

For a number of years 70 Mobile Radar Group (MRG) had maintained an early-warning radar station within the perimeter of the Ondangwa airfield. To extend their coverage farther west they had deployed a mobile radar station at Ombalantu. At a later stage as the emphasis of the war shifted eastwards this group was to deploy another radar station to AFB Rundu.

On 14 February, the aircraft and the MAOT team deployed to Eenhana for the start of Operation *Kwagga*. The next day Operation *Phoenix* was initiated. This contingency plan had been made in late 1982 and was aimed at stopping the expected SWAPO incursion and preventing any of their cadres from crossing the Red Line into the southern farming area of SWA. *Phoenix* was to last until 15 April, the end of the big rains. Fifteen SWAPO companies, each 40 to 50 strong, had commenced their southward trek, crossing the border into SWA on a wide front between Kaokoland and Beacon 34 in the east.

SWAPO had a small elite unit of soldiers which they called their Volcano troops. It was this one group among the 14 that was specifically tasked to penetrate Owamboland through to the south. Our problem was to identify the Volcano group, while trying to prevent all the others from creating mayhem inside Owamboland. Commandant Robin Hook deployed to Oshivello, near Etosha, with a MAOT team, two Alouette gunships, a command and control Alouette trooper and a Bosbok. Throughout Owamboland pamphlets warning the local population about *Phoenix* were dropped from Kudu and Dakota aircraft.

Small shops in Owamboland are called *cuca* shops, after the brand of beer that they sold. Locals would gather at these shops to socialize, much like the English do in their local pubs. If SWAPO wanted to intimidate the local population these were the ideal places to do it. During the day they would dress in the civilian clothes carried in their rucksacks and were indistinguishable from other Owambos. However, at night when they were sure there were no security force units in the immediate area they would don their uniforms and tote their AK-47s, using the power of the gun to scare and intimidate the non-combatants.

Whenever we received intelligence that SWAPO was in the area we would descend, literally out of the blue, and offload soldiers; they would surround the *cuca* and check through the occupants. These *cuca* blitzes rarely produced results as SWAPO were past masters at disappearing into the bush. However, the locals were often very eager to pass on information regarding the presence of 'strangers' in their territory. All they wanted was a peaceful life, to be rid of both SWAPO and the security forces.

On 17 February, acting on 'hot' intelligence, we sent two Pumas carrying reaction force soldiers on a *cuca* blitz, close to Etale in northern Owamboland. On 28 February, another blitz was carried out on a *cuca* shop 20 kilometres north of AFB Ondangwa. Bosboks were used as Telstar to ensure communications.

It was during this type of operation, when we had close contact with the locals that the security forces benefited from the 'ethnic' make-up of our forces. Owambo soldiers could converse naturally with locals facilitating the gathering of information. Koevoet, using only Owambo policemen, were adept in this technique and most of their follow-ups resulted from information gleaned from local Owambos.

Towards the end of February, Major de Bruyn arrived at Ondangwa to carry out *Maanskyn* missions over the full moon period.

March
March was traditionally a very busy month, being in the middle of the annual SWAPO incursion and 1983 proved to be no exception. *Phoenix* was in full swing with ground troops and Koevoet Zulu teams dispersed throughout Owamboland. At times, HQ in Oshakati was monitoring three or four follow-ups simultaneously. Helicopter gunships were being deployed and redeployed as the hunt for the 14 SWAPO companies continued. After each contact SWAPO units would 'bombshell' (split in all directions), increasing the number of spoor that had to be dealt with.

Earlier intelligence reported that a SWAPO camp had been established near Virei. Subsequently intelligence confirmed SWAPO's presence and on the night of 1 March two ten-man recce teams were inserted from Epupa Falls to substantiate the accuracy of this report.

All this time I was busy organizing 100 sacks of cement, 20 cubic metres of crushed stone and the vehicles in which to transport them to Ongiva. I felt it was important to repair the runway at Ongiva that the Angolan forces had damaged in their retreat from the Cunene Province during *Protea*. Work by the SAAF Airfield Maintenance Unit (AMU) was scheduled to be completed by the end of March 1983.

Combined training was carried out by the helicopter and Koevoet crews who were to participate in planned *cuca* blitz operations. Because of the continual change-round of crews it was important that training and retraining take place at frequent intervals.

At 16h00 on 2 March, a Puma dropped off a recce team near Mulemba for Operation *Snoek* and Alouette gunships from Eenhana were tasked to give top cover for the Puma drop. As a general rule we did not allow Pumas to land in unsecured LZs anywhere in the operational area. If ground troops were not present aerial top cover was utilized. The aim of the recce team was to establish the location of SWAPO's eastern area detachment HQ, known to be in the bush near Mupa. If successful the Recces would call in an air strike by Impalas onto the target, followed by the insertion of ground troops by Puma with top cover provided by helicopter gunships. The four Impalas were on crew-room standby, the Pumas were on readiness at Ongiva and the gunships were positioned at the mini-HAG.

Feedback on *Phoenix* was presented to the daily order group at Oshakati on 3 March. Since its inception in mid-February 155 terrorists had been killed. Twenty-five LPs (common abbreviation for local population) had been killed by terrorist intimidation or mine explosions, with a further ten seriously wounded. Forty-five schoolchildren and three teachers had been abducted to Angola. All this in little over three weeks.

On 4 March, radio problems between the helicopters and Recce teams on the ground hampered the continuation of *Snoek* and all aircrew were relaxed from readiness. This problem regarding incompatibility of communication equipment between different service arms continued throughout the duration of the war, causing numerous difficulties. It was caused by the parochial and insular nature of the service arms during peacetime when equipment was ordered to satisfy the needs of that particular service without consideration for joint-operation compatibility.

Arrangements were made with Commandant Steve Ferreira, the operations co-ordinator at AFB Ondangwa, which allowed the stone and cement convoys on their way to and from Ongiva to refuel at the air base. At the same time, problems between AFB Ondangwa and the AFCP at Oshakati were addressed in relation to the sending and updating of 'Mayflys'. A Mayfly is a report which is sent from an air base at predetermined intervals indicating to the AFCP which aircraft are available to fly and in what configuration. This vital information allows the planners at the AFCP to optimize the use of all available aircraft, while at the same time monitoring the maintenance turnaround time between missions. The quicker the maintainers can re-arm and refuel an aircraft the sooner it can be used again in battle. The speed of turnaround is therefore a force multiplier when carried out efficiently. The AFCP is in charge of all air force resources during force employment and thus must be kept informed of the serviceability state of all the equipment. 'Maysee' reports are sent to reflect the state of all radars. The security squadrons tasked with the ground security of air base facilities and installations extended this system to the ultimate by sending 'Maybite' reports, reflecting the health of their security dogs.

On 5 March, Major Neels de Villiers, the SA Medical Services doctor at

Oshakati, warned the daily order group that malaria precautions should be taken by all personnel inside the operational theatre. The number of malaria cases had increased from a monthly average of 50 to 250 in February. There were a multitude of serious implications when severe medical problems occurred which included depletion of manpower, increased medical health care requirements and a substantial increase of flying hours when patients needed to be transported out of the operational area.

The daily statistics revealed that SWAPO had lost 17 men killed in the previous 24 hours, almost all of them in a contact at Tsandi in Owamboland. However, some of the dead were as a result of a fire fight in western Kavango, indicating that SWAPO was really trying to stretch their attacking frontage.

Ondangwa was the permanent base for all Sector 10 aircraft. However, it is interesting to note that on 5 March we had the following aircraft deployed under the command of MAOTs:

- 2 x gunships, 2 x Pumas and 1 x Bosbok at Eenhana
- 2 x gunships and 2 x Pumas at Ongiva
- 1 x SWA commando aircraft at Windhoek
- 1 x SWA commando aircraft at Ruacana
- 1 x Bosbok doing a recce of the Oshigambo area
- 1 x Bosbok doing a recce of the Ombalantu area

These deployments away from base varied on a daily and even on an hourly basis following the ebb and flow of the war.

On 6 March, the interrogation report of a captured terrorist indicated a possibility of a SWAPO ambush along the tar road between Ondangwa and Oshakati. Suitable precautions were taken, even though experience had shown that SWAPO was never keen to take on the security forces directly and the possibility of an ambush was slight. SWAPO used to blow up telephone poles and road culverts at night during the curfew, when there was the minimum risk of encountering a security force patrol.

It is necessary to explain the curfew that existed throughout Owamboland. Earlier in the war it was discovered that SWAPO used vehicles owned by local Owambos to transport their munitions around Owamboland. To stop this, a curfew was imposed, banning all vehicular movement during the hours of darkness. Imagine the implications of that decision. If your child was taken ill during the night you could not transport him to hospital; daily journeys had to start after daybreak and cease before sunset—not an easy arrangement in a region as vast as Owamboland. They affected the security forces as well. If

1983: Anti-insurgency campaign

someone makes a regulation it has to be enforced. How is it possible to control all vehicular traffic at night in an area greater than that of Ireland?

On 7 March, the SAAF had to supply air transportation to fly an interpreter down to Tsumeb to interrogate a terrorist captured in a skirmish in the farming area. It was important to follow up the information immediately as terrorists, who had traversed through Owamboland without being intercepted, must have been of a higher quality and thus a danger to the peace prevailing in the country south of the operational area.

In addition, two psychological operations were planned and activated in all haste. As a result of the interrogation of the captured terrorist a skyshout-fitted Cessna-185 departed from Tsumeb to operate in the Otavi–Grootfontein–Tsumeb triangle. Secondly, a Dakota was tasked to fly after dark on a route 15 kilometres inside Angola from west to east, parallel to the cut-line, distributing pamphlets between Beacons 1 and 28. These pamphlets contained pictorial messages aimed at having the abducted schoolchildren returned to Owamboland.

On 8 March, initial planning was presented to the morning conference for

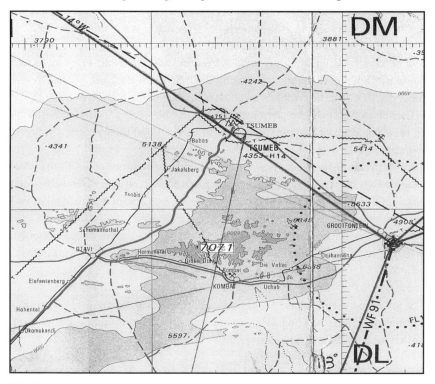

The Otavi–Tsumeb–Grootfontein farming triangle—the target area for every annual SWAPO incursion but rarely reached and never with significant numbers.

243

Operation *Rhubyn*. It was to be a 'large-area' operation covering most of central Owamboland and the shallow area directly northwards into Angola. It was to take place between 23 March and 20 April. Our forces were divided into a Task Force East, under command of Colonel Wouter Lombard and Task Force West, under Commandant Barend van Heerden. Between 18 and 22 March, all our forces operating externally, except those for Operation *Snoek*, were to be withdrawn. The reason for this was twofold—firstly, to ease the pressure on SWAPO to reduce their level of readiness, but mainly to ensure that any armed reaction to the impending operation would only come from SWAPO. Between 23 March and 6 April, intensive reconnaissance activity was to take place internally in central Owamboland, thereby encouraging the terrorists to avert disaster by moving back into Angola. Between 7 and 20 April, both task forces would sweep the shallow external area on a seek-and-destroy mission. During this phase half of Task Force West would operate west of the Cunene River.

On 9 March, it was reported that the terrorist group had reached the farming area around Tsumeb and consisted of 20 to 30 insurgents. These elite troops were called either Volcano or Typhoon groups by SWAPO. It was generally accepted by our own security forces after the war that there was no obvious difference in the standard of training of either type of terrorist. At the time however, this report called for immediate action to the threat posed by this group. Amateurish and lacking training they might have been but no one could say they lacked courage. They knew the dangers facing them before setting off on their yearly incursion, but still they came, which takes courage of the highest order.

Our *Snoek* Recces were obviously having trouble trying to find their target as they asked for their operations area to be extended to cover the Vinticette region.

During the course of the afternoon an in-flight report by one of our Puma pilots indicated a possible terrorist presence in a disused kraal complex halfway between Xangongo and the cut-line. This report was made by Captain Arthur Walker, one of only two air force members to be awarded the Honoris Crux twice.

On 10 March, the death of another security force member was mentioned, bringing to 12 the number killed in *Phoenix* operations. The terrorist total was now 187.

The following night, Impala *Donkermaan* operations began and were to continue through to 16 March. The pilots were majors Abel Grobbelaar and Dick Lewer, both from 8 Squadron in Bloemfontein.

On 12 March, four Pumas and four Alouette gunships were moved to Xangongo to await any developments from Operation *Fakkel*.

1983: Anti-insurgency campaign

On 14 March, Air-Vice Marshall Paddy Menaul, Royal Air Force, visited the sector for briefings and entertainment. We enjoyed visits from professional military personnel as they always had a good understanding of our problems.

A maintenance team had to be sent to Eenhana to repair the NDB beacon. The serviceability record of this particular air navigation beacon was traditionally poor and in this area of minimal terrain features it was vital to keep it as operational as possible.

A report from the *Fakkel* reconnaissance team indicated a strong possibility of two SWAPO bases in the vicinity. They estimated that by 17 March they should be in a position to confirm this report. A company of 32 Battalion was to be prepared to move by air from Ruacana to Okangwati, for possible action on 18 March. As a precaution, the air force flew a Dakota pilot by helicopter in to Xangongo and Epupa to assess the suitability of both runways for DC-3 operations, which could expedite the proposed 32 company's move.

On 15 March, we deployed a five man reconnaissance team by Puma to Chicusse for seven days. Resupply and support was planned to come from Xangongo.

The DC-3 Dragon arrived at AFB Ondangwa from South Africa. This aircraft had a 20mm cannon mounted facing out of the portside cargo door; it was to supplement the Alouette gunships in supplying top cover and battlefield support. The Alouette gunships were without doubt the most successful anti-terrorist weapons in our arsenal. However, the weight of the cannon reduced the amount of fuel that could be carried and so the helicopters could only stay airborne for approximately 90 minutes before having to refuel. It was for this reason all the police Koevoet and army Romeo Mike teams carried drums of avtur (aviation turbine fuel) with them. It was often during critical moments when the helicopters were on the ground that the terrorists could expedite their escape into the thick bush. The Dragon offered us a solution to this vexing operational problem.

The project had been given to Commandant 'Boy' du Preez, OC 44 Squadron at AFB Swartkop, where all the technical aspects regarding the installation were to be completed. He in turn entrusted the operational application to Major Thinus du Toit, an ex-helicopter pilot with 14 years operational and gunship experience. Thinus had to work out the in-flight profiles needed to allow the aircraft to be operationally deployed. A number of problems were immediately apparent.

The aircraft had to be flown in such a way that the gunner would be able to keep the target in the gun sight at all times. With the gun mounted in the cargo and passenger door on the left-hand side of the aircraft it was obvious that the flight profile would be a left-hand orbit. Furthermore it had limitations in its horizontal and vertical travel distances. Too much or too little bank would thus mean that the gunner could lose his visual sighting on the target.

To fly at a pre-determined fixed angle of bank was neither viable nor practical in an operational scenario. A very simple and practical solution was found. If the pilot flew the aircraft from the co-pilot's seat, on the right-hand side of the cockpit, varied the angle of bank to keep the target visual through the small window on the commander's left-hand side of the cockpit, the gunner would have a clear view of the target throughout the action. The only drawback to this solution was that the pilot in the commander's seat following the action on the ground had to lean forward to get a better view. This impromptu movement was usually followed by a brisk smack on the side of his head by the left hand of the controlling pilot—not always good for crew co-operation, especially if it was the commanding officer in the left seat.

Another problem was more of a cultural dilemma. The DC-3, the workhorse freighter of the SAAF, was flown by transport pilots who played an indispensable role throughout the war. However, being shot at was not part of their daily routine. The enemy were armed with AK-47 combat rifles, RPG-7 anti-tank rockets and SAM-7 heat-seeking missiles. Anti-aircraft guns were never part of an insurgent's arsenal when trudging through the bush. Calculations were made around the range of the 20mm cannon, the average height of the Dakota and the muzzle velocity of both the AK-47 bullet and the RPG missile. It was determined that for enemy fire to hit the aircraft the gunner would have to lead the Dakota by between seven and eleven aircraft lengths, which they probably wouldn't do. The threat posed by the SAM-7 was largely negated by the anti-Strela modification fitted to the DC-3 exhaust systems.

An additional capability was added to the DC-3 gunship concept with the installation of a skyshout loudspeaker system to be used in the psychological warfare role. This innovation could transmit prerecorded or live broadcast messages by suitably trained personnel. These personnel were invariably Owambos who addressed the terrorists in their own language. Unfortunately, a Dakota orbiting at low level in conditions of high temperatures and severe turbulence so prevalent over Owamboland invariably resulted in the airborne announcer being unable to perform his required duty, his voice being muffled by the air-sick bag surrounding his mouth. The old Dakota indeed lived up to its infamous nickname 'The Vomit Comet'.

Initial testing of the Dragon concept was carried out from AFB Swartkop by 44 Squadron crews. They included majors Thinus du Toit, Len Haasbroek and Wessel Worst, captains Carlos da Salviera and Melt Pienaar, and Flight Sergeant Daantjie Marneweck.

At 09h00 on 3 August, Commandant Boy du Preez, Major Thinus du Toit and Flight Sergeant Marneweck left AFB Swartkop for AFB Ondangwa where they landed six and a half hours later. At 12h45 the following day, 4 August, the Dragon was scrambled on its first operational flight. On board were the same

1983: Anti-insurgency campaign

crew together with a Koevoet member to operate the skyshout.

Radio contact was soon established with the Koevoet Zulu team who had requested gunship assistance. These men, mounted in their Caspir vehicles, were hot on the trail of an enemy insurgent group. The ground forces were unaccustomed to using the aircraft mission number, in this case L52W, under these circumstances and the first question they asked the DC-3 crew was, "What is your call sign?" The call sign 'gunship' was already in use by the Alouettes, so the crew made a quick decision and answered "Dragon", taken from the well-known American 'Puff the Magic Dragon' aircraft used so effectively in Vietnam.

The Dragon went into a left-hand orbit 1,000 feet above the Koevoet team. At the same time two Alouette gunships, operating anywhere between 50 and 850 feet AGL, arrived on the scene. The ground forces were clearly visible from 1,000 feet. The direction in which they were moving, as well as the most probable route and direction the enemy was taking, was also quickly established. The ground forces were approaching an area of thick vegetation, always a dangerous situation as the enemy were well versed in setting ambush positions. With plentiful supplies of ammunition on board the time had come for the Dragon to prove its operational worth.

The skyshout onslaught began offering the enemy the option to surrender or suffer the consequences. The insurgents ignored the first option and so Flight Sergeant Marneweck was instructed to use flushing fire into the area of thick vegetation in front of the advancing Zulu team. This was most effective; the Koevoet commander reported the fire had fallen very close to the insurgents. The next moment all hell broke loose.

The enemy came running out of the thick bush into an open clearing. Then the Caspirs appeared with Koevoet soldiers running in front. With the enemy in full sight of the Caspir gunners, the Koevoet soldiers, the Alouette gunships and the Dragon, the result was inevitable. It was a short, bloody encounter.

The Dragon concept had proved its worth and became a valuable weapon in the fight against SWAPO. That evening the crew celebrated in appropriate fashion in the Ondangwa pub. For the first time Commandant Boy du Preez, a famous transport and VIP pilot, was seen propping up the counter between all the other fighter jocks, telling war stories with the best of them.

On 16 March, it was reported that 15 terrorists had been killed since 10 March.

The Ondangwa and Grootfontein Dakotas were needed to transport 120 men from Ondangwa to Xangongo in a shuttle service. Because of high temperatures only 20 fully equipped soldiers could be flown on each trip.

Feedback at the morning conference on 21 March indicated that 21 confirmed terrorists visited a *cuca* shop on the evening of 20 March. Unfortunately we could not react because of the unavailability of helicopter crews. This was a command error because we had relaxed the crews from standby before last light, thereby missing a potentially lucrative target.

With the approach of full moon the work load in the AFCP at Oshakati was increasing; a delegation of responsibility was agreed upon to adequately cover all night operations. Commandant Daantjie Beneke was appointed to control the helicopter *Lunar* operations with Major Bernie Sharp in charge of the paradrop resupply; I would handle the Impala *Maanskyn* operations. It must be borne in mind that for each of these operations communications, logistics and comprehensive SAR plans had to be drawn up and executed. With aircraft operating from Ondangwa, Grootfontein and on occasions from forward airfields under the control of MAOTs, involved liaison and co-ordination were always required before any mission could be efficiently and effectively completed.

22 March started as a relatively quiet day with a Puma carrying out helicopter drill training with the army. A Bosbok patrolled the Ondangwa–Oshivello road and an Alouette the Ondangwa–Oshakati road to counter expected ambush threats.

During the late afternoon, a Puma carried out a casevac from an area on the northern edge of the Etosha game reserve. A minefield laid by SWAPO had blown up a Buffel (armoured troop carrier) and severely wounded a member of Koevoet. Second Lieutenant Hendrik le Roux, 61 Mechanized Battalion, entered the minefield, applied a tourniquet to the constable's severed leg and carried him out to the helicopter. For this deed he was awarded the Honoris Crux.

The morning feedback on 23 March reported 24 terrorists confirmed dead since 16 March, including two near Kamanjab, south of Etosha. Three own-forces personnel had been killed since 10 March.

Operation *Rhubyn* commenced, as did the Alouette *Lunar* and Impala *Maanskyn* operations. Impala sorties during the evening were to patrol the Mulondo road and the Cuvelai road. The *Maanskyn* pilots flying over this period were Commandant Steve Ferreira and captains Nel and van Rensburg, together with two Citizen Force pilots, Major Johan Dries and Captain Dave Fish.

On 25 March, one policeman was reported killed in a contact. A Dakota was required to fetch reconnaissance commando personnel from Immelman airfield in the Caprivi Strip and take them to Fort Rev at Ondangwa.

Captain Liebenberg, Airfield Maintenance Unit, gave positive feedback on the progress of the repairs to Ongiva airfield.

A public relations visit was made to the Ongwediva School outside Oshakati. The visit must have been considered important because in the summer heat of Owamboland we had to wear full blues. The senior class consisted of over 450 matriculation students and one wondered if there would be sufficient job opportunities to cater for this yearly output.

On 27 March, a SWAPO press release claimed 28 security force deaths since 1 March. The actual tally was 18 since the beginning of *Phoenix*, against 227 terrorists in the same period.

During hot-pursuit operations Koevoet was famous for following spoor until, as in the tradition of the Canadian Mounties, 'they got their man'. This occasionally resulted in the follow-up moving through the Yati strip into Angola which tended to upset certain authorities as the SA Police were not legally allowed to operate over the border. Warnings were given that in future the 'Zulu' call sign was not to be mentioned if a Koevoet team was involved in a contact north of the border. In a war of attrition if the enemy is allowed to escape he wins. This is unacceptable when one has done all the 'hard yards' finding, fighting and tracking him.

A petty domestic problem arose which required delicate handling. They say an army marches on its stomach—so too the air force. Air force helicopters were utilized to support the army and, as is common with all armies, everything tends to happen at first light. Consequently, the helicopter crews were invariably flying over normal meal times. On completion of their sorties they were understandably hungry and required feeding. Many military establishments left the running of the mess to non-operational staff who tended to abide by normal time schedules and so meals outside of these hours were not provided. Our solution to this thoughtless attitude was to withhold air support from the offending army units until they co-operated for the good of all. I must hasten to add that with the majority of successful army units this problem never arose. The best army commanders realized their entire existence during operations depended on aerial support and therefore nurtured the air force crews.

Over the period 20 to 23 April, 32 Battalion submitted a request to have eight gunships and maximum Pumas available to support their planned action in the Vinticette area of Angola.

On 29 March, Captain Liebenberg (AMU), was flown to Ionde and then to Epupa to inspect the runways. The harsh environmental conditions in this part of Africa caused erosions and washaways, making frequent inspections vital to the preservation of aircraft safety.

Plans were made to fly a continuous patrol using Bosbok aircraft over the Oshakati–Oshivello road during the Easter weekend. Alouette night operations would concentrate on maintaining the curfew. Bosboks would patrol the main arterial roads to and from the south to minimize the threat from ambushes. A Skyshout sortie was scheduled to fly along the cut-line in an attempt to influence children of the local population, who had been abducted by SWAPO, to return to Owamboland.

The Parabat reconnaissance group dropped near Chicusse on 15 March, requested gunships to be available at Xangongo and Impalas on CAS standby at Ondangwa.

On 31 March, it was decided that, because of the threatened ambush, the daily school convoy between Ondangwa and Oshakati would have gunship top cover until further notice. Another point of note is that the children travelled in mine-protected buses with an armed escort, however, before the school convoy could proceed in the mornings the road had to be swept for mines by a patrol.

Commandant Daan Nel, OC 53 Battalion, presented his planning for an area operation. He required gunships on standby at Ondangwa and Bosboks available for night-time flare dropping, on demand.

An interrogation report indicated a SWAPO SAM-7 team had been tasked to an area northwest of AFB Ondangwa. Therefore, for all passenger aircraft operating into or out of the airfield normal top cover was increased to two gunships, or one gunship and one Bosbok. During the critical stages of landing or taking off transport aircraft were protected by circling gunships ready to open fire at any potential SA-7 launch site. Transport aircraft would spiral up or down within the safety diameter above the airport.

April

On 2 April, the Impalas were on standby for assistance in the Vinticette area. We always took these precautions whenever our forces in the field were in a potentially hazardous position. They were very seldom used but always available. One of the principles of war is to maintain reserves which can be rapidly inserted into a battle scenario to influence the result.

The SAAF flew Commandant Borries Bornman to Eenhana. Although the distance between Ondangwa and Eenhana is not very great we used air transportation for moving personnel to and from there, except if a major convoy was planned. Throughout the war Eenhana was probably the most isolated of all the army bases. Situated as it was within a few kilometres of the cut-line it was relatively

1983: Anti-insurgency campaign

easy for the terrorists to lay both vehicle and anti-personnel mines within close proximity of the base. All ground movements required mine-sweeping ahead of a convoy—a long and tedious job. As a point of interest, most victims of SWAP"s mines, during the entire course of the war and for a long while after the cessation of hostilities, were the local population.

Koevoet

At this stage of the war Koevoet was the undisputed leader in the hunt for insurgents. In an attempt to improve their results the army decided to form mobile Romeo Mike (RM) teams, based on the concept of the Koevoet Zulu teams. The task was given to 101 Owambo Battalion and, in an endeavour to expedite their introduction to the war, a liaison meeting was held between Commandant Willem Welgemoed, OC 101 Battalion; Colonel Bertus Burger, OC AFB Ondangwa; and Major Neall Ellis, the senior permanent Alouette pilot in the operational area. This meeting must have borne fruit because, after a slow beginning and many hitches, by the end of the war 101 Battalion was the equal of any operational unit.

The Zulu team concept was based on the principles of mobility, flexibility and offensive action. Four Caspir armoured fighting vehicles made up the fighting unit, with a fifth vehicle carrying the logistic support necessary to maintain the personnel and vehicles during a week long independent patrol through the bush. The team, consisting of Owambo policemen and usually commanded by a Koevoet sergeant, was given an area in which to operate. The team generated its own intelligence by utilizing the Owambo members to talk to the local population. If a terrorist group had passed through the area news of their presence, composition of the group and, quite often, the weaponry with which they were armed, was soon picked up by the Koevoet team. This news, as soon as it was confirmed, would be passed by radio back to Koevoet HQ in Oshakati where a track record would be registered.

A Koevoet Zulu team setting off on patrol in their Caspir mine-protected, fighting vehicles.

The team would then scour the given area until spoor was detected. It takes men skilled in bushcraft to read spoor and the best can do so with remarkable accuracy. From it trackers can estimate the numbers of terrorists, how heavily laden, how quickly they are moving and the age of the spoor. Once locked onto it the team would set off in pursuit. The four fighting vehicles would adopt a formation similar to a fighter squadron's battle formation or combat spread. The lead vehicle and his deputy would straddle the spoor, each being flanked by one of the other Caspir vehicles providing support.

Using this formation, trackers would disembark from the vehicles to enable them to follow the spoor on foot. Generally, these men were so skilled they would run while following the trail. They would be closely escorted by the vehicles containing the rest of the troops. When they tired new trackers would take over the trail allowing the team to close rapidly and keep pressure on the terrorist group. The age of the trail was constantly reassessed and all the information passed back to the tactical HQ.

Koevoet kept the SAAF informed of the progress of the follow-up which allowed us to pre-position aircraft and helicopters as necessary. Using the facilities and security provided at forward bases we could usually have aircraft within a 20 minutes' response time from most tracks. As the countdown to contact decreased aircrews were briefed for the expected mission. Standby times were reduced until the crews were at cockpit standby. When the Zulu team reported they were only 20 minutes behind the terrorists the aircraft would launch. A 20-minute-old spoor relates to about a kilometre between the hunters and the hunted.

Usually, when the terrorists detected they were being followed they would bombshell into smaller groups, heading off in different directions. It was impossible to follow each new track so the Zulu team leader would decide which trail to follow. Very often the terrorist group would bombshell again and again with the groups becoming smaller and smaller. This tactic allowed some of the insurgents to escape but their firepower was reduced and so with each bombshell they became less and less effective.

Koevoet became renowned for their bulldog-type determination and very seldom did their efforts fail. The word *koevoet* is Afrikaans for crowbar. In this case the use of the word was very apt as they would 'lever apart' any resistance.

Visibility in the bush was very restrictive and even as close as a few hundred metres terrorist groups could not be seen. The arrival of the Alouette helicopter gunships immediately altered that scenario in favour of the security forces. From the air movement is quickly spotted; terrorists had to remain stationary under or behind trees to avoid being attacked by the helicopter gunner. This allowed the Koevoet armoured vehicles to accelerate forward with the two flanking cars racing ahead to enclose the enemy within the 'horns of the bull'—the tactic used so effectively by the Zulu king Chaka.

1983: Anti-insurgency campaign

When contact was made between the opposing forces pandemonium ensued. No quarter was asked or given. Four armoured vehicles, filled with troops firing automatic weapons from every port and with the team leader firing his mounted machine gun, crashed their way through the bush and the enemy defences. Apart from the ubiquitous AK-47 each terrorist group was armed with RPG-7s, the standard Soviet-supplied rocket-propelled grenade. To the smoke and flame was added the chatter of the accurate 20mm cannon fired by the Alouette gunners. Most fire fights only lasted for a few minutes but they were violent in the extreme.

The logistics vehicle lagged a short distance behind the offensive unit. It could stop, detach troops to secure the area and then accept helicopters for refuelling and re-arming, allowing them to return into the fight as necessary.

If the terrorist group was assessed as being very large or unusually heavily armed the Zulu team leader had the ability and authority to call for assistance from other teams operating in adjacent areas. On occasions, as many as four Zulu teams co-operated in a joint follow-up and fire fight, very seldom without results. Captured terrorists were brought back for intelligence debriefings and generally provide excellent information on their objectives and modus operandi.

While Koevoet almost always achieved success they too suffered grievous losses. Terrorist groups became skilled in peeling off members to double-back and lay ambushes either side of their original spoor. They made very effective use of POMZ anti-personnel mines which caused many losses and casualties among the on-foot tracking teams.

Each car leader could 'personalize' his Caspir by mounting the weapon of his choice above the driving cab. Ex-air force 20 mm cannons were popular as well as Browning .5-inch machine guns. One car commander, to add to the pandemonium, had a high-powered stereo system fitted to broadcast music as he entered the fray.

The highlight of my week was the day returning Koevoet team leaders attended the order group to present their debriefs. These sessions were very formal and all military staff officers were trained in the art of presenting information. They used overhead projectors and electronic pointers with aplomb. Not so the Koevoet sergeant who had just spent the previous week rampaging through the bush with five armoured vehicles and 40 Owambo policemen. These men were bush fighters of the highest order, with no airs or graces, who presented their story as it was. Whereas we all used a broad sweep of the pointer to discuss the 'big' picture these men stood up close to the huge map and with a stubby finger indicated how they had skirted this *shona* and avoided an ambush as they passed that kraal. Not for them the global picture; theirs was the nitty-gritty of the close encounter, the consequences of an error on their part being fatal.

If I were to offer any criticism of the army RM team it would be the method in which they chose their team leader. A typical Koevoet leader was a 28-year-old sergeant who had been in the force for ten years. He had experience of the criminal mind and had learned how to communicate effectively with the Owambo policemen.

The army decided to select newly qualified lieutenants as their team leaders. At 19 years of age and fresh out of school most of these boys did not have the life skills or experience necessary to effectively lead such a close-knit, mobile fighting team. Once on spoor they would often call for air support too early thereby alerting the terrorist group being followed and allowing them to avoid contact. I am not decrying their courage or enthusiasm, just making the point that it is never easy to control a fluid, violent battle, even with experience.

By 6 April, *Phoenix* seemed to be winding down as the surviving terrorists fled back to the sanctuary of Angola. A decision was made to allow the Alouettes, which had been borrowed from AFB Mpacha during the height of the incursion, to return with their crews to the Caprivi. One of the characteristics of an air force is flexibility as demonstrated below—an ability to redeploy forces as operational requirements demanded.

The SAR plan for the proposed Canberra air strike on Virei was presented for approval at the morning conference. We always paid great attention to this phase of any operation. It was important that the crews at risk were confident of receiving assistance in any emergency situation that might occur.

A long discussion was held regarding the future of the Puma C model in the operational area. This early, under-powered version of the helicopter was not compatible with the later L models. They could not take the same payload, were limited in operational range and had become a thorn in the flesh of the operational planners, as well as the pilots. Standardization of equipment and procedures is a stepping stone to military efficiency.

It was reported that Air-Vice Marshall Menaul, RAF, one of the recent visitors entertained at Oshakati had spoken of his visit to the operational area on BBC radio. As we did not hear it we cannot say whether the message broadcast was positive or not. Normally military visitors appreciated the complexities facing the security forces and their comments were professional, unlike those of some visiting politicians and church leaders.

On 8 April, Alouette gunships and Pumas were deployed forward to Xangongo for Operation *Rhubyn* at the request of Task Force West. As the possibility of contact with the enemy increased we always endeavoured to move our aircraft closer to the expected point of combat to reduce reaction time.

1983: Anti-insurgency campaign

A visual inspection of the dirt runway on the Ionde airfield was carried out which showed it could accept aircraft up to the size of the DC-3 Dakota. Ionde, between Ongiva and Caiundo had, for many years, been disused. The few buildings in the vicinity of the field were in ruins. The walls were daubed by slogans so espoused by liberation movements, 'Viva MPLA' having been crossed out and replaced by 'Viva UNITA' four or five times, indicating that the surrounding territory had changed hands on numerous occasions. Because the mine had always been the favourite weapon of these factions it was assumed that a liberal sprinkling would be in the area.

Before I would grant clearance for aircraft to fly into the field I wanted to be totally certain it was safe for them. I sent a signal to this effect via army channels to our ground troops in the area. The reply, stating that the airfield was safe, arrived back so quickly it aroused my suspicion. Much to the chagrin of the army I insisted that an engineering team be tasked to sweep the entire runway, turning circles and hardstanding areas for mines. In addition, I forwarded a diagram I had drawn of the airfield and its surrounds overlaid by a grid, stating that each grid square had to be signed by the Engineer officer in charge as a guarantee that the area had been cleared. This they did, with obvious ill-feeling towards the SAAF. Their attitude changed after they'd lifted a total of nine mines covering the hardstanding and the narrow entrance to the runway. The mixture included anti-tank TM-46s and TMA-3s, as well as anti-personnel PMNs and POMZs, some of which had been interlinked. A very valuable lesson was learned at Ionde. During the following years the airfield played safe host to a vast number of our aircraft.

Top left: Soviet PMN anti-personnel mine in a non-magnetic plastic casing.
Top right: Yugoslav TMA-3 showing the anti-lift device.
Bottom: Soviet TM-46 anti-tank mine. They were often fitted with anti-lift devices. Chinese variants were often found.

Helicopter crews highlighted a problem when planning their sorties. The quality of intelligence they were receiving from the Intelligence staff at mini-HAGs was below the standard required. In this case a short-term solution was found but the problem continued throughout the war. Senior pilots would easily recognize this lapse and not fly until better intelligence had been obtained. Younger, more junior pilots however, did not recognize the problem and unwittingly flew some very dangerous missions.

On 10 April, four terrorists were killed in western Owamboland. They had been part of the group which carried out the attack on the farm Vergelegen, near Etosha, on the night of 7 March. Only 12 of the original 35 SWAPO detachment members managed to reach the farming area south of Owamboland and, after this contact, all were either killed or captured.

In purely military terms, the only success SWAPO attained during this major incursion was the murdering of two security force soldiers. However, in terms of the attrition strategy they had certainly involved a large number of our troops and aircraft, costing substantial amounts of money. Their presence had been reported in the media, perhaps arousing fears and uncertainty among the civilian population of SWA. More importantly, they could proclaim in world forums that they were making advances in their 'struggle' against the 'Boere' ('the Afrikaaners'—a standard, derogatory term used by terrorist movements in southern Africa for whites). In the global context this was probably what they were trying to achieve.

On 11 April, army live-firing exercises were planned to take place on the range near Mucope for the following week. It was necessary to send a notam (notice to airmen) to all air bases warning crews to stay clear and to the ATC authorities to give in-flight warnings to incoming aircraft from South Africa. This warning included a 21 Squadron jet bringing the Chief of the Air Force, Lieutenant-General Mike Muller, on a visit to AFB Ondangwa.

On 12 April, the light transport Kudu aircraft was tasked out of sector for a few days, so two aircraft from 1 SWA Commando Squadron were put on standby for possible transport requests. The SAAF used a network of commando squadrons to supplement the permanent force. Civilian pilots were encouraged to join this reserve force and were organized into squadrons. These pilots performed admirable tasks and could be relied on to fill the gaps in our force levels.

A DC-4 Skymaster, modified for EW, arrived on deployment for intelligence-gathering operations. Constant reconnaissance of the electromagnetic spectrum was required throughout the war to pinpoint changes or additions to the enemy's order of battle. In this case the enemy referred to was not SWAPO, but FAPLA

1983: Anti-insurgency campaign

and FAPA, the Angolan army and air force respectively, who were gradually becoming the enemy. SWAPO had begun moving their camps from the bush to the close proximity of Angolan establishments, where they could be protected by the defensive umbrella of artillery and air defence systems. This move by SWAPO, allowed by the Angolans, was a major contributor to the escalation of the war. To reach SWAPO we had to come into conflict with Angola's military.

On 13 April, 32 Battalion OC, Commandant Eddie Viljoen, presented his detailed planning for the operation in the Vinticette–Cuvelai areas around 18 April. The air requirement was for eight gunships and six Puma helicopters, with Impala jets on standby at Ondangwa and a Telstar to ensure good communications. Between 13–22 April Mirage F1 aircraft from 1 and 3 Squadrons would deploy from South Africa to AFB Ondangwa. These jets would be on CAS standby for ground attack missions, half in the standard eight-bomb configuration and the others armed with 72 x 68mm rockets apiece. This was possibly the last time 68mm rockets were contemplated for the Mirage F1 force. The advent of the South African-produced new generation pre-fragmented bombs made rockets virtually obsolete.

Colonel Eddie Viljoen, one of the outstanding soldiers of the border war, always worked closely with the SAAF.

On 5 April, *Phoenix*, the operation to counter SWAPO's 1983 incursion into South West Africa, was officially brought to a close. The full results were as follows:

- SWAPO   309 killed
- Security forces   27 killed
- Local population   33 killed
- LP children   161 abducted to Angola

Feedback from Major Neels de Villiers of the SAMS gave the breakdown of casualty evacuations between 28 February and 28 March as follows:

- 149   by air to Oshakati
- 35   medevacs (medical evacuations i.e. malaria, snakebite etc.)
- 7   local population
- 14   dead on arrival (DOA)
- 3   SWAPO
- 123   wounded

The daily intelligence brief included an account of how SWAPO and FAPLA were operating jointly to a much greater extent than at any other time in the war. As mentioned earlier this was a contributing factor in the escalation of the war.

On16 April, a Puma was made available at Oshakati to allow an Italian TV crew to view and photograph the area. By offering assistance and hospitality it was anticipated that positive coverage on our efforts would be screened, but with journalists one could never be sure.

Before sunset, in the Ruacana area, another pamphlet drop had to be completed by a Kudu. According to the pilot the drop was unsuccessful. He released the pamphlets from 3,000 feet AGL in the designated area while on a westerly heading. On completion of the drop, while overhead Ruacana, he spiralled up to 10,000 feet AGL before returning to Ondangwa on an easterly heading. Imagine his surprise when he found he had to take avoiding action from the cloud of pamphlets he had dropped a few minutes earlier. When planning the mission we had not taken the extremely high temperature and strong tropical thermals into consideration. This routine sortie was actually a fairly high-risk mission. An altitude of 3,000 feet AGL placed the piston-powered Kudu well within the engagement zone of the shoulder-launched SA-7 Strela missile.

Impala *Maanskyn* sorties were to be flown every night between 16 and 25 April, over the full-moon period.

On 17 April, an intelligence assessment indicated that SWAPO's actions had shown a temporary shift to the Kavango area. Fortunately these moves were

1983: Anti-insurgency campaign

being satisfactorily dealt with by Colonel Deon Ferreira's troops from Sector 20 at Rundu.

On 20 April, the Administrator General of SWA (AG) Dr Willie van Niekerk, GOC SWA General Charles Lloyd, COM SWAPOL (Commissioner of Police SWA) Geneneral Dolf Gouws, OC WAC Brigadier Bossie Huyser and Colonel Theron arrived in Sector 10 in the late afternoon for an updat on operational situations.

On 21 April, a Puma was sent to Onanjokwe hospital for a visit by OC SAMS, Major Neels de Villiers. Throughout the war this hospital, although receiving great assistance from our medical staff, remained a suspected source of information to SWAPO.

On 22 April, General de Witt of the South African Police visited the police Koevoet and COIN (counter-insurgency) units in Oshakati, accompanied by English-speaking guests. Colonel J. P. Durand, the police chief in Oshakati, invited me to attend the reception. At the time, I was one of only a few English-speaking people living in Oshakati and he wanted me present at such functions to ensure that somebody could converse with the guests.

A joint workgroup was held between Koevoet, the helicopter crews and 101 Battalion Romeo Mike personnel to co-ordinate the introduction of 101 Battalion's mobile force into operations. In peacetime this sort of co-operation would be unthinkable but in our situation any pettiness was forgotten during the quest for combat efficiency in the face of a menacing enemy.

On 25 April, initial planning for Operation *Dolfyn* was presented. This operation was to take place between 30 April and 20 June in eastern Owambo and in the Angolan territory north of beacons 21 to 28. Our forces would operate from Nkongo, internally in Owamboland and from Ionde, externally in Angola.

A report from the Air Force MAOT at Ongiva stated that, although the runway had been repaired and was available for use, our ground forces did not have enough personnel to ensure that the approach paths at either end were clear of SWAPO threats. Until that situation improved we had to halt the use of the Dakota from Ongiva.

On 26 April, the current code list of names and places had to be changed to avoid security leaks. Using codenames for places, people and equipment increased the security of messages transmitted on HF and VHF radios, but only if they were changed frequently. Intelligence reported the possibility of a group of 300-

plus terrorists north of Eenhana and Etale. Although we felt that this was most improbable contingency planning had to be carried out to ensure we had the men, logistics and aircraft available if needed.

On 27 April, feedback on the *Bakkie* operation flown on the evening of 24 April—a bakkie (a pick-up truck) was successfully halted and nine confirmed terrorists were captured. *Bakkie*, *Butterfly* and *Cuca* blitz operations were simply variations on a theme. Reaction Force soldiers, usually Parabats, were flown in two Pumas and air-landed to perform search and interrogation of suspect persons breaking the curfew or visiting *cuca* shops. They weren't always as successful as on this recent operation but kept the terrorists on the move and unable to settle comfortably anywhere in Owamboland.

Bosbok recce missions were flown in the Eenhana–Etale areas and night-flare dropping was carried out around Ondangwa as a precaution, following the terrorist group report of the 26th. Random flare-dropping alerted SWAPO to the fact that security forces knew of their presence, making them think twice before trying to set up a stand-off bombardment with rockets or mortars. The same effect was achieved by the army in all their bases, when at random times during the night they would fire a pre-determined fire plan. (New arrivals to Oshakati were often scared stiff when the 40mm Bofor cannons opened up in the middle of the night.)

Two Pumas were tasked to take medical personnel and equipment to Colonel Viljoen and 32 Battalion at a bush LZ north of Ionde where his forces were deploying for Operation *Dolfyn*.

Our MAOT reported that the helipad at Etale needed maintenance. The army undertook to carry out the necessary work. It was vital that routine inspection and maintenance of aircraft operating facilities was carried out promptly and properly. Loss or damage to aircraft through negligence was absolutely unacceptable.

A misrep (mission report) from an Impala low-level, reconnaissance sortie stated that AAA was drawn from a position close to Ediva. This little hamlet, ten kilometres southwest of Cahama, always acted aggressively towards our aircraft. This type of anti-social behaviour was stored in my memory bank to be addressed on a suitable occasion in the future.

On 30 April, the Air Force Senior Command and Staff course visited the sector for an update on the progress and problems of the war. This visit was considered to be one of utmost importance because the course students would be the next generation of operational commanders. A most comprehensive briefing covering all aspects of the insurgency war was presented.

The Bosbok is a two-seater aircraft with both crew needing to wear parachutes; not an ideal form of medical transport. However, it was used on odd occasions to bring in malaria patients when no other aircraft was readily available.

Fourteen Dakota sorties were flown from Ongiva using 20 flying hours. They air-dropped 13.826 tons of rations at 25 different locations. These 20 Dakota hours probably saved an estimated 100 precious Puma hours. Puma utilization dropped from 411 hours in March to 137 in April. The effects of the war had to be countered in every conceivable manner.

May

On 1 May, Operation *Dolfyn* commenced and the annual Air Force Day memorial service was held at AFB Ondangwa. For me, this service in the operational zone was perhaps more poignant than those held back in South Africa.

On 2 May, a conference was held to discuss the impending visit to the sector of the Minister of Defence. When the minister visited the C SADF, CAF and GOC SWA all attended, making for complex and detailed arrangements. In this instance it was especially involved as all the dignitaries were to be accompanied by their wives. The Oshakati ladies' club was given the task of entertaining the wives—never an easy task given the limitations of a border garrison town.

A wounded terrorist, together with all his weapons, was casevaced to Oshakati. 5 Maintenance Unit was made responsible for securing his equipment and the Recce Commando for his interrogation.

On 3 May, the daily intelligence assessment intimated that there was a possibility SWAPO would attempt to attack a security force target on 4 May, the anniversary of Cassinga Day. It was suggested that AFB Ondangwa was the most likely target with the attack coming from the western side and the insurgents using heavy machine guns. As mentioned earlier, the probability of SWAPO launching a direct assault on the security forces was slight but, nevertheless, precautions had to be taken. It was interesting to note how much emphasis is placed on 'anniversary' days by communist-taught revolutionaries. The counter of course was to ensure that readiness states were raised on those days. A plan was made for a PR sortie of Cuvelai and Tetchamutete to update intelligence for *Dolfyn*, which included an SAR plan.

On 4 May at 17h30, the Minister of Defence, together with other dignitaries, arrived at Oshakati. The evening's activities included briefings, visits to units in Oshakati and a *potjiekos* supper at Driehoek. A *braaivleis* (barbecue) was the traditional form of evening hospitality but on special occasions *potjiekos* was served. This Afrikaans name describes the three-legged cooking pot (the type cartoonists use when missionaries are boiled) carried under the wagons during the famous 1836 Great Trek from the Cape. It is a wonderful way of cooking a full meal in one pot, basically a stew, and the results are always delicious—the Afrikaners are traditionally superb outdoor chefs.

As expected, no SWAPO attack on a security force base materialized and our force reaction states were lowered.

On 5 May, two Pumas, two Alouette gunships, a Bosbok and a Cessna for Telstar duties were deployed to Ongiva.

Two Pumas flew the minister and his entourage to visit Eenhana, Nkongo and Omauni in the east. Two other Pumas took C SADF and his party in the opposite direction to visit Ombalantu, Xangongo and Ongiva. From Ongiva they were flown by Dakota to Rundu.

On 6 May, the MAOT with Task Force West requested that an Alouette trooper be allocated to him. A 'trooper' was a normal Alouette without a gun used to transport officers in the field, or for command purposes when a ground battle was controlled from the air. Aircraft could be redeployed, almost at a moment's notice, for any period of time varying between hours and weeks.

On 9 May, a discrepancy had to be cleared up regarding the distance our forces could penetrate into Angola without clearance from higher HQ. The guidelines and limitations passed down through the air force channel indicated 150 kilometres. Army ground Recces were going farther than this, making 'legal' air support questionable. This incident highlights a most important feature in command and control of forces. On the border, circumstances had proven that a combined headquarters at every level was the only way to prevent anomalies like this. However, back in South Africa, away from the front, peacetime conditions still existed with each service arm's HQ isolated from one another. There is an old military adage which says 'Train as you would fight'.

Butterfly operations were planned for the Ogongo area. The targets were suspected kraals, *cuca* shops and vehicles, the latter to be searched during random road blocks. The name aptly describes the repeated, short-duration activities—like a butterfly interrupting its flight to seek nectar from flowers.

1983: Anti-insurgency campaign

To ease the transportation problem a weekly Dakota shuttle service was instituted between Ondangwa and Ongiva. The distance by road between the towns is only 45 kilometres but, because all roads had to be swept for mines before vehicles were allowed to use them, air transport became the most cost-effective means of transport.

Fuel was urgently required at Ionde and a Dakota was tasked to fly in drums to the airfield. Dakota crews were warned by Intelligence of the dangers of flying the same route between Ongiva and Ionde during the required shuttle. Becoming predictable is an almost certain way of inviting a reaction from the enemy.

The ComOps department asked for a media campaign to be launched in the Tsandi area before commencement of the next *Lunar* helicopter operation. As we had not flown in that area recently, they wanted to remind the local population about the restrictions imposed by the curfew.

32 Battalion passed back a warning order about a possible target they had discovered at the Indungo logistics point.

On 10 May, combined Alouette/Koevoet training continued, under the guidance of Major Neall Ellis.

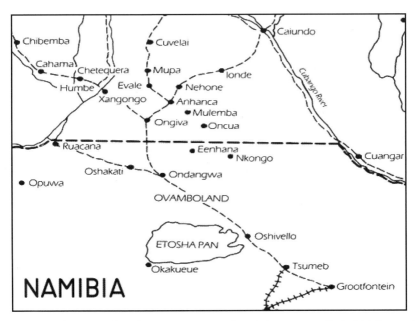

Between Ondangwa and Ionde one can see a number of place names, all of which featured as 'hotbeds' of SWAPO activity. Flying in that particular vicinity required special care on the part of the pilots.

The 32 Battalion plan for Operation *Dolfyn* was presented for approval. Operation *Snoek* fell away and was replaced by *Dolfyn*. The aim was to find and attack the eastern area headquarters (EAHQ) of SWAPO. The ground forces available were 32 Battalion, 4 SA Infantry and 61 Mechanized Battalion. These forces were divided into Task Force West under Colonel Linford, with Major Jannie van de Merwe as the attached air force MAOT. Task Force East was commanded by Colonel Philip Lloyd, with Major Williams as his MAOT. Each MAOT was allocated two gunships and one Alouette trooper.

11 May was an unusually quiet day operationally which allowed attention to be given to pressing domestic problems. Firstly, it was decided that the Joint Information Centre (JIC) was non-productive and required re-organization to improve the quality of its product. Secondly, our analysis indicated that we had to restrict the use of Pumas to operational tasks only. We could no longer afford the luxury of using it for transportation.

On 13 May, a Kudu was dispatched to Tsumeb to fetch five suspected terrorists for interrogation. Information, straight from the mouths of newly captured terrorists often proved to be of immense tactical value.

Koevoet, 101 Battalion and SAAF helicopter crews continued joint training. The more effort we put into training the bigger and better the benefits reaped during operations.

32 Battalion reported that their three companies were positioned near Jaula, northeast of Tetchamutete, for *Dolfyn*. Two companies of Parabats and a mobile force of 61 Mechanized Battalion were in reserve. The reconnaissance, to confirm the position of the Eastern Area HQ, was to commence on 23 May. Full moon was on 26 May and the expected D-Day was to be 28 May. It is worth noting that *Dolfyn* was initially planned to be completed by 20 May. During the entire course of the war we found that a large proportion of all operations had to be extended when initially, the target had to be located by ground recce. Ground reconnaissance deep into enemy territory had to be very carefully carried out to avoid the risk of compromising the attack. The stealth required often extended the planned time allowance.

On 14 May, two Pumas, carrying army spares and equipment, were despatched to rendezvous with army patrols in the bush near Ionde. With troops on the ground to secure the LZ it was not necessary to provide top cover for the Pumas.

An inspector of aviation fuels was sent to Ongiva to check the drums, bladders and refuelling facilities there. He also checked the condition of the fuel in the drums placed at the HAG near Mupa. Periodic inspections had to be carried out on all fuels in the entire operational area to avoid an aircraft accident caused by fuel contamination. Bacterial growth in fuel can cause a type of algae that quickly blocks the micron filters incorporated to protect aircraft engines.

On 16 May, a meeting was held to co-ordinate curfew responsibilities during *Lunar* operations between the army, Koevoet and the air force. The rules governing the curfew imposed in the operational area stated that no movement was allowed on the roads between sunset and dawn and therefore, any detected vehicular movement would be considered hostile. It was this assumption that made it necessary for all the security forces to be informed of who was operating where and when, to avoid dreaded 'friendly fire' or 'blue on blue' incidents. (In military planning and war-gaming friendly forces are always depicted in blue and the enemy in red.)

On 17 May, *Butterfly* bakkie operations were planned for the roads in the Oganjera–Tsandi areas of western Owambo.

An all-day meeting was held to work out the legal aspects of the curfew as pertaining to the five-kilometre circle around both Ondangwa and Oshakati. Being the most densely populated areas in Owamboland it was natural that most breaches of the curfew occurred within these circles. The institution of a curfew could be performed at administration level with the stroke of a pen. Enforcing it was altogether a greater problem. Sudden illness could force householders to head for the nearest hospital. How was the soldier on the ground to differentiate between this 'humanitarian' movement and that of a terrorist intent on causing mayhem?

On 19 May, all aircrew were warned once again about the inherent dangers of continually flying the same routes. Later in the war a Dakota was hit by a SAM-7 en route from western Owambo to Ondangwa.

Wherever they flew in this vast theatre of operations our aircraft were at considerable risk. Constant adherence to safety regulations was a prerequisite. If it was not possible to fly above the 15,000-feet Strela limit we tasked the pilots to fly at low level. We were aided in this strategy by the incredible flatness of the entire area which allowed pilots to fly at 50 feet above the tree canopy with comparative ease. At this low altitude SA-7 operators had insufficient time to acquire the aircraft, gain lock-on and fire, before the low-flying aircraft disappeared from view. Unfortunately, this method was not foolproof.

A DC-3 returning to AFB Ondangwa from western Owamboland proved an

When this DC-3 Dakota was hit by a SAM-7 heat-seeking missile both tail and elevator control surfaces were shot away. Wonderful airmanship by Captain Colin Green and his crew made it possible for them to land the severely damaged aircraft safely at AFB Ondangwa.

exception to the rule. The relatively slow-moving transport aircraft presented an ideal target for the right length of time to a lucky Strela operator. His missile streaked away and exploded as it struck the tail of the Dakota. The pilot heard the explosion and felt the strike as the balance of his aircraft was lost.

The fabric-covered vertical tail fin was completely destroyed and the aircraft immediately started to yaw as directional control was lost. The horizontal elevators had been peppered with holes making height control difficult. With great effort the pilot managed to keep control of his badly damaged aircraft, little knowing that the holes in the elevator fabric were gradually tearing in the airstream. He felt the effect by the increasing sluggishness of his elevator control.

Eventually, he solved the porpoising problem by manoeuvring the position of his passengers. Getting them out of their seats he had them move, in a closely packed group, backwards and forwards to adjust the aircraft's centre of gravity thus allowing him to keep the aircraft more or less level. Fortunately, the passengers included the chief of the navy and his entourage who were on a staff visit. These men, accustomed to a pitching deck, were quite adept at dancing up and down the fuselage at the behest of the pilot. The pilot landed safely at his destination after a demonstration of great flying skill.

On 21 May, a Dakota was tasked to take Echo Victor (Commandant Eddie Viljoen) and twenty 32 Battalion troops from Omauni to Ongiva.

1983: Anti-insurgency campaign

This close-up of the DC-3 Dakota tail shows that the pilot had very little to work with except a quick brain.

On 23 May, a busy morning conference was held during which two plans were submitted for approval. Firstly, *Blouwildebees*. This 52 Battalion Reconnaissance plan called for a Tactical HQ to be set up at Ruacana. Two Pumas were to be used to infiltrate the team on 28 May. If they found the target then an attack would be planned (I did not record the target they were looking for). Two Impalas were to be on CAS standby during the day and another Impala used for Telstar duties during the night.

The second plan was for *Korhaan*. This was to be a high-density, mobile operation in western Owambo. A Tac HQ was to be created at Ogongo from 25 to 29 May and the cut-line sealed by seven platoons while nine Koevoet Zulu teams, supported by five SAP COIN teams, would sweep the area from south to north towards it. Twelve army Romeo Mike teams would sweep from the Xangongo–Ongiva road southward also towards the cut-line. The air force provided a MAOT at Ogongo who was allocated one Bosbok, two Alouette gunships, one Alouette trooper for command and control purposes and two Pumas.

Strike against Mozambique

Also on 23 May Operation *Skerwe* took place. This was the SAAF raid into Maputo in retaliation for the car-bomb explosion outside Air Force HQ in Pretoria at 16h25 on 20 May, which killed 18 people and maimed many others. It was timed to wreak the maximum havoc among the personnel as they headed homewards after normal working hours at 16h15. A cream-coloured Colt Gallant, packed with explosives and parked in front of the main entrance to Air Force HQ, was

From Fledgling to Eagle

The scene of devastation in Church Street, Pretoria, after an ANC car bomb was detonated during rush-hour traffic.

detonated in a massive explosion. Sergeant Leslie Barnes, a member of the Mobile Radar group, was one of three occupants of a car alongside which immediately burst into flames and was severely damaged.

Realizing that the car's petrol tank could ignite at any minute Barnes scrambled out of the vehicle and, despite his severe burns and cuts, released Lieutenant van Wyk's safety belt and carried her to safety. He then returned to the car and freed Captain Clarence who was permanently blinded by the blast, and carried him to safety with the help of bystanders. A few moments later the petrol tank exploded and totally destroyed the vehicle. For these acts of bravery Sergeant Barnes was awarded the Honoris Crux Silver.

A dastardly deed like this could not go unpunished. On Saturday 21 May, Steyn Venter was summoned to Colonel Oosie van der Bergh's office at AFB Pietersburg. Venter was ordered to take four Impala Mk IIs, each armed with four F2 rocket pods, and be at AFB Hoedspruit by 17h00 that afternoon. Venter, then commanding 85 Advanced Flying School, decided to take Norman Bruton, 'Geronkie' Venter and J. P. Gouws in his formation. He also had to send enough ground crew to Hoedspruit to keep 12 Impalas serviceable.

Shortly after the formation landed they were joined by four aircraft from 4 Squadron, Lanseria, and another four from 8 Squadron, AFB Bloemspruit flown by Abel Grobbelaar, Dick Lewer, F. Lategan and Richard Cornelius. All the pilots assembled in the briefing room of 31 Squadron where photographs, taken from a Seeker remotely piloted drone, were available for study. These photos showed houses in a tree-lined street on the outskirts of Maputo, some of them partly hidden by the foliage from trees. The houses were roughly in a straight line

1983: Anti-insurgency campaign

As experienced a bunch of pilots as one could find. Commandant Steyn Venter and majors J. P. Gouws, Norman Bruton and Jeronkie Venter.

running from northeast to southwest. The first obvious reaction from the pilots was that it would be extremely difficult to pick up some of the targets visually during the pitch-up for a 15° rocket attack; the trees would obscure their vision.

Another set of photographs and charts of Mozambique were on their way from Pretoria so in the interim deep discussions were held to work out how best to attack all the targets simultaneously thereby ensuring the aircraft would spend the shortest possible time under fire. It was agreed the best approach would be at low level from the southwest, flying down the river which opens out into Maputo harbour. The 12 aircraft would fly in pairs, line astern and all pitch-up at the same time, attacking to the left. After weapons' release the aircraft would break left while returning to low level, regaining battle formation and heading for the South African border. Then they would climb in safety for their return to Hoedspruit.

The ground crew, after their arrival at Hoedspruit, busied themselves arming each aircraft with 24 x 68mm rockets and 220 rounds of 30mm cannon ammunition. All the aircraft radios had to be re-channelled to ensure the entire formation had the correct frequencies set for the mission. During this frenetic activity the men were drenched by a heavy rainstorm, unusual for late May.

The new photos and charts arrived; it was then decided Venter would lead the attack. Navigation, fuel planning and the SAR plan were all decided upon. The pilots had one nagging thought about the fuel—when they arrived back at Hoedspruit they would not have much to spare. They were also informed that Major Des Barker, flying a Canberra, was to co-ordinate his flight with the attack formation, to contact and inform Maputo Air Traffic Control tower to either keep their aircraft on the ground, or away from Maputo. Two pairs of Mirage F1AZ aircraft would also participate in the operation to ensure the safety of the smaller and slower Impalas. One pair would ensure that the SA-3 missile site in Maputo would be unable to fire during the attack. The second pair was on standby in the remote case that enemy MiG fighters would try and intercept the attacking formation.

With all the planning completed, around 01h00 in the morning, they went to bed on stretchers made up in 31 Squadron's hangar—and it was still raining. Just after 04h30 the ground crew were woken to prepare the aircraft for a 06h40 take-off. The activity in the hangar soon had everyone out of bed. After a bite to eat and a final briefing, the pilots walked out at 06h10 to sign the F700 maintenance book of their aircraft. The rain had stopped but the cloud base was very low. On start-up it was discovered that the maintenance work on the aircraft the night before had drained the batteries and all 12 aircraft required the services of the external Hobart starter. On checking in on the radios the problems of the night manifested themselves; rain had entered the cockpits and radios. Eventually, after a long period trying to get everyone serviceable the formation taxiied out to the runway. At this point, and to great relief of all the pilots, a message postponing the mission was received. After burning off about 200lbs of fuel the aircraft returned to the hardstanding.

Back in the briefing room the crews were informed that the strike had been rescheduled for Monday morning. This delay proved to be a blessing in disguise. The aircraft could be better prepared and the pilots given more time to study their individual targets. TV tapes of the Seeker mission were studied, aircraft topped up to the brim with fuel and, importantly, everyone involved could have a proper night's rest. Most of the pilots spent the available time trying to visualize their targets in a 15° dive. They had been ordered to fire only when they had positively identified them. To restrict collateral damage and avoid unnecessary casualties the use of bombs was precluded because they were not as accurate as rockets.

The next morning, 06h40 on 23 May, the preliminaries worked like clockwork and the entire formation was in the air on time having burned off about 50lbs of fuel. They proceeded to Big Bend on the Swaziland border with Mozambique, where they turned left and descended into the valley leading to Maputo. The turn towards the east produced an uncomfortable situation as the sun was rising dead ahead of the formation. Venter had a wandering PHI (position heading indicator) which had to be reset every few minutes, testing his navigational skills to the limit. At this stage Des Barker joined the formation somewhere astern. Venter can remember thinking how unfair life can be. Barker had a two-seat aircraft with a highly trained navigator while he, Venter, was battling alone in the lead.

Eventually Venter sighted some high-rise buildings on the horizon, far ahead.

1983: Anti-insurgency campaign

Worried about his PHI he called Norman Bruton on the radio to see whether Bruton could identify the buildings as Bruton had spent his honeymoon in Maputo 20 years earlier when it was still Portuguese Lourenço Marques. Despite honeymoon preoccupations Bruton was still able to identify the buildings. The formation was on track and on time. As they entered the riverbed, on a beautiful morning, the formation descended to approximately 30 feet above the water. They accelerated and assumed the correct formation for pitch-up.

Fuel was checked and found to be a trifle below bingo. However, the fuel states were not dangerously low and so the formation pressed on with the attack. At this stage Des Barker was overheard in serious conversation with Maputo Tower saying, "Maputo Tower this is Mike Zero One. We are carrying out strikes against ANC dissidents in your country and request that you keep your air force on the ground as we have no quarrel with the Mozambique government. However, if they do get airborne we will engage them." As an afterthought he added that he would give them clearance to resume normal activities once all SAAF aircraft had cleared the area. After the attack the Canberra returned to AFB Waterkloof.

The formation flashed across the fuel dumps then all 12 aircraft pitched-up for a roll-in to the left. During this time each pilot had about 15 to 20 seconds to search for and find his target and make the necessary adjustments to his flight-path to achieve the correct speed, height and heading, before releasing his weapons. Bear in mind that none of the pilots had ever seen Maputo before, except Bruton, so it was not an easy task.

Venter, whose target was well covered by trees, did not release his weapons but as he pulled out he felt his aircraft shudder as J. P. Gouw's rockets exploded into the target. After all the No 2s had called off the target Venter set heading for base calling for another fuel check. He realized the aircraft's fuel was now critical and started to climb when only 15 miles from the target. In a slow-climbing aircraft like an Impala this is a very uncomfortable thing to do as it becomes easy prey for enemy missiles; all the pilots' heads were on swivels as they desperately scanned the area around them for telltale missile trails.

Levelling at 15,000 feet they had the option of jettisoning the high-drag rocket pods but to their credit retained them. Thirty miles from AFB Hoedspruit the aircraft entered a stream formation as they began the descent to facilitate a straight-in landing for all 12 aircraft. In some cases fuel was so critical a go-round was impossible. The fuel consumption figures used during the planning were those used at 85 ADFS and were renowned for their accuracy. However, this sortie had been flown at sea level, not the usual 4,000 feet of the northern Transvaal—that was the difference.

SADF intelligence had definite information that the Pretoria bombing had been planned by the ANC in Maputo. The targets selected for the SAAF reprisal raids were:

- Gubuze House—the planning office of the 'Transvaal Urban Machinery', the ANC unit responsible for terrorism and sabotage in the urban areas of Transvaal
- September House—planning office of the 'Transvaal Rural Machinery'
- Logistics HQ
- Supply Point
- Command HQ—where final briefings for terrorism missions into South Africa were given
- 'Main Camp'—where training in weaponry and explosives was given

The Mozambican government and the ANC reacted quickly to sanitize the destroyed buildings. In their excellent propaganda they claimed the SAAF had struck a jam factory and a crèche. The SAAF claimed 41 ANC terrorists, 17 Mozambican nationals and eight civilians killed. I suppose the real figures will never be known but it does highlight the fundamental differences between the two attacks—the SAAF attacked legitimate enemy targets. The terrorists attacked a civilian building in the heart of a big city.

The SAAF took every precaution to limit collateral damage by carefully selecting the most accurate weapons and aircraft to deliver them. The terrorist bomb targeted anybody within range and was detonated at a time when Church Street would be most crowded. The SAAF targets were selective while the Pretoria bomb was designed to indiscriminately maim and destroy anyone within range as its aim was to create terror.

On 25 May, everyone was warned about the dangers of loose talk, particularly as it was suspected the Oshakati telephone exchange was manned by SWAPO sympathizers.

May—back in Owamboland

As a direct result of the successful mission on the night of 17 May, another *Bakkie* operation was launched in the Oganjera area. This time though the operation was mounted during daylight. Operation *Korhaan* got underway and the *Maanskyn* night sortie was to be flown along the Cahama–Lubango logistical umbilical.

A Bosbok was flown in the Ongiva area during the evening to act as Telstar for the Dakota resupply sortie. Aircraft flying on their own needed secure radio communications to initiate Mayday calls and to know that a SAR operation had been activated.

The increased use of the Ionde airfield called for runway markers to be installed. These markers allowed the pilots of heavily loaded Dakotas to gauge the progress of each take-off.

SAAF Pumas on the left, Frelons in the background and a Rhodesian Air Force Bell (Huey) helicopter being prepared for Operation *Uric*.

Airborne troops prepare to board a SAAF Puma during Operation *Uric*.

Troops practising rope-assisted landings used in restricted helicopter LZs.

An H2 TV-guided bomb undergoing pre-flight preparation.

Riem Mouton inspecting the pod, mounted under the Buccaneer wing, prior to an operational sortie.

A Buccaneer leaves dispersal on a training exercise.

A rare sight in African skies—six Buccaneers in close formation.

A 24 Squadron Buccaneer with empty pylons returns to AFB Waterkloof after a training sortie.

You can almost hear the distinctive *clap-clap* of the Alouette's rotor blades as it heads for home.

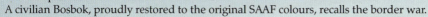

Above: WO Kenny van Straaten firing the door-mounted MAG machine gun as a Puma comes into an operational LZ.
A civilian Bosbok, proudly restored to the original SAAF colours, recalls the border war.

A close-up view from the pilot's seat of the four-barrelled machine gun installed in the earlier Alouette III gunships.

A Puma, backbone of the SAAF air effort, passing a distinctive Owamboland makalani palm tree.

1 Squadron flies line-abreast with Table Mountain as the backdrop.

The SADF made extensive use of paratroops during the war, dropped from C-130, C-160 and DC-3 transport aircraft and air-landed from Frelon, Puma and Alouette helicopters.

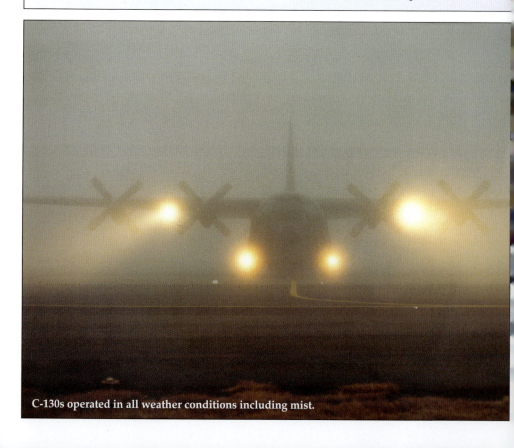

C-130s operated in all weather conditions including mist.

An F1CZ awaits its pilot.

A Mirage F1 carrying out a low and slow flypast over the Roodewal bombing range.

F1CZ in air-combat livery displaying dive-brakes, leading-edge slats and trailing-edge flaps.

The silhouette of a Mirage F1AZ at sunset displaying the distinctive plume from the afterburner.

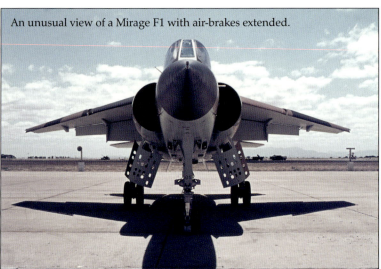
An unusual view of a Mirage F1 with air-brakes extended.

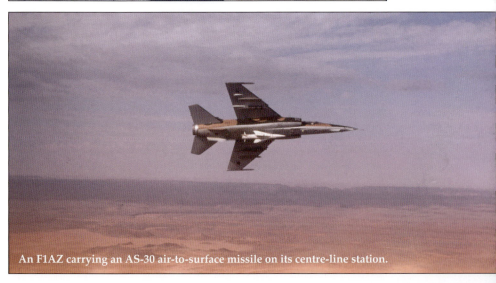
An F1AZ carrying an AS-30 air-to-surface missile on its centre-line station.

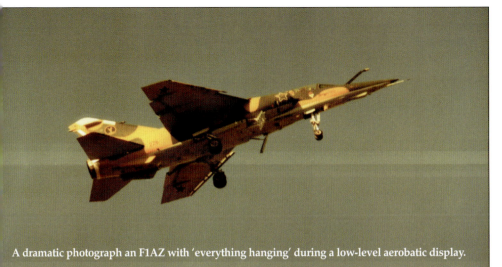
A dramatic photograph an F1AZ with 'everything hanging' during a low-level aerobatic display.

A MiG-21 on a dispersal pan at Namibe airfield, Angola, taken through the window of a departing airliner.

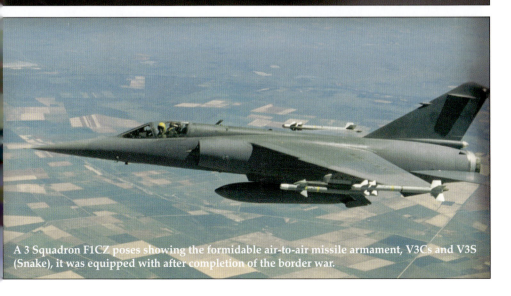
A 3 Squadron F1CZ poses showing the formidable air-to-air missile armament, V3Cs and V3S (Snake), it was equipped with after completion of the border war.

Angolan MiG-23s standing on the line at an air base in Angola.

This 3 Squadron aircraft looks like an ICU as the pilot and ground crew try to shelter from the burning tropical sun.

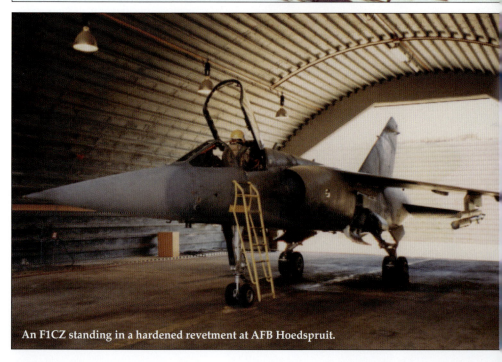
An F1CZ standing in a hardened revetment at AFB Hoedspruit.

The Canberra was a willing workhorse throughout the border war but by the mid-1980s was fast approaching its operational sell-by date.

Buddy-buddy in-flight refuelling between a Buccaneer tanker and a SAAF Cheetah.

A close-up photograph showing the pilot of an F1AZ concentrating on staying 'in the basket'.

An F1 displaying its full weapons capability—unfortunately after the border war had ended.

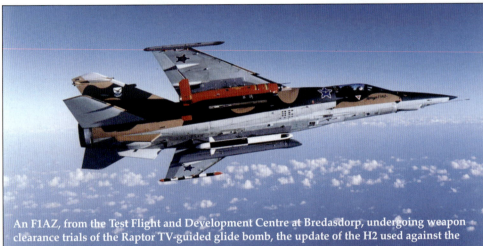

An F1AZ, from the Test Flight and Development Centre at Bredasdorp, undergoing weapon clearance trials of the Raptor TV-guided glide bomb, the update of the H2 used against the Cuito Bridge in Angola.

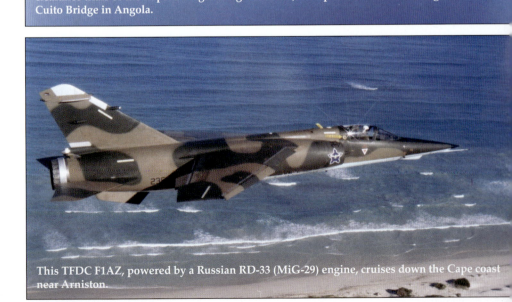

This TFDC F1AZ, powered by a Russian RD-33 (MiG-29) engine, cruises down the Cape coast near Arniston.

1 Squadron aircraft on their way to a target in Angola taxi out from the security area at AFB Grootfontein.

The flame inside the jet-pipe can be clearly seen on engine start-up.

Des Barker flying an F1 during in-flight flutter clearance trials with V3C and V3S air-to-air missiles.

Camouflage schemes varied as the SAAF attempted to find the most effective colour scheme.

Our original camouflage proved to be ineffective as Angolan pilots, flying high over the battlefield, easily detected the bright yellow in the pattern.

It was often easier to see an aircraft's shadow than the aircraft itself.

1983: Anti-insurgency campaign

A notam was sent out informing all aircrew about the 'frozen area' south of Nkongo. A 'frozen area' was one where only one unit of security force personnel operated to prevent any 'blue-on-blue' firing incidents. The unit operating in this area would therefore know they could only expect an enemy presence.

On 28 May, a Dakota was tasked to fly Major Tom Cummings and eight Reconnaissance commandos plus their equipment to Ruacana for *Blouwildebees*. Later that evening two Pumas deployed the team from Ruacana into Angola.

Air transport planning was carried out for the change over of the three 32 Battalion companies who were deployed for *Dolfyn*. On long operations impetus was maintained by the introduction of fresh troops, allowing the others much needed rest and recuperation periods.

32 Battalion informed us that they might be in a position to attack the EAHQ logistical point near Indungo on 2 June. We arranged for four Impalas, permanently based at Mpacha, to redeploy to Ondangwa over this critical time to add fire power to the air strike.

A misrep from a 1 SWA commando pilot indicated the runway at Okankolo was not fit for aircraft operations with tropical downpours and army trucks causing the most damage.

On 31 May, Mr Preisig of the International Red Cross was granted permission to refuel his Islander aircraft at Oshakati. This aircraft was based in Angola but because it belonged to the Red Cross organization it was allowed access to our air space. However, we did not allow him to land for refuelling at AFB Ondangwa. We felt that valuable intelligence regarding this base could have been passed on to the Angolans.

Operation *Kameel* got underway. This operation was a carbon copy of *Korhaan* but situated in central Owambo. The Tac HQ was set up at Etale. The MAOT was allocated four gunships, two Pumas and a Bosbok. OC Task Force Central was Commandant Daan Nel. From 31 May to 4 June, eight RM and ten Zulu teams were to sweep from the south towards the cut-line, which was to be sealed by 3 June. Then, between 4 and 9 June, 16 RMs plus 20 Zulu teams would work southwards from the Ongiva line. Two points of interest here, firstly, 20 Zulu teams would be working externally—they had therefore to be reported as RM teams and secondly, the aim of both these operations required the 'sealing' of the cut-line. Unfortunately, this was an unrealistic aim because the border was too long and the thick foliage provided too much cover. However, there were favourite crossing points used by SWAPO, most of them known to our ground forces, so ambushes were laid in the most likely areas.

June

During the first two days of June Brigadier Joubert used a Puma to visit the UNITA troops in Angola, just north of beacons 16 to 18. His discussions were aimed at delegating areas of responsibility in order to prevent clashes between allies. This visit was a prelude to Operation *Neptune*, when a 60-man force from the Reconnaissance regiment was to move into Angola, north of Beacon 24, for a period of three weeks from 6 June. They required Impala aircraft on standby at Ondangwa and to be resupplied every ten days by Dakota.

Acting on 'B Source' intelligence a *Cuca* blitz was carried out on a shop southwest of Oshakati, with no results. The intelligence community classified their sources according to the alphabet with an 'A Source' being the most reliable. The value of the information declined rapidly as the letter of the alphabet increased and this one produced a 'lemon'.

The sand runway at Ombalantu was situated in a *shona* and was reported to be in a poor state of repair. An investigation was begun to check the feasibility of using a section of the main Ruacana–Oshakati road as a runway. The study was to include the section of road outside the Mahanene army base.

Current operational statistics were presented as follows:

- Week   Internal: 2 SWAPO, 1 Security Force killed, 13 SWAPO wounded
- Month   Internal: 27 SWAPO, 1 Security Forces killed
               External: 17 SWAPO killed
- Jan–May '83 Internal: SWAPO 216, 33 Security Forces killed
               External: SWAPO 115, 7 Security Forces killed

On 4 June, we flew an Impala PR sortie over Oshivello where the army had constructed a simulated terrorist camp for training purposes. We wanted to see if our photographic interpreters could identify the camp, at the same time assessing whether the camp could be identified by using infrared sensors.

The C-160 was used to ferry Major Tom Cummings and 60 Reconnaissance troops from Ondangwa to Eenhana.

On 6 June, the Red Cross Islander again refuelled at Oshakati. This was a real nuisance because we had to transport fuel from AFB Ondangwa to cater for this requirement. The alternative was to allow it to land at Ondangwa, perhaps what the pilot wanted.

1983: Anti-insurgency campaign

On 7 June, we used two Puma helicopters to shuttle the 60 Recce Commando troops from Eenhana to an LZ near Mulemba for Operation *Neptune*. The following day a PR sortie was flown over Cuvelai at the request of Commandant Jackie Snyman, the intelligence officer at Sector 10.

A misrep from the evening of 6 June indicated, at great lengths, that if supplies were to be air-dropped accurately then the DZ had to be properly marked. Obviously the aircrew were protecting their reputations for a drop which had not gone too well. Whenever an operation did not go according to plan it reminded all those involved that joint operations and joint planning were the vital keys to success.

The C-160 Transall was used to carry out the daily Rum Run instead of the Dakota. Close control of the Rum Run was required at Sector HQ level, otherwise the amount of personnel and freight would have grown to such an extent that the Dakota would have become redundant.

The following inputs were given at the morning order group:

Brigadier Dreyer, Koevoet, said that the deep west of Owamboland was firmly under the dominance of SWAPO. He added that he had also received news of a group of 20 to 25 terrorists in the Onessi area.
    A CSI source reported a group of terrorists at Chilombo, 25 kilometres north of Chitado. Commandant Jackie Snyman indicated that it was unclear what was happening in the Dova–Nehone area, but there was a SWAPO sabotage team near Onanjokwe and a spoor of 40 to 50 terrorists northwest of Nkongo.

The night resupply drops were becoming so popular we had to avoid tasking the Dakota crew the night before the Rum Run. The aircraft remained serviceable but the aircrew needed rest.

A Puma was tasked to tour the area to collect air-drop parachutes from the various DZs in the bush.

On 13 June, it was reported that *Blouwildebees* troops had produced a target. Their plan was to open fire with mortars and artillery on H-Hour, at 10h00. At 10h05, the Parabats and the task force would move in, with top cover provided by four gunships. Pumas would place stopper groups to prevent a SWAPO escape.
    This attack on 14 June began as planned but turned out to be a 'lemon'. The army blamed the air force, saying the Pumas had dropped the stopper group at the wrong LZ. The SAAF claimed the FUBAR (foul-up beyond all recognition)

275

was the direct result of communications which, once again, did not work. In reality 'lemons' did occur despite the best intentions of all the participants. It must be remembered that in the bush any unusual sound can be heard for miles and it only takes a matter of seconds for a skittish enemy, like SWAPO, to disappear into the bush. Most experienced operators accepted this while a minority were quick to find a scapegoat.

On 15 June, planning for Operation *Afskeur* was presented for approval. This was to be a high-density area operation against the Far East Detachment of SWAPO in the Nkongo area over the period 8 to 5 July. Commandant Fred Burger would command it from a tactical HQ at Nkongo. The air component would include four gunships and a trooper, two Pumas and a Bosbok. The cut-line would be sealed with ambushes and Claymore mines positioned at known SWAPO crossing points. Maximum available Koevoet Zulu and army Romeo Mike teams would drive the terrorists northwards out of Owamboland. All undetonated Claymore mines were to be retrieved after operation.

On 16 June, the SAAF was placed on high alert when an army patrol reported an unidentified aircraft flying near Namacunde, in southern Angola. It turned out to be an aircraft hired by the SWA Broadcasting Corporation; the pilot had become temporarily unsure of his position.

Planning was received from the *Neptune* forces for a target they had identified at grid reference XM235581 near Mulemba. The operation would be carried out as follows:

- Phase 1   Paradrop from C-160 with a P-Hour of 1620h00 (16 June, 8pm)
- Phase 2   March to the target
- Phase 3   Attack TOT 1707h15
- Phase 4   Extraction
- Phase 5   Recovery of parachutes

On 17 June, news came through early in the day that the attack had once again turned out to be a 'lemon'. The probable reason could have been that the terrorists heard the C-160 during the paradrop and moved their position. There were many recriminations from the higher HQ over the negative result of the operation. I personally believe that not too many of the senior officers who made these derogatory statements really understood the complexities of the bush war.

Intelligence had previously informed us that SWAPO was tasked to attack and destroy high-tension electricity pylons, particularly the ones running southwards

1983: Anti-insurgency campaign

from the Ruacana hydroelectric power station. This non-military soft target was a typical SWAPO objective, with minimal risk of confrontation with the security forces, but potentially attracting maximum media coverage. We showed presence along these widespread power lines by tasking all our aircraft to fly along the grid whenever they were in a position to do so. In addition, Bosbok and Impala aircraft would drop flares at random along the length of the power line in an attempt to discourage SWAPO's night activities. However, this proved to be a poor solution to the problem because if the flares were released too low, the resultant veld fire destroyed valuable grazing. If we compensated and dropped the flares from a higher altitude, the pilots had insufficient illumination to carry out an effective visual reconnaissance. Only SWAPO could have confirmed whether these flare-drops had any real effect.

Three hundred 32 Battalion troops from Operation *Dolfyn* were replaced during a shuttle performed by four Puma helicopters. It required 30 flights and a total of 23.5 hours of flight time to complete the task.

On 23 June, the 800-feet-tall radio mast at Oshakati was the centre of discussion, the red navigational warning light adorning its pinnacle being the cause for concern. Residents of Oshakati wanted the light switched off at night so SWAPO did not have an aiming point for their stand-off bombardments. On the other hand, the mast presented a fatal obstacle (if the warning light was switched off) to many of the aircraft that flew nightly in protection of the same residents. The compromise arrived at was to have the light switched on during flying sorties and then turned off as soon as the aircraft had landed.

The daily intelligence brief reported that at Caiundo, 14.5mm AAA batteries were sited east of the river. They also reported that SWAPO, when moving south to make their infiltration into SWA, was using horses and donkeys to carry their heavy equipment and mines. As a result, orders were given to shoot any animal convoys seen in southern Angola on so-called 'equestrian' operations. Inhumane perhaps, but each POMZ anti-personnel mine detonated in SWA had the potential to kill or maim an average of nine people.

Concentrations of cattle were reported in both the Handebo and Mulemba areas. Ground patrols were tasked to investigate as SWAPO used these herds to eradicate their spoor.

On 24 June, 53 Battalion presented their planning for a sweep operation from Cuamato southwards to the cut-line. The tactical HQ would be at Ogongo and they required the support of two gunships and a Bosbok. The commander appointed for the operation was Commandant Tienie Smuts.

Commandant Daan Nel, 53 Battalion, reported they were to carry out a *Cuca* blitz at Eheke and Okatope.

On the evening of 25 June, Captain Alan Francis was tasked to fly the *Lunar* operations in the Miershoop area.

Every night a Puma crew was placed on casevac standby for emergencies. Occasionally, we would permit the standby to be done from Oshakati. This opportunity was used to ferry non-standby crews to partake of the delights afforded by the Driehoek Steakhouse. On this particular evening the Impala pilots came over for a quiet, pleasant meal. The problem nights were when the helicopter crews visited the steakhouse. Invariably, the following morning, I would be summoned to Brigadier Joubert's office to explain the peculiar habits of helicopter pilots.

On 27 June, lieutenants Richard Cornelius and André Stapa were tasked to fly a low-level armed reconnaissance mission in the Xangongo area of Angola. Captain Frank Vivier carried out the Telstar duties for the sortie. The two armed Impalas were routing just north of Maquete, following a sand road, when they spotted a Ural 375 truck loaded with troops travelling in a northerly direction at substantial speed. By the time Richard's Impala arrived next to it its speed hadn't slackened but there were no passengers to be seen. As the Impala pitched-up to attack the vehicle swung off the road and stopped, making the attack much easier. The now-empty vehicle was destroyed. The next day, on an intercepted message reporting back to the Angolan HQ, the Angolans announced the loss of the vehicle plus a number of dead and injured. These casualties could only have occurred when their troops abandoned the vehicle while it was still moving.

On 29 June, the intelligence assessment indicated that the Alpha, Charlie, Charlie Bravo and Far Eastern Detachments of SWAPO were all inside Owamboland. This was not as serious as it sounded. These terrorists would blow up telephone poles, culverts, plant mines indiscriminately and then flee back into Angola. Not a real military threat, but in terms of an insurgency war they were serving their purpose.

A police report indicated that a small group of terrorists were in the Etananga area, about ten kilometres north of AFB Ondangwa, for the express purpose of shooting down a SAAF aircraft. They were probably part of the Bravo Mike detachment. A possible Strela warning was sent out to all aircrews.

A day later, on 30 June, all army forces operating in the Mupa area of Angola were withdrawn because of the absence of the enemy.

1983: Anti-insurgency campaign

Bernie's elephant

Early one afternoon, the orderly calm of the command post was disturbed by the entry of Captain Sakkie van Zyl of the South African Police. He explained that during an elephant culling programme, a rogue elephant had escaped from the Etosha Nature Reserve and was rampaging northwards through a densely populated area of Owamboland. It was destroying kraals and crops and endangering human life. It had to be shot.

A week earlier I had taken my son to the shooting range at AFB Ondangwa to teach him to shoot. Also at the range was Major Bernie Sharp, my operations officer, who was 'shooting-in' the telescopic sight of his Winchester 300 Magnum. Not being a boffin on rifles I was suitably impressed by the name Magnum. Clint Eastwood, playing Dirty Harry, always carried a Magnum which was supposed to be the biggest hand-gun available. The second impressive fact was that the muzzle velocity of this rifle was 3,100fps, only 100fps less than the 30mm Defa cannon I had fired from a Mirage fighter.

Realizing this elephant had to be shot I immediately thought of Major Sharp and his Magnum. When I asked him if he would like to go on an elephant shoot he jumped at the chance. Then I asked Captain van Zyl if he had a big rifle; he replied in the affirmative. Consequently they were elected the hunters for the expedition. I arranged for an Alouette helicopter to pick us up at Oshakati. I went along as the operation's co-ordinator and to film the event. The Alouette crew consisted of a pilot and flight engineer-gunner, as the aircraft was armed with a four-barrelled, light .303 Browning machine gun. I donned a headset and sat in front to direct operations while the two hunters sat in the back with their rifles.

We found the area and the rogue elephant. From the air we could see both his tusks had been broken off from where they had protruded from the skin. Two police Caspir vehicles had stopped near a school and were surrounded by hundreds of local Owambo. The elephant was striding backwards and forwards in thick bush about 300 metres away. After making a quick tactical appreciation we dropped Major Sharp in a clearing about 200 metres from the elephant. Then we hovered the helicopter directly above the animal while Sharp made his approach.

The close-up view of the elephant flapping his ears and striking out with his trunk at the helicopter was a sight to set the adrenaline pumping. We watched as Sharp stalked to within 70 metres of the agitated animal before taking careful aim and saw his shoulder recoil from the shock as he fired. The elephant collapsed backwards onto his haunches and my immediate thought was one of relief. One shot, one elephant.

Then, to our consternation, the elephant stood up and glared around. If he had been agitated before, he was now downright furious. I shouted at the pilot over the intercom to keep the helicopter in front of the elephant to distract it while

Sharp fired again, this time without any apparent effect on the animal.

Our appointment with fear now began in earnest. Sharp, realizing that his bullets were having little or no effect decided to move closer. From the helicopter we watched aghast as he crept to within 40 metres of the huge creature. From our seat in the grandstand we could see that he was much too close but there was no way we could communicate this fact to him. As if in super-slow motion we saw him raise his rifle, aim and fire again. The elephant did not bat an eyelid. Instead, he turned his massive, angry head and glared straight at Sharp. He realized that here was the perpetrator of all his annoyance and, after a flap of his ears, charged directly at the major.

To give Sharp his due he stood, leaned into the shot, aimed and fired deliberately at the charging elephant. To our horror the elephant did not falter and continued straight at the stationary figure. Realizing at last that discretion was the better part of valour Sharp turned tail and started to run. The monster was now only ten metres behind him, trunk outstretched.

Sharp is a tall man with long limbs and the picture I carry in my memory is the frantic whirling of his arms and legs as he literally ran for his life. When the elephant started his charge I dropped the camera as all thoughts of photography vanished. The pilot started an anguished wail over the intercom and all I could hear was a loud, continuous "Aaaggghhhhh!"

Sharp, in a straight gallop was no match for the elephant and it was gaining at every stride. At this crucial stage fate intervened in the form of a large, tall Owamboland antheap. Sharp took a sharp left around this two-metre-high obstacle. The elephant followed but due to its enormous inertia his turning circle was larger than Sharp's. Dust clouds started to rise as the left-handed scramble around the antheap built up momentum.

I managed to persuade the pilot to manoeuvre his machine to a position directly above the animal and gave Sakkie the order to fire from his side of the helicopter. At the speed that things were happening we only managed to be over the huge head for a fraction of a second. In all the excitement Sakkie had forgotten to cock his rifle and opportunity was lost.

Instructing the pilot to move away from the overhead we managed to get an oblique view of the closing stages of the race. Then I ordered the flight engineer to open fire with his machine gun. He had anticipated this and immediately let fly with a prolonged burst. The elephant collapsed in a cloud of dust but it took me a while to stop the adrenaline-charged gunner firing.

With the elephant immobilized we landed the helicopter and as the engine shut down I heard a single shot ring out as Sharp finally put the poor animal out of its misery. Within minutes the huge carcass was surrounded by a seething mass of locals all exclaiming the characteristic "augh" as they clapped their hands together. They were anxious to reap the benefit of this unexpected windfall. Through the throng I noticed a police Caspir driver who related what had occurred before our arrival.

The Caspir is a mine-protected, armoured personnel carrier built for off-road bundu-bashing, while tracking and chasing terrorists. It is immensely strong and weighs over 13 tons. Interestingly, the name Caspir is an anagram of the initials SAP (South African Police) and CSIR (Council for Scientific and Industrial Research), the two groups who combined to produce this excellent vehicle.

During the course of the morning the elephant had charged one of these vehicles, putting it out of action. Once the elephant had left the scene the other Caspir stopped to give assistance. While all the occupants were standing outside the stationary vehicles discussing the problem, the rogue returned. It came storming out of the bush and ran into the side of the second Caspir. This 13-ton vehicle was physically moved about eight metres sideways by the force of the collision. The policeman I had spoken to was the driver of this second vehicle and although this incident had taken place three hours earlier his face was still chalky white.

About a month after the event I told this story in the pub to General Dennis Earp, then Chief of the Air Force. I spoke about the vision I had of Sharp's limbs whirling all over the place while he was running. On completion of the narrative I felt a tap on my shoulder—it was Sharp who explained the whirling action of his limbs. During his sprint, because he could hear the elephant rapidly gaining on him, he had been trying to shoot backwards over his shoulder.

July

On 1 July, Pumas were sent to recover the Reconnaissance Commando troops who had been working in the Oncocua area of Angola during Operation *Blouwildebees*.

A DC-3 Dakota flew to Omega to collect two sticks of Bushman trackers and fly them to Nkongo for Operation *Afskeur* which was to commence on 8 July. Each stick comprised ten men. These wonderful little people had been removed from Angola by members of the SA Army for humanitarian reasons. The three rival factions in Angola—MPLA, FNLA and UNITA—were fighting to fill the power vacuum created when the Portuguese abruptly left the country in 1975. They all considered the nomadic Bushmen an additional problem which they did not need, practising systematic genocide whenever Bushmen were encountered.

A Bushman settlement was established at Omega in the Caprivi Strip to cater for the extensive Bushman families. Medical facilities and schools were provided and the able-bodied men were recruited into the SA Army and received all the benefits of being in service including, for the first time in their lives, a salary. Previously, living in and off the bush, they had no need or understanding of money. These men were wonderful trackers and could read the bush environment like other people read a newspaper. They were so skilled they could run along a trail left by a terrorist group while leading offensive army or police fighting teams. However, as soon as they slowed down and became visibly nervous it was a sign that a contact situation was imminent, of which they wanted no part. They were gentle people unused to the violence so common among the more 'civilized' populations.

A Cessna 185 delivered vehicle spares to a police Koevoet team stuck at Nkongo. Bundu-bashing took its toll of mine-protected vehicles and constant maintenance and repair had to be undertaken. A team's efficiency was hampered if one of its vehicles was immobilized, therefore the air force assisted, whenever possible, to expedite the return of the offending vehicle to the field.

The successful operations of the half year were celebrated at a joint lunch attended by Brigadier Joep Joubert, Colonel Wouter Lombard and Commandant Borries Bornman from the army and Colonel Dick Lord, Commandant Daantjie Beneke and Major Bernie Sharp from the air force. I mention this function because it was the first occasion of the year we were able to get together on a non-official basis.

On 2 July, an Impala flew a PR sortie over Santa Clara at the request of army Intelligence.

During the afternoon an Alouette trooper flew the Chaplain General to Ogongo. He was to officiate at their church service on Sunday 3 July. The spiritual needs of the men on the border were given the same attention as their physical requirements.

On 4 July, General Geldenhuys, Chief of the Army, was flown by Queen Air from Windhoek Eros to AFB Ondangwa and then by Puma to Oshakati. The air force must shoulder the blame for a most awkward day. At Eros airfield everybody was ready for take-off except the pilot. As a result, the general arrived late at Oshakati and vented his frustration on the staff officers who had to present briefings. Commandants Jackie Snyman and Borries Bornman were told to leave the hall to improve their briefings and Commandant Barend van Heerden's analysis of the mine-warfare situation prevailing in Owamboland, which I thought excellent, was also pulled to pieces. An uncomfortable morning indeed. It only improved when we flew the general up to Ongiva where he learned firsthand of the successes against SWAPO and could see the results of the runway restoration, undertaken by 400 AMU.

The intelligence staff had to update their maps as a new SA-3 site had been positively detected at Jamba, near Lubango. (In Angola, names reoccurred in

1983: Anti-insurgency campaign

several provinces. In our operational theatre there were three places named Jamba; one outside Lubango, one near Techamutete and the third UNITA's headquarters in southeast Angola.)

On 5 July, a function was held at 18h00 to celebrate the opening of the new facilities erected at 5 Maintenance Unit in Ondangwa. Each additional building was seen as a great stride forward in the fight against terrorism. It must be remembered that Owamboland had no facilities to house a modern defence force.

On 6 July, General Geldenhuys left instructions to 'personalize' the war. He felt commanders could develop a better instinct for conducting operations if each was acquainted with the personality traits of his opposing commander. The Angolan Air Force commander opposing me in Lubango was a Major Manuel Dias whom I came to know fairly well and to like, through our meetings at the Joint Monitoring Committee (JMC) in 1984.

On 8 July, Operation *Afskeur* commenced in eastern Owambo with the Tac HQ at Nkongo. Medium-term planning was presented at the daily conference. The annual appearance of Infantry School graduates into the operational area, would take place in early September and they would operate, once again, in the Dova–Nehone area.

From early August, the Force-in-Being (*Mag-in-Wese*) would operate externally on foot because their motorized vehicles were considered too noisy to ensure any success against SWAPO.

On 9 July, brigadiers Joubert and Dreyer and I flew by Alouette to visit the Tac HQ at Nkongo. On the return flight we landed near a Koevoet Zulu team, busy with a follow-up. Never having seen spoor I asked to be shown the tracks they were following. Eventually, all three of us joint-service commanders were on our knees. Only then could we clearly see the outline of a footprint, which the Owambo trackers were following on the run. Each man to his own field of expertise.

On 11 July, *Lunar* operations were planned to take place from 17 July to 2 August. While deployed north of the Red Line 1 SWA Commando Squadron's aircraft were averaging 19 hours flying per week.

On 12 July, planning for Operation *Balpoort* was presented for approval. This was to be a 51 Battalion operation including additional Parabats, under the command of Commandant Gene Basson. It would take the form of an area sweep between

Xangongo and Tetchipelongo, west of the Cunene River, with the Tac HQ and MAOT being sited at Xangongo. Two gunships and two Impalas were available with a restriction of a 20-kilometre radius placed around Cahama. The operation would last between 14 and 24 July.

On 13 July, Captain Chris Clay of the Reconnaissance Commando requested a Bosbok aircraft to act as Telstar for the evening in an attempt to locate his ground troops who had missed a radio schedule. These were some of the forces positioning for *Balpoort*. A missed radio schedule was a fairly common occurrence as the terrain did not lend itself to good radio communications. However, it was always cause for a few anxious moments.

On 14 July, Commandant Stroebel and Captain Liebenberg, from 400 AMU, visited the operational area to inspect the condition of the runways. This was an ongoing task because of the amount of wear and tear on the runways, particularly at the forward bases.

On 16 July, Commandant Steve Ferreira, the operations co-ordinator (Ops Co) at AFB Ondangwa, was requested to ensure the crews flying casevac missions took cameras with them to record the scene and photograph the victims. These photos were needed to counter SWAPO propaganda by showing, in vivid gory detail, the indiscriminate effect of SWAPO anti-personnel POMZ mines. Local population, villagers and children, were the most frequent casualties.

A DC-3 was flown to Ionde taking in much needed ammunition and fresh rations. The hazards of vehicle transportation over mined and ambushed roads was largely overcome by the use of aircraft. It was for this reason that each SWAPO detachment included shouldered-launched SA-7 Strela missiles in their armoury. Flying was done at extremely low level thereby reducing the Strela operator's launch opportunities. Routes were always varied, particularly when aircraft were shuttling to and fro.

On 17 July, the month's *Lunar* operations began and continued until 2 August.

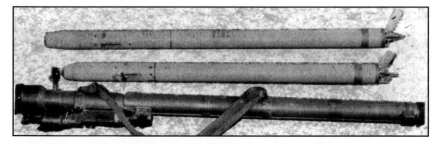

A captured SA-7 launching tube and two Strela heat-seeking missiles.

1983: Anti-insurgency campaign

This was the type of trench used by SA-7 operators when deployed around fixed defensive sites. The shape of the trench allowed the operator all-round freedom of action.

Two SA-7 operators in suitable pose.

Chibembe, between Lubango and Cahama, had been attacked by Buccaneers and Mirages, during Operation *Protea*, to destroy the large air defence radar installations sited there by the Angolans. At the daily briefing on 19 July, intelligence reported there were indications that the Angolans were starting to rebuild the site. Although SWAPO was the enemy, cognizance had to be taken of all developments inherently dangerous to aircraft operating within Angola.

It was also reported that terrorists were present every night at the *cuca* shop at

Oshikwa, north of Ondangwa. They often displayed their 'strongman' image by using their AK-47 as a credit card.

On 20 July, two gunships from Ongiva were tasked to move to Catale at first light. The AMU inspectors ordered 40 cubic metres of crusher dust to complete the surfacing of the Ongiva runway. An interesting problem concerning the building, or refurbishing, of runways, is that in Owamboland there is absolutely no stone whatsoever. The entire surface of Owamboland consists of powdery white sand. Building stone has to be transported into Owambo from the nearest quarries outside Grootfontein for all construction projects.

Planning for Operation *Llama* was carried out. Three motorized companies, an armoured car squadron, one artillery and one anti-aircraft troop (all acting as infantry) and a Parabat company, ex-Operation *Dolfyn*, would be deployed. This force, under Commandant Coetzee, would sweep an area west of the Cunene River to Oncocua and south of the Cahama–Xangongo road. The operation would be carried out between 6 August and 16 September. The 20-kilometre restriction from Cahama, laid down for *Balpoort*, was reduced to 15 kilometres for *Llama*.

These restrictions placed around Cahama were necessary because, over the years, South African army and air force units operating west of the Cunene River felt obliged to annoy the Angolans by firing a few rounds into the military targets round the town. The accumulative effect of these actions was that the Angolans had built Cahama into a powerful defensive position. In addition, the Angolan commander could claim, quite legitimately, that whenever the 'Boere' had attacked his garrison he had sent them packing with his counter bombardments, with their tails between their legs. Ironically, the macho actions of each commander had improved the psychological morale of the defenders of Cahama.

An order was sent to 101 Owambo Battalion instructing them that whenever a helicopter was refuelling during a RM follow-up the logistics vehicle, with the fuel and a stick of ground troops was required to protect the aircraft while it was on the ground.

On 20 July, *Maanskyn* operations commenced and would continue until 28 July. GOC SWA arrived in the sector.

On 21 July, Chief of the Army with entourage visited Sector 10, hence the arrival on 20 July of GOC SWA.

On 22 July, the EW DC-4 Skymaster was back in the area. Commandant Mossie Basson wanted to check transmissions emanating from the Namibe area.

1983: Anti-insurgency campaign

Commandant As Kleynhans, from the ComOps department, requested a Puma to fly an international TV team around the area.

The International Red Cross aircraft visited Ongiva to refuel. This, more than ever, convinced me that despite the ethics of this wonderful organization, a little bit of intelligence-gathering was taking place. Of course, I could have been wrong.

On 23 July, Intelligence reported the withdrawal of SWAPO's Bravo Mike detachment and the western artillery group from their usual areas, armed with the DKZ-8 Grad-P 122mm rocket launchers. A combined mass attack was planned on AFB Ondangwa on 19 August. Contingency orders were issued to have the Fireforce on standby at Ondangwa from 15 August and from that date aircraft dispersal plans had to be executed. This labour-intensive action required all aircraft, normally housed in or around the hardstanding at AFB Ondangwa, to be towed by tractor to positions dispersed over the airfield; also extra ground troops were required to protect the enlarged perimeter. As usual the attack never materialized but the added strain had to be absorbed.

On 25 July, Pumas were required to insert 5 Recce Commando troops into Nkongo for the start of 53 Battalion's operation against the Charlie Bravo detachment of SWAPO, operating in eastern Owamboland. The Tac HQ was sited at Nkongo with a MAOT, four gunships, four Pumas and a Bosbok, with Impalas on standby at AFB Ondangwa. Two parachute companies were placed under command of Major J. P. Snyman, with Major Neall Ellis as the gunship commander. The operation was to continue until 5 August and combined with 5 Recce's Operation *Salmon* in the same area. A mini-HAG was to accompany the ground troops, together with 12 drums of helicopter fuel, a doctor and medical team.

On 26 July, a Dakota was sent to bring 400 AMU personnel back from Ongiva for R&R. Facilities at Ongiva, where these airfield maintenance personnel worked, were particularly primitive and a night or two in the 'splendour and bright lights' of Ondangwa did wonders for their morale.

On 27 July, a source indicated that 200 terrorists were planning to cross the cut-line in small groups by 19 August. They would RV at Oshitaai before attacking Oshakati town ten kilometres to the south.

On 28 July, two Pumas were used to insert Recce teams for Operation *Salmon*.

Two Impalas carried out the last *Maanskyn* operations in the Cahama area for this moon's period.

Mirage III RZ Recce aircraft and F1CZ Mirages deployed to AFB Ondangwa, to combine with Canberras in carrying out PR missions over southern Angola. The faster Mirage IIIs would cover Virei, while the Canberras filmed the area along the Lubango–Menonque railway, Tetchamutete and Cuvelai. Mirage F1s flew escort and CAP missions in the event of MiG intervention.

On 29 July, two gunships were deployed to Ruacana to assist in the search for the body of a soldier who had gone missing while swimming in the Cunene River below the Ruacana Falls. To my knowledge the body was never found, although an extensive ground and air search was carried out for many miles down the fast-flowing river.

An additional plan for the resupply of ground forces during Operation *Llama* was made, which included air-drops from Xangongo by Kudu and from Ongiva by Dakota.

August

By 1983 the war in South West Africa and Angola had developed a predictable cyclical pattern. The rainy season gave mobility to the SWAPO insurgents. It supplied the water they required for their trek to the south and the foliage in the dense bush provided concealment from security forces. The heavy rains washed out the tracks they left making follow-up operations difficult; they also crisscrossed *shonas*, making it increasingly difficult for the trackers. Therefore, the SWAPO insurgency usually commenced in late January of every year and continued until the end of April or early May when the water started to dry up.

The onset of the dry season brought about a change in the tactical situation. SWAPO withdrew its forces to bases in Angola for the so-called 'rehearsals'—the regrouping and retraining of its members prior to the next year's incursion. With SWAPO concentrated in bases it became cost-effective for the SADF/SWATF to launch offensive operations into Angolan territory during the dry winter months. The mobility of vehicles in the torrential rains of summer was always considered a restricting factor.

For many years, up to the spring of 1983, this had been the pattern of the war. A summer incursion by SWAPO's PLAN and a semi-conventional offensive by our security forces into Angola during the winter.

The military results of these activities were overwhelmingly in the favour of the security forces, as can be deduced from the following table of operational losses:

Year	SWAPO	Security Forces
1981	1,494	61
1982	1,280	77
1983	913	96

1983: Anti-insurgency campaign

The economic and socio-political effects on South West Africa and the SADF were appreciable. To counter an insurgency requires the deployment of a large number of forces, in the ratio of about one insurgent to eight security-force personnel. The direct cost factor is therefore considerable as is the insidious effect of keeping able-bodied men out of the economic work force. An additional factor was the war weariness of the population. The war had become so predictable that it was difficult to foresee how this process of violence could be halted.

In an attempt to surprise the enemy and to alter the pattern of predictability, Operation *Askari* was planned. Bearing in mind the difficulties of mobile operations in the wet season, it was decided that *Askari* would be a semi-conventional operation using conventional arms against SWAPO, while they were still massed in their training bases before the start of their 1984 incursion campaign. The timing of the operation proper was set to commence just after the 'little rains' in mid-December 1983.

Operation *Karton*

During this planning I was ordered by Brigadier Bossie Huyser to fly to AFB Rundu forthwith and be prepared to stay for a few days. That's how it was with Huyser; everything was done on the double. On arrival with my Intelligence Officer, Johan Opperman, we were greeted by our chain-smoking commander and hustled into the briefing room. Immediately the door was closed he began his story.

Jonas Savimbi was the charismatic leader of UNITA. His battle was against Angola's governing party, the MPLA, and, like the South Africa government, he was anti-communist. His forces controlled the entire southeastern portion of Angola, preventing SWAPO from entering that region. UNITA controlled almost half of the international boundary between SWA and Angola, an area we, the SA Defence Force, would otherwise have had to defend. Therefore, it was in our interests to support UNITA in their fight.

MPLA forces had captured the town of Cangamba. The airfield close to the little town was seen by both MPLA and UNITA as being of strategic importance. With aircraft based there the Angolan Air Force would be within striking reach of Savimbi's forces in Gago Couthino. Consequently, Savimbi's forces had attacked the Angolans with the aim of driving them out of Cangamba.

At this stage, Savimbi fully realized the important role UNITA was playing in the border war and capitalized on his position. He would inform the South African government on almost all his war planning and whenever he felt it necessary was never shy to request the assistance of the SADF. He realized that all he needed was to arrange a meeting with our government and transport would be provided by the SAAF. On many occasions a Puma, from AFB Rundu, would be flown to Jamba at night to bring Savimbi to Rundu where a HS-125

Mercurius of 21 Squadron would be waiting to fly him to Pretoria or Cape Town. The next thing would be the arrival of a top-secret signal from headquarters in Pretoria detailing the assistance we were to afford UNITA.

In August 1983 the SADF supplied advisors to assist with the planning of the battle for Cangamba. Savimbi anticipated that his forces would need nine hours to capture the town. After nine days of sustained fighting the area around Cangamba had been cleared but the MPLA HQ in the town had not been taken. On his visit to South Africa Savimbi stated that if South Africa did not actively intervene, his forces would be defeated and have to withdraw. This statement was received with much reticence by the South African government. Cangamba was way out of SWAPO's and South Africa's sphere of activity. Any intervention by South Africa would be interpreted by our political antagonists as aggression against the people of Angola.

Huyser attended this meeting and listened to all the arguments for and against. When the negotiations reached stalemate Huyser jumped into the whirlpool with both feet and said, "Give authority to the SAAF for one air strike and UNITA will take Cangamba!" Silence greeted his career-jeopardizing announcement but, after consideration, the authority was given. Hence Huyser's haste and agitation to immediately get down to the job upon our arrival at Rundu.

When Operation *Karton*, the SADF's assistance to UNITA in the Cangamba battle, was originally planned, only the evacuation of casualties by helicopter and possible resupply by C-130 was envisaged. As the Cangamba battle raged on two Puma helicopter flights were needed to take in a South African Tactical HQ team, which included Commandant Mossie Basson, the MAOT. Then four Pumas loaded with much needed ammunition were sent in. Two additional Pumas flew in an air defence team armed with captured Soviet SA-7 Strela missiles and during the nights five C-130 loads of ammunition were flown in and para-dropped to the UNITA forces.

When Huyser made his bid for the air strike, the intelligence picture presented by Savimbi was that the entire area was controlled by UNITA, except for a bunker complex measuring 100 by 100 metres that was still in MPLA hands. However, when Mossie Basson arrived at the Tactical HQ he discovered that the DISA forces (the codename UNITA used at that time) had almost completely withdrawn from the area. Their intelligence picture was completely outdated and they did not know what was happening in the target area. This information could have scuppered Huyser's plans straight away. Fortunately, a captured MPLA soldier provided a complete description of the bunker complex including an accurate sketch. The air force based their plan on this intelligence.

Around the complex and joining the bunkers was an intricate trench system. The bunkers were deeply excavated and heavily fortified overhead by thick tree trunks, making them impervious to UNITA's mortar attacks. The HQ building

On the way to clear a landing zone for the C-130 resupply drop which took place the night before the air strike. Notice the richness of the foliage and the ease with which ambushes could be planned.

and another large bunker, just to the west, were obviously the main targets. However, the entrances were tiny and below ground level, making for very small targets. It was decided therefore that precision-guided AS-30 missiles, launched from Buccaneers, would be used to prise open these bunkers. The remaining bunkers were also fortified so it was decided to fuse half the heavy bombs with 0.06-second delay fuses and the remainder with contact fuses, for maximum explosive effect.

The only aircraft that could comfortably reach Cangamba carrying a full weapon load were Buccaneers and Canberras; it was decided to utilize four of each type. Between them these eight aircraft were loaded with 24 x 1,000lb and

Note the fortified bunkers and the inter-linking trench system used by the enemy in their defence of Cangamba.

36 x 500lb bombs plus eight AS-30 missiles, two on each Buccaneer.

Fortunately, there was no AAA in the target area which meant the aircraft could use low heights of release to achieve great accuracy. The attack direction was to be flown from northeast to southwest, to place the sun directly behind the attackers. The UNITA forces surrounding the target were ordered to remain two kilometres away from the bunkers if they were on the 6 o'clock and 12 o'clock direction of attack. All other forces were to close to 1,000 metres from the target complex at TOT.

The crews from 3, 12 and 24 Squadrons flew their aircraft up to AFB Grootfontein on 13 August. Huyser, Johan and I flew down to greet and brief the crews on the plan of attack, which we were to control from AFB Rundu. The TOT was selected for 08h00 on 14 August, with the attack by the AS-30 armed Buccaneers launching their missiles, aiming at the entrances to the bunkers. The four Canberras would then drop their bombs from a level profile, allowing sufficient height at release for the bombs to achieve a steep penetration angle. The Buccaneers would complete the attack by releasing their bombs in a dive towards the target. The Buccaneer formation was to be led by Major Lappies Labuschagne and Captain Riem Mouton with Commandant George Snyman (recalled off staff course for the mission) and Captain Brian Daniel as No 2. Deputy leader was Major Trevor Schroeder and Major Sandy Roy with Major Pikkie Siebrits and Captain Neil Napier as No 4. Throughout the operation Mirage F1CZ fighters would patrol, giving air cover to the strike force.

Huyser's reputation, as well as that of the SAAF, was riding on this air strike. He spent a sleepless night. Early the next morning he joined us in the command post as we monitored the progress of the aircraft from take-off until they passed

The Buccaneer crews after the strike. *Standing L to R*: Pikkie Siebrits, George Snyman, Trevor Schroeder, Brian Daniel, Lappies Labuschagne, Riem Mouton; *front*: Neil Napier, Sandy Roy.

1983: Anti-insurgency campaign

Rundu. From then onward the flight was flown in radio silence, increasing the tension among those of us waiting on the ground. I was in touch with Mossie Basson by HF radio as he viewed the target from outside the designated safety zone. By 07h55, Huyser was a bundle of nerves. He could not sit still and we could hear his heels clip-clopping as he paced up and down the linoleum-clad passageway outside the operations room.

At 08h00:05 14 August, Basson's voice came bursting through the static of the HF radio announcing the AS-30s had hit the target exactly on TOT. Huyser was so pleased and excited he began thanking me in English—at the best of times Huyser's English was entertaining, but on that particular morning his am's and are's and was's and were's would have astounded any English language student!

This air strike was one of the most effective performed by the SAAF during the war, both in execution and effect. Within a few hours Cangamba was safely in UNITA's hands. The Angolans and Cubans suffered 829 casualties and UNITA captured a further three hundred. UNITA had 63 soldiers killed. At one stage this operation was called *Amsterdam*.

The negative effect of this overwhelming UNITA victory was that the Soviets significantly stepped up the amount and sophistication of replacement weaponry, while the surrogate Cubans committed an additional 25,000 troops to the theatre

Top left: The demolished HQ building.
Top right: All that was left of a URAL-357 logistics truck after a direct hit from a Buccaneer-launched AS-30 air-to-ground guided missile.
Bottom left: A BRDM armoured car in a hull-down defensive position. The cannon in the turret was used to provide defensive fire.
Bottom right: A crater left by a 1,000lb bomb. The size can be gauged by comparison with the soldier standing inside.

The scene on the morning after the battle was reminiscent of Flanders during World War I, where even the trees had lost their leaves and the ground was pockmarked like the face of the moon.

of operations, an alarming development for our forces.

After Cangamba we returned to Oshakati where the planning for *Askari* continued in Sector 10 HQ. There was a considerable lead-in time for any major operation as authority had to be obtained at every level, up to the Cabinet and forces have to be prepared and assembled; all time-consuming activities. Meanwhile, the war continued.

On 16 August, the Fireforce at AFB Ondangwa was tasked to carry out at least one *Butterfly* operation per day within a radius of 25 kilometres of the airfield until 26 August. This was because of an intelligence report indicating SWAPO was planning to attack the base over this time period. In view of the threat a co-ordinating conference was held between the Alouette, Koevoet, Romeo Mike, Dakota gunship and Bosbok crews to ensure compatibility. The Ondangwa protection plan included six army platoons and five Koevoet teams patrolling within 20 kilometres of the airbase and town of Ondangwa. An additional six Koevoet teams were in an area north of Ondangwa.

Helicopter *Lunar* curfew enforcement operations were flown, while Bosboks carried out nightly flare drops around the base and along the power lines. All aircraft on the base were dispersed and the lights illuminating the tower

1983: Anti-insurgency campaign

and obstacles were turned off. The attack did not occur, nevertheless all these precautions had to be taken; complacency leads to disaster.

The following story was sent to me by Bart Hauptfleisch and as I feature in the story I am inserting it verbatim.

>> While doing a tour of duty as Impala Commander at AFB Ondangwa, I received a call from Colonel Dick Lord, the SAAF Commander at Sector 10 HQ in Oshakati. He asked if we had a serviceable dual-seat Impala available as he wanted to do some flying himself. As he was no longer current on type, he requested me to fly with him as instructor. The flight was arranged for the afternoon of 22 August.

At about 16h00 in the afternoon, Colonel Lord arrived and said that he wanted to do some aerobatics and then wanted to fly to Ongiva where we would land for him to attend a meeting. He first wanted to do the aerobatics at altitude and thereafter wanted to do the sequence at low level over Oshakati. As I knew his ability and had flown with him on a number of occasions, I had no problem with what he wanted to do.

We took off at 16h45, climbed to altitude and, after completing all the safety checks, he started with his aerobatics. I was sitting in the back observing all his manoeuvres. He was an old hand at this, thus there were no problems. After a few minutes he said he was ready for nearby Oshakati at a lower level. He proceeded with the same sequence as previously and all went well.

After about 20 minutes we set heading for Ongiva, situated about 50 miles into Angola north of Ondangwa. Although it was in a country where we were involved in a war, it was in an area controlled by the SADF and was thus fairly safe.

The flight at low level to Ongiva took about 15 minutes. En route Colonel Lord told me that the damaged airfield at Ongiva had been repaired by personnel from 400 Airfield Maintenance Unit and he wanted to give them an air show for a job well done. At Ongiva he performed the same sequence he had practised previously. I was sitting in the back cockpit thinking to myself, "Here I am doing aerobatics over an enemy airfield. How strange!" All went well. He then told me we were going to land as he had to attend the function for the airfield maintenance personnel.

After landing we taxiied to the parking area where a number of people were waiting. As we got closer, he cut the engine and let the aircraft roll gently forward through a ribbon of toilet paper held by two people to officially declare the airfield open. When we opened the canopy we were each given a glass of champagne to celebrate the occasion. It was about 17h30 and the sun was setting. It was obvious to me that there was no way we would be leaving before it was dark, so I stayed to check all the aircraft lights etc., ready for the return journey.

Darkness comes quickly in the tropics and it was evident from the cheering of people somewhere in the bushes that the South Africans were having a good party. [Bart does not mention that Bossie Huyser had flown up in a Dakota from Ondangwa arranged by Colonel Bertus Burger. Apart from the personnel the aircraft was loaded with all the necessities for the party. With Huyser, every party was a good party.] While waiting at the aircraft I made arrangements with the drivers of two Land Rovers to use the lights from their headlights to assist us during take-off from this unlit airfield.

It was past 21h00 when Colonel Lord returned to the aircraft while the party quite clearly was still in full swing. Colonel Lord was now the passenger in the back seat. The Impala started on internal power and we set up for take-off with only the vehicle lights for guidance. The asphalt runway had no white lines or distance markers, thus requiring us to taxi at snail's pace to the beginning of the runway, aiming at the middle of the two vehicle lights in the distance. This was certainly my first experience flying a jet aircraft under these conditions.

The next day we were informed by the Intelligence Officer that they had intercepted messages from SWAPO and the MPLA that "the mad South Africans were very noisy at a party in Ongiva". There were rumours afterwards that Chief of the Air Force, General Jan van Loggerenberg, had phoned the OC Western Air Command, Brigadier Bossie Huyser, and told him that "he (Huyser) had made a lot of decisions in his career, but the decision concerning the party at Ongiva was probably the worst he had ever made. <<

On 26 August, Commandant Daan Nel presented the 53 Battalion plan for Operation *Oubaas*. His objective was to destroy the SWAPO Charlie Detachment internally in central Owamboland between 31 August and 16 September. He would be in command of 53 Battalion troops, five troops of armoured cars, four Romeo Mike and six Koevoet Zulu teams and a Fireforce from AFB Ondangwa consisting of two gunships, two Pumas, a Bosbok and a MAOT.

On 31 August, planning was carried out for Operation *Banier*. This was the insertion of two two-man reconnaissance teams into Angola, close to the Namibe–Lubango railway line. The operation would be run from a tactical HQ set up at Epupa Falls and the teams inserted at last light on 19 September. They would stay in Angola until 5 November, unless compromised, and would need to be resupplied after the first four weeks.

September

On 2 September, Colonel Wouter Lombard was assigned as commander of Operation *Javelin*. He was tasked to find and attack the SWAPO camp in the Sopia Sopia area, northeast of Cahama. In air force circles this camp had become known as Joe's camp as Impala pilot Joe van der Berg had spotted it while flying over the area at low level and high speed. Ground reconnaissance would be carried out by 52 Recce Commando and when the SWAPO camp was located troops, allocated for Operation *Llama*, would attack it.

The guidelines given for the operation were that the target had to be confirmed by air photography and ground recce. A first-light attack, preceded by an air strike was planned, with the Pumas placing stopper groups and then bringing in reserves. A mini-HAG would be necessary to allow re-arming and refuelling of the helicopters.

1,250 graduates of the SA Army Infantry School, under command of Colonel Preston-Thomas, were moved into the Dova, Nehone, Mupa and Chiede areas of Angola for Operation *Sefta*. This was a high-density area-sweep lasting from 4 September to 25 September. The MAOT attached for the duration was Commandant Daantjie Schabort. The aim of the operation was to prevent SWAPO from being able to assemble and carry out any activities. These troops would be resupplied by air-drops from Dakota aircraft. Koevoet was tasked to provide a maximum number of Zulu teams internally over the same period. The air force would perform night-flying operations with particular emphasis on patrolling the electrical power lines.

On 6 September, it was learned from interrogation of SWAPO captives that SWAPO cadres were being taught that if they were being pursued by ground teams supported by gunships, their escape tactic was to run back at 45° to the Alouette's line of advance, hopefully avoiding the follow-up ground forces and simultaneously moving out of the gunship's search pattern. This information was passed on to the operators.

On 7 September, the initial operation's directive was given for a proposed infiltration by reconnaissance troops to search the Lubango area of Angola to pinpoint the Tobias Hanyeko Training Camp (THTC). This large training facility, under the shelter of the Angolan defensive umbrella, was responsible for training the terrorists who infiltrated SWA every year. Once located the camp would be attacked by an air strike. The following programme of presentation of plans was laid out:

- 16 September   Operations and air plans
- 23 September   All support plans (logistic, personnel, communications, search and rescue etc.)
- 28 September   Complete presentation to GOC SWA/OC WAC

The result of this directive was Operation *Klinker*, also known as *Rondebosch*, and the air strike occurred on 29 December 1983.

On 8 September, it was decided, because 'Puff the Magic Dragon' had been so successful, to request a second aircraft be converted to the same configuration and allocated to AFB Ondangwa. It was thought two aircraft could dominate Owamboland by enforcing the curfew at night and by so doing save approximately 800 Alouette hours per year.

At the morning order group it was revealed from intelligence that this year's SWAPO infiltration had concentrated on bringing in weapons and ammunition to store in caches for future use. Vehicles had been used from Angola to transport the heavy equipment as far south as they dared. As a direct consequence of this report Impalas were tasked to extend the northern limit of their armed reconnaissance flights to 150 kilometres north of the cut-line and attack any military vehicles they found. The decision by Angola to become a host nation for SWAPO had severe repercussions on the population and infrastructure, particularly in the south of this devastated country.

As the caches were said to contain many SA-7 systems, precautions were taken to prevent a launching in the vicinity of the airfields at Grootfontein and J. G. Strydom Airport.

The intelligence analysis gave Cahama, Oncocua, Mulondo, Cuvelai and Caiundo as the key points through which all SWAPO incursions took place. The point was also made that, because no actions had been taken against them by the security forces, there was no reason to change the routes between their HQ in Lubango and those key points. This analysis sowed the seed which resulted in Operation *Askari* at the end of the year.

On 13 September, the aptly named Operation *Nightingale* took place. Onanjokwe hospital, a traditional SWAPO hotbed, was sealed off at 07h45 and the entire hospital was sifted for SWAPO presence. 53 Battalion troops and two armoured car troops moved into position by road, assisted by four Pumas from AFB Ondangwa, each air-landing a stick of paratroopers. Four gunships and a Bosbok were used to control the surrounding area while medical personnel, interpreters and 'eyes' were used to screen all the people found in the complex. 'Eyes' were captured SWAPO terrorists who were prepared to identify their former comrades providing their own identities were kept secret. To achieve this they were covered in cloth sacks with just a slit at eye level to enable them to carry out identifications, hence the nickname. Their presence had an enormous psychological effect on the terrorists, so much so that many of them gave themselves up before being identified.

On 19 September, Major Corrie Meerholz presented the plan for Operation

Aconite. This was to be an offensive reconnaissance of the Mulondo area, from 21 September until 10 October. A HAG was to be set up at Sequideva, using the call sign 'Sun City', where ten drums of avtur would be placed. Ambushes would be set up at night and enemy vehicle movements recorded during the day. Impalas would be on CAS standby for the entire period and were given the appropriate call sign 'Cavalry'.

Aconite was a very successful operation. The information regarding vehicle movements proved invaluable for the planning of *Askari*. In addition, an overnight stop for vehicles resupplying Mulondo from the north was discovered. It was on the western banks of the Cunene River, north of Mulondo, and therefore fairly safe for the Recces to approach from the east until they had the stop in sight.

I flew into the HAG situated in the bush near Sequediva and, together with Major Meerholz, made a joint plan for a night air strike by Impalas. I only had three night-qualified pilots available and all three were tasked to carry out the strike. The plan was a good one calling for the Impalas to be over their chosen IP, a distinctive bend in the river, exactly at the chosen TOT. On their radio call the Recces were to fire mortars to mark the target and then it would be attacked by all three aircraft. As the last aircraft called clear of the target the mortar bombardment would be continued until it was judged prudent for the small Recce team to withdraw. It worked exactly as planned.

While at Sequediva, I was interested to meet a senior NCO on the Recce team whose name was Jock Hutton. He had dropped with the British forces into Arnhem in 1944 and here he was still going strong almost 40 years later.

On the night of 26 September, a *Cuca* blitz was carried out on a shop just north of Ondangwa. Information had been received that a Blue Ford bakkie standing outside belonged to SWAPO sympathizers. The blitz produced no results, which is hardly surprising when one realizes at that time there were close to 7,000 *cuca* shops in Owamboland and in 1983 blue Ford bakkies were two a penny. Lack of positive results was always disappointing, but in truth it served to keep the security forces sharp and the enemy on the hop.

The same night *Lunar* operations were varied. The motor-cycle reaction force was utilized to apprehend curfew-breaking vehicles. It was worth a try but suffered the same problem as vehicle-mounted troops. The reaction forces had to be prepositioned in the area selected for the night's flying. Unfortunately one could never predict where curfew breakers would appear and Murphy's Law ensured that invariably the ground forces were too far away to make a quick arrest.

On 27 September, SWATF HQ published a statement repudiating the allegations made by religious leaders in Cape Town on 23 September, and by Terry Waite, the Archbishop of Canterbury's special adviser, who had accused the security forces of atrocities. As far as I am aware he was never up on the border and I suspect, like most propaganda, the allegations were based on unsubstantiated claims. Having been personally involved with the war for a considerable time I can vouch for the accuracy of the SWATF repudiation when it stated that "since 1979, SWAPO mines had killed 303 civilians (mostly Owambos) and wounded or maimed a further 513. In addition, SWAPO terrorists had murdered 366 people and abducted 1,341 civilians in the same period".

In a prolonged conflict it is difficult to persuade people by statements—they believe what they want to believe.

On 3 November, General Charles Lloyd, GOC SWA, visited Oshivello. Having a surname similar in pronunciation to that of the GOC opened many doors for me during 1983, particularly when requesting a favour or assistance over the old-fashioned 'slinger' (crank) telephones in use in the defence force. People on the other end thought Lord sounded like Lloyd and it was a case of 'Yes sir, no sir, three bags full, sir!'

On 14 November, we requested the large identification numbers on the roof of Owambo schools be repainted and updated. In the featureless expanse of Owambo these numbers greatly assisted aircrews in determining their position and giving follow-up instructions to ground forces during hot pursuits.

On 20 November, the large ground-reconnaissance programme planned for *Askari* began, with two Pumas flying from Xangongo on Operation *Ringkals*. They inserted a Recce team at a spot 35 kilometres west of Chibembe with their tactical HQ established at Xangongo the previous day. With these Recce teams deployed so far north the Impalas were put on standby to help in any form of emergency and remained on standby until mid-December.

On 25 November, 'Gharra', the codename for the remotely piloted vehicle (RPV), was deployed at Xangongo under the MAOT Major Jinx Botes. This deployment was aimed at monitoring the Cahama area for Operation *Fox*. This sub-operation of *Askari* was designed to detect, locate and then capture one of the SA-8 missile systems known to be deployed in that vicinity.

Commencement of Operation *Askari*

From its inception it was a joint plan. The overall aim of the operation was "to prevent a SWAPO Special Forces incursion to the south". The operation had to begin in November 1983 and the SAAF would support the ground troops. Among the general guidelines were the following:

- the enemy *must* be stopped externally
- deep reconnaissance, coupled with offensive actions, *must* be commenced at an early stage
- maximum use of mobile elements for follow-ups *must* be made
- security forces *must* operate proactively, not reactively
- security forces *must* maintain the initiative
- an infiltration into SWA during 1984 simply *must* not take place; not even ten terrorists *must* successfully infiltrate

The SAAF aims for *Askari* were as follows:

- to gain and maintain a favourable air situation over Cahama–Mulondo–Cuvelai
- to prevent the expansion of enemy air defence capabilities in the Mulondo–Quiteve–Cuvelai areas
- to expand the SAAF interdiction programme up to Chibemba, north of Mulondo and up to Cassinga
- extend *Maanskyn* north of the 150km line
- preference to be given to joint attacks on SWAPO targets

The plan was divided into four phases:

- Phase 1: Deep reconnaissance by Special Forces, followed by a SAAF attack on the Typhoon–Volcano base close to Lubango, between 1 November and 30 December 1983
- Phase 2: Offensive reconnaissance and isolation of Cahama, Mulondo and Cuvelai, from 16 November to mid-January 1984—the aim being to cut enemy communication and logistic lines in the deep area, and to terrorize and demoralize SWAPO to such an extent that they would withdraw northwards
- Phase 3: By the beginning of February 1984, to establish a dominated area from west of the Cunene River, through Quiteve, Mupa, Vinticette, and eastwards through Ionde
- Phase 4: The final stopping of the incursion, internally if necessary

Askari plan approval

The joint army–air force plan was presented to GOC SWA and OC WAC and approved without major alterations. It was then presented at Army HQ in Pretoria to the Chief of the Defence Force. At this presentation the army plan was accepted in toto. The air plan however, was only accepted after much discussion and much alteration. The reasons for these alterations were not given. I personally believe that a personality clash between OC WAC and C SADF had much to do with it. Limits and restrictions were placed on the employment of aircraft so they no longer coincided with the limits of action of the ground forces. In addition, the planned deception air strike on Caiundo was removed from the plan altogether.

After all the alterations and discussions *Askari* was approved, much to the relief of everyone present. At that stage everybody was glad to come away with the authority to proceed. I did not realize it at the time, neither did the 12 generals and one admiral who attended the briefing, that our initial joint plan was now no longer a balanced one. We should have gone 'back to the drawing board', re-hashed the situation and come up with a revised plan. This was a vital lesson.

Askari reconnaissance activities: phases 1 and 2

While I do not intend to go into detail regarding the involvement of the Recces there are a few points which need to be brought up. It must be stated from the outset that *Askari* called for the largest Recce effort of the war. A total of five teams, of varying size, were involved. They were deployed west of Cahama, east of Cahama, in the vicinity of Mulondo, in the outskirts of Cuvelai and were also tasked to reconnoitre the Lubango area.

These teams provided the tactical intelligence on which the battle plans were made and in general they performed a difficult and hazardous task well. However, the command and control of these teams was a bit of a problem from an air force point of view. Each team operated as a separate entity and established its own tactical HQ at Xangongo—in a different location. The air force had provided a MAOT to be co-located with the Army HQ at Xangongo but the air support promised to each of the Recce teams was disjointed. The problem which could have arisen was one of priorities. If all the teams were in trouble who would decide on the priority of air support? The answer was a joint HQ with a representative present from each involved party.

Askari offensive actions: Phase 2

Cahama
Throughout the duration of the war Cahama had remained a tough nut to crack. FAPLA's 2nd Brigade had ensconced themselves in fortified positions in the environs of the little town, to the north and south of the Caculuvar River. Numerous forays and probes by our ground forces during the preceding years had been undertaken against Cahama's perimeters. The air force had attacked radar and AAA sites in the area on many occasions. However, we had never concentrated our effort into taking Cahama. If it had ever been our aim we

1983: Anti-insurgency campaign

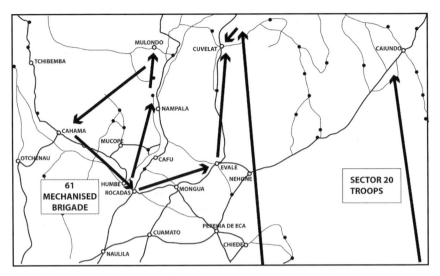

This map traces the routes taken by our ground forces during *Askari*. Note the epic journey of 61 Mech from Cahama to Cuvelai. The Sector 20 troops were surprised by FAPLA forces which resulted in the unplanned bombardment of Caiundo.

would have succeeded.

Interestingly, FAPLA's analysis of these ongoing assaults was that they had always succeeded in chasing the 'Boere' away. Therefore, they were confident of their ability to hold Cahama and, contrary to our own widely disseminated intelligence assessment of their troops in the town, their morale was in fact high.

61 Mechanized Battalion and attached artillery were tasked to pressurize FAPLA's 2nd Brigade, by probes, feints and artillery bombardments. Offensive Recce teams would cut FAPLA's logistic lines between Cahama and Chibemba while the air force carried out strikes against identified targets within the perimeter of the town. The combined result of these actions was to demoralize and terrorize the FAPLA and SWAPO forces to such an extent they would either withdraw, or desert, from Cahama. It was envisaged this *uitmergeling* (squeezing dry) would take place between 16 November 1983 and mid-January 1984. Time was required to allow the desired effects to play their part.

In the event, this was naïve planning in the extreme. Between mid-November and mid-December the Recce forces were indeed active but a brigade garrison, which in their view had successfully beaten off the 'Boere' repeatedly, would not be disturbed by the activities of two small Recce teams. The real offensive pressure started around 16 December with the advance of 61 Mechanized Battalion from the Quiteve area. The defenders in Cahama must have detected this approach and coupled with the continual round-the-clock bombardments, must have had a detrimental effect on them. By the end of December the morale of the Angolan 2nd Brigade was still reasonable but, had the time limit of mid-

303

January been open-ended, then the plan might have been successful.

It was known that SA-8 batteries were positioned about two kilometres southwest of the town, close to the road to Ediva. A sub-operation within *Askari* was Operation *Fox*. This called for a combined programme of air and ground bombardment to be undertaken in such a pattern so that the mobile SA-8 batteries would be forced to change their positions by moving to the south. The idea was to drive them out of the protective ring surrounding Cahama into the vicinity of FAPLA's AAA defensive sites, in the area of Ediva. Once in this area a concerted effort would be made by ground forces (both infantry and recce) to attempt the capture of an SA-8 system. This section of the overall *Askari* plan was given top priority because it was the first time an SA-8 system had been deployed outside of the Soviet Union and would thus be of great intelligence value to us.

This plan was well on the way to succeeding. The SA-8 batteries had been forced to move their position twice, both times towards Ediva, as predicted. However, by the end of December the clamouring in the world media to censure South Africa because of her military presence in Angola had reached a crescendo. Then, a political decision was made to cease all activities on the Cahama front by 31 December 1983.

All forces were withdrawn. FAPLA obviously breathed a sigh of relief and the status quo around Cahama returned to normal. Once again the 2nd Brigade assessed the situation as having beaten off a determined assault by the 'Boere'.

Mulondo

The aim here was to:

- isolate and de-motivate FAPLA in both Quiteve and Mulondo to the extent their troops would withdraw or desert
- monitor the route Matala–Mulondo–Quiteve, to determine if SWAPO was using it as an infiltration route

The time period for this sub-operation was 16 November 1983 to 15 January 1984. The ground forces used were the same utilized to take Cuvelai. The air force would carry out speculative bombing against selected targets in and around Mulondo to heighten the tension prior to the final assault by ground forces.

On their advance towards Cahama 61 Mechanized captured Quiteve almost without firing a shot. This phase was so successful it was decided to detach a small fighting group with artillery support northwards on the western bank of the Cunene River to begin the process of isolating Mulondo.

As a result of the high state of alert throughout Angola FAPLA's 19th Brigade in Mulondo had sent out their own recce teams to protect their front. These troops performed an excellent task for FAPLA in that they pinpointed the position of our fighting team. They never used this intelligence to come out offensively against

1983: Anti-insurgency campaign

our forces but, whenever we moved our artillery into range they proceeded to bombard our positions with their D30 cannons. These guns outranged our artillery by three to four kilometres which resulted in our forces, after firing just a few salvos, having to undertake a quick withdrawal.

This diversion from the original *Askari* plan had repercussions on the air plan. Support had to be flown for the ground forces in that area, thus utilizing aircraft hours and weapons set aside for the Cahama and Cuvelai battles. It had a further tactical disadvantage in that the element of surprise we had hoped to gain from our attack on Cahama was lost. After our Mulondo strikes the entire air defence system of southern Angola was placed on the highest state of alert.

On 23 December 1983, during these support missions two Impala jets attacked targets in the Mulondo area, using 68mm rockets. The weather was atrocious with large cumulo-nimbus clouds. After the fourth attack in the area the wingman's aircraft was hit in the tail by a shoulder-launched SAM missile. Fortunately the pilot managed to land safely back at Ondangwa.

The preamble to the plan to force FAPLA to leave Mulondo was unsuccessful.

Lieutenant Neels Meintjies looking at the jet-pipe of his Impala which had been damaged by one the SAM missiles launched out of Mulondo.

Political considerations in early January 1984 were such that the SADF did not continue with the *Askari* plan for Mulondo. In the eyes of FAPLA's 19th Brigade they too had succeeded in beating off a determined assault by the 'Boere'.

Caiundo

This small stronghold on the eastern bank of the Cubango River was never a part of the original *Askari* army plan. The *Askari* air plan, however, had included a first strike on the FAPLA HQ unit as part of the overall deception plan. The idea was to focus attention in that region while *Askari* proper was undertaken much farther westwards. This request was one of the elements of the air plan that was not approved. Therefore, no operational or logistical planning was carried out for operations in this eastern sector.

Offensive actions of *Askari* commenced around 16 December. Both air and ground forces were engaged in the Quiteve–Mulondo–Cahama areas. Imagine my surprise shortly thereafter when I was casually informed there was an SADF group deployed within 20 kilometres of Caiundo on the western bank. When I inquired about their presence I was told they had been ordered to act as a deception force in that area and were from Sector 20, who otherwise would not have been utilized in Operation *Askari*.

This was never part of the joint plan and as such had a detrimental effect on the outcome of the operation. To everyone's surprise and consternation this force was attacked on the night of 19/20 December. FAPLA recces had discovered one of our force's platoons deployed outside the main defensive perimeter and was much closer to Caiundo than it should have been. During the night FAPLA sent a company to attack them, which they did successfully, killing five and capturing one SWATF soldier, capturing 13 light machine guns, three rifles, three radios, a 60mm mortar and a Unimog vehicle.

This setback resulted in a switch of air activities from the Cahama and Mulondo fronts to the unplanned-for Caiundo area, which continued uninterrupted for the remainder of *Askari*. There was a substantial reduction of air effort over the planned key points which reduced pressure on the enemy and allowed FAPLA to remain in control of their troops in both Cahama and Mulondo.

In spite of a large air effort over a period of 21 days Caiundo was not taken. Despite a heavy air bombardment and a determined ground assault the FAPLA minefields and bunkers remained intact. FAPLA's 53rd Brigade had reason to celebrate their successful defence of Caiundo.

Cuvelai

Phase 2 of the original army operational plan called for the isolation of Cuvelai to take place between 16 November 1983 and 15 January 1984. The threefold aim to:
- isolate, grind down (*uitmergel*) and terrorize Cuvelai to the extent that FAPLA

1983: Anti-insurgency campaign

would either leave of their own accord or their soldiers would desert on a large scale carry out operations against SWAPO elements such as Moscow, Alpha and Bravo battalions in the Cuvelai area
- give early warning of a SWAPO incursion

The air force plan called for:

- extensive photo-reconnaissance of Cuvelai
- speculative bombing both day and night of SWAPO targets in the vicinity
- air attacks on AAA sites that had a direct bearing on ground force operations

In mid-December PR flights obtained up-to-date photography of all AAA sites in Cuvelai. It must be noted that in the history of our activities in Angola PR flights were always understood by the enemy to be the precursor of an attack. Round one of the psychological battle had been won.

At 14h05 on 27 December, two Impalas dropped ten 120kg bombs on a SWAPO

Despite the war, Father Christmas arrived on Christmas Day by Alouette helicopter to distribute his presents. The children enjoyed rides around AFB Ondangwa sitting on a train of bomb-trolleys.

target in the area. At 16h25, four Canberras dropped 600 Alpha bombs, two 460kg bombs and 16 x 250kg bombs on military targets in and around the town.

The following day at 13h35, two Impalas carried out a further recce of the AAA sites in Cuvelai. At 14h39, Canberras carried out attacks on targets close to the

Cuvelai airstrip dropping two 460kg and 17 x 250kg bombs and a further 300 Alpha bombs, obtaining 90 per cent coverage of the target area. At 16h10, eight Impalas dropped 32 x 250kg bombs on various targets in and around the town.

All these flights were undertaken with the aim of achieving results against the enemy's AAA defences, as well as obtaining the psychological advantage while attempting to *uitmergel* FAPLA.

At 09h20 on 29 December, four Buccaneers attacked the THTC base just outside Lubango. This SWAPO training centre had over the years been responsible for training of SWAPO recruits. From this HQ they were posted directly to various front headquarters. The aim of the air strike was to demoralize the recruits before they had even left the safety of their training base. Thirty-two 460kg bombs were dropped into the target area. Approximately half of the bombs exploded on impact, the others were fitted with delay fuses from one to 36 hours, rendering the centre uninhabitable. The air strike was 'on time, on target' and suffered no losses.

Chapter 10

1984: Uneasy peace

Askari continues

The army sent a battle group, consisting mainly of Citizen Force troops, to engage the SWAPO HQ and logistic base five kilometres northeast of Cuvelai. This group was attacked in turn by the FAPLA 11th Brigade and was in real danger of being cut off. It was then decided to re-assign 61 Mechanized Battalion who were then on the outskirts of Cahama, to assist the endangered battle group. In a little over 16 hours 61 Mech moved, under battle conditions, from the Cahama area across the temporary bridge over the Cunene River to the outskirts of Cuvelai. This forced march was itself an epic of determination and perseverance, especially as they had to go straight into battle at Cuvelai when they arrived.

On the afternoon of 3 January, the actual assault on Cuvelai took place. It commenced with a co-ordinated air attack aimed at all the known AAA and artillery sites. Each pilot was equipped with up-to-date enlarged photographs of his particular target. Ten Impalas led the raid, followed by four Canberras. Between them they dropped 60 x 120kg, 18 x 250kg, two 460kg and 600 Alpha bombs. A second wave of Impalas dropped a further 32 x 250kg bombs. This air strike, together with the Cangamba attack, ranks as arguably the two most successful air strikes flown by the SAAF throughout the history of the war.

On completion of the air attack a desperate radio message from the Angolan commander in Cuvelai was intercepted, wherein he pleaded with his Lubango HQ to send help. The gist of his message was "Seventy-five per cent of my artillery has been taken out by the South African Air Force". However, the undoubted success was not without cost.

The Impala strike formation leader was Captain Joe van den Berg, the senior Impala pilot at Ondangwa. His target had been the Firecan radar-guided 57mm

AAA site, just east of Cuvelai. During the pull-out, after bomb release, missile firings were observed and evasive manoeuvres flown. One of the missiles, later identified as a SA-9, struck van den Berg's aircraft in the tail section completely removing the starboard tailplane and elevator.

His aircraft entered the incipient stage of a spin directly above the target he had just attacked. Displaying superb flying skills he recovered to a normal flying attitude and discovered that by reducing speed below 150 knots, the induced roll to starboard could be controlled. Van den Berg also found he ran out of elevator control if his speed decayed below 130 knots. Having established he was able to fly his aircraft within this narrow speed band he set heading for Ondangwa, his home base.

Following the excitement of the previous traumatic seconds he had time to reappraise his predicament. To his consternation he discovered that in the configuration he was forced to fly he could not maintain height and his rate of descent was close to 2,000 feet per minute. Reaching Ondangwa was out of the question and he was diverted to land at Ongiva. This airfield had recently been repaired and resurfaced by the SAAF's 400 AMU for exactly this kind of emergency.

Whenever cross-border operations were taking place a SAR contingency plan was activated. In this case two Puma helicopters were on standby at Xangongo, which had been in South African hands for some time. Because of SWAPO activities a further two Pumas, identically manned, were on standby for emergencies within Owamboland.

The AFCP at Oshakati had initiated the *Askari* plan and was monitoring in real time all the air activities. At the first call concerning Captain van den Berg's emergency both sets of Pumas were alerted and ordered to take off immediately. The Air Defence Controller was asked to work out an interception vector for the Xangongo Pumas to fly to intercept the damaged Impala returning from Cuvelai. The Ondangwa Pumas were directed to proceed to Ongiva to be available, if required, for the emergency around the airfield.

Just after it had been ascertained that with the given rate of descent the Impala would not even reach Ongiva, physical science began to exert its effect. As the aircraft lost height the air closer to the ground became progressively denser. This thicker air allowed the engine to produce more thrust and also improved the aerodynamic qualities of the wing, giving more lift. Therefore, the Impala's rate of descent decreased from 2,000 feet per minute to 1,500, 1,000, 800, 700 and eventually 400 feet per minute. The shallower angle of descent allowed van den Berg to stretch the glide and, with very little height to spare, sneak over the threshold at Ongiva to perform an excellent touch-down.

All the attacking aircraft had been on the same radio frequency. Consequently, the other pilots heard the radio chatter and missile calls and were aware their

1984: Uneasy peace

leader had taken a hit. In the CP at Oshakati attention was focused on the emergency situation which had developed during the 20 minutes prior to the successful emergency landing. Subsequently it was discovered, despite the unexpected SAM threat every pilot had continued with the strike as planned. During recovery from the attacks a voice could be detected giving assistance to the pairs of Impalas returning to base. The voice was that of Joe van den Berg who, despite his own serious problems, still found time to look after the remainder of his formation.

It was a superb achievement with many people displayed a great deal of airmanship, culminating in a wonderful exhibition of flying and leadership by Captain van den Berg. It also demonstrates the effectiveness of a well-prepared SAR plan that, had it been required, could have handled any situation which might have evolved. Fortunately, on this occasion a SAR was not required.

The SAAF played a further important role while supporting the ground forces as they attacked the town after the air strike. The army was faced with two major problems—navigation through minefields and the destruction of the last remaining resistance. Our ground troops approaching Cuvelai from the south came under heavy enemy fire. With complete disregard for his own safety and air force flying regulations, Captain Carl Alberts, flying an Alouette, descended into the heavy fire to mark the enemy gun positions for the ground forces to destroy. At one point he evaded four RPG rockets simultaneously. His actions led to the fall of Cuvelai and he was most deservedly awarded the coveted Honoris Crux.

After being bogged down and losing a Ratel APC in the minefields ground forces entered Cuvelai to find the enemy, both SWAPO and FAPLA, had fled. In fact 32 Battalion, who had troops in the Tetchamutete area north of Cuvelai, used them as stoppers to capture a large number of FAPLA who were fleeing north.

The battle for Cuvelai was a success. A large amount of war matériel was captured. The reason for the success was that for once, during the four major battles that comprised *Askari*, air power was utilized correctly followed by a determined assault by ground forces. The aim was maintained and the concentration of forces, using a joint plan, overcame the enemy. Measured against the principles of war this sub-operation was bound to succeed.

Captain Charlie Wroth, ex-Buccaneer navigator, was appointed as MAOT for 61 Mechanized Battalion during *Askari*. I am including his story of that operation because it gives a different insight into the war—the emphasis changes from the air to the ground. While aircrew are subjected to similar dangers their environment keeps them remote from close range combat, experienced by those on the ground.

>>On a Friday afternoon, early in November 1983, Spof Fee, Russell Espley-

From Fledgling to Eagle

Jones and I landed our C-130 at AFB Waterkloof and made our way to the officers' club for drinks. Here we discovered that one of us was required for a two-month ground tour on the border. Being the youngest I was 'volunteered'. I flew out on Sunday morning to AFB Grootfontein where I learned I was to be the MAOT with 61 Mechanized Battalion, during Operation *Askari*.

At AFB Grootfontein I was issued with a specially equipped command Ratel, an armoured fighting vehicle nicknamed 'Asterix'. My team consisted of my army driver, 'Herman van Fochville', Citizen Force Corporal Paul from Stellenbosch University and a flight sergeant radio operator ex-Rhodesian Air Force. The command vehicle used by the SAAF differed from the Ratels used by the army in two ways— 1) the SAAF vehicle had no armament and 2) the rear section of

SAAF MAOT Charlie Wroth (with beard) and his team, Zulu 41, with 'Asterix', their command Ratel.

the SAAF Ratel was filled with mattresses.

After crossing the cut-line at Oshikango 61 Mech headed towards Ongiva. En route the army commander exercised his unit by shouting the word 'Visgraat' over the radio. This term was used when enemy MiGs were in the vicinity to rapidly disperse the armoured column. Vehicles turn off the road, alternatively left and right, to park under the cover of the nearest suitable tree. The Afrikaans word translates to 'herring-bone' in English and is very appropriate. The reaction appeared chaotic but it worked. Within seconds the 100-vehicle convoy had disappeared. However, getting the column reorganized turned out to be quite a mission.

We continued north from Ongiva towards Mupa, our first target. The attack was led by Ratel 90s, supported by mortar fire and accompanied by a psychological warfare loudspeaker belting out the theme tune from the film *The*

Green Berets. The town was taken in a surreal atmosphere; my first impression was it was something out of the *Kelly's Heroes* movie. Normality returned when two Alouettes rendezvoused with the battle group, piloted by Carl Alberts and Mike Fagin. Sleeping out under Angolan stars was a new experience for the SAAF. Everyone had to dig their own slit-trench to sleep in. Once again the difference between the browns and the blues was obvious. Each SAAF trench had a mattress in it.

The battalion stopped in Xangongo to regroup, giving me the opportunity to see the damage caused to buildings during Operation *Protea*—the target of AS-30 missiles fired from my Buccaneer. Operating off the Xangongo airstrip were two SAAF Pumas, two Alouettes, a Bosbok and a team flying the RPV.

In Xangongo I met a group of soldiers who had found the wreckage of the SAAF Canberra shot down on 14 March 1979. They had organized the digging of a deep trench and had buried the remains of the aircraft. I was touched by this deed as Second Lieutenant Owen Doyle, who was killed in the crash, had been my roommate in the SAAF and we had attended Grey College in Port Elizabeth together.

Crossing the badly damaged Cunene River bridge was like riding on a switchback.

From Xangongo we moved west on our mission to capture a Soviet SAM-8 missile system, near Ediva. At this stage, Major Dudley Wall was allocated to my vehicle. I was never quite sure of his mission, nevertheless we became good friends. After approximately three days we launched an attack near Ediva but were met by Soviet T-54 tanks and BRDM armoured cars, well supported by their mortars. A number of our Ratels had wheels knocked out and a Unimog took a mortar in the back. Casualties were suffered and the attack was called off. While recovering injured soldiers from damaged vehicles the medics took serious shrapnel wounds in their backs and were later decorated for bravery under fire. Light was starting to fade but I called in a Puma to casevac the injured. Escorted by two Ratel 60s, I set up an LZ in a disused quarry. Light was fading fast and the Puma called for 'white phos' (phosphorus grenades) so they could locate the LZ as they were looking straight into the setting sun. With great caution I pulled the pin from the grenade and threw it further than I have ever thrown a cricket ball. Captain Steel Upton landed the Puma and the medics, after stabilizing one of the seriously wounded soldiers, loaded the rest of the injured and the helicopter took off for Ondangwa. Sadly, we learned that the soldier passed away during the flight.

61 Mech then repositioned northeast of Cahama and spent a week in the bush moving between Cahama and Chibemba. [One of the principles of war is that of manoeuvre; this is what 61 Mech was busy with. No commander enjoys having his enemy moving around his flank or manoeuvring in his rear.] On either Christmas Day or the day after, one of our Ratel 90s detonated a triple landmine. The blast split the vehicle's shell and the blast burned the men inside from the

Puma helicopters lifting off from an LZ.

top down. However, although they were all as black as hell, they were casevaced out and survived. The casevac helicopter brought in General Constand Viljoen for a quick flying visit even though we were 350 kilometres inside Angola.

The next day we set up an ambush on the road between Lubango and Cahama. A military Mercedes truck drove into the ambush and was badly shot up. Everyone on board was killed except for an Irish nurse. I was asked to fly her out but due to the late time of day this was not possible. She spent the night with a Special Forces unit. The next day when I briefed her about the helicopter boarding drills, she said there was no need because she already knew the drill—the SADF had ambushed her vehicle exactly a year before.

The ambush was reset and an Angolan reconnaissance team investigating the still-smouldering vehicle entered the killing zone. There was a lot of whispering on the radios trying to confirm it was not our own troops when suddenly all hell broke loose. "*Gat toe, gat toe*" was yelled as we all dived into our slit-trenches, even the SAAF personnel [*gat* is Afrikaans for hole i.e. slit-trench]. Two RPGs were fired in our direction, one exploding against a tree right behind us and the other self-destructing a bit further away. My deafness lasted quite a few days. Once again our troops had the upper hand and destroyed the recce team. The Angolan team leader was buried in a shallow grave next to my Ratel.

At midnight on Christmas Day the Canberras bombed Cahama. To ease their night-bombing problem we fired white phos shells in a line leading to their target. [*Author's comment*: I had planned the Canberra strike from the command post in Oshakati. The Canberras dropped Alpha bombs from level flight, 24,000 feet AGL. Accuracy was not required. We needed a random spread to force

'Asterix' hidden under a tree with camouflage netting making it extremely difficult to see from the air.

the SA-8 batteries to move southward from Cahama towards Ediva where our ground forces were preparing to snatch one. The Canberras attacked from long line astern with the leader's TOT as 23h59. The bombs would take a minute to fall from that altitude so would arrive at the same time as Christmas.]

Using my MAOT radio I was able to exchange Christmas greetings with Dave Knoesen, the leader of the Canberra formation. We had flown together as a Buccaneer crew; now he was at 24,000 feet and I was getting 'stonked' on the ground. The lesson we learned that night was when you fire artillery you give away your position to the enemy and the Cahama troop retaliated very accurately.

Our vehicles took a severe pounding as we bundu-bashed through the veld. Here I have to give praise to the army echelon support crews and 'tiffies' [mechanics] who maintained our vehicles and kept our logistic supply going. Our 'Asterix' required their attention after we hit a low hanging branch over the road and our turret went through a snap 90° turn. Fortunately we were all out of the turret as it would have cut us in half. While our Ratel was being repaired by a tiffie 61 Mech was on the move, so we were towed by another Ratel.

61 Mech was then tasked to return in great haste, through Xangongo towards Cuvelai, to lend support to our other battle group engaged there. During this long drive the armoured column stopped in line astern to celebrate New Year's Day. We did this by firing a burst of tracer simultaneously from all the Ratels towards the north. A very different fireworks display to the one we all grew up with.

We moved north towards Cuvelai and positioned ourselves southeast of the town. The weather was low cloud and rain. The battle for Cuvelai took place on 4 January. Our approach towards the town was hindered by a defensive minefield. Some of our Ratels detonated mines and one was hit by a 76mm shell from the side. This was our single biggest loss as ten guys were killed.

We learned from our experience at Cuvelai that all Angolan towns were surrounded by minefields. What they did was clear the area of bush after cutting the trunks about one metre above the ground, then plant the fields with *muhango*, which looks similar to mealies [maize]. This hid the remaining stumps, which were the right height to sever the hydraulic and brake lines underneath our vehicles.

Once we took the town we appropriately made ourselves comfortable in the blue house, which until a few hours before had been the home of the Soviet commissar. We parked our Ratel in the dining room and set up our communications. We could see the previous occupants had left in a hurry as suitcases had been packed but not taken. The flag which we took off the flagpole is still in my possession as my memento of *Askari*.

To the west of the runway we found a complete SA-9 missile system—a *boere troos* [consolation prize] for not getting the SA-8, our main prize.

1984: Uneasy peace

The SA-9 missile system captured outside Cuvelai. This vehicle was taken into the SAAF inventory.

After the town was secured many people, including members of the press, were flown in for a media briefing. For us it was the end of the operation. I had spent two months in Angola and travelled 3,500 kilomtres in a Ratel. As MAOT I had sent back 21 body bags and 54 serious casevacs.

It was now time for R&R. <<

International pressure

By the first week in 1984 pressure on the South African government reached a peak. Our military presence and operations in Angola were being condemned from all quarters, with threats of even greater boycotts and sanctions. This pressure, plus the relatively slow progress of the weather-hampered operation, made the politicians decide to halt *Askari* on 10 January 1984. Captured equipment was recovered to SWA and all participating forces were stood down.

Askari Phase 3

By February 1984 we established and dominated an area which included all the territory between the Cunene and Cubango rivers, as far north as a line running east–west through Tetchamutete. The area west of the Cunene was still 'Injun territory'.

Askari Phase 4

This phase was to be the final stopping of the incursion internally, if necessary. This always seemed to be a contradiction of the guidelines set for *Askari*. A study of the results of operational losses for 1984 gives an indication of whether this phase was successful or not. SWAPO suffered 916 dead in 1984, of which 361 were killed during *Askari*. The remainder was as a result of the normal SWAPO summer incursion. The one positive factor was the reduction of security force deaths, falling from 96 in 1983 to 39 in 1984, of which 13 occurred during the latter stages of *Askari*.

Despite *Askari*, an incursion in 1984 occurred.

Askari postscript

Over the years *Askari* has been looked on as a major success. This perception began right from the first debrief at Oshakati in February 1984. It is certainly true that:

- masses of war matériel were captured at Cuvelai
- FAPLA suffered a severe defeat in terms of men and equipment lost
- apart from their successful attack on a platoon of ground forces outside Caiundo, SWAPO or FAPLA never achieved any other offensive success

During December 1983 to January 1984, we lost 32 soldiers compared to the 407 SWAPO terrorists that were killed—a ratio of nearly 13:1. The overall figures for 1983 were 96 security force members to SWAPO's 913, a ratio of just under 10:1. The ratio increased in 1984 to 23:1, so in that respect *Askari* reaped benefits and for the remainder of the war this ratio remained over 20:1. SWAPO never succeeded in regaining the offensive capability it had prior to *Askari*.

The overall aim of *Askari*, however, was to prevent an infiltration to the south in 1984. Five hundred and fifty-five terrorists were killed during 1984 in addition to those who died during *Askari*, indicating that although they suffered losses the pattern of the insurgency war continued. We failed to achieve the main aim.

Askari became the watershed in the course of the Angola/SWA war. SWAPO were reduced in military strength and from then onwards no longer posed a major threat. On the other hand, FAPLA grew in stature and evolved into the major factor in our war against SWAPO. Our readiness to attack FAPLA, wherever or whenever they protected SWAPO, provoked them into acquiring an air-defence system to protect their interests that was at the time second only in sophistication to that assembled in the Warsaw Pact countries.

The war had created a surreal situation within the borders of South Africa. All military operations were classified secret or top secret and the government kept a very tight rein on the media. The main reason for the strict control of the press was the excruciating pressure placed on SA politicians by unfriendly nations through the UN. Therefore, they tried to limit the 'ammunition' to be used against them by keeping everything secret.

1984: Uneasy peace

Daily life in SA went on as if there was no war, despite the fact that virtually every family had a brother, son, husband or, because it went on for so many years, a father missing from the family at frequent intervals. In my own case, if I was not at home when my eldest brother telephoned he would listen to the SABC news and, if Foreign Minister Pik Botha stated definitely that the SADF was *not* in Xangongo or Cuvelai, then he knew exactly where I was.

In the mid-1983 national service intake, my sister's 18-year-old son, David Goodhead, was called up to the School of Armour in Bloemfontein. He was trained as a loader in Oliphant tanks. He took this to be a 'cushy number' as South African tanks were not involved in the war at that stage—much better than being in the PBI.

In the aftermath of *Askari* a number of almost brand-new Soviet T-55 tanks had been captured from the Angolans. As mentioned earlier, Angola had become our most reliable arms supplier and these tanks were considered useful additions to our order of battle.

Young Goodhead, playing volley ball at the School of Armour, was shaken out of this pleasant routine when, early in 1984, 18 volunteers were requested to "go up to SWA for three weeks to fetch some tanks". Being young and unaware of the old army maxim, 'never volunteer for anything', he leapt at the chance to increase his travel experience and volunteered.

A day or two later 18 national servicemen, a second lieutenant, two tiffies, a corporal and Major Louw (an Angola veteran) departed by Flossie (C-130) for Grootfontein. The next day they departed by road to Ondangwa on the back of a SAMIL 100 with live ammunition loaded in their rifles. They were under the impression that the tanks which needed collecting would be waiting at Ondangwa. However, their convoy bypassed the Ondangwa army base and entered the gates of AFB Ondangwa and headed straight to a waiting Dakota. The doors were closed, the aircraft took off and 20 minutes later landed at Ongiva. This was the first time they realized SWA was not their real destination.

They spent the night in tents in Ongiva and the next morning, after finally being properly briefed by Major Louw, two Pumas flew them north to Mupa. For most of them it was their first experience of flying in a helicopter skimming along just above the treetops. Even the disembarkation was an experience as the pilot hovered about six feet above the ground and they had to jump out quickly, kit and all.

Their location was a derelict farmhouse about one 'click' (kilometre) south of Mupa where the tanks were parked. They were tasked to familiarize themselves with the four T-55 tanks and then proceed northwards to use them against the enemy. This never occurred, as the negotiations begun after *Askari* led to South Africa's withdrawal from Angola.

After two weeks they had mastered all aspects of the Soviet tanks with the exception of the communication system. They solved this problem by using portable South African radios. Interestingly, David Goodhead found the T-55 to be a superior tank to the Oliphant in a number of aspects—speed, manoeuvrability, height and in secondary firepower. The T-55 mounted two machine guns, one inside the tank as in the Oliphant, and the other on top of the turret.

The inside machine gun had a calibre of 7.62mm the same as the SA weapons. However, the mechanism of the Soviet weapons was far simpler than ours. They also used thick yellow-type grease as lubricant as opposed to the oil used in the Oliphant. The Soviet guns had far fewer stoppages or malfunctions than their South African equivalents.

The machine gun on the turret was a 14.5mm whose loading and firing procedure took a while to sort out. To load the South African machine gun the procedure was to pull back the cocking mechanism and release it to the front by pulling the trigger; it was then ready to fire. Goodhead tried it on the Soviet gun but when he pulled the trigger to 'release the cocking mechanism' it fired off a quick burst of ten shells, only 30 yards left of the staff sergeant tiffie who was busy with a call of nature.

While at Mupa, intelligence reported a strong SWAPO presence in the vicinity of the little town. Therefore, all the tank crews took turns to stand guard at night. Goodhead and Glen Grundy were on guard when, in the early hours of the morning they spotted someone smoking away to the east of the house.

This photograph shows a South African tank crew on a T-55 tank. The 100mm main armament is covered while the crew exercises the 14.5mm turret-mounted cannon.

1984: Uneasy peace

Quietly they woke the entire contingent who completed the defensive circle around their camp. Only then, to the disgust of the major, did they realize the 'smoking' was actually fire-flies going about their nightly business.

They eventually left Mupa in convoy with UNITA troop carriers and headed for the SWA border. On the way they really put the T-55s through their paces— bundu-bashing over trees, driving through mud and water and even straight through a bombed-out house, in one side and out the other. At the border they drove the Soviet tanks onto tank- transporters from 61 Mechanized Battalion for the journey to Omuthiya, near Namutoni. Their three weeks' tour ended after 13 months. As the only SA tank force in SWA, they had earned the nickname 'The Moscow Maniacs'.

Two significant events occurred after *Askari*. Firstly, initiatives were taken to bring the South Africans and Angolans to the negotiating table. South Africa, being in the position of strength welcomed the proposal as did the Angolans, who were suffering militarily and psychologically at this stage. South Africa saw the opportunity as a chance for peace in the region. Angola on the other hand seized the opportunity as a stalling tactic. Communist-inspired organizations have a history of going to the table whenever they are in trouble and utilizing the breathing space to replan, re-arm and re-equip. This is precisely what they did during the protracted life of the Joint Military Commission (JMC), brought into being for the purposes of negotiations.

During the regular meetings of the JMC we had the unusual situation of hosting our Angolan enemies in their own country. Most of the discussions were of a political nature, however, at this time I did get the opportunity to meet my opposing Angolan Air Force commander face to face. It is interesting to note that the two of us got on very well. Both sides arrived for these meetings in helicopters and in a matter of minutes opposing aircrew were swapping stories, mementoes and aquavit—a menacing looking liquid that the Angolan pilots carried in their helicopters. It would appear that members of both military organizations bore little or no malice toward their opponents. Each man did his duty as required by his superiors; that was it.

Away from the negotiating table Major Manuel Dias and I had interesting and friendly discussions and exchanged gifts. I supplied him with some Cape grapevines to plant outside the Angolan Air Force HQ in Lubango. Understanding how much I enjoyed fishing he brought me a magnificent fish as a present. This monster was a tarpon, or silver king, described in the encyclopaedia as a 'great and powerful fish'. Standing on its head it was nearly as tall as I and provided a superb meal for everyone at 10 AFCP, including our families. We braaied the fish over the open coals at Oshandira, the SAAF pub we had built at Oshakati and, in their absence, toasted our opponents who had given us this wonderful gift. Unfortunately, despite the best efforts of the military peace was not to be.

Left: An Angolan An-26 at Ongiva. When the JMC meetings were held at Ongiva the Angolan delegation flew in one of these aircraft.
Right: The author in front of the braai at the SAAF pub in Oshakati, holding the fish presented by FAPA's Major Manuel Dias.

The JMC, composed of members from both Angola and South Africa, was formed under the auspices of Operation *Sclera*. Their task was to monitor the 'area in dispute'—basically from the border to Cuvelai. South Africa was to withdraw in stages from Angola, the Cuban forces would remain north of the 'area in dispute' and the Angolans would ensure this area was kept free of SWAPO terrorists. A joint monitoring force, composed of South African and Angolan troops, would patrol the area to ensure that both sides kept to the terms of the agreement.

South Africa adhered to all the conditions laid down and by the end of the year had withdrawn from Angola. The Angolans, manipulated by their communist masters in Moscow and Havana, failed to honour any of their obligations. SWAPO passed without hindrance through the 'area in dispute', suspected they were once again aided logistically by the Angolan defence force. This yearly

Left: Angolan Mi-8 helicopters arrive at the JMC HQ near Cuvelai.
Right: Colonel Dick Lord and Commandant Daantjie Beneke deep in conversation with Major Manual Dias.

incursion into SWA cost SWAPO 584 lives and the security forces thirty-nine.

However, the intensity of the war decreased significantly during the JMC period removing the need to constantly deploy the Mirage F1, Buccaneer and Canberra squadrons. The introduction of SA-8 mobile ground-to-air missile batteries and the suspected presence of SA-6 systems changed the combat scenario. SAAF flying tactics and attack profiles were seriously affected. The lull in the air war allowed our squadrons valuable training time to counter the new threat.

It has been my experience that western ethics are no match for the deviousness of the communists, of which there are innumerable examples. One only has to think back to Stalin in World War II, the protracted negotiations over the 38th Parallel with the North Koreans between 1950 and 1953 and the bloody 1968 Tet offensive launched in the middle of peace negotiations in Vietnam, to realize westerners have always come off second best. I put the problem down to the use of a French word *détente* in political negotiating circles. The exact meaning of the word, according to the dictionary is, 'relaxing of tension between states'. To westerners this is interpreted as a cessation of hostilities and means getting around a table in an attempt to resolve issues with the aim of returning to a situation of normality. However, communists see détente as an excellent opportunity to seize positions of power while the military presence has been conveniently removed.

In Angola the situation developed according to the instructions laid out in Mao's 'Little Red Book'. The South Africans relinquished all their gains in Angola and withdrew according to the terms laid down by the JMC. Angola blatantly ignored every restriction placed on her and, in fact, encouraged and assisted SWAPO logistically to re-occupy the territory vacated by South African forces. By mid-1984 it was a situation of 'back to the drawing board'.

The second significant occurrence was the subtle change in the whole structure of the war. FAPLA gradually replaced SWAPO as our main enemy and the war entered a phase of greater sophistication. The low intensity, counter-insurgency bush conflict was to escalate over the next four years into a high-intensity, undeclared conventional war between the armed forces of the South Africa, South West Africa and UNITA on the one hand and FAPLA, SWAPO, the Cubans and their Soviet advisors on the other.

The war was no longer a regional conflict. It had become internationalized and as such the solution was no longer in the hands of the South Africa or SWAPO. An international solution had to be sought, with all the accompanying complications.

I do not believe that the consequences of *Askari*, in terms of factors other than SWAPO, were originally envisaged. The four years from 1984 to the culmination of hostilities outside Cuito Cuanavale and Calueque in 1988, were to stretch our reserves and capabilities severely. The wholesale build-up of Soviet arms within this time period created a situation that was becoming daily more difficult to handle. The cost factor in terms of men and matériel was placing a critical burden on our resources.

The internationalization of the conflict led us to become increasingly involved in extricating UNITA from situations they could not handle. These unmanageable situations for the guerrilla forces of UNITA were brought about by their inability to counter heavy equipment such as tanks, artillery and helicopter gunships that FAPLA had acquired specifically to counter South African attacks. These factors supported the belief that the conventional attacks on FAPLA during *Askari* caused repercussions which affected the entire course of the war.

Up to this stage the border war had taken place mainly in Owamboland, north and south of the cut-line. It had been fought primarily against SWAPO insurgents, with sporadic incidents involving the forces of SWAPO's host, Angola. Now, however, the conflict began in earnest on two fronts—Angola's 5th Military Region, north of Owamboland and the 6th Military Region, north of Rundu.

Tosca

Since the first armed clash with SWAPO insurgents in 1966 the population of Oshakati had grown as the police, and later the army, began deploying counter-insurgency personnel. By 1983 the air force, medical services, engineers, signallers and workshop artificers ('tiffies') had joined the swelling ranks of South African and SWATF soldiers and policemen, transforming the settlement into a military garrison.

In an operational area where ambushes, landmine and anti-personnel mine detonations and stand-off bombardments were an everyday occurrence daily activities of the population took place within the confines of the town's defended perimeter. This curtailment of social, sporting and leisure opportunities led to a conservative life style.

Without museums, theatres, cinemas or discos life was pretty much a humdrum affair—except for Tosca. Tosca was the star attraction and focus of conversation in the war-torn town. No visit to Oshakati was complete without a drive past Tosca's house. Tosca was a full grown, magnificent male lion, and yes, he did live in a house, in the main street of Oshakati.

A patrol, while operating in the bush, had come across an abandoned lion cub. Separated from its mother and suffering injuries to its hindquarters it was in a desperate state. Realizing that the minute bundle of fur would not survive on its own the men brought it back to Oshakati and christened him Tosca. All kittens are adorable and none more so than a lion cub. Captivated by this little lion his master approached the Department of Nature Conservation and explained the predicament. He asked if he could keep the lion instead of having it put down; its injuries were such that it could not be released back into the wild.

1984: Uneasy peace

Nature Conservation agreed to his keeping and rearing the animal provided proper rules of conduct and safekeeping were followed. Abiding by all the regulations and guidelines he raised Tosca in Oshakati. Although his entire backyard was enclosed Tosca also had the run of the house. He grew up with humans, probably thinking he was one, and apart from a slight limp matured into a magnificent specimen.

As air force commander, my family and I moved into a house that backed directly onto that of the Army commander, Brigadier Joep Joubert. Two back gardens away on the left lived Tosca. Coming directly from AFB Hoedspruit, close to the Kruger National Park, we felt we were accustomed to wild animals. However, when Tosca roared at night 60 metres from our open windows we awoke with hair erect and palpitating hearts.

Tosca loved company and enjoyed his many visitors. Friends of the family allowed their children into the yard to play with and pet him. He was huge, with enormous paws and a long, thick, dark mane. I often stroked him and permitted my two boys to do the same, but always through the bars of his enclosure. My lack of faith in his amicability would not allow me to enter his enclosure. Tosca was not only the king of the beasts but also of Oshakati and I felt he deserved the right to roam his 'kingdom' on his own.

With the intensification of the war in the early 1980s came the requirement of additional personnel to handle the increased load. The air force solved this problem by seconding personnel from their home units and sending them to the operational area on bush tours. These tours were usually three months in length resulting in an ever-changing work force.

Each new member had to be fully briefed and trained to ensure the maintenance of standards. Each briefing contained at least a passing reference to Tosca, as was the case when Flight Sergeant Nicky Havenga arrived from the Cape to commence his tour at 310 AFCP.

Havenga was a specialist cryptographer and as the majority of the signal traffic was classified his services were in great demand. He arrived in Oshakati late one Friday afternoon with just sufficient time to be briefed before suppertime. He was accommodated with other air force personnel in the bungalows alongside the Oshakati runway. From his bungalow to the CP was a walk of one kilometre along the main road and past Brigadier Joubert's house, two doors away from where Tosca lived.

Brigadier Joubert owned a large collie dog, Oubaas, on whom he lavished tender loving care. This beautiful animal had a coat like Lassie with a long mane around his neck, typical of this breed. Oubaas slept outside serving as a faithful watchdog, a lovely animal without a vicious hair on its body whose greatest desire was to be fussed over. His days were spent being petted by the hundreds of troopies he came into contact with. Oubaas did, however, have one bad habit.

He liked to greet passing pedestrians by running and bounding up at them.

On the evening of Havenga's arrival, at 22h00, he was asked to return to the CP to decode a top-secret signal. As he walked back to work he wondered where Tosca lived. He eventually left the CP around midnight to make his way back to the airfield. It was very dark, because to avoid being a target for a SWAPO stand-off bombardment no lights were left on in the town. It was also very silent because the roads were not tarred, all the surfaces being thick sand. So, there he was in the pitch dark with not a sound to be heard. Once again his thoughts turned to Tosca. Havenga knew he must be in the vicinity of the lion's 'house'.

Just then Oubaas, never one to miss an opportunity, raced out of the brigadier's garden, silent as a shadow on the powdery sand, and sprang into the air onto Havenga. Just before the dog landed Havenga glimpsed the long flowing mane around the collie's neck and thought it was Tosca.

Havenga ran the remaining kilometre back to his bungalow despite discovering that his 'lion' was nothing more than a big friendly dog.

The Koevoet 'zoo' in Oshakati—the two elephants eventually found a home in the Pilanesberg National Park in South Africa.

1984: Uneasy peace

The Iko Carreira document

At about this time in early 1984, Major Johan Opperman entered my office and laid a document before me, saying, "What do you think of this, sir?"

>>*TEXT-SEGMENT-LYNNOMMER*09000
1. Colonel Henrique Carreira, head of the Angolan Air Force, was in Belgrade in February for talks with Admiral Branko Mamula, the Yugoslav Defence Minister. Before going to Yugoslavia Carreira had been in Moscow where he participated in the Soviet–Cuban–Angolan talks. Carreira gave Mamula an account of the Moscow talks as these affected him and he also answered questions put to him by Mamula.
2. Sokolov told Carreira [*author*: and presumably the other participants but this is not clear from Mamula's report] that in the policy review being made the situation in Angola must be considered within the context of Angola's future role in the struggle that will have to come, to complete the liberation of southern Africa by bringing to an end rascist rule in South Africa and therewith the imperialist intrigues based upon South Africa.

*TEXT-SEGMENT-LYNNOMMER*10000
3. As seen from Moscow, Sokolov said, Angola will have an important function in the preparation for the final struggle by providing back-up support for Zimbabwe in co-operation with Zambia.
4. This will be of exceptional importance during the first stages, Sokolov said, until the stage is reached where Zimbabwe will be in a position itself to take up a greater burden for what promises to be an intensive and possibly prolonged struggle.
5. The fact that Zimbabwe is not yet ready for that role, Sokolov said, is no reason to neglect the preparations in Angola; the more so, Sokolov added, because it would be an encouragement for Mugabe if he realized the scale of support which will be available to him when the preparatory work is completed.

*TEXT-SEGMENT-LYNNOMMER*11000
6. ... [*text garbled*] ... soon as the internal situation in the country had been secured and 'normalized', much would depend, Sokolov said, upon decisions still to be taken regarding Savimbi and UNITA; the key decision on this matter, Sokolov said, whether to seek to 'neutralize', 'absorb' or 'defeat' UNITA.
7. Sokolov described the probability of extensive future US aid for UNITA as possible, a positive development in so far as it would help to overcome existing differences of opinion within the MPLA and also in the Soviet Union about how to deal with UNITA.
8. Carreira then told Mamula about the aspect of the Moscow talks that concerned him personally.

*TEXT-SEGMENT-LYNNOMMER*12000
9. More effective air power would be needed n southern Africa for the final defeat of rascist rule in South Africa, Sokolov said; so far as the Soviet Union saw this need in respect of Angola, there would therefore have to be two separate but parallel phases, Sokolov explained. The one being the provision of adequate air support for the MPLA and fraternal forces in the struggle to secure Angola, and the other preparations for a southern African strategic build-up of air power. These two requirements would have equal priority and the one need not detract or interfere with the other.
10. Sokolov also told Carreira that a comprehensive assessment of South Africa's air power, which through a serious omission had never before been made, is now in progress. Though not yet completed, Sokolov said, the information already analyzed indicated some potentially serious shortcomings in South Africa's ability to face

*TEXT-SEGMENT-LYNNOMMER*13000
a future challenge in the air; for instance, Sokolov said. South Africa is short of long-range air potential and this is considered to be unlikely to change in the foreseeable future, and there are several other shortcomings that are likely to become evident if South Africa was put under real pressure.
11. One conclusion which already seemed almost certain, Sokolov said, is that South Africa's air potential has so far been generally overestimated and that a counter to it can realistically be considered as feasible. Given time and enough co-operation from other southern African countries with Angola as a starting point, and also as an example to others, of what can be achieved [sic].
12. It cannot be disputed, Sokolov said, that a fundamental need for all southern Africa is air power to provide not only

*TEXT-SEGMENT-LYNNOMMER*14000
protection against South African aggression but also for "whatever needs may arise in the future". Angola would be the logical place to start the necessary ... [text garbled] ... including the first stages of the needed infrastructure; what will follow in other countries in southern Africa will almost certainly depend to a large extent upon the success achieved in this respect in Angola.
13. Sokolov asked for Carreira's full support and co-operation in this war that now lay ahead; it would have to start once the 'anti-South Africa all potentiality study' had been completed.
14. However, Sokolov also said that the final decision would be taken by Gorbachev but that Gorbachev would be guided by the recommendation being prepared and others in the course of policy review.

1984: Uneasy peace

*TEXT-SEGMENT-LYNNOMMER*15000

15. In a comment to Mamula, Carreira said that he himself and the other MPLA members who participated in the Moscow discussions were "not too happy" about the prospects of Angola being developed as a prototype air base but that although their approval would be needed it would not be Sokolov's prognosis ... [*text garbled*] ... appeared to be a ... [*text garbled*] ... should probably not reach implementation stage until after the next presidential election.<<

How our intelligence system came to be in possession of this document I did not try to find out. Apparently the document had arrived at HQ in Pretoria but, to our knowledge, nothing constructive resulted from it; it probably ended up in File 13.

Like our HQ in Oshakati, during the course of any one day hundreds of snippets of information were received from intelligence sources, army or police

The tall man on the extreme right inspecting a Soviet-supplied ZPU-4 towed anti-aircraft cannon is Iko Carreira.

patrol reports and aircrew debriefings. Many of these snippets on their own seemed to have little or no relevance to the situation prevailing in the immediate war theatre and tended to be summarily disregarded.

However, Opperman and I were both convinced of the importance of the document we christened the 'Iko Carreira Plan'. Opperman had his intelligence staff clear an entire wall of the intelligence office so these seemingly unimportant snippets of information could be displayed on a matrix, constructed by using the contents of the document as a guide. Within a very short time we realized these 'irrelevant' snippets when placed into the matrix started revealing a very clear picture of what was really taking place along the length of South Africa's northern borders. These pieces of information had become useable intelligence. What we were faced with in SWA was not just a show of resistance by disgruntled inhabitants. SWAPO's activities were clearly part of a far larger orchestration and the man wielding the baton was situated in Moscow. The percussion section was made up of 50,000-plus Cuban ground troops and air force pilots, many of whom were very competent indeed.

Perhaps the easiest demonstration of the importance of our matrix is to study the following diagram of the radar chain being established right around South Africa at that time.

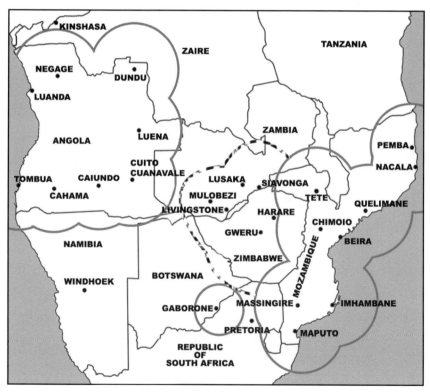

Early-warning radar cover surrounding southern Africa at 20,000 feet.

1984: Uneasy peace

The solid circles display the detection range of Soviet-supplied radars against fighter-sized targets which existed in July 1984. The hatched lines indicate the range of the radars planned to become operational at Mulobezi in Zambia and Gweru in Zimbabwe. However, the most significant position to note is how the circles just touch between Mulobezi, Zambia and Cuito Cuanavale, Angola. The actual gap existing between Livingstone radar and Cuito Cuanavale radar was the gap exploited by the SAAF to fly behind enemy lines. This gap was, I believe, the real reason for the Angolan attempts in 1985 and 1987 to capture the small town of Mavinga. In the Soviet planning that gap had to be filled before their plan could progress to the next level.

During SAAF staff courses a study was made of Soviet military doctrine. An absolute step in their waging of war was to provide their aircraft with radar cover before they embarked on military adventures. Their radar cover extended well into Owamboland. However, they did not have adequate cover over the SAAF base at Rundu or Grootfontein. This was the second major reason for their attempts to capture Mavinga. People have often speculated why the Angolan Air Force never tried to attack AFB Ondangwa or any other targets in Owamboland. I firmly believe it was this strict adherence to Soviet doctrine that prevented them from carrying out air attacks, despite their aircraft being flown by very capable Soviet and Cuban pilots. They certainly had the capability but it never happened.

A look at the radar coverage chart for aircraft flying at only 2,000 feet AGL highlights this obvious shortcoming. Most combat flying in the war theatre took place at low levels.

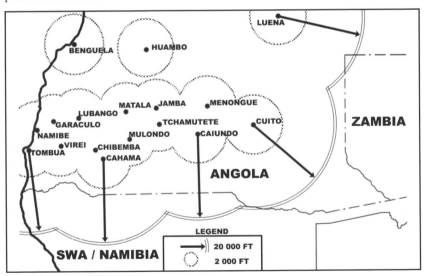

This is the coverage of Angolan radar at 2,000ft AGL. The gap up the Zambian border was vital for both sides.

331

At night, the gap along the Zambian–Angolan border was used by SAAF C-130 and C-160 transport aircraft giving support to UNITA forces who were harassing Angolan government forces throughout central Angola.

After Operation *Askari* in 1983/84 the nature of the border war changed from a low-intensity insurgency conflict to that of a fully fledged conventional war. This transformation was made when it was obvious that SWAPO could no longer achieve its desired military aim. Therefore, the communist triumvirate of the USSR, Cuba and the MPLA Government of Angola decided to escalate their involvement by pumping in massive amounts of Soviet military hardware and Cuban surrogate forces in an attempt to win a military victory.

Baby elephant

During the planning for the operation I had occasion to visit Omega, the Bushman Battalion base in the Caprivi Strip of northeastern South West Africa. Colonel Brian Adams, commander of the base and old friend of mine, met me at the airstrip and drove me down to his officers' mess. En route we stopped to watch the sun set in a blaze of glorious red, orange and blue, one of the splendours of this remote part of the world and during our conversation he told me about the newest inhabitant of Omega—an elephant.

Fortunately, this one turned out to be a baby. One of the patrols had found the abandoned orphan and, not wanting to leave it in the bush to die, brought it back to Omega. Of course I expressed a desire to see it which Adams said he would arrange after we arrived at the mess. Built in an open-plan design with a thatched roof the officers' mess was a very pleasant place to enjoy a sundowner. Without side walls the air could circulate freely and it was most refreshing after the heat of the day.

Suitably equipped with long, cold glasses in our hands Adams called for the regimental sergeant-major (RSM) and asked him to arrange for the elephant to put in an appearance. Stamping his foot and exclaiming loudly "Yes, sah!", as soldiers are wont to do, the RSM stepped outside and hollered, "McClaren, bring your elephant!"

It turned out that McClaren, a national serviceman, was a lad who had caused the RSM much grief. The RSM had seen the arrival of the baby elephant as a godsend and had installed McClaren as its mother, nursemaid, friend and cleaner. After a few minutes McClaren arrived, out of the now darkened bush, looking for all the world like a modern day Quasimodo. His left arm looked decidedly misshapen as it dangled away from his side while his right arm stretched across his chest to his left. As he walked into the light we could see that he was being closely followed by the tiniest, most charming, infant elephant imaginable.

The resourceful young man had accepted his new role as a mother and applied considerable thought to his unusual position. Realizing most babies need constant nurturing he had armed himself with cardboard cartons of long-life milk. After making an opening in the top of a box he poured the milk in a steady trickle down his left forearm; his left hand dangled downwards with fingers pointing backwards acting as teats. Wherever he walked the elephant followed suckling on his fingers and oblivious to barstools, tables or anything that might be in its way. He was no more than a metre tall, his hide still covered by the bristles characteristic of newly born elephants. In a lifetime spent in the military I had visited many messes and witnessed unusual happenings, however, none matched the one I had just witnessed. Unfortunately, this delightful little elephant was not able to remain in the mess for long; the repair bill would have been exorbitant.

Omega

Omega was always an interesting base to visit. As mentioned earlier it had been established to accommodate an entire Bushman community. During South Africa's earlier forays into Angola during the mid-1970s, interestingly at the bidding of the United States, it was discovered that all warring factions in that strife-ridden country used the opportunity to rid Angola of the Bushmen through systematic genocide. South African forces came across groups of these little people wandering aimlessly around Angola in an attempt to avoid conflict and stay alive. In a humanitarian act the South Africans offered these groups protection and gave them sanctuary. Bushmen maintain strong family ties and often their families included grandparents and up to eight or ten children. Omega therefore grew in leaps and bounds.

When it was appreciated that the Bushmen had skills that could be fully utilized by our ground forces an ethnic Bushman battalion was raised, in the British tradition. The men were enlisted into the South African Army, receiving the same pay and benefits as other members. After basic military training they were set to work as trackers with infantry patrols. They were magnificent in the bush and their skills soon led to an increase in contacts with the enemy. They would run along an enemy spoor and give accurate estimates of how old the tracks were from days, hours and minutes. Ground troops could tell by watching the little men at work whenever a fire fight was imminent. At this stage the trackers would indicate the direction of the enemy then change places with the regular soldiers, taking up a position in the rear. They knew their own strengths and weaknesses and fighting was an unfamiliar skill for these gentle people.

Omega, where the total Bushman community exceeded 10,000 souls, covered a vast area. The army erected a large open-air cinema screen on which nightly movies were shown. Apart from army vehicles and the airstrip alongside the base these people had been exposed to nothing else. It is difficult to understand they had never seen a mountain, train, double-storeyed building, snow or a neon light—all the things they could now see on the screen. They could not follow the dialogue; only stare at the moving images. Of course their reactions were understandably different to those of more sophisticated audiences.

There were no chairs in front of the screen; the people sat in the sand as they had done for centuries. In spite of their limitations they could still recognize the good guy from the bad. Whenever the good guy, or the beautiful girl, was on the screen they all edged nearer and nearer the front. However, when the bad guy appeared they all scampered into the protection of the surrounding bush until the coast was clear. This description is not meant to be patronizing, just an attempt to illustrate the lovely innocence of a people uncontaminated by so-called civilization.

Unfortunately, in real life, every story does not have a happy, Hollywood ending. In a sincere attempt to save these little people from annihilation and to improve their lot the South African Army tried their very best, but did not really achieve the results we all hoped for. The Bushmen, who never knew what money was and had never needed any, suddenly discovered that with their army pay they had become wealthy overnight. They bought fridges and TV sets, without realizing they needed electricity to make the appliances work. They also discovered that with money they could buy hard liquor or beer, substances they had no previous experience of or need for. Within a relatively short time they started losing their traditional bushcraft skills and became increasingly dependent on, and in some cases addicted to, western material goods and brews.

The last thing I want to mention about Omega concerns the large water tower built on pylons, which dominated the camp area. It was needed to supply water, at pressure, to the spread-out community. On the sides of this steel tank, in huge white letters, was painted the word OOPS. It appears the tower, erected by the Public Works Department, had been built in the wrong place far away from the water source and the people wanted a permanent reminder of the error.

Casevac matters

Almost every day the routine of the command post was interrupted with the necessity to cater for critical situations. We attached absolute priority to casualty evacuation because there is a 'golden hour' between injury and hospitalization which drastically affects the chances of survival. A casevac call-out during wartime is a very involved procedure. The standby helicopter crew has to be briefed of all the circumstances, a doctor and his orderly must ensure they have the correct equipment on board and a section of Parabats is required to secure the helicopter while it is on the ground. In some situations top cover helicopter gunships must accompany the ambulance helicopter as protection from ambush during the critical pick-up. Long-distance flights require additional fuel, which can be taken in extra fuel tanks loaded inside the helicopter cabin, or the helicopter has to land at forward bases or HAGs to refuel. All these arrangements have to be made after the flight has been thoroughly planned.

In Owamboland we worked hard to reduce the average casevac time to approximately 40 minutes. Worldwide, the Israeli Defence Force was the benchmark used to compare efficiency; they had a remarkable reaction time of about 20 minutes. When we considered that their theatre of operations was about the size of the Etosha Pan we felt we were doing pretty well recovering most patients within the 'golden hour'. Unfortunately, situations existed where wounded soldiers had to wait hours before they could be recovered. Often this was because we had to wait for cover of darkness to protect the unarmed and vulnerable helicopters.

However, it was not only casevac flights that provided the break in routine. During major terrorist incursions SWAPO would send up to 14 or 15 detachments across the border at the same time. The incursion routes would cover almost the entire border from the Kaokoland in the west, through Owamboland and Kavango, a distance of nearly 900 kilometres. Each group would consist of between 40 and 100 men carrying the ubiquitous AK-47 rifles, vehicle and anti-personnel mines, mortars, at times Katyusha rockets and, almost always, a number of Strela SA-7 shoulder-launched SAM missiles.

Kudu problems

It was 24 June and Mario Vergottini was on his first bush tour in SWA, flying the light transport Kudu aircraft. Just three weeks before the Kudu had been cleared to return to duty on the border after a series of technical problems. They had been withdrawn from service because of engine cuts and propeller blade tips flying off. After undergoing rectification programmes it was felt the aircraft was ready to re-enter the war with a bunch of brand-new 'loots', straight from conversion course, in command.

A Kudu about to touch down on a sand strip in the bush

The previous day Vergottini had flown to AFB Grootfontein via AFB Rundu, bringing Major Wessel Worst, Mpacha's commanding officer, Mrs Worst and Lieutenant Mark Hill to attend a function at the huge logistic base. He was now preparing to return them direct to Mpacha. In the three weeks he had been in the bush he had flown 31 hours and had a grand total of 188 hours on the Kudu.

Major Worst's meeting dragged on through the morning and Vergottini could only take off just before noon. He realized it would be a very 'hot and high' take-off as the aircraft was heavily loaded with night-stop kit and stores, urgently required by the army at Katima Mulilo. The pongos loaded the back of the Kudu as if it was a Samil truck. Vergottini eventually offloaded all the kit and re-weighed everything to ensure his aircraft remained within the centre of gravity (C of G) limits. After removing some of the freight he was ready to go. This precaution was the result of an overloading scare he had experienced with Captain Dave Upfold, during his conversion course. The only factor in his favour was the runway at AFB Grootfontein 'went on forever' and he knew he would eventually get airborne.

While manning up, he ensured that Mrs Worst and Mark Hill were seated directly behind the pilots' seats, to ensure the aircraft would have a slightly forward C of G for the take-off. He taxiied out, did his pre-take-off checks, lowered 15° of flap and, after receiving take-off clearance, lined up and commenced the take-off roll.

Climbing through 500 feet AGL he came back on his take-off power when suddenly the control yoke shot forward out of his hands into the instrument panel. The aircraft stood on its nose and dived for the ground. He grabbed the control column and pulled back with all his strength, at the same time trying to use the electric trimmer to get the nose up, but nothing happened. He put his left arm around the yoke and pulled as hard as he could while trying to manually trim the aircraft with his right hand, but the trim wheel just would not move and had no effect on the forces Vergottini was fighting. They were still heading for the ground, but at a slightly lower rate, so he pushed the engine controls fully forward to get as much speed as possible in an attempt to raise the aircraft's nose.

He declared an emergency over the radio, informing the tower he was flying a tight left-hand circuit. By this time Major Worst was helping to maintain backward pressure on the yoke, easing the rate of descent to about 200 feet per minute. Vergottini decided to land using full speed, about 130 knots. He did not want to chance closing the throttle and having the aircraft enter another dive. He knew his high speed was above the tyre rating but felt a ground incident would be preferable to a crash.

He touched down at high speed and slowly closed the power and let the control yoke move forward. Only after he managed to get the tail onto the ground did he realize he had been standing on the rudder pedals while pulling back on the yoke, trying to keep the aircraft in the air. His legs developed an uncontrollable shake during the long taxi back to dispersal.

After shutting down he exited the cockpit, only to see the entire moveable tail surface of the elevators was facing down. After inspection it was found the trim cable had snapped, allowing the entire tail to travel into the fully nose-down position which was the reason for the sudden nose-dive.

There were two things which saved the aircraft that day. The first, the runway at Grootfontein was very long. The second, Vergottini, at 6 foot 2 inches and 210lbs is a big man, whose adrenaline-induced strength physically manhandled the errant Kudu safely back onto the ground.

The King Air

On 11 and 12 August, 3 Squadron returned to AFB Ondangwa where they escorted a Canberra carrying out a PR mission over southern Angola. The Canberra crew were tasked to acquire photographic evidence of a FAPLA build-up in contravention of the rules laid down by the JMC.

The Canberra–Mirage F1CZ formation took off from Ondangwa at 12h05 on 12 August and routed via Jamba, Cassinga, Tetchamutete, Cuvelai and Cuito Cuanavale. Unfortunately, it did not cover the evidence we were looking for but did allow us to update our photography of large areas of the theatre.

The SAAF had a small contingent stationed in Windhoek called SAAF Detachment Eros. In the late 1960s this unit had started off with two Alouette helicopters which were later moved north, closer to the border. They were replaced by Kudu light communications aircraft and then, after the independence of Angola in 1975, the unit grew with the addition of two Beechcraft Queen Air and two Piper Aztec aircraft. Aircrew for these aircraft were supplied on a rotation basis from 27 Squadron in Cape Town. In 1984, the SAAF acquired a Beechcraft Super King Air 200C to complement the Eros fleet as a high-speed, high-altitude, pressurized VIP communications and casevac aircraft. The cargo door allowed stretcher cases to be loaded directly into the cabin.

Initially the King Air, registered as ZS-LAY, was flown by crews from 21 Squadron at AFB Waterkloof, the SAAF's VIP squadron. The novelty soon wore off and a more satisfactory arrangement was introduced in July 1984 when a permanent King Air commander was appointed from 25 Squadron, AFB Ysterplaat as OC, SAAF Det Eros. Three co-pilots from 25 Squadron rotated every two weeks to make up the crew for ZS-LAY.

Flying intensity was extremely high. Major Anton Kriegler, the first King Air commander flew 728.2 hours in ZS-LAY during his 18 months' posting in Windhoek. At present (2008), ZS-LAY still flies as King Air 652 at 41 Squadron, AFB

Waterkloof and Kriegler still flies it occasionally. On a personal note I flew in and tasked this King Air on innumerable flights. When General Jannie Geldenhuys was on board I even flew it. Kriegler, or Andy Anderson his replacement, often had to make up a bridge foursome with the general and I, as a non bridge-playing passenger, was despatched up front to keep an eye on things. This aeroplane was one of 18 SAAF aircraft types that General Geldenhuys played bridge in, which must be a record.

On 19 September, Anton Kriegler and Lieutenant Mario de Gouveia took off from Eros at 15h00 on a flight to Ondangwa, 290 miles north of Windhoek. On board was General Georg Meiring, the GOC SWATF and his staff. They were on their way to a late-afternoon briefing at Oshakati, a further 20 kilometres by road from the Ondangwa airbase. The following morning they would continue their flight to Okaukuejo, on the southwestern corner of the Etosha Pan.

Kriegler and de Gouveia spent the early evening with other Ondangwa aircrew around the pool. Around 21h00 the public address system announced that the standby Puma crew were to report immediately to the operations room. Upon hearing this Kriegler and de Gouveia remarked to each other that this probably heralded a casevac and they wondered if they would also have to fly later that evening.

ZS-LAY on the apron of the sand strip at Buffalo, the 32 Battalion base.

About 20 minutes later the Puma took off and at low level disappeared out to the west. Shortly thereafter they could see activity in the sick bay/trauma centre which was right next door to the aircrew enclosure. Just after 22h00 the King Air crew were turning in for the night when public address loudspeaker blared, "Would the King Air crew report to Ops immediately."

On arrival the ops officer explained that there had been an ambush near Concordia base, a few miles east of Ruacana. A vehicle had detonated a landmine and in the ensuing fire fight there had been several casualties. The Puma was returning with four stretcher cases, one of whom was critical. This patient would be stabilized by the doctors at Ondangwa and then airlifted to 1 Military Hospital, 832 nautical miles or 3h20min flying time from Ondangwa. Kriegler

1984: Uneasy peace

reminded the ops officer that he had a 08h00 flight planned for General Meiring and was told that Colonel Dick Lord wanted to speak to him on the telephone. According to Kriegler the conversation went something like this:

"Good evening, colonel."

"Hi Anton, how are you and Mario feeling for a flight to Waterkloof?"

"Sir, we are okay, but what about General Meiring tomorrow?"

"Man, we are actually in a spot of bother as the general has a very tight schedule over the next three days. We have to get him to Okaukuejo or it will bugger up his entire schedule. Could you possibly fly to Waterkloof, return here and then take the general to Etosha? You will be back in Windhoek by lunchtime and can then go and sleep."

"We are okay with that sir, as we only flew one hour, thirty minutes today and did not drink this evening, so we're well rested. However, we will need some top cover because we will be breaking some rules."

"How many rules?"

"The eight hours of sleep before flight as well as the on-duty time and we will not be able to make the 08h00 take-off tomorrow. It is now nearly 23h00 and it's three and a half hours either way. If we get airborne at midnight and take an hour to turn around at Waterkloof the earliest we could be back will be 08h00 tomorrow morning."

"Anton, if you are happy to go, I will give you all the top cover you need and we will postpone your take-off tomorrow to 09h00."

"We are happy with that, sir."

"What a player! Many thanks and good luck."

De Gouveia was already busy with the pre-flight. As Kriegler walked out to the King Air he could hear the Puma approaching from the west and the ambulances moving out to the helicopter dispersal. The Puma landed and the on-board doctor conferred with the Ondangwa medical team, who made the decision to load the critical patient straight into the King Air with additional medical support staff. The cargo door was opened and the seriously wounded soldier, who had sustained multiple bullet wounds, was slowly and carefully loaded. Drip bags were hooked into supports from the cabin roof, drainage bags positioned and medical support kit and documentation loaded while the two doctors exchanged notes outside on the tarmac.

As is usual in a long casevac flight over different countries, Kriegler enquired as to the condition of the patient. He was told the soldier was critical but stable but needed to reach the Intensive Care Unit at 1 Military Hospital as soon as possible. Kriegler conferred with the doctor and told him to remember that should the patient die during the flight he must be declared dead in the ambulance on the way from Waterkloof to the hospital. This was to simplify the issue of the place of death and the magisterial district in which it occurred. A permit is required to transport a deceased person from one magisterial district to another. The King Air in its flight over South West Africa, Botswana and the Transvaal would traverse possibly 200 magisterial districts. The doctor said he understood.

Finally, with everyone loaded, the doors were closed and de Gouveia ran through the familiar checklist as they started ZS-LAY. They took off as the global navigation system, a GNS 500 VLF/Omega system, showed the time to be 16 minutes past midnight. The aircraft was cleared to route overhead Grootfontein at FL250 and then direct to Waterkloof. It was a no-moon night, described by Kriegler as being "as dark as the inside of a cow". There were no visible lights or fires until they passed overhead Tsumeb and Grootfontein. Nearly two hours later the lights of Gaborone, Botswana were the next visible feature.

In the back of the aircraft it was quiet although they could see the doctor and medic monitoring the patient. ZS-LAY was on auto-pilot which allowed Kriegler to gaze at the incandescent purple-blue flame coming out of the fluted exhaust of the Pratt and Whitney PT6A-41 engine. This purple-blue flame, invisible during the day, extended from the exhaust along the beautifully slender and curved nacelle and over the top of the wing.

After an uneventful flight the King Air landed at Waterkloof at 03h20 local time. The medical personnel carefully transferred the patient to the waiting ambulance. The doctors thanked the crew for the flight and told them that the patient's prospects for survival were good, before they departed for 1 Military Hospital.

Ground crew refuelled the aircraft while Kriegler and de Gouveia had a cup of coffee. Then they were off again on the return leg to AFB Ondangwa. A few minutes later they were established at FL240 on course and on auto-pilot. At that time of the morning nothing stirs. It was quiet in the cockpit and the radios were silent. To assist the crew with fuel management the GNS 500 had a page where actual fuel flow and actual total fuel on board could be inserted. This started a countdown timer which after 20 minutes ignited a message light on the primary GNS 500 page to remind the crew they had to check and correlate the fuel flow and fuel total with the actual readings on the instruments.

There was absolute silence in the cockpit as conversation dried up and slowly but surely weariness started affecting both pilots. As the orange MSG light illuminated to show 'Please update fuel status', Kriegler told de Gouveia that, as they were both tired, one of them should doze for 30 minutes and then let the other man do the same. In the military, rank has its privileges, so Kriegler decided to sleep first and asked de Gouveia to wake him after the stipulated half an hour. Before nodding off Kriegler re-entered the fuel data, knowing the warning light would ignite ten minutess before he was due to be woken up. He then slid back his seat and immediately drifted off into a well-deserved nap.

He woke up with a start. Next to him de Gouveia was sleeping like a baby.

Kriegler scanned all the instruments to find they were on track, on altitude and the engines were purring in perfect synchronization. The GNS indicated Grootfontein was 220 nautical miles ahead and it was still pitch black outside. Kriegler woke de Gouveia who stammered apologies. The illuminated orange MSG light indicated 64 minutes had elapsed since the last update. Both pilots were deeply shocked and silent as they realized they had traversed almost the entire breadth of Botswana fast asleep, with ZS-LAY flying all by herself.

They landed at Ondangwa at 07h45. The aircraft was refuelled while the crew hastily made themselves presentable before rushing back to ZS-LAY. They arrived as General Meiring and his entourage were climbing out of their vehicles. Kriegler immediately apologized to the general for delaying his take-off. The flight to Okaukuejo was uneventful as was the ferry leg back to Eros Airfield in Windhoek. The weary crew handed over ZS-LAY to WOI Fats Booysen and retired to bed. They had flown 10h15mins since the previous afternoon and logged 7h17mins of night flying, which included five hours of actual instrument time, excluding the lost 64 minutes.

As a finale to the account, I want to say that in my entire flying career, ZS-LAY was the most incredible, individual aircraft I ever came across. During my five years of association with it I can only recall one take-off that was delayed for mechanical reasons. Every other sortie it flew on time. It was a flying tribute to Beechcraft who built it and the SAAF who maintained it so wonderfully well.

*****

Between 1 and 5 October, a Canberra photographed the area of Mongu in Zambia, also the Zambezi River from Kazankulu to Katima Mulilo. Excessive cloud cover forced the Canberra to re-fly the mission between 16 and 19 October. On completion of the task the Canberra crew flew a small area coverage (SAC) of the Shakawe area in northwest Botswana. It was from this area that trigger-happy Botswanan gunners used to fire at SAAF aircraft entering the narrow Caprivi Strip.

This was an interesting mission because Mongu was being developed as a Zambian fighter airfield—another intelligence snippet which lent credibility to the Iko Carreira plan.

Chapter 11

1985: Internationalization

The extent and complexity of the border war had increased since the completion of *Askari* and *Sclera* in 1984. We were now actively engaged on a western front, north of AFB Ondangwa in Owamboland and an eastern front, north of AFB Rundu in Kavango. The western front remained an anti-terrorist war against SWAPO; it contained no major military threat to us, purely nuisance value as it still had to be contained. However, the eastern front contained a conventional military threat of a very different nature from that posed by SWAPO. This was a civil war between the government forces of Angola and the rebel UNITA movement. The opposing ideologies ensured that it was in South Africa's own self-interest to support UNITA.

There were decided advantages and disadvantages in this situation. UNITA controlled over half of the border line between South West Africa and Angola; without their presence South Africa's resources would have been extremely stretched. However, the big disadvantage was that we, the SADF, were in support and not in control of the military situation.

To maintain continuity in this history of the war I have decided to cease the purely chronological recording of events and split the events into a Western and Eastern Front.

EASTERN FRONT

Mavinga Triangle

The world-famous Bermuda Triangle has achieved notoriety due to the many unexplained disappearances of aircraft and ships. For a few hours in 1985 it seemed that the mysteries surrounding Bermuda had been transposed to the

1985: Internationalization

Angolan bush around the little town of Mavinga. The following account was related to me by Major Ray Barske:

>>During the height of the bush war Major Barske, an experienced helicopter pilot, was on a tour as operations officer at AFB Rundu. Round-the-clock operations were being run from the base against SWAPO and in assisting UNITA in its struggle against the Angolan MPLA government. The operations staff was the hub around which all these activities took place.

During the evening of 5 January, Barske phoned WAC to report an aircraft accident. A Puma, flown by Captain J. C. Linde, had hit trees with its tail rotor. Linde had been on his way to fetch a casevac from 32 Battalion at a place called Luenga, in the bush, 60 kilometres south of Menonque. There were no injuries to the personnel in the helicopter but a new tail rotor needed to be flown out as a replacement for the damaged one. Colonel Dick Lord, SSO Ops in Windhoek, who took the call, thanked Barske for his report and gave the instruction, "Ray, you sort it out and keep me posted on progress."

Puma, workhorse of the border war.

Being short of Pumas, Barske requested one from Colonel Hap Potgieter in Oshakati. Potgieter dispatched a Puma flown by Major 'Slinger' Swart, accompanied by a maintenance-work team, from Ondangwa to Rundu early on the Saturday morning. Enemy MiG fighter activity prevented helicopter day sorties into Angola so Slinger and his crew had to wait until last light before taking off, and so the Puma did not arrive at 32 Battalion at its expected ETA. However, because there were thunderstorms in the vicinity, it was decided to wait until the aircraft either radioed in its position or arrived back at Rundu, before initiating overdue action. When the total planned flight time had elapsed and there was still no sign of Slinger and his Puma, Barske reported the missing aircraft to his HQ in Windhoek. Once again Colonel Lord said, "Ray, you sort it out and keep me posted."

Full of initiative, Barske then instructed a C-160, during its resupply run into Mavinga, to perform an electronic search for the missing Puma. The C-160 disappeared northwards, but no call came from Mavinga to announce its arrival. The Mavinga Triangle had struck! A Puma disabled in the bush, another Puma and a C-160 missing without trace.

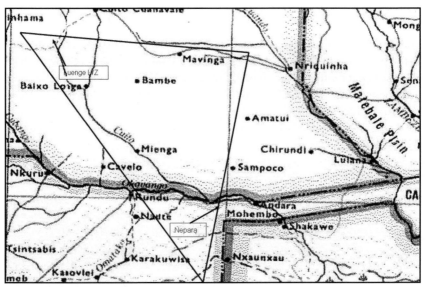

The Mavinga Triangle.

Barske, questioning his bad luck, phoned Windhoek with his report of yet another aircraft missing. Colonel Lord's words of wisdom were, "Ray, you sort it out and keep me posted."

Wondering what to do next Barske was delighted to hear the drone of the C-160 on approach to land. The communications gap between Rundu and Mavinga was responsible for the supposed loss of the big transport aircraft. Within minutes an army officer ran in to the command post to inform Barske that he had just received a radio message from the army base at Nepara; it reported the arrival of an air force officer, in full flying kit, without an aircraft.

Slinger's flight to 32 Battalion had been badly disrupted by the storms. Being forced way off track, with his Puma very short of fuel, he had eventually landed on the Golden Highway, the sand road stretching the whole length of the Caprivi Strip. Flagging down an extremely surprised local he had cadged a lift for the ten kilometres to Nepara.

Slinger's aircraft was refuelled on Sunday morning. By evening the mission was finally accomplished. The spares were flown in for J. C. Linde's aeroplane which, fitted with its new tail rotor, was flown back to a much-relieved Ray Barske. Barske then sent Slinger's Puma back to Hap Potgieter, having already returned the C-160 to AFB Grootfontein. His final action, after successfully laying to rest the myth of the Mavinga Triangle, was to report back to his headquarters in Windhoek. After hearing his long explanation over the phone, Colonel Lord said, "Thank you Ray, well done."<<

The nightly ration, ammunition and personnel resupply to Mavinga was going full-steam ahead to keep up with the demands of the fighting forces in the front line. Every night C-130 and C-160 aircraft shuttled between Rundu, Grootfontein and Mavinga. The fast turnaround schedule meant the aircraft never switched off their engines, even while offloading at Mavinga. The lack of a suitable loading ramp at the airfield necessitated this task being carried out on the turning circle at the end of the runway.

Logistics are always a headache for commanders in the field. To co-ordinate 32 Battalion's supplies and requirements Major Johan van der Vyver, their logistical officer, flew in to Mavinga on the first aircraft on the night of 12 September. He was to hold discussions and a planning session throughout the night, returning to Rundu on the last aircraft out.

That night Commandant Chris Rabie was the C-160 pilot of the last sortie to Rundu. The offloading went as planned with the aircraft's engines still running. On completion the aircraft loadmaster indicated to the gathered passengers to enter the aircraft via the opened back ramp. It was closed once all the passengers were on board; van der Vyver arrived just as it was closing. Not wanting to miss the flight back he ran to enter by the aircraft's side door which was still open.

Unfortunately, his path took him through the propeller arc of the port engine. Rotating blades are difficult to see during daytime and virtually impossible at night. He was struck and killed by two of the blade tips. Rabie immediately shut down the engine because it began vibrating very badly due to the damaged propellor.

The approaching dawn complicated the situation on the ground. The C-160 was too large to successfully camouflage and would attract the attention of the daily flights by Angolan MiGs. Also, it was blocking the runway halting any further flights to Mavinga. It was not possible to attempt a take-off from the confined, narrow, sand strip using just one engine.

Although very shaken by the accident Rabie made a decision to take the aircraft out. Unloading everything possible to reduce weight he started both engines and took off, despite the vibration. On gaining safe flying speed he immediately switched off the port engine and flew on one engine back to Rundu.

'Murphy' now decided it was time to put in his appearance. On final approach, with the plane's wheels down in a high-drag configuration, the runway lights at Rundu went out. Somehow Rabie managed to get the damaged aircraft to overshoot. He then had to circle the airfield until the base's standby generator came on line and restored the runway lights. Then he was able to make a safe one-engined landing. This was fine airmanship from Rabie and his crew which saved the aircraft from almost certain destruction at the hands of the Angolan Air Force, FAPA.

On June 10, aircraft from AFB Rundu were used to deploy two seven-man teams into the Luena and Bie areas of Angola. These teams assisted UNITA in demolition, medical and reconnaissance training over a four-month period.

Intelligence inputs regarding the build-up of Angolan forces in the Menonque and Cuito Cuanavale region increased dramatically throughout the first half of the year. This prompted the requirement for photography of the area. On 27 June, a pair of Canberras flew a most successful PR sortie covering Cuito and Baixa Longa, in excellent weather. The enemy had decided that Mavinga was to be their initial prize. Firstly, it had a runway suitable for supporting their push against UNITA. Secondly, it was an ideal location to position one of their radar sites, effectively closing the yawning gap in their existing radar coverage. If they could not take Mavinga, then Baixa Longa was the second prize; hence the required photographic coverage.

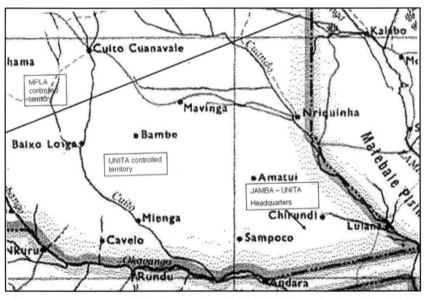

The straight line in the top left of the map roughly denotes the separation between MPLA and UNITA territories. Ideally, the Angolan government wanted Mavinga, with its airstrip, from which to attack Jamba. The second choice was to establish a radar site at Baixo Longa.

Operation *Second Congress*

Ever since the MPLA party came into power in 1975, they had tried to destroy UNITA militarily and politically. Despite all these actions UNITA had, by 1985, succeeded in extending their area of influence and control over large parts of rural Angola.

General Constand Viljoen and Jonas Savimbi after a meeting at UNITA Headquarters in Jamba, southeastern Angola. These meetings invariably led to additional assistance being required from the SADF.

In 1985, the Angolan armed forces were tasked to undertake massive operations simultaneously in the Moxico and Cuando Cubango provinces which were under UNITA's control. The aim of the operation, named *Second Congress*, was to launch a two-pronged advance, the first into the Cazombo Bight (3rd Military Region) and the second to capture Mavinga (6th Military Region) by 2 September. They would then continue the offensive in a final assault on Jamba, UNITA's HQ in southeast Angola.

UNITA controlled the Cazombo enclave on Angola's eastern border with Zambia. The eastern thrust of *Second Congress* was an attempt, which proved successful, by the MPLA government to recapture this vast territory. South Africa only became involved in this campaign when requested by UNITA. We were required to fly in large numbers of UNITA reinforcements to the airfields of Gago Couthino and Cazombo. The SAAF plan formulated for this operation was called Operation *Magneto*. We positioned MAOT teams at both airfields to control the flying, all of which was done at night because of the threat of MiG interception. Between 23 August and 10 September, SAAF C-130/C-160 aircraft flew 220 hours on delivery flights and the Pumas another 30 hours. A possible record load aboard a Lockheed Hercules was flown one evening, when a total of 183 soldiers were airlifted from one sand strip to another. It was during this hectic evacuation period from the Cazombo enclave that a truly remarkable search and rescue took place.

Long-range casevac

In South Africa, all people with the surname Labuschagne are called Lappies. As the name is not uncommon this can lead to problems. To sort out the confusion a qualification is usually added to the name if the person is not present. For example, '24 Lappies' happens to be Major-General Frans Labuschagne, ex-CO of 24 Squadron.

'Lang (Afrikaans for long because of his six-foot-plus stature) Lappies' was the permanent Puma pilot based at AFB Rundu throughout 1985. Being a permanent member of staff his family was with him and they lived in Rundu town. On the evening of 16 September, he had just started his evening braai and poured drinks for his South African guests. Being on casevac standby Lappies poured himself a soft drink … as the call-out came.

Arriving at the airfield he was briefed by Major Jannie van der Merwe. Two casevacs needed to be flown from a place near the Angolan town of Lunga. Lappies and his co-pilot, Lieutenant Mark von Zorgenfrei, planned the mission, their first task being to locate Lunga. It turned out to be situated in the Cazombo enclave, a rectangular block of territory protruding into Zambia on Angola's eastern border. This discovery came as a shock to Lappies. Security was so good he was unaware South Africans were involved in operations that far north of the SWA border.

After finding a set of maps covering the entire route they started their navigational planning. After the charts had been stuck together the locking bar from a steel filing cabinet was needed to draw in the tracks, a normal navigational ruler being too short. Appreciating the extreme distances involved Lappies asked the two flight engineers, flight sergeants Christo Botes and Ken van Straaten, to fit four long-range ferry tanks into the helicopter's cabin. This was to be the only occasion that Lappies ever flew with the maximum of four extra fuel tanks on board.

They planned to fly direct to Lunga and land, to obtain further clearance before continuing to pick up the casevacs. Gago Coutinho was the alternate refuelling point. After adding a doctor to the crew they lifted off at 20h15 into a very dark, moonless, night sky. The darkness and lack of visual landmarks added to the tension of the long flight. The Pumas, based in the bush, were notoriously difficult to compass-swing within the acceptable limits. The navigation was dead reckoning (DR), with the help of the ground speed and drift modes given by the Doppler radar.

After the first hour thunderstorms on the horizon began to add interest to the low-level flight. The vivid lightning strikes had the advantage of momentarily illuminating the area, therefore, it became possible to pick up the major rivers and in that way keep track of distance flown. Within radio range of Lunga they started calling on radio, without success. At the Lunga airstrip the air force had a MAOT under the command of Major 'Budgie' Burgers. Fortunately,

1985: Internationalization

Harry Gilliland and Fred Frayne, flying a Dakota in the same area, heard the Puma calling and told them to change frequency in order to pick up Burgers. Thankfully, they did this and made contact. Burgers sent up a flare to guide them in and they landed just after 23h30.

Burgers told them that the two casevacs were not yet in a position to be picked up. At night, radio communications on HF radio were poor and the UNITA soldiers, being chased by FAPLA, had to keep on the move. Breaking out a tin of pickled fish from a ration pack they settled down to wait. Botes and van Straaten used this interlude to refuel the helicopter, to avoid having to refuel on the return flight. Studying the route they had just flown they realized they had violated international airspace, inadvertently overflying a small portion of Zambian territory.

The Dakota, whose crew had assisted them on the radio, landed and Lappies discovered that Gilliland and Frayne were taking out UNITA casevacs from the battle which had been raging in the area for the past few days.

Around 02h00, Burgers briefed the Puma crew on the co-ordinates of the LZ and shortly thereafter they took off. The LZ was another 60 nautical miless northeast of Lunga which they found after half an hour, and was marked by the pre-briefed three fires. When UNITA was requested to make fires they always did this very well.

The distance to Lunga was just over 400nms and the pick-up point another 60nms farther, making this one of the longest helicopter casevacs on record. Compare the distance flown to the positions of Mavinga and Cuito Cuanavale.

The trees around the LZ were appreciably higher than the bush in southern Angola. The enclave is only 11° south of the equator, hence the lush climatic conditions. Lappies had to perform a steeper-than-normal approach into the confined LZ. On landing, UNITA soldiers indicated by hand signals that the casevacs were being brought from a temporary base to the helicopter. Lappies kept the motors idling to avoid a possible starting snag at this remote location and after 15 minutes the two casevacs were loaded and the helicopter took off on its return flight to Lunga.

At Lunga, it was decided not to transfer the casevacs to the Dakota as the doctor had stabilized them and was happy with their condition. Around 04h00, Lappies took off for the long flight back to Rundu, landing there shortly after 07h00. On shut-down, Lappies remembers overhearing the one patient saying to the other, "When we get back to the States we are going to have the biggest steak meal we can get, washed down by lots of rum." (The 'States' was troopie slang for South Africa.)

Lappies assumed, on overhearing this conversation, that the two men were not too badly injured. Subsequently, the doctor told him at that stage the men were still living on the adrenaline flow brought on by their traumatic experiences. The night after their return to Rundu was the critical one, with both men requiring intensive care treatment to keep them alive.

Both patients survived. They were awarded the Honoris Crux for their actions in the contact where they had been seriously wounded. Major Theunis Coetzee and Lieutenant Leon Phillipson were driving along a dirt road when an enemy ambush of about 40 men opened fire. Both men were wounded, Coetzee in the left thigh and Phillipson in the foot. In trying to rescue a badly wounded medical orderly Theunis was shot again, this time through the shoulder.

Lappies was awarded the Southern Cross Medal for his dedication and determination in helping to save the lives of these two soldiers.

On his first bush tour as a Puma commander Lappies had been tasked to fly Puma 156 north from Eenhana to a *shona* inside Angola. On this flight on 13 September 1980, his flight engineer was Ken van Straaten. They were trooping soldiers from 32 Battalion, working under the operational command of Commandant Deon Ferreira. As they touched down they felt a tremendous shudder throughout the aircraft followed by heavy vibrations. They immediately shut down the engines. Looking backwards out of the cockpit Lappies could see that the entire tail rotor was missing.

The date probably had something to do with this incident. He can consider himself very unlucky to have lost his rotor on the 13th, however, they were all extremely fortunate that it occurred on touch-down, not a moment before

The complete Puma tail boom was removed and replaced with a serviceable unit, in the bush, under combat conditions. The infantry was called in to literally

Left: This close-up shows the damage to the Puma after the tail-rotor disintegrated.
Right: Maintenance in the bush. Major Labuschagne, far left, anxiously supervises the reconstruction of his aircraft.

lend a hand, as the entire tail section had to be lifted manually into position. After a test run suitable adjustments were made and a valuable aircraft was returned to service.

Operations *Wallpaper* and *Weldmesh*

UNITA guerrillas and their reinforcements did not have the capability to withstand Angolan government forces supported by tanks and armoured vehicles. Realizing their position had become untenable UNITA, once again, requested our help. They needed to withdraw their threatened troops from Cazombo and have them flown to Mavinga to bolster their defences against the southeasterly leg (the left hook) of the Angolan advance.

Operation *Wallpaper* was planned and between 11 September and 8 October C-130/C-160, L-100 and DC-4 aircraft flew 310 hours, again at night, to return UNITA troops to Mavinga. In a parody of the children's rhyme we had, like the Grand old Duke of York, 'marched our men to the top of the hill and then marched them down again'. That is the nature of war when the future is difficult to predict. Historians find it much easier to pass judgment after the event.

An important point to note here is that none of these airfields bore any resemblance to airfields in the 'First World'. They all had sand runways, hacked out of the African bush during the time of the Portuguese occupation. There were no approach or navigational aids and air traffic control was exercised by the SAAF MAOT commander using a portable VHF radio. Runway lighting was provided by beer or cold drink tins, half-filled with sand doused with paraffin and placed at intervals to outline the runway. On command they were lit to illuminate the runway on which the heavily laden aircraft would land.

In the turning circle at the end of the runway the aircraft ramp would be lowered to disgorge or load UNITA troops while the aircraft engines were kept running. We could not afford to have engine problems at these airfields as the aircraft had to be back in SWA by dawn; patrolling MiGs would make short work of any aircraft left on the ground. The cargo aircraft had been stripped of seating and the troops were packed like sardines into the cavernous holds. As the pressure of war increased the record for passengers carried was often exceeded on successive flights.

All these flights, carried out under extreme operational pressure, were successful because they occurred in the all-important 'gap' which existed in the enemy radar chain. It is my belief that plugging this hole with a suitable early-warning radar system was more important to the enemy triumvirate than capturing Savimbi's HQ at Jamba.

Jonas Savimbi persuaded the South African government that his forces could not prevent the Angolans capturing Mavinga and, inevitably, Jamba, without active intervention by the SADF. UNITA's presence in southeastern Angola was of tremendous value to South Africa. They effectively controlled 600 kilometres of the international border between Angola and SWA along the Caprivi Strip. The opening up of this border to SWAPO would create an almost impossible situation for the already stretched South African defences. Therefore, it was not surprising that the SADF was ordered to prepare a plan to provide air support to UNITA in order to assist them in stopping the Angolan advance from Cuito Cuanavale to Mavinga. This plan, known as Operation *Weldmesh*, lasted between 16 September and 9 October 1985.

In the Angolan 6th Military Region there were only two airfields suitable for sustained air operations—Menongue and Cuito Cuanavale. During *Second Congress*, Menonque was used for both fighter and helicopter operations while Cuito Cuanavale operated only helicopters. As the operation progressed they were forced to withdraw all their aircraft to Menonque. The helicopter deployment at Cuito Cuanavale consisted of four Mi-25, two Mi-8 and four Mi-

An Mi-17 transport helicopter showing rocket pods on the side of the fuselage and the large loading door in the rear. The rockets were not used offensively but to clear landing zones in the bush.

17 helicopters, plus an unknown number of Alouette IIIs.

Southeast Angola is extremely flat with trees reaching up to 100 feet in height. The relief does not change by more than 300 feet for 300 nautical miles northward from AFB Rundu. The rivers are situated in open grassland areas called *shonas*. Navigation is difficult as there are no outstanding hilly features. The safest method of air navigation is to follow river lines or the few roads to be found in the area. The term 'roads' is used loosely as they are normally just sandy tracks through the bush.

The FAPLA advance towards Mavinga developed into a two-axis pincer movement after their brigades crossed the Cuito River. The southernmost route rounded the source of the Lomba River, west of Mavinga, allowing their forces to advance towards the UNITA-held town on the southern side of the east–west-orientated Lomba River.

Transport helicopters were used to resupply FAPLA brigades running short of supplies, caused by aggressive UNITA actions against FAPLA resupply convoys. These missions were flown on a daily basis providing critical items such as vehicle spares and medical supplies. Casevac missions were flown when necessary.

Mi-25 gunship helicopters were used to escort transport helicopters as well as CAS for ground forces. They would often be used to provide flushing fire onto LZs during troop deployments. On these missions 57mm rockets would be fired using a shallow dive profile and on rare occasions, cannon fire.

An Mi-25 helicopter gunship in flight over Angolan bush, presenting the type of target sought by SAAF Impala pilots.

The helicopter formations would transit at 3,000 to 6,000 feet AGL with the escort helicopters one to two kilometres in the rear. The transport helicopters would fly in a line-astern formation and the escorts in a loose echelon about 500 metres apart. They had probably assessed that the threat from ground fire was greater than an air threat and this was the reason for flying such a vulnerable formation. Soviet advisors believed the main threat to the helicopters was from RPG-7 and small-arms fire. Depending on the threat the helicopter formation would often be escorted by MiG-23 fighters flying at approximately 15,000 feet AGL and orbiting to the rear.

We assessed that, in general, the standard of enemy flying was poor. Their navigation abilities were extremely weak and it was noted they always used physical features such as river lines and roads to enable them to reach their destinations. They would seldom fly a direct route to any point. This lack of competence was another reason for flying at height and pilots often failed to find their LZs. Furthermore, because their missions tended to be planned for the same time of day our intelligence community was able to easily predict these sorties.

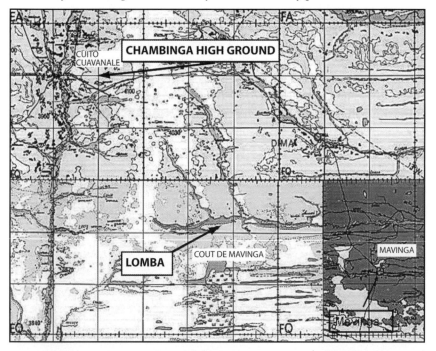

This compilation of maps shows Cuito Cuanavale at the top left and Mavinga at bottom right. The Lomba River running east–west between the two towns can be clearly seen. The Cuzizi and Cunzambia are the two tributaries running into the Lomba from the north. It was these two outstanding features the Angolan pilots used as navigational aids.

Radio discipline and procedures were poor. However, these improved as losses were incurred or when Soviet pilots flew as formation leaders. Only two radio frequencies were used, one for fighter and helicopter operations and the other for transport aircraft operations. Night operations were not flown; helicopters returned to base before at dusk.

A major aerial bombardment by Canberra, Buccaneer, Mirage and Impala fighter-bombers decimated the FAPLA brigades, forcing them to retreat back towards Cuito Cuanavale. The following table gives an idea of the intensity of the battle:

Aircraft type	Hours flown
Mirage F1CZ	33
Mirage F1AZ	171
Buccaneer	37
Canberra	69
Impala	241
Puma	71

I hasten to add, the SAAF aerial attacks were in addition to accurate and heavy artillery bombardment from the South African ground force, deployed to counter the Soviet-built armoured vehicles used by the Angolan government forces. A number of South African soldiers were attached as advisors to UNITA battalions. Members of our Special Forces and 32 Battalion were used in active reconnaissance and ambush roles.

Helicopter shoot-down

During this retreat the guerrilla forces of UNITA harried the Angolans. The enemy had suffered severe losses both in personnel and equipment and were in a pitiful state. By intercepting enemy broadcasts it became known that FAPLA had requested assistance from their helicopter force to remove the many casualties back to their medical centres.

Another radio intercept was received shortly after the helicopter shuttle began. In this message it became obvious that, whereas the Angolans wanted to evacuate their wounded their Soviet advisors had a totally different aim. The patients were ignored and the Soviets themselves used the air transport to escape to safe havens. This callous disregard of their allies was seen as an opportunity by the South Africans.

The impetus behind Angolan operations was provided by Soviet advisors. They had planned, led and orchestrated *Second Congress*. Suddenly a golden opportunity presented itself for the SAAF which could seriously affect the conduct of the campaign.

A planning session for an attack on these enemy helicopters was initiated. It was later established they were operating from Menongue at this stage of the campaign.

All enemy helicopter activities occurred well below SAAF radar cover. To enable a DR plan to be formulated accurate helicopter lift-off times from the enemy airfield at Menongue were required. A ground force team was needed to be in visual contact with this airfield, who could then radio the required information back to the SAAF command post in Rundu. A small professional team from 32 Battalion volunteered for this dangerous, but essential task.

Deployed at AFB Rundu were Mirage F1CZ fighters and Impalas to supply CAS to ground forces. A decision was made to employ the Impala rather than the more sophisticated and faster Mirage for the envisaged task, the turning ability of the slower Impala being considered better suited for attacking helicopters.

Once the communication relay plan had been formulated the ground force team set off to find a suitable vantage spot from which to view the airfield. This was not easy. Because the terrain was as flat as a pancake it meant that the communications team had to find a hiding position very close to the airfield's perimeter. During the time they required to get into position the SAAF set up a training programme. Suitable *shonas* south of Rundu in SWA were selected to simulate those north of the border. Puma helicopters were tasked to fly along these routes at 2,000 feet above the ground.

Then Impalas were launched to fly at very low level, also along these routes, with the idea of visually locating the Pumas and carrying out dummy 30mm cannon attacks on them. The Pumas simulated the flying techniques and formations used by the Angolan aircraft.

The main problem the Impala pilots had to contend with was the ingress at 50 feet AGL. This was required to keep them below enemy radar cover to ensure surprise and to prevent the MiG-23 escort fighters from being pre-warned of the SAAF's intentions. The profile decided upon was to attack the helicopters from the rear quarter and from slightly above. With underwing stores the little Impalas bled speed very quickly in a rapid pitch-up from low level, leaving them vulnerable at the top of the pitch to the MiG escort. It was found, when the attack was initiated, that by reducing the rate of pitch and flattening the peak of the pitch a suitable overtaking and manoeuvring speed could be maintained.

For the actual operation the Impalas would fly in pairs and, during the attack, a type of scissors pattern would be used with the lead Impala attacking the rearmost helicopter first. The wingman would then attack the next helicopter. Four pairs of Impalas would be used for each sortie, three to carry out the armed reconnaissance and the fourth to act as back-up for SAR if necessary. During each intercept mission a pair of Pumas would be airborne for SAR recovery.

From AFB Rundu the combat zone was 35 minutes' flying time for the Impalas, therefore, timing for the operation was critical. Pairs of Impalas would be launched at four-minute intervals to fly the same route to the combat area. This allowed an eight-minute coverage window along the anticipated helicopter routes. This window was considered to give the most area coverage without placing the pilots' lives, or aircraft safety, in jeopardy. The pilots were instructed to make one pass over the route; they were not to remain in the area if there

1985: Internationalization

were no helicopters on the scene and radio silence was to be maintained at all times. However, a fixed-wing aircraft would fly at high level, overhead Rundu, to relay code words informing the Impala pilots on the status of enemy helicopters and escorts. Impala crews were placed on cockpit standby to be scrambled immediately word was received regarding enemy helicopter movements. Enemy flights were so regular they were reasonably easy to predict.

Numerous missions were aborted, either before take-off or after the scramble, when the mission controllers realized the timing of the flights was wrong. However, each aborted mission provided a refinement of the parameters until finally at approximately 16h00 on the afternoon of 27 September the first successful mission was scrambled.

The SAAF CP received news from the ground force team that two Mi-25 attack helicopters were airborne and heading for the war zone. The Impalas were scrambled and soon in the area, with the wingman of the second pair of Impalas making visual contact with the helicopter formation. The helicopters were flying at 2,000 feet AGL. As he was in the most favourable position to attack the wingman pitched-up towards the rearmost helicopter. He attacked, as practised, from the rear and above the helicopter and his burst of fire was observed to strike towards the rear of the fuselage. After a short period of time the helicopter started to burn and the helicopter pilot initiated a controlled descent towards the ground. Then the helicopter started to burn furiously and the pilot fired off his FFAR (forward firing air rockets) rockets carried in the underwing pods and also jettisoned all his underwing stores.

As the Impala leader began his quarter-attack he saw the lead helicopter initiate a steep descent so he approached it from below and to the side. As the helicopter turned the Impala closed range until, with his pipper on the exhaust port, he fired 19 rounds. Strikes were observed on the side of the helicopter exactly where the pipper indicated. A side panel was seen to detach from the helicopter, which immediately adopted a high nose position and the rotor blades separated. The helicopter went into a tail slide, hit the ground nose-high and exploded.

The wingman had by this stage repositioned for a second pass on his target and shot it down. With the second burst of 30mm cannon the rotor blades separated and the helicopter crashed, exploding on impact with the ground.

Two days later the 32 Battalion ground team again informed SAAF operations of another helicopter formation which had lifted off, bound for the battle zone. This mixed formation consisted of two Mi-8/17 transport helicopters escorted by two Mi-25 gunship helicopters. The Impalas were again scrambled and similar tactics and procedures used as on the previous operation.

A helicopter formation was observed flying along the Lomba River at 3,000 feet AGL. The Mi-8/17 formation was in a trailing echelon about 1,000 metres apart. A further 1,000 metres astern were the Mi-25s, also in an echelon.

The first pair of Impalas initiated the attack which was continued by the second pair, resulting in all four helicopters being brought down. Interestingly, the third pair of Impalas noticed two MiG-23 fighters flying at 200 feet AGL over the burning wreckage, after which they swept their wings and zoomed up to a safer altitude.

It was soon apparent that the Angolans had entirely ceased all helicopter resupply/rescue/evacuation operations. Also of note, it was the first time Impala aircraft had destroyed enemy aircraft in aerial combat.

General Meiring presenting the Jakkals Trophy to Western Air Command's Brigadier 'Thack' Thackwray and Colonel Dick Lord. This trophy was awarded every quarter to the unit, or individual, who has shown the best *veglus* and *veglis*—fighting skill and enthusiasm. The trophy was presented to acknowledge WAC's effort in destroying enemy helicopters.

*****

In 1986, to discourage the Angolans from attempting another advance towards Mavinga an entire series of operations was planned under the overall codename *Asterix*. Most of these contingency plans were not used although a few of the smaller operations did take place.

During October, our Special Forces carried out Operation *Cerebus*. A SAAF C-130 was used to fly two captured SA-9 systems into Mavinga. From there the BRDMs were driven to a position within the Menonque–Baixa Longa–Cuito Cuanavale triangle. This deployment was assisted by UNITA. Perhaps the enemy got wind of the deployment because all FAPA aircraft avoided the once very busy area; no aircraft were shot down.

During December, Operations *Jerry 1* and 2 were launched to harass and disrupt FAPLA preparations in the 6th Military Region. The operation used multiple rocket launchers to carry out stand-off bombardments of Angolan positions. The many engagements that took place were attributed to UNITA.

On 8 December, a single SAAF Buccaneer carried out successful LOROP (long range oblique photography) of the Cuito bridge and Angolan brigade concentrations, east and west of the river. The camera pod was mounted within the rotating bomb bay of the aircraft.

On 18 December, SAAF C-130 aircraft transported seven Unimog Sabre vehicles and 50 Reconnaissance force troops into Mavinga for Operation *Abrasion*. This operation was planned to last until mid-February 1986. In co-operation with UNITA this team was tasked to carry out offensive hit and run operations against the enemy between Menonque and Cuito Cuanavale. At AFB Rundu Pumas were on casevac standby throughout the operation. Impala aircraft were used in a Telstar role to maintain radio contact between the team and HQ in Rundu.

This photograph taken from a Buccaneer cockpit illustrates the type of terrain found in the combat theatre. If the picture is studied carefully the leading Buccaneer can be seen just right and below the IFR nozzle, the correct height to fly in combat.

WESTERN FRONT

Telstar

On 8 February, Captain Mario Vergottini, on his fifth bush tour and stationed at AFB Ondangwa, was called to the ops room. He was tasked to fly his Kudu on a Telstar mission. The Bosbok which usually performed these duties was unavailable. The Pumas, known by bush operators as 'Giants', were tasked for a night mission into Angola. These flights were usually conducted in radio silence apart from the 20-minute 'ops normal' calls. Vergottini was tasked to relay these progress reports back to 310 AFCP at Oshakati and, in the event of the Pumas picking up an emergency, to be on hand to initiate the SAR plan.

He took off at 20h30 and headed for the selected Telstar position, just north of Eenhana, at 10,000 feet. On arrival he settled into a gentle 5° banked turn to orbit the position. It was a beautiful, clear, calm night. He had the aircraft well-trimmed and was enjoying a sense of wellbeing. As per the briefing the Giants called in at their reporting points and Vergottini promptly relayed the message to Dayton and X-Ray 2 at Oshakati.

During this tranquil period Vergottini kept an eye on the ADF (automatic direction finding) needle, ensuring that it corresponded with the position of Ondangwa. However, after an hour, with everything perfect, Vergottini decided to while away the long wait by reading his book. Thirty minutes later he noticed a blanket of cloud moving in and decided to climb above it to 12,500 feet; he levelled off and continued to orbit. The onset of the cloud upset the flying conditions and the Kudu started to buck and bounce. Vergottini could see lightning flashing underneath him as the intensity of the approaching storm increased. The Giants' final call came in forty minutes later and he relayed the message as required. Feeling chuffed with himself at having successfully completed his first Telstar mission he turned and headed for home.

At this point, the ADF needle which had been extremely steady throughout the flight broke lock and started to revolve—one of the limitations of this equipment is that electricity, generated in thunderstorms, seriously affects the accuracy of the indications. He checked the NDB frequency which was correct and still the needle just revolved. He then switched his radio to the AFB Ondangwa frequency but received no answer. He tried both the Dayton radar and X-Ray 2 frequencies but had no joy on either. Feeling uneasy he called the Giants but without success. He began to feel anxious. He was above cloud at night with a severe electrical storm beneath him, could no longer tell where he was in relation to Ondangwa, had no idea whether he was inside Angola or SWA and was unable to make radio communications with anyone. During the war, while the curfew was in force throughout Owamboland very few, if any, lights were seen on the ground. It was a very dark country to fly over.

Vergottini decided his best option would be to fly southward while trying to make contact on both VHF and HF radios. On this heading he checked the fuel remaining in his tanks. He had used quite an amount during his two hours of flying but knew that if he leaned the mixture for endurance flying would have another two hours of flight time available.

After 30 minutes on his southerly heading he found himself inside the storm clouds and opted to descend in an attempt to fly below them. This would allow him to fly at a reduced power setting to save a little fuel and, hopefully, see some distinguishing feature on the ground.

He broke cloud at 8,000 feet in the pouring rain after a hectic descent. It was pitch black with nothing to be seen in any direction. He had used up more than one hour of his remaining fuel. Vergottini started to consider about how, when and where he could make a landing in the dark. He was hoping to find a stretch of road and land while there was still enough fuel to control the descent. He did not want to make a dead-stick landing under such circumstances. He commenced a slow descent and levelled off at 1,000 feet AGL, from where he began descending very gradually in an attempt to identify ground features with his landing light.

Suddenly he heard a radio call from a Dakota which had entered the Ondangwa area. Vergottini tried contacting him but there was no reply. The Dakota then called, "Base leg, turning finals" and to Vergottini's delight he saw the sky light up in his 5 o'clock position. Although it was very faint he knew it had to be the Dakota's landing lights. He turned his Kudu towards the light, praying he had sufficient fuel remaining to reach the base. After an extremely anxious half an hour he was back, safe and sound on the ground.

When he landed the base was in a state of pandemonium. Vergottini understood why after chatting to an ATC officer. For some inexplicable reason, after the Giants had landed, the tower had forgotten the Kudu was still airborne and switched off the radios and NDB beacon. The next expected arrival was the Dakota, just before midnight when the radios and navigation aids would be switched on again. The pandemonium was caused by the radar monitoring a very slow blip moving towards Ondangwa and Dayton was busy scrambling Impala jets to investigate. No one knew whose aircraft it was until Vergottini called the tower ten minutes before he landed.

The following morning, one of the Kudu maintenance personnel discreetly called Vergottini aside. He showed Vergottini that 633 pounds of fuel had been needed to fill the Kudu's tanks. The pilot's notes for the Kudu warn all pilots they can rely on only 642 pounds of useable fuel. Vergottini had been a very, very lucky pilot.

*****

On the night of 28 June, SWAPO terrorists sabotaged a culvert near Oshakati and blew down some telephone poles. In great haste, Sector 10 planned and executed Operation *Boswilger*, to follow up and destroy the insurgents. Ondangwa Puma and Alouette helicopters assisted the army and Koevoet ground forces in a follow-up which extended from Oshakati to 40 kilometres within Angola.

From Fledgling to Eagle

SWAPO knew they were no match militarily for the security forces therefore they concentrated their attacks against soft targets from which they could make safe their escape. This is not a criticism, as it took great courage for them to undertake these missions and the results achieved the media attention they sought.

The SADF warned the Angolan authorities they were pursuing SWAPO into Angola and wisely the Angolans refrained from trying to stop us. This was a most successful operation over 29 and 30 June, during which 57 SWAPO were killed in 36 different contacts for the loss of one of our soldiers.

On 15 September, Operation *Egret* was launched as a pre-emptive external operation against the SWAPO Charlie Detachment in the Evale, Aanhanca and Dova area of the 5th Military Region. The aim of the operation was to disrupt the expected SWAPO incursion. Puma, Alouette and Impala aircraft supported 500 men from 101 Owambo Battalion, organized into mobile Romeo Mike teams, who combed the selected area. This was another successful operation which led to nine separate contacts and at least one air strike, in which 15 terrorists were killed and 103 captured.

This operation was curtailed early as our forces were required to assist in the battle to stop *Second Congress*, the Angolan advance towards Mavinga.

Marienflüss: 17 October 1985

A reconnaissance team of Special Force commandos had to be deployed deep into the southwestern corner of Angola. The obvious place from which to run the operation was Okangwati, a military base in northern Kaokoland. The sand runway allowed the use of fixed-wing aircraft and there was a strategic fuel storage facility for avtur (helicopter fuel) and avgas (aviation petrol for piston-engined aircraft).

1985: Internationalization

Colonel Dick Lord standing on one of the revetment walls, raised to protect the army base at Okongwati from stand-off bombardments.

The operation was planned at the Sector 10 HQ in Oshakati where it was decided Major Brian Williams would deploy to Okangwati as the MAOT commander. He would be in tactical charge of the air force contingent which included three Puma helicopters and a Bosbok. Two Pumas would deploy the soldiers while the third helicopter would serve as a back-up for them. The Bosbok would fly at altitude in a holding pattern over the Cunene River, the border between SWA and Angola, to act as the Telstar. The penetration would take place at low level below Angolan radar cover. VHF radio range is limited to line of sight only, hence the necessity for a relay facility.

The final tactical planning was carried out at Okangwati. The route decided on was northwest to the Marienflüss, then north across the Cunene into Angola. The drop was planned to take place after dark. During the late morning of 17 October the weather conditions started to deteriorate to the extent the SAAF wanted to postpone the operation. Because of the critical timing involved in their part of the operation the Special Forces team persuaded the air force to go ahead with the drop. However, they compromised by accepting a last-light insertion instead of the night drop. This adjustment to plan was acceptable to all parties and the operation commenced late in the afternoon.

The Pumas departed on their planned route with Major Manie Geldenhuys as flight leader and Lieutenant Nardus Meyer as his co-pilot. The flying conditions were typical of those associated with the Inter-Tropical Convergence Zone (ITCZ), the area between the tropics of Cancer and Capricorn where the trade winds from both hemispheres converge. This convergence causes huge upward development and results in a line of cumulo-nimbus clouds extending roughly east to west over thousands of miles. Airline passengers travelling between South Africa and Europe are often woken somewhere over mid-Africa by the aircraft's captain telling them to fasten their seat-belts. This is invariably caused by the presence of the ITCZ.

This weather did not greatly hamper the helicopters en route as they flew below the cloud base, necessitating only a few minor deviations to the planned track to avoid the heaviest rain showers. The intended LZ was reached and the reconnaissance team were successfully inserted. Although radio silence between formation aircraft was maintained, every 20 minutes Geldenhuys would send a quick 'ops normal' call on a predetermined frequency. This burst transmission was relayed to Brian Williams at Okangwati who was then able to keep track of the helicopters on their planned route.

The Bosbok, flown by Lieutenant Chris Rautenbach on his first bush tour, had taken off just after the helicopters, climbed to 9,000 feet and entered the holding pattern as arranged; he was now ready to relay all radio messages. Unfortunately, the ITCZ weather seriously affected the light aeroplane at this height. The first 'ops normal' call was the first and final message Brian Williams received from him.

The moisture content of the cloud mass was very high and the freezing level had lowered to around 8,000 feet. Icing on the aerials degraded the reception and transmission power of the radios, although this was not initially suspected. The other area where a piston- engined aircraft is very susceptible to icing is in the carburettor. Engine manufacturers know this and all such aircraft are fitted with a carburettor heating facility. The drawback of using 'carb-heat' is fuel consumption is greatly increased.

Always a lonely job—a solitary pilot doing his pre-flight check on his Bosbok.

As the operation continued Williams became more and more uncomfortable. Since the first 'ops normal' call he had not heard a further word from any of his aircraft. Suspecting radio problems with the Bosbok he decided to scramble the standby Puma to re-establish radio communications. This plan failed as the Puma also could not establish contact. By this time it was almost dark, the cloud base was covering the hilltops and the Puma that had gone instrument meteorological conditions (IMC) could not recover to Okangwati. There were no navigation aids in Kaokoland and because the terrain resembles the rugged craters of the moon was no place to attempt an unguided let-down. The Puma skipper diverted his aircraft farther south to Opuwa where the weather conditions were slightly better.

Williams was now frantic. All his aircraft were airborne, he hoped, but he could not talk to any of them. To add to his woes he could not report his problems to his higher HQ in Oshakati because the HF link was also disabled due to the bad weather. He spent an anxious, sleepless night not knowing what had happened to his entire force.

Unaware of the drama unfolding at Okangwati Geldenhuys and Captain Steve Whiting, the other Puma commanders, were heading back to South West Africa. The weather had worsened since their departure. With the cloud base lowering, visibility in the increasing showers was bad. Because the helicopters could land anywhere they were not particularly worried, especially when they re-entered the Marienflüss right on track. As they neared the river and moved closer to the Bosbok they re-established VHF radio contact with Rautenbach and were reasonably happy their mission had gone according to plan.

The Marienflüss is a unique geological phenomenon in the otherwise rugged Kaokoland terrain. It is a wide, flat valley running south to north, with the Cunene River at its northern extremity. It has a reasonably flat, sandy surface which allowed for the scraping of a sand runway for emergency purposes. This south–north runway lies in the western half of the valley and is demarcated by old petrol drums. A windsock is the only aid to pilots wishing to land there.

Geldenhuys led his formation into a left-hand turn as they exited the Flüss bound for Okangwati. It was already dark and they were flying with navigation and formation lights on. To get out of the Flüss the formation had to climb and Geldenhuys immediately realized that Okangwati, located in a bowl surrounded by high hills, was unapproachable. As they did not have sufficient fuel to fly anywhere else he made a decision to about-turn and led his formation back into the Flüss. A long, uncomfortable night lay ahead of them but all the crew preferred this rather than risk trying to get back to base.

On re-entering the Flüss Geldenhuys called up Rautenbach in the Bosbok and told him about the weather at Okangwati. He suggested Rautenbach divert to Opuwa. Rautenbach, being on his first tour thanked Geldenhuys and then asked, "Where is Opuwa?" Geldenhuys explained and Rautenbach found Opuwa on his map. He then realized, to his horror, that because of the increased fuel consumption while using carb-heat he did not have sufficient to reach Opuwa.

Geldenhuys, remembering the old runway in the Flüss suggested the only alternative possible. He told Rautenbach about the runway and described the setting—high mountains east and west, with the valley running south to north. He determined the height of the valley floor and passed the same pressure setting to Rautenbach to reset his altimeter.

While he was talking both helicopters were still airborne, air-taxiing across the valley trying to find the runway. Normally a runway, being a large, flat surface, is fairly easy to find. In the Flüss however, a very infrequently used sand runway is the same colour as the valley floor. At night, under the illumination of the aircraft's landing lights the search was doubly hard. Finally, Steve spotted the windsock and using it as a reference eventually located the runway.

Rautenbach, following Geldenhuys's talk-down, performed a spiral descent out of the clouds. On breaking through the cloud base he spotted the helicopter's landing lights which orientated him in the valley. The two helicopters now adopted a technique used by vehicles when assisting light aircraft to land on bush strips. They hovered on either side of the runway threshold with their landing lights pointing at 45° angles in the landing direction. Rautenbach made his approach between the two helicopters and landed his Bosbok safely on the runway, followed by the two Pumas.

At 06h00 the next morning, after an uncomfortable, but safe night they managed to communicate with Okangwati for the first time, much to the relief of Brian Williams. He arranged for the third Puma at Opuwa to take fuel to the stranded aircraft after which they all returned to base.

This unique rescue of Chris Rautenbach and his Bosbok from a potentially hazardous situation in a very hostile environment resulted from mutual concern between the crews and quick creative thinking.

Chapter 12

1986: Taking a breather

After *Weldmesh*, the intensity of the war diminished, allowing both sides time to plan for what was to come. With the SAAF it was a period of training, training and more training. Lessons learned from previous operations were analyzed and improvements were tried, tested and introduced. Pilot skills were polished and readiness levels were maintained so squadrons were prepared when called upon.

Fixed-wing battle-formation flying

The basis of all jet operations was the ability to fly impeccable formation under all conditions. When combat flying began during World War I it was soon realized that in a hostile environment an aircraft flying on its own was easy prey. Machine guns were fitted into the wings or nose of the fighters so in effect the pilot had to aim his aircraft at the enemy to have any hope of hitting the moving target. Head-on approaches almost always led to collisions; attacks from the side were difficult as the pilots had to judge how much 'lead' to use on the fast-moving target; sneaking up astern provided the most practical solution, particularly if the attacker approached by concealing himself below the tail of the target. The answer lay in the self-protection provided by flying in formation.

Flying abeam of each other, 300 metres apart, allowed each pilot to watch the other aircraft's tail, for that was the dangerous area. When machine guns were replaced by longer-ranged 20mm or 30mm cannons the fighters had to spread out to around 800 metres. With the advent of heat-seeking missiles, like the Soviet Atoll or American Sidewinder, the formation spread to 1,500 to 2,000 metres. Pilots had to be able see far enough astern to warn formation members of threats approaching from the rear. Good lookout and instant reactions were essential to counter enemy fighters which could be approaching at near supersonic speed.

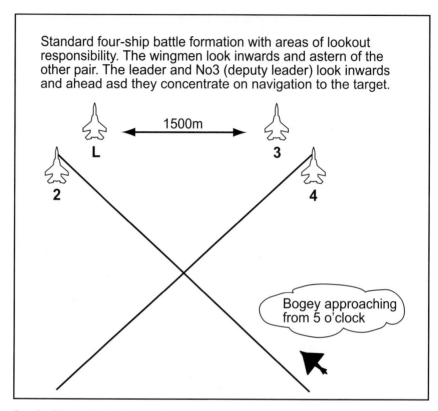

Standard four-ship battle formation.

This was the situation which prevailed during the border war.

The standard SAAF battle formation was a division of four aircraft flying as two pairs: the leader with his No 2 as wingman; No 3, the deputy leader with No 4 as his wingman. Lead and No 3 concentrated on lookout ahead and navigation, with the deputy leader being in a position to assume leadership at any stage of the flight if necessary. The wingmen flew looking backwards and inwards, as they were responsible for picking up any threat approaching from the dangerous 6 o'clock position.

Navigational turns were accomplished by the second pair crossing the leader's flight path to end up on the completion of the turn once again on the leader's beam. At altitude, the second pair could slide high or low to achieve this position.

At altitude the formation would be separated in the vertical plane as well, making it more difficult for an attacker to locate all the aircraft in the formation. However, when operating at low level all aircraft had to stay underneath the enemy radar cover during navigational turns. It was essential they maintained the same speed and so pilots had to use geometry to stay on the beam by sliding just above or behind the leader during turns. It was essential at this crossover

1986: Taking a breather

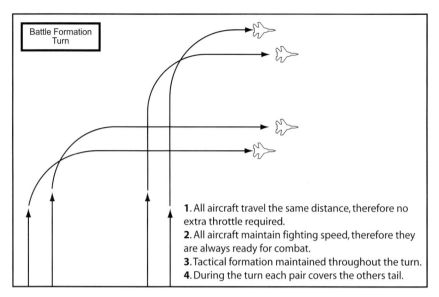

A standard 90° battle formation turn.

point to avoid passing through the slipstream of another aircraft, particularly when so close to the ground.

Using these formations allowed our pilots to visually cover each other right up to the moment they pitched up into the attack. After releasing their weapons and breaking off from the attack it was judicious to regain battle formation as soon as possible for the flight back to base.

During fighter combat this same formation allows the leader freedom to manoeuvre as hard as he likes and to use the second pair (Nos 3 and 4) to sandwich any attacker. Any pilot in the formation can assume tactical leadership of the formation if he sights a 'bogey' in a threatening position. He will continue to control the situation until the leader can see the enemy and takes over control once again. Good battle formation is the basis of good command in the air.

Navigation

Aerial navigation is fraught with difficulties. The crew of a slow-flying aircraft has plenty of time for map-reading and the mental arithmetic required to keep the aircraft on track and on time. However, they are more affected by the vagaries of the wind which affects both track and time-keeping. The effects of the same wind on fast-flying jets is identical except that the reduced time spent flying each leg of the mission decreases the time the wind can affect the aircraft.

A pilot flying an aircraft at 180 knots has a 'relatively' longer time to look for significant features on the ground compared to a crew flying at 540 knots—the aircraft covering nine miles per minute. The faster one flies, the greater is the effect of time errors. Every six seconds the aircraft covers one nautical mile on

From Fledgling to Eagle

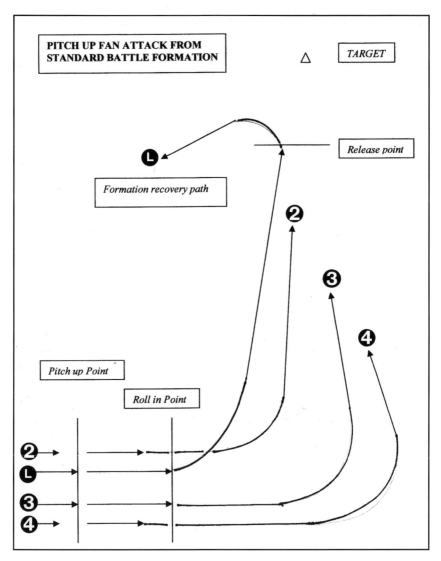

Pitch-up fan attack from standard battle formation.

the ground. At the extremely low levels our strike aircraft were forced to fly for safety's sake, vision is blurred except directly ahead along the aircraft's flight path. Each leg of the navigation route is timed in minutes and seconds. It is as critical as that.

All air strike missions are flown at speed increments of 60 knots to ease the navigation problem. Sixty nautical miles per hour equals one mile covered per minute. After take-off, while on the 'safe' side of the cut-line, the speed flown by the formation leader would be 360 knots (six miles per minute). This allowed

1986: Taking a breather

ample opportunity for the tail-end-Charlie to catch up and join into the correct battle formation. The other benefit of flying relatively slowly is its effect on fuel consumption. As in a motor car, the faster one drives the more fuel used.

However, after crossing the cut-line into 'Injun territory', speed is increased to allow less time for enemy AAA or SAM operators to acquire and fire their weapons. Threats for every leg of the navigation are assessed and, as the threat increases as the aircraft approach their targets, the formation speed will be increased appropriately.

The route is planned via suitable way-points—significant navigational features from which crews assess their progress. Approaching the target the formation leader aims for an IP (initial point). This point is selected as an exact point over the ground from which all crews can update their navigation. It is also used as a 'hack' point, from where pilots start their cockpit stopwatches. From this point the aircraft should be on the correct heading and flying at the planned speed towards the pull-up-point (PUP).

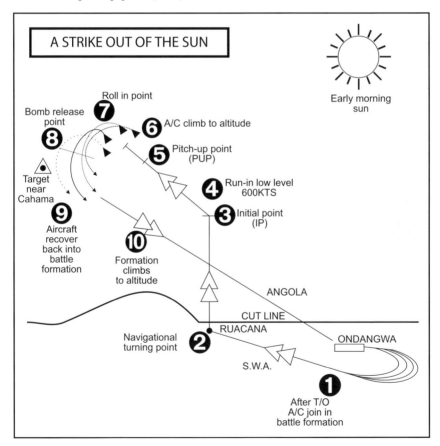

Diagram illustrating a strike out of the sun.

At the PUP the leader applies 4G (four times the effect of gravity) and pulls his aircraft's nose up into a steep climb. If the plan calls for a dive-bombing profile the leader climbs to the roll-in-point—the altitude that will give him the required dive angle onto the target. At this altitude the leader calls "Rolling in left" or "Rolling in right"—radio silence is no longer necessary as the enemy will very shortly be in no doubt as to the formation's presence.

As the formation rolls-in the pilots fan out in an echelon (all aircraft on one side of the leader), so there is approximately a 10° difference in attack heading between aircraft. This separation forces enemy AAA gunners to select individual targets thereby dispersing the AAA barrage. The fan manoeuvre also separates the aircraft from each other, allowing the pilots to concentrate on their aiming and release conditions.

After weapon release the aircraft break away from the dive path and head for low level. The faster pilots can reach treetop level the less time there is available for a misfortune to occur. The next problem for the pilots is to regain battle formation as they egress towards base. At this time they are vulnerable to enemy fighters so their lookout capabilities, offered by flying in the correct formation, become all important.

Toss-bombing sorties were flown into high-threat target areas where the enemy was equipped with anti-aircraft artillery including the very effective ZSU 23-4 Shilka systems. These four-barrelled, Gun Dish radar-guided 23mm cannons, mounted on a tank chassis were very mobile. Their exact presence was difficult to predict which, coupled with their very high rate of fire, made them extremely

This close-up of the tank-mounted ZPU-23-4 AAA system shows the four barrels and the Gun Dish radar dish of the integrated system.

1986: Taking a breather

dangerous. In addition, these target areas were also protected by mobile SAM systems such as the heat-seeking SA-9 and Land-Roll radar-guided SA-8 batteries. The SAAF had first-hand experience of SA-2 and SA-3 SAM systems during our strikes on targets near Lubango. These huge missiles were fired from fixed sites and, provided our intelligence information was accurate, the threat they posed could be avoided. Mobile systems that could withstand the effects of bundu-bashing through the African veld were equally dangerous to any aircraft visible for more than a few seconds. To achieve minimum time under fire and stay safe from the enemy defensive systems the SAAF changed over to toss-bombing.

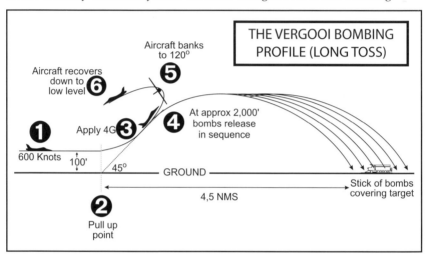

Despite errors inherent in toss-bombing, the pattern normally fell within the target area.

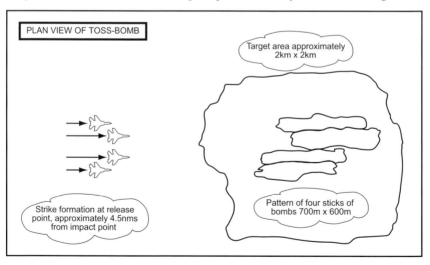

Three four-ship strikes into the same target with 250kg pre-frag bombs was certain to damage most vehicles and personnel in the area.

Navigational planning stayed exactly the same except a pre-IP was often inserted before the IP. The fast-flying formation would then be in a perfect position as the IP was reached and the timing hack begun. At PUP all four aircraft would apply 4G in two seconds and hold it as their aircraft shot upwards. When the angle of incidence reached 45° nose-up the bombs would be independently released at the pre-set intervalometer setting. This fractional delay was designed to allow a selected distance between bombs over the target to be achieved. Therefore each aircraft would throw a stick of bombs. Immediately after bomb release, the pilot would roll on 130° of bank, keeping the 4G on the aircraft as he rolled back down to the safety of low level.

EASTERN FRONT

28 Squadron 'long drop'

On the night of 4 April, 28 Squadron was tasked to fly a supply mission deep into Angola. As usual, the operations board had 'WK-GF-X-WK' written in the mission column. This meant the formation would fly from Waterkloof to Grootfontein. There, they would refuel and receive the operational briefing for the leg Grootfontein to X, the designated drop zone. After the drop the aircraft would return direct to Waterkloof.

This particular evening the formation was led by Commandant Bob Hewetson with Major Adrian Woodley flying as No 2. Woodley, one of the squadron's instructors, was carrying out an operational check on Captain Marc Bignoux who had been recently upgraded to aircraft commander of the Hercules. Also in the cockpit was Major Louis van Wyk who had just completed his C-130 conversion and was going along for the ride.

They departed Waterkloof at 16h10 and had an uneventful flight to Grootfontein where they attended the army–air force intelligence briefing. This consisted of an overview of the prevailing situation, a list of the known 'hot spots' to be avoided and details of the drop zone. Then a detailed route briefing was given by the lead navigator. These missions were only undertaken during no-moon periods to add to the difficulties of the Angolan defenders.

The briefing was followed by a meal after which the crews could relax until take-off. Woodley used this time to sit quietly in the cockpit, fully kitted up in his survival jacket, swatting mosquitoes and contemplating the abrupt change in his life style. Earlier that morning he had taken his children to school, arranged a game of golf for the coming weekend and forgotten to clean the pool. Within an hour or two he would be in the middle of an extremely hostile environment where 28 Squadron was a major thorn in the enemy's side and one they badly wanted to extract. Hopefully, providing the drop was successful, the return flight to Waterkloof would be uneventful.

1986: Taking a breather

C-130 Hercules aircraft on the ramp prior to a sortie.

At the appointed hour the pair of heavily loaded aircraft took off and headed north in a loose formation. Approaching the Angolan border they descended to the briefed operational height of 500 to 1,000 feet AGL. C-130s have small, purple-coloured formation lights on the top of their fuselage and wings. They were also equipped with Tacan, which provided directional and distance information from a transmitting station either on the ground or in the air. With the two aircraft operating on the same Tacan frequency the procedure was for the No 2 to fly slightly stepped up and spaced out at about 0.2 to 0.3 nautical miles on the Tacan read-out. The cockpits were usually very quiet on these trips as flying on this type of information required great concentration and constant cross-referring between the Tacan information in the cockpit and the formation light on the lead aircraft.

Woodley remembers flying one of these missions as co-pilot of the lead aircraft when the Tacan read-out closed to 0.1 and then 0.0 nautical miles. Looking out of the right-hand side of the cockpit he saw the huge plan-form silhouette of a C-130 filling all the cockpit windows at 90° angle of bank as it broke away. Tinky Jones, one of the SAAF's most experienced pilots, had sneaked in for some close-formation flying.

The flight proceeded normally via the pre-planned routing points and altitudes which kept the formation below enemy radar cover. Pinpoints appeared on time and the formation turned, climbed or descended without any radio calls being made. Eventually they approached the DZ and the atmosphere in the aircraft intensified as they identified the fires marking it.

The supplies, mounted on thick plywood pallets with parachutes attached, were to be dropped using the platform extraction delivery system (PLEDS). Each pallet held up to four 200-litre drums and there were two rows of pallets running the length of the cargo compartment. As soon as the pallet locking system was released the load exited from the rear of the aircraft by the force of gravity aided by the nose-up attitude of the aircraft. This was a very noisy, dusty and windy affair, created by the open ramp and door.

The PLEDS drop was similar to this, although each pallet was smaller and had its own parachute attached. Noticed how the aircraft has adopted a very nose-down attitude just as the load leaves the aircraft. This violent attitude change close to the ground requires a very alert crew, particularly on a dark night.

Just prior to reaching the DZ the formation eased into a longish line-astern so each aircraft could complete their drop individually. The aircraft were at their most vulnerable during the run-in and overhead the DZ—straight and level at 1,000 feet AGL at 130 knots—while being illuminated by the parallel flares marking the DZ.

At release, as the load departed, the pilots had to maintain aircraft stability. The centre of gravity (C of G) temporarily shifted so far aft that the control column had to be pushed hard forward against the stops. In spite of this the nose still pitched way up. Suddenly, in the few seconds that it took for the load to exit everything was reversed. The DZ fires were underneath the aircraft and no longer visible from the cockpit. In the pitch dark, with no visible horizon, these fairly extreme pitch movements had to be controlled on instruments alone. As soon as the aircraft was stable they descended to 500 feet AGL while cleaning up, closing up, speeding up and reforming formation.

At some point after the drop Woodley was looking out of the right-hand window into complete darkness and was surprised to see what he thought was a flare. It looked to be about two miles away and was travelling in the same direction as the aircraft. He turned his head back into the cockpit to tell the crew what he had just seen when he noticed a green glare lighting up the left side of the aircraft. Before he could say anything a missile accelerated past the left-hand side between the two engines. They felt and heard a large *thump* which caused the aircraft to roll briefly, much the same as when encountering turbulence, and he could smell the exhaust gases from the missile's motor coming through the air-conditioning system. Within about five seconds the bright green light of the missile's rocket motor disappeared as it streaked away into the night sky.

Woodley thought his aircraft had been hit and made a brief call to his leader saying, "I'm going down," (meaning he was going to fly really low level) and he descended to 200 feet AGL. At this stage, all the crew were wide awake and looking out of every available window to see if there were any more telltale green glows. After a while, when heart rates had returned to normal, an inspection of the aircraft was made but no damage could be seen. For safety's sake they diverted to AFB Rundu where an external check ascertained the aircraft had suffered no damage at all. They concluded the *thump* was probably caused by the shockwave of the missile as it passed very close to the C-130. It was a very quiet and pensive crew who arrived back at AFB Waterkloof after a total flying time of ten hours 50 minutes.

After numerous debriefings it was concluded the flare Woodley had initially seen was probably some kind of signal to the ground troops. Based on the shockwave, exhaust smell and incredible speed with which it streaked away, the missile was possibly an SA-2, a medium-to-high-altitude missile. It probably had insufficient time to lock-on properly because of the low altitude the aircraft was flying. For the same reason the proximity fuse failed to detonate the missile as it passed the C-130. Woodley's radio call, 'I'm going down' was probably heard by enemy listening posts and misinterpreted to mean, 'I'm crashing'. The Angolans claimed in newspaper reports they had shot down one of our aircraft.

SADF denies its plane shot by Angola

STAR 7/4/86

A Defence Force spokesman today denied Angolan allegations that a South African Air Force transport plane allegedly ferrying supplies to Unita was shot down by Angola on Thursday night.

The Angolan news agency Angop claimed the plane was one of three Hercules C—130s dropping supplies by parachute to the rebels over the central province of Bie.

An Angolan Defence Ministry communique said a second plane was hit.

The communique said some of the supplies, described as war materiel, were captured by Angolan troops.

It gave no details of what had happened to the crew of the downed plane.

South Africa has in the past acknowledged giving the rebels what it called moral, material and humanitarian aid.

Today a South African army spokesman in Pretoria denied the Angop report.

"We deny categorically this allegation. I don't know what they shot down, but it wasn't one of ours," he said.

The communique said Angolan air force fighters intercepted the planes about 45 minutes before midnight on April 3 after they had been detected flying west of Andulo.

Star newspaper report, 7 April 1986.

This incident did not change the resupply schedule. The C-130s continued to penetrate deep into Angola without incurring a single loss—testament to the professionalism and skill of the crews involved.

On 19 May, 3 Squadron deployed to AFB Mpacha to escort a Canberra on a PR sortie, north of the cut-line. The mission was uneventful and all the aircraft returned to Waterkloof the same day.

Extended-range operations

At this stage the B-707 tankers of 60 Squadron were becoming operational. The increased tanker capacity of the Boeing and additional refuelling points added impetus to the extended-range operations practised by 1 and 24 Squadrons.

This Mirage F1AZ is tanking from the starboard wing station of a 60 Squadron B-707. This flying 'service station' had two more fuelling points, one under the tail and the other under the port wing.

Motoring authorities recommend drivers stop every two hours for a rest and to stretch their cramped limbs. Flying-safety experts had voiced concern over aircrew remaining firmly strapped into ejection seats for long periods. While fatigue was an area of concern the most pressing issue was over bladder control. However, following advice to alleviate these problems, from doctors at the Institute of Aviation Medicine, operational ranges and airborne times were greatly increased.

Bombing sorties were flown, using the Jacob's Reef target off the Western Cape coast, with Mirage F1AZs taking off and returning to AFB Hoedspruit. The rendezvous and top-up from tankers became second nature—involved, satisfying sorties, although still trying on the bladder.

1986: Taking a breather

While Commandant Rankin concentrated on extended-range operations, Major Nic Oosthuysen and Captain Rikus de Beer continued developing the night-attack capability of 1 Squadron. The combination of these efforts culminated in the squadron flying four-ship night sorties including in-flight refuelling from B-707 tankers, in radio silence. A typical night-strike mission flown out of AFB Hoedspruit followed this pattern. Four F1AZs, each loaded with six bombs and two fuel tanks, would fly a tactical navigation to Roodewal to deliver four of their bombs. Then, they would rendezvous with the tanker, top up with fuel and before heading back to base return to drop the last two bombs.

An infamous pair of 1 Squadron panty-rippers, Moolies Moolman and Wassie Wasserman, wearing evidence of their crimes around their necks.

In May, history was made as the first night toss-bomb (called *vergooi* in the SAAF) attacks were carried out with very reasonable results. Day time *Gatup* attacks were producing miss-distances of between four to eleven metres—excellent results when the effect of a 500-kilogram high-explosive bomb is considered. The *Gatup* profile was developed by 1 Squadron specifically to be used against heavily defended targets. The approach was flown at very low level and high speeds, both elements crucial to aircraft survival in a hostile environment. A high-G pitch-up and roll-in onto the target is used and a laser shot fired the moment the sight is pointed at the target. The pilot pulls up, the bombs release automatically at the optimum instant as calculated by the computer and the pilot is then clear to escape from the combat zone.

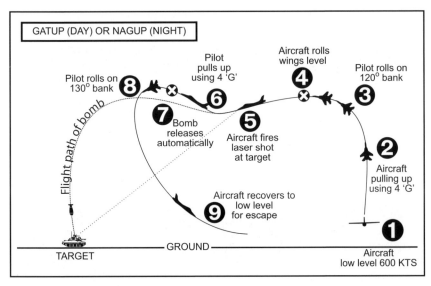

Gatup (day) or *Nagup* (night) profile.

*****

During 1986, the Angolans were licking their wounds after the pounding they had received the previous year. This period of respite was used by both sides to catch up with training and much-needed aircraft maintenance. Operational planners on both sides of the border analyzed the battles of 1985 and began planning for the next inevitable round.

The effectiveness of SAAF ground-attack strikes increased due to the availability of the new pre-fragmented bombs and because the low-level *Vergooi* bombing profile had proved operationally sound. However, concern existed over the lack of radar cover for our own aircraft and the limited facilities for operating fighter aircraft out of AFB Rundu.

The Angolans, with their Soviet and Cuban mentors, investigated the reasons for their 1985 defeat, of which there were many. The main problem was their lack of suitable air-defence systems, allowing the SAAF freedom of movement over the brigades. Another simple omission, which caused their ground troops dreadful hardship, was water. They began their operation in the dry season and did not carry sufficient water reserves with them. Morale among their soldiers suffered accordingly. The passive air-defence measures taken by the brigades against attacks by the SAAF were almost non-existent because their vehicles were not dug in and were exposed to shrapnel.

Winning a battle, but not ending the war, is a double-edged sword. Victory brings euphoria and confidence. However, it is tinged with the certain knowledge

1986: Taking a breather

Brigadier 'Thack' Thackwray and the staff of Western Air Command, responsible for the implementation of all operational doctrine.

that the next battle will be more difficult and dangerous. This was a pattern of the war. Every time we beat the opposition and captured tons of equipment they came back for more, better equipped and better trained.

With this knowledge the SAAF initiated corrective actions over a large spectrum, ranging from an updated command post to the deployment of mobile radar at AFB Rundu. Extensions and improvements to Rundu airfield were started. Unfortunately, these were not completed before the next offensive began in 1987.

WESTERN FRONT

Under Operation *Rickshaw* a pamphlet-dropping programme from Kudu and Dakota aircraft was continued over Owamboland throughout 1986 and 1987. It was considered the best way to reach the local population with important messages.

As in all other years an entire series of counter-insurgency operations were carried out designed to keep SWAPO unsettled. Operations such as *Pyp, Fagot,*

This Sukhoi Su-25 Frogfoot is in Soviet livery, but is similar to the aircraft delivered to Angola. It is a formidable ground-attack aircraft. In this photograph, four of the eight weapon stations can be seen under the port wing. *photo* Sergey Riabsei

Cinema, Jabber, Pannikin, Slade 7, Flouriet, Duxes, Enol and *Accrete* continued throughout the year. They were all small-scale operations, either in Owamboland or Angola, and were supported by air force helicopters and light aircraft. Few of them rendered major results but they had to be performed. SWAPO was perpetually harassed and, consequently, their actions and successes were few and far between.

On Saturday 28 June, Commandant Labuschagne/Major Mouton and majors Siebrits/Napier flew their Buccaneers, configured for PR, up to AFB Grootfontein. The aim of Operation *Shanty* was to confirm the presence of SU-25 fighters on the airfield near the coastal town of Namibe. The SU-25 was a subsonic ground-attack fighter used with great success by the Soviet military in Afghanistan.

Namibe was well-protected by a SAM-3 site and batteries of AAA guns of various calibres. The weather forecast was good and the flight was scheduled for Sunday—the traditional day of rest. As part of the SAR plan a MAOT (Major Tristan la Grange) would be placed near Virei together with two Puma helicopters and two sticks of paratroopers. Each Buccaneer carried a LOROP (long-range oblique photography) pod. The profile selected was a low-level penetration of Angolan airspace with a last-minute pop-up to 21,700 feet AGL. This would give a slant range of 12 nautical miles from the airfield with a depression angle of 16 degrees. The stand-off distance was to keep the aircraft outside range of the known AAA.

The pair of Buccaneers took off at 11h15 from AFB Grootfontein and flew to a point just west of Ruacana, then to the MAOT position at Virei where they saw the waiting SAR Pumas as they flashed past. They continued to the western edge

1986: Taking a breather

of the vast Angolan escarpment before turning west for the final approach and run-in to the target.

As they approached the target they could see it was covered by a bank of low coastal cloud with a base of 2,500 feet AGL. Commandant Labuschagne asked his navigator Riem Mouton to recalculate the distance out and the height to fly, so they could stay clear of the cloud below the base and still complete the PR run. Exactly the same actions took place in the second aircraft. As always, all operational sorties were flown in complete radio silence. Approaching the target Lappies began heading closer because of the much lower height of the PR run. Pikkie Siebrits followed as No 2. At the correct new distance out they pitched quickly to 2,000 feet and with the airfield just about under their wings they flew past it with both cameras running. The RWRs remained silent—they had achieved complete surprise. On completion of the run they plunged back to low level until crossing back into SWA and then once again climbed.

The Buccaneers returned to AFB Waterkloof and the rolls of film were taken to JARIC for developing and interpretation. Later, the aircrew received the good news that their rapid reappraisal of the conditions had been correct. SU-25s could be seen housed in revetments, on both rolls of film. The bad news was the dressing-down they received from AFHQ for flying so close to the airfield thereby increasing the danger to both aircraft and crew. You can't win them all.

*****

Between 14 August and 10 September, the SAAF supported Operation *Chappy*. A small team of Special Forces soldiers was inserted deep into Angola close to the Namibe– Lubango railway line. The air side of the mission was controlled by a MAOT deployed at Okangwati. Four Pumas were allocated for the task, although only three were used for the infiltration and exfiltration; the fourth helicopter was for contingencies. An Impala was placed on standby at Ondangwa for Telstar duties during these flights.

The SAAF ran Operation *Bernico* on 3– 4 September. This was an EW elint-gathering flight, parallel to the cut-line but inside the 'shallow area' of Angola. The aim was to excite the Angolan air-defence system while recording all their electronic emissions for analysis at the debriefing. The mission was led by two Mirage III R2Zs with active radar receivers, escorted by two Mirage III fighters. By this stage we were becoming quite adept at plotting recorded intelligence and increasing our intelligence picture of the enemy.

The army requested the SAAF to assist in a reconnaissance of the Calueque area from 25–29 September. They were interested in locating suitable vehicle crossing points. Two Pumas carrying a ground recce team, supported by the top cover of two Alouette gunships, were used for the mission.

Between 1 November and 12 December, Operation *Colisseum* (later changed to *Kakebeen*) was launched to disrupt SWAPO command and control in the deep external areas. Ground forces, supported by Puma, Dakota and Impala aircraft from AFB Ondangwa, moved into the area 40 kilometres northeast of Cassinga on 1 November. They were tasked to locate and attack the SWAPO Eastern and Central Detachment HQ. Initially, this operation achieved success but was curtailed after our troops suffered a number of casualties.

Intelligence inputs indicated the Angolan air force was trying to establish an airfield closer to the SWA border. The SAAF deployed a ground-based Comint (Communications Intelligence) team under the name Operation *Moonraker*, on 4 November. These men set up a communications post on a mountain in Kaokoland to listen to VHF transmissions from Angolan and Cuban pilots. It was from this information we learned of the building of an airfield at Cahama.

Operation *Bakeliet*, an EW mission, was flown by an ECM-equipped DC-4 Skymaster between 1 and 4 December. These flights, from the mouth of the Cunene River right up the west coast of Angola, were tasked to verify the intelligence emanating from *Moonraker*.

Zimbabwe

SAAF support for Rhodesia had ceased when Robert Mugabe was installed as premier and the country's name changed to Zimbabwe. Optimism over the progress of the new country soon changed to pessimism and by 1986 it was clear that good neighbourliness was not part of Mugabe's agenda. The Iko Carreira document indicated that the Soviets had planned their main thrust against South Africa to be made simultaneously from Zambia and Zimbabwe. Consequently, Zimbabwe was under the close scrutiny of our intelligence department.

On 14 September, the SAAF launched Operation *Mandrax* to update photographic coverage of strategic installations in Zimbabwe. Two Canberras took off from AFB Waterkloof to photograph the road and rail system between Beitbridge, Bulawayo and Victoria Falls. Upon completion of the operation they landed at AFB Mpacha to refuel before returning to base.

At the same time, four Mirage III RZ photo-reconnaissance aircraft took off from AFB Hoedspruit and photographed the airfields at Bulawayo, Harare and Mutare. The SAR plan for this combined operation included a C-160, five Impalas and six Pumas, on standby at various places.

Chapter 13

1987: Conventional warfare

WESTERN FRONT

Although SWAPO activity had decreased significantly it was still necessary to prevent the organization from being able to assemble any worthwhile attack force. In January, Operation *Uitspring* was carried out in the Ogongo–Ruacana area. Between 13 and 27 January *Rondomtalie* was launched in Angola aimed at the logistic routes used by SWAPO's Central and Eastern detachments.

On 25 and 26 January, seven Alouette gunships and four Impala jets carried out attacks on a target identified at Mongua. On 31 January, 1 Reconnaissance Regiment set off on Operation *Markotter* to attack and harass SWAPO elements known to be in the western area. These troops were supported by Puma helicopters with an Impala being used in the Telstar role to ensure communication contact between the ground team and the tactical HQ at Okangwati

The SAAF deployed a MAOT team to Okangwati in Kaokoland on 2 February for Operation *Ale*. Puma helicopters were used to infiltrate a Special Force reconnaissance team into Angola. This team was tasked to carry out a recce on the Lubango airfield and to sabotage aircraft and facilities. The team remained in Angola until 25 March when they were collected once again by Pumas.

Two area operations, *Perske* and *Kraai*, were carried out in February and March to seek and destroy SWAPO's Western Area HQ in southern Angola. Often these operations, particularly in the recent years since *Askari* in 1984, produced no tangible results. However, in terms of the insurgency war SWAPO was attempting, the effect of all these operations was vital. One of the fundamental principles of an insurgency campaign is to establish bases within the country being attacked. The next step is to expand one's campaign from the security of these bases. Our operations kept SWAPO on the move, not only within SWA, but also in the 'shallow areas' of Angola. By this stage, SWAPO cadres could not spend more than three days across the border without their presence being reported. Our reaction to these reports, almost always from locals, was to launch an immediate follow-up operation. These hot pursuits by Koevoet Zulu teams or the Romeo Mike teams of 101 Battalion were often successful.

In April, the SAAF initiated operations to attempt to ambush aircraft of the Angolan Air Force. The reason was to actively discourage them from encroaching anywhere near the border with SWA. The idea was to establish a mock tactical HQ that would hopefully attract the attention of their aircraft. When this occurred, Mirage interceptors from 1, 2 and 3 Squadrons, stationed at AFB Ondangwa, would be scrambled to intercept them.

Operation *Bellombra* was launched in an attempt to curb the newfound aggression noticed in the flying patterns of enemy MiGs. The idea was to scramble pairs of Mirages to designated low-level holding points whenever the MiGs were in the air. Our radar controllers would watch the MiGs and, if they came into the area of one of the holding points, would give the Mirages a radar vector and a time to pitch-up. Our aircraft would accelerate to 600 knots-plus before pitching-up. The idea was to climb to 4,000 feet below the targets. Airborne radar was only switched on during the pitch to give the enemy minimum warning before missile launch was achieved. When our aircraft appeared on Dayton's radar they would be vectored onto the bogeys.

Numerous attempts were made but none was successful. The closest we came to success was when we managed to position Commandant Norman Bruton, of 2 Squadron, behind and within two nautical miles of Angolan MiGs. However, as our radar lacked height information the controller could not help Bruton acquire the MiGs visually and we had to break off the attack. The problem was passed to SAAF HQ, who in turn tasked 3 Squadron and Devon radar to investigate the problem and come up with a suitable solution.

Snakebite

During low-intensity periods forces needed to remain on the alert. The bush war showed no signs of ending; a war of attrition is like that. You have to persevere until your enemy cracks. Therefore, every night a Puma crew was kept on standby at AFB Ondangwa to cater for any eventuality. After more than 20 years of conflict the novelty of this particular duty had long since worn off.

The weather on the evening of 28 July was atrocious, black as pitch and whatever moon there was concealed behind the billowing clouds of an unusual winter storm; all flying had been stopped due to the weather conditions. This was another unusual occurrence—cessation of flying during the war was virtually unheard of and gives one an idea of what the weather was like.

Major Martin Kruger was on his first Puma bush tour and in keeping with operating procedures had to fly as co-pilot to familiarize himself with conditions on the border. He was down to fly with the 'Silver Fox', an experienced instructor with 33 bush tours behind him. Major Dave Owen had been an instructor since 1974; this probably accounted for the colour of his hair from which his nickname was aptly derived. They were the duty crew that evening and even though the weather was 'clampers' they only drank Coca-Cola in the pub, another strict procedural requirement.

Around 20h00 a call came through from X-Ray 2, the AFCP at Oshakati, from a young operations officer inquiring if they could do a casevac sortie down to the Kaokoveld as an army lieutenant had been bitten by a snake. The way the system worked in Owamboland was Oshakati tasked the crews to carry out missions; this polite request was Oshakati's way of trying to shift the onus of responsibility onto the pilots. Oshakati had cancelled all flying so they knew exactly what the weather was like. It was such a polite little inquiry from an obviously very young ops officer. The Silver Fox replied there was no way they could fly and hinted it was a bloody silly question to ask. About 20 minutes later the same young officer was on the line again. This time he was pleading, saying Colonel Louis Lourens, the Oshakati commanding officer and himself a helicopter pilot, had asked them to please try and carry out the sortie as "the Browns were crying" and the lieutenant's condition was deteriorating fast.

Not being able to resist this bended-knee approach Owen agreed to give it a go. During the war low-level flying was the saviour of helicopter operations. With AK-47s, RPG-7s and SA-7s the customary arsenal of SWAPO, the lower one flew the more protected the aircraft was from ground fire. However, that evening ground fire was the furthest thing from Major Owen's mind. He decided to fly at a flight level above the calculated terrain safety height for the mountains in the Kaokoland, possibly the only time during the war one of our helicopters operated like this.

They took off at 21h15 in their Puma, climbed to FL80 on instruments and set heading for Ruacana. Overhead Ruacana they reset their Doppler navigation computer before continuing to Epupa Falls on the Cunene River where the army patrol and the casevac were waiting. Flying at high level they were amazed at how early radio contact was made with the people on the ground. They requested the soldiers to listen out for the Puma approaching and to call when the helicopter was overhead.

Prior to taking off, Owen had asked Oshakati to relay a request to the army at Epupa to build four fires around the LZ and light them on request. Fortunately, the cloud cover broke as they flew west and as they were approaching overhead the four fires were lit and visually picked up by the Puma crew.

There are no navigation aids in Kaokoland and the terrain is mountainous.

Epupa Falls, in the riverbed, has the Zebra Mountains immediately south of it running parallel to the Cunene River. These unusual mountains have a definite striped appearance during the day but on a pitch-black night are invisible. A normal approach to the LZ was out of the question.

Owen decided to position exactly overhead, reduce his speed to 60 knots and then enter a 20° banked, right-hand, spiral descent. He would keep the fires in sight, relying on the principle that if he could see them there could not be any *solidus granitus* between them. He warned Kruger to stay on instruments as he would be flying on a visual reference from the ground and to 'patter' him all the way down. Once the radio altimeter came alive Kruger was to call out every 100 feet interval.

With the helicopter's landing light on they planned to come out of the last turn straight into the hover and land before becoming enveloped in the dust cloud. This procedure worked well and after making a good touch-down Owen kept a little power on the collective to keep the dust away from the aircraft.

The doctor accompanying the casevac flight jumped out with the flight engineer. Between the two of them and with the help of the soldiers the stretcher with the snakebite victim was quickly loaded aboard the helicopter. Owen spent these moments on the ground devising a plan of how to get out of the area. It was still pitch black and the mountains were invisible. They decided to fly out the same way as they'd flown in. After lift-off they transitioned out of the dust; when the indicated airspeed registered 60 knots, they entered a 20° banked, climbing spiral to the right. There was a difference however, which created a serious difficulty. Descending, they had used the fires as reference points; climbing into total blackness there was no reference to keep them from drifting.

Owen briefed the flight engineer to keep the landing light on and watch ahead of the spiralling helicopter. Such attention to detail paid dividends. Shortly after take-off the engineer shouted a warning that he could see a mountain entering the illumination beam of the landing light. Fortunately, its conical shape provided greater clearance as the helicopter gained height.

After a few tense minutes the helicopter reached a safe flight level and headed back towards Ondangwa. The irony of the situation became apparent when en route back to base the doctor, who had been attending his patient, came onto the intercom saying, "Don't worry, the patient is fine. There's no problem from the snakebite."

Bellombra development

Back in South Africa, 3 Squadron and Devon controllers developed a new profile in the general flying area of the eastern Transvaal, using 2 Squadron as the 'enemy'. Loskop Dam wall, Piet Gouws Dam wall and Pietersburg were the chosen holding points, closely simulating the distances between AFB Ondangwa, Oshikango and Ongiva. Initially, they named this attack method UNCIP (unconventional intercept profile). Later the name changed to LIP (low-level intercept profile). Success in training was surprisingly high until the 'enemy' targets were given a close escort and supported by roving CAPS. On pitching-up our pilots were never too sure which formation they were attacking. There was always the real danger of ending up sandwiched between enemy aircraft.

On 23 June, 3 Squadron and a dedicated team of Devon radar-controllers deployed to AFB Ondangwa. Here they employed the interception profiles operationally they had trained for over the eastern Transvaal highveld. By first light the following day the pilots were on cockpit standby. Radar controllers were positioned at their consoles at 140 Radar Squadron, situated on the edge of the airfield. The waiting began. By mid-morning MiG activity was detected and shortly thereafter Mirage F1CZs were scrambled. An important aspect of this plan was to ensure its security; unless a kill was guaranteed our aircraft would not pitch-up into enemy radar cover. In retrospect this was a harsh limiting factor and numerous unsuccessful scrambles were performed.

Another unsuccessful scramble to the Ongiva area occurred on 28 June, where our controllers, wisely, did not allow our aircraft to pitch-up. The reason being, radar controller Commandant Delport picked up a total of 22 blips operating in the same area, instead of the usual one or two MiG formations. On analysis after landing it appeared the Angolans were aware of our plan and had created their own trap. In the event neither side had any success.

Meanwhile, back in South Africa on 23 June, General Jan Geldenhuys was invited to fly in the Boeing 707 to experience the capability-enhancement in-flight refuelling provided. Four F1AZs from AFB Hoedspruit rendezvoused with the 60 Squadron B-707 which had taken off from AFB Waterkloof. After refuelling from the tanker the Mirage formation flew to Hopefield bombing range, north of Cape Town where a bombing attack was carried out. On the return flight

A 60 Squadron Boeing 707 tanker busy refuelling Mirage F1AZs from all three refuelling stations.

another refuelling rendezvous with the tanker allowed the formation to land back at Hoedspruit four hours after take-off.

On 24 June, 3 Squadron pilots at AFB Ondangwa were tasked to escort a Canberra PR mission over southern Angola which proved uneventful. After the sortie the Mirage F1CZs were refuelled for the return flight to AFB Waterkloof. Commandant Gagiano noticed that instead of refuelling from the customary bowser the underground fuelling installation was used. This change of procedure made Gagiano uncomfortable and he asked for the condition of the fuel to be checked before allowing his F1s to take off.

His doubts were justified as the fuel was badly contaminated. All the F1s had to be checked, fuel drained, engine fuel filters changed and the pilots returned home in the back of a C-130 transport aircraft. Gagiano was awarded a 'Well Done' certificate from the Air Force Safety Board for professionalism which probably prevented a serious accident,

3 Squadron deployed to AFB Ondangwa from 15 to 22 July but not a single operational sortie was flown. As the next serious conflict drew inexorably closer tension increased. In the fog of war the commencement of hostilities is often difficult to predict.

Although the threat from SWAPO had declined and the emphasis of the war shifted to the Eastern Front forces in Owamboland which had remained at readiness. The SAAF still had a MAOT positioned at Ruacana with 51 Battalion and from October to December the commander of this detachment was Major Cobus Toerien. During his Alouette flight to clear-in at Ruacana the helicopter crew explained how the 'IRR' (Independent Republic of Ruacana) was considered

Colonel Spyker Jacobs handing over a new bakkie (pick-up truck) to the helicopter crews at AFB Ondangwa in October. L to R: Polla Kruger, J. R. Redelinghuys, Arie Korf, Mario Vergottini, hidden unknown, Wynand Malan, Jonnie Laing, Ronnie Johnsson, Spyker and Cynthia Jacobs.

one of the better MAOT tours as SWAPO had been inactive in the area for such a long time. Ruacana owes its existence to the hydroelectric plant buried inside the mountain and run by Swawek. The official name of the utility company was Suid-Wes Afrika se Elektrisiteitvoorsieningskommissie, which probably explains the use of the acronym.

51 Battalion was under command of Commandant Lampies Lambrecht and sited in the little town. Attached to the army base was the SAAF MAOT team, a contingent from SWA Special Forces under Lieutenant Fires van Vuuren, Koevoet and a detachment of troops from 201 Battalion. Toerien had one Bosbok, two Alouette aircraft and their crews allocated to him. The helicopter operated from the base itself but the Bosbok was housed at Hurricane, the small tarred airfield just to the east of the town.

Although stationed inside the army base the SAAF MAOT team maintained its independence from the army mess, the airmen preferring the safety of their own food to army stew. MAOT C fell directly in the line of command from 310 AFCP which was at that time commanded by Colonel Louis Lourens. The main task of the Ruacana aircraft was to patrol the power lines running southward from the hydroelectric scheme. A rumour circulating through Ruacana concerned the importance of these power lines, which connected into the national grid of South Africa. Every Tuesday afternoon Swawek ran up its standby turbine to produce the extra electricity required to satisfy the extra power demand caused by the TV show 'Dallas'.

The SAAF worked well with all the units based at Ruacana but, even at this late stage in the war, the army and Koevoet still had their differences. The air force, once again, became the ham in the sandwich.

Early one morning in December, 51 Battalion Ops requested urgent air support for a section of the army drawing heavy enemy fire to the north of Beacon 1. The Alouette crews were scrambled while Toerien notified Oshakati of the request, and to obtain authority for his helicopters to cross the cut-line. A few minutes later another frantic call came from Koevoet Ops requesting gunships to assist one of their Zulu Teams engaged in a heavy contact. Toerien noted that the grid reference given for both contacts was precisely the same. The helicopters were recalled and messages sent to both army and Koevoet units to cease fire as they had engaged each other. Fortunately, no injuries were sustained. 'Blue on blue' (the colour used on military maps denoting own forces) incidents should not happen, particularly when operations are being run from a joint HQ.

The SAAF contingent caused trouble of a different kind. There is a lot of truth in the old proverb, 'The devil makes work for idle hands'. It was all to do with the Christmas party. The SAAF members channelled all their activities into ensuring the party would remain etched in Ruacana's memories for many years. The air force was aided and abetted by the very able 2IC of the army base, Major

Werner Sott. This huge man had worked well with the SAAF during his time in 32 Battalion and, like the rest of that superb battalion, had formed strong bonds with the airmen.

The party, based on an 'Asterix' theme, included the open-air roasting of the biggest pig in all Owamboland and was an undoubted success. The Asterix magic potion had been a little stronger than expected and the next morning those who weren't still asleep under the trees were reeling about like casevacs.

Unfortunately, the camp commandant in charge of discipline and security decided that a 09h00 parade was required. This is what the army does when no other course of action is apparent. This did not directly affect the air force members on the base as they had, years before, excused themselves from this strange habit, until the base loudspeaker blared forth urgently summoning the MAOT commander to the parade ground.

Toerien thought it was a matter of life and death so, dressed only in SAAF battle kit—T-shirt, shorts, *plakkies* (flip-flops) and Rayban sunglasses—he jumped onto a SWASPES 500cc motorbike and sped onto the parade ground where the base troops were formed up. He did not hear the chuckles emanating from the lines of soldiers—he imagined there must be a serious casevac required. Then he noticed the 6'4" Werner Sott standing next to a furious and red-faced base OC. Sott was shaking while trying to suppress his laughter and Toerien realized he had not been summoned for a casevac. In front of the full parade ground, Commandant Lampies shouted, "How the hell must we hoist the national flag?"

Toerien, still a little confused, looked up to the top of the flag pole. The head of the huge pig from the previous night's spit-braai was sitting firmly atop the pole and surrounded by every insect in Owamboland. Toerien remembers wondering how he fitted into the picture until he remembered some furtive whispering late the previous night between Alouette flight engineers and the SWASPES sergeant-major. The bottom line was that Toerien had to retrieve and dispose of the pig's head while the parade dissolved in laughter.

A month or two later Toerien was back with 3 Squadron at AFB Ondangwa. The Cubans had been posturing in the Cahama and Oncocua areas and SAAF Mirages were used as a show of force to prevent any enemy delusions of grandeur. The pilots had been tasked to patrol between the Skeleton Coast and Beacon 1 and Toerien used this opportunity to extract revenge on the residents in the Independent Republic of Ruacana for his parade-ground humiliation. He persuaded his leader, Captain Rudi Mes, of the necessity to restore SAAF honour in the outpost and the two of them roared over the base parade ground at 50 feet AGL in full afterburner. Toerien's ally, Werner Sott, later informed him that a mixture of framed pictures, dust, trophies, medals and cups descended on Lampies and Sott as they were having coffee in the commander's office.

Revenge is sweet.

EASTERN FRONT

Between 28 and 30 June, 1 Squadron's Johan Rankin, Chris Skinner, Rikus de Beer and Willie van Coppenhagen deployed to AFB Grootfontein for electronic-intelligence-gathering (elint) flights. On one of these flights Chris and Rikus flew at low level to a position northeast of Cuito Cuanavale. Turning onto a southwesterly heading they pitched to 2,000 feet as they passed just south of the enemy positions around the town. Before the enemy missiles could react, both aircraft had plunged to very low level for the return to base. Recordings from the RWS equipment in both aircraft verified the presence of SA-3s and SA-8s.

1986 and the early months of 1987 were used by the Angolans to retrain and rearm. Huge amounts of modern Soviet weaponry poured into Angola including air-defence radars, surface-to-air missiles, MiG-23 fighters and Mi-25 attack helicopters. Cuban troop strengths were increased to around 50,000 men. Over 1,000 Soviet advisors boosted the planning and command capabilities of FAPLA. It was obvious they were about to repeat their attempt to capture Jamba and destroy UNITA. However, the air-defence weaponry included in their advancing columns indicated they realized that, if they were to succeed, they would have to counter the SAAF.

As soon as we detected the build-up of forces beginning again in Menonque and Cuito Cuanavale we planned Operation *Asterix*. Under the overall name of *Asterix* we produced a series of contingency plans to pre-empt the Angolans and to cover all eventualities. We used names such as *Ministerix* and *Hagar*—comics

An Angolan MiG-23 during pre-flight inspection. The swept-wing capability plus the two large engines gave it superior straight-line performance over the SAAF Mirage force.

Angolan Mi-25 attack helicopters could pack quite a punch with their turret-mounted cannon and underwing rockets and missiles, as well as carrying a dozen troops inside the cabin.

must have been the flavour of the month in the intelligence department whose members selected the names for operations.

We also produced a plan which called for an advance of our forces up the western side of the Cuito River to take Cuito Cuanavale. This plan was turned down by the South African government as being too aggressive and would result in even greater pressure being put on our politicians by the United Nations. They were possibly correct but it would have prevented the seven-month-long conventional war that was soon to start.

Operation *Moduler*: 22 June to 26 November 1987

In mid-1987, the Angolans, encouraged by their Cuban allies, crossed the bridge at Cuito Cuanavale and headed off towards Mavinga in the southeast. The strategy and approach routes were almost identical to the ones utilized in 1985 which ended disastrously for them when they were repulsed. However, this time they were better prepared logistically and in air-defence weaponry.

Once again, the Angolans decided on a pincer movement. The Defence Force was asked to stop the enemy right-hook against the key town Mavinga which consisted of two Angolan brigades. As in 1985, UNITA did not have the capability of stopping the advancing armour and requested assistance from South Africa. Cabinet approval was only granted at a late stage when the enemy 47th Brigade was south of the Lomba River. This is where the similarity to Operation *Weldmesh* ended.

The communist brains-trust had corrected their 1985 errors. They brought water- and air-defence missile systems with them. MiG-21s, -23s and SU-22s were deployed at Menonque. They stationed their helicopter force, consisting of Mi-8s, Mi-17s, Mi-25s and Mi-35s, at Cuito Cuanavale.

Protecting Menonque were static SA-3 missile batteries. Within the advancing brigades were included mobile SA-6, SA-7, SA-8, SA-9, SA-13, SA-14 and SA-16 batteries as integral units.

1987: Conventional warfare

The Su-22 ground-attack aircraft supplied to the Angolan Air Force, FAPA.

An SA-2 missile being prepared for launching.

Their armoured fighting force was made up of 40 T54/55 tanks, BM21 multiple rocket launchers (the famous 'Stalin Organ'), BRDM, BMP and BTR fighting vehicles. Their artillery support came from D-30 and M-46 cannons, with firing ranges up to 30 kilometres.

General Konstantin Shagonovich, the Soviet commander of the Angolan and Cuban troops massed at Cuito Cuanavale, had waited until July before launching five brigades on an advance towards the UNITA-held town of Mavinga. This slow advance through thick bush and deep sand began by crossing the Cuito River bridge just east of the town. This bridge, the only structure capable of supporting vehicles, was vital for the logistical backup of this ambitious advance.

Top: BRDM armoured car.
Bottom: Different view of the SA-13 system mounted on a MT-L3 tracked chassis, making the machine ideal for the thick sands of Angola. It was probably this system that succeeded in shooting down Major Ed Every in his Mirage F1AZ.

Operation *Coolidge*

The importance of this key point did not go unnoticed by UNITA and its allies. An audacious plan, Operation *Coolidge*, was conceived which called for a team of commandos to be flown into a safe area about 40 kilometres north of Cuito. This was done without any problems on the evening of 24 August, after which the helicopters withdrew. The following evening at last light the combat team entered the water and, after a combination of swimming and rowing, reached the bridge about five hours later.

The placing of the demolition charges did not proceed without problems. The low state of the river and the unexpected alertness of the bridge guards combined to compromise the swimmers. A fire fight ensued with the enemy using small arms and hand grenades to drive off the team, but not before the charges had been set.

Withdrawing down the river the team was pursued and fired at but for the Reconnaissance commandos this was all in a day's work. Enter 'Murphy', in the guise of crocodiles. They were understandably upset by this unusual invasion of their privacy. Having had their slumbers rudely disturbed by grenade explosions in the water they extracted their vengeance on the rapidly fleeing swimmers. One of the scuba-divers had to fight off his three-metre assailant with a knife,; another had his flipper bitten.

Despite hot pursuit from enemy soldiers, gunshot wounds and crocodile bites, the team managed to temporarily evade their pursuers. They had a further twenty kilometres to trek through the bush, carrying their equipment and assisting their wounded, before they reached their designated helicopter rendezvous point. Re-enter Murphy, this time in the form of thunderstorms—during the dry winter months.

Captains Koos Myburgh and Lionel Sawyer were the crew of one of four Pumas to fly in and fetch the commandos on the evening of 26 August. The helicopters, flying at 150 feet AGL on the radio altimeter, encountered severe thunderstorms en route with headwinds that reduced their ground speed from 120 to 45 knots. Running out of fuel they had no option but to return to Rundu. After refuelling there was insufficient time left to fly again before daybreak. The pick-up was rescheduled for the following evening. Enemy MiG activity precluded a daylight rescue attempt.

The next evening at last light the four Pumas set off again. Aircraft problems forced one Puma to return to Rundu but Myburgh and the remaining two Pumas continued. The pick-up problem was now aggravated by the enemy's persistence during the day in following the Recces. Using Mi-8 and Mi-24 helicopters they had been leap-frogging pursuit troops to keep on the track of the commandos, who had to vacate the pre-planned pick-up point.

It was very difficult for the commandos to provide a grid reference for a rendezvous because they had been running through thick bush. The aircraft navigated towards the Cuito River, then flew northward parallel to it and five kilometres to the east. As the aircraft were reaching bingo fuel they managed to make communications with the team by FM radio. The commandos heard the aircraft and illuminated an 'instant light' which fortunately the helicopter crews saw and homed in on.

Then the soldiers fired a pencil flare through the trees and parallel to the ground to indicate a landing area. They could not fire it skyward because of the proximity of the following Angolans. The grassy area selected for touch-down was just large enough for the Pumas to land in line astern.

The unserviceability of the fourth Puma led to severe overloading of the three remaining aircraft. Myburgh, at the head of the line, loaded 16 men plus a casevac. Equipment had to be thrown out to allow the aircraft to lift off. Andy Freeman, pilot of the second aircraft, also took his maximum load while Steve Gallineti, in Puma number three, took the remaining 21 soldiers. Being last to land he had a slightly longer take-off run in which to transition to normal flight and therefore could accept the extra weight. All the aircraft landed back at AFB Rundu with their fuel low level warning lights burning brightly.

Twelve of the commandos were awarded the Honoris Crux for their deeds. The bridge was damaged to such an extent that vehicular traffic was stopped. The enemy had to use a helicopter air-bridge to ferry supplies over the Cuito River.

By this late stage in the war the SADF realized success in warfare depended on joint actions based on a joint plan, therefore all resources available to the security forces were optimally utilized in a combined effort to achieve success. The selected aims of Operation *Moduler* were to:

- watch and harass FAPLA forces when they deploy
- monitor and harass the FAPLA force as it advances
- halt the advance of FAPLA on Mavinga
- destroy the FAPLA forces involved

To assess the magnitude and composition of the Angolan forces was priority number one. To allow intelligence assessments of the composition of the enemy force to be accurately determined a PR programme was launched using Mirage R2Z PR aircraft. These assessments indicated that the force was mobile and included tanks, armoured cars and self-propelled SAM missile batteries and a huge logistic tail to sustain the front-line brigades.

Political restrictions prevented direct SADF intervention in the Angolan advance. Only if the little town and vital airstrip of Mavinga were directly threatened could SADF forces become involved in the direct fighting. However, small numbers of SADF personnel were being used as advisors to the UNITA guerrilla forces who were harassing the FAPLA advance.

A circle with a radius of 50 kilometres was drawn around Mavinga and only if and when the Angolan forces breached this circle would Operation *Moduler* be initiated. This political restriction severely hampered the principles of offensive action, manoeuvre, surprise and flexibility. However, it must be appreciated that in warfare political restrictions are a fact of life.

A major problem for the SADF was the lack of suitable targets as the enemy brigades moved through the thick bush. The brigades were spread over vast distances (within a five- to eight-kilometre square), making air attack and even artillery bombardments non-cost-effective. It was only as the 'right-hook'

1987: Conventional warfare

brigades rounded the source of the Lomba River that an attack became viable. 21 Brigade positioned itself north of the Lomba while 47 Brigade circled round to its southern bank. While the river itself is not particularly wide, the flatness of the terrain extends the flood plains on either side making them formidable obstacles to vehicular movement. These two brigades thus became isolated and could no longer effectively support one another. By the skilful use of harassing tactics by UNITA, advised by the SADF, both these enemy brigades were squeezed against the Lomba River. Their personnel and vehicles were concentrated into areas less than two square kilometres.

During the many years of involvement in the bush war the SADF had come to grips with the problem of aiming weapons in thick bush and on sandy surfaces. Contact-fused bombs or shells penetrated the soft, sandy ground surface before detonating. The result was an enormous crater but nothing else. Under these conditions air-burst bombs and shells were far more efficient. In addition, the new generation SAAF bombs were filled with thousands of ball-bearings instead of having a heavy metal casing and were called pre-fragmented anti-personnel bombs. When they detonated in the air patterns of fragmentation were scattered, covering large areas of ground. A stick of eight bombs could effectively cover a strip 70 metres wide by 400 metres long and any person or lightly armoured vehicle within this area would suffer damage. A formation of four aircraft each tossing a stick of eight bombs into brigades concentrated in the bush could and did cause huge amounts of damage.

It was during these battles we deployed a detachment of RPVs (remotely piloted vehicles/aircraft). They assisted in the identification of suitable targets as the Angolan brigades advanced through the dense bush. Despite overhead foliage, tanks and armoured vehicle tracks were easily identified. The Angolans

The remotely piloted Seeker has a pusher-propeller and a seeker-dome underneath the forward fuselage. The camera can be operated from the control cabin to focus on anything of interest. It is an excellent intelligence-gathering system because all the captured data is recorded.

placed these RPVs at the top of their list of targets to be destroyed and using SA-8 missiles they achieved success, shooting down three of the little aircraft.

Two days after the first RPV was destroyed a signal arrived at our HQ from UNITA. Their message was one of deep sorrow, expressing their grief at the event they had witnessed. They heard the SA-8 explode and saw the aircraft crash to earth. After a lengthy search they found the wreckage and then spent two days trying to find the pilot, without success. We thanked them for their efforts and concern and explained these aircraft were fortunately unmanned.

A number of years earlier we had deployed the RPV system at Xangongo airfield to carry out surveillance of Cahama. It was during this deployment we discovered for the first time that mobile SA-8 batteries had entered the war. I can vividly recall watching video footage, taken from the RPV while it was on a pass near the town. The drone received a salvo of three SA-8 missiles; fortunately, all three missed by the narrowest of margins. Everybody in the room automatically ducked as the video showed the missiles flashing past the seeker dome. This intelligence led to our abortive attempt to capture an SA-8 vehicle during Operation *Askari*.

During the night of 3 September, Lieutenant Richard Glynn was tasked to fly a Bosbok on a night artillery-spotting mission south of the Lomba River. In his back seat he carried an artillery officer who was to co-ordinate the nightly artillery barrage. Unfortunately, the aircraft was struck by a missile, presumed to be an SA-8, and crashed with the loss of both occupants.

On 4 September, 3 Squadron was deployed to AFB Rundu for air-defence duties together with a Rodent mobile radar unit. The base itself was in chaos because the

3 Squadron pilots on crew-room 'readiness' in 'Little Siberia'. *L to R*: Frank Tonkin, Mark Raymond, Arthur Piercy, Anton van Rensburg.

runway was being extended and a large building programme was in progress. Facilities were at a premium. This led 3 Squadron to christen their readiness tent at the end of the runway 'Little Siberia'. An arrestor barrier had been installed at the end of the runway but there was no available power to raise it.

Hygiene left a lot to be desired and within a week of arrival everybody was suffering from diarrhoea. Squadron strength was often down to four fit pilots, causing an extremely stressful situation. Air defence required pilots to be strapped into aircraft throughout the day, seven days a week. Under glass canopies temperatures often soar to over 40°C and the pilots endured gruelling conditions. The hardship was amplified by the perennial problem of war—the impossibility to forecast when it would all end.

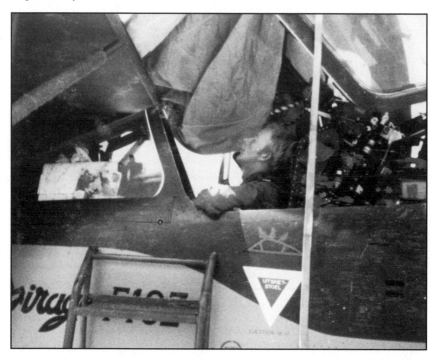

Mark Crooks on cockpit standby at 'Little Siberia'. Makeshift canopies were rigged to protect the pilots from the debilitating effects of the tropical sun.

Because of substantial MiG activity over the advancing enemy brigades 3 Squadron pilots and the radar controllers decided to modify the LIPs profiles to suit the area north of Rundu. The AR3D radar was sited on a ridge ten nautical miles north of AFB Rundu and used the call sign Sunset Radar.

Holding points were worked out and cockpit standby became the order of the day. The distances involved were so vast that, although a number of scrambles were made, our aircraft only arrived in the area after the MiGs had left. It must be pointed out Rundu's radar could only see aircraft in the combat area above approximately 24,000 feet because of the limits of the radar horizon. However, because of their radar at Cuito Cuanavale and Menonque the enemy had coverage from the ground upwards. As the majority of air activity took place below our radar horizon our pilots were going in blind—like taking a knife to a gunfight.

Because of the realistic training programme they had undergone 3 Squadron pilots were full of confidence. They were tasked to escort the Mirage III RZs of Leon Burger and Keith Page during the many PR missions flown prior to the real outbreak of hostilities. At the back of their minds was the desire for a dogfight. Everybody wanted a MiG. Carlo Gagiano and Anton van Rensburg always seemed to fly together, while Pierre du Plessis, Frank Tonkin, Mark Raymond, John Sinclair, Jaco de Beer, Rudi Mes and Arthur Piercy used to rotate.

On 10 September, the *Bellombra* training paid off. Commandant Thinus du

3 Squadron pilots pose formally with their Honorary Colonel.
Left to right back: Les Bennett, Mark Raymond, John Sinclair, Rudi Mes, Arthur Piercy, Anton van Rensburg; *front:* Clive Turner, Pierre du Plessis, Carlo Gagiano, Honorary Colonel Pik Botha, Dries Wehmeyer, Johan Barnardt, Pete Cooke.

Toit, at 320 FACP, authorized the scramble of three pairs of F1CZs. Shortly after arriving at their holding point Commandant Carlo Gagiano and Captain Anton van Rensburg were told to pitch-up into an intercept. The interception procedure sounded as calm and as cool as any training exercise. Carlo asked for a height check on the bogeys and climbed above them. As the range decreased he called "Tanks" and both aircraft jettisoned their empty drop tanks.

Moments before the cross on the head-on intercept profile van Rensburg screamed he had a visual on one of the two MiG-23s. The MiG pilot had turned to the left exposing his aircraft's tailpipe and Anton immediately spiralled down behind him. Within seconds he achieved firing parameters and launched a Matra 550 missile. It guided but exploded in the heat plume behind the MiG-23. He launched his other missile which also tracked the descending MiG. Not knowing where the second MiG was caused van Rensburg to break off before seeing his second missile detonate early, a failing of that generation of missiles.

Gagiano, who had missed the frantic action, joined up with van Rensburg as the MiGs fled back to Menonque. After the engagement both Mirages returned 163 nautical miles to AFB Rundu. Following this incident the pilots were full of confidence and everyone volunteered for the next cockpit standby.

Meanwhile, 1 Squadron had ferried to AFB Grootfontein. The opening sortie of the operation was scheduled for 16 September. Major Norman Minne, being the new boy on the block, was allocated the only unserviceable aircraft. Persuading the ever-willing ground crew to pull out all stops he was finally airborne for a night test flight (illegal in peacetime) at 22h30 on 15 September. After an engine change the test schedule required acceleration past Mach 1.4, to check the operation of the engine overspeed system. Minne carried out a full afterburner climb, levelled out, achieved the M1.4, then cut the afterburner and returned to land. He reported the aircraft serviceable.

Next morning, after an extensive briefing regarding the possibility of encountering SA-6s and SA-8s the formation, including Minne, was airborne at 05h45. After his last experience over Lubango when 1 Squadron had two aircraft damaged by missiles, Minne flew the sortie with a certain amount of trepidation. As it turned out this first sortie was a non-event as no enemy fire was experienced.

Despite initial South African artillery fire accounting for a number of tanks and over 200 casualties, the enemy continued to advance. On 16 September, the SAAF opened the air offensive with a combined air strike against 47 Brigade delivering 100 x Mk 82 (250kg) pre-frag bombs.

The success of the Mk 81 (120kg) during 1985 had prompted the designers to modify the original American Mk 82 (250kg) bomb. The casing was modified to contain larger-diameter ball-bearings. The greater inertia of these heavier balls allowed them to penetrate the light armour of the enemy's fighting vehicles.

During the early strikes against the enemy brigades, deployed near the Lomba River, Commandant Johan Rankin led an attack that nearly proved to be his last. As planned his formation pitched-up for a *Vergooi* delivery. After bomb-release, the profile called for a rapid application of 130° of bank to return to the comparative safety of low level as quickly as possible. As Rankin rolled into this turn a 'missile launch' call was heard on the radio.

Swivelling his head to the rear he soon picked up numerous smoke trails coming towards his aircraft. Distracted by the approaching missiles he retained too much bank while pulling the nose down to avoid the missiles. As the danger receded he looked forward, only to see treetops filling his windscreen. Rolling wings level and pulling maximum G, he entered an open *shona* where the absence of trees provided the extra 50 feet he needed to recover. Leaving a plume of dust, he flashed below the spreading tops of a clump of makelani palms, before returning to more normal conditions for the return flight to AFB Grootfontein.

At the debrief when the situation was analyzed it was discovered Captain Reg van Eeden had ended up in a similar predicament. All subsequent strike briefings included a reminder of priorities during an attack sequence:

- accurate bomb release
- avoidance of missiles
- a safe recovery

Speed of sound

Despite the intensity of the war visiting groups from South Africa continued to make their appearance on a daily basis in the operational theatre. Time had to be set aside to brief each group, a tedious, but necessary part of the war. However, a welcome sight at AFB Rundu was the arrival of members of the senior joint staff course who were to be updated on the progress of the war.

During the briefing Brigadier Thackwray, a renowned practical joker, quietly whispered instructions in my ear. Slipping out of the side door I hurried across to 3 Squadron's operations room. At 10h00 the guests would break for tea, served under the trees outside the briefing room, and Thackwray wanted to give them a surprise.

I briefed Captain Arthur Piercy to take off shortly before tea-time. At precisely 10h10 he was to make a high-speed, low-level pass over 32 Battalion HQ where the briefing was being held. On the second, just as tea had been poured, Piercy's F1 arrived. When an aircraft travels at supersonic speed no warning sound indicates its approach. Piercy's arrival was unheralded, although he claims his aircraft was flying below Mach 1. Well, Piercy was obscenely low when he flew over the tea party. Cups, saucers and people fell to the ground as if pole-axed. Minutes later some semblance of order was restored outside. However, inside the HQ consternation reigned. General Georg Meiring, GOC of the theatre, instead of going outside for tea had been called to the office of Colonel Eddie Viljoen to take an urgent phone call. He was deep in conversation when the shockwave from the Mirage F1 struck the building. Neon lighting tubes and ceiling panels fell down. The accumulated dust of many years swirled through the building like advection fog on the Skeleton Coast. A very shaken general appeared out of the gloom looking like a figure from Cape Town's famous Coon Carnival with only his eyes not covered in dust. Being the man he is he took the prank in the spirit it was intended, most fortunately for Piercy.

MiG surprise

During the morning of 27 September, a PR sortie escorted by 3 Squadron was flown over the Lomba River area without incident. At 15h30, three pairs of Mirage F1CZs, Carlo Gagiano and Arthur Piercy, Pierre du Plessis and Frank Tonkin, and Rudi Mes and Jaco de Beer, were scrambled. The first two pairs set off in trail to a holding point. Mes and de Beer, the last pair, were vectored 40° off to the left to act as a cut-off in the event other MiGs entered the area while the first pairs were occupied with the main intercept.

The centre-line tank can be jettisoned to transform the Mirage F1CZ into a sleek fighter.

Gagiano and Piercy were given the order to pitch-up and once again the intercept occurred as if in training. The range closed in a head-on profile, drop tanks were jettisoned and at the cross Gagiano saw an aircraft and called, "Su22, correction MiG-23." Both pairs then entered left-hand turns to approach again in a head-on posture. It was difficult for the pilots to maintain visual contact with the MiGs at the extreme range of the turning circles.

As they were nearing the head-on position Piercy shouted "Missiles!" as three front-sector missiles, probably AAM-8s, were launched from the MiGs. One missile, which could be seen in Gagiano's camera-gun film, passed directly over his canopy. The other two guided onto Piercy, one of which exploded on the left-hand side of his aircraft alongside the tailpipe.

"Arthur, you've been hit. Go down, go down, go down," Gagiano shouted.

At this, Piercy disappeared from view.

"Where are you, Arthur?" Gagiano asked.

"Among the trees going like the clappers," Piercy replied.

The MiGs had disappeared and Gagiano joined up with Piercy to help assess the damage. Meanwhile, Piercy had his hands full coping with all sorts of emergencies, hydraulics and fuel being the cause of greatest concern. Gagiano's first comment to Piercy when he flew alongside was possibly the understatement of the war—"Arthur, you've had your tail feathers ruffled." After that, as they flew back to Rundu he nursed Piercy through all the emergency procedures. The drag 'chute had been shot off, fuel was leaking from holes on the right-hand side of the aircraft, hydraulics had failed and Piercy was using the emergency throttle to control engine power.

The deficiencies at AFB Rundu airfield now assumed major proportions. After a fine exhibition of piloting skills Piercy managed to land the aircraft safely. Unfortunately, the lack of hydraulic pressure used to work the aircraft braking system, coupled with the loss of the braking drag 'chute, made the aircraft unstoppable. Because of the lack of an arrestor barrier the aircraft shot off the end of the runway at high speed. A heavy impact on the rough surface caused the ejection seat to fire, throwing Piercy out of the cockpit. Unfortunately, because of insufficient time his parachute did not deploy and when he was found was still strapped into his seat. He sustained severe, permanent damage to his lower back—an unjust reward for a superb display of airmanship. (*See* Appendix 3)

A step into the third generation

This incident brought home the fact that the technological advantage now lay in the hands of our enemies. While the facts were being analyzed 3 Squadron was restricted to base defence and escort duties. *Bellombra* sorties were cancelled.

Commandant Mossie Basson, an ex-1 Squadron pilot, played a very important role in altering the entire air-combat manoeuvring programme with regard to fighting against front sector missiles. He gathered information relating to performance of the AAM-7 and AAM-8 missiles. He brought in tactical changes to our fighting doctrine, explaining why and when to cut afterburner to reduce the infrared signature of our aircraft. Training started at AFB Rundu, but without practice missiles it was a difficult and inexact science. Initially, we were hopeful of acquiring the Matra Magic missile but the international arms boycott eliminated that possibility.

On 1 October, a Buccaneer returned to base with some of its bombs still attached which had not released during the attack. Sergeant Phillipus van Dyk, an experienced armourer on 24 Squadron, noticed that the safety arming wire which primed the delay pistol mechanism—which detonated the bomb—had been pulled out. He knew the pistol allowed for a one-hour delay and the aircraft had been flying for over one hour. Knowing this he opened the tail panel of the bomb and removed the pistol. The smell of acetone confirmed his suspicion that it had been activated. The firing pin went off five minutes later. His quick thinking and brave reaction prevented a catastrophe on the flight line. He deserved his award of the Honoris Crux.

On 4 October, Commandant Rankin led a four-ship F1AZ *Vergooi* strike against the Angolan 59th Brigade situated in the bush near the Lomba River, northeast of Mavinga. Digby Holdsworth, Norman Minne and Paulus Truter were the other pilots. Critical fuel factors limited the attack direction for the strikes from the south. Also, a shortage of navigable features further reduced the attack options open to the pilots. On this strike, because of these factors, they planned to use a pitch-up point previously used. This disregard for the principle of surprise almost resulted in drastic consequences.

The attack plan required two pairs of Mirage F1AZs, 15 seconds apart, to use the same pitch-up point (PUP). As Norman Minne, leading the second pair, released his bombs he thought he saw a smoke trail passing over his cockpit. Breaking down for the recovery a second SA-7 passed over the aircraft. Digby Holdsworth was called into a break as a third SAM guided onto his exhaust plume and exploded in the trees behind his F1. At the mission debrief Minne asked Paulus Truter if he had seen the missiles. Truter said yes, but because it was his first missile sighting he had been too tense to call. The enemy's clever deployment to the previously used PUP nearly paid dividends for them and a sobering lesson was re-learned.

SA-8 recovery

On 5 October, Commandant Johan Lehmann succeeded, under heavy enemy fire and difficult conditions, in recovering a Soviet-built SA-8 ground-to-air missile system and other complex weapons for the SA Defence Force. While the enemy attempted to destroy their abandoned vehicles using mortar and artillery fire Lehmann, driving a captured enemy tank, crossed two kilometres of open terrain on the mud-flats of the Lomba River, three times, to tow away three enemy vehicles stuck in the mud.

The recovery of these weapon systems greatly assisted South African engineers to build suitable counter-measures against them. For his bravery Lehmann was awarded the Honoris Crux.

Cuito bridge PR

On 11 October, Major Giel van den Berg and Captain Peter Kirkpatrick were tasked to carry out an oblique-angle PR on the Cuito Cuanavale bridge. This was at a very busy time; 24 Squadron had just flown 14 strikes in a nine-day period and 1 Squadron had been as equally involved. The PR was to take place at the same time as a combined Buccaneer–F1AZ strike sortie on a target between the Lomba River and Cuito Cuanavale. Chances were high MiG-23s would be in the area.

Unlike the Mirage F1AZ, the Buccaneer had plenty of fuel and could cruise at 480 knots at low level for close on two and a half hours. This meant the lone aircraft could approach from a totally different sector giving them a safety factor. In addition, the Buccaneer was fitted with full chaff and flare dispensers as well as carrying two active radar-jamming pods. The photographic pod was carried internally in the bomb bay, significantly reducing drag.

Kirkpatrick, the navigator, planned to go around the combat area and then run up the Cuando River, staying low in its flood plain. At their IP they would turn left to approach the target from the northeast, accelerating to 580 knots but remaining at 100 feet AGL. This approach from behind the Chambinga high ground would shield the Buccaneer from the enemy radars at Cuito until the last minute.

During their transit, well east of Rundu, the crew conducted normal checks on the camera system. Van den Berg rolled the bomb door open, deployed the starboard sight for the camera and set up the sight angle to coincide with the camera setting which was about 10° to starboard. Everything checked out so the bomb door was closed and the sight stowed away.

There are inherent difficulties taking oblique-angled camera shots. The camera lens is fixed at 10° below the horizontal wing-level position, pointing out of the right-side of the photo-pod. To aim the camera the pilot has to raise a sight fixed to the cockpit rail, run the target through the sight, at the same time pressing the camera button to run the film. This manoeuvre is difficult enough during training but exceptionally difficult under operational conditions.

The crew were used to operating under conditions of radio silence but on this occasion found it disconcerting to be on their own and not in the comforting surroundings of a battle formation. This isolation caused Kirkpatrick to develop a healthy respect for the pilots of 2 Squadron Mirage III single-seat reconnaissance aircraft. They never had the comfort of someone to talk to on the intercom.

Shortly after they crossed the cut-line they turned into the Cuando River valley and were amazed to find it nearly four kilometres wide. The Buccaneer was fitted with a good (for its day) navigational system but required updated information at each of the planned turning points. They turned left as planned at the IP and accelerated. As they hit the PUP van den Berg pulled 4G and, almost immediately, as the aircraft shot past 2,500 feet he inverted it and pulled the nose down to level off at 5,000 feet AGL, at the same time rolling the bomb door open. This was 12 seconds after he initiated pitch-up.

At this point their RWR (radar warning receiver) was very busy with several SA-8s and an SA-3 making themselves heard. They were not in missile launch-mode but their presence could attract the MiG-23s. Kirkpatrick switched on the camera and van den Berg lined up the sight with the bridge which was exactly in the correct place.

The run was completed, the film had been taken and now was the time to escape. Van den Berg plunged towards the deck opening the 'barn doors' (split-

1987: Conventional warfare

tail dive brakes) to increase the rate of descent and closing the bomb bay while Kirkpatrick switched off the camera. By now the RWR was screaming its head off with all the radar activity being received from Cuito and Menonque.

Safely back at low level and heading south the crew were startled to hear over the radio, "We are in your seven o'clock." It took them a few startled seconds to realize it was the voice of Major Pikkie Siebrits talking to Captain Mike Bowyer on the way out from their strike to the southeast

The return flight was uneventful and they landed safely back at AFB Grootfontein. The film was removed for developing and analysis and the crew headed for the pub for some well-deserved refreshment. That was the good news. The bad news was instead of the bridge lying in the lower third of the photo it was positioned near the top. Although usable, the intelligence staff and photographic-interpreters required better photos for later operations so the crew had to repeat the mission.

Van den Berg and Kirkpatrick double-checked their planning but could not

The bridge is clearly marked but the PIs wanted it in the lower part of the frame.

find any faults. When they pitched-up the bridge was exactly where it should have been. On 14 October, they boarded the same aircraft and set off again. During transit they re-checked their equipment. It was when van den Berg raised the starboard camera sighting arm he noticed it was slightly loose and had vibrated itself to 12° instead of the required 10°. After some choice words he corrected the problem.

The second pass over the target was exactly the same as the first, even to the amount of noise generated by the radar warning receivers, only this time the photos were perfect.

After the first heavy SAAF strike against the Angolan brigades south of the Lomba River, the enemy did not begin their retreat as expected. Further bombardment by aircraft and artillery continued until October when the remaining enemy soldiers fled on foot. Later, clearing the battlefield, it was discovered their vehicles had been decimated by the larger ball-bearings in the new Mk 82 pre-fragmented bombs. Engines, radiators and tyres had been punctured and the vehicles were immovable.

The fighting when it had started was heavy, intense and conventional. Artillery bombardments on both 21 and 47 Brigades were accurate and prolonged. SAAF air strikes by Buccaneers, Mirages, Canberras and Impalas, using air-bursting pre-fragmented bombs, decimated both brigades. Within a few days the enemy suffered tremendous casualties and their will was broken. 47 Brigade personnel abandoned whatever vehicles were still roadworthy and retreated on foot across the Lomba River to join the retreating 21 Brigade. The threat to Mavinga, Jamba and UNITA was thwarted once again.

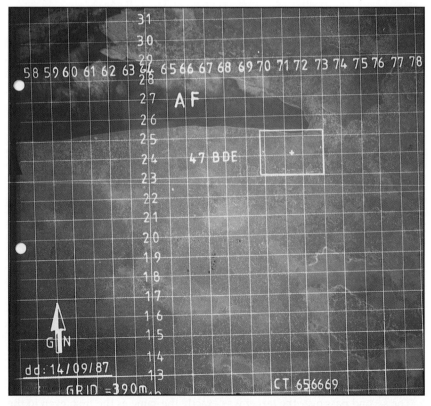

This photograph, taken on 14 September 1987, shows the position of 47 Brigade. They had advanced to this position from the west along the edge of the flood plain. A look at the scale shows the whole brigade was crammed into an area of 1,200 metres by 800 metres—a perfect target for the application of pre-fragmentation bombs.

When the battlefield was finally cleared it was established enemy equipment losses had been 61 tanks, 53 BTR-60s, seven BMP-1s, 23 BRDM-2s and 20 BM-21 rocket launchers. The enemy lost 1,059 killed and 2,118 wounded. South African losses were 17 killed and 41 wounded. The SAAF lost one Bosbok and four RPVs to SAM missile fire.

Assessed against the selected aim Operation *Moduler* was completely successful. The joint plan had been well executed with predictable results.

The 'mayor' of Mavinga

At this time, Major Eddie Brown, a renowned helicopter pilot, found himself as the MAOT commander for the air force at Mavinga. As the senior SAAF representative Eddie looked on himself as both the mayor and airport manager of the town. Angolan MiG fighter activity precluded the use of SAAF transport aircraft during the day. At night, however, the skies belonged to our Hercules and Transall aircraft. Brown's job, late every afternoon, was to ensure the sand airfield and its limited facilities were fully prepared for the night's activities. He carried out his daily airfield inspection on a 350cc off-road Honda scrambler.

As 'mayor', Brown was very aware of enemy MiGs and during daylight hours they were never far from his mind. However, because they were on the ground shortly before sundown Brown could make the most of his airfield inspection. Every evening he set off on his motorcycle on an adrenaline-pumping, full-throttle charge to the end of the runway, ostensibly to check the surface, before returning more sedately to inspect the rest of the airfield.

Because Angola lacks navigational features the 'Vlammie' pilots tended to use Mavinga airfield as a definite IP to update their en-route navigation. Whenever an offensive strike by Mirages or Buccaneers was planned Brown was informed beforehand by radio. This was necessary to ensure our own aircrafts' safety from UNITA's anti-aircraft artillery.

On one particular occasion Brown did not receive the customary early warning and had just reached 120kph on his Honda when four Mirages and two Buccaneers, travelling at high speed and very low level, reached their selected IP. The sudden noise and the fact he had not received any warning led our motorcyclist to react as if they were MiGs. A quick 45° turn took him into cover of the bush, where he was promptly unseated by a large branch and propelled into the Angolan dust.

Fortunately he was unhurt but to this day, nearly two decades later, he is still suspicious of air force communications and exhibits signs of anxiety in the presence of 'Vlamgat' pilots.

By late October the enemy brigades had been savaged at the Lomba River and were in full retreat. UNITA and its allies were engaged in the decisive battle

Commandant Eddie Brown, an excellent helicopter bush pilot but nervous motorcyclist.

northwest of Mavinga. South African artillery was increasing pressure on the Angolans with an almost continuous bombardment of their forces, using batteries of Valkiri multiple rocket launchers and 155mm howitzer fire. The SAAF was carrying out air strikes on a daily basis in support of the ground forces.

Initially, we had made use of the pre-fragmented Mk 82 bombs with air-burst fuses. These were extremely effective on troops exposed at the time of the strike but less effective against troops in foxholes. They also proved the designers' forecasts, causing havoc against trucks and light armour, especially the vehicles' radiators and tyres. Intercepted enemy radio messages indicated food and ammunition had to make way for radiators and tyres on the convoys sent from Menonque to support their troops.

Whenever one of the enemy brigades got bogged down, unable to continue their retreat until the arrival of the convoys, the SAAF would switch to dropping conventional 'iron' bombs, half of which would be fitted with variable-delay fuses. On contact half the bombs would detonate and the others disappear into the sandy surface to explode at irregular intervals during the following 48 hours, making it very uncomfortable for the Angolan forces in the area.

Buccaneer strike

On 30 October, Commandant 'Lappies' Labuschagne and Major Neil Napier led a three-ship Buccaneer formation on a strike southeast of Cuito Cuanavale. Their plan was to approach up the Cuito River past Vila Nova del Armada, find the pre-IP, turn east to reach the strange-shaped pan selected for their IP and then turn north to the target. The break-off was to be to starboard and the return low-level to the south. This approach plan was chosen to avoid the SA-9 and SA-8 batteries known to be on the southern and western flanks of the brigade to be attacked. This route would give ample clearance from the four Mirage F1AZs whose TOT was just 30 seconds before that of the Buccaneers. The odd-looking pan was also the only usable IP in the otherwise flat terrain.

Left: Giel van der Berg and Peter Kirkpatrick pre-flighting their Buccaneer prior to an operational sortie.
Right: The big smile on Peter's face tells us that this photograph was taken after a sortie.

The aircraft took off at 14h05, settled into battle formation and set heading for the Cuito River. Major Giel van den Berg and young Peter Kirkpatrick were flying in the No 3 slot, farthest aircraft away from the leader, sometimes 2,000 metres on the beam. This position makes it difficult for the crew to accurately update their navigation system as only the lead aircraft passes directly overhead each selected turning point. To solve this problem van den Berg and Kirkpatrick developed a technique. They would lag behind the deader during formation crossover turns so van den Berg could position his aircraft accurately over the turning point and Peter update the navigation system. This was particularly important the closer they got to the IP, especially if it was a pan in the middle of an otherwise featureless area and they were only 100 feet AGL, flying at a speed of 480 knots.

As the formation arrived at the planned turning point on the river van den Berg expected an 80° turn to the right, allowing Kirkpatrick to update the system accurately. However, the formation leader turned only 30° then levelled out. They were now heading directly for the target via the SA-8 defences and closing on the track planned for the Mirage formation.

The mission was being flown in complete radio silence. On the intercom

Kirkpatrick told van den Berg they were heading for disaster. Van den Berg concurred and agreed Peter should break the imposed silence. Peter called the formation leader and questioned the change of heading.

Commandant Labuschagne realized things were going horribly wrong with his navigation system and immediately handed over leadership to van den Berg, who initiated a 270° turn to the left to take the formation back on track. The pilots heaved the heavily loaded aircraft into a high-G turn and Kirkpatrick gave van den Berg a new heading for the IP point. Thanks to the accuracy of their navigation update they arrived at the IP, albeit 30 seconds late, hacked (started stop-watches and navigation system) and accelerated to 540 knots for the attack. The other two Buccaneers dropped into echelon astern.

Van den Berg rolled the bomb door open and Kirkpatrick started the chaff running just before pitch. By now the SA-8s had been confirmed by the amount of noise coming over the RWRs. Van den Berg was flying the aircraft at 80 feet AGL and at 540 knots, following the weapon system commands in the head-up-display (HUD). In these conditions the beauty of a two-man crew is the pilot can concentrate solely on flying the aircraft while the navigator manages the weapons' system. He arms the weapons, fires the protective chaff and flares, controls the active EW-jammer and checks for missile trails, AAA fire and MiGs.

They hit the pitch at 4.7 nautical miles from the target and van den Berg followed the HUD commands pulling up at 4G, and six seconds later the bombs were automatically released in sequence as the aircraft passed through 35° to 40° nose high. Once the bombs were released they rolled hard right and commenced the break-off manoeuvre to the south and the relative safety of low level and 580 knots. At the apex of the turn Peter released the flares to deal with any infrared, heat-seeking missiles such as the SA-7, SA-9 and SA-14. At this stage, although the SA-8 warnings were becoming very loud the system had still not locked-on into the missile-launch mode. Thirty seconds after pitch the entire formation was safely back at low level and heading back to base, all heads swivelling as the crew watched for MiG interceptors. Only when they were south of the cut-line did the crews relax.

C-160 Transall—battlefield transport

At this stage of the war, 28 Squadron, the SAAF's premier transport squadron, was required to keep one of their aircraft permanently at AFB Grootfontein. The compromise they had reached was to deploy one aircraft every week alternating between the C-130 and C-160. This allowed the bush aircraft to return to AFB Waterkloof for maintenance and servicing. These aircraft were worth their weight in gold; they were worked extremely hard in the tough bush conditions. The record for one week's bush flying was 74 hours, held by a C-160 crew.

1987: Conventional warfare

On 5 November, a Transall took off from AFB Waterkloof at the start of one of these weekly tours. The aircraft commander was Major Ockie Engelbrecht, Major Anton Kriegler co-pilot, Captain Malan Pienaar navigator and WOI Neels Theron flight engineer—an experienced and battle-hardened crew.

The following day at 07h50 they left Grootfontein on a four-hour five-minute flight ferrying troops between AFB Rundu and Okongo, an army base approximately 150 nautical miles west of Rundu. Upon returning to Rundu they were tasked to carry out a night flight to Gago Coutinho, some 285nm northeast of Rundu, in Angola and close to the Zambian border. Here they were to pick up 40 UNITA soldiers and a Soviet SAM-8 missile system captured from the Angolans. They were briefed to land at Mavinga on their return, offload freight carried from Rundu and pick up a further 20 South African soldiers from UNITA. Then they had to offload the soldiers and SAM-8 system at Rundu before returning to Grootfontein after a typically long, hard day's border duty.

28 Squadron had laid down a set of SOPs for flying in and out of Angola which their crews adhered to. All the sand strips they flew in and out of were held by UNITA. Due to the clandestine nature of their operations they only flew during the periods of half-moon or less, in complete radio silence, with all exterior and interior cabin lights extinguished and at 1,500 feet AGL. The four-engined Hercules was allowed to shut off its engines at each destination because it was possible for the large aircraft to take off on three engines in the event of a starting problem. The C-160, with only two engines, was never shut down for the same reason. In the event an aircraft could not take off before sunrise it had to be completely burned out. This was to prevent embarrassing satellite photos from the Soviets or Americans showing a South African aircraft in Angola where, according to official sources, we were not.

All routings out of AFB Rundu were to the northeast, to a point on the Cuando River where it intersects the Angolan–Zambian border. The northward leg of

The high tail gives space for the rear ramp to lower. The large undercarriage nacelles house the main wheels required for operation off dirt strips.

the flight would parallel the international border with the aircraft staying just within Angolan airspace until abeam of the destination airfield. All the runways in southern Angola and northern SWA lie in an east–west direction to cater for the prevailing winds. However, at night the winds usually dissipate. This allowed 28 Squadron crews to always land towards the west and to take off to the east, keeping the aircraft away from hostile Angolan territory to the west.

Ground forces at the destination airfields were informed via encrypted radio messages of the ETA of each aircraft which would coincide with a pre-planned roster. Five minutes before the ETA ground troops would ignite used food tins, half-filled with sand and soaked with paraffin, to mark the sides of the runway. All these lights were extinguished immediately the aircraft had landed and re-lit only for take-off. From experience the transport crews knew that the last few tins towards the end of the runway were never lit on time, so they never really knew where the runway ended.

The C-160 had a maximum all-up weight (MAUW) of 99,000lbs on a gravel/sand runway while the four-engine C-130 could lift off at 155,000lbs. However, there were two reasons the C-160 was specially selected for this particular task. Firstly, the main wheels of the C-160 were housed in nacelles on the outside of the fuselage, giving a cargo space of larger dimensions than the stronger C-130 and could thus accommodate the SAM-8 system. Secondly, the C-160 had the ability to 'kneel' while cargo was loaded on board. This was accomplished by partially retracting the main wheels while the aircraft was on the ground, thereby lowering the ramp onto the ground. The beauty of this capability was the ramp and aircraft floor remained on one plane allowing vehicles to be driven straight into the back of the aircraft and lashed securely in place. The aircraft was then 'un-kneeled', the ramp closed and the aircraft ready to taxi.

This gave the Transall a huge tactical advantage over the Hercules in these situations, as the 'Herc' would have to shut down all its engines with freight and vehicles manhandled into and out of the cargo compartment. Also in the Transall, when palletized cargo was unlashed the pallets would slide down the ramp under the effect of gravity. With the aircraft taxiing slowly all the cargo could be dumped in under three minutes and, if no freight needed to be loaded, the aircraft airborne again within five minutes of landing. Between Rundu and Mavinga a single C-160 could fly four trips a night delivering a total of 42,000lbs of freight, while a single C-130 with longer turnaround times at both airfields could only fly two sorties, delivering a total of 30,000lbs of freight. Another advantage of using the C-160 on sand strips was its ten main wheels did far less damage to runway surfaces than the four-wheeled C-130.

However, being a similar size and empty weight to the C-130, and having only two engines the C-160 had fewer options than the C-130 between the fuel weight and the available payload—155,000 to 99,000lbs MAUW.

The C-160 Transall was designed as a battlefield transport aircraft and proved to be a magnificent workhorse.

At the flight briefing the first question the crew asked the Intelligence Officer was, "How much does the SAM-8 system weigh?" He replied very confidently that it was 7,500lbs. Navigator Malan Pienaar calculated the routing for the night, checked the fuel required to complete the trip and checked the expected weather forecast. Four to five-eights of cumulus cloud was expected at 3,500 feet, the moon was waxing and would set at 23h30. It was going to be very dark.

Sunset was at 18h45 and while standing underneath the wing of the Transall waiting for take-off time the crew discussed the missile system they were to carry. Anton Kriegler remarked that the SAM-8 was a huge machine which appeared to have almost amphibious capability. Knowing something about the philosophy of Soviet design he thought it would be built along the lines of a steam locomotive. The rest of the crew agreed, having had first-hand experience of other Soviet fighting vehicles. The consensus was that the estimated 7,500lbs of the system was probably closer to 7,500kgs; it was going to be a tight squeeze staying within the 99,000lb MAUW.

The flight north was uneventful except for the ever-present veld fires burning in hundreds of places along the route and the occasional flashes of lightning in the distance. Reaching their calculated turning point they headed west for ten minutes to a plotted position five nautical miles out on the extended centre line of the Gago Coutinho airfield.

When 28 Squadron started flying dark-moon sorties into Angola they soon realized that an approach and line-up on two distant and very faint rows of tiny canned fires against a pitch-black backdrop, afforded the pilot very few visual clues as to the orientation of the aircraft. In order to keep the runway lights visual the pilot had to focus all his attention outside the cockpit. Many times this had caused endless weaving while trying to line up at low level and using excessive bank angles. It was obvious, after one or two crews had returned with 'horror' stories, that a safer procedure had to be instituted. The SOP called for the navigator to take the aircraft on the runway heading to a point five nautical miles on the extended centre line with the aircraft configured for landing. The co-pilot kept his eyes outside the cockpit and talked the commander, flying on instruments, onto the centre line and glide slope, almost like a radar-controlled GCA (ground controlled approach). At approximately one mile, with the aircraft settled on the approach, the co-pilot took over and made the landing. This procedure turned out to be very safe and worked well.

On this occasion it was a good approach with Engelbrecht on instruments and a combined effort between Kriegler and Pienaar giving the information for the 'talk down'. As the landing lights were switched on Kriegler took over for the landing as they all noticed the vegetation flashing past under the nose. Kriegler allowed the superbly designed three double-wheeled main bogeys to settle firmly on the ground before he called for reverse thrust, then braked and handed over the nose-wheel steering to Engelbrecht as they slowed to 40 knots. Completing the after-landing checks they taxiied to the western end of the runway while all around them soldiers scurried about extinguishing the tin-can lights.

Reaching the tiny parking area they turned the aircraft around, facing back down the runway and with the propellers still turning opened the rear ramp, 'kneeled' the aircraft and unloaded the freight. Neels Theron disembarked to drive the SAM-8 into the hold of the Transall. In the dust kicked up by the propellers Engelbrecht, Pienaar and Kriegler were aware of people milling around the aircraft. This was one of the peculiarities of these night sorties—the aircraft would stop, the crew would open the ramp, offload, load up, close up the aircraft and take off without knowing who had climbed aboard. They just kept their fingers crossed it was the 'good guys', not having spoken to anyone on the ground during the turnaround.

Then the pilots heard the noise of the SAM-8 as it was driven up the ramp and onto the aircraft's floor. The Transall shuddered and seemed to sink an inch or two. The pilots exchanged anxious glances and made a few comments about the 7,500lbs quoted by the Intelligence Officer. When the SAM-8 was in place its engine was cut and the crew could hear UNITA soldiers talking and shouting above the aircraft noise.

Theron returned to his seat and the loadmaster gave the signal for the crew to 'un-kneel' the aircraft. One of the pilots noticed Theron was dripping with perspiration and when questioned, he answered, 'Major, that thing is fokken heavy!" One of the tasks of the navigator is to compute the take-off weight of

An SA-8 system as it was abandoned on the battlefield. The tyres had been punctured by ball-bearings from pre-fragmented bombs.

the aircraft, then calculate the V_1 (take-off refuse speed), V? (rotation speed) and V^2 (single-engine safe climb speed). Anton Kriegler remembers Malan Pienaar sticking his finger in his mouth then holding it out as if he was gauging the wind and said, "Take-off weight 99,000 pounds," simply because the aircraft manual stated that that was the MAUW for a gravel runway. He passed a paper forward to the pilots indicating that V_1 = 60 knots IAS (indicated air speed) and the rotate speed was 85kts IAS.

The crew went through the pre-take-off check list which included a section on the management of the water–methanol power augmentation system. This system automatically injected a water–methanol mixture into the combustion chambers of the Rolls Royce Tyne 6100 SHP (shaft horse power) engines during MAUW take-off when the power levers were advanced beyond the 97 per cent power setting. This injection increased the engine output by up to 15 per cent during the critical lift-off period of flight. The additional power boost could be clearly felt. In the border area with the general elevation of approximately 3,500 feet and the ambient temperatures normally above 30°C, even during the night, all take-offs above 97 per cent power were water–meth assisted.

If the aircraft was lightly loaded and the runway long, as at Grootfontein, the commander could choose to do a 'dry' take-off. The flight engineer would tap the pilot's hand to remind him to stay below the 97 per cent power setting. Should water–meth be required for take-off the engineer had to monitor two black-and-white-striped windows on the instrument panel to ensure both engines were receiving the mixture. Asymmetric feed could present the commander with a very awkward swing towards the 'dry' engine.

The 200-litre water–methanol tank was situated in the aircraft's tail section above the ramp. Because the fluid was very corrosive replenishment was normally only done at a base where the necessary ground-support equipment was available. Careful management of the system allowed for three take-offs before the tank was empty. This was achieved by crew co-ordination—when the commander called "Gear up", the co-pilot selected the undercarriage lever to 'up' and while the gear was cycling the flight engineer would retard both power levers to just below 97 per cent power.

For this take-off the crew paid particular attention to these details as they waited for the last few 'lights' to be lit at the far eastern end of the runway. Engelbrecht advanced the power levers to fully forward with his right hand while his left hand was holding the nose-wheel steering. Kriegler turned on the landing lights and checked temperatures and settings. He kept his right hand on the yoke to keep it in the wings-level position until the commander released the nose-wheel steering; Kriegler's left hand was on top of Engelbrecht's right hand ensuring that full power stayed selected throughout the run. Theron called "Water–meth on both" and had his hand below the pilots' on the short fuel-trim levers. Most turboprops have three sets of engine controls: fuel-flow levers, propeller levers and throttles, however, the C-160 has only one. The large power levers control all three areas via an engine-management computer. To ensure the torque and/or engine temperatures are within limits on take-off the two small fuel-trim levers are manipulated by the flight engineer. Pulling them back reduces the fuel flow and, therefore, also the torque and/or temperature of the affected engine accordingly.

On releasing the brakes they were all instantly aware of the C-160's extremely sluggish acceleration and Theron immediately called, "TGT high on both, trimming fuel flow."

Engelbrecht grunted over the intercom, "Neels, if you touch the fuel trimmers I will smash my elbow through your forehead."

Theron answered very politely but with anguish in his voice, "Major, you are going to cook my engines."

"Neels, even if we melt the fokken engines we need all the power we can get so let GO of those levers," Engelbrecht retorted.

On they trundled, the anguished silence on the flight deck ever intensifying, with three pairs of eyes glued to the TGT gauges. When Kriegler called "V1", they had already passed three-quarters of the runway lights. Engelbrecht took over the stick as he let go of the nose-wheel steering. Slowly the speed built up and they reached 80 knots as they passed the last row of lights. In the 150-metre range of the bright landing lights they could still see runway but had no idea what lay beyond. Finally the IAS reached VR and Engelbrecht, smoothly and gingerly, eased the heavy Transall into the air.

They could see bushes flashing past seemingly very close to the underside of the labouring aircraft. They watched the VSI (vertical speed indicator) and ASI (air speed indicator) with trepidation as the speed was stuck on 105 knots and the VSI was trembling on zero. They were in that very unforgiving bubble of the flight envelope where, if they checked forward to increase the speed, they would descend and strike the ground. If they eased the nose higher to climb the speed would decay and the aircraft would stall before hitting the ground. Everyone in the cockpit was sweating and breathing hard.

Their next target was V^2 120 knots where the undercarriage could be retracted, the drag reduced and the aircraft climb away at the single-engine safety speed but this did not happen. Kriegler had his hand on the undercarriage selector lever when Engelbrecht said, "Stand by, stand by ..." as the speed crept up to about 115 knots.

"Gear up," barked Engelbrecht. The wheel doors opened, the speed stuck on 115 knots, and they were very still very low. As the undercarriage completed its cycle the main-wheel doors closed, followed shortly thereafter by the scary thump of the nose-wheel door closing immediately below the crew's feet. The thump sounded exactly like a tree smashing into the nose of the aircraft. They slowly inched their way out of the 'bubble' and started a shallow climb away from the threatening trees.

"Come out of water–meth Neels," ordered Engelbrecht.

"Major, the tank was sucked dry about five minutes ago," Theron replied.

The C-160 settled into its climb and the crew started breathing normally again. They ran through their check lists. Pienaar steered the aircraft safely onto its proper course, while Theron nursed his engines like a mother watching over first-born twins. The next obstacle was the landing at Mavinga, about 40 minutes' flying time away, followed by a dry take-off after loading another 20 soldiers.

Over the intercom Engelbrecht asked the two, up to now, very quiet loadmasters in the back, "Boys, are you okay?" When they replied shakily in the affirmative, he asked, "What do we have in the back?"

After a while one of the loadmasters replied, 'Major, beside this fokken machine we have 43 soldiers and all their kit."

After a stunned silence and some choice expletives on the flight deck it was decided to offload all the personnel with their kit at Mavinga and take off with nothing but the 'fokken' machine in the back.

Thirty-five minutes later they picked up the two thin rows of small fires marking Mavinga's runway and, after repeating the landing procedures they had used at Gago Coutinho, were soon safely on the ground. Engelbrecht sent Theron out with the instruction to find the senior South African officer present and explain to him why they were not taking any freight or passengers on the next take-off.

After five minutes Theron re-entered the cockpit saying, "Major, they didn't like it, but don't worry, nothing was loaded."

They lined up again as Pienaar said, "Same speeds as before."

They wound up the engines and Engelbrecht said, as they released the brakes, "Okay, Neels, this time you can trim the TGTs."

Once again the acceleration was slow, particularly as there was no water–meth assistance. Fortunately, the soldiers at Mavinga were organized and all the tin cans were burning brightly. They lifted off, went through the 'bubble' with little or no trouble and set course for AFB Rundu where they landed an hour later. They stopped, 'kneeled' the aircraft and Theron went back to drive the 'fokken' machine out of the Transall. The tired crew disembarked and walked back to look at the SAM-8. They were greeted by hordes of cheering SADF personnel—just reward for a once-in-a-lifetime take-off.

After refuelling and a cup of SAAF coffee they flew back to AFB Grootfontein and finally collapsed into bed at 02h00.

While writing this narrative Anton Kriegler recalculated the MAUW using exact figures of the weight of the SAM-8 system plus the estimated weight of the 43 soldiers and their kit aboard the Transall that night. The MAUW of a Transall flying off 'exceptionally surfaced runways' was 112,400lbs. Off 'well-prepared runways' the limit was given as 108,400lbs and off gravel runways the MAUW should not exceed 99,000lbs. The night they were stuck in the 'bubble' the C-160

The G5 155mm howitzer. This gun can fire a 47kg shell out to a range of 39,000 metres at a rate of three rounds per minute.

Transall lifted off at an MAUW of 116,000lbs, exceeding all the given limitations, and yet still brought the crew safely home. It is a wonderful aircraft.

Deep daylight casevac

Early on 11 November, the breech block of a South African G5 cannon exploded, causing two instant deaths and severe injuries to eight gun-crew members. The casevac call-out arrived at AFB Rundu around 08h00. Helicopter flights were forbidden into the battle area during daytime because of the presence of Angolan/Cuban MiGs. This time, however, because of the severity of the wounds of the injured soldiers, a single Puma was tasked to fly to the scene with Mirage F1 fighters for escort—normally, two helicopters would fly in formation to provide support for each other but on this occasion the risk from enemy fighters was assessed to be so high that only one Puma was authorized.

Captain Koos Myburgh, with Captain J. R. Redelinghuys as his co-pilot, took off in Puma 187 at 10h00 for the artillery position about 15 kilometres south of the Lomba River. Two F1CZs were scrambled to stay within five kilometres of the Puma at low level. An Impala jet was flown at medium altitude overhead Rundu to act as the Telstar communications link with the low-flying aircraft.

Twenty minutes after leaving Rundu friend 'Murphy' put in his appearance. The Puma crew lost radio communication with the Impala and the Mirages but decided to press on with the rescue. After 75 minutes radio contact was made with the artillery group who ignited orange smoke to indicate its position at the previously given, very accurate grid-reference point. The helicopter landed.

Myburgh kept his motor idling for the ten minutes it took to stabilize and load the casevacs. Before taking off for the return flight, as he still could not raise the Telstar, he asked the artillery troop to notify Rundu of his position. After lift-off, surrounded by the drifting smoke from the battle, Myburgh turned south and set heading.

Feeling vulnerable and conspicuous he flew at very low level, telling his crew to keep an exceptionally sharp visual lookout. Imagine the suspense in the Puma when three fighters were seen heading south on their beam. If it had been the F1s there would have been only two aircraft. The Angolan fighter pilots were looking for them. Myburgh went from 'very' low level to 'very bloody' low level, while following the course of a riverbed. Normal flight was resumed after 15 hair-raising minutes. Myburgh landed at Rundu after an elapsed time of two hours ten minutes in an aircraft that had a two-hour-fifteen-minute endurance.

Unbeknown to Myburgh, when reports of the enemy MiGs were received, the command post at Rundu scrambled a pair of Mirage F1s into enemy radar cover to divert their attention from the escaping helicopter—a ploy that obviously worked. The casevacs were all loaded onto a waiting C-160 and taken to 1 Military Hospital in Pretoria.

Front-line reinforcement

During the continuous bombardment of Angolan positions normal wear and tear on the huge guns also took its toll. One day, an urgent appeal from the front informed us that a small component in a G5 breech-block mechanism needed replacing. This delicate operation could not be performed at the front because only someone with factory experience could make the necessary precise adjustments. Not wanting to withdraw the gun from the front line an expert from the factory in Pretoria was dispatched in all haste. This poor man received his instructions when he returned to his workbench from lunch. He barely had time to collect his tool-bag, the required component and an overnight case before rushing off to AFB Waterkloof. At the huge air base he dashed out to a C-130 whose propellers were already spinning. Moments later this excited civilian found himself on the long haul to AFB Rundu.

It was already dark when the freighter landed. As soon as the engines stopped the mechanic, clutching his tool-bag, G5 component and overnight case, was escorted across the hardstanding to a Puma helicopter. The rotors were turning and noise from the engine made conversation difficult. However, before the mechanic strapped into a canvas seat and the helicopter lifted off his guide did manage to give him the instruction: "Make sure you get out on the third landing."

A few short hours previously he had been going about his daily business in peacetime Pretoria. Now he was crossing the border in a darkened helicopter, filled with fully armed fighting men. At Mavinga, the Puma's first landing, a number of the soldiers were offloaded within 30 seconds. At this time the helicopter crew was requested to urgently airlift a seriously wounded soldier. Because casualty evacuation took precedence over everything the helicopter was re-routed. At the second landing, a medical doctor climbed aboard and the helicopter then set heading for the front line. At the third landing, stretcher-bearers were waiting to load the casevac, while a bewildered civilian passenger alighted. No one had informed the unfortunate man about the change of route.

All of these activities occurred in almost complete darkness, the enemy's proximity precluding the use of illumination. Everyone, apart from the civilian, was dressed in camouflage, heavily armed and with their faces covered in black camouflage cream. Only after the helicopter had disappeared into the night did the man discover, to his horror, he had alighted in the wrong place. He was not at artillery deployments but with the infantry who were face to face with the enemy on the front line. He spent a most uncomfortable and anxious 24 hours dodging bullets and explosions, waiting for the following night's helicopter to arrive to rectify the problem.

*****

1987: Conventional warfare

Moduler was an astounding success. The enemy advance on Mavinga had been stopped and all their brigades were retreating towards Cuito Cuanavale. It was at this juncture that adrenaline replaced reason. The aim of the operation changed and orders were issued, contrary to advice from the SAAF planners, to harass the enemy during their retreat.

Operation *Hooper*: 27 November 1987 to 13 March 1988

A plan was made for Operation *Hooper* with the selected aim 'to destroy FAPLA forces east of the Cuito River by 31 December 1987'. The luckless Angolans retreated under very difficult conditions until they eventually reached the Chambinga high ground just east of the Cuito River. It was at this juncture, when the SADF was in pursuit that, the reservations raised by the SAAF became apparent.

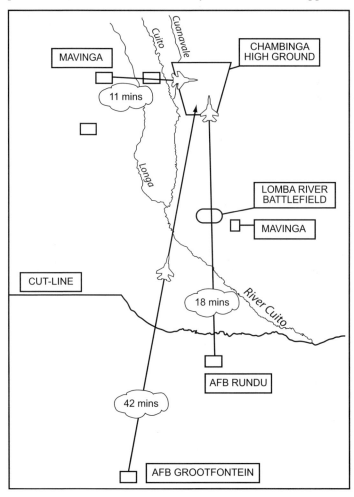

Aircraft reach and reaction times.

The SAAF objections to the plan were based on geography and physical science, not a reluctance to fight. Operation *Moduler* had been fought alongside the Lomba River. On a map it can be seen the battleground is almost equidistant between Rundu and Menongue. Opposing fighters had to fly approximately the same distance to reach the combat area, therefore, combat fuel allowance for both opponents was similar.

Radar beams are restricted to line of sight. SAAF air-defence radar coverage of the battle theatre from the radar site at Rundu was very similar to the enemy coverage from their radar site outside Cuito Cuanavale. These limiting factors ensured that aerial combat would be undertaken over the battlefield under conditions of parity.

With the battle arena shifting to the Chambinga high ground immediately east of the Cuito River, the aerial battle advantages shifted completely into the enemy's favour. Mirage F1AZ fighter-bombers flying from AFB Grootfontein required 42 minutes' flying time to reach the target area, leaving the aircraft with only two minutes of combat fuel in the high-threat area. MiG-23 fighters, flying out of Menonque reached the area in less than eleven minutes, ensuring a combat fuel allowance of around 45 minutes.

The horizon from Rundu limited SAAF radar cover over Chambinga to 24,000 feet and above. Below that our radar was blind. Angolan radar could see clearly from ground level upwards. If they were not to be detected too early SAAF pilots had to approach the target area at extremely low level. As they did not have excess fuel to allow them to vary their lines of lines of attack they became predictable.

The Mirage aircraft were equipped with large underwing fuel tanks which allowed them to reach and recover from the target area. Underwing stores seriously affect aircraft performance during aerial fighting. The MiG-23s could fly in clean configurations, increasing their already considerable performance margin over the Mirages. Flying within their own radar cover also protected them, while the SAAF pilots were flying blind. The situation was aptly described by one SAAF pilot as being "akin to playing with a lion's testicles".

The situation around the Chambinga high ground reached a stalemate. The aim, as laid down by the SADF for *Hooper*, had not been achieved so the operation was extended to 13 March 1988.

Escalation in the numbers and sophistication of enemy aircraft seriously concerned SAAF planners. Angolan aircraft were able to stay for over an hour above the ground battle before having to return to base to refuel. This situation led to justifiable complaints from ground forces embroiled in the battle that enemy MiGs were overhead all day but the SAAF never appeared.

Enemy pilots, both Angolan and Cuban, were delighted with the situation. For the first and only time in the entire war they controlled the air. Their confidence was gained from the knowledge that they flew with positive radar cover from ground level up. Radar at Cuito Cuanavale, two minutes from the battlefield, ensured this advantage. The analogy can be compared to two boxers in a ring, one of whom is blindfolded. It's a dangerous situation when aircraft closing speeds over 1,000mph occur and guided missiles are the favoured weapons.

However, the enemy still lost the battles, a testimony to the excellent training our pilots received and the care and meticulous work that went into planning operations and to the extreme skill and enthusiasm of the pilots themselves. During seven months virtually all the flying was carried out between 500 and 600 knots at extremely low level. Way back in the 1970s, Commandant, now General Rtd, Hechter had concentrated fighter training on not gaining height during steep turns close to the ground. 24 Squadron practised similar techniques, utilizing the advantage of having two crewmen in each aircraft. While the pilot concentrated on looking forward and flying very low the navigator would swivel his head to watch astern of the bomber. In steep turns this meant looking out of the back of the glass canopy. Dave Knoesen and Charlie Wroth practised this while flying along the Zululand coast. They flew their Buccaneer down to 40 feet on the radio altimeter, in the V where the waves break onto the shore. In the operational area they were confident to counter at 80 feet and not hit the trees. This was excellent farsightedness when one considers the missile environment which was to prevail inside Angola at a later date.

Visionaries had foreseen the need to develop a low-level toss-bomb (*Vergooi*) profile. Low-level navigation, while travelling at speeds approaching 16 kilometres per minute, was perfected with the assistance of finely tuned onboard computer systems. To ensure maximum effect correct weapons were designed for the prevailing situation in Angola and brought into service.

On 11 November, Captain Chris Skinner was the leader of two three-ship F1AZ formations, from AFB Grootfontein, on a strike sortie to a target east of Cuito Cuanavale. On this occasion a Boeing 707 tanker was used to refuel the aircraft before the strike which allowed the pilots to vary their ingress routes and attack the enemy from the north. Previously, tankers had been used to allow aircraft to refuel after strike sorties to avoid diverting to alternate airfields. At this stage, the B-707 only had a centre station and the F1 pilots were not practised in refuelling with such heavily loaded aircraft. Mini-afterburner had to be used just to stay in the basket. The attempt was only partially successful.

The plan was for all the Mirages to top up before passing over AFB Rundu, however, turbulence and very heavily loaded aircraft forced the refuelling to take place at a higher altitude than anticipated. For all six aircraft, the delay in taking on fuel resulted in the second three-ship formation having to abort the sortie and return to Grootfontein. It was necessary for Skinner and his two wingmen to plug a second time before they detached and carried out a successful attack.

On 25 November, four F1CZs were tasked to escort three Buccaneers on an

The angle of incidence indicates this Mirage F1AZ is heavily loaded with bombs under both wings and fuselage, two large drop tanks and wing-tip missiles.

H2 guided-bomb mission to cut the runway at Menonque. A planning session had been held at AFB Grootfontein where co-ordination between formations was finalized. After a delay the Mirages were airborne from Rundu at 08h20. A radio-silent rendezvous was made with the Grootfontein Buccaneers. Previous combined training paid dividends. Their entry was at low level to avoid warning the enemy radar and SAM-3 missile systems defending the base.

At the pitch one pair of the F1s dropped chaff carried in their dive-brakes; dispensers were not yet ready for operational use. Only the lead F1 was equipped with a CRWS ECM radar-warning receiver. However, it was installed in all the Buccaneers. Levelling off at altitude all aircraft homed towards Menonque. Although they were inside SAM-3 range the time gate was such that the guided-bombs should have been launched before any defensive missile was fired at the formation. Unfortunately, a technical hitch prevented both bombs from launching and the formation homed to almost overhead Menonque before Commandant Lappies Labuschagne, leader of the Buccaneers, called the abort, turned for home and plunged to low level. The second pair of F1s dropped chaff at the top of descent before screaming down to treetop level. Our GCI radar detected a MiG scramble and interception of the chaff blips after all our aircraft were out of range.

On 8, 12 and 13 December, Mirage F1AZs were used to escort a Buccaneer on H2 guided-bomb strikes on the bridge at Cuito Cuanavale.

The H2 weapon system on the Buccaneer S MK 50

The weapon
The H2 was a 460kg pre-fragmented, folding-winged glide-bomb controlled after release by means of a TV link between the bomb and the controlling aircraft. The weapon had a guidance unit in the nose with its own power generator, driven by

1987: Conventional warfare

Mike Bowyer and Riem Mouton flank the H2 bomb prior to take-off for their attack against the Cuito bridge on 13 December 1988. The TV nose, folding wings and power-generating impeller can be clearly seen.

an impeller at the back of the weapon.

A communication pod was carried under the opposite wing to establish the TV link. Communication was effected through either a front or rear antennae, ensuring the weapon could be controlled after release from the parent aircraft. This allowed the carrier aircraft to turn through 180° to escape the target area during a rapid descent to low level.

The weapon had a maximum glide range of 50 to 60 kilometres, depending on the head- or tailwind, when released at 30,000 feet AGL at Mach 0.83.

After release from the carrier aircraft the weapon would fall away with wings folded. Once safely away from the aircraft the wings would unfold and it would climb initially to bleed speed and glide at 250 knots IAS to the target.

The weapon had an accuracy of three metres CEP.

Controlling the weapon

The Buccaneer navigator controlled the H2 by means of a joystick, numerous buttons and a mini green-and-white TV screen. Various audio signals to the crew indicated the serviceability status and flight progress of the weapon.

The weapon's flight was recorded by means of a tape recorder positioned in the comms pod. For debriefing purposes this included the weapon's audio and crew's intercom conversations, as well as the TV picture from the camera in the bomb's nose as it flew towards the target.

Left: The H2 in-flight with wings spread showing the TV guidance head and the impeller generator at the back between the twin tails.
Right: An H2 in the 'bunt phase' just before impact during development trials.

A single Buccaneer could carry, release and control its own H2 weapon autonomously. However, in the 'buddy mode' it could carry and release a weapon to be controlled by a navigator in a second Buccaneer flying at low level outside the high-threat environment.

The attack profile

The Buccaneer would run in low level at 480 knots ground speed to an IP 50 to 60 nautical miles short of the target. Just before the IP the aircraft would accelerate to 540 knots for the pitch to 30,000 feet AGL. During the pitch the navigator had to identify the planned release point and the track checkpoints on the TV screen, then lock the H2's TV 'eye' onto these features. Before launch, the Buccaneer crew had to determine the drift that would affect the weapon during its flight; they had to offset for this, prior to release, as the weapon's navigation reference was taken from the aircraft's last heading.

To protect the launch aircraft against enemy missile fire, AAA or interceptors, an ACS-pod (ECCM) was carried on the outside station of the same wing on which the H2 was carried. The ACS-pod was programmed to automatically suppress enemy missile and fire-control radars when they were sensed. A blanking pulse, placed on the frequency on which the H2 was communicating with its controlling comms pod, prevented jamming of the weapon.

Overhead the release point the navigator would call for the pilot to launch the H2; the counters on the TV screen would start ticking away the weapon's flight time in seconds. The typical flight time for an H2 was three to three and a half minutes.

The navigator would then 'navigate' the weapon from the track checkpoint to checkpoint of the H2 run on a 1:60,000-scale photo strip.

When the navigator had identified the target he would lock the TV crosshairs to it and press the 'target acquired' button. This would trigger the final phase of flight for the weapon where it enters a 45° bunt. The primary mode of homing in on the target, known as auto-tracking, was done by locking the crosshairs on the bottom left-hand corner of the target. However, in the event of break-lock the navigator had to revert to flying the weapon manually onto the target, a nerve-wracking exercise.

As soon as the weapon was released the pilot would commence a fairly gentle 180° descending turn. This turn was away from the side on which the comms pod was fitted, thus maintaining control of the weapon while switching from the fore antennae to the aft antennae took place. Until weapon impact the pilot would have to remain at an altitude which would allow line-of-sight communication with the weapon. Only then could he make a rapid descent to the safety of the treetops.

The navigator would have his head inside the cockpit from the time the aircraft pitched until the bomb impacted—some six to seven minutes. During this period the pilot was responsible for lookout and cockpit management.

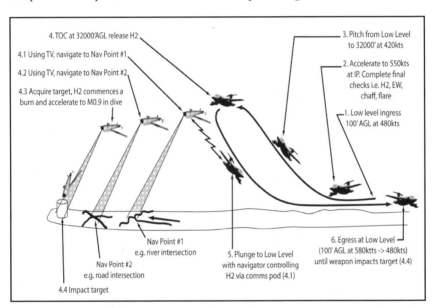

The H2 attack profile as used by the Buccaneers.

*****

After repeated bombing attempts success was finally achieved, although the Cuito bridge was never totally destroyed.

By late December the enemy were busy trying to reinforce their position around Cuito Cuanavale. Huge logistical convoys were operating from Menonque. To hamper this build-up it was decided to launch attacks against their resupply route. At great risk to themselves, ground force reconnaissance teams infiltrated

From Fledgling to Eagle

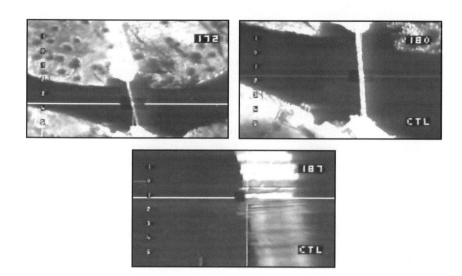

Three still photos taken from the TV tape of the H2 bomb dropped by Major Pikkie Siebrits and Captain Neil Napier. Note the time of flight read-out in seconds in the top right-hand corner of each photo.
Top left: The weapon locked-on to the centre of the bridge during the cruise stage of flight.
Top right: The weapon locked-on during the bunt stage.
Bottom: The weapon as it missed the left-hand edge of the bridge within the three-metre CEP specification.

This Angolan photograph clearly shows the damage inflicted by the H2 bomb that narrowly missed the span. Ferries can be seen high and dry on the far bank.

1987: Conventional warfare

the area and passed back by radio information on the position and composition of these convoys and where they stopped for the night.

This valuable intelligence was used to plan air attacks to be usually flown either at last light or early dawn. These extreme times were selected to reduce the threats faced by our pilots. The Angolan air force did not operate well in the dark and was seldom seen. The poor visibility at dawn or nightfall was the only advantage our pilots had in their favour.

After incoming intelligence had been assessed at Sector 20 FACP plans were made and aircraft tasked to carry out the required strikes. Invariably, these orders only reached 1 Squadron pilots during the evening prior to the planned attack. The crews designated for the sortie would then carry out the pre-strike planning before going to bed. A wake-up call at 03h00 the next morning ensured the crews were tired as well as tense. Grootfontein had no meteorological station to provide updated weather information and very few navigational aids were available in this remote area. After briefing the pilots would emplane and, in complete radio silence, start up and taxi out. After line-up on the runway a green light from the tower would clear pilots to take off.

It was planned that the formation would set heading overhead a distinctive old mine dump northeast of Grootfontein, the heavily loaded aircraft starting their take-off roll using ten-second intervals between each succeeding aircraft. On a number of these pre-dawn strikes aircraft would lift off and disappear into cloud before the undercarriage was locked away. Each pilot was allocated a height difference of 300 feet. Nevertheless, it was an uncomfortable feeling knowing there were six or eight aircraft, all in the same piece of cloud, within 300 feet of each other. No pilot wanted to break radio silence or climb above the cloud because these actions would warn the enemy of the approaching formation. Normally only after they had crossed into Angola was it light enough to visually acquire the rest of the aircraft and settle into the briefed attack formation.

Then the anxiety of the take-off and join-up was replaced by the excitement of really low flying. Five minutes before strike time this thrill altered to an adrenaline rush. At this juncture the formation would accelerate to 540 knots. Armament switches would be checked and rechecked and EW equipment turned on. Approaching the initial point (IP) the speed was stabilized at 600 knots. Pilots would hold their aircraft level at 50 feet on the radio altimeter. Navigation was by reference to maps giving maximum feature references.

Directly overhead the IP the formation leader 'hacked'. This procedure begins the final precise flying to the release point using heading and ground speed obtained from the roller map and the navigation computer. At the PUP, usually around 5.2 nautical miles from the centre of the target, the pilots apply 4G to their aircraft. Keeping the wings level they pull the aircraft's nose skyward, monitoring the fly-up light in the head-up display (HUD). At 2,000 feet the horizontal green light in the HUD illuminates and the pilots manually press the bomb-release button. The bombs release in sequence according to the preset intervalometer settings to give the required bomb-stick length.

A standard practice among the pilots was to press the bomb-jettison button immediately after the manual release to rid their aircraft of any bombs that might be hung up. The extra drag on the return flight often made the fuel situation extremely critical. Therefore, it was advisable to ensure that all the bombs had left the aircraft.

After release it was necessary, from a safety point of view, to return to low level as soon as possible. Each aircraft would bank away from the target and the pilot pull the nose down as quickly as possible. Each pilot had a different escape heading to ensure safety between aircraft and to make it difficult for the enemy defences to track the formation. Going down, the pilots look backwards to watch for anti-aircraft fire or the telltale smoke trails from surface-to-air missiles.

Summer in Angola brings weather conditions known locally as the 'big rains'. Enormous tropical thunderstorms create extreme flying conditions with heavy rain, strong wind gusts and severe turbulence. Not knowing the positions of these storms often meant that pilots, running in at low level, pitched-up for the attack right into these enormous clouds. Bomb release would be done on instruments together with recovery to a normal flight attitude. But inside the cloud the aircraft were safe from the enemy but in danger from the elements.

One of the unfortunate characteristics of attacking under poor daylight conditions was the fact that enemy anti-aircraft fire and the flame emitted from the ground-to-air missiles were easily visible. Therefore, to the pilot, under these conditions, the targets always appeared more dangerous.

Chapter 14

1988: Negotiated settlement

Operation *Moduler* ended in November 1987; the forces were now engaged with *Hooper*. The end of every year created problems for the army because it was based on the national service system. Soldiers at the end of their two-year service period had to be withdrawn from operations and replaced with a new intake. This change-over caused a hiccup in operations, much enjoyed by the permanent force members of the SAAF. Over the festive season, while the army completed their reshuffle, 1 Squadron left five pilots and aircraft at AFB Grootfontein in a caretaker role while the remainder enjoyed the comforts of home.

By early February the battle resumed in earnest and air strikes were flown against the Angolan 21st, 25th and 59th brigades. On 6 February Buccaneers, escorted by F1AZs, again attacked the bridge over the Cuito River using the H2 guided-bomb.

In order to present some degree of air defence around the vital runway at Mavinga the SAAF launched Operation *Arnot* on 8 February. The Air Defence Artillery Group (ADAG) deployed two Cactus SAM firing units, one SA-9 system and six 23mm anti-aircraft guns to the Mavinga area. The SA-9 and the 23mm guns had been captured from the Angolans who, since sanctions, had become our most reliable source of arms procurement. The unit had limited direct success, firing four missiles and damaging one MiG. Indirectly they must have been a deterrent because Mavinga was never attacked by enemy aircraft.

At 18h17 on 18 February, 12 F1AZs took off from AFB Grootfontein for the third strike of the day. After the attack the aircraft had to divert to AFB Rundu because bad weather had closed the runway at Grootfontein. Three four-ship formations, low on fuel, arrived at Rundu in the dark; Rundu had not been built for this amount of traffic. Like most remote airfields no taxi strips had been constructed.

Dumbbells at the end of the runway allowed landing aircraft to turn off, then back-track up the runway. The arrival of 1 Squadron certainly tested the theory.

Being short of fuel there was no time for the aircraft to individually clear the runway as planned during the airfield's construction. The Mirages landed from west to east and had to stack themselves one behind the other down the side of the runway. Major Willie van Coppenhagen, landing behind Norman Minne, had a drag 'chute failure but managed to stop.

When all 12 Mirages had landed safely they had to wait for the Impala Telstar aircraft which was also desperate to land. The Impala pilot, in the illumination of his landing light, saw aircraft blocking one side of the runway for close to half its length. This alarming sight made him very heavy-footed on the brakes and in his attempt to stop promptly burst the main-wheel tyres. After an uncomfortable night in makeshift accommodation the pilots returned to Grootfontein the following morning.

WESTERN FRONT

Lubango again

19 February, Colonel John Church, OC 310 AFCP, reported a bomb explosion in Oshakati town, initiated by SWAPO. A reprisal raid on two targets within the SWAPO Tobias Haneko Training Centre was planned. Mission planning at Grootfontein went on late into the night.

Eventually retiring to bed the tired crews were then kept awake by the noise of a wedding party in full flow at Grootfontein. Before 06h00 the next morning Johan Rankin, in a fit of pique, led his eight aircraft at low level and in full afterburner over the town. Presumably the wedding party woke up with a bang, perhaps a little earlier than anticipated.

Landing at AFB Ondangwa they received a pleasant surprise. Colonel Koos Botha, the base OC, had laid on transport, breakfast and briefing facilities for them in a show of organization they had not previously experienced when arriving at a base in the bush.

At 08h00, after refuelling, the aircraft took off from Ondangwa. Major Norman Minne led the combined strike, flying F1AZ 218. This aircraft's excellent navigation system was giving errors of less than one mile at all the way points. Approaching Lubango from the southeast the compact radar warning receiver (CRWS) started picking up indications of the Soviet-built Barlock and search radars being on the air. He took his formation lower and lower. Because his navigation system was proving so accurate Minne tucked away his standby map and prepared for the attack.

A famous quotation from the Second World War states: 'Battles always take place on the joins of the maps', indicating there is always a 'buggerance' factor

1988: Negotiated settlement

The Soviet Barlock search and GCI radar had a circular scan, an aerial rotation period (ARP) of 10–20 and a pulse repetition frequency of 288–788.

in the fog of war. This strike was no exception. The two targets were either side of the join of the map. Unbeknown to Minne this join caused ten minutes of a degree error in the measured target co-ordinates. With his perfect navigation system he led Trompie Nel and Johan Rankin straight over the edge of Lubango airfield before initiating the *Vergooi* attack. Their bombs landed in the bush ten miles from the target. Each minute of a degree equates to one mile on the ground.

Fortunately, the co-ordinates of the target for the second formation were correct and a successful *Gatup* attack was carried out. During this attack only three aircraft dropped their bombs. Major Willie van Coppenhagen, realizing his sight conditions were not correct for an accurate release, performed a second attack on his own with his bombs landing as planned. Probably the most dangerous act in aerial warfare is to carry out a repeat attack on a target,;fortunately van Coppenhagen got away with it. Most of the aircraft flew directly back to Grootfontein while others, for safety reasons, refuelled at Ondangwa.

EASTERN FRONT

Around midday, Major Minne led a four-ship strike on a target near Baixo Longa. Later that afternoon Commandant Rankin and Captain Reg van Eeden, returning from another mission, also flew close to the little town. Their flight was rudely disturbed when a large, smoke-trailing missile, probably an SA-9, flashed between the two aircraft. The residents of Baixo Longa were obviously a little touchy after Major Minne's midday visit.

Mirage F1AZ shoot-down

During the early afternoon a message from a 32 Battalion reconnaissance detachment in the bush reported a large convoy moving on the Menonque–Cuito Cuanavale road. Planning was carried out and at 16h30 Norman Minne, Ed Every, Frans Coetzee and Trompie Nel took off to attack the convoy using a *Vergooi* profile and dropping sticks of pre-fragmented air-burst bombs. Over the previous five or six days a number of sorties had been flown in the same area.

After releasing their bombs Minne and Every broke out to the left while the other pair went right. Minne heard Every shout "Break left" which Minne did. Seconds later he heard Trompie shouting "Eject, eject." Reaching the safety of low level Minne could see the plume of smoke where Major Ed Every's aircraft had crashed. Flying over the crash site it was obvious the aircraft was totally broken up. Because no emergency calls were picked up on the Pelba beacon it was presumed Every had been killed. It was his second tour; he was aged thirty-one. During the seven-month deployment, squadron personnel were continually rotated to allow for rest and recreation back at Hoedspruit. Ed Every had volunteered to stay at Grootfontein over this crucial period. He was shot down that weekend.

Mirage F1AZ conversion course, 1980. *L to R*: Ronnie Knott-Craig, Frans Coetzee, Dick Lord, Bill Collier and Ed Every, the pilot who was shot down.

Because of the static nature of the war it was presumed the enemy had studied our tactics; an air defence battery had been moved close to the pitch-up point. After bomb release, as Every broke off, the missile system locked-on to the aircraft's exhaust plume. The missile successfully tracked and struck the aircraft as it reached low level.

An immense SAR operation was launched. Captain Dave Stock flew a Telstar mission listening for possible emergency radio transmissions. A C-160 scoured the region with a Parabat team aboard who, if any sign of Every was found, were ready to jump into the hostile area. However, it was clear from Trompie's description that Every had not survived. That night the air- and ground crew joined in what could only be described as a very emotional farewell.

Ed Every.

The continuous presence of enemy MiG fighters over the battlefield became a real source of concern. Ground troops could only move their vehicles at night and the artillery were not able to give supporting fire during the day, the blast from each salvo being a perfect aiming point for patrolling enemy aircraft.

1 Squadron was tasked to show presence over our own troops as a confidence builder. Unfortunately, the F1AZs were configured for ground-attack sorties with large fuel tanks and bomb pylons giving a high-drag index. This made the Mirages inferior to the MiG-23s armed with forward-sector air-to-air missiles.

Two quick dogfights

On 25 February, two of our sorties were intercepted by MiG-23s. In the first engagement Major Willie van Coppenhagen, and captains Dawid Kleynhans and Reg van Eeden turned to fight. The MiGs immediately broke away.

On the second sortie, Commandant Rankin, Major Frans Coetzee and Captain Trompie Nel received a warning they were being stalked by a Cuban MiG-23 formation. Major I. C. du Plessis, an ex-F1AZ pilot, was monitoring enemy radio frequencies at the electronic-warfare control centre. Positioned with him were two Chilean pilots interpreting the Cuban MiG pilots' Spanish. They passed on the information by radio that the MiGs, flying at medium altitude, had spotted Rankin's three F1s flying at low level.

They were accurately describing the yellow-green camouflage of the F1s while descending and positioning themselves behind the Mirage formation. Rankin called the F1 pilots to jettison their fuel tanks and, at precisely the correct range, broke into the fast-approaching enemy. In the turn Rankin saw two MiG-23s flash overhead and he manoeuvred to position the Mirage formation behind them.

Rolling out astern and out of firing range was frustrating. The high-drag-configured Mirages could not close into firing range behind the fleeing MiGs. In a vain attempt to force the MiGs to turn Rankin fired his missiles and cannons, to no effect. He also watched as Nel's missile was outdistanced by the MiGs.

A Mirage camera-gun photograph of a MiG-23 accelerating out of range of the pursuing F1AZ. Configured for a bomb attack the drag index of the Mirage was too high to really threaten the clean MiG whose afterburner flame can be clearly seen.

1988: Negotiated settlement

When the intercepts were analyzed at the debriefing it was obvious the MiG pilots were picking up our aircraft visually by looking down on them. The yellow in the F1AZ camouflage scheme was probably too light. Rankin decided to modify the yellow to a darker brown. It was altered overnight in the hangar, without authority, with the pilots assisting the ground crew. Lieutenant Jimmy Spies, the squadron's technical officer, nearly had a heart attack. He was convinced General Frikkie Bolton, the logistics head of the air force, would court martial Rankin. Whatever the repercussions were at HQ the matter was resolved when Chief of the Air Force, General Dennis Earp, backed Rankin's decision.

A project was then registered to develop a camouflage scheme best suited to the Mirage F1AZ in its various roles. Aircraft 243 was painted dark blue underneath. This colour was later applied to both sides of the vertical fin and the sides of the fuselage. The aircraft's upper surfaces became dark brown and green. (*See photos on the last page of the colour picture section*)

On 2 March, the squadron was stood down from operations. All the aircraft were flown back to AFB Hoedspruit where, as an interim measure, they were officially modified to a dark-earth and matt-green colour scheme.

*****

By 12 March, the aim of Operation *Hooper* had not been achieved so the operation was replaced by *Packer*. The aim set was similar to *Hooper* and was given as, 'To destroy FAPLA forces east of the Cuito River, by 20 March, or to drive them off the east bank by that date'. This aim was not achieved and the date was later extended to 12 May 1988.

Loss of Mirage F1AZ in Angola
On 19 March, six F1AZs returned to AFB Grootfontein from Hoedspruit. At 22h00, Commandant Rankin and Major Willie van Coppenhagen took off for a Darkmoon diversionary strike on an area target near the town of Longa. The aim was to draw enemy attention away from the Cuito Cuanavale battlefield. The flight was the first complete *Nagup* sortie to be flown—the night variation of the *Gatup* profile.

Crossing the cut-line into Angola the weather became marginal but as the raid was only diversionary the pilots continued. Van Coppenhagen flew on his own, trailing Rankin by three nautical miles. He maintained this distance by using readings from the Tacan beacon switched to the air-to-air mode.

Commandant Rankin returned from the flight at low level. For security reasons these flights were flown in radio silence. Shortly before crossing back into South West Africa Rankin saw a momentary flash of fire that he thought was a bomb exploding. On landing, it was found van Coppenhagen was missing.

Commandant Thinus du Toit, OC of Rundu FACP, organized a massive SAR operation. He utilized all the aircraft available to him, including Impalas and the C-160, in a search pattern which lasted for three days, without success. The dense bush had obscured all traces of the missing aircraft.

On the fourth day, 24 March, realizing visual reconnaissance was proving futile, Thinus adopted a new plan. He briefed the crews of two Alouettes to fly to the point where Johan had crossed the river. There, they were to separate—one aircraft working westward and the other east. Each crew would be accompanied by a Kavango soldier to act as an interpreter. The helicopters were to land at each kraal or settlement to inquire whether an explosion or loud bang had been heard during that fateful night.

Almost immediately this change in tactics met with success. Captain Rob Sproul and Sergeant-Major Bachus Rautenbach, the crew of the eastern helicopter Alouette 61, located a family who had heard the crash and indicated the direction from where the noise had come. Following this information the helicopter flew from kraal to kraal until, eventually, they found the impact point of the Mirage F1. Unfortunately, a rescue was unnecessary as van Coppenhagen had been killed in the crash.

His fighter had descended at a very shallow angle until it struck the treetops. It continued through the trees before impacting with the ground. The shallow angle embedded the wreckage underneath a leafy canopy of trees over a distance of one and a half kilometres, removing the possibility of it ever being found directly from an air search. The subsequent board of inquiry offered a number of possibilities as to the cause of the crash. One was that fuel pipe corrosion could have caused the engine to flame-out. At low level the disaster would have been almost immediate.

*****

On 21 and 22 March, while the search continued, a 600-foot cloud base and 7/8ths cumulo-nimbus cloud over the battle area prevented offensive operations. During the enforced lull, Captain Dawid Kleynhans arrived from AFB Hoedspruit in F1AZ 220 sporting its latest colour scheme, with the upper surfaces green and brown and the underneath and sides dark blue/grey.

On 23 March, after a 06h03 take-off in poor weather conditions, Major Norman Minne led Captain Chris Skinner and Major Frans Coetzee on a *Vergooi* attack at 100 feet. Between the initial point (IP) and the pitch the weather deteriorated so quickly Minne decided to abort the attack. Staying at low level the aircraft turned through 180° and returned to AFB Grootfontein. This was the last sortie flown by the Mirages in the bush war. On 25 March, the squadron was stood down and returned to AFB Hoedspruit.

On the border the stalemate at Cuito Cuanavale continued with opposing

1988: Negotiated settlement

ground forces facing each other in an uneasy peace over the Chambinga high ground.

For combatants on both sides this final conventional battle had been tough. SAAF pilots had contended with the full spectrum of Soviet air-defence missile systems which included SA-2, -3, -6, -7, -8, -9, -11, -13, -14 and -16. They reported sighting 112 missiles fired at them, flew 794 strike sorties and dropped nearly 4,000 bombs. Enemy personnel losses (killed and wounded) were estimated by our intelligence department to have been between 4,000 and 6,000. In a speech to his parliament in Havana, Fidel Castro quoted 9,000 losses.

The Angolan Air Force had flown approximately 1,200 sorties and for over seven months were almost continually overhead the Chambinga battlefield. At the culmination of the battle, despite their overwhelming advantages, our casualty figures were four personnel killed and a further seven wounded from air attack.

Operation *Moduler* had been a complete success. The intensity and ferocity of the combined artillery and aerial bombardment surprised both the 47th and 21st brigades and success was ensured. All facets of the aim had been achieved. However, both *Hooper* and *Packer* were unsuccessful in terms of the set aim. The surprise element had been lost during the seven-month duration of both these operations. The battle dragged on into a costly war of attrition.

The geographical location of the combat theatre during *Hooper* and *Packer* restricted the SAAF's ability to manoeuvre and use flexible tactics. The resultant predictability significantly increased the dangers to our aircrew. The Mirage F1AZ lost to missile fire was almost certainly the result of the enemy being able to predict the approach paths of our low-flying attack aircraft.

Rommel learned to his cost at El Alamein that long logistics lines make it almost impossible to support operations properly with the matériel required for war. Napoleon outside Moscow suffered the same situation which was exacerbated by freezing weather. The SADF had similar difficulties keeping its ground forces resupplied during the long battle outside Cuito Cuanavale. A major air-transport effort was launched using the sand airfield at Mavinga from where supplies were convoyed by vehicle to the battle front. Helicopters were extensively used to transport key personnel and necessary spares to critical parts of the combat zone.

The airstrip at Mavinga was as important to us as it was to the enemy. The single sand runway was vital. Transport aircraft were very vulnerable to roaming MiGs, effectively preventing resupply operations during daylight hours. At nightfall Mavinga came to life with a shuttle service of C-130 and C-160 transports bringing in the vital matériel of war. Only one aircraft at a time could use the strip because it had no taxiways or loading ramps. It was a runway with turning circles at either end for light aircraft, built during the Portuguese colonial period.

The loading parties at Mavinga developed a slick routine which allowed the freighters to be offloaded in the minimum amount of time. Then they had to remove the cargo, ammunition or food from the dumbbell so the next aircraft had space to turn and unload. It was extremely hard, physical work but their efforts were appreciated by the aircrew who felt very vulnerable while the aircraft was parked on the ground. This procedure occurred every night of the seven-month campaign with an average of three to four flights offloading every night. During intense periods six or seven flights were made, with the last flight sneaking home in the rapidly breaking tropical dawn.

Any electricity Mavinga might have had in the past was non-existent by 1988. Normally, when approaching to land a pilot uses homing instruments to guide him to the airfield which he can see visually by reference to lights of nearby towns. In Mavinga's case there was no electricity, town lights or navigational homing beacons. The deployment of a mobile beacon would have eased the problem for our pilots but could also have been used by the Angolans so the idea was dismissed.

To find the airfield at night was a difficult task and the aircrew had to rely on onboard systems to position their aircraft on an extended, long final approach. Only then could they request, over the radio, for runway lights to be illuminated. These lights would be used for the shortest possible time to allow the aircraft to land, after which they would be extinguished immediately. Prowling MiGs were a threat that had always to be considered. When the lights illuminated the pilot would, hopefully, acquire them visually, adjust his flight path and land. On touch-down, the propellers were put into reverse thrust and power applied to slow the heavily laden aircraft. This reverse thrust caused clouds of dust from the dirt runway to billow into the air, which was another reason the strip could not be used during daytime. Dust clouds always attract the attention of roving fighter-bomber pilots.

Unlike Heathrow or O. R. Tambo today, Mavinga runway did not possess the luxury of row upon row of lead-in lights, making line-up in the total blackness of darkest Africa extremely difficult. The lack of a visual horizon often caused an induced oscillation in the yawing plane as the aircraft tended to move from side to side as it approached. The technique used by the crews was for the pilot to fly visually using outside references while the co-pilot closely monitored the flying instruments and pattered the captain on the aircraft attitude. All landings were successful, some being harder than others, but no aircraft was damaged to the extent it could not fly out of Mavinga the same night, despite all the difficulties involved in the operations.

At a later stage of the operation a generator and mobile landing lights were deployed to improve the situation but initially these were not available. A plan was made where beer and cool-drink cans, half-filled with sand and soaked in

1988: Negotiated settlement

paraffin, were placed at equal intervals alongside the runway. UNITA soldiers were used to man these cans and when the pilot requested lights the soldiers would light their cans.

This worked very well—for the first landing. Unfortunately, when pilots applied reverse thrust, not only was dust blown into the air but the cans were dispersed far and wide, much to the disgust of the soldiers. The tins had to be retrieved, refilled and repositioned ready for the next take-off. To alleviate this tedious task the UNITA runway illuminators decided on a modification to the system. They tied the cans to shoulder-height sticks which they could hold onto while the aircraft passed, thus preventing the frantic search after every landing. This evolutionary step seemed, at first, to have solved the problem but no R&D (research and development) had been carried out on the new modification.

With the introduction of the new 'UNITA Flare-path Illuminating System' (UFIS) the pilots started reporting severe cases of spatial disorientation and even vertigo when on their final approach to land. After an in-depth investigation the cause was established. Invariably after the lights were illuminated the pilot found his aircraft to be off centre line. He had to bank the aircraft to fly towards the line and then apply opposite bank to stop the crossing movement. This is straightforward and happens on every approach to land but put yourself in the position of the man holding the stick on the edge of the narrow runway. After setting fire to his can he looks up in the direction of the approaching aircraft. He sees the aircraft's landing light and instead of coming straight down the middle of the flare path it appears to be heading directly towards him. This impression is magnified when one remembers that there is no depth perception on lights at night. Therefore, holding onto his pole he moves away from the runway until he notices the aircraft making the bank correction onto the centre line, then he moves back to the edge of the runway. The soldiers on the near side of the runway were quite happy when, initially, the aircraft seemed to be heading towards the far side. However, when the pilot banked to turn onto the centre line it suddenly appeared as if the aircraft was flying at them. They in turn, holding their poles, also moved away from the runway until they detected the danger had passed and only then would they return to their original position.

The aircrew's spatial disorientation problem was induced by the 'ebb and flow' of the moving flare path when seen against the complete blackness of the surroundings. The poles had to be anchored firmly into the ground. This third modification remained in use until the arrival of the generator and mobile lights brought a vestige of civilization to this dark corner of Africa.

Hooper and *Packer* had been initiated in haste without proper consideration of all the factors, while disregarding the restrictions and warnings of the SAAF inputs. The plan was approved in the heat of battle after the success of *Moduler*, while adrenaline was flowing freely. The seven-month battle saw an escalation of personnel and armaments on both sides. The SADF introduced tanks into the campaign for the first time in the 23-year history of the conflict. G5 and G6 cannons were also used, although they had not yet been fully cleared for service. The SAAF utilized the RPV system while it too was still in its development stage; all hasty actions on our part.

Clausewitz, the renowned warfare analyst, described a logical point at which a successful attack should be called off, which he termed the 'point of culmination'. It is that stage of battle where the effort being put in is not commensurate with the gains being achieved. It is therefore important, in Clausewitz's words, "to detect the culminating point with discriminative judgement". In aerial combat fighter pilots are taught to attack with aggression but to maintain situational awareness, i.e. to know when enough is enough.

Before Operation *Packer* we had reached the logical point of culmination. We were at the end of a long and arduous supply line with our enemy compressed back onto their logistical infrastructure—we were risking much for very little in return. Although we were never in any danger of losing the campaign after the spectacular success on the Lomba River, we had reached a point where any effort expended in terms of men and equipment outweighed any possible benefit we might still accrue.

Gradualism, the evil that besets every war, affected both sides in this protracted conflict. The SADF had begun their operations by supplying advisors to UNITA. Forces were then introduced regularly to supplement requirements. They had been introduced a little at a time, which allowed the enemy to counter each new addition.

In this battle, as in the *Second Congress* débâcle in 1985, the numerically superior might of the communist ground and air forces was repulsed by South African and UNITA ground forces, assisted by the SAAF's conventional air power. It was this situation that eventually instilled reason into the minds of the politicians on both sides and which culminated in the peace settlement under United Nations Charter 435, which was eventually achieved in SWA.

Much has been said by political leaders in the aftermath of the war, with politicians from both sides claiming ultimate victory. Perhaps this sort of posturing is necessary to save face in the political arena. However, from a purely military point of view, it is important to add a list of losses suffered by both sides in the ultimate struggle around Mavinga and Cuito Cuanavale during the seven-month battle of 1987/88 which essentially ended the border war.

SADF losses during Operation *Moduler/Hooper/Packer*
(to 9 April 1989)
- Killed: 40
- Wounded: 114

- Killed in air attacks: 4
- UNITA killed in air attacks: 2
- Armoured fighting vehicles: 3

Enemy losses

(to 14 February 1988)
- Personnel (killed and wounded): 4392
- Logistic vehicles: 377
- Armoured fighting vehicles: 84
- SA-8: 7
- SA-9: 3
- SA-13: 5
- BM-21: 10
- Radars: 5

During the battles around Chambinga the SADF lost three Oliphant tanks, later recovered by the Angolans. The ability to display the tanks to the foreign press was a major propaganda coup. It was on these three tanks that the Angolans and Cubans based their entire claim of victory. A close study of the actual losses suffered by both sides tells the real story.

Towards the end of Operation *Packer* the Cuban 50th Division, from Lubango, launched a strong armoured thrust in the direction of Calueque and Ruacana. Much publicity was given to this and it was taken very seriously by the SADF. Simultaneously, their aircraft began appearing on our radar screens during the day and at night. Some of their flights approached within 30 kilometres of the border north of Kaokoland and one or two actually crossed the Cunene River.

However, I believe these were the results of navigational errors rather than deliberate attempts to provoke us.

Despite the banners and headlines accorded it in Havana, in a purely military sense it was only a feint. They stopped near Oncocua, 50 kilometres from the border, without any persuasion from the SADF. To enter SWA from that direction would have entailed a crossing over the large, fast-flowing Cunene River—a difficult military task. Had they decided to take the risk their forces would have been at the end of a long and tenuous logistic line, much like Rommel, Napoleon and the SADF outside Cuito Cuanavale. Once inside our border the full might of the SADF would have been unleashed upon them. This time the campaign would have been on our home turf with all the attendant advantages. I firmly believe Castro, despite all his proclamations and announcements, would not have risked the substantial Cuban losses that would inevitably have ensued.

As a deterrent to any foolhardy adventure and further displays of bravado from north of the border, it was decided to hold the SAAF's annual *Golden Eagle* training exercise in Owamboland. 1 Squadron deployed to AFB Grootfontein while 2 and 3 Squadrons as the 'enemy' operated from AFB Ondangwa. The resultant battle took place over the pans north of the Etosha National Park, well within range of the enemy's long-range radar. The situation was defused—the border war, for so long part of our lives, appeared to have fizzled out.

The political powers on both sides had finally had enough and, along with international facilitators, the bargaining for an equitable peace began in earnest. The gist of these negotiations was South Africa would withdraw from Angola and SWA and the Cubans would return to Cuba. UNITA and the MPLA would cease hostilities, while a plan was drawn up to allow both factions in the civil war to be accommodated in the government of Angola. All these arrangements would be monitored by UNTAG (United Nations Transitional Agreement Group), the UN force to be deployed to the theatre. The date set for the implementation of the 'peace process' was 1 April 1989.

Readers may wonder why, if the war had ceased, I have continued with this account. Unlike a novel where the author can reach a happy-ever-after ending, this was not to be the case in South West Africa. We didn't know there was to be a twist in the tail.

The lull after the storm

Between April and September the SAAF ran another unsuccessful operation. It was decided to try and ambush Angolan aircraft to discourage their presence over our own troops outside Cuito Cuanavale. Operation *Labotomy* used PR missions as lures to attract enemy fighters. The following units were involved:

- 70 Mobile Radar Unit (MRU) controllers to monitor our aircraft

- PR aircraft from 2 and 24 Squadrons as bait
- Impala aircraft for Telstar radio communication links
- Mirage fighters from 2 and 3 Squadrons
- Pumas on SAR standby

Intelligence reports indicated large-scale reinforcements being moved into southern Angola. To monitor this activity and update our photographic coverage two Canberras were tasked on a PR mission. At 10h20 on 2 May, the Canberra formation took off from AFB Waterkloof. They crossed the cut-line at Okalongo flying at FL430, photographed Xangongo and Humbe then covered the Mongua–Ongiva–Oshikango road as they left the area, bringing back excellent photography. This mission did not lure the Angolan MiGs away from their bases.

In order to discourage and prevent the enemy from attempting another advance towards Mavinga from Cuito Cuanavale the SADF initiated Operation *Displace*. The east bank of the Cuito River was prepared as 'an obstacle' to movement by sowing a long minefield with anti-personnel and vehicle mines, orientated north to south. The operation was obviously successful because no attempt was made to breach the minefield, allowing the South African forces to withdraw from Angola by 27 August.

The SAAF ran Operation *Assassin* from 2 June to the end of the year. This was a programme of EW elint (electronic intelligence) flights covering the southern Angolan coast and the railway line between Namibe and Lubango, paying particular attention to the area between Menonque and Cuito Cuanavale. The aircraft utilized were B-707s from 60 Squadron and DC-4 Spooks from 44 Squadron. This was a most successful programme as it pinpointed a new fixed SA-2 site at Xangongo and the presence of SA-6 mobile units in Techipa.

The SAAF EW programme included the deployment of ground-based Sigint (signals intelligence) teams. In June 1988, one of these teams was encamped on a mountaintop in Kaokoland monitoring the progress of the Angolans. The team, which included Portuguese and Spanish interpreters, was protected by a group of 51 Battalion soldiers from Ruacana. This team confirmed the existence of the jet airfield at Cahama, when they listened to professionally sounding Cuban pilots calling for landing instructions there.

Operation *Assassin* was planned in support of *Hilti*, its aim to expand the UNITA liberated area and retake the old 'area of dispute' east of the Cunene River, by 31 December 1988. Preparations were made for improving the necessary infrastructure within Owamboland but the operation was never initiated because the political climate had begun to change. For security reasons, in August, the operation's name was changed to *Prone*. This would have been a large operation, including the sub-operations *Excite, Faction, Florentine* and the autonomous SAAF

Operation *Placable*. The forces earmarked for the operation were:

- South West African Territorial Force
- 81 Brigade
- 71 Brigade
- 61 Mechanized Battalion
- 32 Battalion
- 101 Battalion
- 44 Parachute Brigade
- South African Air Force

Before the final SADF withdrawal from Angola a contingency plan was made to supply UNITA with equipment. Between 21 and 30 August, 28 Squadron flew in 1,100 tons of supplies to Mavinga and Licua. The total flying time of these night flights was 62 hours for the C-130s and 66 hours for the C-160s.

*****

During 1988, modifications so desperately needed during the bush war finally reached the F1 fleet. All the aircraft were fitted with compact radar warning receivers (CRWSs) and chaff and flare dispensers, which would have relieved the pilot load during the battles over the Lomba River and Cuito Cuanavale. Matra 550 missiles, with fuses modified to prevent ineffective detonations in exhaust plumes, became available from Kentron.

Between 8 and 14 November, Mirage AZs were used in a series of weapons trials. Potentially dangerous profiles were flown from which Condib bombs were dropped. (The Condib, or 'concrete dipper', air-launched runway-cratering bomb was developed by the Israelis.) When the bomb is released from level flight, 300 feet above a runway, a rocket motor ignites, driving it through the hardened runway surface. A delayed-action fuse detonates the bomb after it has buried itself, causing an enormous crater that renders the runway unusable. The downside of the weapon is the delivery profile. No one in his right senses would, by choice, fly straight and level above the enemy's runway, airfields usually being the most heavily defended installations. During the Gulf War, Royal Air Force Tornado bombers were lost using similar tactics.

Cluster bombs were delivered from both *Vergooi* and *Gatup* profiles. As the name suggests, the bomb consists of numerous bomblets which are strewn along the flight path of the mother bomb. These cause widespread damage to personnel and lightly armoured vehicles.

1988: Negotiated settlement

Aiming

I feel it is an appropriate time to explain a little about delivery techniques and the problems associated with aiming. The term 'ground-attack' refers to weapons delivered by air against surface targets. Precision bombing using guided missiles, or guided bombs, is by far the most cost-effective means of delivery because success is almost guaranteed.

The SAAF used AS-30 guided missiles successfully during Operation *Protea* and with extreme accuracy during the battle at Cangamba. We also used the H2 TV-guided bomb with mixed success against the bridge over the Cuito River. This system was still in the proving state of development and had not been cleared for squadron service when we used it in battle.

A Buccaneer with an H2 bomb on the inner pylon and an EW pod on the outer pylon under the port wing. The H2 communications pod is under the starboard wing.

When delivering 'dumb' weapons (unguided bombs or rockets) the aircraft has to overfly the target while the crew offset the sight to allow for the effect of the forecast wind. If the forecast is wrong the weapons will miss the target. This was the problem when medium-level (15,000 feet) bombing was attempted. The time of flight for the dropping bombs was comparatively long and any unexpected wind would drift the weapons away from the target. The accuracy of these bombs was insufficient to guarantee the desired results.

Dumb weapons were more accurately delivered from a traditional dive-bombing profile. Range to target at the pre-determined release altitude is all important because weapons released too high fall short of the target and those released too low fall over it. Similarly, if the dive angle is too shallow the weapons fall short of the target; too steep and they fall over it. Only the Mirage F1AZ had

451

When fired in salvo all the rockets leave the aircraft travelling in the same direction but at millisecond intervals. Each pod carries 18 rockets, so four full pods deliver 72 rockets into an area of 60 x 60 metres, with devastating effect.

laser-ranging to assist the pilot with an accurate release point.

During an operational attack, using 68mm rockets, full pods are fired in salvo. They leave each pod at millisecond intervals to avoid possible collision. Each rocket is affected by the turbulent slipstream from the rockets ahead, giving a random dispersal as they hit the surface. This actually compensates for possible small aiming errors as the pods tend to saturate the target area. Although rockets are very accurate the downside of this method of attack is that the aircraft has to encroach well into the defensive range of all of the enemy systems, including small arms.

The SAAF made rockets obsolete when the 120kg pre-fragmented bomb was produced in 1985. A standard Mk 81 250lb bomb was used as the model. By using the same shape and weight of bomb the SAAF was able to bring the pre-fragmented version into service without having to repeat the stringent series of flutter tests required to prove new underwing stores. The bomb casing was thinner than the standard bomb, thus allowing 17,000 small ball-bearings to be encased around the explosive. Using an air-bursting fuse the bomb detonated about six metres above a surface, causing the full weight of the explosion to be focused down and outwards. The ball-bearings would spread in a pattern about 40 metres along the track and 35 metres to either side of the point of explosion. As an anti-personnel weapon it was superb as any unsheltered body within range would receive at least four to five hits. It was reclassified as the 120kg pre-fragmented bomb.

The success of this bomb led to the development of a 250kg pre-frag bomb. This bomb held fewer but larger and heavier ball-bearings. The kinetic energy of these larger fragments was sufficient to puncture lightly armoured vehicles and

1988: Negotiated settlement

This crater was created by the explosion of a 250kg general purpose bomb. The sandy soil is similar to that found in Owamboland and Angola and demonstrates the reason for the development of our pre-fragmented bombs. In this case, unless the bomb actually hit the target very little damage would be experienced. In the upper portion of the photograph craters caused by the next two bombs in a stick can be seen.

caused havoc amongst the B-echelon support vehicles.

However, to achieve good results the pilots had to see the targets they were aiming at and this was a problem. Enemy brigades moving through thick bush are virtually invisible to the naked eye and we could not hit what we could not see.

After long discussions with soldiers and reconnaissance commandos a solution was found. These brave men told us they were prepared to recce enemy positions and send back co-ordinates of where these brigades were dispersed. When on the march each Angolan brigade would be spread over an area of two square kilometres or more. At this stage, it was almost impossible for our recce troops to pinpoint the moving brigades. However, when the enemy was hunkered down for the night our soldiers were prepared to sneak in to determine their position.

This information was passed by radio to the SAAF as soon as it was available and, provided the area was within two square kilometres, an air attack was planned using the toss-bomb or *Vergooi* delivery mode.

Ironically, this method of bomb delivery was inherently the most inaccurate of all other systems. It was also the one most used during the final seven months of conventional battles of operations *Moduler, Hooper and Packer*.

Originally, the toss-bomb profile was developed for use in the Cold War against heavily defended Soviet targets. It was planned for allied aircraft, armed with a single tactical nuclear weapon, to penetrate Soviet airspace at very low level to avoid radar cover. Using the techniques previously mentioned they would pull-up into a low-altitude bombing system (LABS) manoeuvre and toss the bomb about five nautical miles towards the target. With a nuclear explosion aiming errors of up to 300 metres were acceptable.

The SAAF used this technique for a number of reasons. The first was to ensure the greatest safety for the delivery aircraft and its crew. Isolation and a full arms embargo prevented us from replacing any combat losses. We had no alternative but to protect our aircraft. Secondly, even if we had overflown the target, through the thick bush we probably would not have seen anything to aim at. The third reason was the proven ability of our ground forces to determine a brigade's presence within acceptable limits.

When ground intelligence was positive attacks were launched. The aircraft would fly in battle formation and at PUP be spaced laterally about 200 metres apart. The bombs would fly off in sticks of eight towards the target causing four swathes of damage, each 140 metres wide by about 400 metres long, within the designated target area. Any person, weapon system, logistic vehicle or lightly armoured fighting vehicle within this blast area was destroyed or damaged. On occasions we missed badly, but when we hit we caused mayhem. This compromise between inherent inaccuracy and invisibility of the target was almost perfect for the situation. Enemy losses in 1987/88 bear testimony to the effectiveness of these air strikes.

Electronic warfare

One of the major advantages the Buccaneer possessed over the Mirage was having a two-man crew. The navigator doubled as the weapon system operator, bombardier, rearward lookout specialist, radio operator, ECM monitor and chief cook and bottle-washer, which allowed the pilots to concentrate solely on flying the aircraft—which they did well. On numerous occasions I tasked 24 Squadron to perform some of our more difficult missions and they never disappointed me. My boast was that you could set your watch by their strike times.

In the ECM role the Buccaneer navigators used considerable initiative extracting as much intelligence as possible from each operational mission. One of the Buccaneers was fitted with a more up-to-date prototype RWR which included a recording facility. Every time a warning appeared on the aircraft's RWR the signal would be automatically recorded. After landing the navigators would play-back these recordings and at each event-marker plot their aircraft's heading, the type of warning, bearing, frequency, pulse repetition interval (PRI) and signal power. By converting all this information to navigation charts they were able to plot the position of any enemy radar detected during the flight.

By cross-referencing this information between all the aircraft in the formation fairly accurate intelligence was developed regarding the position of Angolan radars, radar-guided AAA systems and numerous SAM sites.

Often during briefings, intelligence officers would warn the aircrew of enemy radar and weapons en route and in the target area. Sometimes these positions differed from those plotted by the navigators. The navigators decided to combine the Buccaneer's information with that derived from the RWRs aboard the Mirage F1AZs. These inputs coincided remarkably and accurate positions were plotted of the SAM sites hidden in the bush.

On one occasion at a briefing for a combined strike on an Angolan brigade, both Buccaneer and Mirage crews were warned of a deadly SAM-8 site close to the target. The position plotted at the intelligence briefing differed by about 500 metres from the position plotted using the combined ECM recordings. At a discreet meeting between Paulus Truter and Riem Mouton (1 and 24 Squadron EW specialists respectively), one of the four Mirage pilots was asked to change his aiming point onto the position of the SAM-8 (taken from the recorded plots) for his stick of eight bombs, as the Mirages were to be first onto the target.

With the crews listening intently to their RWRs they all picked up the audio warning from the active SAM-8 site as they approached the target. The Mirage formation delivered three sticks of bombs onto the briefed target while one stick landed 500 metres away. On detonation of these bombs the deadly SAM-8 system suddenly went off the air making the strike safer for all the attacking crews and proving the accuracy of the pilots.

In his account of the introduction of 'Puff the Magic Dragon' to operational service, Colonel Thinus du Toit asked me to include a statement, which he feels very strongly about. He said, "We in the SAAF did not always have the latest and best equipment available but we did what we had to do with what we had."

*****

By November, the border war had apparently ended. However, the peace was fragile and forces had to be kept at readiness. The year ended with both 1 and 3 Squadrons working hard to master the intricacies of third-generation ACM. The all-aspect capability of the new air-to-air missile called for immense co-ordination and practice. Air fighting became a succession of into afterburner, out of afterburner, firing self-defence flares, rolling the aircraft and pulling G while maintaining a constant lookout and commentary between aircraft. It was a handful!

Chapter 15

1989: Breach of promise

And that should have been that. The SADF, after a collective sigh of relief and suitable celebrations, began on a new and equally daunting task of returning 23 years of logistics supplies to South Africa. By the end of March 1989, 257 freight trains had been loaded with arms, ammunition, armoured and logistic vehicles and despatched back to receiving depots in South Africa. With the withdrawal of front-line personnel the SADF's presence in South West Africa only consisted of the logistic teams responsible for the final handing-over of bases and facilities to the SWATF.

Although the SADF had adopted a more defensive posture they still maintained an eye on developments north of our borders. The SAAF initiated Operation *Wedge*, to run continuously through 1989. Using B-707 and DC-4 EW aircraft the programme was designed to monitor all transmissions in the electromagnetic spectrum (EMS) that could affect South Africa. The flights extended from Kosi Bay on the east coast, across our northern borders to the southern Angolan coast. During this withdrawal phase particular emphasis was placed on known Cuban radar systems.

Between 9 February and 16 March, SAAF Airfield Maintenance Units upgraded UNITA's runways at Jamba and Liuana in what was probably our last direct support to them. As a tribute to SAAF transport crews I am including a summary of the flights undertaken in support of UNITA. Most of these flights were to DZs in the 3rd and 4th Military Regions of Angola, north of the Benguela railway line:

Year	Missions	Hours
1978	2	10.45
1979	25	157.55
1980	20	130.10
1981	66	341.55
1982	71	538.30
1983	84	724.45
1984	69	595.25
1985	43	439.25
1986	8	81.05
1987	13	129.35
1988	20	193.10
Total	**421**	**3,342.40**

These 'long-drop' flights had required effort from so many people, thus:

- Stores and equipment securely packaged for air-dropping
- Pallets attached to parachutes
- Parachutes carefully packed to ensure proper opening
- Aircraft loaded
- Load masters secure loads to the floors of transport aircraft for the flight and then ensure a clean drop once DZ sighted
- Every flight undertaken at night
- Navigational aids in Africa are still not readily available even today. In those days there were no electronic aids, so aircrews had to rely on first-class navigation over very hostile territory under extreme pressure
- Aircraft maintenance units ensure aircraft fully serviceable and in a high state of preparedness

Not one aircraft was lost despite the vagaries of the weather, the hostile intent of the enemy or bad airmanship on the part of the flying crews. These people were magnificent.

Resolution 435 and UNTAG

In March, UNTAG finally began arriving in dribs and drabs to become the interim authority, commencing 1 April. Although they were willing and certainly had excellent equipment, they were inexperienced, un-acclimatized and completely out of their depth. SWAPO and the SADF had just been involved in a long bush war; the UNTAG forces were green by comparison. The SADF went out of its way to accommodate and assist the newcomers and to demonstrate how they were abiding by every stipulation laid out in UN Resolution 435.

Who said size doesn't count? UNTAG arrived and the difference between a global and a regional power was made very obvious.

April Fools' Day

It was our own fault! After 23 long years of border war against communist-trained and brainwashed opposition, we should have seen it coming. As soon as peace had been negotiated we reverted in our thought patterns to the reasoning and logic of the western world. Peace had been agreed upon, signed by all parties and it was all over bar the shouting. We even missed the biggest hint—1 April, April Fools' Day, had been chosen as the first official day of peace.

True to form, SWAPO, the communist 'liberation' movement, launched the largest incursion of armed fighters into South West Africa of the entire war. They knew the SADF, in accordance with UN 435 resolution, had all but left the territory. SWAPO had undertaken to remain inside Angola at least 200 kilometres from the border. To their everlasting shame they blatantly violated every aspect of the agreement. Subsequently, they claimed they were just returning peacefully to the land of their birth. This they could have done under the terms of the settlement. In truth, they were heavily armed and each of their fighters had orders to pin the following notice onto the body of any member of the SWATF whom they killed:

>>
NAMIBIAN CITIZENS IN SWATF
You fell prey to PLAN Combatants. Why?

Because
- You are traitors, betraying your own land and people
- You agreed to fight us on behalf of the racist white foreign colonialists from South Africa and delay freedom and independence of our people
- You are killing our people, burning their houses, destroying their crops and stealing their cattle
- You are raping our mothers, sisters and women of old age
- As a rule, rest assured, you shall have to pay the price for your evil deeds

Remember
- To be a traitor, as you are, you are assured of a foreshadowed future. There is no hope for a happy life. As you know, one day, the people will decide to hang or put you before a firing squad. So much for a traitor … <<

On 31 March, SWA police patrols started picking up the spoor of large numbers of insurgents crossing the cut-line from north to south into South West Africa. These experienced police trackers could tell the insurgents were heavily laden. As soon as these indications were reported the SWA police and the few remaining representatives of the SADF entered into planning sessions in an attempt to muster a viable defence strategy.

Under the terms of UN 435 all SADF forces remaining in South West Africa were restricted to their bases. By early morning on 1 April, it was clear SWAPO had violated every clause of the settlement and had launched the largest incursion of the entire war. Around 1,500 heavily armed SWAPO terrorists had crossed the border. Apart from the first small base SWAPO had established at Ongulumbashe at the very start of their insurgency campaign in 1965, they were never able to dominate any territory within South West Africa. In fact, during the last few years of the war none of their insurgents could stay inside South West Africa for more than three days; any longer, and they risked being hunted down and killed by the security forces. Interestingly, it was information given by the local population to Koevoet and the Romeo Mike teams of 101 Battalion which led to the rapid demise of any terrorist outstaying his welcome.

The plan formulated to counter the insurgency was called Operation *Merlyn*. The aim was 'to stop the SWAPO's infiltration into SWA at the implementation of Resolution 435 on 1 April 1989'.

On 27 March, Captain Mario Vergottini arrived at AFB Ondangwa for his first bush tour as an Alouette pilot. He had completed numerous stints in the operational area flying Kudu and Bosbok light aircraft over the previous five years, knew Ondangwa and the area very well but was 'the new boy on the block' as far as gunship flying was concerned. He had flown from both AFB Mpacha and AFB Rundu but Ondangwa was traditionally the place where it all happened. However, UN 435 was so far advanced by this stage that his chance of gaining any real combat experience appeared to be virtually zero.

Ondangwa and the border bases were reduced to skeleton staffs and all offensive aircraft and weapons shipped back to South Africa in preparation for handing over the reins to UNTAG. Vergottini replaced Captain Lionel Sawyer, who had spent his tour not doing much more than providing top cover to incoming transport aircraft. Between 28 and 31 March Vergottini flew seven and a half hours, all of it as top cover. Sawyer's forecast looked to be accurate. On his last flight on 31 March Vergottini and his flight engineer, Sergeant Marne de Rouxbaix, decided to fire a few rounds from the Alouette's 20mm cannon because they knew as from the next morning the bush war would be officially over. They wanted to make the claim of firing the final shots of the war, even though they were not fired in anger.

The night of 31 March was a very sombre and morbid affair for the helicopter aircrew. The main topic of conversation revolved around the bush war which had become a way of life for an entire generation of South Africans. There was a great deal of reminiscing about 'absent friends' and wondering whether all the sacrifices had been worth it. Vergottini's elder brother had been killed in a

Mario Vergottini and Marne de Rouxbaix lifting off from AFB Ondangwa during the April Fools' Day incident.

1989: Beach of promise

Harvard accident just 18 months earlier and Vergottini was still affected by his loss. In the end, not really having all the answers they did what helicopter pilots had been doing for decades; they solved the problems of the world with the aid of a healthy consumption of alcohol.

It was a rather sad bunch of helicopter aviators who finally staggered off to bed in the knowledge that from the next morning UNTAG would be taking over and the SAAF would begin disarming the gunships.

At about 07h15 on 1 April, the landline telephone in Vergottini's room shrieked and the ops clerk on the other end informed Vergottini he had received orders from Oshakati to scramble two Alouette gunships to Ruacana. "Sure," Vergottini replied, "and a happy April Fools' Day to you too." Replacing the phone he climbed back into bed in the hope of sleeping off a massive hangover. During the next 15 minutes the ops clerk rang Vergottini a further three times, each time receiving the same reply. On the last occasion Vergottini even threatened him with physical violence if he persisted with this April Fools' nonsense. The calls stopped and Vergottini settled down to sleep.

It was not long before Major Mac McCarthy walked in and suggested Vergottini get dressed and join him in the briefing room. Vergottini chuckled and turned over saying, "Bloody good joke, major!" Using all his persuasive powers, which included a direct order, McCarthy finally got Vergottini out of bed and into the shower. Shortly thereafter, he was in his flying suit and in the briefing room. The crews were told that there were problems in the Ruacana area and Alouettes were urgently required to give assistance to the SWA police (SWAPOL).

Vergottini listened with half an ear as he waited for the point when someone would say "April Fool" and they would all laugh and return to bed. Nothing like this happened so they signed the authorization book and went out to the DD700 hut where they were assigned their aircraft. Although halfway through the pre-flight inspection Vergottini was still convinced it was all a joke engineered by Commandant John Church. The commandant was probably rolling with laughter somewhere on a floor in Oshakati.

While completing his pre-flight he saw the Bosbok pilot climb into his aircraft and start up. Thinking he too was being made fun of Vergottini watched the Bosbok taxi out to the end of the runway, expecting to see it turn around and return to the hardstanding. Finally, when he saw the Bosbok lift into the air he began to think perhaps it was not a joke after all. McCarthy and Vergottini took off at 10h15 and headed to Ruacana, not knowing what to expect. According to UN 435 it was the beginning of peace in South West Africa and UNTAG were supposed to be in control.

About an hour later the two Alouettes landed at Ruacana and the crews were briefed by Captain Keith Fryer regarding the existing situation on the ground. Fryer and Vergottini had flown together in 41 Squadron in 1986 and were good friends. Fryer was the MAOT at Ruacana and the sitrep (situation report) from him outlined what had transpired during the morning. SWAPOL patrols had encountered huge groups of heavily armed SWAPO insurgents and fighting had ensued. Captain Alan Slade, flying a trooper version of the Alouette had gone to their assistance. He was now on the ground at a HAG not far from where Fryer had requested McCarthy and Vergottini go. Fryer informed them to look out for the insurgents but they were not allowed to engage them, the main reason being Margaret Thatcher and a number of high-ranking politicians were all in Windhoek for the peace talks and no one wanted to see UN Resolution 435 derailed.

At 11h30, McCarthy and Vergottini were airborne and headed out towards the mountains west of Ruacana. It is interesting to note that 23 years earlier the border war had started not far from Ruacana. Before taking off the pilots had discussed ways to ensure they did not mistake SWAPOL for SWAPO terrorists. Ten minutes after take-off they reached the area where the terrorists had been reported, and began orbiting. A few minutes later they sighted a group of 40–50 insurgents moving up the side of a riverbed into the mountains. The SWAPOL representative, a passenger in the Bosbok circling 500 feet above them, got very excited and asked McCarthy and Vergottini to engage immediately. Major

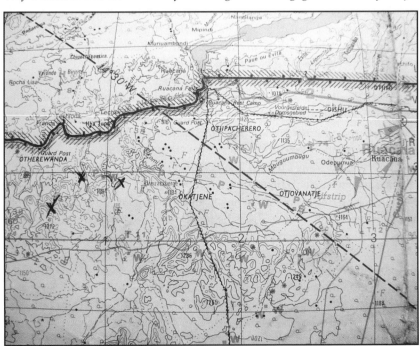

Mario Vergottini's map showing the position of the first three contacts. Despite the element of complete surprise SWAPO groups never managed to get any distance from the border before they were found and attacked.

1989: Beach of promise

McCarthy radioed back to Fryer, reported what they were seeing and asked if the order to 'not engage' was still valid. Fryer replied in the affirmative as the aircraft remained in orbit and in sight of the slow-moving terrorists.

For the next hour and a quarter McCarthy had to deal with a very frustrated SWAPOL representative who had received clearance from the highest level in his organization to open fire. Unfortunately, the SAAF chain of command had said an emphatic no. A great deal of cursing took place in the cockpit because the crews knew the insurgents had the potential to inflict real damage if they ambushed our forces. Repeated requests to engage were turned down, although Fryer did radio to say they could return fire if fired at. At one point during the orbiting, out of frustration, Vergottini called McCarthy and said he was being fired at. McCarthy disagreed and as mission leader told Vergottini to behave. Nothing came of it except for years afterwards Vergottini was continually 'accused' of trying to start 'Revolution 435'.

By this stage both helicopters were running short of fuel and Vergottini was instructed to refuel at the HAG while McCarthy remained on station. While refuelling Vergottini spoke to Slade who told him SWAPOL were extremely agitated because the SAAF were doing nothing to help. A number of their policemen had already been killed or wounded; they were angry and wanted to take the fight to SWAPO. The SAAF aircrew sympathized but their hands were tied. This emotional frustration was vividly displayed to Vergottini as he strapped in prior to returning to relieve McCarthy. A SWAPOL policeman, with tears streaming down his cheeks, knelt at the open door of the helicopter and pleaded for Vergottini's active assistance. Some of his friends had just been killed and he begged Vergottini to ensure that no others would be lost. For 23 years the combination of SAAF gunships and Koevoet policemen had been the most successful anti-terrorist system in South Africa's armoury. It went totally against the grain to have to refrain from fighting.

Just as Vergottini started his engine Slade ran over to announce that there were casevacs needing urgent pick-up. Slade said he would lead in his trooper and land to pick up the wounded men while Vergottini gave top cover overhead. At the position given by SWAPOL Slade and his flight engineer, Theo Fredrikson, landed their helicopter and loaded the wounded policemen. Their helicopter came under intense enemy fire as the wounded were lifted out. Later that day the Alouette returned to Ondangwa because of the severe damage it had sustained from the small-arms fire. That night Fredrikson worked until dawn to repair the helicopter.

After Slade's departure, Vergottini headed back towards the area where he had last seen the terrorists. He had not flown very far when suddenly he heard explosions behind his helicopter. He looked out to the right and saw SWAPOL vehicles coming down the dry riverbed. He banked left and saw a large SWAPO group right below him. It appeared as if the terrorists had seen the SWAPOL vehicles heading in their direction and thought the helicopter was directing the policemen so they'd decided to eliminate the threat posed by the helicopter. A number of RPGs were fired at Vergottini's Alouette as well as small-arms fire. Vergottini immediately called Fryer on the radio, informed him that the helicopter was drawing fire and that they were engaging the enemy.

By this time SWAPOL were fairly close to the enemy so de Rouxbaix had to be careful when firing the 20mm cannon. The aircrew could see sparks as the 20mm shells struck the rocks and were sure there was a lot of shrapnel and pieces

Left: The 20mm cannon mounted in an Alouette III transformed the tiny helicopter into the most feared anti-terrorist weapon.
Right: The seating arrangement in the gunship shows the pilot on the left and the flight engineer-gunner on the right.

of rock flying around close to the ground.

After the initial burst from the aircraft's 20mm cannon they saw a number of the terrorists fall. However, their immediate attention was focused on the group who were firing RPGs at the helicopter, particularly one terrorist who seemed determined to knock their helicopter out of the sky. Vergottini told de Rouxbaix to focus on eliminating this imminent threat, which he did with a well-placed burst of fire. As the man tumbled backwards his last action must have been to pull the trigger, firing the rocket into the mountainside about 100 metres from him. The impact of the explosion was like a scene from a Hollywood action movie.

By now there was absolute chaos beneath the circling helicopter. The insurgent group had broken into smaller units of five to eight terrorists and each one had to be identified and engaged. After 15 minutes of frenetic combat the 20mm cannon ran out of ammunition. Vergottini called McCarthy on the radio and told him to return to the area pronto. In fact, McCarthy was already airborne so the two helicopters were able to hand over on station. As Vergottini left RPGs were still exploding in the air. He also passed Alan Slade in the trooper Alouette rushing in to support McCarthy.

Vergottini landed back at Ruacana, refuelled, re-armed and was airborne again just after 14h00, heading back to the contact area. By this time the fighting had subsided somewhat, although RPGs were still being fired at the helicopters. The task had become one of seek and destroy as the terrorist group had 'bombshelled' and run off in different directions. During the next hour they had three or four successful contacts as they flushed out hiding groups before having to return to Ruacana again.

At 15h45, McCarthy and Vergottini were once again airborne, this time carrying SWAPOL policemen as passengers. They assisted in a sweep operation being run by the ground forces which successfully routed the three remaining SWAPO groups. By this stage the flight engineers were being very careful not to waste ammunition as there was a critical shortage of live rounds. In fact, during these last sorties of the day, the helicopters were firing solid-shot practice rounds and they only had 40 rounds of these. This shortage had resulted from our strict compliance with the terms of UN 435 as the SADF had sent most weapons, aircraft, vehicles and ammunition back to South Africa. I believe it was this knowledge that persuaded Sam Nujoma to attempt to take advantage of the situation.

After refuelling yet again, Vergottini and de Rouxbaix were tasked to carry out a casevac which went without a hitch. That evening it was a tired and hungry bunch of aviators who settled down to get some much-needed rest. However, none of them could really relax because they knew there were more than a thousand heavily armed terrorists in the area with a greater firepower than was now available at Ruacana, to defend themselves.

The next morning, unlike April Fools' morning, the team was up at 06h00 and airborne by 08h00 to give top cover to Pumas arriving from AFB Ondangwa. These large helicopters were tasked for the grisly job of collecting the bodies and equipment from the scene of the previous day's battle. The SADF wanted to present evidence of the breaking of UN 435 to the world media.

At 09h45 the Alouettes were again in the air, this time taking out food and water supplies to the hard-pressed SWAPOL forces on the ground. Once again, back at Ruacana, the crews were delighted to discover they could refill their ammunition trays with live explosive rounds. Captain Chris de Jager had taken an enormous risk by overloading his Kudu aircraft and flying in the much-needed ammunition. This turned out to be just in the nick of time as the helicopters' next call-out turned into a no-holds-barred engagement.

The helicopter crews had just completed preparing their helicopters when the order came to fly to the eastern side of Ruacana, in the area of the Concor Dam. A large group of about 150 terrorists was being followed by SWAPOL who urgently required top cover. Shortly after midday McCarthy and Vergottini flew to the co-ordinates given. Accompanying Major McCarthy was an overweight SWAPOL policeman whose weight seriously affected the speed of McCarthy's Alouette. Vergottini found staying in formation to be almost impossible as McCarthy's aircraft staggered along. As they neared the given co-ordinates SWAPO must have plainly heard the *tak-a-tak* (the name SWAPO called the Alouettes) as they laboured through the air and started firing early in an attempt to scare them off. Black explosions from detonating RPGs filled the air, resembling the flak shown in World War II movies.

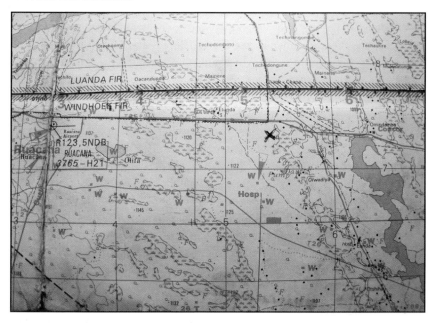

Coincidentally, this contact, marked by the X, one of the last fire fights of the war, occurred only a few kilometres north of the first SWAPO clash of 1966 at Ongulumbashe.

A greater problem than the flak was the two helicopters staggering along at 800 feet AGL at just over 50 knots. McCarthy then made a wise decision and radioed that he was going to drop off his passenger. As he turned off course Vergottini heard the SWAPOL forces on the ground radio say in alarm, "*Die helicopters draai weg!*" (the helicopters are turning away). Vergottini called them and explained that the lead ship was landing but he was continuing on towards them.

Vergottini watched as McCarthy turned and descended to the left. As he looked forward again he saw a smoke trail which had passed between the two helicopters. Before he could say anything to de Rouxbaix a second smoke trail streaked past, this time much closer to the helicopter. Vergottini followed the smoke trail back down to its source and saw a group of terrorists in a *shona* who were responsible for the second smoke trail. He tried to turn the nose of his helicopter by pushing on the right-hand anti-torque pedal to give de Rouxbaix the opportunity of a shot. He managed a few shots during this violent manoeuvre but they landed well wide of the group.

The next minute Vergottini saw the launch of what he knew was a SAM-7 missile. The smoke trail stayed low-level, moving very quickly, then suddenly pitched heavenwards and headed straight towards them. He remembers being mesmerized by the sight. It reminded him of something bubbling profusely with an eye at the centre of the bubbles—something akin to dry ice being dropped into water. The missile was approaching the Alouette at an increasing rate and Vergottini realized it was going to hit the helicopter dead centre. He banked hard right and felt the shockwave as it passed over them. As he rolled out he shouted to de Rouxbaix to reply with all the cannon fire he could. Vergottini reduced speed and hoofed in rudder, yawing the helicopter so de Rouxbaix could get a bead on the terrorists. He opened fire and they started to run. A few men fell but about five or six continued. Then they made the mistake of trying to hide behind a tree; after one orbit of the tree de Rouxbaix had neutralized the threat. During this short episode RPGs were still exploding around the helicopter but the crew's focus remained on the offending group.

By this time McCarthy had entered the fray, although he was east of Vergottini's helicopter. The two joined forces and engaged the fleeing groups of terrorists. The combat zone covered a very large area and was strewn with burning vehicles and bush fires running wild. Although de Rouxbaix was out of ammunition, Vergottini stayed in the fight to support McCarthy. McCarthy and his gunner, Flight Sergeant Steyn, were doing a fine job with some very accurate shooting.

Then SWAPOL radioed for casualty evacuation. McCarthy told them to throw a smoke flare to mark their position and with that four smoke clouds suddenly appeared. While McCarthy provided top cover Vergottini headed for the nearest smoke and found a suitable landing spot within 50 metres of it. Because no one met them on landing Vergottini instructed de Rouxbaix to jump out with his R5 rifle, find the SWAPOL casevacs and bring them to the helicopter.

As de Rouxbaix disappeared into the bush Vergottini realized he was sitting alone and defenceless in a helicopter in the middle of a huge fire fight. The few minutes de Rouxbaix was away seemed like an eternity. It gave Vergottini time to reflect this was not the best way of celebrating his youngest son's birthday. Just then de Rouxbaix reappeared. He said he had found numerous dead bodies but no casualty and so they lifted back into the air and made for the HAG. Just then a Puma arrived bringing in much-needed ammunition and to assist with casevacs. While refuelling and helping de Rouxbaix load the ammunition belts Vergottini noticed an uncharacteristic shaking of his hands—the near miss with the missile must have been closer than he had at first thought.

The rest of the day passed in a blur of refuelling, re-arming and fighting. It had been another day of seven hours' intense flying followed by another night of one-eye-open sleep. By 07h00 the next morning the rather dirty, smelly bunch of aviators were once again airborne on flights in the Ruacana area. It had been two days without shaving or changing clothes and they were looking and feeling very ragged. Before the next call-out they heard the sound of helicopters approaching. Four gunships landed at the base and out climbed Kobus Swart, Pierre Steyn, Chris Opperman and Jamie Burger. They informed McCarthy and Vergottini they were being relieved and could return to AFB Ondangwa.

In all, nine days of intense fighting and bloodshed occurred. Seven hundred and fifty SWAPO insurgents, almost half of the original incursion force, were killed or wounded while we had 22 security force members killed. In addition, 21 Caspir and Ratel fighting vehicles were hit by SWAPO RPG-7s. The brunt of the fighting was borne by members of the Police Koevoet units who once again proved outstanding in this decisive conflict. Owambo members of 101 Battalion were reinstated to enable them to join in the fighting. Alouette helicopter gunships were rushed back to the border inside the cavernous holds of C-130 and C-160 aircraft. The aircrews of these machines won eight Honoris Crux medals for valour during the battles of that tumultuous time. Captain Alan Slade and Sergeant Theodore Fredrikson were each awarded the Honoris Crux Silver; Major Alan McCarthy, captains Mario Vergottini and Etienne Eksteen, Flight Sergeant Esias Engelbertus, and sergeants de Rouxbaix and Gerhard Fourie the Honoris Crux. These men had flown an average of seven hours a day, the bulk of which was in action against SWAPO.

I had a very personal interest in the proceedings. My son had been newly commissioned as a second lieutenant on 30 March 1989, before proceeding directly to the border as a new SAAF intelligence officer. Within a day or two, because of the acute shortage of personnel he was deployed to Eenhana as the air force representative in the very front line. He gave an intelligence briefing to a Koevoet team at 07h00, before they departed the base on the spoor of SWAPO. By 10h00, he had answered a call for volunteers to donate blood for casualties just brought in to the base. He had the chilling experience of having his blood being connected in a direct feed to a young policeman he had briefed a few hours earlier. This young man had gone into action in his Caspir manning the mounted machine gun. A SWAPO RPG struck and entered the vehicle at his feet, detonating an ammunition tray. Unfortunately, the transfusion was in vain despite the excellent work of Dr Wilson, a young national-service doctor from Cape Town, as the trauma and loss of blood the youngster had suffered was too severe. It was yet another futile loss.

The fighting around Eenhana was intense. Every afternoon Alouette helicopters would fly 'base-plate recces'. Their mission was to search and find the mortar firing positions that SWAPO had installed prior to their evening's bombardment of the base. From the air it was fairly easy to detect the V-shaped scrape marks indicating the firing direction towards Eenhana. The terrorists would decide on the mortar position and then anchor the base-plate ready for the next evening's firing. All they had to do once darkness fell was to silently move into the pre-determined spot, attach the mortar tube to the base-plate and the bombardment could begin. When these aiming positions were located the helicopters would land and remove the base-plate.

The day the Caspir was hit the MAOT at Eenhana called out an Impala strike, just west of the base, to assist the hard-pressed Koevoet teams. Four Impalas fired salvos of rockets into the SWAPO defence lines, one of the extremely rare occasions that SAAF fighter jets had struck targets on South African soil.

The terrible thing is this battle was unnecessary. Peace had been negotiated, agreed and signed by all the parties concerned. This was further proof that communists are taught to use every opportunity to gain an advantage over their western opponents. They realized it was abhorrent to a westerner to break his promise. SWAPO leadership may hail their dead fighters as martyrs but in truth they were sacrificed by the peculiar logic of their leaders.

Although the fighting ceased after ten days normal spoor follow-ups continued while hastily arranged 'peace talks' took place. Fighting had spread along the Kaokoland and Owamboland borders and the SAAF, flying mainly helicopters from 16 and 17 Squadrons, had operated from Ondangwa, Eenhana and Ruacana. By Day 4 of the emergency, 15 x Puma and 22 x Alouette helicopters were flying in action out of AFB Ondangwa. These aircraft had been dismantled in Pretoria, loaded into C-160/130 transport aircraft and flown to Ondangwa where they were reassembled, tested and put into service.

Perhaps it was fitting that SAAF helicopter crews who had been involved in the first contact in 1966, also fired the last shots in anger in April 1989.

Finally, after the dust had settled once again, the long-awaited peace arrived in the arid, semi-desert regions of South West Africa and Angola.

Chapter 16

Conclusion

From a purely air force perspective there were a number of factors which led to our success during the border war, one of which was real-time command and control. In 1983 a computerized system, known by its codename Jampot, was introduced at 310 AFCP in Oshakati, which allowed for the professional utilization of our aircraft. Another major factor was the superb level of training of our air- and ground crews who maintained the highest standards of flying and ground maintenance.

In the latter stages of the war SAAF aircraft and their missile systems were outperformed by those of the MiG-23. Air superiority of the battlefield which the SAAF had achieved for most of the war was seriously threatened. What kept our pilots in the conventional battle around Cuito Cuanavale for seven months, against serious challenges, was a combination of what is known in Afrikaans as *veg lus en veg lis*—literally clever tactics and a desire to get to grips with the enemy. Every quarter GOC SWA presented the Jakkals Troffee to the unit or individual in South West Africa who showed the greatest initiative during the war. It was a coveted trophy with the winners receiving miniature lapel pins adorned with a broken AK-47. There were a number of SAAF winners.

There can rarely be a military victory in a counter-insurgency war. It is not over as long as one AK-47-toting enemy soldier is still in the bush. For this reason a negotiated diplomatic solution satisfying all the aggrieved parties has to be achieved. Actions of the entire SADF, supported so effectively by the air- and ground crews of the SAAF, finally produced the required conditions for peace to be declared.

The SADF, renowned for inter-service bickering during peacetime, cast those squabbles aside in the face of the enemy and reached a standard of unsurpassed

Conclusion

'joint-ness' (inter-service co-operation) in the latter stages of the war. By employing all the resources available to the army, air force, navy, medical corps and police, the enemy had been presented with an unbeatable force.

Explanation of the title—*from fledgling to eagle*
In the early 1960s the SAAF was feeling the effects of the post-World War II recession. South Africa was desperately trying to catch up on the six years of development it had lost between 1939 and 1945. Any available money was being spent on economic recovery and defence spending had been reduced to a trickle. The Korean War between 1950 and 1953, where the SAAF's famous Cheetah squadron won well-deserved accolades, provided a temporary boost to the air force, allowing it to transform into the modern era of jets and helicopters. However, funds for replacing aged aircraft were not forthcoming.

During the Second World War the SAAF had proven itself on the world stage. Major components of the famous Desert Air Force, the Balkans Air Force and the Allied air forces in Italy consisted of SAAF squadrons. As part of the Empire Aircrew Training Scheme flying training schools sprung up like mushrooms all over South Africa. South African-trained pilots were to be found in all theatres of the war. However, by 1960 the SAAF had shrunk to a tiny organization, a phenomenon not only applicable to South Africa but worldwide.

But size was not the only factor. In terms of global defence agreements South Africa was envisaged as part of the British defence infrastructure and the SADF was organized to fulfil particular needs within this overall structure. Therefore, it was not a balanced force on its own. In addition, Britain was the traditional arms supplier from where most of our defence requirements were met.

In 1961 the status quo changed and South Africa soon found herself standing alone and cut off from armament supplies. Fortunately, visionaries foresaw the problems the SAAF would encounter in the future and began an extensive campaign to re-equip and turn it into a viable force. At a crucial period in South Africa's military history France replaced Britain as our major supplier of arms. Training programmes for air force personnel were intensified. Industry was tasked to design, develop, test and produce the equipment denied us by the rest of the world and with gathering momentum South Africa and the SAAF were ensured of the resources to face the challenges that lay ahead.

To utilize these material resources the SAAF needed high-quality, trained and disciplined personnel. South Africa has a history of producing fine fighting men and women and in this case it was no different. It is common for old men to imply that the youth of today are not a patch on those of yesteryear. In the time of the border war our youngsters were as good, steadfast, disciplined and determined as the best of them. I believe the situation which prevailed on April Fools' Day 1989, was an excellent example of the discipline required of an air force. Under extreme pressure our youngsters never opened fire until they received the order to do so. This is the discipline which forges a superb fighting force. It was our people who can take the credit for turning the SAAF, once again, into an 'eagle' air force.

How the transformation was effected

It started at Ongulumbashe in 1966 with Alouette helicopters and a SAAF DC-3.
- Initially we armed the Alouette with one 7.62mm machine gun, then quadruple mountings, then a 20mm cannon, turning the little Alouette into the most effective anti-terrorist weapon in the armoury.
- We armed the DC-3 with 20mm cannon and skyshout.
- We built air filters for helicopter engines, allowing them to operate in sandy, gritty environments.
- We converted the exhaust systems of aircraft to reduce the infrared signature from the engines, reducing the effects of Strela-type, heat-seeking missiles.
- We constructed safety revetments to protect aircraft on the ground from Katyusha rockets and mortar fire.
- SAAF helicopter crews refined the Fireforce concept used by the Rhodesian Air Force, to fly troops into 'hot engagement' with the enemy in the quickest possible time. In concert with both Koevoet and the Romeo Mike teams of 101 Battalion, Alouette gunships formed a most successful anti-terrorist team.
- We perfected the use of MAOTs, allowing aircraft control right in the heart of the battle.
- By using a HAG and mini-HAG system we could keep our helicopters engaged in a fight for as long as the ground forces required them.
- By using the combined talents of the SAAF, Parabats and SAMs, the casualty-evacuation system saved many lives and was, I believe, on a par with the best in the world. SAAF helicopter crews excelled in this vital operation.
- The advanced fighter school at AFB Pietersburg produced fighter, bomber and recce pilots of the highest quality.
- The transport crews, flying out of rough and ready makeshift sand runways day and night, created the lifeline which sustained many SADF operations by bringing much-needed food, ammunition and personnel right to the front line.
- Dedicated air force intelligence teams predicted and detected enemy intentions, providing the details on which good operational planning could be done.
- Logistics and maintenance, under extremely trying conditions, was of the highest standard. I have flown aircraft in the RAF, Fleet Air Arm and the United States Navy and state unreservedly the SAAF aircraft were superbly maintained.

Conclusion

- We began the war using WWII 3-inch rockets and general purpose HE bombs. Both types of weapon were satisfactory for attacking densely packed buildings in Europe but against targets scattered through dense bush and standing on soft sandy soil, they were soon found to be practically useless. Through dedicated engineers and weapon effort planners (WEPs), like Mac Macatamney, a new set of bombs and fuses were designed, tested, and introduced, which proved the difference between the SAAF and our enemy.
- Many hard-pressed soldiers, policemen and injured civilians will attest to the bravery and skill of SAAF helicopter crews who 'fetched and carried' at all hours of the day and night.
- SAAF recce crews and skilled photographic interpreters combined skills to continually locate the enemy, one of the most difficult jobs of this kind of warfare. Recce missions using the complete range of aircraft from Cessna-185, Bosbok, Impala, Mirage, Buccaneer and Canberra were carried out. These recce tasks varied from low to high level, from visual to armed recce, using hand-held and installed cameras, covering vertical, tail and oblique photography, to electronic surveillance.
- South Africa produced a full range of chaff and flare dispensers, ECM and ECCM airborne equipment.
- The SAAF equipped Buffel, Ratel and Caspir vehicles with command-compatible radio and communication systems for both operational and intelligence uses.
- All SAAF command posts, bases and squadrons were interconnected with a computer-based, real-time command-and-control system, improving aircraft utilization and turnaround times and effectively acting as a force-multiplier. Instead of using aircraft twice a day four sorties could be flown, effectively doubling our capability. In a period of isolation where we could not obtain any new or replacement aircraft this was a major factor.
- South African industry transformed the Mirage III into the Cheetah series of fighters. A programme was started that transformed Puma transport helicopters into Oryx helicopters with increased capability. In another programme the Rooivalk attack helicopter was built. Unfortunately, it arrived too late to be used in the border war as did other South African innovations.
- The SAAF command-and-control structure delegated Western Air Command the responsibility of running the air involvement in the war. The SAAF then had the wisdom to appoint some great air force commanders, for example Bossie Huyser and Thack Thackwray, to command operations during the hectic periods of the war.

The threat

The SAAF began the war in 1966 using light helicopters. When it ended in 1989 it had supported the SADF in a seven-month-long conventional battle against enemy forces from Angola and Cuba, advised and assisted by the Soviets, East Germans and sundry others. The enemy were better equipped than the SADF, having access to copious quantities of the latest and best Soviet armour, surface-to-air missile and anti-aircraft artillery systems. They had built a radar chain of immense proportions which stretched around South Africa's border, from Angola in the west to Mozambique in the east. During the final battle around Cuito Cuanavale they deployed a force which was numerically four or five times superior to that deployed by South Africa.

Major Soviet Equipment Delivered to the Third World 1980-1985*					
	Near East & South Asia	Sub-Saharan Africa	Latin America	East Asia & Pacific	TOTAL
Tanks/Self propelled Guns	3,600	630	505	280	5,015
Light Armour	6,565	1,000	280	250	8,095
Artillery	3,810	2,050	895	390	7,145
Major Surface Combatants	26	4	4	5	39
Minor Surface Combatants	27	21	49	48	145
Submarines	7	0	2	0	9
Missile Attack Boats	16	9	6	6	37
Supersonic Aircraft	1,340	340	135	270	2,085
Subsonic Aircraft	120	5	0	5	130
Helicopters	695	190	80	75	1,040
Other Combat Aircraft	250	70	40	80	440
Surface-to-Air Missiles	10,400	1,890	1,300	430	14,020
* Revised to reflect current information					

The vast majority of the equipment listed under sub-Saharan Africa was poured into Angola.

At no time did the SAAF or the SADF have all their forces deployed on the border, nor were any of our fast-jet or bomber squadrons ever permanently stationed there. They were deployed whenever required for particular missions.

The war ended after the political masters, on both sides of the border, finally came out of their starting blocks and negotiated a settlement to the long-standing and bitter conflict. The fighters on both sides, including the SAAF, gave a collective sigh of relief and returned to more peaceful and humanitarian activities.

Not so the politicians. Posturing, gesturing and laying claim upon absurd claim became the order of the day. There were those in Angola, Cuba, the newly independent country of Namibia and people with leftist leanings inside South Africa, who made headlines by claiming a massive military victory over the SADF forces at Cuito Cuanavale. As the facts in this book relate nothing could be further from the truth. They can certainly claim they won the political settlement but they lost militarily. The fighters on the field of battle know very well whether the battles they participated in were won or lost.

Conclusion

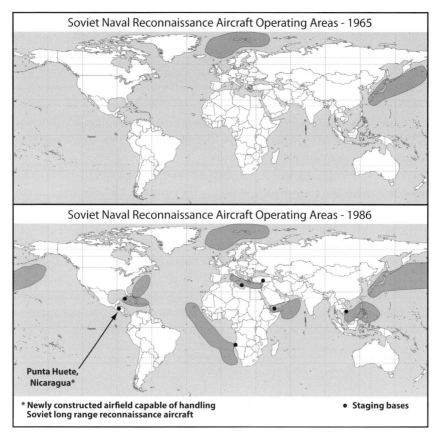

This graphic, taken from the US Defense Summary for 1986, illustrates Soviet expansionism across the globe. SADF actions in Angola assisted in stopping this advance.

Let me illustrate the fundamental difference between politicians and military personnel. In 1984, after Operation *Askari*, the JMC was formed in what turned out to be a futile attempt at a settlement. This was a joint committee of Angolans and South Africans tasked to monitor the situation as both sides tried to withdraw from combat. Every week the two delegations would meet to discuss progress. The meetings, held in 16 x 16 canvas tents and chaired by senior military personnel from both sides, were always formal, polite and structured. However, they often degenerated into long, heated and sometimes obstructive debates when the political representatives were given the opportunity to speak. Sitting through some of these interminable discussions I would often look outside to where the respective helicopter aircrews were sitting under the shade of big trees. The difference was chalk and cheese. Inside the ten, the diplomats were being most undiplomatic, trying to score petty political points. Outside, the fighters who by circumstances beyond their control had been set at each others' throats were engrossed in deep conversation, often discussing the pros and cons of their respective aircraft, sharing bottles of aquavit, which seemed to be an important part of the Angolans' survival equipment, and generally enjoying each other's company—this is the way of professional people.

During the second half of the twentieth century Soviet expansionism was rampant right across the globe. One country after another had succumbed to the rhetoric and coercion of communist pressure. Soviet doctrine, expounding the theory of revolution, exhorted revolutionaries to foment unrest and 'where they struck butter, go right through'. On the other hand, 'if they struck steel they were to withdraw and try somewhere else'.

From 1950 to 1985 they had struck nothing but butter. However, in the 1980s, most unexpectedly they struck steel in Afghanistan. The Soviet economy suffered because of the economic burden of the campaign and Soviet mothers campaigned against the rapidly rising casualty figures. They withdrew and, in the last throw of their dice, tried again—this time in Angola using surrogate troops. To their dismay and bewilderment they again struck steel in the form of a resolute, determined composite force of South African soldiers, policemen and airmen. Revolutionary warfare is based on a long, drawn-out campaign which leads to the collapse of a nation's will to continue the fight—as happened with the Americans in Vietnam. On the border between South West Africa and

The arrow indicates the Soviet plan, as outlined in the Iko Carreira document for the long-term take-over of South Africa. Angola was to be the' war of attrition' which weakened the SADF, in particular the SAAF. The final thrust was to be from Zimbabwe and Zambia into the industrial heartland of South Africa.

Conclusion

Angola they never broke our will. In fact, we outlasted, outmanoeuvred and militarily defeated the so-called revolutionary forces. This is the legacy of the border war.

Thankfully, since the last shots of the border war were fired there have been almost two decades of peace. However, in my opinion, the history of this conflict is being manipulated for political expediency, my primary reason for writing this book. I wanted a factual document to be published, recording as accurately as possible what actually occurred in order to counter the propaganda and embroidered falsehoods being expounded for political reasons.

Secondly, I wanted to produce a document as testimony to those who stood shoulder to shoulder to stem the communist tide. I hope I have illustrated adequately the magnitude of the threat the security forces faced and the enormity of the defeats suffered by the combined enemy. This was what the border war was all about.

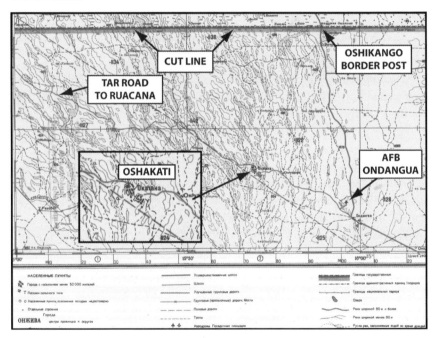

Soviet aeronautical chart of Owamboland.

If, after all this, there are still doubting Thomases, a close study of the map above might be of interest. It is a map of central Owamboland showing the tar road running from Ondangwa (bottom right), through Oshakati (centre), towards Ruacana (off top right). Ondangwa airfield with its runways is clearly visible just to the northeast of Ondangwa town. In the blow-up of Oshakati the layout of the town is clearly marked. For two years, 1983–84, my family and I resided in one of these houses.

```
>                    = FREE TEXT MESSAGE =              9406301115
FROM: 40NWM
TO: ALL

MESSAGE: " AND SO IT CAME TO PASS THAT ON THE THIRTIETH DAY OF JUNE 199
         DICK LORD SHOULD BE TAKEN OUT OF THE PLACE OF COMMAND, AND B
         PUT OUT TO PASTURE.

         HERE ENDETH THE LAST LESSON."

         I WANT TO THANK ALL OF YOU FOR YOUR SUPPORT AND FRIENDSHIP
         DURING MY YEARS IN THE AIR FORCE AND PARTICULARY IN THE
         COMMAND POST.

         I LEAVE WITH THE KNOWLEDGE THAT THE AIR FORCE AND THE COUNTR
         ARE IN YOUR VERY GOOD AND CAPABLE HANDS.

         WITH ALL MY THANKS.

         BRIG DICK LORD
```

My final Jampot message on the day I retired from the SAAF.

Now take a close look at the script on and surrounding the map. This is a Soviet map printed in 1977, clearly indicating both their preparations and expectations for their advance into southern Africa.

*****

'Unadjusted impressions have their value, and a road to a true philosophy of life seems to lie in humbly recording diverse readings of its phenomena as they are forced upon us by chance and change'
—Thomas Hardy
Preface to *Poems of the Past and Present*, 1901

'It isn't over, till the paperwork is finished'

Glossary

AAA – anti-aircraft artillery. Triple A was the overall term used to describe the anti-aircraft guns that were employed in limited numbers by SWAPO, but extensively by the Angolan defence force. These guns covered the complete spectrum of Soviet-supplied weaponry and included the following:

- 12.7mm
- 14.5mm
- 20.0mm
- 23.0mm*
- 37.0mm
- 57.0mm**

*This included the towed, twin-barrelled version that was probably the most widely employed and effective gun used in the entire campaign by either side, both in the ground-to-air and ground-to-ground mode. The four-barrelled, tracked version (Shilka) was also encountered. The 23mm cannons used by 32 Battalion, Koevoet and the SAAF were some of the many captured in operations over the years. Ironically, Angola became probably the biggest arms supplier to South Africa throughout the difficult years of arms boycotts

**These radar-guided guns were originally equipped with the Fire-can radar system and later updated with the Flap-wheel version

ACM – air combat manoeuvring, modern name for old-fashioned dog-fighting

Adhemar – French word meaning angle of attack indicator (AAI), sometimes irreverently referred to as ADI (angle of dangle indicator); ADD in the Buccaneer

AFB – air force base

ADF – automatic direction-finding navigational instrument which locks onto an NDB

AFCP – air force command post. The SAAF uses a system of command posts to efficiently command and control all of the resources available to it. This includes aircraft, personnel, radars, air-defence systems and ground security squadron specialists with their dogs. An AFCP controls the air force involvement in its designated area of responsibility, which includes both ground and air battles. An FAC, forward air command post, is subservient to an AFCP but handles all the equivalent operations, except it does not control the air battle

AGL – above ground level, the height in feet that the aircraft flies above the ground

AI – air interception

AK-47 – Automat Kalaschnikov type 47, the standard, and ubiquitous, Soviet-designed automatic assault rifle

Alouette III – single-engined light helicopter, the aerial workhorse of the border war. In the trooper role it could carry a crew of two plus four soldiers, or two stretchers when used in the casevac role. In the offensive role as a gunship it carried a 20mm cannon firing out of the port side

Alpha bomb – circular-shaped anti-personnel bomb weighing six kilograms that when dropped by the Canberra from level flight, gave a natural dispersion pattern. The bomb would strike the surface activating the fusing mechanism and then bounce into the air to detonate about six metres above the ground. This bomb was an improved version of that used by the Rhodesian Air Force, and 300 of them could be loaded into the bomb bay of a Canberra

ANC – African National Congress

ATC – Air Traffic Control

ATCO – Air Traffic Controller Officer

avtur – aviation turbine fuel used in helicopter and fixed-wing jet-turbine engines

bakkie – pick-up truck (Afrikaans)

Bakkie ops – SWAPO insurgents were known to utilize the vehicles of sympathizers for the conveyance of personnel, equipment and explosives throughout Owamboland. As these vehicles were usually of the light pick-up variety, operations launched to combat this illegal use of vehicles became known as *Bakkie* ops

bandit – an aircraft identified as hostile

beacon – the cut-line designating the border between Angola and Owamboland stretched in a straight line the 420kms from the Cunene River in the west to the Kavango River in the east. Every ten kilometres a concrete beacon was built to identify position in an otherwise featureless terrain. Beacon 16 was therefore 160km east of the Cunene River.

blue job – anybody serving in the air force (slang)

BM-21 – 122mm 40-tube multiple rocket launcher, mounted on a Ural-375 truck, with a maximum range of 20,000 metres

boere – a general-usage, normally derogatory term used by both SWAPO and the Angolans to describe the South Africa/SWATF security forces (from the Afrikaans *boer* meaning farmer)

bogey – an unidentified aircraft

bombshell – guerrilla tactic of splitting up during flight (slang)

Bosbok – single-piston-engined, high-wing reconnaissance aircraft flown by two crew seated in tandem. In the bush war it was utilized in many roles, including visual and photographic reconnaissance, Skyshout, pamphlet dropping and Telstar

braai – barbecue (Afrikaans)

brown job – any soldier; variations were 'browns' or the more commonly used 'pongos' (slang)

Glossary

Buccaneer – S-50 version of the British-built naval strike fighter; twin-engined, subsonic two-seater that could carry the full range of bombs plus AS-30 air-to-ground missiles

C-130 – four-engined turboprop heavy transport aircraft otherwise known as the Hercules. Used extensively throughout the bush war to support the actions of both ground landing and air-dropping of personnel and freight (*see* Flossie)

C-160 – twin-engined tactical transport aircraft. Although limited in payload when compared to the C-130, it had the decided advantage of a larger-dimensioned freight compartment, allowing easier and quicker transporting of helicopters to the battle area. Known by NATO as the Transall it had the dubious distinction of being probably the most difficult and expensive aircraft to maintain in the inventory of the SAAF, owing to the extreme difficulties imposed by the international arms embargo

Canberra – English Electric twin-engined, medium jet bomber, used as such and also in PR roles. Armament included Alpha bombs, World War II-vintage 500lb and 1,000lb general purpose (GP) bombs plus the South African-manufactured 120kg and 250kg GP and pre-fragmentation bombs

CAP – combat air patrol. The armed mission air-defence fighters fly to ensure safety of own aircraft in the battle area

CAS – close air support. Aircraft supporting the ground forces in close proximity to the immediate battle line are termed to be giving CAS

casevac – casualty evacuation

Caspir – mine-protected, armoured personnel carrier

CEP – centre of error probability. A mathematical method of determining the miss-distance of a number of weapons from the centre of a target

Cessna 185 – A single-engined, four-seater tail-dragger used in the communication, Skyshout, pamphlet-dropping and Telstar roles, by day and night

CFS – Central Flying School

clampers – visibility and cloud base below the minimum required for safe flying operations (air force slang)

COIN – counter-insurgency

coke – the centre or bull's-eye of the target (air force slang)

ComOps – communications operations. The type of activity performed to influence our own and the enemy forces positively, as well as the local population. Although the members of our ComOps teams did sterling work, the successes they achieved with the enemy and the local population were negligible compared to the effort they put in

contact – a fire fight, i.e. when contact is made with the enemy

CO – commanding officer

cuca – small shop/stall in Owamboland, derived from a popular brand of beer, Cuca.

***Cuca* blitz** – security force raids on cuca shops. These raids were mostly carried out after the receipt of intelligence but ad hoc raids were also undertaken to keep the enemy guessing. Most raids were carried out by the ground forces alone, but joint air force, army and police raids were also mounted. These raids were generally unsuccessful but a few did

481

result in the arrest of important insurgents, and presumably kept SWAPO guessing.

curfew – within the military operational area of Sector 10, i.e. Owamboland, a curfew was imposed on all movements of people and vehicles between sundown and sunrise, to inhibit SWAPO's nightly activities

cut-line – the border between Angola and Owamboland, so named from the graded strip cut through the bush to indicate the international border

D-30 – Soviet-built 122mm cannon with a range of 15,000 metres; also used in an anti-tank role

Dayton – the radio call sign of the radar station situated at AFB Ondangwa. All matters concerning air defence were the responsibility of Dayton

density altitude – aircraft aerodynamic and engine performance are adversely affected by high temperatures and low pressures. Because these criteria vary from airfield to airfield and on a daily basis, the term 'density altitude' is used to determine aircraft performance. At a sea-level airfield in Europe during winter, a jet aircraft will produce more thrust and lift than it will at AFB Waterkloof, 5,000ft AGL, during the 30°C-plus temperatures of summer

dominee – padre (Afrikaans)

DR – dead reckoning, when navigating without electronic aids

DZ – drop zone designated for any parachute delivery, whether personnel or supplies

ECM/ECCM – electronic counter measures/electronic counter counter measures, part of EW (*see* EW)

ERU – explosive release unit The device which ensures clean separation of bombs from the carrying aircraft

EW – electronic warfare; covers all aspects of warfare involving use of the electromagnetic spectrum

FAC – Forward Air Controller

FAPA – *Forças Aeria Popular de Angola,* People's Air Force of Angola

FAPLA – *Forças Armadas Populares de Libertação de Angola,* People's Armed Forces for the Liberation of Angola

FFAR – forward-firing air rockets

Fireforce – an airborne offensive force comprising combinations of the following:

- gunships
- offensive firepower
- troopers
- command and control
- Bosboks
- recce or Telstar
- Pumas
- insertion of stopper groups
- troops—usually highly trained Parabats

Flossie – C-130 Hercules used as the air link between South Africa and South West Africa during the border war. A term of endearment as this aircraft took the troops home. (SADF slang)

FLOT – forward line own troops. A very necessary requirement during close air support operations, which ensures safety of own forces

FNLA – *Frente Nacional para a Libertação de Angola*, National Front for the Liberation of Angola

FTS – Flying Training School

G – gravity. Under normal circumstances everything on earth is affected by the pull of gravity, called 1G. In tight turns or loops, centrifugal force effectively increases the pull of gravity. A G meter in the cockpit registers this increase. Readings of -2 to +7G are the usual range experienced during a typical fighter sortie. At =7G, the body's blood effectively becomes seven times heavier than normal and hastens the onset of blackout as blood drains towards the pilot's feet. At -G readings, blood is forced to the head, sometimes resulting in red-out as the capillary blood vessels in the eyes burst due to the increased pressure

G-suit – the inflatable garment, zipped around abdomen and legs that inhibits blood flow to the pilot's feet as aircraft G-loading is increased

Gatup – a high-G manoeuvre developed by 1 Squadron pilots which affords maximum safety for an aircraft in a hostile environment. A 4G pull-up is followed by 120–130° banked turn, as the pilot pulls the sight onto the target. Immediately thereafter he fires a laser shot to accurately measure range to the target. The pilot then pulls the nose skyward. The laser input allows the computer to predict an automatic release of the bombs during the pull-up. After bomb release the pilot reapplies G, over-banks and pulls the aircraft's nose down toward the ground. The escape from the target area is flown at low level. When this manoeuvre is performed at night it is termed *Nagup*

GCA – ground controlled approach. Radar talk-down used to guide pilots to a safe landing in bad weather or at night

GCI – ground controlled interception

GIB – guy in the back i.e. Buccaneer navigator (air force slang)

GOC SWA – General Officer Commanding South West Africa

Grad-P – single-shot 122mm Soviet rocket launcher. Mounted on a tripod and could fire a 46kg rocket with an 18.3kg warhead, a maximum distance of 11,000 metres. Much used by SWAPO for their stand-off bombardments

Guns free – the state prevailing when all guns are allowed to fire at designated targets as and when they are ready; only ordered when no own-forces' aircraft are in the area

Guns tight – the order given to cease own forces' artillery firing when own forces' aircraft are operating over a battlefield

HAG – *helikopter administrasie gebied*, Afrikaans for helicopter administration area (HAA). A designated area, planned and secured by ground forces, from where helicopters operated to expedite operations. Very often it was co-located with a forward headquarters where immediate tactical plans were co-ordinated. Fuel in drums or bladders was available to refuel the helicopters, with extra gunship ammunition available. The HAG could be stationary for two or three days depending on the area, but longer than that was considered dangerous, as SWAPO could be expected to locate the HAG in that time. On the border, the Afrikaans HAG was always used as the sound came more easily to the tongue.

HC – Honoris Crux. The highest decoration for military valour that could be awarded to members of the SADF. There were three classes, namely: HC Bronze, HCS Silver and HCG Gold

HE – high explosive

HF – high frequency (radio)

hopper – a high-frequency radio that has the facility for hopping from one frequency to another during broadcast, thus improving the security of messages and signals

HQ – headquarters

HUD – head-up display. The sighting system mounted in the front windscreen of a cockpit. Information displayed relieves the pilot of having to look inside the cockpit during critical manoeuvres

IAS – indicated air speed

IEC – Independent Electoral Committee

IFR –in-flight refuelling/instrument flight rules, when flying in bad weather or at night

IMC – instrument meteorological conditions. Used when it is mandatory to fly with sole reference to aircraft instrumentation

Impala – a single-engined, light jet ground-attack aircraft used very successfully throughout the bush war, by day and by night. Armed with 68mm rockets, bombs and 30mm cannon

interdiction – offensive mission flown with the aim of disrupting the enemy's logistical lines of communication

IP – initial point. A well-defined navigational position, from where navigation or attack profiles can be commenced with accuracy

IRT – Instrument Rating Test. An annual requirement for all pilots

ITCZ – Inter-Tropical Convergence Zone

JARIC – Joint Air Reconnaissance Intelligence Centre

JPT – jet-pipe temperature

kill – during simulated ACM, missile launch or gun firing is expressed as a 'kill'

KIAS – knots indicated air speed

klap – smack, hit (Afrikaans)

kraal – either a single hut or a complex of huts, used as dwellings. In Owamboland the kraal complex (village) was usually surrounded by a thorn-bush fence that offered security to the cattle and goats owned by the occupants

kts - knots

Kudu – a single-piston-engined, high-wing battlefield communication aircraft with capacity for six passengers (provided the temperature was not too high) or a limited quantity of freight

Glossary

LABS – low altitude bombing system. The system was originally designed to 'throw' tactical nuclear weapons in a toss-type manoeuvre. The launch aircraft pulls up from low level at high speeds and releases the bomb as the nose passes 45° above the horizon. The aircraft continues in a looping manoeuvre to escape the detonation, while the bomb flies nearly five miles before exploding. Never a very accurate method of delivery but sufficient for a nuclear blast

lemon – a futile operation (military slang)

LIP – low intercept profile (later changed to UNCIP, *see* UNCIP)

LMG – light machine gun

LP – local population. A more common usage was PB, from the Afrikaans *plaaslike bevolking*

LZ – landing zone. An area designated and secured by ground forces for the landing of helicopters

Mach – as the speed of sound varies with temperature and altitude, Mach + number is used to refer to the aircraft's speed as a per centage of the speed of sound, e.g. Mach 1.0 = speed of sound and Mach 0.9 = 9/10ths of that speed (which also equates to 9nms per minute)

MAOT – mobile air operations team. The air force team usually comprised an OC (pilot), an operations officer, an intelligence officer, a radio operator and one or two clerks. The team plus their equipment could be airlifted into a tactical headquarters co-located with the army or police, or could move with the ground forces in mine-protected vehicles, as an integral part of the command headquarters. The OC of the team was often called 'the MAOT'

Mayday – international distress call

medevac – medical evacuation. Differs from casevac as the patient is already under medical supervision, being transported to a more suitable medical centre

MF – medium frequency (radio)

MHz – megahertz, to denote frequency band

MiG – Mikoyan-Gurevich, the Soviet-designed family of jet fighters. The Angolan Air Force (FAPA) was equipped with the delta-winged MiG-21 and later the swing-wing MiG-23 variety

Military Region – for military purposes the border areas inside South West Africa immediately adjacent to the Angolan border were divided into the Kaokoland, Sector 10 Owamboland, Sector 20 Kavango and Sector 70 Caprivi Strip. The Angolans, however, divided their country into military regions. The 5th Military Region faced Kaokoland and Sector 10, while the 6th Military Region faced Kavango and Caprivi

Mirage – French-built Dassault, the family of supersonic fighters used by the SAAF

misrep – mission report. These reports had to be completed by the intelligence staff after debriefing the aircrew after every mission. Often a source of irritation to the aircrew and the communications department who had to encode and decode all these documents, but possibly the best source of intelligence for the successful prosecution of operations

MPLA – *Movimento Popular de Libertação de Angola*, Popular Movement for the Liberation of Angola

MRG – master reference gyro. The main gyro which controls all the flying instruments in a Buccaneer. Failure of the 'master' can, under certain circumstances, cause the crew instant dyspepsia, hysteria and can be accompanied by uncontrollable tears

MTBF – mean time between failure. A term used to describe the time period, usually in flying hours, that a component could be expected to remain serviceable

Nagup – the night equivalent of *Gatup* (*see Gatup*)

NDB – non-directional beacon. A navigational aid which transmits a signal in all directions, except immediately overhead. Pilots using their ADF instrument can lock-on to the NDB to receive directional information from the beacon

nms – nautical miles

notam – notice to airmen. The standard form of warning message sent to all operators of aircraft, informing them of air-related information that could affect the safe passage of the aircraft

OC – officer commanding

OC WAC – Officer Commanding Western Air Command

OCU – Operational Conversion Unit

Ops Co – operations co-ordinator

Ops normal – a radio transmission made at regular intervals (usually 20 minutes), allowing command post staff to monitor the progress of low-level missions

orbat – order of battle, the force levels of protagonists

panty – the name given to the canvas spreader that surrounds an in-flight refuelling basket. A pilot who breaks this material while attempting to refuel earns the reputation of being a 'panty-ripper' (air force slang)

Parabat – Parachute Battalion soldier, qualified to wear the famous red beret

PBI – poor bloody infantry (British slang)

PI – photographic interpreter

PLAN – People's Liberation Army of Namibia, SWAPO's military wing

PNR – point of no return

POMZ – Soviet anti-personnel mine, commonly known as 'the widow-maker'

pongo – an infantryman, a brown job (SADF slang)

PR – photographic reconnaissance

Pro-Patria – general-service medal awarded to those who had been involved in the fight against terrorism

Puff the Magic Dragon – the gunship version of the Dakota, fitted with a 20mm cannon and Skyshout facilities. More commonly referred to as 'the Dragon' (US/Vietnam der.)

Puma – a twin-engined transport helicopter that carried a crew of three and 16 lightly

Glossary

armed or 12 fully armed troops

PUP – pull-up point

QFI – qualified flying instructor

R&R – rest and recreation

RAMS – radio-activated marker system

recce – reconnaissance, as in ground recce, an airborne visual recce, a photographic recce or an EW (electronic) reconnaissance of a point or area

Recce – Reconnaissance Commandos or Special Forces

Romeo Mike – from the Afrikaans *Reaksie Mag*, the army's mobile reaction force. This force usually consisted of four Caspir fighting vehicles plus a fifth logistical back-up vehicle. This force could act independently while searching for spoor, but became most effective in follow-up operations when used in concert with additional RM teams that could be summoned by radio, when a contact was imminent. The RM concept was copied from the Zulu system expounded so effectively by the Police Koevoet units. 101 Battalion, the so-called Owambo Battalion based at Ondangwa, supplied the RM personnel

RP – rocket projectile

RPG-7 – rocket-propelled grenade. An anti-tank, tube-launched grenade of Soviet origin, with a maximum effective range of 500 metres, and an explosive warhead weighing 2.4kg. It is robust, 'soldier-proof', easy to use and much favoured by insurgents worldwide

RSA – Republic of South Africa

RV – rendezvous. The chosen point was usually a grid reference on a map, an easily recognizable ground feature, or a bearing and distance from a navigational facility

RWR/RWS – radar warning receiver/system

SAAF – South African Air Force

SADF – South African Defence Force

SAM – surface-to-air missile. A missile, guided by infrared or radar, fired from a launcher on the ground at an airborne target. By the end of the war FAPLA had an array of missiles which included the following:

- SA-2 fixed site
- SA-3 fixed site
- SA-6 mobile, tracked
- SA-7 shoulder-launched*
- SA-8 mobile, wheeled
- SA-9 mobile, wheeled
- SA-13 mobile, tracked
- SA-14 shoulder-launched
- SA-16 shoulder-launched

  *SWAPO used only the SA-7 but FAPLA was equipped with the entire range

SAMS – South African Medical Services

SAP – South African Police

SAR – search and rescue

SATCO – Senior Air Traffic Control Officer

scramble – traditional air force term used when fighter aircraft are ordered to take off immediately

shona – a shallow pan or an open area in the bush that fills with rain during the rainy season and is invariably dry during the winter months. Also *chana* in Angola

Sir Ponsonby – nickname given to the very sophisticated automatic pilot fitted in the Mirage F1. Abbreviated to Sir Pons and used in preference to the more common George

SOP – standard operating procedure. Common parlance for anything that is a standard, recognized drill

Souties – from *soutpiel*, a derogatory name for Englishmen, originating from the Afrikaans idea that English immigrants to South Africa had one leg in Africa and the other in Britain. The piece between, known as a *piel*, was said to dangle in the salty (*sout*) sea

Spook – nickname for the DC-4 Skymaster fitted with EW equipment used for intelligence-gathering purposes. The Dakota that was later fitted with an EW suite became known as 'Casper'—the friendly ghost

sprog – a new, or trainee, pilot. Also known variously as studs, shirt-tails, second lieuts or bicycles (air force slang)

SSO Ops – Senior Staff Officer Operations

States – military slang referring to the Republic of South Africa, probably originating from the pilot who, when asked what type of aircraft he flew, answered, "I fly Cans in the States." What he actually flew were Spamcans (Harvards) in the Orange Free State

stonk – to attack or bomb (military slang)

Strela – Soviet-made shoulder-launched SA-7 surface-to-air missile. Each SWAPO detachment was issued with three or four of these missiles as an integral part of its armament. Rough handling and extremes of temperature in the field ensured that these weapons were unreliable. However, because they were so freely distributed, cognizance had to be taken of their presence. All flying in the operational area was affected by the need to minimize the chance of taking a Strela hit

SWA – South West Africa, now Namibia

SWAPO – South West Africa People's Organization (a misnomer as the organization only represented the Owambo people)

SWATF – South West African Territory Force. Both the SADF and SWATF were commanded by GOC SWA

Tacan – tactical air navigation facility

Tac HQ – a tactical headquarters instituted for the running of an operation close to the combat zone, commanded by a subordinate commander with guidelines and limitations delegated by a sector headquarters

tail-dragger – any propeller-driven aircraft that has two main wheels and the third under the tail. This aircraft requires different techniques when approaching and taking off, than those used by the more usual tricycle-configured aircraft

Glossary

Tally ho! – The fighter pilot's call used when the enemy has been spotted, usually the precursor to a few minutes of mayhem

Telstar – an aircraft flown at medium altitude to relay VHF messages from aircraft on low-flying operational missions

THTC – Tobias Hanyeko Training Camp, SWAPO's training base outside Lubango

tiffie – a mechanic, from the word artificer (military slang)

terr – a terrorist; also known as a freedom fighter in some circles (military slang)

TOD – top of descent

top cover – aerial cover. Aircraft were considered prestige targets by the SWAPO insurgents. Aircraft are at their most vulnerable when taking off or landing in the vicinity of airfields. At Ondangwa, therefore, an Alouette gunship was airborne for all movements of fixed-wing transport aircraft. The gunship carried out a wide left-hand orbit of the airfield to counter any attempt by terrorists to fire at the transport aircraft. The concept was also used in combat areas to cover own ground troops or to make-safe landing zones for troop-carrying helicopters in the bush

TOT – time on target

transonic zone – the speed band where the airflow over the aircraft alters from subsonic to supersonic flow, usually between Mach 0.9 to 1.1. As the aircraft transits through this zone, changes to the centre of pressure can affect stability

Typhoon – SWAPO's elite group of highly trained troops whose specific task was the deep infiltration of South West Africa. Although highly esteemed by SWAPO they did not achieve any more notable successes than the ordinary cadres. They were also referred to as Vulcan troops

UNCIP – unconventional interception profile

Unimog – a 2.5-litre 4x4 Mercedes Benz transport vehicle, that bore the brunt of bush operations until SWAPO mine-laying hastened the introduction of mine-protected vehicles

UNITA – *União Nacional para a Independência Total de Angola*, National Union for the Total Independence of Angola. The breakaway party led by Jonas Savimbi, supported by the western powers, including South Africa, in the fight against the communist-backed MPLA in Angola

UNTAG – United Nations Transitional Agreement Group

Vergooi – a long-toss bombing profile used by F1AZ aircraft. From a high speed, low-level approach, the pilot pitches-up the aircraft at the pull-up-point (PUP). At about 2,000ft AGL, when the aircraft's nose is at 45° above the horizon, the bombs are released according to settings pre-set on the intervalometer. The bombs then follow one another in a parabolic flight path, flying a distance of around 5nms. The bombs detonate in a stick, hopefully spread evenly through the target. The aircraft recovers to low level and escapes from the combat zone. The manoeuvre affords the enemy missile systems minimum time to lock-on and fire. Inaccurate against pinpoint targets but very suitable against enemy brigades spread out in the bush

vertical manoeuvre – flying an aircraft to rapidly change height, as in a loop

VHF – very high frequency (radio), limited to line-of-sight communication

Visgraat! – the order to rapidly disperse convoy vehicles under threat from air attack (der. Afrikaans for herring bone)

Vlammie – a South African jet-fighter pilot. From the Afrikaans *vlamgat*, literally flaming hole, the afterburner flame produced by a fighter

Volcano – SWAPO's training base for their specialist Typhoon troops, 14km northeast of Lubango

Vrystaat! – the radio call made immediately prior to an attack, warning pilots to select their armament switches to the live or hot position (Afrikaans der. the Orange Free State)

VT fuse – variable time fuse that allows bombs to be detonated at selected heights above targets

WAC – Western Air Command

white phos – a grenade or shell containing phosphorus which, when detonated erupts in a distinctive white cloud, utilized mainly to identify positions on the ground, but also as a grenade in close-quarter combat

Yati Strip – one kilometre south of the cut-line another strip was graded through the bush parallel to the cut-line. This one-kilometre strip of land was known as the Yati Strip and was originally designed as a no-go area but was largely ignored

Zulu call sign – *see* Romeo Mike

Appendix 1

"One of our aircraft is missing"
—SAAF aircraft and crew losses to the enemy during the bush war

---

Date	14 August 1974	
Aircraft	Alouette III	Side number 111
Crew	Pilot	Lt Ray Houghton
	F/Eng	Sgt Ray Wernich

Aircraft was struck by an RPG and crashed in the Madziwa Tribal Trust area of Rhodesia. 111 was the leader of two Alouette helicopters landing in a bush LZ. As the wheels touched the ground an RPG, fired from no more than 20 metres, exploded as it struck the aircraft. The pilot and flight engineer fell out of the wreckage, suffering from minor shrapnel wounds. Lt Erasmus, flying the second helicopter, dropped his troops and then returned to evacuate the downed crewmen

---

Date	25 November 1975	
Aircraft	Cessna 185	Side number 739
Crew	Pilot	2/Lt K. W. Williamson (KIA)
	Pax	2/Lt E. B. Thompson (KIA)
	Pax	Capt D. J. Taljaard SA Army (KIA)

Aircraft failed to return from a reconnaissance flight for Task Force Foxbat during Operation *Savannah*. On 27 November an intercepted enemy radio message indicated that the aircraft had been shot down north of Ebo. Three months later a correspondent of the London *Times* reported that he had seen the wreck of the aircraft north of Ebo.

Date	22 December 1975	
Aircraft	Puma	Side number 134
Crew	Pilot	Capt John Millbank
	Co-pilot	Maj Chris Hartzenberg
	F/Eng	F/Sgt Piet O'Neill du Toit
	Pax	Medic cpl

During Operation *Savannah*, the Puma was hit by Cuban AAA from a hillside 18 kilometres northwest of Cela. The pilots carried out a forced landing fewer than three kilometres from the AAA site. The crew then evaded capture for 22 hours before returning safely.

Date	22 February 1977	
Aircraft	Alouette III	
Crew	Pilot	Lt Neil Liddell (KIA)
	F/Eng	Sgt Flip Pretorius

Operating out of AFB Mpacha, Lt Liddell's helicopter was struck by enemy small-arms fire as it overflew a SWAPO detachment operating in Zambia. A bullet entered the floor of the aircraft and wounded the pilot after passing through the bottom of the pilot's seat. Lt Liddell made a forced landing and the flight engineer ran off to get aid. Lt Liddell succumbed to his wound before help arrived.

Date	14 March 1979	
Aircraft	Canberra	Side number 452
Crew	Pilot	Lt Dewald Marais (KIA)
	Navigator	2/Lt Owen Doyle (KIA)

A formation of four Canberra bombers attacked a target close to Cahama in Angola. Immediately after bomb release, the Canberras descended from 500 feet to low level. It was noticed that Lt Wally Marais' aircraft remained with bomb doors open. Radio calls failed to establish contact with either occupant. Detaching from the formation, Capt Roly Jones closed in on 452. He could see no outward sign of damage to the aircraft. Flying above 452 he noticed the pilot slumped over the controls. 452 climbed slowly up to 2,000 feet while decreasing speed to around 200 knots. The aircraft then banked gently to port before adopting a 10° nose-down attitude. It descended to extremely low level before suddenly pitching up into an almost vertical attitude. The aircraft stalled before plunging into the ground.

Date	6 July 1979	
Aircraft	Mirage III R2Z	Side number 856
Crew	Pilot	Capt Otto Schür

Capt Schür, flying a reconnaissance aircraft, was tasked to take post-strike damage-assessment photography of a target near the Angolan town of Omapande. At 600 knots and 190 feet above the ground, he began his filming run. Seconds later he was struck by AAA that caused a total electrical failure. Clearing the target, he zoomed to gain altitude as he turned back towards base. Passing 8,000 feet and 500 knots, the Mirage flicked into a high-G, right-hand descending spiral, from which he could not recover. He ejected, evaded capture and was recovered to AFB Ondangwa.

Date	6 September 1979	
Aircraft	Puma	Side Number 164 (?)
Crew	Pilot	Capt Paul Vellerman (KIA)
	Co-Pilot	Lt Nigel Osborne (KIA)
	F/Eng	F/Sgt Dick Retief (KIA)
	Pax	14 Rhodesian troops (KIA)

Capt Vellerman was flying as No 4 in a formation of Rhodesian Air Force helicopters during Operation *Uric* in Mocambique. His helicopter was struck by AAA as the formation circled over a terrorist camp, whose position was unknown before the operation. Without a radio call the helicopter crashed killing all the occupants.

Date	18 October 1979	
Aircraft	Impala Mk II	Side number 1033
Crew	Pilot	Maj Aubrey Bell

On an armed reconnaissance mission near Omapande in Angola, Aubrey Bell's Impala was hit by AAA slightly below and behind the cockpit. The aircraft started buffeting, warning lights began flashing and the smoke in the cockpit persuaded him to eject close to the town. After a combined rescue mission involving Impala jets, Puma helicopters and Parabats, the pilot was recovered. Maj Polla Kruger's rescue Puma returned with 22 bullet holes.

Date   24 January 1980
Aircraft   Impala Mk II   Side number 1056
Crew   Pilot   Capt Leon Burger

During an armed reconnaissance mission near Aanhanca in Angola, Capt Burger's Impala was struck by a SA-7 missile while at low level. The missile entered the jet pipe from the lower right-hand side and detonated against the bottom of the vertical tail fin. Despite the loss of the entire vertical fin, Capt Burger managed to fly the aircraft back to AFB Ondangwa. As night had fallen by the time he arrived overhead, he was ordered to eject rather than attempt a landing. The airfield was packed with aircraft and it was decided not to risk landing the Impala with severely reduced directional control.

Date   23 March 1980
Aircraft   Impala Mk II   Side number 1050
Crew   Pilot   Capt Sarel Smal

With fuel filters blocked with very fine white powder, suspected to be an accumulation of Ondangwa sand, Capt Smal's engine lost power while he was on a mission in Angola. Smal ejected at very low level. Angola propaganda claimed they had shot down this aircraft. They produced publicity photographs demonstrating their skill, with pictures of their soldiers standing on the tail and near the cockpit in victorious poses. They claimed that they had killed the pilot, Capt J. H. Henning. Capt Henning's name was painted on the aircraft but he is still very much alive.

Date   25 April 1980
Aircraft   Impala Mk II   Side number 1029
Crew   Pilot   Lt Pete Hollis (KIA)

A pair of Impala aircraft on an armed reconnaissance mission in Angola found and attacked an enemy target. While pulling out from the attack, Impala 1029 was struck by ground fire and flames were seen coming from the tail section as

Appendix 1

Lt Hollis ejected. His neck broke on ejection. The Board of Inquiry found that the pilot's head struck the canopy before the canopy breaker on the seat, causing the fatal injuries. The ejection seat had not been lowered prior to the ejection.

Date 20 June 1980
Aircraft Impala Mk II Side number 1037
Crew Pilot Lt Neil Thomas

On an army support mission during Operation *Smokeshell* Lt Thomas's aircraft was struck by a 23mm shell in the region of the cannon barrel. Debris passed through the engine compressor and with 98 per cent power selected minimal thrust was produced. The aircraft descended until it was striking the treetops when Lt Thomas ejected. He was rescued by Lt André Hattingh and flown to the HAG near Evale in Angola. En route the Alouette red fuel-warning light illuminated, indicating a fuel-filter blockage. After a forced landing in enemy territory, the crew cleared the filter before the rescue mission was completed. The aircraft was recovered by Frelon helicopter and returned to Atlas Aircraft Corporation. It was repaired and returned to service with the same side number.

Date 23 June 1980
Aircraft Alouette III Side number 24
Crew Pilot Capt Thinus van Rensburg
  F/Eng Sgt Koos Celliers (KIA)

Aircraft was struck by enemy fire while providing top cover for landing Pumas and crashed 12 kilometres east of Xangongo in Angola. After exiting the burning wreckage Sgt Celliers was shot by Swapo terrorists. He was confirmed dead by Capt van Rensburg. No pulse could be found. Capt van Rensburg managed to escape and evade capture and reached safety by foot. He was found by ground forces near Cuamato, suffering from compression fractures of the vertebrae, superficial scratches and dehydration. Radio intercepts indicated that SWAPO had taken the body of Sgt Celliers to Lubango.

Date 10 October 1980
Aircraft Impala Mk II Side number 1042
Crew Pilot Lt Steve Volkerz (KIA)

Lt Volkerz, a Mirage III pilot on 2 Squadron, was still current on Impalas and volunteered to do an operational tour on Impalas at AFB Ondangwa. During a mission 20 kilometres southwest of Mupa in Angola, Lt Skinner, the other pilot in the formation, saw Impala 1042 hit by two SA-7 heat-seeking missiles. He saw Lt Volkerz eject and the aircraft explode as it hit the ground. Circling the scene, he saw Lt Volkerz land in his parachute, stand up and wave to indicate that he was uninjured. Radio messages intercepted from the enemy the next day, indicated that Lt Volkerz had been shot and killed by SWAPO.

Date	25 August 1981	
Aircraft	Alouette III	Side number 48
Crew	Pilot	Lt Bertus Roos (KIA)
	F/Eng	Sgt Clifton Stacey (KIA)

During Operation *Protea*, Alouette 48 was involved in a CAS (close air support) mission with the ground forces 20 kilometres NNW of Cuamato in Angola. The aircraft was struck by 14.5mm anti-aircraft fire. Smoke was observed coming from the helicopter as it crashed, killing the crew.

Date	29 December 1981	
Aircraft	Alouette III	Side number 30
Crew	Pilot	Lt Serge Bovy
	F/Eng	Sgt A. J. Janse van Rensburg

Alouettes were operating with the ground forces during Operation *Vlinder* near Evale in Angola. On 29 December, ground forces were in contact with the enemy who were armed with SA-7s and RPGs. A serious casevac from an enemy 82mm mortar blast needed to be picked up. Lt Arthur Walker led a two-ship Alouette formation to the scene. He provided top cover to Lt Serge Bovy's helicopter that was to carry out the pick-up. After calling for the ground troops to mark the LZ with 'white phos', Lt Bovy approached to land. During the approach he saw Lt Walker's helicopter veer sharply as it drew heavy AAA fire. Lt Bovy also drew tracers as he flared to land. On touch-down, two troops loaded the casevac into the helicopter while the rest of the platoon formed a defensive semi-circle around the helicopter. On lift-off, because of the extra weight, it took a long time for the Alouette to pass through the transition from vertical to forward speed. As Bovy started to bank away from the enemy positions he saw two 14.5mm AA guns firing at him from a little over 100 metres away. His aircraft was hit with rounds going through the door, another removing the top part of the instrument panel and one passing through his flying overall but missing his leg. Turning away

Appendix 1

from the AA site, Bovy tried to fly below tree level, barely keeping his rotors clear of the branches. There was a smell of burning and several electrical sparks in the cockpit. The AAA continued and further hits were felt in the port forward door and the co-pilot's seat. Bovy's armoured seat was also hit and he was bounced briskly forward several times. The engine started losing power, causing the rotor blades to slow down. Realizing they were about to crash when the controls stiffened up, he flared harshly to dig the tail in. Looking up, he realized that the helicopter was going to hit a big tree so he deflected the cyclic and rudder to the right. After impact the helicopter came to rest. Dolf van Rensburg, the flight engineer, was lying in the small space between Bovy's chair and the door. Although a lot of blood was streaming from his mouth, he indicated that he was otherwise fine. Bovy unstrapped and, apart from a very sore back, was able to exit the helicopter by punching out the window. The casevac showed no signs of life and was trapped in the wreckage. Seconds later, mortars started falling around them and the two men ran off in a northerly direction. During their escape Bovy noticed a terrorist with an AK-47 about 50 metres away. Dolf wanted to make a stand but Bovy persuaded him to keep silent as the terrorist hadn't seen them. He was looking up at the gunship helicopter firing from above. Soon AK-47 rounds and other larger-calibre shells started bouncing off the trees around the two men. It sounded as if the terrorists were running on the aircrew's spoor. Sgt Botes in the overhead gunship spotted the escapees and, despite heavy AAA, Arthur Walker landed in a confined LZ. The two airmen jumped aboard as Arthur pulled all the instrument panel needles into the red to get the heavily loaded helicopter into the air and on track for base.

Date	5 January 1982	
Aircraft	Puma	Side number 168
Crew	Pilot	Capt John Robinson (KIA)
	Co-pilot	Lt Michael Earp (KIA)
	F/Eng	Sgt Kenny Dalgleish (KIA)

While trooping, the helicopter was struck by small-arms fire. All hydraulic pressures were probably lost and the helicopter struck the ground inverted.

Date	1 June 1982	
Aircraft	Impala Mk II	Side number 1052
Crew	Pilot	T/Maj Gene Kotze (SD) (KIA)

Diving to attack an enemy target, Maj Kotze's aircraft was hit by AAA and crashed.

Date	9 August 1982	
Aircraft	Puma	Side number 132
Crew	Pilot	Capt John Twaddle (KIA)
	Co-pilot	Lt Chris Pietersen (KIA)
	F/Eng	Sgt Grobbies Grobler (KIA)

At 13h20 on 9 August, eight Pumas took off from a HAG, trooping a company of 32 Battalion for a follow-up operation. The formation, flying at very low level, came under heavy AAA and small-arms fire as it crossed an open *shona*. Puma 132, the fifth Puma in the formation, had its tail shot off. The helicopter inverted and crashed into the ground, killing all the occupants.

Date	3 September 1987	
Aircraft	Bosbok	Side number 934
Crew	Pilot	Lt Richard Glynn (KIA)
	Pax	1 (KIA)

During operation *Moduler*, Lt Glynn was tasked to fly a night artillery-spotting mission south of the Lomba River in Angola. The aircraft was struck by a missile, presumed to be an SA-8, and crashed, killing both occupants.

Date	20 February 1988	
Aircraft	Mirage F1AZ	Side number 245
Crew	Pilot	Maj Ed Every (KIA)

During a *Vergooi* bombing mission near Cuito Cuanavale, Maj Every's aircraft was struck by a SA-13 missile as the pilot was levelling out at low level. The aircraft was seen to crash into the trees.

Unmanned remotely piloted vehicles/aircraft (RPVs)

Operation *Askari*: November 1984 to January 1985

The Scout system was deployed to Xangongo in southern Angola and flew missions in the Cahama area in an attempt to locate SA-8 batteries located in that region. During one mission, three SA-8 missiles were captured on video as they were fired at the RPV. Shrapnel from the third missile damaged the camera's protective dome. Approximately 250 rounds of 23mm AAA were also fired at the drone, but it was recovered safely.

Appendix 1

Operation *Moduler*: September 1987

The system was transported to Mavinga where a runway was graded and compacted for the deployment. The poor quality of the runway resulted in damage to four propellers before the runway was improved. On the second operational mission, 16 SA-8 missiles were fired at the drone before it was finally shot down. UNITA soldiers witnessed the shooting and found the wreckage. They then spent three days searching for the pilot, not knowing that it was an unmanned aircraft. Two more RPVs were lost to missile fire before the deployment was curtailed.

Summary

During 15 years of bush war between 1974 and 1989, the South African Air Force lost 22 aircraft as a direct result of enemy action. This period included operations in Rhodesia, Mozambique, South West Africa and Namibia. Lost were:

- 1 x Mirage F1AZ   No 245
- 1 x Mirage III R2Z   No 856
- 1 x Canberra   No 452
- 5 x Impalas Mk II   Nos 1056, 1029, 1042, 1052, 1033
- 1 x Bosbok   No 934
- 1 x Cessna 185   No 739
- 4 x Pumas   Nos 134, Vellerman, 168, 132
- 5 x Alouettes   Liddell, 111, 24, 48, 30
- 3 x RPVs (RPAs)

During this time many aircraft were struck by hostile fire but all landed safely, were repaired and returned to service. The list includes:

- Two F1AZs hit by SA-3 missiles near Lubango (Majs Du Plessis and Pretorius)
- A Mirage F1CZ struck by AA-8 missiles in combat near Cuito Cuanavale (Capt Piercy)
- A Mirage III hit in the tailpipe by an SA-7 over Ongiva (Capt Keet)
- An Impala struck by a SA-7 over Mulondo (Lt Meintjies)
- An Impala had its starboard rear tail plane removed by an SA-9 over Cuvelai (Capt van den Berg)
- A DC-3 Dakota's entire tail section was shredded by a strike from an SA-7 missile (Capt Green)
- A DC-4 Skymaster's fuselage was punctured by small-arms fire north of Ruacana (Maj Rybicki)
- The helicopter fleet, flying close to the fire fights, naturally received the

greatest attention from enemy small arms-fire, 12.7mm, 14.5mm and 23mm AAA, as well as RPG and SA-7 missiles. Many helicopters were hit, often suffering multiple strikes, but apart from those listed as destroyed, all returned to service. Perhaps the record belongs to Maj Polla Kruger whose Puma returned to AFB Ondangwa sporting 22 bullet holes after he had rescued a downed Impala pilot.

Other aircraft destroyed in the operational areas as a result of maintenance and aircrew errors but not enemy fire. The list includes:

- Two Impalas that impacted the ground while pulling out after firing at enemy targets (1074 and 1024)
- An Impala that crashed after take-off on a night mission after the canopy blew off (1096)
- A Mirage F1AZ that crashed while returning from a night mission inside Angola (223)
- A Puma that spiralled into the Cunene River after a mechanical failure (135)
- A Puma that crashed while landing in thick dust at night at Oshakati (174)
- A Puma that crashed after take-off while trooping near Cassinga (155)
- A Kudu, with engine trouble, that forced-landed in an enemy-infested area of Rhodesia (975)
- An Alouette that crashed into high-tension cables in Rhodesia
- An Alouette that crashed into Lake Kariba after an engine cut. The aircraft was salvaged from the lake and placed onto a low-bed truck for transportation back to a repair depot. The truck was destroyed en route when it detonated a landmine
- An Alouette that crashed at Okankolo at night after striking an antenna (43)
- A Cessna 185 that crashed on take-off from Impalela Island in the Caprivi Strip (743)

Appendix 2

Chronology of operations

1966
Blouwildebees   26 August

1971
Mexer (Portuguese)   21–29 January
Anniversaria (Portuguese)   3–10 February
Dragon (Portuguese)   25 June–1 July

1972
Nacala (Portuguese)   5 May–8 September
Junction (Rhodesian)   26 June–8 September

1973
Zorro (Portuguese)   25 June–3 July
Zurzir (Portuguese)   12–31 July
Zorba (Portuguese)   20 August–2 September
Speedway (Portuguese)   22–29 September

1974
Gramophone   20 April–4 May
Liza   7 May–4 November
Shangombe   13–20 May

Blanket (Rhodesian) 14–27 August

1975
Savannah July–March 1976

1977
Kropduif 28 October

1978
Bruilof April (replaced by Reindeer)
Reindeer 4 May
Maanskyn ongoing
Donkermaan ongoing
Cotton 22–26 August
Senator 13–23 November

1979
Vanity (Rhodesian) 25–26 February
Rekstok 6–13 March
Saffraan 6–13 March
Mulungushi (Rhodesian) 10–12 April
Saffraan II 4–14 July
Rekstok II 6 July
Cucumber (Rhodesian) 7–8 July
Placid I (Rhodesian) 22 August
Sponge (Rhodesian) 22 August
Placid II (Rhodesian) 22 August
Motel I (Rhodesian) 23 August
Motel II (Rhodesian) 23 August
Uric (Rhodesian) 1–8 September
Driepoot 24–27 September
Miracle (Rhodesian) 27 September
Tepid (Rhodesian) 18 October
Senanga 5 November
Capsule (Rhodesian) 23–26 November & 8–12 December

1980
Chitumba 7 January
Chitumba II 15 February
Smokeshell (QFL) 10 June
Sceptic 8–21 June

Sceptic II   7 June
Klipkop   30 July
Wishbone   19 December

1981
Interrupt   17 March
Konyn   21 August–22 September
Knife   21 August–8 September
Protea   24 August–22 September
Daisy   2–13November
Vlinder   29 December

1982
Super   13 March
Rekstok III   25 March
Meebos   8–25 August
Bravo   4–8 October
Volcano   14 December

1983
Gepetto   24 January–10 February
Bantam   28–31 January
Kwagga   14–28 February
Skyshout   ongoing
Groundshout   ongoing
Phoenix   15 February–15 April
Trallies   March–April
Phoenix   March–April
Rhubyn   23 March
Fakkel   1–21 March
Lunar   ongoing
Bakkie   ongoing
Butterfly   ongoing
Cuca blitz   ongoing
Snoek   3–4 March
Rhubyn   23 March–20 April
Dolfyn   30 April–20 June
Skerwe   23 May
Korhaan   25–29 May
Blouwildebees II   28 May
Kameel   31 May–9 June

Neptune	6–27 June
Afskeur	8–15 July
Balpoort	12–24 July
Salmon	5 August
Karton	10–14 August
Amsterdam	13–15 August
Oubaas	31 August–6 September
Sefta	4–25 September
Llama	6–16 September
Javelin	1–17 September
Banier	13 September–15 November
Nightingale	13 September
Aconite	19 September–10 October
Kopswaai	16 November–15 December
Fox	17 November–31 December
Ringkals	19 November– 5 December
Askari	20 November–14 January 1984
Shark	20 November–15 December
Blesbok	21 November–6 December
Adolfi	5–13 December
Gypsey	15 December
Klinker	29 December
Rondebosch	29 December

1984

Sclera	February–December

1985

Catamaran	6–15 May
Sea Warrior	10 June–mid-October
Boswilger	28–30 June
Magneto	23 August–10 September
Wallpaper	11 September–8 October
Egret	15–22 September
Weldmesh	16 September–8 October
Cerebus	5 October–3 November
Jerry I & II	2–27 December
Ministerix	8 December
Abrasion	18 December–mid-February 1986

Appendix 2

1986

Rickshaw	ongoing to 1987
Pyp	23 February
Abduct	29 March–21 April
Fagot	April–May
Cinema	1 April–16 September
Jabber	9–30 April
Kenwood	21 April–early June
Herbal	22 April–early June
Pannikin	9 May–6 June
Slade 7	14–18 May
Cuadad	17–19 May
Leo	18–19 May
Anergi	18–19 May
Drosty	23–30 May
Flouriet	18 June–2 July
Duxes	20 June–7 July
Shanty	28–30 June
Enol	7–11 July
Grebe	18–25 July
Accrete	20–25 July
Barbour	22 July–5 August
Hermione	24 July–2 August
Alpha Centauri	28 July–5 August
Annaras	1–14 July
Chappy	14 August–10 September
Killarney	14 August–10 September
Bouval	23 August–6 September
Ceramic	30 August–6 September
Cannabis	2–20 September
Bernico	3–4 September
Denounce	7 September–18 October
Muffel	9 September–10 October
Charm	10–17 September
Mandrax	14 September
Afasi	17 September–31 December
Catapult	19 September–13 October
Deville	19 September
Pergola	25 September–20 October
Cartwheel	25–29 September
Jairus	5 October–11 November

Tremor	15–26 October
Deodar	17–20 October
Colisseum	1 November–12 December
Kakebeen	1 November–12 December
Moonraker	4–11 November
Nigel	28 November–1 December
Dorsan	1 December–30 April 1987
Bakeliet	1–4 December

1987

Uitspring	January ongoing
Rondomtalie	13–27 January
Jupiter	15–19 January
Paternoster	25–26 January
Markotter	31 January–20 February
Ale	2 February–25 March
Perske	27 February–11 March
Kraai	27 February
Batten	7 April (changed to Benzene)
Benzene	9 April (changed to Bellombra)
Bellombra	April–May
Rolio	16–23 April
Ale II & Southgo	5 May–3 June
Asterix	May
Hagar	May
Moduler	22 June– 6 November
Hunter	15 July continuous
Firewood A	15 July–August
Coolidge	24–26 August
Gwarrie	25 August–25 September
Impact	29 August–1 September
Komeet	16 October
Firewood B	26 October–12 November
Bagdon	26 October–7 November
Variato	9–20 November
Hooper	27 November–13 March

1988

Prone	January ongoing
Arnot	8 February–30 March
Packer	14 March–12 May

Appendix 2

Labotomy	April–September
Displace	13 May–27 August
Excite	June– end August
Assassin	2 June–31 December
Hilti	3 June–31 December
Coronation	21–30 August
Faction	1–30 September
Florentine	1–31 October
Placable	1–31 October

1989

Wedge	3 January–31 December
Coronation II & III	9 February–16 March
Merlyn	1 April– 5 May

Appendix 3

ACM diagrams

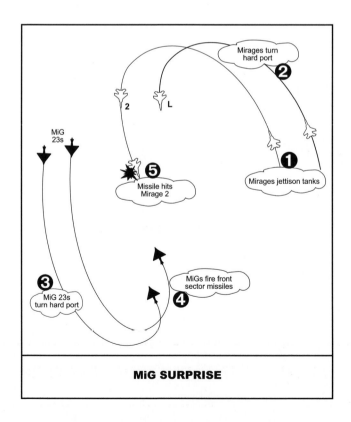

Appendix 3

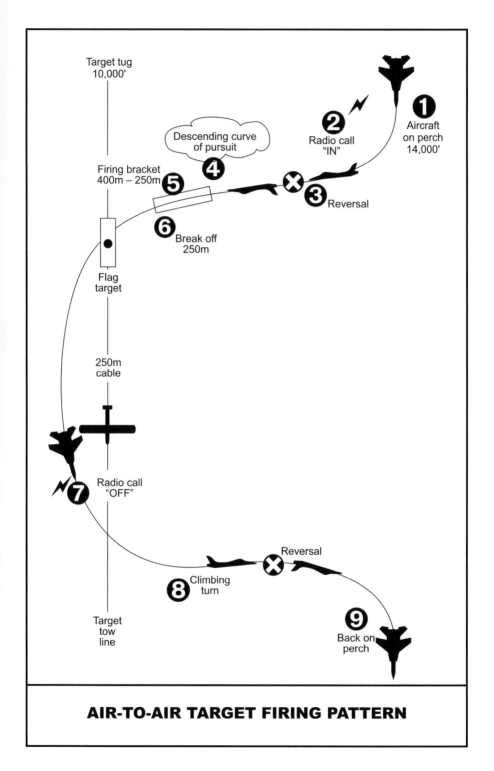

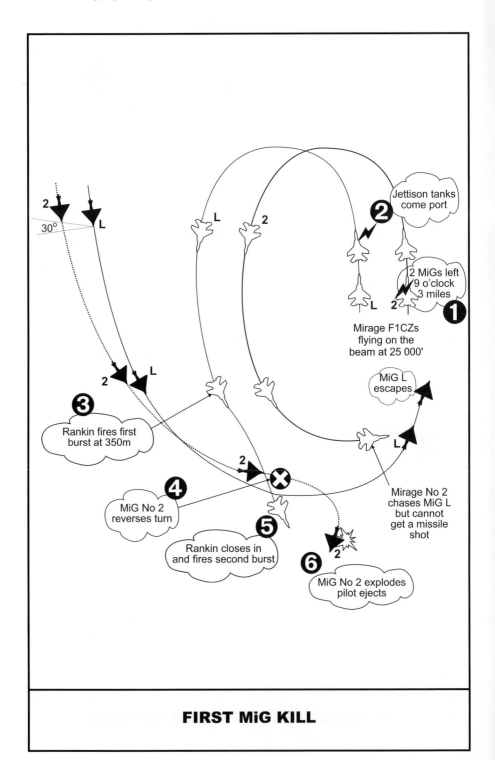

Appendix 3

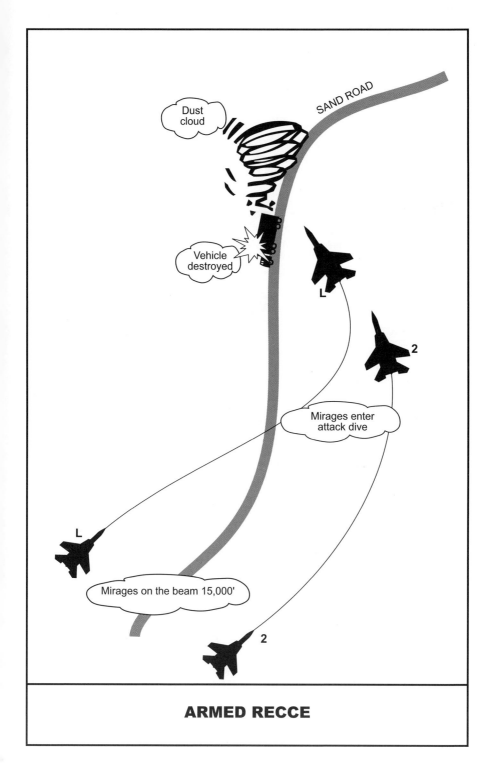

From Fledgling to Eagle

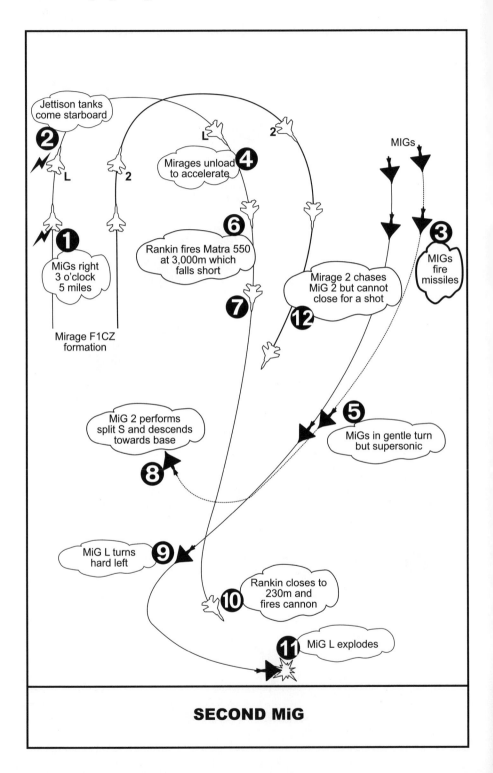

Appendix 4

V3 air-to-air missiles

1973: V3A
First local air-to-air missile. Built in three sections, which was found to be a poor technique. Based on Sidewinder D. Solid state. Limited to 30° angle off firing under low G conditions. Integrated on the F1CZ before the aircraft left France.

1977: V3B
Improved version. Went into production and was carried operationally on the F1. Same category as Sidewinder J. Gimbal limits 34°. No bias ahead of the plume—like the Matra 550, it tended to detonate on the plume. Used an I/R detector fuse, which could be triggered by decoy flares or hot patches on the ground. There was, therefore, a low-level limitation. Fired in anger during the bush war but did not achieve a kill because it detonated on the enemy aircraft's heat plume.

1986: V3C
Greatly improved version. Category similar to Sidewinder L. Gimbal limits 55°. Short reaction time. Laser fuse. 17kg tungsten cube warhead. Lead bias optimized from 20°–160° using a colour guidance system to distinguish between aircraft and decoy flare. The bush war ended before it could be used operationally.

1988: V3S
Acquired as an interim measure but not used operationally.

1992: V3P
Successful integration trials completed but missile not brought into SAAF inventory. Combination of helmet sight and missile gave lock-on up to 75° with a keep-lock ability up to 80°. Missile lock-on was achieved on a 180° pass. Turning diameter at sea level with a Mach 0.9 launch speed was 200 metres. Not in SAAF inventory owing to budgetary constraints.

Appendix 5

The Billy Boys' song

(To the tune of *Ghost Riders in the Sky*)

The Billy Boys were loading up
One dark and windy night
Six bombs each, Mark 82s
It was a fearsome sight
To strike at dawn, that was their task
Against the Swapo swine
To kill the commies in a group
Before they crossed the line

Chorus
AZs high, AZs low, AZs in the sky

The sun was rising in the east
The boys were on the go
Nav computers working well
They crossed the cutline low
The Swaps were stirring from their sleep
To make the morning meal
Just before the Billys dropped
Their load of burning steel

Appendix 5

Chorus

They reached the IP in good time
Their final run began
They pitched-up in the early dawn
The bombs were right on line
The Swaps were taken by surprise
Death came so quick and fast
No more would they terrorize
They'd met their end at last

Chorus

The AZs pulled out from the dive
Their deadly load now gone
With engines screaming low they flew
Into the morning sun
The Billy Boys are known throughout
Wherever men may roam
The task complete, a job well done
The Billy Boys flew home

Chorus

Note: The words to this song were written by Rick Culpan during the dark days of the bush war. They reflected the sentiments of those who had been at risk from the enemy war machine.

Bibliography

Ad Astra – SAAF magazine

Angola Operasie Savannah 1975–1976, Spies, Prof. F. J. du Toit (1989), Pretoria: SADF

FAPLA: Bulwark of Peace in Angola, Edição: Departmento de Agitação e Propaganda – DPN/FAPLA

High Noon in Southern Africa, Chester A. Crocker, Jonathan Ball, Johannesburg

Nyala – SAAF Aviation Safety magazine

Paratus – official monthly periodical of the SADF

Salut – official monthly periodical of the SANDF

South Africa's Border War, Steenkamp, W (1989), Ashanti Publishers, Gibraltar

The SAAF at War, Louw, Martin & Bouwer, Stefaan, Chris van Rensburg Publications, Johannesburg

Index

Aanhanca, Angola 138, 362, 494
Ackerman, Lt Johan 206
Adams, Col Brian 332
African National Congress (ANC) 13, 28, 42, 109, 268, 271, 272
Alberts, Capt Carl 311, 313
Alexander, Col Mac 71
Allison, Capt Sandy 64
ANC *see* African National Congress
Andara 21, 44
Anderson, Maj Andy 336
Anderson, Capt Harry 121-123, 212, 214
Angolan Air Force (FAPA) 106, 156, 167, 193, 196, 215, 257, 283, 289, 320, 321, 327, 331, 346, 358, 384, 386, 393, 395, 433
Arnoldi, Capt Ben 175, 176
Atlas Aircraft Corporation 140, 160, 495

Badenhorst, Ben 48
Badenhorst, Maj Daantjie 53
Bagani 38, 43
Bailey, Lt Keith 53
Barker, Maj Des 100, 269-271
Barnardt, Maj Johan 402
Barnes, Sgt Leslie 268
Barragem, Mozambique 128
Barron, Cadet Gary 60
Barske, Capt Ray 343-345
Bartlett, Cmdt Russell 41
Basson, Cmdt Gene 223, 283
Basson, Cmdt Mossie 150, 179, 286, 290, 293, 406
Baumgartner, Capt Hugh 111
Bekker, Maj Hannes 94, 100, 127
Bell, Maj Aubrey 90, 91, 132-135, 493
Beneke, Lt Daantjie 44-48, 93, 248, 282, 322
Bennett, Capt Les 151, 206, 402
Bester, Capt George 238

Beukes, Capt Roelf 69
Bignoux, Capt Marc 374
Billy Boy *see* Faure
Blaauw, Brig Jan 46
Bolton, Maj-Gen Frikkie 441
Bomba, Lt (MAF) 74
Bornman, Cmdt Borries 165, 225, 250, 282
Bornman, Capt Gavin 105, 106
Botes, Cadet Anton 60
Botes, Sgt 'Boats' 164, 198
Botes, Sgt Christo 348, 349, 497
Botes, Maj 'Jinx' 48, 225, 300
Botes, Cadet Lewis 60
Botha, Lt André 124
Botha, Lt Gerrie 60, 93
Botha, Capt Hans 53
Botha, Maj Koos 111, 133, 189, 436
Botha, Pik 94, 319, 402
Botha, Sgt Willem 200
Bovey, Lt Serge 198
Bowie, Capt Bill 63
Bowyer, Capt Mike 409, 429
Bradstreet, Cadet Arthur 60
Brand, Col Mickey 189
Branders, Capt Thys 48, 51
Brent, F/Lt Ted (RhAF) 99
Brett, Cmdt Monty 83
Breytenbach, Col 'Breyty' 36, 93, 128, 129
Breytenbach, Col Jan 38, 48, 83
Brits, Cadet Buks 60
Brits, Maj Chris 239
Brits, Sgt Stan 44
Brown, Maj Eddie 411, 412
Bruton, Capt Norman 84-86, 158, 268, 269, 271, 386
Buchanan, Maj Buck 236, 237
Burger, Col Bertus 69, 215, 236, 251, 296

Burger, Cmdt Fred 223, 276
Burger, Capt Jamie 468
Burger, Capt Leon 138, 400, 494
Burgers, Capt 'Budgie' 74, 155, 160, 161, 348, 349

Cahama, Angola 108, 111, 143, 167, 169, 170, 171, 184, 185, 190, 192, 208, 209, 212, 214, 215, 232, 233-235, 260, 272, 284-287, 296, 298, 300-306, 309, 314-316, 384, 392, 400, 449, 492, 498
Cabinda enclave, Angola 54
Caiundo, Angola 174, 255, 277, 298, 302, 303, 306, 318
Calonga River, Angola 214
Campbell, Lt Colin 53
Cape Town 290, 299, 337, 389, 468
Caprivi Strip, SWA 21, 38, 40, 43, 44, 52, 88, 90, 136, 248, 254, 281, 332, 341, 344, 352, 500
Carolan, Capt Paddy 74, 139, 178, 207
Cassinga, Angola 81, 82, 84-87, 167, 185, 189, 192, 206, 207, 214, 261, 301, 337, 384, 500
Castro, Fidel 28, 443, 448
Cazombo Bight, Angola 347, 348, 351
Cela, Angola 65, 66, 492
Celliers, Sgt Koos 160, 495
Central Flying School (CFS) 49
CFS *see* Central Flying School
Chambinga, Angola 408, 423, 426, 443, 448
Chetequera, Angola 82, 85
Chibembe, Angola 170, 174, 285, 300
Chiede, Angola 123, 124, 126, 132, 297
Chitado, Angola 160, 275
Church, Col John 86, 436, 461
Clarence, Capt 268
Clay, Capt Chris 284
Cloete, Col Clive 225
Cloete, Capt Joos 47, 48
Clulow, Capt Mark 110, 157, 188
Coetzee, Capt Frans 74, 188, 438, 440, 442
Coetzee, Brig Gerrie 286
Coetzee, Sgt Stephen 204, 205
Coetzee, Maj Theunis 225, 350
Coetzer, Maj 'Knoppies' 189
Collier, Capt Billy74, 188, 438
Conradie, Capt Frans 215
Cook, Cadet Howie 60
Cook, Capt HP 189, 191
Cooke, Maj Peter 90, 91, 231, 402
Cornelius, Capt Richard 268, 278
Cronjé, Lt 'Hojan' 60

Crooks, Capt Mark 158, 401
Croukamp, Cmdt JCR 225
Crous, Lt Terry 200
Cuamato, Angola 117-120, 132, 164, 277, 495, 496
Cuban forces 65, 66, 96, 184, 185, 206, 208, 210, 293, 322, 323, 330, 331, 380, 384, 392-395, 423, 426, 440, 447-449, 456, 493
Cubango River, Angola 20, 21, 306, 317, 347
Cuito Cuanavale, Angola 52, 53, 58, 323, 331, 337, 346, 349, 352, 355, 358, 359, 393-395, 400, 407, 413, 423, 426-428, 431, 439, 441-443, 446, 448-450, 470, 472, 474, 498, 499
Cuito River, Angola 21, 44, 353, 394, 395, 397, 398, 413, 423, 426, 435, 441, 449, 451
Culpan, Rick 515
Cummings, Maj Tom 273, 274
Cunene River, Angola/SWA 20, 22, 23, 173, 186, 193, 202, 203, 244, 285, 286, 288, 299, 301, 304, 308, 313, 363, 365, 384, 387, 388, 447-449, 500
Cuvelai, Angola 143, 205, 206, 213, 214, 219, 232, 235, 238, 248, 257, 261, 275, 288, 298, 301-311, 316-319, 322, 337, 499

da Salviera, Capt Carlos 246
Dalgleish, Sgt Kenny 200, 497
Daniel, Capt Brian 208, 292
Dar es Salaam, Tanzania 43, 52
Dayton radar station *see* SOUTH AFRICAN AIR FORCE (SAAF) UNITS/70 MRU
de Beer, Capt Jaco 400, 403
de Beer, Capt Rikus 379, 393
De Brug range 140, 141, 143
de Bruyn, Capt 'Punchy' 90, 240
de Gouveia, Lt Mario 338, 341
de Jager, Capt Chris 465
de Rouxbaix, Sgt Marne 460, 464-467
de Swardt, Brig 'Blackie' 36
de Villiers, Capt Dirk 74, 151, 152, 188
de Villiers, Cmdt 'Div' 129
de Villers, Maj Neels (SAMS) 223, 241, 258, 259
de Waal, Lt 'Os' 63
de Wet, Cmdt 'Speedy' 110
de Witt, Gen (SAP) 259

Index

Deans, Maj 'Dizzy' 48
Delport, Cmdt 'Dellies' 389
Delport, Sgt Jan 44
Devon radar centre 386, 388, 389
Dias, Maj Manuel (FAPA) 283, 321, 322
Dillon, Sgt Alan 200, 201
Dillon, Gen Pat 46
Dixon, S/Ldr Chris (RhAF) 95, 97, 99, 100
Domingos, Rfn Bernardo 205
Doyle, Lt Owen 95, 100, 109, 313, 492
Dracula, T/Sgt Victor 205
Dreyer, Elmarie 174
Dreyer, Brig Hans (SAP) 224, 275, 283
du Plessis, Cmdt Herman 225
du Plessis, Capt IC 153, 155, 156, 188, 440
du Plessis, Capt Jan André (Air Rhodesia) 94
du Plessis, Lt Johan 91, 193, 194, 206
du Plessis, Capt Pierre 149, 152, 159, 400, 402, 403
du Preez, Cmdt 'Boy' 245-247
du Toit, Col Fred 140
du Toit, Lt Boesman 48, 49, 51
du Toit, Maj Thinus 245, 246, 402, 441, 455
Durand, Col JP (SAP) 224, 225, 259
Dutton, Lt Mark 93

Earp, Brig Dennis 63, 281, 441
Earp, Capt Errol 53
Earp, Lt Michael 200, 497
Ebo, Angola 65, 492
Ediva, Angola 109, 209, 238, 260, 304, 314, 316
Eenhana, SWA 102, 159, 223, 229, 231, 236, 237, 239, 240, 242, 245, 250, 260, 262, 274, 275, 350, 360, 468, 469
Einkamerer, Capt Bill 188, 238
Eksteen, Cmdt Chris 22, 24
Eksteen, Maj Etienne 468
Eksteen, Sgt Mike 57, 144, 145
Elifas, Filemon 44
Ellis, Capt Neall 203-205, 213, 215, 251, 263, 287
Eloff, Cmdt 48
Engela, Cmdt Tom 111
Engelbertus, Sgt Esias 468
Engelbrecht, Maj Ockie 415, 418, 420-422

Epupa Falls, Angola/SWA 20, 21, 240, 245, 247, 296, 387, 388
Erasmus, Capt Lourens 60, 62, 491
Espley-Jones, Capt Russell 311, 312
Esterhuizen, WOI Barend 91
Ethel, Jeff 146
Etosha National Park/Pan 40, 58, 168, 201, 239, 248, 256, 279, 335, 338, 339, 448
Every, Capt Ed 188, 396, 438, 439, 498

Facer, Maj Marsh 193
Fagin, Capt Mike 313
FAPA – see Angolan Air Force
FAPLA (Forças Armadas Populares de Libertação de Angola) see People's Armed Forces for the Liberation of Angola
Faure, Hannes 188
Fee, Capt Spof 311
Ferreira, Cadet Danie 60
Ferreira, Cmdt Deon 14, 112, 259, 350
Ferreira, 'King' 36
Ferreira, Maj Steve 69, 70, 71, 104-106, 113, 241, 248, 284
Fish, Capt Dave 110, 248
Fitzpatrick, Capt Ray 143, 144
Flatow, Maj JCR 225
FNLA (Frente Nacional para a Libertação de Angola) see National Front for the Liberation of Angola
Foote, Cmdt Dudley 110, 248
Forças Aeria Popular de Angola (People's Air Force of Angola) see Angolan Air Force
Fourie, WOI Daantjie 200
Fourie, Sgt Gerhard 468
Foxcroft, Cadet Gavin 60
Frayne, Maj Fred 48, 349
Freeman, Col 48
Freeman, Capt Andy 398
Frelimo (Front for the Liberation of Mozambique) 130
Fryer, Capt Keith 461-464
Füss, Maj Hubs 117, 238

Gagiano, Cmdt Carlo 160, 390, 400, 402, 403, 405, 406

519

Gago Coutinha, Angola 58
Gallineti, Capt Steve 398
Gardiner, Maj Peter 201
Garrett, Capt Geoff 238
Geldenhuys, Lt-Gen Jannie 282, 283, 338, 389
Geldenhuys, Maj Manie 363-366
Geraghty, Capt 'Spook' 205, 207, 216, 218
Gerhard, Capt Dieter (SAN) 92, 137
Gibson, Rfn Brian 135
Gilliland, Col Harry 349
Glynn, Lt Richard 400, 498
Golden Eagle exercise 448
Gomez, Lt (FAPLA) 232
Goodhead, Lt David 319, 320
Gouws, Gen Dolf (SWAPOL) 259
Gouws, Capt JP 268, 269
Green, Capt Colin 266, 499
Grobbelaar, Maj Abel 244, 268
Grobler, Sgt 'Grobbies' 213, 498
Groenewald, Brig Tienie 190
Gründling, Cmdt Jack 149, 158, 206

Haasbroek, Maj Brand 141
Haasbroek, Capt Len 93, 97, 246
Harare, Zimbabwe 60, 384
Hart, Maj Errol 155
Hartebeespoort Dam 110
Hartogh, Maj Skillie 69, 70
Hartzenberg, Maj Chris 65, 492
Harvey, Maj Pete 133
Hattingh, Capt André 159, 165, 495
Hauptfleisch, Lt Bart 295, 296
Havenga, Maj Gert 64, 66, 93, 111, 136, 165, 170, 182
Havenga, Sgt Nicky 325, 326
Hechter, Lt-Gen Willem 75, 140, 427
Henning, Capt Jan 74. 111, 207, 494
Hewetson, Cmdt Bob 374
Hill, Lt Mark 336
Hill, Lt Mike 213
Hoebel, Sgt 'Ziggie' 133, 135
Hoffman, Sgt 'Hoffie' 44
Holland, Cadet Roy 60
Hollis, Lt Pete 139, 148, 494, 495
Holmes, Cmdt Ollie 69, 84-86, 121, 139, 152, 189
Hook, Cmdt Robin 239
Hoon, Maj GJ 225
Hougaard, Cmdt Jan 205
Houghton, Cadet Ray 60, 62, 491
Humbe, Angola 121, 172, 185, 449
Huyser, Brig 'Bossie' 141, 192, 223, 224, 259, 289, 290, 292, 293, 296, 473

Inggs, Capt John 152, 205, 206
Ionde, Angola 174, 180, 189-193, 197, 212, 249, 253, 255, 259, 260, 263, 264, 272, 284, 301

Jacanin, Lt Jake (USN) 216
Jackson, Lt Henry 102, 103, 110
Jacobs, Col Spyker 69, 201, 390
Jamba, Angola 187, 207, 208, 210, 282, 283, 289, 337, 346, 347, 352, 393, 410, 456
Janse van Rensburg, Sgt AJ 496
JG Strydom Airport 44, 298
Johannesburg 48, 72
Jones, Capt Roly 94, 95, 109, 492
Jones, Lt Tinky 48, 158, 375
Joubert, Brig Joep 224, 225, 278, 282, 283, 325

Kaiser, Lt Vic 102, 110, 188
Kaokoland, SWA 25, 39, 40, 43, 57, 58, 145, 201-204, 226, 235, 239, 335, 362, 365, 384, 385, 387, 447, 449, 469
Kapoo, Clemens 44
Kapp, Col Andy 103
Katima Mulilo, SWA 40, 52, 88, 223, 336, 340
Kavango, SWA 38, 40, 43, 164, 207, 242, 258, 335, 342, 442
Kay, Capt Laurie 90
Keet, Capt Rynier 169, 175-177, 499
Kentron missile factory 450
Kerr, Maj Jock 139
Kieck, Capt Koos 110
Kirkland, Cmdt Derek 160, 238
Kirkpatrick, Capt Peter 407-409, 413, 414
Kleynhans, Cmdt As 287
Kleynhans, Capt Dawid 439, 442
Klomp, Dr Anton 48
Knoesen, Maj Dave 52, 136, 174, 316, 427
Knoetze, Capt Kallie 171
Knott-Craig, Capt Alan 74, 91, 188, 438
Koning, Cadet Hans 60
Korf, Capt Arrie 390
Kotze, Maj Gene 91, 110, 210, 497, 498
Krieger, Capt Israel 206
Kriegler, Maj Anton 71, 337, 341, 415, 417-422
Kritzinger, Maj Rudi 139
Kruger, Maj CH 225
Kruger, Cmdt Martin 387, 388
Kruger, Maj Piet 90, 91

Kruger, Maj 'Polla' 132-135, 390, 494, 500
Kwando River, Angola/Zambia 21, 43, 52

la Grange, Capt Tristan 91, 139, 207, 382
Laas, Maj JJ 225
Labuschagne, Gen Frans '24' 72, 348
Labuschagne, Capt 'Lang' 144, 182
Labuschagne, Cmdt 'Lappies' 72, 94, 95, 126, 208, 209, 292, 350, 351, 382, 383, 413, 414, 428
Laing, Capt Jonnie 390
Lambrecht, Cmdt 'Lampies' 391
Lategan, Lt F 268
Laubscher, Capt Daanie 173
le Roux, Lt Hendrik 248
Lee, Capt Darryl 149, 151, 159
Lehmann, Cmdt Johan 407
Lennox, Capt Gordon 48
Lewer, Maj Dick 171, 244, 268
Lewis, Cmdt Casey 123
Liddell, Lt Neil 70, 492, 499
Liebenberg, Capt 248, 249, 284
Liebenberg, Lt Sakkie 53
Linde, Capt JCR 343, 345
Linford, Col 264
Lithgow, Lt Andy 133, 134
Lloyd, Maj-Gen Charles 223, 259, 300
Lloyd, Col Philip 264
Lobito, Angola 109, 113
Lomba River, Angola 53, 354, 357, 394, 399, 400, 403, 405, 407, 410, 411, 423, 426, 446, 450, 498
Lombard, Col Wouter 225, 244, 282, 296
Lomberg, Capt Les 215
Lord, Col Dick 74,139, 149, 161, 181, 224, 225, 238, 239, 282, 295, 296, 300, 322, 339, 343-346, 359, 363, 438
Loskop Dam 388
Loubsher, Maj 'Gooks' 46-48
Lourens, Cmdt Louis 387, 391
Louw, Capt Hennie 74, 151, 188
Louw, Cmdt Johan 189
Louw, Capt Martin 205, 206, 318
Luanda, Angola 54, 59, 65-67, 144, 145, 210, 221
Lubango, Angola 69, 92, 123, 137, 149, 153, 159, 161, 165, 169, 185, 189, 193, 222, 233, 272, 282, 283, 285, 288, 296-298, 300, 302, 308, 309, 315, 371, 383, 385, 403, 436, 437, 447, 449, 495, 499
Luso, Angola 94-96, 99, 100

Macatamney, Mac 473

Malan, Capt Wynand 390
Mapai, Mozambique 128
Maputo, Mozambique 267-271
Marais, Lt Dewald 95, 101, 102, 109, 492
Marais, Capt Dries 86
Marais, Cadet Kiewiet 60
Maritz, Maj 'Mitz'189
Marneweck, Sgt Daantjie 246, 247
Martin, Maj Dave 90
Martin, Lt-Gen Kalfie 50, 51
Mavinga, Angola 53, 331, 342-347, 349, 351-354, 358, 359, 362, 394, 395, 398, 407, 410-412, 415, 416, 421, 422, 424, 425, 435, 443, 444, 446, 449, 450, 499
McCarthy, Maj Mac 461-468
Meerholz, Maj Corrie 298, 299
Meintjies, Lt Neels 305, 499
Meiring, Maj-Gen Georg 338, 339, 341, 358, 404
Menaul, AVM Paddy (RAF) 245, 254
Menonque, Angola 52, 69, 137, 185, 188, 288, 343, 346, 352, 358, 359, 393, 394, 400, 401, 409, 412, 426, 428, 431, 438, 449
Mes, Capt Rudi 392, 400, 402, 403
Meyer, Lt Nardus 363
Meyer, Col PJ (SAP) 225
MILITARY SECTORS
    Sector 10: Oshakati 40, 186, 223, 224-226, 242, 259, 275, 286, 294, 295, 361, 363
    Sector 20: Rundu 40, 164, 223, 259, 303, 306, 433
    Sector 30: Otjiwarongo 40
    Sector 40: Luipaardsvallei 40
    Sector 50: Gobabis 40
    Sector 60: Keetmanshoop 40
    Sector 70: Katima Mulilo 40, 223
Millbank, Capt John 65, 492
Minne, Capt Norman 74, 149, 152, 178, 179, 188, 214, 403, 407, 436-438, 442
Mongua, Angola 109, 160, 173, 185, 186, 385, 449
Moody, Capt Barry 69, 139
Moolman, Lt 'Moolies' 144, 379
Morton, Sgt George 44, 45
Morton, Capt Mathew 64, 65
Moses, Capt Mark 238
Mouton, Lt Riem 53, 94, 95, 97, 99-101, 165, 182, 208, 292, 382, 383, 429, 455
MPLA (Movimento Popular de Libertação de Angola) *see* Popular Movement for the Liberation of Angola

Mt Darwin, Rhodesia 59-62
Mugabe, Robert 137, 327, 385
Mulemba, Angola 159, 240, 275-277
Muller, Lt-Gen Mike 131, 256
Mulondo, Angola 22-24, 143, 208, 232, 235, 248, 298, 299, 301, 302, 304-306, 499
Mupa, Angola 161, 212, 241, 265, 278, 297, 301, 312, 319-321, 496
Myburgh, Capt Koos 397, 398, 423

Namacunde, Angola 185, 276
Namibe, Angola 69, 92, 188, 286, 296, 382, 383, 449
Namolo, Gen Charles (NDF) 71
Nampala, Angola 23
Napier, Capt Neil 292, 382, 413, 432
National Front for the Liberation of Angola (FNLA) 38, 53, 59, 66, 281
National Union for the Total Independence of Angola (UNITA) 23, 38, 53, 59, 104, 185, 219, 255, 274, 281, 283, 289, 290, 292, 293, 321, 323, 324, 327, 332, 342, 343, 346, 347, 349-353, 355, 358, 359, 393-396, 398-400, 410, 411, 415, 418, 445-450, 456, 499
Nefdt, Capt Les 225
Nehone, Angola 275, 283, 297
Nel, Cmdt Daan 225, 250, 273, 278, 296
Nel, Brig Gert 71
Nel, Col Jan 36
Nel, Lt Petrus 205
Nel, Capt Trompie 248, 437, 438, 440
Nell, Maj Theo 74, 150, 151, 156, 188
Nepara, SWA 344
Nestor (SWAPO cadre) 238
Newham, Maj Basil 135
Niewoudt, Maj Johan 110, 238
Nkomo, Joshua 94, 137
Nova Catenque, Angola 111
Nujoma, Sam 41, 465

O'Neill du Toit, Sgt Piet 65, 492
Okavango River, SWA/Botswana 21
Omapande, Angola 106, 123, 124, 126, 133, 134, 493
Ombalantu, SWA 151, 239, 242, 274
Omega base 38, 40, 281, 332-334, 340
Oncocua, Angola 109, 281, 286, 298, 392, 448
Ongiva, Angola 82, 104-106, 123, 132, 139, 143, 144, 162, 166, 167, 174, 175, 177-181, 183, 185, 211, 240-242, 248, 255, 259, 261-264, 266, 267, 272, 273, 282, 286, 287, 288, 295, 296, 310, 312, 319, 322, 389, 449, 499
Ongulumbashe, SWA 37, 42, 46, 459, 466, 472
Oosthuizen, Lt Francois 53
Oosthuizen, Paul 44
Oosthuysen, Capt Nic 124-126, 377
OPERATIONS
  Abrasion 359
  Accrete 383
  Aconite 299
  Afskeur 276, 281, 282
  Ale 385
  Amsterdam 293
  Anniversaria (Portuguese) 53
  Arnot 435
  Askari 219, 289, 294, 298-306, 309-312, 316-319, 321, 323, 324, 332
  Assassin 449
  Asterix 358, 393
  Bakeliet 384
  Bakkie 260, 272
  Balpoort 283, 284, 286
  Banier 296
  Bantam 227, 228
  Bellombra 386, 388, 402, 406
  Bernico 383
  Blouwildebees 45
  Blouwildebees II 267, 273, 275, 281
  Boswilger 361
  Bravo 213, 214
  Butterfly 260, 262, 265, 294
  Capsule (Rhodesian) 137
  Cerebus 358
  Chappy 383
  Cinema 382
  Colisseum 384
  Coolidge 396, 397
  Cotton 90
  Cuca blitz 239, 240, 260, 274, 278, 299
  Cucumber (Rhodesian) 126
  Daisy 187-197
  Displace 449
  Dolfyn 259-261, 264, 273, 277, 286
  Donkermaan 89, 143, 231, 235, 238, 244, 441
  Dragon (Portuguese) 53
  Driepoot 129
  Duxes 382
  Egret 362
  Enol 382
  Excite 449

Faction 449
Fagot 381
Fakkel 244, 245
Florentine 449
Flouriet 382
Fox 300, 304
Gepetto 227
Hagar 393
Hilti 449
Hooper 425-428, 433-435, 441, 443, 446, 453
Interrupt 164
Jabber 382
Javelin 296
Jerry I & II 359
Kakebeen 384
Kameel 273
Karton 289-292
Klinker 298
Knife 168
Konyn 167
Korhaan 267, 272, 273
Kraai 285
Kropduif 70
Kwagga 228, 236, 239
Labotomy 448
Llama 286, 288, 297
Lunar 248, 263, 265, 278, 283, 284, 294, 299
Maanskyn 89, 140-143, 161, 231-235, 240, 248, 258, 272, 286, 287, 301
Magneto 347
Mandrax 384
Markotter 385
Meebos 211, 213, 214 Merlyn 459
Mexer (Portuguese) 53
Ministerix 393
Miracle (Rhodesian) 102, 130
Moduler 394-426, 435, 443, 445, 446, 453, 498, 499
Moonraker 384
Motel I & II (Rhodesian) 127
Mulungushi (Rhodesian) 116
Neptune 274-276
Nightingale 298
Oubaas 296
Packer 441, 443, 445-447, 453
Pannikin 382
Perske 385
Phoenix 239-241, 244, 249, 254, 258
Placable 450
Placid I & II (Rhodesian) 126
Prone 449
Protea 166-181, 184-187, 190
Pyp 381
Reindeer 81-87, 220
Rekstok 102, 109, 123
Rekstok II 123
Rekstok III 205, 206
Rhubyn 244, 248, 254
Rickshaw 381
Ringkals 300
Rondebosch 298
Rondomtalie 385
Saffraan 110, 114
Salmon 287
Savannah 65-67, 76, 491, 492
Sceptic 148, 159
Sclera 322, 342,
Second Congress (FAPLA) 347, 352, 355, 362, 446
Sefta 297
Shanty 382
Skerwe 267-272
Skyshout 175, 233, 236, 237, 250
Slade 7, 382
Smokeshell 148, 149, 495
Snoek 240, 241, 244, 264
Sponge (Rhodesian) 126
Super 203, 204
Tepid (Rhodesian) 135-137
Trallies 235
Uitspring 385
Uric (Rhodesian) 93, 127-129, 495
Vanity (Rhodesian) 102
Vlinder 198, 199, 496
Wallpaper 351
Wedge 456
Weldmesh 351-355, 367, 394
Wishbone 162, 163
Zorba (Portuguese) 58
Zorro (Portuguese) 58
Zurzir (Portuguese) 58
Opperman, Capt Chris 468
Opperman, Maj Johan 224, 225, 232, 289, 327, 330
Opuwa, SWA 40, 57, 230, 365, 366
Orr, Capt John 84-86, 158
Osborne, Lt Nigel 128, 493
Oshakati, SWA 25, 36, 40, 58, 72, 80, 88, 103, 104, 118, 121, 129, 135, 148, 189, 192, 205, 224, 225, 228, 229, 235, 237, 238, 240-242, 248-251, 254, 258-262, 264, 272-274, 277-279, 282, 287, 294, 295, 301, 311, 315, 318, 321, 322, 324, 325, 329, 338, 343, 360, 361, 363, 365,

387, 391, 436, 461, 470, 477, 500
Oshikango, SWA 42, 102, 312, 388, 449
Otto, Cadet Piet 60
Owamboland, SWA 21, 25, 26, 37, 39, 42-47, 81, 88, 93, 102, 133, 139, 149, 155, 164, 201, 205, 207, 223, 226, 227, 234, 235, 239, 240, 242-244, 246, 249, 250, 256, 259, 260, 265, 272, 275, 276, 278-280, 282, 283, 286, 287, 296, 298, 299, 310, 324, 331, 335, 342, 360, 381, 382, 387, 390, 392, 448, 449, 469, 477
Owen, Capt Dave 165, 387, 388

PAC *see* Pan Africanist Congress
Paetzold, Maj 46
Page, Capt Keith, 400
Paine, Capt 'Hug' 70, 133-135
Palela, SWA 162
Pan Africanist Congress (PAC) 28
Pansegrouw, Capt G 225
Parsonson, Capt Mike 135
Pearce, Cadet Mike 60
Penhall, Maj Rod 189, 191, 192
Penzhorn, Cmdt 'Ertjies' 131
People's Armed Forces for the Liberation of Angola (FAPLA) 144, 171, 173, 185, 207, 256, 257, 302-306, 308, 309, 311, 318, 323, 324, 337, 349, 353, 355, 359, 393, 398, 423, 441
People's Liberation Army of Namibia (PLAN) 288, 459
Perold, Lt Faan 48, 51
Peu-Peu, Angola 172, 185
Petter-Bowyer, Gp Capt Pete 97
Phillipson, Lt Leon 350
Pieksma, Cadet Frits 60
Pienaar, Capt Malan 415, 417-419, 421, 422
Pienaar, Capt Melt 246
Pienke, F/Lt Kevin (RhAF) 102
Piercy, Capt Arthur 400, 402, 404-406, 499
Piet Gouws Dam 388
Pietersen, Lt Chris 498
PLAN *see* People's Liberation Army of Namibia, *see also* SWAPO
Platter, Capt Ralph 126
Popular Movement for the Liberation of Angola (MPLA) *see also* FAPLA 23, 38, 59, 65, 66, 104, 117, 160, 255, 281, 289, 290, 296, 327-329, 332, 343, 345-347, 448
Port Elizabeth 313

Potgieter, Col Hap 343, 345
Potgieter, Lt Johan 238
Preisig, Mr (ICRC) 273
Preston-Thomas, Col 297
Pretoria 29, 35, 37, 38, 45, 84, 111, 126, 144, 148, 267-269, 271, 272, 290, 301, 329, 423, 424, 469
Pretorius, Col (SAP) 44
Pretorius, Lt Dewald 182,
Pretorius, Sgt 'Flip' 70, 492
Pretorius, Maj Frans 74, 150, 152-155, 188, 499
Pretorius, Chap JJ 225,
Pretorius, Capt 'Muis' 70
Pretorius, Pierre 50
Prins, Maj Anton 225,
Prinsloo, Cmdt Dolf 206
Prinsloo, Capt Hannes 110

Quiteve, Angola 143, 193, 232, 301, 303, 304, 306

Rabie, Maj Chris 345, 346
Radloff, Maj Gerrie 84-86, 157, 206
Rankin, Maj Johan 193-195, 206, 215-217, 377, 393, 403, 407, 436, 437, 440, 441
Ratte, Capt Willem 190
Rautenbach, WOI Bachus 442
Rautenbach, Lt Chris 364-366
Raymond, Capt Mark 400, 402
Red Line 40, 239, 283
Redelinghuys, Capt JR 390, 423
Renfree, Brig 46
Repsold, Cmdt Zach 75
Retief, Sgt Dick 128, 493
RhAF *see* Rhodesian Air Force
Rhodesian Air Force (RhAF) 54, 60, 93-95, 116, 126, 310, 472, 493
Rhodesian Light Infantry (RLI) 60, 128
Riemvasmaak range 113, 139, 170
Ritchie, Cadet John 60
RLI *see* Rhodesian Light Infantry
Roberto, Holden 59, 66
Roberts, Capt Gordon 70
Robinson, Capt John 145, 200, 497
Robinson, Maj Robbie 91
Rochat, Maj Graham 75, 110, 114, 117-120, 158
Ronne, F/Lt Mike (RhAF) 97
Roodewal bombing range 51, 81, 83, 97, 98, 119, 158, 379
Roos, Lt Bertus 173, 496
Roos, Capt Pieter 60, 139, 176

Index

Rosseau, Lt Philip 64, 65, 93
Roy, Maj Sandy 170, 182, 208, 292
Ruacana, SWA 22, 46, 47, 58, 115, 117, 130, 155, 156, 160, 168, 209, 214, 223, 225, 242, 245, 258, 267, 273, 274, 277, 288, 289, 338, 382, 385, 387, 390, 391, 392, 447, 449, 461, 462, 464, 465, 467, 469, 477, 499
Ruacana Falls, SWA/Angola 20, 21, 277, 288
Rudman, Capt Les 171
Rudnick, Capt Charlie 133-135
Russell, F/Lt Jim (RhAF) 95, 97, 100
Rybicki, Maj 499

SAMS *see* South African Medical Services
SAN *see* South African Navy
SAS *see* Special Air Service (Rhodesian)
Savimbi, Jonas 59, 289, 290, 327, 347, 352
Sawyer, Capt Lionel 397, 460
Schabort, Cmdt Daantjie 297
Scheepers, WOI 'Skippy' 200
Schickerling, Cadet Reg 60
Schmidt, Maj Errol 90, 91
Schmulian, Capt Eric 70
Schroeder, Capt Trevor 123-126,182, 183, 208, 292
Schür, Capt Otto 70, 123-126, 149, 150, 189, 493
Sequediva, Angola 299
Sevenster, Capt Derek 117, 119, 120
Shakawe, Botswana 21, 341
Shalli, Gen (NDF) 71
Sharp, Maj Bernie 225, 248, 279-282
Shiyagaya, Toivo 44
Siebrits, Capt Pikkie 161, 162, 292, 382, 383, 409, 432
Sinclair, Capt John 402
Singalamwe, SWA 21, 43
Skinner, Capt Chris 161, 393, 427, 442, 496
Slade, Capt Alan 462-464, 468
Smal, Capt Sarel 144-146, 464
Smit, WOI FH 225
Smit, Sgt Johnny 121, 122
Smith, Ian 94,
Smuts, Cmdt Tienie 223, 277
Snowball, Maj Ken 64
Snyman, Maj George 111, 182, 183, 208, 292
Snyman, Cmdt Jackie 223, 275, 282
Snyman, Maj JP 287,

Snyman, Capt Piet 48
Snyman, Sgt Thys 45
Solomon, Capt Ian 189
Somerville, Capt John 53
Sott, Maj Werner 392
SOUTH AFRICAN AIR FORCE (SAAF) BASES
Bloemspruit 48, 49, 140, 142, 201, 268
Eros, Windhoek 44, 48, 49, 123, 282, 337, 338, 341
Grootfontein 49, 64, 69, 72, 111, 121, 123, 149, 156, 157, 162, 164, 168, 174, 183, 186, 191, 208, 214, 222, 227, 230, 243, 247, 248, 286, 292, 298, 310, 319, 331, 336, 337, 340, 341, 345, 374, 382, 393, 403, 404, 409, 414, 415, 419, 422, 426-428, 433, 435-438, 441, 442, 448
Hoedspruit 104, 145, 148, 149, 168, 200, 201, 205, 214, 217, 268, 269, 271, 325, 378, 379, 384, 389, 390, 438, 441, 442
Mpacha 70, 79, 80, 88-91, 110, 114, 136, 254, 273, 336, 376, 378, 384, 460, 492
Ondangwa 55, 57, 58, 69, 72, 80, 84, 85, 92, 102-104, 109, 110, 114, 117, 121, 123-126, 129-131, 135, 137-140, 142-145, 148-151, 154, 155, 157, 159, 161, 162, 168, 169, 176, 179, 181, 184-186, 192-194, 197, 200, 201, 205-208, 212-215, 222, 228, 236, 238-242, 245-248, 250, 251, 256-258, 260, 261, 263, 265, 266, 273, 274, 278, 279, 282-287, 294-296, 298, 299, 305, 309, 310, 314, 319, 331, 337-343, 359-361, 383, 384, 386, 388-390, 392, 436, 437, 448, 459, 460, 463, 465, 468, 469, 477, 493, 494, 496, 500
Pietersburg 72, 74, 77, 81, 83, 91, 98, 119, 129, 176, 193, 268, 388, 472
Rooikop, Walvis Bay 45, 48, 122, 123, 129
Rundu 40, 48, 52, 53, 80, 87, 164, 239, 259, 262, 289, 290, 292, 293, 324, 331, 336, 342-346, 348, 350, 353, 356, 357, 359, 377, 380, 381, 397, 398, 400, 401, 403, 404, 406, 408, 415, 416, 422-424, 426-428, 435, 441, 460
Swartkop 44, 48, 245, 246
Waterkloof 54, 62, 65, 69, 84, 90, 94, 96, 111, 117, 129, 136, 137, 138, 148, 157, 184, 205, 271, 310, 337-340, 374, 376, 377, 383, 384, 389, 390, 410, 415, 424, 449
Ysterplaat 95, 337

SOUTH AFRICAN AIR FORCE (SAAF) SQUADRONS
1 Squadron: Hoedspruit (Mirage F1AZ) 73-75, 114, 148-150, 153, 168, 180, 188, 200, 201, 205, 207, 212, 218, 377, 379, 393, 403, 406, 407, 433, 435, 436, 439, 448
2 Squadron: Waterkloof (Mirage III CZ & R2Z) 69, 70, 84-87, 90, 92, 104, 161, 168, 169, 171, 176, 220, 386, 388, 408, 495
3 Squadron: Waterkloof (Mirage F1CZ) 109, 121, 137, 148-150, 184, 193, 205, 215, 218, 206, 337, 376, 386, 388-390, 400-402, 405, 406
4 Squadron: Swartkop (Impala) 90, 92, 110, 132, 140
8 Squadron: Bloemspruit (Impala) 48, 110, 140, 172, 244, 268
12 Squadron: Waterkloof (Canberra) 53, 94, 126, 168, 218
17 Squadron: Swartkop (Alouette) 48
21 Squadron: Waterkloof (VIP Transport) 256, 290, 337
24 Squadron: Waterkloof (Buccaneer) 64, 65, 72, 129, 136, 140, 165, 168, 219, 220, 348, 406, 407, 427, 454, 455
25 Squadron: Ysterplaat (Dakota DC-3) 337
28 Squadron: Waterkloof (C-130 & C-160) 66, 81, 374, 375, 414-417, 450
41 Squadron: Swartkop (Cessna185) 337, 461
44 Squadron: Waterkloof (DC-3 & DC-4) 93, 245, 246, 449
60 Squadron: Waterkloof (Boeing-707) 378, 389, 449
85 Squadron: Advanced Flying School (Impala, Sabre & Mirage III) 77, 268
SOUTH AFRICAN AIR FORCE (SAAF) UNITS
301 FACP (Forward Air Command Post), Grootfontein 69
310 AFCP (Air Force Command Post), Oshakati 35, 121, 205, 222, 325, 360, 391, 436, 470
400 AMU (Airfield Maintenance Unit) 240, 248, 282, 284, 287, 295, 310
70 MRU (Mobile Radar Group), Dayton, Ondangwa 92, 105, 109, 111, 118, 129, 142, 144, 152, 154, 169, 193, 196, 215, 360, 361, 386, 448
70 MRU (Mobile Radar Group), Sunset, Rundu 401
JARIC (Joint Air Reconnaissance Intelligence Centre), Waterkloof 53, 54, 70, 383
SAAF HQ, Pretoria 139, 186
SAC (Southern Air Command), Silvermine 35
WAC (Western Air Command), Bastion, Windhoek 35, 36, 121, 139, 224, 228, 232, 233, 259, 296, 297, 301, 302, 343, 358, 381, 473
SOUTH AFRICAN ARMY UNITS
32 Battalion, Bagani 14, 15, 39, 53, 70, 71, 112, 180, 190, 201, 203, 205, 245, 249, 257, 260, 263, 264, 266, 273, 277, 311, 340, 343, 344, 345, 350, 355-357, 392, 404, 438, 450, 498
44 Parachute Brigade ('Parabats') 85, 110, 116, 124, 126, 133-135, 197, 214, 260, 264, 275, 283, 334, 472, 494
51 Battalion, Ruacana 283, 390, 391, 449
53 Battalion, Ondangwa 250, 277, 278, 287, 296, 298
61 Mechanized Battalion 190, 191, 197, 248, 264, 303, 304, 309, 311, 312, 314, 316, 321, 450
71 Brigade 450
81 Brigade 450
Army Infantry School 283, 297
Reconnaissance Commandos (Special Forces) 15, 70, 111, 112, 117, 130, 241, 244, 262, 267, 273, 274, 281, 284, 299, 301, 302, 315, 355, 358, 359, 363, 383, 385, 391, 397
School of Armour 319
South African Medical Services (SAMS) 57, 135, 258, 259
South African Navy (SAN) 35, 92, 138, 266, 471
SOUTH AFRICAN POLICE (SAP)
SAP COIN 42-44, 46, 60, 267, 279
SAP Koevoet 22, 41, 224, 227, 240, 245, 247-249, 251, 252-254, 259, 263-267, 275, 276, 282, 283, 294, 296, 297, 361, 386, 391, 459, 463, 468, 469, 472
SAP Reaction Force 40, 41, 46
South West Africa People's Organization (SWAPO) 21, 23, 28, 29, 37-39, 41-47, 70, 75, 77, 78, 81, 84-88, 90, 104, 106, 109, 110, 112, 114, 121, 123, 129, 131, 135, 136, 138, 139, 144, 146, 148, 149, 152, 159-162, 164-167, 171, 181, 184-187, 190-193, 196,

197, 201, 203, 205, 207, 208, 211, 212, 214, 221-223, 226, 227, 229, 231, 232, 234-245, 247-250, 256-262, 264, 272-278, 282-285, 287-290, 294, 296-301, 303, 304, 307-311, 318, 320, 322-326, 330, 332, 335, 342, 343, 352, 361, 362, 381, 382, 384-387, 390, 391, 436, 457-459, 462, 463, 465, 466, 468, 469, 492, 495, 496

SOUTH WEST AFRICAN MILITARY/ PARAMILITARY UNITS
1 SWA Specialist Unit, Otavi 40
1 SWA Commando Squadron, Eros 40, 256, 273, 283
101 Battalion, Ondangwa 40, 41, 251, 259, 264, 386, 450, 459, 468, 472
102 Battalion, Opuwa 40
2 SWA Specialist Unit, Windhoek 40
201 Battalion, Omega 40, 190, 191, 391
202 Battalion, Rundu 40
203 Battalion, Mangetti Dunes 40
701 Battalion, Caprivi 40
911 Battalion, Luipaardsvallei 40
SWAPOL (South West African Police), Windhoek 259, 459, 461-467
SWATF (South West African Territory Force) 37, 39, 41, 288, 299, 300, 306, 324, 338, 456, 458, 459
Special Air Service (Rhodesian) (SAS) 128
Spies, Lt Jimmy 441
Sproul, Capt Rob 442
Stacey, Sgt Clifton 173, 496
Stannard, Maj Crow 128, 129
Stapa, Capt André 278
Stead, Capt Dave 139
Steenkamp, Cmdt 'Brick' 53
Steenkamp, Capt 'Stony' 53
Steyn, Capt Pierre 468
Stock, Capt Dave 438
Stroebel, Cmdt 284
Strydom, Lt JJ 53, 100
Swanepoel, Col Theuns (SAP) 45-47
Swanepoel, Maj WJ 225,
SWAPO *see* South West Africa People's Organization
Swart, Maj 'Blackie' 70
Swart, Capt Kobus 468
Swart, Maj 'Slinger' 343

Taljaard, Capt 65, 491
Terrace Bay, SWA 45
Tetchamutete, Angola 85, 212, 235, 261, 264, 288, 311, 317, 337
Thackwray, Brig 'Thack' 146, 358, 381, 404, 473
Thatcher, Margaret 462
Theron, Col 459,
Theron, WOI Neels (SAMS) 415, 418, 420-422
Thomas, Lt Neil 159, 495
Thompson, Lt EB 65, 491
Thorne, F/Lt Dave (RhAF) 60, 61
THTC *see* Tobias Hanyeko Training Camp
Tobias Hanyeko Training Camp (THTC), SWAPO base, Angola 123, 149, 150, 297, 308, 436
Toerien, Lt Cobus 91, 102, 103, 110, 139, 206, 215, 217, 390-392
Tonkin, Capt Frank 400, 403
Tooth Rock range 141
Truter, Maj Paulus 407, 455
Truter, Lt Piet 139
Tsumeb, SWA 43, 121, 123, 130, 243, 244, 264, 340
Turner, Capt Clive 206, 402
Twaddle, Capt John 213, 498

UNITA (União Nacional para a Independência Total de Angola) *see* National Union for the Total Independence of Angola
United Nations (UN) 39, 65, 94, 234, 318, 394, 446, 448, 457-462, 465
United Nations Transitional Agreement Group (UNTAG) 94, 448, 457, 458, 460, 461
UNTAG *see* United Nations Transitional Agreement Group
Upfold, Capt Dave 336
Upington 48, 49, 90, 104, 148, 149, 168
Upton, Capt Steel 144, 314

van Buuren, Lt Vince 45, 46, 48
van Coppenhagen, Capt Willie 393, 436, 437, 439, 441, 442
van den Berg, Capt Giel 407-409, 413, 414
van den Berg, Capt Joe 309-311, 499
van der Bijl, Maj Dawid 90
van der Merwe, Maj Jannie 60, 348
van der Merwe, Cmdt Mac 158, 169,
van der Merwe, Maj Willem (SAMS) 225
van der Vyver, Maj Johan 345
van der Waals, Cmdt Wim 48

van der Westhuizen, Cadet Ben 60
van Eeden, Capt Reg 404, 437, 439
van Eeden, Maj Sarel 91
van Garderen, Cmdt Simon 140
van Heerden, Cmdt Barend 223, 225, 244, 282
van Heerden, Sgt 'Whitey' 165
van Loggerenberg, Lt-Gen Jan 217, 296
van Niekerk, Dr Willie (AG SWA) 259
van Onselen, Maj DM 225
van Rensburg, Capt Anton 400, 402, 403
van Rensburg, Sgt Dolf 198, 497
van Rensburg, Capt Thinus 160, 248, 495
van Rooyen, Maj John 139
van Straaten, WOI Kenny 93, 348-350
van Vuuren, Lt 'Fires' 391
van Wyk, Lt 268
van Wyk, Maj Louis 374
van Zyl, Cadet 'Flip' 60
van Zyl, Lt Piet 124, 125
van Zyl, Capt Sakkie (SAP) 279
Vellerman, Capt Paul 128, 493, 499
Venter, Maj Chris 74, 200
Venter, Lt Jakes 181
Venter, Capt 'Jeronkie' 269
Venter, Maj Steyn 48, 49, 51, 75, 90, 91, 102, 103, 110, 111, 114, 132-135, 140, 161, 268-271
Vergottini, Capt Mario 122, 335-337, 359-361, 390, 459-468
Vermaak, Capt Frans 110, 139, 175, 176
Vermeulen, Capt Giep 132-135
Viktor, Johan (SAP) 48
Viljoen, Gen Constand 315, 347
Viljoen, Col Eddie 70, 71, 257, 266, 404
Viljoen, Capt Frik 74, 188
Viljoen, Lt Herman (SAN) 60
Viljoen, Col P (SAP) 225, 260
Vinticette, Angola 238, 244, 249, 250, 257, 301
Virei, Angola 214, 235, 240, 254, 288, 382
Visser, Lt 57
Vivier, Capt Frank 278
Vivier, Capt Pete 75, 206
Vogel, Capt Koos 139
Volcano, SWAPO base/troops 222, 239, 244, 301
Volkerz, Capt Steve 161, 495, 496
von Zorgenfrei, Lt Mark 348
Vorster, John 78
Vos, Lt 'Vossie' 48

Waite, Terry 299

Waldheim, Kurt 94
Walker, Capt Arthur 122, 164, 198, 199, 244, 496, 497
Wall, Maj Dudley 314
Walls, Lt-Gen Peter 94
Walsh, Cadet Rocky 60
Ward, F/Lt Clive (RhAF) 62
Wasserman, Capt 'Wassie' 188, 379
Wehmeyer, Cmdt Dries 195, 206, 402
Welgemoed, Cmdt Willem 251
Wellington, Col Doug 71
Weltehagen, Des 48
Wenela Base 43
Wepener, Col J 223, 225
Wernich, Sgt Ray 61, 491
Wesley, Lt John 48
Wessels, Capt JP 238
Whiting, Capt Steve 365
Williams, Maj Brian 264, 363-366
Williams, Lt Glen 60, 110
Williams, Capt Kenny 145
Williamson, Lt KW 65, 492
Wilson, Dr (SAMS) 468
Windhoek, SWA 35, 36, 39, 40, 43, 44, 48, 49, 51, 103, 121, 122, 123, 141, 223, 233, 236, 242, 282, 337-339, 341, 343-345, 462
Winterbach, Lt Tobie 44, 45
Woodley, Maj Adrian 374-377
Worst, Maj Wessel 246, 336
Wroth, Lt Charlie 136, 137, 174, 182, 311, 312, 427

Xangongo, Angola 23, 82, 105, 143, 160, 162, 166, 167, 172, 173, 185, 186, 211, 233, 234, 244, 245, 247, 250, 254, 262, 267, 278, 284, 286, 288, 300, 302, 310, 313, 314, 316, 319, 400, 449, 495, 498

Yati strip, Angola/SWA 143, 249

ZANLA *see* Zimbabwe African National Liberation Army
Zambezi River, SWA/Zambia/Zimbabwe 21, 136, 341
Zeeman, Cmdt Dan 64, 65, 69, 91
Zimbabwe African National Liberation Army (ZANLA) 102, 130, 137
Zimbabwe People's Revolutionary Army (ZIPRA) 94, 96, 126, 127, 135, 137
ZIPRA *see* Zimbabwe People's Revolutionary Army
Zunckel, Maj Zack 189